18

SENECA
AGAMEMNON

SENECA

AGAMEMNON

EDITED WITH A COMMENTARY

BY

R. J. TARRANT

Associate Professor of Classics,
University of Toronto

CAMBRIDGE UNIVERSITY PRESS

CAMBRIDGE

LONDON · NEW YORK · MELBOURNE

Published by the Syndics of the Cambridge University Press
The Pitt Building, Trumpington Street, Cambridge CB2 1RP
Bentley House, 200 Euston Road, London NW1 2DB
32 East 57th Street, New York, NY 10022, USA
296 Beaconsfield Parade, Middle Park, Melbourne 3206, Australia

First published 1976

Printed in Great Britain
at the
University Printing House, Cambridge
(Harry Myers, University Printer)

This book was published with the aid of a grant from the
Humanities Research Council of Canada, using funds provided
by the Canada Council.

Library of Congress Cataloguing in Publication Data

Seneca, Lucius Annaeus. Agamemnon.

(Cambridge classical texts and commentaries; 18)
Bibliography: p.
Includes indexes.

1. Tarrant, Richard John, 1945–II. Title.
PA6664.A6 1976   872'.01   76–15668

ISBN: 0 521 20807 6

CONTENTS

TO
MY PARENTS

PREFACE

When Friedrich Leo published his edition and critical studies of Seneca's tragedies a century ago, he made little effort to conceal his scorn for the author whose interpretation he had advanced so greatly. This attitude toward Seneca no longer seems appropriate, since literary critics of the past two generations have provided a more adequate framework for the evaluation of his work. Released from unequal competition with his Greek predecessors, Seneca can now be judged on his own merits as a powerful, though limited, poet, whose depictions of disordered personalities in a violent and unstable world have taken on a new interest in the present century.

In this edition of *Agamemnon* the text has been constituted directly from the manuscripts. The introduction devotes most attention to sources and manuscripts, and is brief on subjects about which much has already been said or on which little may usefully be said. The commentary has a twofold purpose: to discuss what Seneca wrote and what his words mean, and to place his work in a wider context. I have tried in particular to illustrate Seneca's debt to Greek and Latin drama, Augustan poetry (that of Ovid above all), and declamatory rhetoric, in an effort to isolate more clearly what is characteristic and original in his writing. Because of this double aim, and also because of the almost complete absence of modern commentaries on the plays, I have made the commentary rather full. Even so, it is far from exhaustive; some omissions are deliberate (p. 156 below), but many others are the result of ignorance or lack of perception. I hope that by analysing a single play in detail I have made some contribution to the general understanding of the plays.

This book is based on an Oxford thesis for which I received the degree of Doctor of Philosophy in 1972. The typescript was first sent to the Press in August 1974, but references to works which have reached me since then have been inserted where possible.

PREFACE

For financial support or assistance I wish to thank the Marshall Aid Commemoration Commission, the Danforth Foundation, Corpus Christi College, Oxford, and University College, Toronto. I am particularly grateful to Corpus for providing me with splendid facilities for research while I was P. S. Allen Junior Research Fellow. I must also thank the Institut de Recherche et d'Histoire des Textes in Paris for supplying microfilms of several manuscripts. The staff of the Cambridge University Press have dealt expertly and patiently with an often trying author and typescript.

That I was able to write this book at all is due to the help given me by my supervisors. Professor R. G. M. Nisbet suggested *Agamemnon* as a subject for research, and my commentary derives much of its approach as well as many specific ideas from him. Sir Roger Mynors led me to take an interest in the medieval transmission of the tragedies and guided my work on the text. I owe a great deal to their instruction and their friendship. The examiners of my thesis, M. E. Hubbard and Professor E. J. Kenney, removed numerous errors from the work and offered useful suggestions for its improvement. Professor H. D. Jocelyn very kindly read a late version of the commentary and made many suggestions, almost all of which I have gratefully adopted. Professor C. O. Brink and Professor F. H. Sandbach gave me valuable comments on a draft of the entire book. For criticism, advice, and information of various kinds I am indebted to L. E. Boyle, G. P. Goold, A. P. MacGregor, R. H. Rouse, D. A. Russell, O. P. Taplin and Otto Zwierlein.

There is one scholar whom I hesitate to name here, since he neither directed nor read my work on Seneca. But I should feel less than honest if I did not record my gratitude for the encouragement, the teaching, and the example of Eduard Fraenkel.

R.J.T.

May 1976

INTRODUCTION

THEME AND STRUCTURE

Modern criticism of Senecan tragedy has produced two sharply distinct approaches to the fundamental question of unity. The harsh, but not baseless verdict of Leo, 'istae uero non sunt tragoediae, sed declamationes...in actus deductae',[1] has found more moderate and refined restatement in the work of Friedrich[2] and Zwierlein,[3] who have acutely demonstrated Seneca's lack of interest in organic structure and his subordination of large-scale unity to the interest of the individual scene. The majority of recent writers on Seneca, however, find a unity in recurrent themes or images and minimise the diversity of the episodes.[4] The unitarian and analyst positions need not exclude each other, and the debate between them has at times proceeded at cross-purposes; in discussing *Agamemnon*, which has attracted much unitarian[5] and little analyst[6] criticism, I shall try to indicate the proper sphere of each.

The play lacks the most obvious agent of unity, a dominant central figure or pair (compare *Medea* and to some extent *Oedipus, Phaedra* and *Thyestes*). Indeed, no character dominates even two consecutive acts; Cassandra's tenure of centre stage is the longest (659–807, 868–909). The title character is the most shadowy of all, visible only long enough to suggest a pious but fatally dim-witted *imperator*. One should not attempt to fill out his characterisation by adding to his one brief scene all references

---

[1] *Obs.* 158.
[2] *Untersuchungen zu Senecas dramatischer Technik* (1933).
[3] *Die Rezitationsdramen Senecas* (1966), also *GGA* ccxxii (1970) 196ff.
[4] Among representatives of this approach may be named G. Müller, E. Lefèvre, W. Steidle, B. Seidensticker; for the 'imagist' interpretation cf. N. T. Pratt, *TAPA* xciii (1963) 199ff., D. J. Mastronarde, *TAPA* ci (1971) 291ff.
[5] E. Lefèvre, *Hermes* xciv (1966) 482ff.; G. Streubel, *Senecas Agamemnon* (diss. Wien, 1963); Seidensticker 119ff.
[6] Zwierlein, *Rezitationsdramen* 105–7 treats points of detail. An extensive account of earlier criticism (of both types) is now available in Liebermann 207–31.

made to him by other persons of the drama;[1] these opinions are shaped by the *affectus* of the speaker, and characterise their source more than their object.

The insignificance of Agamemnon is striking. If it is taken as part of Seneca's design, important consequences follow, for it is clear that, on a notional rather than a theatrical level, Agamemnon (or, more precisely, his death) is the central and unifying point of the drama. Every figure in the play is affected by it and reacts to it, each from a distinct and personal point of view: Thyestes looks forward to Agamemnon's murder as his revenge on Atreus; Clytemestra plots the deed to avenge Iphigenia and to satisfy her own sexual vanity; Aegisthus aims solely for power, using Clytemestra as his instrument; Cassandra welcomes the event as a recompense for Troy's sufferings; Electra can see only the momentary triumph of evil; Strophius (928) and the Chorus (57ff.) recognise implied moral lessons about the impermanence of human happiness and the risks of power. These attitudes are presented *seriatim* and largely in isolation; the autonomous outlook of each character is carefully preserved, and the play does not compel choice among them. Only the moral seriousness and prominent place of the first chorus suggest that its implied response to the action is meant to be the most valid.

On a larger scale, these varied approaches to the central event are presented within a bipartite structure. The first two acts present Agamemnon's murder in a familial setting; the themes stressed, known to us from Aeschylus, are the self-perpetuation of crime[2] and the danger of high position. The second part of the play, from the entrance of the Trojan chorus (589), places the murder against the background of Troy's fall, developing a Euripidean equation of conqueror and conquered[3]

---

[1] As is done, for example, by Lefèvre, who makes Clytemestra's description of Agamemnon in 162ff. the basis of his reading.

[2] Note *sanguine alterno* (44), *scelus alternum* (77), *scelera semper sceleribus uincens domus* (169).

[3] Most notably in 752ff. *haec hodie ratis | Phlegethontis atri regias animas uehet, | uictamque uictricemque*, 870f. *resurgis, Troia: traxisti iacens | pares Mycenas*; also 730ff., 791ff., 1007ff.

and so demonstrating the emptiness of power under another aspect. Between these main sections comes the narrative of Eurybates describing Agamemnon's return from Troy to Greece (421–578); since it has no close connection with the action in either of its phases, it is an apt transitional element.[1] It is noteworthy that Seneca does not use it in Aeschylean fashion to involve the gods in Agamemnon's death; the only prominent appearance of a god is connected with the death of Ajax (527ff.).[2] Gods matter less in the play as a whole than *fortuna* and *fatum*: *fortuna* afflicts the exalted, including both Agamemnon (57ff.) and the Trojans (589ff.), while the action of a symmetrical, if not just, fate is a subsidiary theme in the 'Trojan' scenes.[3]

A unity of theme, then, is evident, to which almost every part of the play can be significantly related.[4] But this thematic consistency must not be mistaken for organic structure, nor must mere complexity be confused with success. Each part of the play is developed more for its own interest than for the light it casts on the central themes; a good example is the last choral song (808ff.), whose relation to the central action (Hercules the blameless captor of Troy as a foil to Agamemnon) is only an occasion for a colourful excursus on a congenial mythic *topos*. Seneca is equally unconcerned to produce close connections between scenes or to maintain tension: witness the separation of the prologue from its natural sequel (226ff.) and the resulting division of the second act into two unconnected episodes (108–225, 226–309), the presence of Eurybates' leisurely narrative in the central act,[5] the space given Cassandra's fevered visions in the fourth act, and the fragmented action of the finale.

---

[1] It introduces the equality of Greeks and Trojans in 511, 521ff.

[2] The allusive phrase *postquam litatum est Ilio* (577) cannot be compared with Aesch. *Ag.* 650ff.

[3] Note *fata se uertunt retro* (758), *uenere fata* (885), *ut paria fata Troicis lueret malis* (1008).

[4] Only 310–411 seem entirely ornamental (*pace* Seidensticker 131 n.163).

[5] Described by M. Coffey (*PACA* 1960, 16) as 'an enormous rhetorical cadenza, intrinsically brilliant, but too long to be accommodated to a dramatic structure'.

Seneca seems in fact most successful when his imagination is engaged by a thematically irrelevant aspect of the plot: the tormented self-awareness of Thyestes, the conflicting emotions of Clytemestra and their cool manipulation by Aegisthus, the rhetorical possibilities of the storm-narrative. By contrast, where theme is close to the surface, most notably in the dialogue between Agamemnon and Cassandra (791ff.),[1] the writing is both dramatically and rhetorically threadbare.

The combination of thematic unity with episodic structure may be paralleled in certain plays of Euripides,[2] and may indeed be one of Seneca's many indirect legacies from that dramatist. The result for *Agamemnon* is that the parts are of considerably greater interest than the whole, and that dramatic coherence and tension are relatively slight. The play is also curiously restrained; it cannot match the gross excesses of, for example, *Medea* and *Thyestes*, but as a consequence it does not arouse the revulsion characteristic of Senecan drama at its most effective.

DATE

Nothing useful can be said about the date of *Agamemnon*, and very little about that of the tragedies in general.[3] The genuine fixed points are few, and give only *termini ante quos*: 54 for *HF*, parodied in the *Apocolocyntosis*, and the early sixties for all the plays, imitated by Lucan, the writer of the Einsiedeln Eclogues, and perhaps Petronius.

The other evidence that has been adduced will not bear inspection: *Medea* 364ff. need not refer specifically to the conquest of Britain under Claudius and, even if it did, might be a later insertion; the controversy between Seneca and Pomponius Secundus over Pomponius's tragic diction (dated by

---

[1] Made the basis of his interpretation by Seidensticker (119ff.).
[2] Notably the *Phoenissae*; see the thematic analysis by E. Rawson, *GRBS* xi (1970) 109–27.
Bibliography and short discussion in M. Coffey, *Lustrum* ii (1957) 149–51.

Quintilian to his own youth, therefore *ca.* 50)[1] need not have been simultaneous with the composition of Seneca's own tragedies; the gibe reported by Tacitus[2] that Seneca *carmina crebrius factitauit* after Nero had developed a fondness for them would better fit the epigrams attributed to Seneca in the Latin Anthology than the plays. *Agamemnon* contains no visible allusions to contemporary events; it is surely misguided to suggest that the plot of regicide by a queen could only have occurred to Seneca after similar events had taken place in the Julio-Claudian house.[3] Parallels with Seneca's other works, though ubiquitous, are not close or specific enough to permit conclusions about priority.

Two of the most perceptive modern students of Seneca, Leo and Stuart, thought the plays were youthful productions; this is inherently plausible, and nothing speaks against it, though it cannot be proven. What should be clear, however, is that the fashionable interpretation of these works as 'Neronian' has no secure basis in fact; they could with equal justification be regarded as Claudian, Gaian, or even Tiberian.[4]

PRODUCTION

In interpreting *Agamemnon* I have assumed that Seneca wrote with recitation, not stage-production, in mind; by 'recitation' I mean public reading either by one person or by several persons dividing the roles among themselves. This is, I think, the most probable view, but its truth cannot be demonstrated. The most recent and best treatment of this old question[5] makes

---

[1] *Inst.* 8.3.31; Cichorius (*Römische Studien* (1922) 426-9) suggested a date shortly after 51.

[2] *Ann.* 14.52.

[3] The approach is exemplified by O. Herzog, *Rh. Mus.* lxxvii (1928) 51-104.

[4] 'In general the tragedies may have belonged to any stage of Seneca's literary career' (Coffey 150).

[5] O. Zwierlein, *Die Rezitationsdramen Senecas* (1966). Although some of Zwierlein's arguments and assumptions have been rightly criticised (cf. for example E. Lefèvre, *Gnomon* lx (1968) 782-9), attempts to refute his

it clear that Seneca deviates in many ways from the dramatic technique of fifth-century Greek tragedy, and that some Senecan scenes would be difficult or even impossible to stage within classical Greek conventions.[1] It is, however, dangerous to assume that notions of acceptable theatrical technique remained static between Euripides and Seneca; no complete tragedy survives from the Hellenistic, Republican, or Augustan period, and the pronouncements of theorists cannot compensate for this lack of evidence. I think it likely that Seneca followed the example of Ovid, and not that of his contemporary Pomponius Secundus,[2] in abandoning the theatre for the more refined atmosphere of the reciting hall.[3] His tragedies, however, even if not meant for the stage, have at least the appearance of drama, and at times its spirit as well. They require dramatic analysis, and I have on occasion used language appropriate to the theatre in speaking of events on Seneca's 'pseudo-stage'.[4]

SOURCES

A series of accidents has preserved some of the works of three Greek dramatists of the fifth century B.C. and ten plays written in the first century A.D., while no complete tragedy from the intervening half-millennium survives.[5] This coincidence, combined with Seneca's use of the same mythic plots as the Attic tragedians, helps to account for the widespread belief that

---

central positions have been unavailing (cf. B. Walker, *CP* lxiv (1969) 183–7). Discussion of the matter is not advanced by W. M. Calder III, *CP* lxx (1975) 32–5.

[1] A stage-production of *Agamemnon* would expose *lacunae* in the action at 108ff./125ff., between 225 and 226, at 780f. and after 909.

[2] It seems clear from Tac. *Ann.* 11.13 (*is carmina scaenae dabat*) that Pomponius composed for the theatre at least on occasion; for his probable involvement in recitation cf. p. 7 n.1.

[3] It is, of course, quite possible that Seneca's plays were given performances of some sort in or shortly after his own time, just as they are on occasion performed in theatres today.

[4] This useful term is that of W. S. Barrett (*Hippolytus*, p. 44 n.4).

[5] With the possible exception of the *Rhesus*.

fifth-century tragedy was Seneca's primary model and source of inspiration.[1] Even where the influence of a later writer must be admitted (as in the case of Ovid's *Medea*), it is often treated as a secondary source to be placed beside the Attic original.[2] Manifest differences between Seneca's plays and their putative models are at times implausibly explained as the result of contamination of more than one Greek source, even when this postulates an almost Alexandrian learning on Seneca's part.[3] Such knowledge of Greek tragedy would not have been typical for an educated Roman of the time;[4] it is, furthermore, nowhere displayed in Seneca's voluminous prose writings, where citations from tragedy are generally restricted to well-known *sententiae*.[5] A similar reticence is found in Quintilian, most of whose Euripidean citations are taken at second hand from Cicero,[6] and in Pliny the Younger, who mentions the tragedians not at all and Menander only once;[7] even Statius, well versed

---

[1] Cf. M. Coffey, *Lustrum* ii (1957) 144–9, H. J. Mette, *Lustrum* ix (1964) 183–5; e.g. C. Zintzen, *Analytisches Hypomnema zu Senecas Phaedra* (1960), B. Snell, *Scenes from Greek Tragedy* (1965) 23ff., Mazzoli 172 (with bibliography).

[2] The most recent editor of *Medea* remarks that 'so far as we can judge, Seneca's chief model was Euripides' play' (p. 8).

[3] E.g. Q. Cataudella, *REG* xciii (1966) 38–63; W. Braun, *de Senecae fabula quae inscribitur Troades* (1870); C. K. Kapnukajas, *Die Nachahmungstechnik Senecas* (1930) 3ff.

[4] H. I. Marrou, *Histoire de l'éducation dans l'antiquité*[6] (1965) 404–6, 248, 566. Ovid's list of tragic love-plots (*Tr.* 2.381ff.) might suggest that a learned Roman of his time had access to a large body of tragic texts, but his catalogue might also derive from an anthology, such as those of Timon of Phlius (Diog. Laert. 9.113). On Cicero's use and knowledge of Greek tragedy cf. H. D. Jocelyn, *YCS* xxiii (1973) 61–111.

[5] *Clem.* 2.2 (*adesp.* 513.1 N²), *Epist.* 31.11 (Eur. 1018 N²), 49.12 (Eur. *Phoen.* 469), 115.14 (*adesp.* 181.1, 461 N²; Eur. 324 N²), *Apocol.* 4.2 (Eur. 449 N²). The *Realien* in *NQ* 4.2.16 presumably derive from indirect tradition.

[6] *Inst.* 1.12.18 (from Cic. *de Or.* 2.187, *Tusc.* 2.47), 5.10.31; also 3.1.14 (Eur. 796 N²), in Aristotle's paraphrase, probably from Cic. *de Or.* 3.141; cf. A. Gwynn, *Roman education from Cicero to Quintilian* (1926) 226ff., A. Vergeest, *Poetarum Enarratio* (1950) 62.

[7] *Epist.* 6.21. The *Graeca tragoedia* written by Pliny at fourteen (7.4.2) may have had little relation to Attic tragedy (note the depreciatory phrase *tragoedia uocabatur*); there is no reason to accept Sherwin-White's suggestion that Pliny wrote a tragedy in the Senecan manner.

at Naples in Menander and the lyric poets, is silent concerning tragedy.[1] Ovid is perhaps the last Roman poet with a wide and deep knowledge of Greek tragedy.

In the case of *Agamemnon*, at least, no fifth-century play can be shown to have served as Seneca's model. Perhaps because of the prestige of Aeschylus' *Oresteia*, there is evidence of only two other Agamemnon-plays before 400, one by Ion of Chios and the other a work by an unknown poet perhaps produced at the Lenaea for 420/19.[2]

It seems incredible that the *Agamemnon* of Aeschylus could ever have been thought Seneca's source.[3] The basic outline of the plot is similar, but this Seneca need not have derived from Aeschylus; on the other hand, characterisation, structure, and themes are all quite unrelated. The only parts of Aeschylus' play which find a parallel in Seneca are the arrival of a herald with the news of the storm and a scene in which Cassandra foresees the murder of Agamemnon and herself; even here the similarity of situation is heavily outweighed by diversity of content and treatment. Nothing in Seneca's play requires direct knowledge of Aeschylus.[4]

The *Agamemnon* of Ion of Chios has received less attention in this context than it deserves;[5] it was famous enough in later centuries to elicit a commentary from Didymus,[6] and Ion him-

---

[1] *Silu.* 2.1.113f., 5.3.151ff. The *Thebais* contains no certain Aeschylean or Sophoclean influence (cf. D. W. T. C. Vessey, *Statius and the Thebaid* (1973) 69f.).

[2] *IG*² II.972 (Kohler); only ΑΓΑ is preserved. For the pretige of Aeschylus' play, cf. Pearson, *Fragments of Sophocles* 1.219.

[3] As maintained or implied by (e.g.) Buecheler, *Zentralblatt für Deutschland* xxx (1879) 965f.; Strauss (36); E. Paratore, *Dioniso* xv (1952) 210; Giomini (7); Runchina (192); Mette, *Lustrum* ix (1964) 183; Heldmann (2); Liebermann (216). See now W. M. Calder III, *CP* 71 (1976) 27ff.

[4] The 'fast wörtliche Übereinstimmungen' adduced by Buecheler, e.g. Seneca 83ff. and 96ff. with Aeschylus 461ff. and 470ff., do not bear inspection.

[5] For Ion cf. Bentley, *Epist. ad Jo. Millium* (304ff. Dyce), Diehl, *RE* ix.1861–8, T. B. L. Webster, *Hermes* lxiv (1936) 263ff. His *Agamemnon* was produced between 452/49 (Ion's first competition) and 421 (when he is spoken of as dead in Arist. *Pax* 835ff.).

[6] Athenaeus 468d.

self enjoyed high regard among the Alexandrian critics, who ranked him (and Achaeus) with Aeschylus, Sophocles, and Euripides. The fragments support the following inferences: a messenger entered in haste to inform Clytaemestra that Agamemnon had arrived;[1] Agamemnon himself probably entered on a ἅμαξα;[2] Ion seems to have returned to the Homeric account of Agamemnon's death;[3] finally, a verse of uncertain meaning[4] has been referred to a scene in which Aegisthus and Clytaemestra plot the death of Agamemnon[5] and to a scene after the murder in which Aegisthus (or Clytaemestra) threatens a recalcitrant Electra with protracted torment;[6] either suggestion, if true, would establish an important link between Ion and a non-Aeschylean element of Seneca's treatment. Direct imitation of Ion by Seneca is extremely unlikely, but Ion's play should be taken seriously as a potential influence on later Greek (and, conceivably, early Roman) treatments of the myth.

No positive evidence connects a post-classical Greek tragedy with a play of Seneca, and it is unlikely that the productions of this period were widely known at Rome at any time later than the second century B.C.[7] In many aspects of dramatic economy and technique, however, Senecan tragedy is the heir and only surviving exemplar of innovations which seem to have become canonical between the death of Euripides and the introduction of tragedy at Rome.[8] Among these developments are a five-act

---

[1] Fr. 1 N², perhaps also fr. 60 N²; the character who enters may be the watchman stationed by Aegisthus in *Od.* 4.524f. (The fragments have been collected and commented on by A. von Blumenthal (Stuttgart, 1939).)

[2] Fr. 3 N² ἱππικὸν χλίδος.

[3] Phot. *Lex.* p. 143.26 Reitzenstein: ἀπροσδοκήτως [γὰρ] καὶ ἄνοπλοι πορθούμεθα (κἄνοπλοι Reitzenstein).

[4] Fr. 2 N² κακῶν ἀπέστω θάνατος ὡς ἤδη κακά (κακῶν) ἓν κακόν Nauck).

[5] So von Blumenthal, Webster (266).

[6] K. Stackmann, *Class. et Med.* xi (1950) 219.

[7] Fragments and *testimonia*, cf. F. Schramm, *Tragoediae Graecae Aetatis Hellenisticae Fragmenta* (diss. Münster, 1929), B. Snell, *Tragicorum Graecorum Fragmenta* 1 (1971) 259ff.; survey, K. Ziegler, *RE* s.u. 'Tragoedia', VI.A.1971ff.

[8] The following paragraphs present the conclusions of an argument I hope to develop in another place; the discussion must be conducted with

structure, recommended by Horace (*A.P.* 189f.) and visible in Menander,[1] to which Seneca adheres in all the genuine plays except *Oedipus*; several elements of dramatic technique such as entrance-monologues,[2] asides,[3] handling of the chorus,[4] and small details of stage-business;[5] an interest in the development of individual scenes even to the occasional detriment of a coherent and unified structure.[6] Many of these 'post-classical' features can be seen first in the latest plays of Euripides and then in Menander; they probably characterised the tragedy of the fourth century as well and were absorbed into the Roman dramatic tradition by the Republican writers of tragedy and comedy.

The influence of Republican Latin tragedy must also be considered, although in my view Seneca is not likely to have used Republican tragedies as his immediate models. The tragedians of the Republic did not restrict their repertory to the works of Aeschylus, Sophocles, and Euripides; it is clear that they also adapted plays by other writers of the fifth century and by major figures of the fourth,[7] but the role (if any) played by Hellenistic tragedy is still debated.[8] Even if the Romans did not use Hellenistic plays as models, though, they could hardly have escaped the influence of Hellenistic literary criticism and attitudes; what they imitated and adapted was not fifth-century

---

reference to the Senecan corpus as a whole, and is thus unsuitable in an introduction to a single play.
1 See Brink's note *ad loc.* for details.
2 Zwierlein 67–72; cf. my note on 226ff., 918ff.
3 Zwierlein 63–7.
4 Leo, *Rh. Mus.* lii (1897) 509ff.; Jocelyn 19 n.4; Sifakis, *Studies in the history of Hellenistic drama* (London, 1967) 115 n.2.
5 See notes on 308f., 788.
6 O. Regenbogen's influential term was 'Auflösung des Dramenkörpers' (*Vorträge der Bibliothek Warburg* vii (1927/8) 187ff.); cf. also W.-H. Friedrich, *Untersuchungen zu Senecas dramatischer Technik* (1933), Zwierlein 85ff.
7 Leo, *Geschichte der römischen Literatur* (1913) 70f., 227–9, 396–9; H. J. Mette, *Lustrum* ix (1964) *passim*; H. D. Jocelyn, *Entretiens sur l'antiquité classique* xvii (1972) 46ff.
8 S. Mariotti, *Livio Andronico e la traduzione artistica* 63ff.; Jocelyn, *Tragedies of Ennius* 7–12.

tragedy itself, but classical tragedy as understood in the Hellenistic world.[1]

It is on general grounds improbable that Seneca knew Republican tragedy well or thought highly of it.[2] His prose works cite in general only well-known tags or passages also attested in intermediate writers (most often Cicero).[3] In addition, his poor opinion of Ennius (known from a passage preserved by Aulus Gellius[4]) makes it likely that Seneca shared the scorn for old drama expressed by several Augustan, Neronian, and Flavian writers.[5]

While most of the specific connections alleged between Seneca and the Republican dramatists will not bear inspection,[6] there are clear similarities of plot between *Agamemnon* and Livius Andronicus' *Aegisthus* and Accius' *Clytemestra*.[7] Livius' play (whose Greek source is not known) coincides with Seneca's in several deviations from Aeschylus: a messenger reported the Greek homecoming in a leisurely narrative;[8] Agamemnon was apparently murdered at a banquet,[9] and this was also reported in third-person narrative; Electra taunted her mother with Agamemnon's murder[10] and took sanctuary, from which either

---

[1] I. Mariotti, *MH* xxii (1965) 206ff.

[2] Leo, *Rh. Mus.* lii (1897) 510; *Monolog* 40 n.2; *Plautinische Forschungen*[2] 24; *Geschichte* 70 n.5. Leo's position was elaborated by his pupil F. Strauss (*de ratione inter Senecam et ueteres Romanas fabulas intercedente*, diss. Rostock, 1887). Many writers take a different view, cf. Mazzoli 195 n.46.

[3] For example, *Ira* 1.19.4, *Epist.* 102.16, 8.8f.; Mazzoli 188–98.

[4] *N.A.* 12.2.11.

[5] Hor. *Epist.* 2.1.18ff., Persius 1.76ff., Mart. 11.90, Tac. *Dial.* 20.8, cp. Cic. *Brutus* 71 (on Livius Andronicus).

[6] For example, Sen. *Med.* 176 – Acc. 619 R[2] (cf. Eur. fr. 1066 N[2]); Sen. *HF* 338ff. – Acc. 272 R[2] (and *inc. inc. fab. com.* 128 R[2]), cf. Philemon fr. 180 Kock; Sen. *Oed.* 86 – Acc. 460 R[2]; Sen. *Thy.* 992ff. – Acc. 223ff. R[2], *Thy.* 221ff. – Acc. 205, 229ff. R[2]; Sen. *Med.* 845f. – Enn. 235 R[2] (cf. Eur. *Med.* 1069f.).

[7] Accius's *Aegisthus* has also been compared (cf. Ribbeck, *Römische Tragödie* 465), but this play was probably about the return of Orestes (cf. Leo, *Obs.* 159; Strauss 44 n.1).

[8] Fr. I (1) R[2], cp. Seneca 421; fr. II (2–4) R[2], cp. Seneca 449ff.

[9] Fr. VI (10–11) R[2] *in sedes conlocat se regias:* | *Clytemestra iuxtim, tertias natae occupant;* fr. VII (12) R[2] *ipsus se in terram saucius fligit cadens;* see note on 875.

[10] Fr. III (7) R[2] *iamne oculos specie laetauisti optabili?*

Clytemestra or Aegisthus ordered her to be removed.[1] The fragments of Accius' *Clytemestra* supplement the outline of Livius' play to a remarkable degree, and no fragment of Accius is incompatible with what can be known about Livius' *Aegisthus*;[2] it has been suggested that both plays depend on the same Greek source. Together their fragments provide a precedent for several non-Aeschylean features of Seneca's treatment, but not even here is there sufficient evidence to justify speaking of a direct Republican influence on Seneca.

The loss of Augustan tragedy has deprived us of the greatest Roman achievements in this genre, Ovid's *Medea* and Varius' *Thyestes*.[3] In addition, it has distorted our view of an important episode in dramatic history: many aspects of Senecan dramatic procedure probably derive from Augustan precedent and inspiration, and the Augustans may have been responsible for the synthesis of classical myth, Hellenistic canons of form, elements of archaic diction, and great stylistic refinement which we associate with Senecan drama. No Augustan treatment of the Agamemnon-story is known, but this is no reason to doubt the existence of such a work. The play at which Tiberius took offence for its vilification of Agamemnon[4] is not likely to have dealt with the material of Seneca's tragedy; if it was not the *Atreus* of Mamercus Aemilius Scaurus,[5] an *Ajax* or *Iphigenia* are more plausible subjects.

---

[1] Fr. VIII (13–14) R² *quin quod parere* [*mihi*] *uos maiestas mea | procat, toleratis temploque hanc deducitis?*

[2] Storm-narrative (fr. III–V (32–5) R², *inc. inc. fab.* 21); solemn arrival of Agamemnon (Cic. *Fam.* 7.1.2); scene in which Cassandra foresees her own death (fr. VII (38) R²); encounter after the murder between Electra and Clytemestra, possibly involving Aegisthus (fr. I (28) R²?, x (41); *inc. fab.* 6, *inc. inc. fab.* 67–8).

[3] Quintilian, *Inst.* 10.1.98, Tac. *Dial.* 12; Leo, *Obs.* 147ff.

[4] Tac. *Ann.* 6.29, Suet. *Tib.* 61.3.

[5] As asserted by Dio Cassius 58.24.3f.

SOURCES

INTERNAL EVIDENCE

A writer's use of a source can at times be revealed by internal analysis, since inconsistencies within a work may be the result of deviations from the order of an earlier treatment. This approach has frequently been applied to Seneca's tragedies, but often with insufficient tact and understanding; it is surely unsound method to assume, as several writers seem to have done, that every offence against logic in a Senecan play betrays deformation of a flawless Greek model.[1] With the danger of misplaced subtlety in mind, I have tried to make the following discussion brief and appropriately tentative.

Two arguments combine to suggest that the first scene of the second act (108–225) is a Senecan addition:[2] the close link between Thyestes' address to Aegisthus (48ff.) and Aegisthus' first lines (226ff.);[3] the absence of transition between the two scenes of Act II and the different attitudes of Clytemestra in

---

[1] The dangers of this approach are well illustrated by K. Stackmann's ingenious but quite unconvincing treatment of *Agamemnon* (*Class. et Med.* xi (1950) 180–221). The inconsistencies adduced are trifling, when not illusory: Clytemestra's awareness of Helen's return in 273ff. and her inquiry about Menelaus and Helen in 404a (but the earlier passage is textually suspect, the later one certainly corrupt); the long intervals between the arrivals of Eurybates, the Trojans, and Agamemnon (parallels are available in Aeschylus' *Agamemnon* and Sophocles' *Trachiniae*); the ability of Clytemestra (586) and Electra (950) to identify Cassandra, whom they have not previously seen (but Clytemestra at least knows that Cassandra is to return with Agamemnon, cf. 189ff.). As Seneca's source Stackmann postulated a lost Greek play in which Clytemestra had been told of Agamemnon's infidelities by Oeax (cf. Hyg. *fab.* 117, implausibly used in reconstructing Accius' *Clytemestra* by Welcker and Ribbeck), and was then convinced of his adultery by the arrival of Cassandra, sent ahead on a separate ship. His only evidence for the latter variation is Dracontius, a notoriously unsure guide to the shape of his sources (cf. P. Langlois, *Real-Lexicon f. Religion u. Ethik*, s.u. 'Dracontius', pp. 263ff.), and even in Dracontius Cassandra's early arrival does not play the part assigned to it in the hypothetical source.

[2] This is one of Stackmann's valid observations; see also E. Paratore, *Dioniso* xv (1952) 210f.; Giomini 55; Runchina 292.

[3] In Attic tragedy prologue-speakers address characters about to enter and speak, cf. Eur. *Hipp.* 51, *Hec.* 58, *Tro.* 36, *Ion* 78, *Ba.* 55.

each.[1] In adding the scene Seneca may have wished to present a more sympathetic and complex portrait of Clytemestra, based on Euripides and Ovid.[2] The scene is a typical specimen of a favourite Senecan form of exposition and character-drawing;[3] the problems which the opening speeches would pose in a stage-performance are also characteristically Senecan.

The first three acts of the play offer little ground for further speculation. The moralising first chorus might be a Senecan addition, like the scene which follows; the stronger characterisation and religious language of the second ode make it a suitable *parodos*.

The subsidiary chorus of captives might also be an interpolation.[4] It is imperfectly integrated into the play's action, as is shown by the problem of knowing when, if at all, the Trojans leave the stage after their first entrance;[5] such ambiguity would be surprising in a tragedy written for the classical stage. Seneca's fondness for the captive chorus is evident from *Troades*,[6] and the author of *Hercules Oetaeus* clearly saw this as a Senecan characteristic.

In the fourth act two points require discussion. L. Strzelecki[7] has alleged the influence of Euripides' *Alexandros* on the prophetic speech of Cassandra (720ff.), principally because of its allusion to the judgement of Paris (730ff.). The *Alexandros* did contain a prophetic speech of Cassandra, but both its place in

---

[1] See p. 217 below.

[2] *Ars* 2.399ff. Ovid need not have had any source for his handling of the story, since he is writing to exemplify the maxim *ludite, sed furto celetur culpa modesto* (2.389); in a comparable passage dealing with Paris and Helen (2.359ff.), however, his *color* has Euripidean precedent (*Tro.* 945ff.), and for the portrayal of Clytemestra cf. Accius 38–9 R².

[3] See introduction to Act II.

[4] J. Lammers (*Die Doppel- und Halb-Chöre in der antiken Tragödie* (diss. Paderborn, 1931) 133ff.) suggests that Seneca took the Trojan chorus from a post-classical *Agamemnon*, but offers no evidence for this view.

[5] See note on *Agam.* 775ff.

[6] Leo, *Obs.* 97.

[7] *De Senecae Agamemnone Euripidisque Alexandro* (*Travaux de la Société des Sciences et des Lettres de Varsovie*, ser. A, no. 33, 1949). Strzelecki's assertions have been accepted by Runchina (pp. 220–6) and Webster (*Tragedies of Euripides* 168).

the play and its contents are unclear; several writers have doubted that it described the judgement in detail,[1] and Strzelecki's only reason for believing that it did is the alleged imitation by Seneca. His other parallels are so dubious or slight that they would carry weight only if Seneca's debt to the *Alexandros* had been established on other grounds; as proof of such a connection they are worthless.[2] The *Alexandros* cannot be ruled out as a source for the speech (if it indeed has a source, and is not a free composition based loosely on Virgilian themes), but nothing more positive can be said.

The maladroit handling of Agamemnon's arrival (780f.) also calls for comment. Seneca elsewhere avoids comparison with the set-pieces of Greek tragedy by omitting or curtailing scenes from a Greek antecedent,[3] but this may also have been a characteristic of Hellenistic or Augustan tragedy. Perhaps the only clue the scene offers is the description of Clytemestra's movements in 780f.; would a dramatist uninterested in staging have troubled to account for Clytemestra's actions in such an awkward way if he were not following a source? These lines, and the allusions to Clytemestra in the ensuing dialogue (794f.), make it plausible that her part has shrunk from one of greater prominence in an earlier treatment.[4]

The last act of *Agamemnon* contains the clearest parallel to Republican drama; a scene after the murder involving at least

---

[1] So Snell (*Hermes* Einzelschriften v (1937) 53f.), supported by Jocelyn (217–20), who attempts to show that the explicit references in Enn. 54 R² (47 J) *eheu uidete: iudicauit inclitum iudicium inter deas tris aliquis* is an Ennian insertion; T. C. W. Stinton puts the case for a detailed prophecy of the judgement in *Euripides and the judgement of Paris* (1965) 68–71.

[2] For example, he compares Sen. *Ag.* 707–8 with *fr. inc.* 968 N² Ἑκάτης ἄγαλμα φωσφόρον κύων ἔσῃ; but the fragment is not certainly from *Alexandros*, the myth was widely known and referred to, and the situation in Seneca is quite different.

[3] Note the compression of *Oed.* 764–83 (cf. Soph. *O.T.* 698–862) and the omission of the Theseus–Hippolytus *agon* (Eur. *Hipp.* 902–1101) in *Phaedra*; cf. C. Lindskog, *Studien zum antiken Drama* II (1897) 14ff.

[4] W.-H. Friedrich (*Untersuchungen* 124 n.1) cites Accius *inc. fab.* 36 R² *cur me miseram inridet, magnis compotem et multis malis?* as evidence for a scene in Accius' *Clytemestra* in which the title character appeared as in Aeschylus (cf. *Agam.* 1035ff.).

Electra and her mother (and perhaps Aegisthus and Cassandra as well) is certainly attested for Livius and Accius.[1] Such a scene therefore occurred in a Greek tragedy. Sophocles' *Electra* has often been cited as Seneca's model,[2] but the resemblances are in fact slight and could be due to the similarity of situation;[3] alternatively, Sophocles may have been himself influenced by an Agamemnon-play of another dramatist.[4] No firm conclusion seems possible.

Strophius' appearance as a speaking character has no surviving Greek or Roman parallel; the dramatists keep his protection of Orestes on the periphery of the action,[5] and the only references to an episode in which Electra herself gives Orestes to Strophius come from mythographers and scholiasts.[6] Seneca may have dramatised what he found narrated in Sophocles or Euripides,[7] but it is more economical to suppose that the lost source of Livius and Accius contained this scene as well.

The awkward 'joins' at 909f., 950, and 1001 suggest that Seneca has grafted scenes involving Cassandra on to a structure originally dominated by Electra. If in the source Cassandra died with Agamemnon (as in Aeschylus), her clairvoyant narrative (867ff.) would be a Senecan innovation; so, too, would be the last lines of the play, in which Cassandra's defiant exultation is expressed in language ultimately derived from Euripides.[8]

---

[1] See above, pp. 13f.

[2] As early as the time of Daniel Heinsius (cf. ed. Scriveriana, pp. 332ff.).

[3] The closest parallels are between *Agam.* 988ff. and Soph. *El.* 379ff.; see commentary on 988ff.

[4] Ion's *Agamemnon* must have been produced before 421, and Sophocles' *Electra* is almost certainly later than that date.

[5] Aesch. *Ag.* 88of., Soph. *El.* 11ff. (cf. Eur. *El.* 539f.).

[6] Ps.-Apoll. *Epit.* 6.24, Servius on *Aen.* 4.471; but Hyg. *fab.* 117 implies an agent.

[7] Runchina (283).

[8] Sen. *Agam.* 1005, cf. Eur. *Tro.* 445, 46of.

APPENDIX: *NARRATIVE OF EURYBATES* (421–578)

Seneca's account of the storm owes nothing to Aeschylus.[1] A narration of the event formed part of the post-Aeschylean play adapted by Livius and Accius, but Seneca had other sources for this part of the play, and drew on non-tragic material as well.[2]

Seneca's narrative comprises three distinct episodes: the storm which overtook the Greeks on the return voyage from Troy, the death of Ajax Oileus at the hands of Athena and Poseidon, and the deceit of Nauplius. Each of these stories is quite old, and both the storm and the death of Ajax are found in the *Odyssey*. Homer, however, does not relate the incidents at length, nor does he connect Ajax's death with the great storm or with Athena's revenge for the rape of Cassandra.[3] Nauplius does not appear in Homer.

It is often alleged that all three episodes were narrated in the Cyclic *Nostoi*;[4] the evidence, however, is not conclusive. Proclus refers to the death of Ajax 'at the Capherean rocks',[5] but the Euboean coast was the traditional setting, and so no allusion to Nauplius need be inferred. Nothing rules out a role for Nauplius in one of the numerous and lengthy *nostos*-poems,[6] but his story may have been quite separate from that of the storm and death of Ajax.[7]

The Cyclic poems did connect the impiety of Ajax and the storm,[8] a theme further developed by Alcaeus,[9] who contains the earliest preserved record of a motif often found in later writers: the Greeks are shipwrecked because of one man's fault, which they share for not killing him on the

---

[1] See commentary on lines 421ff.
[2] For example, Cic. *Diu.* 1.13 and Virg. *G.* 1.356ff., 458ff. for *Ag.* 462ff.; Virg. *Aen.* 1.81 ff. and Ovid, *Met.* 11.480ff. for many details of the storm.
[3] Cf. 3.130ff., 3.276ff., 4.495ff., 5.108f.; Strabo 13.1.40, p. 600.
[4] So Frazer on ps.-Apollod. *Epit.* 6.7, Pearson, *Fragments of Sophocles* II.80, Rzach in *RE* s.u. 'Kyklos' XI.2.2424, G. L. Huxley, *Greek epic poetry* (1969) 165; F. Vian (*Recherches* 79), however, is properly cautious.
[5] P. 53 Kinkel; cf. *Od.* 4.495ff., Eur. *Tro.* 84, 89ff.
[6] Cf. Rzach 2422.
[7] The explicit statement of ps.-Apollodorus (*Bibl.* 2.1.5) that the writer of the *Nostoi* called the wife of Nauplius Philyra is the best evidence for his appearance in the work.
[8] Cf. Proclus's summary of Arctinus's *Iliupersis* (pp. 49f. Kinkel).
[9] P. Colon. 2021 + P. Oxy. 2303 fr. 1 (a); cf. R. Merkelbach, *ZPE* i (1967) 81ff., W. Barner, *Neuere Alkaios-Papyri aus Oxyrhynchus* (= *Spudasmata* xiv (1967)) 187ff.

spot.[1] Alcaeus seems to have made Athena alone responsible for the storm, and to have used the story as a παράδειγμα for the inevitable punishment of arrogance;[2] Nauplius can have played no part in such an account. Stesichorus also treated the *nostos* in an apparently long poem, but almost nothing is known of its contents.[3]

The subject was popular with tragic poets in both the fifth and fourth centuries, but there is no clear evidence that the three incidents of Seneca's narrative were ever combined. Aeschylus[4] describes only the storm, ignoring both Ajax and Nauplius; the storm was foretold by the ghost of Achilles in Sophocles' *Polyxena*[5] and described in his *Teucer*,[6] probably the source of Pacuvius's famous storm-narrative in a popular play of the same name.[7] The fragments of Pacuvius include several details which also appear in Seneca's account,[8] suggesting that Sophocles (or Pacuvius) had at least an indirect influence on Seneca's narrative;[9] there is no sign, though, that Sophocles mentioned Ajax or Nauplius in *Teucer*. Each of these figures was the subject of a Sophoclean tragedy; *Nauplius Pyrcaeus* is more likely than *Ajax Locrus* to have contained a comprehensive narrative,[10] but no positive evidence survives. The prologue of Euripides' *Troades* treats the storm as Athena's revenge for the impiety of Ajax, but mentions neither Ajax's death nor Nauplius; in *Helen*, on the other hand, Nauplius is touched on twice in isolation from the other events.[11] The *Nauplius* of Timotheus contained a storm-narrative which excited ridicule in a contemporary,[12] and Naupliusplays were also composed by Astydamas[13] and Philocles.[14] It should also be

---

[1] Cf. Eur. *Tro.* 65ff., Lycophron, *Alex.* 365f., Virg. *Aen.* 1.42f., Quint. Smyrn. 14.419ff.

[2] Cf. Merkelbach 81, Barner 199–201.

[3] A brief summary in J. Tzetzes' *Posthomerica* 750ff.

[4] *Agam.* 650ff.

[5] Fr. 525 P (= 482 N²); on the play cf. W. M. Calder III, *GRBS* vii (1966) 49.

[6] Fr. 578 P (= 520 N²); cf. also Arist. *Nub.* 583f.

[7] Cf. Cic. *de Or.* 1.246, 2.193; Ribbeck, *Römische Tragödie* 223ff.

[8] (a) Smooth sailing marked by the sight of dolphins (Pac. 408–10 R², Sen. 431–55); (b) outbreak of storm at sunset (Pac. 411 R², Sen. 46off.); (c) unnatural darkness broken only by lightning (Pac. 412–13 R², Sen. 47off., 494ff.); (d) struggle of conflicting winds (Pac. 415f. R², Sen. 474ff.); (e) damage to the ships (Pac. 333–6 R², Sen. 497ff.).

[9] Direct use by Seneca of either Sophocles or Pacuvius is less likely than imitation of an intermediate source, possibly Augustan.

[10] The structure of both plays, however, is conjectural.

[11] 767f., 1132ff.

[12] Athenaeus 338a (where Ναυπλίῳ is Casaubon's correction for Ναυτίλῳ, cf. Suidas IV.557.1 Adler); cf. Haupt, *Opuscula* III. 611f.

[13] Cf. Nauck² 779.   [14] Suidas IV.727.25 Adler.

noted that the unknown Greek source of Accius' *Clytemestra* contained a report of the storm which incorporated the death of Ajax.[1]

One or more lost tragic messenger-speeches may have combined for the first time the storm, the death of Ajax, and the treachery of Nauplius; the loose sense of dramatic relevance presupposed by such a sprawling narrative may point to a fourth-century play.

The earliest surviving work containing the complete series of events described by Seneca is Lycophron's *Alexandra*;[2] the action must be seen through the distorting-mirror of Lycophron's style, but the outlines of the story are quite clear.[3] Lycophron's treatment seems to have been without influence; this is not likely to have been so for a nearly contemporary work, Callimachus' *Aetia*, which presented the storm and death of Ajax as the consequence of Athena's anger.[4] There is no evidence that Callimachus included Nauplius, but if he did so, it must have been before narrating Ajax's death (as in Lycophron). A third Hellenistic witness emerges from an unexpected source, a puppet-show described in Hero of Alexandria's *Automatopoetica* (and perhaps taken from Philo of Byzantium).[5] Some unique features of this handling result from the special limitations of the puppet-theatre: for example, Nauplius appears together with Athena because both are seen at a higher level than the ships (which are out of sight during this scene); this rearrangement may explain why Ajax's death is shown last, and the similarity to the order of events in Lycophron (and Callimachus?) may be fortuitous. When allowances have been made for the special character of the performance, the following elements can be recognised: the Greeks prepare to depart and launch their ships; at first the weather is fair and they encounter some dolphins, but then the sea grows rough; Nauplius raises his beacon, and the ships are wrecked; Athena threatens with the thunderbolt and strikes Ajax, drowning him. The show clearly has its basis in a literary account, but no certain identification of the source seems possible. A tragic messenger-speech has been suggested, and indeed the similarity to what can be surmised of Sophocles' *Teucer* is noticeable,[6] but a later tragic handling or a Hellenistic poem such as the *Aetia* are equally plausible sources. Most important is the clear evidence that the structure of Seneca's account

---

[1] For the fragments cf. above, pp. 13f.; those relating to the storm show that Jupiter was active (*deum regnator nocte caeca caelum e conspectu abstulit* 32 R²) and that Ajax was struck by a thunderbolt, cf. 36f. R², Virg. *Aen.* 1.42.

[2] 361–97.

[3] The order 'storm–Nauplius–death of Ajax' may be rhetorical and thus not derived from an earlier handling.

[4] Fr. 35 Pf. (= schol. AD on *Il.* 13.66).

[5] 22.3–6 (p. 264 Schmid).

[6] Sophocles' *Nauplius Pyrcaeus* was suggested by Schmid (praef. lxi), cf. Tittel, *RE* VIII.1.1051.

appeared in an important literary work of the third century B.C. or earlier.[1]

Only one other detailed poetic treatment of Seneca's material survives, in the last book of Quintus of Smyrna's *Posthomerica*. Inspection reveals numerous points of contact with Seneca, which have most often been referred to a common source,[2] while a minority view, with eminent support, holds that Quintus used Seneca himself, as well as Virgil and Ovid.[3] Imitation of Virgil raises no problem, since the *Aeneid* had been translated into Greek as early as the first century A.D.;[4] Quintus' alleged borrowing from Ovid is a rhetorical *color* which may have been familiar to him from Greek declaimers.[5] Knowledge of Seneca's tragedies by a fourth-century Greek, however, remains hard to credit, even though the awareness of Latin literature by Greek writers of late antiquity has recently been shown to be greater than previously supposed.[6] Probability therefore inclines toward the hypothesis of a common source, and comparison of the two accounts strengthens this view: the same events appear in different contexts;[7] similar situations are narrated in unrelated ways;[8] each account contains many narrative elements not found in the other;[9] finally, while Quintus' borrowings from Homer, tragedy, Apollonius and Aratus are often demonstrable by exact verbal correspondences, there is no Senecan *color* in the whole of Quintus.[10]

---

[1] I do not propose to discuss in detail here the accounts preserved in the mythographical works attributed to Apollodorus and Hyginus: the sources and dates of composition of these collections are too uncertain to permit secure conclusions to be drawn; it is also possible, in particular for 'Apollodorus', that the comprehensiveness of the narrative does not reflect the structure of any single source.

[2] Liedloff 17; R. Wagner, *Epitoma Vaticana* (1891) 262; R. Heinze, *Virgils Epische Technik*[3] 77f.; F. Vian, *Recherches* 98f., 101ff., *Notice* 171ff.

[3] R. Keydell, *Würzburger Jahrbuch* iv (1949/50) 81ff., *Gnomon* xxxiii (1961) 278ff.; also L. Ferreri, *Osservazioni su Quinto Smirneo* (1963) 34.

[4] Sen. *Cons. Pol.* 8.2, 11.5.   [5] Quintus 5.218ff., cf. Ovid, *Met.* 13.121f.

[6] A. Cameron, *Claudian* (1970) 19f., 316; knowledge of Ovid by Nonnus is suggested by Diggle, *Phaethon* (1970) 9, 180ff.

[7] Quintus 394/Seneca 458f.; Quintus 460ff./Seneca 470ff.; Quintus 602ff./Seneca 485ff.

[8] Quintus 370ff./Seneca 421ff.; Quintus 497ff./Seneca 507ff.

[9] Quintus 383ff., 419ff., 505ff., 519ff., 551ff., 614ff.; Seneca 431, 442, 444ff., 476ff., 517ff., 547ff., 558ff.

[10] Characteristic Senecan *colores* would include 446ff., 495f., 499f., 510, 513ff., 517ff., 532, 547ff. In the only place where Quintus and Seneca make a similar rhetorical point (Quintus 588f./Seneca 553ff.), the additional parallel in Ovid, *Ibis* 340f. suggests that the point may derive from the common source.

The common source of Seneca and Quintus cannot be identified with confidence, but a poem extensive enough to have provided both writers with much of their material and well-known enough to have influenced them both[1] is not likely to have been written later than the third century B.C. The most plausible candidates are a tragic rhesis such as that of Sophocles' *Teucer* or a Hellenistic poem such as the *Aetia*. The structure of the source is probably better reflected by Quintus than by Seneca, who has clearly recast much of the material to suit his method of schematic exposition arranged by topics.

THE MANUSCRIPTS

A complete account of the MS tradition of the tragedies would fill a large book and cannot be written at all in the present, incomplete state of knowledge. The census of MSS compiled, though not published, by C. E. Stuart in the years 1906–8 listed slightly more than 300; this already large number is being significantly increased by the current researches of A. P. MacGregor. Until all these late medieval and Renaissance copies have been examined, an editor's view of the transmission and the conclusions drawn from it for recension must be to an extent provisional.[2] The working hypothesis now generally accepted[3] includes the following basic points: the text is preserved in two branches (E and A), each of which may in a given passage offer a true and authentic reading; where E and A differ, therefore, the recension is open; the A branch survives in two subdivisions, one (δ) represented by P alone (and by G in *Octauia*),[4] the other (β) comprising virtually all remaining

---

[1] And perhaps Virgil as well, cf. Vian, *Recherches* 80 and *Notice* 175 on *Aen.* 1.37ff.

[2] This text of *Agamemnon* is based on personal collation of slightly more than sixty MSS and excerpt collections.

[3] Recent syntheses: W. Woesler, *Senecas Tragödien. Die Überlieferung der α-Klasse dargestellt am Beispiel der Phaedra* (1965); R. H. Philp, *CQ* N.S. xviii (1968) 150–79.

[4] A. P. MacGregor has called attention to Paris B.N. Lat. 8031 (s. xv), which has some striking agreements in error with P and G (most notably at *Octauia* 669ff.); it is, however, not yet clear whether or not this manuscript should be regarded as a member of the δ-group. See Addenda.

MSS, of which CS are the purest specimens known; the reading of A can be recovered (1) when P CS agree, (2) when P or CS agree with E against the other.

In the following pages I take these as points of departure, directing attention to areas where uncertainty persists or where new information is available. I have not attempted to write a history of the text, since this, too, requires much further investigation of the fourteenth- and fifteenth-century material; R. H. Rouse's brilliant treatment of the thirteenth-century transmission[1] may serve as both a model and an incentive for such a study.

CATALOGUE OF MSS CONSULTED[2]

E Florence, Biblioteca Medicea-Laurenziana, plut. lat. 37.13: generally called 'codex Etruscus' (formerly Florentinus and Marcianus): vellum: late eleventh century, central or North Italy: 233 × 155 (185 × 105 ruled); originally larger (fourteenth-century headings cut off): ff. iv + 165 + iv (one vellum and three paper fly-leaves at each end; f. 160 a slip, 165 × 155): 33 long lines (except ff. 81^r, 100^r, 151^r, which are double-columned), ruled in drypoint with double vertical and horizontal bounding lines; writing begins above top ruled line: collation 1–19^8, 20^8 (+1 (f. 160) inserted after 7), 21^4; quire-signatures in red at end from f. 24^v onwards: catchwords visible on f. 8^v, 16^v, 72^v, 80^v, 88^v, 120^v (others presumably cut off): plain red lettering used for headings, *personarum notae*, metrical descriptions, first letter of each scene (2–4 lines high), and first letter of each line (in ff. 25^v–77^v red and black alternate); on f. 1^r the list of

---

[1] *Revue d'Histoire des Textes* i (1971) 93–121.

[2] With the exception of the Scorialensis (S), the Milanese *recentiores* (M1–4) and the Brussels Excerpts (Brux), I have inspected all MSS in this catalogue *in situ*. The form of the descriptions is based on that used by A. C. de la Mare in her catalogue of the Lyell MSS in the Bodleian (Oxford, 1971, cf. xxxi–xxxiii).

titles of the plays is enclosed in a double ovoid frame, in red: binding, thick boards covered with red leather, with red leather clasps and brass corner guards and bosses bearing the Medici coat of arms (possibly fifteenth-century).

2° fo. fractum atque domitum est (*HF* 33).

Contents: f. 1ʳ (1) Definition of tragedy derived from Isidore (18.45 and 8.7.5): *tragedi sunt qui antiqua gesta*... *imaginem fictis*. (2) 'Epitaphium Senecae' (*P.L.M.* v.386 Baehrens): *Cura labor meritum*...*Reddimus ossa tibi*. (3) List of titles in decorative frame. (4) Metrical note: 'metrum verbicum Archiloicum constat trimetro acatalectico'.

Above these texts are two *ex libris* notes. The higher is now nearly illegible: a transcription done by E. Bertagno in 1916 records only '........de .....ban...ex p(ar)te Occide' (tear), while Giardina (praef. viii) gives 'liber iste traiediarum. de ???? bancho Ex parte Occide ////' (my own inspection of the MS did not reveal any more than was seen by Bertagno). The lower note is better preserved: 'iste liber e(st) co(n)uentus ṣ/// marci de flo(renti)a ordinis p(re)di̧c(atorum) h(ab)itus de heredi-tate [N]icolai ///// uiri do̧ctissimi (et) flore(n)[tissimi'.

f. 1ᵛ–22ʳ *Hercules Furens* ('HERCULES')
f. 22ʳ–40ʳ *Troades* ('INCIPIT FELICITER TROADVM', f. 22ʳ)
f. 40ʳ–50ᵛ *Phoenissae*
f. 50ᵛ–67ᵛ *Medea*
f. 67ᵛ–86ʳ *Phaedra*
f. 86ʳ–102ᵛ *Oedipus* ('OEDYPPVS' f. 86ʳ; 'OEDIPPVS' f. 102ᵛ)
f. 102ᵛ–118ᵛ *Agamemnon* ('AGAMENNON')
f. 118ᵛ–136ʳ *Thyestes*
f. 136ʳ–165ʳ *Hercules Oetaeus* ('HERCULES')

The text is written by a single scribe throughout, in a good late Caroline minuscule (*HO* 182–225 were omitted, and are written on a slip pasted in following f. 159, i.e. after *HO* 1712). At least two later hands can be distinguished: the earlier (fourteenth-century?) entered the titles of the plays at the top of each page and added marginal notes, often quite substantial, all of which were later erased; those on f. 93 and f. 106 are partially visible (script and colour of ink match those of the effaced *ex libris* on f. 1^r). The later hand (fifteenth-century cursive) has noted variants in the margin (e.g. f. 25^v *hysmenos* for *lyrnesos* in *Tro.* 221; *caicus* for *calchus* in 228). It is uncertain whether the hand which has entered readings (usually those of A) in the text in places where E's original reading has been erased is to be identified with either of these later hands; the script is clumsy and ill-spaced, and might represent an attempt by the fifteenth-century corrector to write an old-fashioned book-hand.

The later history of E has long been known. It was willed to the library of San Marco in Florence by Niccolò Niccoli (*ex libris*, f. 1^r), and was seen and consulted there by Poliziano.[1] The origin and early history of the MS, however, are still unclear. Billanovich has suggested that E is the very MS of the *Tragedies* registered in the 1093 catalogue of the monastery of Pomposa,[2] and that Lovato Lovati discovered E at Pomposa shortly before 1300.[3] Though widely accepted,[4] the hypothesis appears to rest on a chain of circumstantial evidence: Lovato's use of a Pomposa MS of Justin's *Epitome* (B.M. Add. MS 19906), the presence of Lovato's metrical notes in two MSS (F N) descended from a lost MS (Σ) closely connected with E, and the convenience with which the date of E matches that of the Pomposa catalogue.[5] Further, this evidence,

---

[1] *Misc.* cent. i.xvii (on the text of *HF* 83): '*alias* enim codex habet uetustus ex publica Mediceae familiae bibliotheca, non *altas* ut in uulgariis exemplaribus' (cf. Sabbadini, *Scoperte* 1.152, A. Perosa, *Catalogo della Mostra del Poliziano nella biblioteca Medicea-Laurenziana* (1955) 49f.). On the identification of the 'publica Medicea bibliotheca', cf. S. Rizzo, *Il lessico filologico degli umanisti* (1973) 86 n.2.

[2] Cf. G. Mercati, *Opere Minori* I (= *Studi e Testi* 76) 358ff.

[3] Gius. Billanovich, *I primi umanisti e le tradizioni dei classici latini* (1953) 18ff., 40ff.

[4] L. D. Reynolds, for example, speaks of Pomposa as 'that very monastery which is known to have housed the most important manuscript of Seneca's *Tragedies*' (*Medieval Tradition of Seneca's Letters* (1965) 100).

[5] The 'conferme sicure' which Billanovich promised in support of his suggestion (based on the work of A. Campana) have yet to appear.

even if accepted, would not exclude the possibility that Lovato had access to a twin, an apograph, or even to the exemplar of E instead of E itself. All that may be stated with confidence is that the MS at Pomposa in 1093 belonged to the E-branch of the tradition. To trace its history further, it is important to note that the 1093 catalogue describes a library only recently enriched by rare and valuable accessions, not an ancient repository like Verona or Bobbio. The Pomposa MS of the tragedies was very likely one of those copied at the instigation of abbot Hieronymus (1079–1100), of whose zeal for enlarging the library the 1093 inventory speaks at length. For this purpose texts would have been borrowed from older libraries, and as possible sources of Pomposa's books Billanovich suggested Verona and Monte Cassino. No evidence links Seneca's plays and Verona, but for Monte Cassino a suggestive, though inconclusive, connection is established by the citations of Eugenius Vulgarius.[1] Writing at Teano (the refuge of the monks of Monte Cassino) *ca.* 900, Eugenius shows more familiarity with the text of the tragedies than any other figure from the end of antiquity until the thirteenth century; more interesting, Eugenius's citations agree with the text of E in at least one, and possibly two, wrong readings.[2] The evidence is not sufficient in quantity to support definitive conclusions, but a Monte Cassino origin for the Pomposa MS of the E-family must be considered a strong possibility.[3]

---

[1] Cf. P. von Winterfeld, *Poetae Latini Medii Aeui* iv.1 (1899) 406ff., H. Bloch, *Dumbarton Oaks Papers* iii (1946) 168f.

[2] In *HF* 661 E and Eugenius have *loqui*, A the correct *eloqui* (the error arose by haplography from the preceding word, *impune*); in *HF* 192ff. Eugenius cites the lines in the order 192–194a–195b–197 and E in the order 192–194–193–195. Brugnoli (*Tradizione Manoscritta* 216ff.) makes an unconvincing attempt to relate Eugenius's citations to a stage of transmission before the division of E and A.

[3] That E's parent came from Monte Cassino was suggested by Manitius (*Geschichte d. lat. Literatur im Mittelalter* i (1911) 436); he, however, regarded the Pomposa MS as a second descendant of the Monte Cassino MS.

Bibl.: Leo, *Obs.* 16–41; Sluiter 3–4; Viansino, *prol.* 4–25; Giardina, praef. vii–ix; Axelson, *Korruptelenkult* 7–25; Philp, *CQ* N.S. xviii (1968) 151, 172f. Plate of *Med.* 898–930 in E. Chatelain, *Paléographie des classiques latins* II (no. CLXXIII.2); of *Oed.* 12–44 in Sluiter, facing p. 22.

F Paris, Bibliothèque Nationale, Lat. 11855. Vellum, fourteenth century, Italy: 420 × 255 (290 × 175, 300 × 180 in tragedies): 288 numbered leaves: 2 columns, 50 lines to a column, ruled in pencil (three vertical bounding lines at left of each column, one at right): collation 1^{10} (lacks 1), 2–4^{10}, 5^8, 6–26^{10}, 27^8, 28^{10}, 29^{6+1}, 30^8 (lacks 8): catchwords visible in almost all cases: decoration, elaborate and consistent (except in *Oedipus*, in ff. 282ʳ–287ᵛ); left side of each column bordered with red and blue streamers flourished at top and bottom (not in tragedies); at beginning of each play (or book of the prose works) are miniatures within large gold initials, sometimes with borders including gold balls (in some places a marginal hand has left instructions for the miniaturist, e.g. f. 240ᵛ 'hic debet fieri figura de auro quae sit anima hominis mortui', 276ᵛ 'hic debet esse figura de auro mulieris'); especially noteworthy illuminations in f. 91ʳ, 122ʳ; the final leaves (ff. 282–7) lack most of these decorative elements: binding and flyleaves, modern (watermark on flyleaf: crown over rose, with D63 at bottom).

2° fo. -tores quoque ipsos

Contents: Miscellaneous works by or attributed to Seneca: f. 1ʳ *de quatuor uirtutibus* (inc. *quatuor uirtutum species...deficientem premat ignauiam*); f. 2ʳ *epistulae ad Lucilium* (1–124); f. 81ʳ *de prouidentia*; f. 84ʳ *de constantia sapientis*; f. 87ᵛ *ad Polybium de consolatione*; f. 91ᵛ *de beneficiis*; f. 122ᵛ *de clementia* (incomplete); f. 129ᵛ *de remediis fortuitorum* (cf. *Opera* ed. Haase III.446ff.); f. 131ʳ *de tranquillitate animi*; f. 137ʳ *de breuitate uitae*; f. 142ʳ *ad Heluiam de consolatione*; f. 147ᵛ *ad Marciam de consolatione*; f. 154ʳ *de uita beata* (and *de otio*, which follows with no break); f. 161ᵛ *de ira*; f. 178ᵛ *naturales quaestiones* (incomplete);

f. 210^r *declamationes* (i.e. *controuersiae*, incomplete); ff. 225^r–227^v blank; 228^r *Hercules Furens*; 234^v *Troades*; f. 240^v *Agamemnon*; 245^v *Thyestes*; f. 251^r *Hercules* (*sc.* *Oetaeus*); f. 261^r *Phoenissae*; f. 264^v *Medea*; f. 269^v *Phaedra*; f. 276^r *Octauia*; 281^r list of contents; 281^v *ex libris* (see below); unnumbered blank leaf; f. 282^r *Oedipus* (on 287^r at end of play: 'in hac tragedia Senece in carmine chori qui | incipit *effusam*, post uersum *te senior* (429) et | ante uersum *sensere terre* (472) uidentur esse infrascripti uersus', followed by 430–71); f. 288 Trevet's *argumenta* of the tragedies (inc. 'liber tragediarum Senece decem continet tragedias quarum prima est de hercule furente...in celum translatus est').

The MS is written in a large, upright Gothic script by two, possibly three good hands. On f. 281^v (originally the last folio of the codex) an ownership note in a hand close in style to that of the text has been nearly obliterated, but can be recovered from the impression left on the facing blank leaf (transcription in Fohlen 86, Megas (1967) 197 n.36). It reveals that the book belonged to the Dominican order (no house is named) and had been loaned (*concessus*) to a certain Ugolinus, whose *curriculum uitae* is given: he served as *socius* (= secretary and travelling companion) to a number of prelates and masters general of the Dominicans, the latest being Aymericus Placentinus, who was master general from 1304 to 1311 and died in 1327. The mark is consistent with a date for F of 1300–25, which is both palaeographically and textually plausible. Ugolinus himself has not yet been identified; his surname has been erased and is invisible to the naked eye (Megas, using ultraviolet light, reads it as Varcha or Vaccha; my own examination suggests that Parcha is also possible).

Bibl. W. Hoffa, *Hermes* xlix (1914) 465f.; A. Megas (1967) 196–8; J. Fohlen, *Revue d'Histoire des Textes* i (1971) 83ff.

M   Milan, Biblioteca Ambrosiana, D 276 inf. Vellum, fourteenth century, Italy: 350 × 250 (285 × 190): iii + 48

+i (paper flyleaves have watermark, hand surmounted by six-pointed flower/star): two columns, 64 lines to a column, ruled in ink with double left vertical and horizontal bounding lines: collation $1-4^{10}$, 5^{12} (9–12 cancelled), catchwords at end of first four quires: decoration, large coloured initials (six or more lines high) at beginning of each play (those on ff. 13^v, 35^v, 43^v not executed), and smaller initials in alternating red and blue at the start of each scene; scene headings, *personarum notae*, and metrical descriptions in red: binding perhaps original, parchment over thin boards with paper pastedowns, spine of worn calf.

2° fo. uirtus uocatur (*HF* 252)

Contents: f. 1^r *Hercules Furens*; f. 6^r *Troades*; f. 10^v *Phoenissae*; f. 13^v *Medea*; f. 17^v *Phaedra*; f. 22^v *Oedipus*; f. 27^r *Agamemnon*; f. 31^r *Thyestes*; f. 35^v *Hercules Oetaeus* (*Hercules* only in colophon on f. 35^v); f. 43^v *Octauia*; f. 47^v definition of tragedy (from Isidore), 'tragedie sunt... ymaginem fictis'; f. 47^v 'Planctus of Oedipus' (cf. Walther 4511, P. M. Clogan, *Mediaevalia et Humanistica* N.s. i (1969) 233ff., who does not record its occurrence here), *in patris infausta pignora...quem patitur gens miserabilis* (introduced by passage in prose, 'Thebarum rex laius...ut infra in rithmis continentur').

The MS was written by three scribes (ff. $1-35^v$, 36^r-43^v, 44^r-48^v); variant readings and other marginalia (mostly instructions to the rubricator and metrical comment) have been added in a small, neat hand not that of any of the scribes; another hand, later and more florid, has added lines missing in the original text (e.g. *Med.* 948–50). The MS was purchased by the Ambrosiana in 1606 from the heirs of Rovidius, a Milanese senator.

N Rome (Vatican City), Biblioteca Apostolica Vaticana, Vaticanus Latinus 1769. Vellum, fourteenth century, Italy: 370×235 (280×155): leaves cut at bottom (some catchwords sliced): ff. 247 (139–49 numbered twice, 204 skipped): two columns, 62 lines in a column, ruled in drypoint: collation $1-4^{10}$, 5^4, $6-8^{10}$, 9^4, $10-26^{10}$, 27^{10}

(wants 9 and 10), catchwords not visible on f. 30^v, 40^v: decoration, consistent and elegant; red and blue flourished initials for beginning of new chapters (scenes in the tragedies), headings in red, in tragedies first letter of each line stroked red; no running titles: binding and flyleaves, modern (seventeenth/eighteenth c.?).

2° fo. cuius admittet

Contents: (1) ps.-Quintilian, *Declamationes* (f. 1^r–44^v); (2)–(18) Various authentic and spurious works of Seneca (for details, see Nogara; the selection resembles that in F, p, and a; no *Ludus*), ff. 45^r–192^r; (19) Publilius Syrus (inc. *Alienum est*...exp. *uitiosum est*), f. 192^v–194^r; (20) 'Sentencie ex uariis philosophorum dictis collecte' (inc. *Cum quidam stultus*; also in p), f. 194^r–195^v; (21) Isocratis Oratio in Dimonicum (inc. *In pluribus quidem, o Dimonice*; also in p), f. 195^v; (22) Fragment of Theophrastus, *de Nuptiis* (from Jerome, *PL* 23.288–91), inc. *Fertus aureolus Theophrasti liber*, f. 196^r–197^r; (23) ps.-Seneca, *de paupertate* (inc. *honesta inquit Epicurus*... exp. *diuitie insolentiam*; also in p and a), f. 197^{r-v}; (24) Tragedies, f. 197^v–246^r. A note on f. 197^v gives order and titles as follows: 'Marci lutij annei senece tragedie no-|uem. hercules troades. phenissa medea. | phedra. oedipus. agamenon. thiestes. | hercules. octauia. feliciter incipiunt.' The real order, however, is: *HF* (197^v–203^r), *Tro.* (203^r–208^v), *Med.* (209^r–213^r), *Pha.* (213^r–218^r), *Oed.* (218^r–222^v), *Pho.* (222^v–225^r), *Agam.* (225^r–229^v), *Thy.* (229^v–234^r), *HO* (234^r–242^r), *Oct.* (242^r–246^r); (25) f. 246^{r-v}: (*a*) Life of Seneca (inc. *Lucius Anneus Seneca Cordubensis Neronis preceptor*...*si sapiunt intellegere licet* (cf. Haase, *Opera* III.482, Megas (1967) 104); (*b*) Metrical note of Lovato Lovati (inc. *Seneca in decem istis tragediis*...*non memini me legisse*), cf. Megas 105; (*c*) Transcript of an inscription naming Lucan, discovered in Rome in 1303 by Rolandus de Plazola (=*C.I.L.* VI par. v, p. 9*.6*); inc. *M.CCCIII°. mense Januario*...*FAMA SERVATA* (cf. Megas 106).

The MS was written by a single scribe in a neat upright Gothic hand. Annotation is generally light, but in ff. 99–115 a distinctive small hand has made many marginal notes.

Bibl. B. Nogara, *Codices Vaticani Latini* III (1912) 229–31; A. Ch. Megas (1967) 92–113; Leo, *Obs.* 6–15.

P   Paris, Bibliothèque Nationale, Lat. 8260. Vellum, thirteenth century (first half), North France: 200 × 122 (140 × 50; margins wide at bottom, narrow at top); leaves have been cut at the bottom: v + 156 + iii, 38 long lines, ruled in pencil (three vertical bounding lines at left, one at right); writing begins below top ruled line: collation 1⁶ (1 a fragment), 2–15⁸, 16⁸ (1 missing), 17–20⁸, 21⁸ (7, 8 cancelled); quires 6 and 7 were interchanged in binding; catchwords visible on f. 73ᵛ, 121ᵛ (others cut off): decoration, headings in red, initial letters of scenes in alternating red and blue, occasionally flourished in the contrasting colour: binding, modern (red morocco); end papers and paper flyleaves also modern.

2° fo. mediusque collo (*HF* 72, second time)

Contents: f. 1ʳ *Hercules Furens*; f. 18ᵛ *Thyestes* (to 1111, f. 33ᵛ; rest of play on f. 42ʳ); *Phoenissae* (*Thebais*), ff. 42ʳ–49ᵛ (to 602), f. 34ʳ⁻ᵛ (603–end); f. 34ʳ *Phaedra* (*Hippolytus*), to 554, f. 41ᵛ; rest of play on 50ʳ–59ᵛ; f. 59ᵛ *Oedipus*; f. 73ᵛ *Troades* (*Troas*); f. 89ᵛ *Medea*; f. 103ʳ *Agamemnon*; f. 116ᵛ *Octauia*; f. 130ᵛ *Hercules Oetaeus*. The MS once contained the *Ludus de Morte Claudii* (cf. note on last flyleaf at front, 'Tragedie Senece *et ludus eiusdem*', italicised words scored out and 'detractus est' added in later hand), the first leaf of which is probably f. 73 in Par. Lat. 8624. The script, decoration, and *mise en page* match those of 8260; the page size, 220 × 135, is presumably that of 8260 before cutting.

The MS was written by a single scribe;[1] in a very few

---

[1] The hand is apparently to be identified with that of Leiden, Voss. Lat. Q.38 of Propertius (= A).

places variant readings and lines missing in P (e.g. *HF* 18–19a and 21b, *HO* 838–46) have been added by a later hand. P was copied for the library of Richard of Fournival, and is no. 129 in his *Biblionomia*; after his death it passed, through the mediation of Gerard of Abbeville, to the library of the Sorbonne, where it appears in the 1338 catalogue.[1] It came into the Bibliothèque Nationale from the collection of Colbert (in which it had the number 5961).

Bibl.: C. E. Stuart, *CQ* vi (1912) 1–12; T. Düring, *Hermes* xlvii (1912) 186–98; T. H. Sluiter, *Mnemosyne* ser. iv.1 (1948) 139–60; Woesler 24–42; Viansino, *prol.* 71–5; Philp, *CQ* n.s. xviii (1968) 155–9; R. H. Rouse, *Revue d'Histoire des Textes* i (1971) 95ff. A plate of f. 66^r (*Oed.* 515–52) appears in Sluiter's *Oedipus*, facing p. 22 (no. 2); plates of f. i^v, f. 1^r (*HF* 1–39), and f. 39^r (*Pha.* 326–62) in Rouse, after p. 96.

C   Cambridge, Corpus Christi College 406. Vellum, early thirteenth century, England (?): 210–215 × 155; ff. 77–100 have been cut down at top, often removing part of the text (written area varies; for tragedies 180 × 135): iv + 144 (144 a pasted-in fragment): 3 columns (for tragedies; two elsewhere), *ca.* 50 lines to a column, ruled in ink; writing consistently above top ruled line: collation 1–9^8, 10^4, 11–13^8, 14^{10} (10 cancelled), 15^4 (1 cancelled), 16–19^8; quire signatures in form i^9, ii^9, etc.; second and fourth quires interchanged in binding: decoration, alternating red and blue initial letters, red headings (most extensive in tragedies): modern (1971) binding and end papers (eighteenth century?).

2° fo. sceptra obtinentur (*HF* 342)

Contents: (1) f. i^i medieval list of contents with incipits, in hand resembling none of those in the body of the MS, but perhaps that of the scribblings on ff. 142–4 (thirteenth

---

[1] On the origin and early history of P, see Rouse 95ff. The absence of P influence in later stages of transmission may be due to the restrictive lending policies of the Sorbonne library (cf. Rouse, *Scriptorium* xxi (1967) 42–71, 227–52); it apparently escaped the attention of Petrarch on his visit to Paris in 1333.

century, according to James); (2) *Tragedies*: f. 1ʳ *Hercules Furens*; f. 5ʳ *Thyestes* (to 986, f. 8ᵛ; rest of play f. 25ʳ); f. 9ʳ *Medea* (from 387; 1–386 on ff. 23ᵛ-25ʳ); f. 11ʳ *Agamemnon*; f. 14ʳ *Octauia* (to 761, f. 17ʳ; rest of play on f. 33ʳ⁻ᵛ); f. 17ʳ *Oedipus* (from 285; 1–284 on ff. 32ʳ-33ʳ); f. 19ᵛ *Troades* (*Troas*); f. 25ʳ *Phoenissae* (*Thebais*); f. 27ᵛ *Phaedra* (*Ypolitus*); f. 33ᵛ *Hercules Oetaeus*; f. 40 blank; (3) John of Hautville, *Architrenius* (ed. T. Wright, *Satirical Poets of the Twelfth Century* (1872) 1.240ff.); ff. 41ʳ-64ᵛ; (4) Bernardus Silvestris, *Megacosmus* (ed. Wrobel and Barach, *Bibliotheca Philosophica Medii Aeui* (Innsbruck, 1875) 1); ff. 65ʳ-74ʳ; (5) Joseph of Exeter *De Bello Troiano* (in MS.: 'Frigii Daretis Yliados Liber') (ed. L. Gompf, Leiden, 1970); ff. 74ᵛ-86ᵛ; (6) Alan of Lille, *Anticlaudianus* (ed. R. Bossuat, Paris, 1955); ff. 86ᵛ-100ᵛ; (7) Geoffrey of Vinsauf, *Poetria Noua* (ed. E. Faral, *Les arts poétiques du xiiᵉ et du xiiiᵉ siècle* (Paris, 1924) 194ff.); ff. 101ʳ-112ᵛ. (The 'poem exemplifying *colores*' noted as a separate item by M. R. James is in fact a misplaced section of the *Poetria Noua*, whose proper place is after f. 109ᵛ); (8) Walter of Châtillon, *Alexandreis* (ed. Migne, *PL* 209.460ff.); ff. 113ʳ-141ᵛ; (9) ff. 142ʳ-144ᵛ miscellaneous scribblings and mnemonic verses (e.g. on the sacraments, 'unda calix pallax cinis unctio tonsio lectus'; 'saepe sibi moneat confessor ne recidiuet').

The MS is written in several good small hands, of which that of the tragedies is perhaps the most careful and elegant. Occasional corrections and variants have been added in a hand closely resembling that of the scribe. The MS was given to Corpus Christi College in 1575 by Archbishop Parker.

Bibl. As above, for P, with these additions: M. R. James, *Catalogue of the MSS in Corpus Christi College Cambridge* (1911), 288–91; L. Gompf, *Josephus Iscanus* (Leiden, 1970) 27ff. A plate of f. 32ʳ (*Oed.* 1–138) appears in Sluiter's *Oedipus* following p. 22 (no. 3).

S   Escorial, Biblioteca Real. 108 T.ɪɪɪ.11. Vellum, fourteenth century (second half), Italy: 260 × 200: ff. 164:

two columns, fifty lines to a column: decoration, flourished initials in alternating red and blue (especially elaborate at start of each play), headings in red: binding, not original.

Contents: (1) *Tragedies* (order and titles as in P and C) (ff. 1ʳ–60ᵛ); (2) Terence, *Comoediae* (a separate codex bound together with the Seneca at the Escorial) (ff. 61ʳ–164ᵛ).

The text is written by a single scribe with great care; occasional corrections in margins or above the line.[1] The MS later belonged to Alfonso, duke of Calabria and king of Naples (1448–95); I owe this information to Otto Zwierlein. For its further history cf. G. Antolín, *La Ciudad de Dios* cxxi (1920) 117ff.: it was willed by Alfonso to Gonzalez Perez (d. 1566), who willed it to Philip II.

Bibl. G. Antolín, *Catálogo de los códices latinos de la biblioteca real del Escorial*, vol. IV (Madrid, 1916) 145; Stuart, *CQ* v (1912) 17ff.; Philp, *CQ* N.S. xviii (1968) 152, 155ff., 172.[2]

V   Rome (Vatican City), Biblioteca Apostolica Vaticana, Lat. 2829. Vellum, fourteenth century. Origin uncertain, but script exhibits features not normally found in Italian MSS (e.g. *et* and *g*); MacGregor's comparison of the hand of M seems unjustified. 340 × 240 (270 × 160): ff. ii + 52 (f. 42 numbered twice) + i: two columns, *ca.* 60 lines to a column, ruled in pencil: collation 1·3¹², 4¹⁶ (catchwords f. 24ᵛ, 36ᵛ): decoration, sparse and inelegant (red initials and headings, no flourishing): binding, not original.

2° fo. in cuius urbem (*HF* 264)

Contents: (1) *Tragedies*, A order and titles (i.e. = P CS) (ff. 1–49ᵛ); (2) Definitions of tragedy and abbreviated *argumenta* of Nicholas Trevet (see pp. 81ff. below) (ff. 49ᵛ–51ᵛ). The definitions on f. 50ʳ are largely based on Trevet's *accessus* (Franceschini 35); that on f. 49ᵛ is not, and this is

---

[1] S adds no *lacunae* of its own to those of β (MacGregor, *Survey*).

[2] My account of S is based on Giardina's, corrected against the photographs in Göttingen and a microfilm loaned by the IRHT.

the only part of the extraneous material written in the same hand as the text (inc. 'Tragedia est sermo siue scriptura commemorans illustrium personarum prosperitatem in calamitatem finaliter declinantem'; there is no connection, as tentatively suggested by MacGregor, between this definition and that in M, f. 47^v, which derives from Isidore and is found as well in E, f. 1^r).

The text is written in a single hand; other hands have added comments, notably a small, precise hand first seen on f. 31^v.

> *Bibl.* A. P. MacGregor, *TAPA* cii (1971) 327ff. (especially 331ff.); *idem*, 'Survey', *passim*. The MS was not seen by Stuart, who was presumably misled by the incorrect description 'recollecta in tragoedias' in the handwritten Vatican catalogue (reproduced by Kristeller, *Iter Italicum* II.314).

d   Naples, Biblioteca Nazionale iv.e.i. Italian, late fourteenth century. Parchment, ff. 146, 2 columns (contains tragedies and Sallust's *Catilina*); marginal glosses to f. 23^r, the oldest from Trevet. The MS later belonged to Cardinal Antonio Seripandi (*fl.* 1475; cf. Cosenza 3252). *Bibl.* Franceschini 93; Philp 160ff.; MacGregor, *TAPA* cii (1971) 343ff., *Survey*.

p   Padua, Biblioteca Antoniana i.9. Italian, late fourteenth century. Parchment, ff. 344, 320 × 230, 2 columns, no glosses or commentary. A miscellany of Senecan and pseudo-Senecan material, similar in contents (though not in text) to F, N, and a (like N, it contains a Latin version of part of Isocrates' speech against Demonicus and a collection of 'Sententie uariorum philosophorum', inc. *cum quidam stultus*), but with the addition of the *Ludus de morte Claudii*. Described in A. M. Iosa, *I codici manoscritti della biblioteca Antoniana di Padova* (1880) 203f.

m   Venice, Biblioteca Marciana xii.25 (previously 685 at SS. Giovanni e Paolo). Italian, fourteenth/fifteenth century. Parchment, ff. 191, single columns. Contains tragedies and Mussato's *Ecerinis*. No glosses or commentary; clearly a deluxe book. *Bibl.* Philp 163f.

q   Brescia, Biblioteca Queriniana B.1.13. Italian, late
fourteenth century. Parchment, ff. 78, two columns;
glosses to *HF* 1250 only. Contains tragedies with miscellaneous peripheral material: (1) a prooemium suggesting
that each play is named for its principal 'persona passio-
nata' (inc. 'Tragediarum librum Euripidem et Sopho-
clem'), in a hand similar to that of the glosses on *HF*;
(2) an incomplete copy of Coluccio Salutati's letter of
15 October 1371 on the authorship of the tragedies and
the letters to St Paul (Novati, *Epistolario* 1.150), a letter
found in several other Seneca MSS, e.g. B.M. Add. MS
11986 (by the scribe of Add. MS 11990, a Lucan written
in Ferrara in 1378 for Feltrino de' Boiardis by Jacopo
Giuliano da Portiolo), MS Burney 250 (1387, San
Gimignano), Venice Marc. x.147 (1420, Padua), Vat.
Lat. 1645 (*s.* xv), Vind. Pal. 3121 (a Florentine miscellany, probably before 1450), cf. Ullman, *Studies* 210; (3)
at end (f. 79ʳ) the hexameter *argumenta* of Pietro da
Moglio, in their most common form (inc. 'Herculis insani
fert prima tragedia strages...Herculis Oethei summas
canit ultima flammas'). For Pietro (teacher of Coluccio
Salutati and professor of rhetoric at Bologna, 1347–62)
cf. G. Billanovich, *IMU* vi (1963) 203–34; for the different forms of his *argumenta* in MSS of the tragedies, cf.
G. Billanovich, *IMU* vii (1964) 293-7 (to the MSS cited
by Billanovich may be added Oxford Canon. Class. Lat.
93 and Laud. Lat. 71; Vat. Lat. 1643 conflates his
versions I and II, cf. Nogara, *Codices Vaticani Latini* III
(1912) 126; other versions of the *argumenta* are found in
Vat. Lat. 1642, 1646, 1648, Florence Strozz. 134, Naples
B.N. iv.d.46, and Rehdigeranus 10 (I owe the references
to this last group to A. P. MacGregor)). *Bibl.* A. Beltrami,
SIFC xiv (1906) 67f.

a   Paris, Bibliothèque Nationale Lat. 6395. Italian, fourteenth century. Parchment, ff. 309, 370 × 245 (245 × 175),
2 columns, 50 lines each. A miscellany of Senecan
material generally similar in content to F, N, and p; like

37

p it contains the *Ludus de morte Claudii* (f. 221ᵛ–223ʳ, under the title *liber de ludis*). The tragedies appear last, as is customary for such collections (ff. 252ʳ–309ᵛ); they are completely integrated into the MS. Few variants or glosses, but systematic correction in *HF* (replacement of A readings with E). *Bibl.* W. Hoffa, *Hermes* xlix (1914) 466f., Philp 164. (Called p by Philp.)

l   Florence, Biblioteca Medicea-Laurenziana plut. 24 sin. 4. Written between October and December 1371 in Pisa and Florence by Tedaldo de Casa, O.F.M., a friend of Coluccio Salutati (for whom cf. Méhus, *Historia Litterarum Florentina* 334f., Voigt, *Wiederbelebung³* 1.397, Cosenza 910); his books went in 1406 to S. Croce, whence thirty passed to the Laurenziana. Parchment and paper, ff. 162, single columns; abbreviated version of Trevet's commentary in the margins. *Bibl.* Düring, *Hermes* xlii (1907) 113ff., 579ff.; Sluiter, preface to *Oedipus* (1941) 14f.; Woesler 54–7; Viansino, *prolegomena* 77–81 (full description, with much erroneous and irrelevant matter); Philp 159ff.; MacGregor, *Survey*.

n   Naples, Biblioteca Nazionale iv.d.47. Written in 1376 at Lucca by Francesco da Camerino (f. 168ᵛ; over *Franciscum* is written *Petrutii*, presumably a reference to the correspondent of Salutati, cf. Méhus 305). Paper, ff. 168, 290 × 220, single columns. Contains almost the entire commentary of Trevet (called 'Altraveth', f. 168ᵛ). *Bibl.* As above for l; described by Franceschini 88–90.

r   Rome (Vatican City), Biblioteca Apostolica Vaticana Reg. Lat. 1500. Written in 1389 in N. Italy. Parchment. Classed with ln by Düring–Hoffa (and derived from a common parent called by them γ), it is too heavily contaminated from an E source to be useful. *Bibl.* As above for l; G. Richter, *Kritische Untersuchungen* (1899) 25f.

K   Cambrai, Bibliothèque Municipale 555 (513). The hand is generally said to be N. French (though Rouse 118 n.1 tentatively suggests that an Italian exemplar was

used), but an Italian origin may be possible (note open
a, r superscript); early to middle fourteenth century. A
collection of Senecan material, ff. 246 (tragedies ff. 166–
236), 2 columns, 39 lines each, 330 × 230.

Q Monte Cassino, Biblioteca dell'Abbazia 392 P. Italian,
ca. 1350 (so Rouse 117 n.1, from decoration; similarly on
the basis of the script, a good *rotunda*); wrongly dated
to the thirteenth century by M. Inguanez, *Codicum
Casinensium Manuscriptorum Catalogus* II (1928/34) 258f.
Parchment, ff. 258, 355 × 275, 2 columns. A composite MS containing the tragedies (ff. 1–120), the *Ludus*
(ff. 121–6), and Vegetius (ff. 127–258). Text heavily
corrected.

e Eton, College Library 110. N. Italian, *ca.* 1350 (so
Stuart: 'I should not myself have dated it earlier than
1330–1340', Trinity College Add. MS C.67, p. 64; Rouse
117 n.1); the thirteenth-century dating by M. R. James,
often cited in previous discussions, should be abandoned.
Register of births on flyleaf, earliest date 1391; purchased
in Vicenza in 1450 by a dependant of Giovanni Fran-
zigine. Ff. 58, 2 columns (3 on ff. 1–7). Contains tragedies
only. *Bibl.* Giardina, preface xi–xiv, *Bollettino* 91–101;
Philp 167–9; Zwierlein, *Gnomon* xli (1969) 761–3;
MacGregor, *Survey.*

Ox. 1 Oxford, Bodleian Library Canon. Class. Lat. 93. North
Italian, fourteenth century. Ff. 123; contains tragedies
with *argumenta* of Mussato in augmented form. *Bibl.*
Megas (1969) 1ff.

Harl London, British Museum Harleianus 2484. Italian,
mid-fourteenth century, ff. 126. Contains tragedies with
a commentary which draws on Trevet, but which frequently corrects his errors of interpretation or discusses
variant readings (Trevet is consistently called 'Trauech');
this commentary appears in shortened form in Laur (see
below), which is dated 1368. The Harley commentary
can thus be placed between 1316 and 1368; the MSS
which contain it suggest a central Italian origin (i.e.

Florence–Bologna). It is tempting to connect the Harley commentator with the Augustinian Dionigi de' Roberti da Borgo San Sepolcro, a friend of Petrarch (cf. *ad Fam.* 4.1) who is known to have produced a commentary on the tragedies, but the identification is not proven.[1] *Bibl.* Philp 167–9; MacGregor, *TAPA* cii (1971) 347; *Survey.*

Laur   Florence, Biblioteca Medicea-Laurenziana plut. 37.6. Written in 1368 in central Italy (Stuart thought Florence possible). Owned by Francesco Sassetti, Medici agent (1420–91), cf. Sabbadini, *Scoperte* 1.165. Contains abridged form of Harley commentary. *Bibl.* T. Düring, *Hermes* xlii (1907) 122–5.

Vat   Rome (Vatican City), Biblioteca Apostolica Vaticana Lat. 1647. Written in 1391/2 in Italy (f. 156^r) in *littera Bononiensis* (MacGregor compares Vat. Urb. Lat. 165, pl. 2 in Ullman, *Origin and development of Humanistic script*). Parchment, 360 × 260, ff. 186. No commentary or glosses

---

[1] For Dionigi cf. Cosenza, 1234–6, Sabbadini, *Scoperte* 1.36–44, Ullman, *Studies* 38, 51f., R. Weiss, *Italian Studies* x (1955) 40–2. He was a master in Paris, but visited Italy several times between 1328 and 1333; in 1339 he moved to the court of Naples, where he died in 1342. His commentary on Valerius Maximus survives in at least 32 MSS (critical edition of book one by John W. Larkin, S.J., diss. Fordham (New York) 1967), and shows him to be a man of wide reading and critical judgement. The Seneca commentary contains at least one reference to Valerius Maximus (f. 98^r, note on *Agam.* 37: '*sed sera* sera iuxta illud ualerii in primo de neglecta religione...'). Both the Seneca and Valerius commentaries appear in the Ossinger catalogue of the Bibliotheca Augustiniana in Ingolstadt–Augsburg (1782).

Other possibilities, however, cannot be ignored. MacGregor (*Survey*) has called attention to Giovanni Segarelli, friend of both Petrarch and Salutati (cf. Cloetta ii.90); the other figures he names, however, are either too late or not known to have written on the tragedies. I owe to my wife a reference to yet another known commentator on the plays, Bartolomeo da San Concordio, O.P. (1262–1347), whose life was centred around the convent of S. Caterina in Pisa; his *Ammaestramenti agli antichi* reveals a wide classical culture, and his treatise *de Orthographia* (cf. A. Marigo, *ALMA* xii (1938) 1–26) recommends classical usages; for further details cf. A. Teetaert in the *Dictionnaire de Droit Canonique* ii.213–16, C. Segre in the *Dizionario Biografico degli Italiani* vi (1964) 768–70.

(except on f. 1); a few variants were added by the first hand. See Nogara 129f.

Cant Cambridge, University Library Nn. 11.35. Italian, fourteenth/fifteenth century. A composite MS written by several hands and copied from more than one exemplar; in some plays (including *Agam.* 1–517) probably a copy of Laur.

Bo Bologna, Biblioteca Universitaria 2485 (formerly 583 at S. Salvator in Bologna). Italian, late fourteenth century. Heavily contaminated, but not in the group I call 'AE'.

Florence, Biblioteca Medicea-Laurenziana

F1 Plut. 37.1. Italian, fourteenth century. Later belonged to Leonardo Dati (bibliophile and scholar, pontifical secretary to Paul II in 1467, cf. E. Hauler, *WS* xvii (1895) 105ff.). Contains many marginal variants, with others grouped at the foot of the page in a primitive *apparatus criticus*; with *argumenta* of Trevet and Mussato (cf. MacGregor, *Survey*).

F2 Plut. 37.3. Italian, fourteenth century; cf. MacGregor, *Survey*.

F3 Plut. 37.9. Italian, fourteenth century, in a hand similar to that of Bo; corrections in several other hands. Called 'pure A' by Hoffa; described as 'goodish but no value' by Stuart.

F4 Plut. 37.11. Italian, early fifteenth century; copied by Poggio Bracciolini (cf. Leo, *Obs.* 42ff., Ullman, *Development of Humanistic script* 25ff.). Leo thought it a copy of plut. 37.1 (F1), but the Poggio MS has left more *lacunae* intact than its alleged parent (cf. MacGregor, *Survey*).

F5 Plut. 37.12. Italian, late fourteenth century. In *Agamemnon* 1–604 close to, though probably not a copy of, Bo; in rest of play from a source related to KQ.

F6 Plut. 91 sup. 30. Italian, 1385. Heavy but unsystematic E contamination. MacGregor, *Survey*.

F7 Florence, Biblioteca Riccardiana 527. Italian, fourteenth century (*ca.* 1375 or somewhat earlier). Parchment, ff. 182, 250 × 200. Belonged to Boccaccio, but apparently lacks any trace of his writing, cf. A. Mazza, *IMU* ix (1966) 55, Franceschini 78, MacGregor, *Survey*.

For   Foroiuliensis (San Daniele del Friuli, Biblioteca Communale) 75 (formerly 72). Italian, fourteenth century. Tragedies precede a collection of prose works of Seneca. Text shows some similarity to π, but is more heavily influenced by E contamination than are mpq. MacGregor, *Survey*.

Sal   London, British Museum Add. MS 11987. Italian, fourteenth century; written in his own hand by Coluccio Salutati (cf. Ullman, *Humanism of Coluccio Salutati* (1963) no. 103; plate of *HF* 715ff.), presumably before 1370; in March of that year Salutati wrote to Cecco Romano thanking him for the loan of a Seneca MS with which to correct his own (Novati, *Epistolario* 1.124). The MS contains the tragedies and Mussato's *Ecerinis* and *Somnium*; for Salutati's admiration of Mussato cf. *Epistolario* III.408ff. Like other Salutati MSS, the Seneca contains numerous variants and conjectures in a variety of inks, apparently entered at different times. The conjectures are of generally low quality (cf. MacGregor, *Survey*), but there are occasional signs of acuteness (his *nubam* in 290 anticipates Bentley). Unlike his Catullus (Vat. Ottobon. Lat. 1829 = R), Salutati's Seneca does not seem to have exerted a significant direct influence on the late fourteenth-century transmission; its conjectures remain for the most part isolated (Leiden Voss. Q.31 is the only exception known to me). Salutati's own Senecan interests, however, may have stimulated the circulation of the plays; his letter on their authorship (*Epistolario* 1.150, 15 October 1371) is found in many MSS (see above, p. 37), and the verses of Sidonius Apollinaris cited therein appear in Laur. plut. 24 sin. 4, copied between October and December 1371.

L1   London, British Museum Arundel 116. Italian, fourteenth century. Extensive notes in several hands; at end, 'Franciscus Lucharelli de eugubio scripsi' (so catalogue; MacGregor reads the name as Ceccharelli or Caccharelli, and suggests that the commentary is that found in Vat. Pal. 1675; *Survey*).

L2   London, British Museum Kings 30. Italian, late fourteenth century (contains at beginning epitaphs of Francesco Bussone of Carmagnola, d. 1432 and of Francesco Foscari, Doge of Venice 1423, d. 1457); cf. G. F. Warner and J. P. Gilson, *Catalogue of Western MSS. in the Old Royal and King's Collections* III (1921) 10.

L3   London, British Museum Burney 250. Written by a Bartholomaeus in San Gimignano in 1387; described in *Catalogue of the Burney MSS. in the British Museum* (1840) 64f.; plate in *Palaeographical Society Facsimiles* ser. 2 (1884/5) pl. 95. A contaminated MS, but not on the scale of the 'AE' group. See MacGregor, *Survey* (who calls it a copy of Milan, Trivulziana 809).

Leid.1   Leiden, University Library Voss. Lat. F99. Written in 1447 (cf. *Manuscrits datés conservés dans les Pays-Bas* 1.94, no. 218; pl. 262.3); two hands, of which the first (ff. 1–170, including *Agamemnon*) may be South French. Owned by Dreux Ier Budé, later by Paul Petau (cf. K. de Meyier, *Petau* 126). Text shows significant agreements with d.

Leid.2   Leiden, University Library Voss. Lat. Q 31. Written in 1456 (cf. *Manuscrits datés* 1.95, no. 222; pls. 256–7) by Johannes P..ss.n (other letters illegible) for Henry de Marle (d. 1495); later owned by his son Jerome (d. after 1538) and thereafter by Petau (cf. de Meyier 74–6). Text shows significant agreements with Salutati's MS (London B.M. Add. MS 11987).

M1   Milan, Biblioteca Ambrosiana A118 inf. Italian, fifteenth century. Paper, ff. 155; 280 × 210. Contains tragedies and (on f. 151^r–152^v) a 'tragedia quedam de casu cesene' attributed to Coluccio Salutati; cf. Viansino, *Prolegomena* 88–90, Franceschini 73f.

M2   Milan, Biblioteca Ambrosiana G89 inf. Italian, late fourteenth century. Paper, ff. 174. Viansino 90–3, Franceschini 75f.

M3   Milan, Biblioteca Ambrosiana H77. Written by Giovanni de Gadio (Gudio?) of Cremona, in Verona in 1380/1 (cf. Megas (1967) 233). Parchment, ff. 246, 240 × 180. Viansino 93ff., Franceschini 62, MacGregor, *Survey*.

M4   Milan, Biblioteca Trivulziana 809. Italian, fourteenth century. Parchment, ff. 127, 320 × 225. Contains Trevet's commentary in margins (= Z in editions of Trevet). Viansino 85–8, Franceschini 46 n.1, C. Santoro, *I Codici miniati della biblioteca Trivulziana* (Milan, 1958) no. 100 (p. 93).

Ox.2   Oxford, Bodleian Library Ashmole 1791. Fifteenth century. Noteworthy for several agreements with EP against CS; not elsewhere subject to E-branch contamination.

Ox.3   Oxford, Bodleian Library d'Orville 176 (= Madan 17054). France (or England?), fifteenth century. Text heavily influenced by C (Trevet); possibly a copy of London, Society of Antiquaries 63 (for which cf. N. R. Ker, *Medieval manuscripts in British libraries* 1 (1969) 302).

Ox.4   Oxford, Bodleian Library Laud Lat. 71. Italian; belonged to Thebaldo de' Thebaldeschi. Contains verse *argumenta* of Pietro da Moglio (see above, p. 37).

Ox.5   Oxford, Bodleian Library Bodleianus 292 (= Madan 2446) vol. 1.368f.). English, early fifteenth century. Text and commentary of Trevet (ff. 1–119); also contains Trevet's commentary on Augustine's *de Ciuitate Dei* (for which cf. R. J. Dean, *Speculum* xvii (1942) 243–9) and on the elder Seneca's *Declamationes*; also a commentary on the *Ludus de morte Claudii* (ff. 156ᵛ–160ᵛ) of the fourteenth century, which circulates in other Oxford MSS (cf. C. F. Russo, *Parola del Passato* vii (1952) 48–65; P. T. Eden, *C & M* xxi (1960) 29–30).

The other Oxford MSS listed in the *sigla* were selectively examined; they appear to be undistinguished *recentiores*, and are cited rarely if at all.

Rome (Vatican City), Biblioteca Apostolica Vaticana

R1 Ottobonianus Latinus 1749. German (?), fifteenth century. Paper. The work of several hands, and full of reckless conjecture.

R2 Urbinas Latinus 356. Italian, fourteenth/fifteenth century. Parchment, ff. 159; 335 × 250. Fine illuminations. See C. Stornajolo, *Codices Urbinates Vaticani* I (1902) 329f.

R3 Vaticanus Latinus 1642. Italian, fifteenth century. Paper, ff. 190; 335 × 235. Contains (f. 188^v) verse *argumenta* based on those of Pietro da Moglio (see above, p. 37). For description cf. B. Nogara, *Codices Vaticani Latini* III (1912) 126.

R4 Vaticanus Latinus 1649. Italian, written in 1395 (f. 167^r). Parchment, ff. 168; 390 × 285. Ownership note on f. 166^v in later hand ('iste tragedie sunt mei Marij Ser. Ugolini de Amelia'). See Nogara 130f.

R5 Vaticanus Latinus 2827. Italian, fourteenth/fifteenth century. Several hands. Numerous glosses.

R6 Vaticanus Latinus 2828. Italian, fourteenth/fifteenth century. Marginal commentary in early plays only.

R7 Vaticanus Latinus 7319. Italian, fifteenth century. Contains tragedies and letters.

R8 Vaticanus Latinus 7620. Italian, late fourteenth century. Marginal commentary, much conjecture. MacGregor, *Survey*.

V1 Venice, Biblioteca Marciana 12.26. Written in Padua for Francesco Zabarella in 1395 (cf. Franceschini 17; Richter, *Kritische Untersuchungen* 11 n.2). Fine illuminations.

Vi.1 Vienna, National Library (formerly Hofbibliothek) 61 (211 Endlicher). Italian, fourteenth century; ff. 154. Single columns, with Trevet's commentary in margins.

The MS was collated in full by Stuart; the order of plays on f. 1 is that of MN (i.e. the E order with *Octauia* in tenth place), but this arrangement is not followed in the MS. The influence of an E-branch text is strong in the early plays, but declines sharply thereafter (Stuart, *Dissertation* 177, confirmed by MacGregor, *Survey*). The MS is also noteworthy for numerous conjectures, some of which betray more than mediocre acuteness.

Vi.2 Vienna, National Library 122 (210 Endlicher). North Europe (France or Flanders), early fifteenth century. Illuminated on a lavish scale by three Flemish masters for Charles VII of France while still Duc de Bourges (hence before 1422). Trevet's commentary in margins, text and glosses on alternate lines. Ff. 369; 285 × 205. For description and plate of f. 206ᵛ cf. F. Unterkircher, *Abendländische Buchmalerei: Miniaturen aus Handschriften der österreichischen Nationalbibliothek* (1967) 200–3.

COLLECTIONS OF EXCERPTS

L Leiden, University Library 191 B (variously called Excerpta Leidensia, Eclogae Lugdunenses, Anecdoton Lugdunense). North Europe, mid-fourteenth century (the hand is very similar to that of another text in 191 B, William of Bolonselle's *Peregrinatio ad terram sanctam*, dated on f. 182 to 1351). The MS comprises several unrelated texts and was assembled at St Jacques in Liège in the late fifteenth century. See G. I. Lieftinck, *Manuscrits datés conservés dans les Pays-Bas* (1964) 1.81 (no. 186), II pl. 144 (plate of f. 170). The Seneca excerpts appear in ff. 155ʳ–159ᵛ; they were first published by Leo in 1873. See also Woesler 44ff.; Philp 170.

Brux Brussels, Bibliothèque Royale 20030–2 (van den Gheyn 1508). Written at the Cistercian house at Villers in the mid-thirteenth century. The Senecan excerpts on f. 133ᵛ–134ʳ and f. 176ʳ–177ᵛ form part of a large *florilegium* called the *Flores Paradysii*; the Senecan material has previously been cited from a less complete text of this collection in MS 4785–93 (van den Gheyn 970) of the early thirteenth century (f. 140^v–142^r). See Rouse 98ff.; Woesler 44ff.; Philp 169f.

Exon   Exeter, Cathedral Library 3549B. North France (?), first half of the thirteenth century. Contains excerpts from nine plays (f. 194), complete text of *Octauia* (ff. 190^v–194^r) and *Ludus de morte Claudii* (ff. 257–9); description and complete contents in C. J. Herington, *Rh. Mus.* ci (1958) 353, 375ff. Owned by John Grandisson (1292–1369; bishop of Exeter 1327–69). See Rouse 97f.

Gon   Cambridge, Gonville and Caius College 225. Thirteenth century (second half), from Bury St Edmunds (f. 1^v 'liber monachorum sti Edmundi'). Excerpts appear on ff. 7^r–9^r and are taken from nine plays (*Phoenissae* is not represented), in A order (i.e. with *Octauia* and *Hercules Oetaeus* in that order at the end).[1] For description cf. M. R. James, *Descriptive catalogue of the manuscripts in the library of Gonville and Caius College* (1907) 1.263–6; Rouse 115f. The excerpts were presumably taken from the MS of the tragedies which was at Bury St Edmunds at this time (it is recorded as a Bury book in the Franciscan *Registrum Anglie de libris doctorum et auctorum*, composed between 1260 and 1306; I have consulted MS Oxford Tanner 165 and MS Cambridge Peterhouse 169) and which is described in greater detail in the Bury catalogue of Henry of Kirkestede (mid-fourteenth century):[2] the incipit and explicit in Kirkestede's list show that the MS began with *HF* and ended with *HO* (whose last line appears in the form *fulmina montes*), and the catalogue also specifies nine plays, thus giving an exact correspondence with the formation of the excerpts in

---

[1] The statement of Rouse, 'the extracts are taken from eight plays (there are none from *Hippolytus* and *Agamemnon*') (p. 115) is mistaken.

[2] For the catalogue, formerly attributed to 'Boston of Bury', cf. Rouse, *Speculum* xli (1966) 471–99; for the classical authors cf. R. A. B. Mynors in *Memorial essays for Fritz Saxl* (1957) 199–217.

Gonville and Caius 225.[1] This same Bury MS was probably the source of another set of excerpts (now lost) in the Bury MS British Museum Royal 12 C VI (*s*. xiii/xiv).

Par   Paris, Bibliothèque Nationale Lat. 8049. Italian, fourteenth century (for the Seneca excerpts on ff. 28^r–45^v; the MS is a composite also containing Persius in a good Caroline hand, part of Cicero's *de Diuinatione*, and excerpts from Petronius), 260 × 200 (190 × 150); two columns, 37 lines each. The excerpts from the tragedies are grouped in an alphabetical collection of material from the prose works, Publilius Syrus, and other writers; the plays come at the end of each letter (cf. Rouse 116 n.5); they were printed by R. Peiper, *De Senecae tragoediarum uulgari lectione constituenda* (1893) 17ff.

Vin   Vincent of Beauvais, excerpts from the tragedies in *Speculum Historiale* 9.113–14 (published by Leo in 1873 together with the excerpts in Leiden 191 B, pp. 39ff.), themselves drawn from an excerpt collection (cf. Rouse 99 and 105). Before 1244, when Vincent completed the work.

Hieremias   Hieremias de Montagnone (1250/60–1321?), Paduan lawyer and jurist; excerpts from the tragedies in his *Compendium moralium notabilium* (after 1295). See B. L. Ullman, *Studies* 88ff., R. Weiss, *Primo secolo dell'umanesimo* (1949) 15–50; the excerpts were printed by Peiper, *op. cit.* 171–8.

The excerpt collections have no importance for the constitution of the text, since they contain no reading not already known through E P CS which is not attributable either to conjecture or to corruption. They are, however, of interest in tracing the transmission of the plays, and since they do not derive from E P CS, they merit citation in the few passages they contain.

The Leiden collection contains the most extensive corpus of

---

[1] The Bury MS thus offers no evidence for the interpolation of *Octauia* into the corpus (as suggested by MacGregor, *Survey*).

material: *flores* are taken from nine plays (*Octauia* is unrepresented), and are divided into *cantica* and *diuerbia*. The order of plays is basically that of A, but *Phaedra* is used instead of *Hippolytus* and in the *diuerbia* excerpts from *Phoenissae* follow those from *Oedipus* (an arrangement found again in Vat. Lat. 1769 = N). Although the immediate source of L was probably also a *florilegium*,[1] the collection seems not far removed from a complete MS, judging from the careful notation of line-endings in the *cantica*.[2] The text of L clearly has an A origin, but is independent of the errors of both δ and β and agrees with E against P CS in eighteen true and four false readings. The most satisfying explanation of the facts is to conclude that L derives from A before the division into δ and β; its agreements with E in error and with *recentiores* may be regarded as coincidental.[3] Contamination from an E source is, while not impossible, unlikely in north Europe at this time. If this placing of L is correct, the omission of *Octauia* may be significant.[4] The Leiden collection has no known relatives or descendants.[5]

The Brussels and Exeter collections may be connected on both textual and codicological grounds.[6] The text of *Octauia* in Exeter 3549 B derives from the same hyparchetype (δ) as P, and the Brussels material (i.e. the *Flores Paradysii*) also gives clear indications of a δ source; the evidence for the excerpts in Exeter 3549 B is less compelling because of the small quantity of material, but it too points to a source within δ.[7] The place of origin for the Exeter excerpts was presumably also that of the Exeter text of *Octauia*, and thus probably that of P (or its

---

[1] Woesler 95 n.5.

[2] Richter, *Kritische Untersuchungen* (1899) 34 n.1, noted that *HF* 174b–194 appear in L with correspondence of sense- and line-units. The notation of line-endings, however, is general.

[3] The use of *Phaedra*, regarded as a counter-argument by Woesler, may conceivably reflect an alternative still present in A.

[4] See below, pp. 52ff.

[5] Brugnoli's attempt (in *Annali della Facoltà di Lettere dell'Università di Cagliari* (1960) 156–61) to connect the excerpts in Rehdigeranus 73 Ziegler (*s.* xv, f. 108ᵛ) to L is misguided.

[6] In this paragraph I am in general summarising the full discussion by Rouse (99–112). [7] Woesler 44–6; also Philp 169f.

parent) as well. Since P is firmly located in northern France and the Exeter MS, the *Flores Paradysii*, and Vincent's *Speculum*[1] all have certain or plausible north French origins, this yields a fairly precise temporal and geographical context for δ: 'in sum, text δ of the *Tragedies* and the collection of extracts made from it may well have appeared in Paris between the late twelfth and mid-thirteenth centuries'.[2]

The Bury excerpts, however, are an English product and appear closer to β than to δ.[3] This fits well with the β character of Corpus Christi (Cambridge) 406, a probably English MS of the early thirteenth century.[4] It is remarkable that, while δ is securely located in north France, there is no specimen of the β text from this area; β appears in thirteenth-century England and fourteenth-century Italy. Since, however, there is no certain evidence of a Seneca MS in England before the end of the twelfth century,[5] it is reasonable to suspect that the β text was imported from the continent. The twelfth-century texts in the Corpus MS were school readings in Paris as well as Oxford, and two Englishmen of the early thirteenth century who display an awareness of the tragedies, Alexander Neckam and Gervasius of Melkley, had studied or taught in Paris.[6]

---

[1] The place of Vincent is less easily fixed, owing to the inconsistency of some readings in passages cited more than once and the lack of a reliable critical edition; the agreements with δ sources cited by Rouse (100f.), however, make a δ origin of Vincent's material likely.

[2] Rouse 112.

[3] The clearest example is *Thy.* 307 *miserias* E P L Brux Exon Vin: *miseris* C S Gon.

[4] See above, pp. 33f.; the hand of the Seneca is not beyond doubt English, and the English provenance rests primarily on the script of the other texts.

[5] No Seneca MS appears in the mid-twelfth-century Bury catalogue (Rouse 116 and n.1), and the identification of the MS described in a late fourteenth-century Peterborough catalogue with the *Epp. Senece cum aliis Senece in uno uolumine* in a late twelfth-century book list of Peterborough abbey is uncertain (Rouse 114 n.1). The two citations of Seneca by Aldhelm (*c.* 639–709) probably derive from a grammatical source rather than a complete MS (cf. J. D. A. Ogilvy, *Books known to the English 597–1066*[2] (1967) 240).

[6] Neckam, in a list of school-texts composed between 1200 and 1211, notes 'tragediam ipsius [sc. Senecae] et declamaciones legere non erit inutile'

The Italian branch of β furnishes the sources for the excerpts in Paris B.N. Lat. 8049 and Geremia de Montagnone. The Paris excerpts lack interest, but Geremia's collection of more than two hundred lines illustrates a new phase of the transmission. It is related to no other surviving *florilegium*[1] and its composition suggests an independent selection made directly from a complete MS. The text is clearly A in origin; agreement with E is limited to right readings, suggesting either contamination or independent conjecture (or both).[2] Within A the closest links appear to be with the η MSS KQ e, but the publications of Geremia's material by Peiper and Giardina are based on partial and conflicting MS evidence, making a firm conclusion impossible. In general, though, it may be said that Geremia's collection reflects the type of contaminated β MS which

(cf. Rouse 113 n.1 with further bibliography). MacGregor (*Survey*) now ingeniously suggests that the singular *tragediam* refers to the *Octauia* and supports the hypothesis of its separate circulation until the twelfth century; the evidence, however, will hardly bear the weight of this connection. For Gervasius's two allusions to the tragedies in his *Ars Poetica* (written around 1216), cf. Rouse 113 n.2; they concern Seneca's use of multiple *antilabe* and of *anticipatio* in disputes, and can hardly be based on excerpts. A third thirteenth-century English citation has been noted by R. W. Hunt (I owe the precise reference to R. H. Rouse). In New College MS 21 (f. 31ʳ), as an addendum to a gloss on Isaiah 22.13 (*comedamus et bibamus; cras enim moriemur*), lines 394–406 of *Troades* have been transcribed and introduced with the words 'hanc sententiam epicuri ponit seneca in tragedia que troas inscribitur his uerbis'. The text of the lines avoids three peculiar errors of the Corpus MS (396 *tegimur*, 404 *cerebrus*, 406 *pars*) and contains four unique errors (396 *hoc*, *effluens*; 403 *trenera* (?), 404 *exitu* for *ostio*); it also contains *mors* in 397, a word omitted by L. Unfortunately, the passage offers no basis for assigning the text to δ or β. Independence of C is virtually certain, and the Bury excerpts cannot have been the source; the glossator probably used a complete MS (line-endings are scrupulously observed), and his reference to Epicurus betrays noteworthy familiarity with the matter of the plays. Finally, lines 407–8, wrongly placed after 399 in E² P CS, do not appear in the New College citation.

[1] Brugnoli ('Tradizione manoscritta' 232f.) suggested L as Geremia's main source, but there are only two agreements in errors against the paradosis, both insignificant and easily accounted for as independent trivialisation (omission of -*que* in *Tro.* 259, *lapsis* for *lassis* in *Thy.* 616), while Geremia agrees with E P CS (or E or P CS) against a reading of L seven times.

[2] Geremia includes *Med.* 156, missing in P CS KQ but found in the Etonensis (and E).

dominates the fourteenth-century transmission. The *Compendium* was written after 1295, which is very close to the time of Lovato's alleged discovery of E at Pomposa, and the presence of E readings in it may be due to Geremia's Paduan connections. The work shows that contamination of a β text had begun in Italy shortly before or after 1300.

ORIGINS AND CHARACTER OF
THE E AND A BRANCHES

Leo's *Obseruationes Criticae* begins with these words: 'nouem Senecae tragoedias ante extinctas Romanorum litteras data opera homo aliquis non indoctus interpolauit. idem Octauiam praetextatam, primis Flauiorum temporibus scriptam, nouem tragoediarum corpori iniunxit mutatique ordinis locum tenere iussit nonum.' This characteristically lapidary assertion draws together and to a degree confuses three logically distinct questions: when in the transmission did the division into two branches, E and A, occur? (put otherwise: what is the date of the archetype, or is there an archetype later than the author's own text?); when did the thorough stylistic interpolation visible in A take place? when was the *Octauia* added to the genuine plays?[1] Leo answered all three questions in the phrase 'ante extinctas Romanorum litteras' (i.e. before the end of the fifth century), but in at least two of the three cases this now seems doubtful. Only the division of E and A may with confidence be dated to late antiquity; the main A interpolation and the incorporation of *Octauia* may both be as late as the twelfth century. The following discussion is brief, since much important evidence was gathered by Stuart and recently promulgated by Woesler and Philp;[2] some arguments have been modified and others added to produce what I hope is a more firmly based and clearer synthesis.

---

[1] The *HO*, though equally spurious, seems to have been part of the corpus from a very early date.
[2] Woesler 73–82; Philp 172–9.

First, the old view[1] that E and A descend *recta uia* from two editions of the plays by Seneca himself may be dismissed. Even if the majority of A readings could plausibly be regarded as author's variants, the two branches agree in scores, perhaps hundreds, of common errors.[2] Such agreements are hardly to be explained as coincidences; the existence of an archetype (i.e. a common ancestor of all surviving MSS later than the author's own MS) is beyond doubt.

External evidence offers little aid in dating this archetype. A secure *terminus ante quem* is supplied by the excerpts in the tantalising *florilegium* Paris Bibl. Nat. Lat. 8071 (the so-called *Codex Thuaneus* = T); these agree with E in several wrong readings and thus attest the existence of an E branch as their source.[3] The MS itself was written in the second half of the ninth century in France, possibly at Fleury,[4] but several of the texts it contains (Martial, the Latin Anthology, Grattius's *Cynegeticon*, the ps.-Ovidian *Halieutica*, and Nemesianus) were copied from a Carolingian court MS of the late eighth century, Vienna Nationalbibliothek 277 (= *CLA* x.1474, ff. 55–73). It is impossible to date the source of the Seneca excerpts; their remarkably corrupt state is not necessarily a sign of long separation from a complete MS, since other texts in T suffer from comparably negligent copying.[5] Even on a conservative reckoning, however, the *terminus* imposed by T is probably closer to 750 or even 700 than to 800.[6]

---

[1] Propounded by Siegmund and Kunst; cf. Woesler 105 n.2.

[2] Philp's assertion (177) that 'far from sharing widespread corruption... they [i.e. E and A] only seldom concur in error' is slightly misleading; the Seneca transmission is not comparable with those of Catullus and Propertius, but more emendation is required than most previous editors have allowed.

[3] Woesler 105 n.1; Philp 170f.

[4] On the MS cf. H. Schenkl, *NJb* suppl. xxiv (1898) 399f., J. A. Richmond's edition of the *Halieutica* (1962) 6–9. I owe the information regarding a possible Fleury origin to R. H. Rouse, who is currently investigating the history of the MS.

[5] Of the three MSS of the *Peruigilium Veneris*, for example, Par. Lat. 8071 is by far the most inaccurate.

[6] The only other early medieval witness to the E branch, Eugenius Vulgarius (see above, p. 27), may be situated near 900.

An earlier *terminus ante quem* has been sought in several late antique citations in which E contains errors not in A or the source of the citation.[1] Richter[2] and more recently Brugnoli[3] have taken these passages as evidence for the existence of A in late antiquity, but agreement in true readings is, of course, worthless for this purpose. Each author may have been citing an A text,[4] but three other possibilities are equally valid: each may have used (1) a MS which antedated the division of E and A, (2) a MS belonging to a third branch of tradition which was not copied in the Middle Ages and so is not otherwise preserved, or (3) an E-branch MS in which the errors present in the Etruscus had not yet been made. The first is perhaps the most likely and the third hardly more than a theoretical possibility, but when the evidence is so meagre none may be excluded.

The few citations from the early Middle Ages[5] have been similarly misinterpreted by Brugnoli.[6] He asserts that these centuries ignored the E text[7] and knew the tragedies only in an 'uninterpolated A' version; since he places the division of E and A in the tenth century, any reference to A before this point, uninterpolated or not, is clearly nonsensical. This apart, the mere absence of E errors in early medieval citations proves nothing about the existence of an A tradition; the same four possibilities exist here as for the late antique citations just mentioned. A branch of tradition can only be identified as such by significant errors,[8] and no characteristic A error has been

---

[1] Texts in Woesler 106 n.3; the authors involved are Augustine, Ennodius, Priscian, and Lactantius Placidus.

[2] *Kritische Untersuchungen* (1899) 6; cf. Philp 175 n.10. Richter avoided the fault of method by wrongly thinking the A readings were errors.

[3] 'Tradizione manoscritta' *passim*.

[4] Augustine's citation, however, avoids an error present in P CS; his source, if A, contained a purer state of that branch than is preserved in our MSS.

[5] Texts conveniently assembled in Franceschini 3–8.

[6] The defects of his study have been pointed out by Zwierlein, *Rezitationsdramen* 212ff.; surprisingly, the essential point of Brugnoli's hypothesis is endorsed by Philp (175).

[7] He misinterprets the evidence of T and of Eugenius Vulgarius.

[8] In the case of A, 'errors' must be carefully distinguished from interpolations.

discovered in the secondary tradition until the end of the twelfth century.[1]

In determining the date of the archetype, and consequently of the division of the E and A branches, the evidence of the fifth-century Ambrosian palimpsest (R)[2] is clearly relevant. Unfortunately, R's testimony is difficult to interpret: Giardina[3] regards it as a witness to the pre-archetypal, undivided tradition, Philp[4] as the earliest evidence for the separate existence of A, and Zwierlein[5] as a third offshoot of the archetype, independent of both E and A. Both the second and the third hypothesis entail placing the archetype in the fourth or fifth century at the latest (i.e. R becomes a *terminus ante quem* for the archetype itself), while the first merely requires that the archetype be later than the source of R and therefore establishes no criterion for precise dating.

The evidence consists of a handful of R's agreements with E and A and of independent readings in R. In such a case one cannot speak of proof: the most economical hypothesis deserves preference. Previous discussion has rightly concentrated attention on two passages. In *Medea* 204, R and A agree in the corrupt (and meaningless) *caput*, while E preserves the true reading, *putet*. In the absence of RE agreement in an error of comparable weight, this is strong evidence for R's derivation from the A branch. In *Medea* 226, however, R alone has the correct *Graeciae* and EA agree in *gloriae*.[6] If R and A have a common source which is not a source of E, R's unique good

---

[1] Brugnoli's reconstruction of A is also defective in not resting exclusively on P CS.

[2] Milan, Biblioteca Ambrosiana G 82 sup.; for description cf. E. A. Lowe, *Codices Latini Antiquiores* III (Oxford, 1938), nos. 344–6. The transcription of the Senecan material done by W. Studemund for Leo (cf. Leo's text volume, xv–xxix) is the basis of all modern discussions.

[3] *Vichiana* ii (1965) 38ff.; *Bollettino* 64ff.

[4] *CQ* N.S. xviii (1968) 173ff., 177f.

[5] *Gnomon* xli (1969) 763f.; see also Woesler 77.

[6] R's two other correct readings where both E and A are corrupt (*Med.* 220 *eripuit exilio* R: *eripuit et exilio* EA, 267 *feminae* R: *feminea* EA) carry less weight individually. Either or both might have been corrected by a reasonably alert copyist or reader.

reading is best accounted for by considering *gloriae* the archetypal reading[1] and *Graeciae* a variant imported into the A hyparchetype from another source; R made the correct choice between the variants, A did not.[2] *Graeciae* and *gloriae* are both intelligible; it is plausible that they might have circulated as alternatives, and that two copies of a MS containing both readings might have chosen differently between them. Neither of the competing hypotheses (R as prearchetypal; R, E, and A as independent copies of the archetype) can explain the evidence without recourse to much less probable assumptions.[3] The balance of plausibility favours regarding R and A as descended from a common source; the archetype of E and A is therefore to be dated earlier than R.

Internal criteria for dating the division of E and A must also be considered, in particular the palaeographical evidence. Here caution is required, since in any transmission the causes of error are numerous and complex, and the misreading of scripts a relatively infrequent factor.

It has often been observed[4] that E and A contain virtually no common errors traceable to the misreading of minuscule script; indeed, in this case 'virtually' may be an unnecessary qualification. Of the three examples alleged by Brugnoli, not one is certain: in *Tro.* 633 the true reading is in doubt (E has *sicre*, i.e. *scire*; P CS *sero*), but it is surely not Paratore's *ferre* (presumed true by Brugnoli); in *Pha.* 428 the change from *iussa* to *iusta* (E P CS) might be psychological, induced by *scelus* in the previous line, and thus not palaeographically based; in *Oed.* 243 where E P CS give *querit*, the true reading may be, not Avantius's

---

[1] *Graeciae* may have been corrupted to *gloriae* by anticipation of the following *florem*; certainly *Graeciae* poses no difficulty which might have prompted interpolation.

[2] It is also possible that *Graeciae* (and R's two other correct readings) entered R's immediate ancestor or R itself, rather than the A hyparchetype, but this would make the failure to correct the obviously corrupt *caput* harder to explain.

[3] In particular the assumption that either A, or R and A chose the meaningless *caput* from the variant-pair *caput–putet*.

[4] Woesler 78; Philp 176; Zwierlein, *Gnomon* xli (1969) 764.

queritur, but Wilamowitz's *curat* (omitted because the following line begins with *curam*, and replaced by the makeweight *qu(a)erit*.[1] Philp has added a fourth, *sors* for *fors* in *Pho.* 632, but this too may be an unconscious trivialisation without a palaeographical basis. My analysis of EA errors in *Agamemnon* reveals none which clearly derives from a misreading of minuscule, and indeed none which is without doubt purely palaeographical. This is in itself a minor argument for an early division of E and A; had the tradition remained unified through many copyings, a larger number of palaeographical errors might be expected.[2]

It is illegitimate, however, to conclude from the lack of shared minuscule errors that the archetype was not written in minuscule script.[3] The presence of common minuscule errors would require their derivation from the archetype, and would thus indicate at least one pre-archetypal MS in minuscule. Were the archetype itself in minuscule, but copied directly from a capital or uncial MS, one could expect each of its descendants (in this case E and A) to display individual minuscle errors, but not shared minuscule errors (since the latter would have to have been made twice independently).[4] In fact, both E and A do contain individual minuscule errors.[5]

To rule out a minuscule archetype, therefore, more than the absence of shared minuscule errors is required. If E and A each contained individual majuscule errors, an archetype in majuscule script (capital or uncial) would be indicated;[6] this appears

---

[1] For this type of error, cf. Housman, *Manilius* i.livff.

[2] The corruption of *iuncta* to *inuita* (307) and of *alio* to *alto* (500) might have a palaeographical cause, but in neither case is this certain. Philp (177) argues that 'the most cogent proof of an early division of the tradition lies in the wide separation of the two texts'; but since A has been thoroughly interpolated, this separation could have been created largely at one time, perhaps as late as the twelfth century.

[3] The argument is so used by Woesler 78; Philp 176; Zwierlein 764.

[4] For the principle, cf. S. Timpanaro, *La genesi del metodo del Lachmann* (1963) 100–11.

[5] For E, cf. Woesler 107 n.6 (drawing on Stuart, *diss.* 31), for A see below, p. 61.

[6] Separate minuscule errors in E and A would then be derived from minuscule hyparchetypes.

to be the case. E's majuscule errors are more numerous and obvious,[1] perhaps because it has been less often copied and never systematically corrected; they include confusions of L and I and L and T (*HF* 1123 *uili* for *ulti*, *Ag.* 576 *illo* for *Ilio*), E and F (*Ag.* 201 *perfunde* for *pereundo*, *Tro.* 817 *et hie* for *fthie*), C and G (*Med.* 382 *iunget* for *uincet*, 549 *signatos* for *sic natos*), and AI and M (*Ag.* 538 *magis* for *Aiacis*; also C–G).[2] For A the material is frankly meagre: the C–G confusion in *Med.* 132 (*incestum* for *ingestum*) may stand, though it is also an example of trivialisation; the other examples adduced by Stuart,[3] involving confusion of C and P, appear doubtful at best. These letters are occasionally (though not often) confused in capital script,[4] but in these three cases the A reading either is or may be correct (*Tro.* 395 *dissicat* E: -*pat* P CS; 457 *expulit* E: *excutit* P CS, *recte*; 1115 *impulsu* E: *incursu* P CS, perhaps a genuine *lectio difficilior*?). In spite of A's failure to display unmistakable majuscule errors, the clear presence of such errors in E suggests that E and A descend independently from a capital archetype. The evidence of R makes it likely that the division of E and A had taken place by the fifth century, and so points to an archetype of the fourth or early fifth century at the latest.[5]

Despite its early date, the archetype had already suffered considerable damage; in *Agamemnon* I have corrected it in approximately fifty places, which suggests that the entire corpus

---

[1] Leo, *Obs.* 8f. (though his assertion that E is a direct copy of a capital MS has been disproven).

[2] I disallow Philp's instance of an L–R confusion (*Tro.* 634, *lustrare* for *lustrale*); the exchange is not easy in capital scripts, and the error might be a trivialisation. I also place no weight on errors of faulty word-division in E (and, less often, in A); some early minuscule MSS are as difficult to read in this respect as MSS in capital scripts.

[3] Philp 177 (and n.2); two examples cited by Philp are illusory, since in *HF* 504 A's *remolito* is correct (*demolito* in E) and in *Pha.* 336 A's *c(a)erulus* is correct, E's *peruius* a corruption perhaps induced by recollection of line 88, where *peruius* is used of Nereus.

[4] See L. Havet, *Manuel de critique verbale appliqué aux textes latins* (1911) 160 sect. 607.

[5] It has been noticed that the E and A hyparchetypes each contained 42 or 43 lines per folio (i.e. 21–2 lines to a side), cf. Woesler 105 n.2; such a physical arrangement fits a late antique date for the hyparchetypes.

(excluding the *Octauia*) may harbour nearly five hundred errors. Furthermore, the most extensive corruptions, involving the omission, displacement, or insertion of whole lines, are largely archetypal;[1] the individual interpolations of the E and A branches are more limited in scope and more modest in purpose.

In addition to large-scale corruption, the archetype contains errors due to the ordinary vagaries of scribes,[2] for example trivialisation of unfamiliar words or forms (515 *Agamemno*, 648 *Hecabe*, 566 *Chalcida*), insertion of glosses or explanatory notes (542 *in se*, 785 *Troia*, perhaps 898 *prius*), perseveration (529 *et* changed to *aut* under the influence of the preceding *aut*, so also the first word of 530; 888 *negat* for *negant* because of *uestis* earlier in the line).

It also seems probable that archetypal error may be present in places where E and A differ and neither offers a satisfying text. In 551, for example, E has *pepulerunt gradu* (repeated from 549) and A *mitti dextera*; E may have reproduced an archetypal error which A attempted to heal by interpolation. In such cases (which are perhaps not rare, but seldom as easily recognised as this one), A's text has no authority and the editor is free to accept a more elegant conjectural correction.

The second and third questions posed at the start may now be more briefly touched on. Although the absence of *Octauia* and of systematic interpolation in E might suggest that *Octauia* was added when the A-branch was subjected to interpolation, there is no connection in logic between the two. No external evidence suggests that *Octauia* circulated with the other plays in late antiquity or the early Middle Ages,[3] nor is any characteristic A interpolation cited in the secondary tradition before the end of the twelfth century. It is thus possible that both the interpolation of A and the incorporation of *Octauia* took place

---

[1] For possible omissions, cf. commentary on 13f., 159, 273ff., 290; displacement, cf. 471; insertion, cf. 545–6, 548, 755, 934.

[2] Here and in the sections on E and A only selected examples are cited.

[3] The alleged imitations of *Octauia* by Boethius cited by Woesler (106f. n.3) are unconvincing.

at a relatively late point in the transmission, shortly before the appearence of the earliest A MSS in the first half of the thirteenth century. Two pieces of external evidence support this hypothesis, at least as regards *Octauia*: the early thirteenth-century Exeter MS (3549 B = G) contains *Octauia* alone (the only MS which does so), and the Leiden Excerpts, which probably derive from A before the division into δ and β, contain no excerpts from *Octauia*, although they are the most extensive and orderly surviving collection of extracts.

Given the silence of the secondary tradition, the dating of A interpolation must rest on an evaluation of the variants themselves. My own impression is that very few, if any, exceed the capabilities of a bold and learned twelfth-century scholar. A smattering of exceptions[1] would not disturb this hypothesis, since interpolation seems to have been constantly at work in the Seneca transmission; the thorough and deliberate interpolation which has left its mark in A, however, may have been a product of the twelfth rather than of the fourth or fifth century.

The E and A branches separately contain many examples of error (mechanical and psychological) and of interpolation. E is distinguished for errors perhaps resulting from misreading of capital script and for faulty word-division; A's most note-worthy feature is its widespread and wilful interpolation. A short (and selective) list follows.[2]

Omissions. E: 182; 131 *ut*; 569 *e* (haplography). A: 194; 694; 279 *uita*; 604 *-ue*.

Misreading of script or abbreviation. E: possible capital errors 51 *timet* (*temet*), 81 *faciunt* (*fugiunt*), 201 *perfunde* (*pereundo*), 538 *magis* (*aiacis*), 650 *deferre* (*deflere*), 737 *alta* (*alia*), 889 *inuli* (*inuii*);

---

[1] A's interpolation *Briseidam* for *Lyrnesida* (186) would require a close familiarity with Ovid, Seneca's source for the learned epithet; this is not impossible in the twelfth century, and in this instance the A reading may be the result of a gloss's having been substituted for the original reading.

[2] The true reading (or in some cases the archetypal reading) appears in parentheses. Controversial passages are generally omitted.

minuscule errors 133 *iuxtus* (*mixtus*), 483 *eteoeo sonus* (*et eoos sinus*), 702 *exhaustu* (*-sta*; note also a–u confusion in 81 *faciunt* for *fugiunt*),[1] 867 *per annos* (*par annis*; misreading followed by accommodation), 959 *semitam* (*feminam*).

A: minuscule errors 403a *artamur* (*attamen*), 428 *regimen emouit* (*remigem monuit*), 701 *fratrum* (*fraterni*), 756 *migrantis* (*nigrantis*),[2] 760 *uerba* (*uerbera*), 938 *demum* (*donum*).

Wrong word-division. E: (with no further alteration) 234 *periclis otia* (*-cli socia*), 358 *tibi abuxo* (*tibia b.*), 418 *mensae gratantis* (*mens aegra t.*); (with further alteration) 298 *sub rupe reductus* (*subripere doctus*), 301 *regia* (*regi ac*; corruption induced by preceding *haec*), 439 *ualidam subracchia* (*ualida nisu b.*), 846 *seuistrinxitque* (*s(a)euis tinxitque*).

Accommodation to surroundings. E: 428 *summa* (*summas*). A: 503 *populata* (*-o*), 593 *impotens* (*-ntis*). Adjustment of syntax. E: 411 *regis* (*regi*), 480 *ad* (*ac*), 485 *reuellit* (*reuelli*). A: 36 *miscuit* (*miscui*), 477 *mittunt* (*mittit*), 702f. *regiam...uacuam* (*-a...-a*).

Anticipation. E: 262 *aliquis* (*-quid*), with *uictor* following; 291 *generoso* (*-a*), followed by *exuli*; 413 *classa* (*-e*), influenced by *tanta*; 597 *minas* (*minaces*), with *iras* following. (Note also 14, 620, 683, 764, 851.) A: 326 *phebe* (*pace*), with *Phoebe* following; 409 *gerens* (*ferens*), by influence of *gerit* immediately below; 429 *aurora* (*aurata*), because of *prora*; also 689, 727.

Perseveration. E: 126 *consilia* (*-ii*), with *tacita* preceding; 257 *nollet* (*nolet*), from *illa*; 298 *tori* (*-os*), under influence of *genialis*; 596 *coetos* (*-us*), from *nullos*. A: 52 *an* (*ad*), from earlier *an*; 580 *laeter* (*-or*), from previous *laeter* (579); 664 *lacrimas lacrimas* (*-as -is*); 915 *fugis* (*times*), because of preceding *fugis*. (Note also 400, 702, 849.)

Introduction of glosses or marginal notes. E: 397a *lacrimas mesta eternum marmora manant*, 450 *id* (*iam*), 933 *quid sit* (*caesus*), 907 *dixi* (*iustae*), 973 *tibi* (*uolens*); perhaps also 162 *dolet* (*piget*),

---

[1] It is tempting to take these a–u confusions as indicating the type of minuscule in which E's exemplar (or a more remote ancestor) was written, but the evidence is too meagre and the possibilities too numerous.

[2] This might also be an interpolation, though *migrantis poli* is hardly a *lectio facilior*.

300 *nostrae* (*clarae*), 742 *testis uel* (*te sequor*). A: 186 *Briseidam* (*Lyrnesida*), 526 *simul* (*uehet*), 667 *enim* (*tu*), 786 *cur* (*quid*).

Trivialisation. Tenses. E: 753 *uehit* (*-et*), 821 *mouet* (*-it*); A: 365 *cadit* (*-et*), 659 *petit* (*-et*), 887 *tradet* (*-it*). Persons. E: 871 *resurgit* (*-is*). Moods. A: 204 *temptas* (*-es*), 875 *spectamus* (*-emus*).

Interpolation. In E unmistakably conscious alteration is quite rare. The false attribution of 288ff. to the Nutrix is an example (caused by the problem of *nubet* in 290 if spoken by Clytemestra), and in 745–8 interpolation has been used to cope with a damaged or illegible exemplar. Other places in which at least half-conscious change may have occurred include: 45 *securem* (*-es*), 162 *peperi* (*-it*), 172 *alio* (*Aulis*), 220 *uictrix* (*ultrix*), 240 *referemus* (*remeemus*), 315 *stirpis Inachiae* (*stirps Inachia*), 475 *infimum euerso polo* (*infimo euersum solo*), 689 *furit* (*ferit*), 730 *Idae* (*Idaea*), 872 *parens* (*pares*).[1]

In A, on the other hand, there are more than sixty instances of wilful alteration, usually to remove an allusively or idiomatically expressed point, or to enliven a passage which appeared flat to the interpolator. In 38 *incertae* was improved to *incestae*; Seneca's generic or restrained epithets were replaced by more expressive ones (84 *tumidas* for *nimias*; 738 *uexatus* for *sublimis*; 747 *fortes* for *illos*, 818 *candida* for *pallida*);[2] the puzzling *addimus* (297) was replaced by *aduocas*, the archaic *facesse* (299) by *secede*, the rare *putem* (694) by *reor*. The aims of the interpolator are syntactical regularity and simplicity of expression; in his intolerance of what appeared anomalous he recalls Bentley at his worst.

Wherever E and A differ, the editor must accord their variants equal stemmatic value; the choice between them must be based on internal grounds alone. (Where E P agree against CS or E CS against P, however, this normally gives the reading of the archetype.) The process of *selectio* is significantly complicated by the thorough interpolation of A; while in many places its

---

[1] From other plays Woesler (110 n.10) cites *Tro.* 472 *rediuiua* (*recidiua*), *Pha.* 769 *comae* (*rosae*), *Oed.* 45 *die* (*nouo*).

[2] Similar is A's Ovidian *misso fregere* for *uictos uidere* (340).

readings are better because they are authentic, in others the attractions of A are specious and E's difficulty or obscurity are genuinely Senecan. Striking the proper balance between E and A is the most persistent problem in editing Seneca's tragedies; while Leo's professed contempt for A was overdone, an awareness of its interpolated character is a legitimate and necessary factor in the weighing of E and A variants.[1]

E AND Σ

Only three manuscripts – F M N – have so far been identified as belonging to the same branch of tradition as E.[2] These three MSS derive from a common ancestor, traditionally called Σ: none is the parent of another, and MN appear to have in common a source which was not a source of F. It is important for an editor to decide whether F MN are descended directly from E itself, or whether Σ was an independent copy of E's exemplar; if their independence could be established, the agreement of F MN with P CS would in theory distinguish *lectiones singulares* of E from readings of its exemplar.

The only editor to have considered the matter seriously, Leo, dismissed M and N as directly descended from E.[3] This judgement has not been formally contested, although several editors have either pronounced or treated M or N or both as independent of F.[4] In addition, the significance of F for recon-

---

[1] See commentary on lines 38, 161f., 220, 340, 414, 738, etc.

[2] Giardina has attempted to identify a fourth descendant of Σ in Neap. Orat. CF 4.5 (= O), cf. *Bollettino dell'Accad. Naz. dei Lincei* xiii (1965) 61ff., praef. ix–x. O's descent from Σ cannot be ruled out, since it contains the plays roughly in the E order and with the E titles (the clearest external signs of the E tradition); it has, however, an E-branch text in only two complete plays (*HF, Tro.*) and parts of three others (*Pho.* 1–213, *Med.* 709–end, *Pha.* 1–359), and even in these sections shows a high degree of A contamination (cf. *Bollettino* 99 for *HF*). The value of O in the study of Σ is therefore small (see also Zwierlein, *Gnomon* xli (1969) 760).

[3] *Obs.* 6ff.; this view was accepted by Stuart and has recently been restated by Woesler (72), Philp (153) and Zwierlein (*loc. cit.* (760)).

[4] So, for example, in the stemma of Brugnoli ('Tradizione manoscritta' 274), in Giomini's *Phaedra* and *Agamemnon* (but cf. *Phaedra* pref. p. 14), in

structing and evaluating Σ, though shown by Hoffa in 1914,[1] has not been fully realised. F is by far the closest of the three MSS to E in both true and false readings, and appears the least affected by conjecture and contamination.[2] In the following places F alone agrees with E:

> 9 alte *E F*: alti (*recte*) *P CS N*: alto *M*
> 76 soluet *E^{ac}* (*ut uid.*) *F*: soluit (*recte*) *P CS MN E^{pc}*
> 81 faciunt *E F*: fugiunt (*recte*) *P CS MN*
> 182 om. *E F*: habent *P CS MN*
> 186 Lyrnesida (*recte*) *E F*: briseida *MN*: briseidam *P CS*
> 201 perfunde *E F*: pereundo (*recte*) *P CS MN*
> 597 minas *E F*: minaces (*recte*) *P CS*: nimias *MN*
> 655 flectent *E F^{ac}*: flent (*recte*) *P CS MN*
> 772 furore *E^{ac}* (*ut uid.*) *F*: futuro (*recte*) *E^{pc} P CS MN*
> 855 lamna (*recte*) *E F*: lamina *P*: flamma *CS MN*
> 915 quid (*recte*) *E F*: quos *P CS MN*

Neither M nor N can produce similar instances of fidelity to E in manifest error.[3]

The most reliable basis for a study of Σ's relation to E will be the unanimous testimony of F MN. The question is complicated from the start by the obvious presence of A material in the Σ MSS (i.e. the A-text of *Pho.* in F MN, of *Med.* 1–700 in F and of *Med.* entire in MN, and of *Oed.* in F).[4] The three extant Σ MSS were written in Italy in the fourteenth century, and Σ itself may have been an Italian MS of the same century; long before 1350, copies of the A-text of the tragedies were circulating in Italy. In addition, F and N contain the note of

---

Viansino, cf. *prol.* 26f., and in Giardina, praef. ix–x (modified on xxvi–xxvii and in *Bollettino* xiv (1966) 68f.).

[1] *Hermes* xlix (1914) 465f.

[2] A readings have been entered in F by the hand of the corrector; the process seems to have affected the common parent of MN.

[3] For further agreements of E F, cf. Hoffa 465f.; M and N alone agree with E either in correct readings or in places where corruption is not obvious (e.g. 545 *nunc* E N: *nunc se* P CS F: *tunc se* M; did Σ and the parent of MN have *nunc* with *se* written above the line or in the margin?).

[4] The presence of *Octauia* in F M N cannot, of course, serve as a sign of A influence in Σ until it is shown that the Σ text of *Octauia* derives from an A source; it is in theory possible that *Octauia* was present in E's exemplar, but was not copied by the scribe of E. See below, pp. 68ff.

Lovato Lovati on the metres of the tragedies, which suggests a connection between Σ and a MS owned or used by Lovato himself or another member of the Paduan circle.[1] The relation of Σ to such a MS or to the MS seen by Lovato in Pomposa must remain imprecise,[2] but the link with the Paduans makes Σ's combination of a basically E-type text and A corrections thoroughly explicable.[3]

Since contamination of Σ and its descendants from A sources is plausible, even likely, on historical grounds, it should not be surprising that standard stemmatic procedures do not yield a clear result. Thus, for example, F MN have remarkably few peculiar errors in common; in *Agamemnon* I know of only two:[4]

188 et *F MN*: en *E P CS*
873 furor *F MN*: fruor *E*: et fruor *P CS*

This scarcity of peculiar Σ readings is probably to be explained by the high degree of contamination and conjecture in MN, processes in which peculiar errors of Σ were replaced by E or A readings. Similarly, the Σ MSS offer only a handful of true readings not in either E or A,[5] and those they contain may be the result of conjecture. This rarity of good readings unique to Σ, while limiting the practical value of Σ in the constitution of the text, is not in itself fatal to the hypothesis of Σ's independence from E: the number of readings independently corrupted in E and A is not large, and E's general fidelity to its

---

[1] M differs in format and contents from F N, which may explain the absence of Lovato's note.

[2] The Paduan material in N (f. 246) has been carefully analysed by Megas (1967, 93–112). He notes (181f.) that Lovato cites *Med.* 433 with the (correct) text of E, *remedia quotiens*, while F MN agree with P CS in *remedia totiens*. This points away from Σ as Lovato's source (a possibility entertained by Megas 233) and toward either E or E's exemplar.

[3] Megas has shown (1969, 137ff.) that Mussato used an A text as the basis for his own commentary on Seneca.

[4] Hoffa (*loc. cit.*) noted three for *HF*: 688 *stigis* (for *strigis*), 1277 *tibi*, 1312 *letede* (for *letale*). It may be worth noting that one of these (688) and both those listed in the text are to be found in *recentiores*.

[5] The most recent tabulation is given by Zwierlein, *Gnomon* xli (1969) 760.

exemplar makes it natural that a second witness to that exemplar would not have a great deal to contribute.[1]

The heart of the matter is the agreement of Σ with errors of E and A. If, in a vertical transmission, Σ were a copy of E, it should contain all errors of E except those which the scribe of Σ might have corrected. In fact, Σ does not share a number of E's wrong readings. Some of these, to be sure, are patent blunders for which the remedy was obvious:

> 127 consilii *P CS F MN*: consilia *E*
> 161 langore *P CS F MN*: lango *E*
> 190 troica *P CS F MN*: troiaca *E*
> 386 errantem *P CS F MN*: errante *E*
> 413 classe *P CS F MN*: classa *E*

The absence of these E errors in Σ poses no serious obstacle to regarding Σ as a copy of E. Other E readings are (or might have been to a scribe) clearly defective, but the solution might not have been as obvious:

> 120 trabe *P CS F MN*: graue *E*
> 134 pectus *P CS F MN*: cecus *E*
> 188 paridis *P CS F MN*: rapidis *E*
> 579 leter an *P CS F MN*: an letaere *E*

Still other readings of E would have appeared wrong only to an acute reader with a grasp of Senecan metre:

> 63 uexatque *P CS F MN*: uexat *E*
> 131 ut *P CS F MN*: *om. E*
> 158 equidem *P CS F MN*: et quidem *E*
> 411 regi *P CS F MN*: regis *E*
> 525 sistite *CS F MN*: siste *P*: et sistite *E*
> 569 e summo *P CS F MN*: summo *E*
> 730 idea *P CS F MN*: idae *E*
> 904 exanimem *P CS F MN*: exanime *E*

---

[1] The principle recently formulated by M. L. West (in *Textual criticism and editorial technique* (Leipzig, 1973) 44), 'there must be a correlation between lack of individual good readings and lack of independent sources', while generally valid, may be modified by the circumstances of an individual transmission.

If the circumstances of transmission excluded contamination and resourceful conjecture, the foregoing examples would suffice to establish the independence of Σ from E. At this point in the transmission, however, there is reason to believe that both contamination and conjecture were present, and it may therefore be argued that Σ was a copy of E in which some of E's errors were corrected either by recourse to A or by conjecture.

It is no objection to the foregoing argument that Σ shares wrong readings with E in a number of passages, and that some of these are manifestly wrong;[1] such agreements would weaken the case for Σ being a contaminated copy of E only if contamination is misconceived as an unremitting scrutiny of E and A readings by a gifted textual critic. On the more realistic hypothesis that the scribe of Σ entered A readings in a sporadic and inconsistent way, it is not implausible that a number of erroneous E-branch readings should have escaped correction.[2]

If A was used by Σ in the manner suggested, we should expect to find examples of plausible but wrong A readings introduced where E was apparently corrupt. Such is in fact the case at 281, where Σ agrees with A in *et a tanto uiro* in place of E's nonsensical *eurotantum* (from which Gronovius elicited

---

[1] So, for example, 213 *immixta* (*immixte* P CS); 229 *permitti* (*perniciem* P CS); 236 *pariter* (*pater* P CS); 240 *referemus* (*remeemus* P CS); 247 *innocens* (*impotens* P CS); *aliquis* (*aliquid* P CS); 324 *sacri* (*sacris* P CS); 538 *satisque* E^ac F MN (*ratisque* E^2pc P CS); 625 *Troia* om. (habet P CS); 867 *per annos* E MN: *par annos* F (*par annis* P CS). Further telling examples would be added if, as is likely, the omission of 182 (F) and of 550–1 (F M) faithfully reflect the state of Σ. The scribe of Σ also failed to correct the clear signs of corruption in 745f.

[2] Since Σ can be securely reconstructed only from the consensus of F MN, it is possible that Σ itself entered A readings in places where they were not adopted by all its descendants. (An A reading found only in MN, for example, lies under suspicion of being a product of contamination at a stage later than Σ.) Such a process can be seen at work in places where only one Σ MS shows a reading made up of both E and A elements, e.g. 507 *ars cessit malis* E F M: *in magnis malis* P CS: *ars in magnis malis* N; 932 *quid sit* E F N: *c(a)esus* P CS: *quid cesus sit* M; 970 *iust(a)e* P CS MN: *dixi* E: *iuste dixi* F; cf. also *HO* 477 (M). Such composite readings probably took their origin from the presence of interlinear or marginal readings in Σ.

Eurotan tuum), and in 577, where Σ has A's *in lucem* – itself a corruption caused by dittography – instead of E's *illo* (corrected to *Ilio* by Gronovius). In addition, at 394 Σ has the trivialisation *sisiphi* where E and P preserve the correct *sipyli* (*syphili* P); here the Σ reading is not that of A, but of CS (= β), a fact of some importance for determining the type of A text used by Σ.[1]

To justify the inclusion of the Σ MSS as independent witnesses to the E-branch of the tradition, it is not enough to show that Σ *might* be independent of E; independence must appear as either a necessary or by far the most probable hypothesis. Neither is true of Σ; it *can* without difficulty be regarded as a contaminated copy of E,[2] and the editor is therefore free (perhaps even obliged) to exclude it.[3] The readings of F MN are as a result not cited in the apparatus, except where they might help establish the original reading of E when it has been corrected or lost through damage, or where they contain a variant of critical interest (presumably the result of conjecture).

A note on the Σ-text of *Octauia*[4]

The absence of *Octauia* in E makes it possible to test the conclusions reached above, and raises the hope of locating Σ more precisely in the transmission.

---

[1] An argument used by Leo against Σ's independence must be discarded: Σ does at times show traces of a false word-division also found in E (e.g. *HO* 1230 *pesti satis*] *pestis at est* E: *pestis adest* F MN; 589 *gradu serperet aequo*] *graduŝeper et aequo* E: *gradus semper et aequo* N: *gradu aequo semper* M (*gradu semper et aequo* in Σ?)), but mistakes of this kind could easily occur twice in the same passage in transcribing a difficult exemplar.

[2] To account for the A-text of certain plays in F MN, it is to be assumed that Σ suffered damage before F and MN were copied from it.

[3] Cf. R. A. B. Mynors (*C. Valerii Catulli Carmina* (Oxford, 1958) praef. viii): 'quod ad ceteros codices attinet...omnes a codicibus *OGR* originem aut duxerunt aut, quod nobis idem ualet, duxisse possunt.' Note that, even if Σ were demonstrably independent of E, its agreements with A could not be mechanically applied to isolate *lectiones singulares* of E, since the possibility of A contamination would have to be reckoned with in every case. The *recensio* would still, in other words, be consistently 'open'.

[4] These observations are based on my own collation of F and N for lines 1–376 of *Octauia*, supplemented by Viansino's account of M for those lines; they are therefore tentative.

It is in theory possible that *Octauia* was in E's exemplar and was omitted by the scribe of E; if so, the presence of *Octauia* in F MN would be a mark, not of A contamination, but of fidelity to the original state of the E-branch text. This possibility can be put to the test, for, if Σ's text of *Octauia* were derived from an E-source, F MN ought to contain approximately the same number and quality of true readings not in P CS as E does in the other nine plays. They do not: in more than a third of the play F MN offer only six good readings not in the major A MSS (PG CS):

19 lux *F MN KQ e O*: nox *PG CS*
46 uenenis *F MN KQ e^c*: ueneris *PG CS*
80 omina *F MN S KQ^{bc} O*: omnia *PG C e*
87 fera quam *F MN e S^{bc} Q^{bc}*: feraque *P CS^{ac} KQ^{ac}*: fera *G*
105 grata *F MN KQ e O*: grate *PG CS*
360 credent *F MN e O*: credunt *P CS KQ*

This is but a small fraction of the number of good E readings in any of the other plays. Even more important, all of these true readings involve minor corrections of the A text, easily attainable by conjecture. There is, therefore, no reason to believe that Σ owes its text of *Octauia* to an E-source, or to an otherwise lost third branch of tradition independent of both E and A; the source of Σ is to be sought within A.

As might be expected, F MN show no significant affinity to the rare, northern branch of A represented by PG. Agreement of F MN with PG against CS is limited to correct readings:

83 dabit *F MN PG KQ e O*: dabis *CS*
186 uetat *F MN PG*: uetat uetat *CS KQ e O*
315 resonant *F (M?)N PG K e O*: resonent *CS Q*

These are probably to be added to the six good readings of Σ listed above; like them, all are easy corrections of the β text.

Agreement with CS against P(G) is considerably more frequent, and includes these shared errors:

90 superbos humilesque *F MN CS KQ e*: superos hominesque *G* (superbos hominesque *P*), *recte*

232 cometam *F MN CS KQ e O*: cometem *PG*
252 et *F MN CS KQ e O*: est *P* (*de G non liquet*)[1]

Agreement with C alone is absent. Σ does show indirect affinity to S in some shared readings,[2] but the relationship is almost certainly not with S itself; in such cases both Σ and S betray the influence of the strain of conflated tradition preserved in KQ and e.

It will have been noticed that in the instances cited so far F MN are almost always in agreement with one or more of KQ e.[3] This close relationship extends to shared errors not found in PG CS:

308 lacerosque *F MN KQ e O*: laceroque *PG CS*
331 est *PG CS*: *om. F KQ e*: huic *MN recc.*

On the other hand, Σ agrees with PG CS against KQ e in several places, showing that it does not derive its text of *Octauia* directly from this group:[4]

207 fluxit *F MN PG CS*: fulsit *KQ e O*
234 bootes *F MN G CS*: boetes *P KQ e O*
317 profecta *F MN PG CS*: perfecta *e*: profectum *KQ*
333 hec *P C F M*: hoc *S N KQ^{ac} e O*.

Although close and stable affiliations are hard to identify among such MSS as KQ e, it is noteworthy that F MN consistently avoid the peculiar errors of KQ, e.g.:[5]

---

[1] Shared good readings include 63 *quem* (*quam* PG O), 140 *praeferre* (*perferre* PG), 157 *quis* (*qui* PG), 186 *ipse* (*ipsus* G: *ipš* P), 234 *arctoo* (*-eo* PG), 346 *feriunt* (*ferunt* PG). In each of these agreements F MN are joined by KQ e.
[2] For example, the error *uiolenta* in 254 (*uiolenti* PG C) and the true readings *omnia* in 80 (*omnia* PG C) and *fata post fratris* in 112 (also in P: *fratris post fata* G C, more likely to be the original A reading?).
[3] The only true reading in F MN which is not also in one or more of the group KQ e is *uetat* in 186 (also PG: *uetat uetat* CS KQ e O).
[4] F MN also contain peculiar errors not shared by either PG CS or KQ e: 36 *uno* (*subito* (*recte*) PG C: *sub uno* C^{mg}S KQ e O), 49 *qui secreta* (*quem s.* PG CS KQ e: *secreta* (*recte*) recc.), 166 *tuque* (*tu quoque* (*recte*) KQ e O: *tuo quoque* PG CS), 238 *tithoea* (*tithona* PG CS KQ e O), 260 *incerta* (*incesta* CS KQ e O: *inf-* P), 346 *luctus* (*fluctus* PG CS KQ e), 376 *fudit* (*reddit* PG CS KQ: *dedit* e).
[5] F MN also side with PG CS e against KQ in one place where KQ have the true reading: 181 *expectat* KQ e^{pc} (*-et* O): *-as* F MN PG CS e^{ac}.

41 en *F MN PG CS e^{ac}*: et *KQ e^{bc}*
222 saeua sideribus freta *F MN PG CS e*: syderibus freta *KQ O*
261 coniugis *F MN PG CS e*: coniugii *KQ*: coniugium *M^{mg}*
310 nati *F MN PG CS e*: nostra *KQ O*
322 uagatur *F MN PG CS e*: uocatur *KQ^{ac}*
343 merui *F MN P C e O*: merū *S*: meru *Q*: metum *K*

There is no example of F MN agreement in a peculiar error of KQ. With e, on the other hand, the facts are more complex: while F MN (always in company with all or some of PG CS) agree with KQ in avoiding some *lectiones singulares* of e,[1] the following exceptions are to be noted:

13 manet *F MN e*: remanet *PG CS KQ*
121 inerti *F MN e*: inherenti *PG CS KQ*
159 potentis *F^{ac} e*: petentis *F^{2bc} MN PG CS KQ*
193 est ausa *F e*: ausa est *PG CS MN KQ^{bc}*
311 scelera *F e^{ac}*(?): saecula *PG CS KQ e^{2bc}*

This affinity of F MN (and of F in particular, the MS most faithful to Σ) to e suggests that Σ or a descendant might be the source of E-branch readings in the conflated MSS (of which e is the most interesting representative).[2]

To conclude: the Σ-text of *Octauia* belongs to the β-branch of the A tradition, and shows clear affinities to the MSS KQ e and to e in particular. Σ deserves no more consideration in *Octauia* than in the other plays, and is to be cited only as a source of successful conjectures.[3]

---

[1] 209 *residet* (*sedet* e), 269 *lapsam* (*lassam* e), 305 *tarquinio* (*tarquino* e O), 317 *profecta* (*perfecta* e).

[2] Further study might reveal similar links between Σ and the so-called 'AE' MSS (Vat. Lat. 1647, Harleianus 2484, Laur. 37.6 in particular).

[3] Much the same may be said of Giardina's O. It differs from F MN in being even more closely related to the KQ e group (it has their correct reading in 36 and 166, their wrong reading in 207, 234, and 333), and within that group it exhibits shared errors with KQ (222 *sideribus freta*, 310 *nostra*). O's two agreements with e against F MN are almost certainly due to coincidence (254 *violentam*: -*nta* F MN S KQ: -*nti* (*recte*) PG C; 305 *tarquino*: -*inio* F MN PG CS KQ).

THE A MSS

The most intricate task facing an editor is the reconstruction of the common parent of the A-branch, since there are more than 300 potential witnesses, most of which have not been more than cursorily examined. Stuart's discovery of P CS first placed the question on a firm basis,[1] and these three MSS are still considered indispensable. Of the three, P offers the purest text; several hundred agreements with E in true readings suggest that P escaped a phase of interpolation which affects all other A MSS.[2] P is the only complete MS descended from this purer A-strain; its witness is, however, supplemented on occasion by the excerpt collections and it is joined in the *Octauia* by the Exeter MS (G). Unfortunately, P was carelessly copied and abounds in superficial corruption (a feature it shares with other Fournival books); except in *Octauia*, these cannot be distinguished from the errors of its exemplar (δ). C is by far the earliest and best witness to the strain of A (β in my stemma and discussion[3]) which in the fourteenth century, in a somewhat debased form, became the vulgate text.[4] Although written with greater care and accuracy than P, C naturally contains peculiar errors; to distinguish them from errors of β, an independent β MS is needed. For this purpose Stuart selected S, and no better MS has since been located.[5] More than a century later than P and C, and Italian where P and C are north French and English, S shows clear signs of the growth of a vulgate text from β; in twenty of thirty places in *Agamemnon* in which S has a wrong reading not in E P C, it agrees with one or more later A sources

---

[1] *CQ* vi (1912) 1–20.

[2] Woesler 24ff. (who refutes the suggestion of Herington, *Rh. Mus.* ci (1958) 353ff., that P was contaminated from E).

[3] I have replaced Woesler's γ, since this *siglum* has long been used to designate the common parent of the secondary A MSS lnr; I thus follow Philp (cf. stemma, p. 171).

[4] C itself was not the basis for the vulgate; very few MSS reveal a close relationship with C through shared errors (Paris B.N. Lat. 6395 and Bodley D'Orville 176 are the only examples known to me).

[5] Stuart's discussion of S (17ff.) has not been superseded.

(Trevet, lnr, KQ e, Vd mpq). S is thus a less reliable witness to β than is C, and it contains virtually no reading definitely that of A which has been lost in both P and C;[1] the few cases in which it alone of the three agrees with E in a true reading are perhaps best regarded as fortunate blunders or conjectures.[2] The value of S, therefore, lies not in its own readings but in its independent derivation from β and its freedom from E contamination. Where S agrees with (E)P against C, it will usually give the reading of β and A, and so isolate a *lectio singularis* of C; this happens slightly less than twenty times in *Agamemnon*. (Agreement of P and C, of course, will usually give the reading of A.)

Stuart thought that P CS were sufficient to permit an editor to reconstruct with reasonable confidence the readings of δ, β, and thereby A; all other A-branch MSS could be ignored, since they represented a β text debased by further stages of copying, contamination from E, and conjecture. Editors and writers on the subject have not shaken Stuart's case, but they have been slow to emulate his austere judgement. Düring and Hoffa conceded that P CS yield the entire witness of A,[3] but cited lnr sporadically in their draft apparatus; these MSS form the basis of A in Moricca and Giomini and are consistently reported by Viansino (along with MSS of far less worth[4]); Ussani has argued for the independent status of the MS used by Nicholas Trevet for his commentary;[5] Giardina has given complete citations of three conflated MSS, KQ e;[6] Philp has called attention to d (Neap. Bibl. Nat. iv.e.1), a 'pure A' MS, and has suggested that it might serve as an additional witness to A in

---

[1] Stuart could adduce only *HF* 543, where, he said, S indicated the loss of a line while P C did not; but Giardina notes '543 *om. A* (*spatio relicto C P S*)'; Philp (163) cites only *Med.* 608, where P is missing.

[2] Philp 159 n.2; I have found no significant E S agreements in *Agamemnon*.

[3] See below, p. 92.

[4] See below, p. 93.

[5] 'Per il testo delle tragedie di Seneca', *Accad. Naz. d. Lincei, Memorie* ser. viii vol. viii (1959) 489–555.

[6] He has not, however, asserted their independent status, see below, p. 94.

doubtful cases;[1] finally, MacGregor has altered the picture by his discovery of Vat. Lat. 2829 (= V), a 'pure A' MS unknown to Stuart which stands as close or closer to S in value as any other MS.[2]

Much clearly remains to be learned about the transmission of the tragedies in the later Middle Ages, particularly in fourteenth-century Italy, and further investigation in this area may alter or modify current views on many points.[3] The editor of Seneca, however, must determine whether, on the basis of what is now known, any of the witnesses which have found favour with editors and scholars since Stuart deserves to be placed on a par with P CS in the reconstruction of A. It is my view that no A MS apart from P CS merits full reporting, and my apparatus is constructed accordingly; in the following pages I briefly discuss the most important issues.

The later A MSS (I refer in particular to V, d, lnr, KQ, e, and mpq) show no trace of derivation from the δ-branch represented by P, and (with the exception of Trevet and a handful of other MSS) no sign of direct descent from the form of β preserved in C. The state of β found in S, however, does contain numerous agreements with the secondary A sources under discussion; in 1912 Stuart acutely remarked that 'quite a number of false readings of Scor., not in c or p, are very common in ψ',[4] and concluded that S, or its parent, was much used in the fourteenth century. Most recently MacGregor has applied an expanded form of Düring's *lacuna*-criterion to the secondary A MSS, and has found that the pattern of *lacunae* in V is shared by a large number of MSS apart from P CS; since V is also the

---

[1] Pp. 160–3; p. 172: 'It is well to have one or two other independent witnesses when there is disagreement between CPS. d will be our best supplementary witness, and ln may be retained for any further reference.'

[2] *TAPA* cii (1971) 327ff.

[3] One should not hope for significant positive gains for the text from such study; even Stuart's discovery of P CS unearthed a mere handful of good new readings (Stuart 20).

[4] P. 19.

least contaminated A MS now known after P CS, MacGregor concluded, perhaps injudiciously, that V itself was the last common ancestor of the vulgate tradition.[1]

The presence or absence of *lacunae* is widely recognised as a criterion useful in dealing with contaminated traditions; a *lacuna* is less likely to have been horizontally transmitted than an attractive variant.[2] By themselves, however, *lacunae* serve only to establish broad groupings of MSS; within these groups more precise relationships can only be determined by other methods, in particular by observing patterns of shared errors. Futhermore, purity alone is no guarantee of stemmatic priority or of ancestral status; of five independent copies of the same exemplar, each may exhibit either no contamination or varying degrees of contamination, depending on the circumstances in which each copy was made and on the character of the individual scribes. I do not believe V to have been the direct ancestor of the other secondary A MSS being considered: as I shall show, there are many errors peculiar to V of which the other MSS show no trace. What may be said on the basis of present knowledge is that V, of all extant MSS, most closely resembles the last common ancestor of the later A tradition (the MS I call η).

I have attempted to define the relationships of S and the secondary A MSS by the traditional procedure of noting conjunctive and separative errors.[3] In a highly contaminated tradition this method cannot be applied with the neatness and confidence possible in a purely vertical transmission, but when used cautiously it does seem to reveal certain stable and plausible affiliations.

---

[1] *TAPA* cii (1971) 341; in his *Survey* the case is restated in a more considered form, and the language is less exact ('in V, then, and in no other MS, we have the A-MS ancestral to the vulgate tradition'), but the claim is essentially the same.

[2] For the principle, cf. P. Maas, *Textual criticism* (1958) 8; G. Pasquali, *Storia della tradizione e critica del testo*[2] (1952) 182 (citing Knoche); M. L. West, *Textual criticism and editorial technique* (1973) 42.

[3] My information is complete only for *Agamemnon*; in other plays I must rely for KQ e on Giardina's selective accounts.

(a) S V d mpq lnr KQ e agree in errors not present in P or C:[1]

Agam.   31 hausi] ausi *S V d K e^{ac} n*
177 iam tum] tantum *S V d mpq l^{2pc} n* (tamen *KQ*)
233 sata] fata *S KQ V d mp*
395 flebile] flexile *S KQ^{ac} e^{ac} V d ln q* (flexibile *p*)
457 parent] patent *S V d mpq lnr KQ e Trevet*
868 eheu] heu *S Q e nr mpq*
964 posthac] post hec *S V d mpq lnr* (post *e^{ac}*) *Trevet*
972 iugulo] iugulum *S V d p KQ^{ac} e l^{ac}n* (iugul *m*)

Pho.   174 tum] cum *S KQ^{ac} e ln V m*
506 festas] letas *S KQ lnr V m*

Pha.   20 fete (V)] fere *S KQ e lnr m*
1074 fluctum] fluctus *S KQ e lnr V m*

Oed.   806 he (V)] hee *S l e^{ac} m* (hec *KQ*)
991 et] it *(recte) S KQ e^{2pc} l V m*

Thy.   732 armenia] armena *S KQ lnr V m*
864 egoceros] egloceros *S KQ lnr V d mp Trevet*

These readings presumably derive from a common ancestor within the β branch which is not an ancestor of C (I call this MS θ). S, the purest MS of the group, cannot be the direct ancestor of the others since there are many wrong readings unique to S.[2]

(b) V d mpq KQ e lnr agree in errors from which S is free:

Agam.   14 ter/trigemina] tibi gemina *V d KQ^{ac} n mq*
429 prora] prore *V^c d p KQ* (pro *m*)
667 quamuis] qualis *V d mpq KQ e^{ac}*
736 amazonium] amazonum *V d p ln KQ e* (*Trevet*)
806 pecore] pectore *V d q n Q e* (*Trevet*)
807 fibra] fibras *V d mpq l^{ac}*: fibrias *KQ^{ac}*
839 hesperium] hesperiumque *V d mpq ln KQ e*
903 illinc] illic *ln KQ e^{ac}*: illuc *d pq*

---

[1] I list places where all or virtually all members of this group agree; if the views presented here are correct, it is to be expected that η errors will have been on occasion corrected in one or more of η's descendants.

[2] *Agam.* 380 *reddunt*] -ent (+e); 406 *abauusque*] -oque; 436 *sigei*] -ea; 541 *fluctusque rumpit*] *fluctus rumpitque*; 610 *par superis*] *par et superis* (+e); 904 *recedunt*] -ent. S also lacks the *lacunae* shared by V and many other late A MSS, as MacGregor has shown (*Survey*).

(ante) 918 strophius] strophilus *V d p Q ln* (*tit. om. K e*)
    960 forte] *om. V d mpq KQ ln*

HF   528 exagitet] exaggeret *V d²ᵖᶜ mpq lnr* (*Trevet*)
    1037 cecidi] occidi *V m lnr KQ e* (*Trevet*)

Med.   681 pestes] pestesque *V m KQ lnr* (*Trevet*)

Thy.   370 dahas/dachas] dachos *V d pq Q e lnr* (*om. m*)

These readings are to be attributed to a common ancestor of V d mpq KQ e lnr which is not an ancestor of S (I call this MS η). (It will be seen that no MS of this group can plausibly be identified as the direct source of the readings common to all the members.) The errors on which the preceding two deductions are based are for the most part small, and taken singly would carry modest weight. As a group, however, they seem numerous enough to permit the MSS involved to be placed in a significant relationship.[1] Their slightness may indeed commend them for this purpose, since they might have survived all but the most thorough contamination.[2]

The intermediate position of S between C and the η-group is clearly illustrated by two passages in which it preserves pairs of variants also found in C: *Oed.* 289 *genu* E P: *genu uel gradu* C S: *gradu* η; 683 *loqui* E P: *sequi uel loqui* C S: *sequi* η. The pairs were present in θ, from which S faithfully transcribed them; the scribe of η, however, chose one reading and suppressed the other, with the result that all η's descendants show no trace of *genu* or *loqui*. The conclusion that θ at times contained pairs of variants is significant; if in other places these were copied into η, or if η absorbed readings from other sources and entered them as variants, this would help to explain passages in which the η-MSS fail to act as a unified group.[3]

---

[1] Complete collation of V d mpq lnr KQ e for all plays would undoubtedly uncover a number of additional shared readings.

[2] D. S. Avalle, *La letteratura medievale in lingua d'oc nella sua tradizione manoscritta* (1961) 172; cf. S. Timpanaro, *Maia* xvii (1965) 398 and n.14.

[3] For example, the occasional agreement of S with KQ (e): *Agam.* 99 *currant*] *certant* S KQ eᵃᶜ; 114 *incita*] *mota* S KQᵃᶜ; note in particular 250 *rere* (E P C) V d S²ᵖᶜ e²ᵖᶜ: *tere* Sᵃᶜ: *tereat* S¹ᵘˡ: *tere uel tereat* KQ. Other anomalous (and inconsistent) groupings include: *HF* 1232 *at*] *ac* V lnr:

(*c*) V d mpq share errors from which KQ e lnr are free:[1]

Agam. 117 impos] inops *V d p*: impios *m q*
125 inclitum] solitum *V d mpq*
200 exigatur] erigatur *V d mpq*
279 honesta] honestas *V d mpq*
281 spartem num (*CS*)] sparten nunc *V d*: sparta nunc *m*: si partem
nunc *q*: si partem mei *p Q* (*ut uid.*)
419 refugit] respicit *V*: despicit *d*: displicet *p*
515 cadere] eadem *V d mpq*
962 tuus est] tuus *V d mp*

Therefore these MSS have a common ancestor which is not an ancestor of lnr KQ e (called π in my stemma). Among the descendants of π should perhaps be numbered the MS copied by Coluccio Salutati (B.M. Add. MS 11987), which contains the characteristic readings at 125, 279, and 515 as well as other signs of similarity to V d mpq; because of its closeness to d, Leiden Voss. F 99 (Leid. 1) also belongs here.

(*d*) Within this group V and d share errors from which mpq are free to an extent not matched by any other grouping:

Agam. 206 frygas] fricat *V d*
248 tumidos] tudos *V^{ac}*: tutos *d*
334 sed (set)] superet *V d*
474-7 *om.* *V d*
591 libera] liberos *V d*

These agreements (particularly the omission of 474-7) justify postulating a common source for V d; neither can be the parent of the other, since each contains significant errors from which the other is free (errors of d, 42 *duo*, 150 *domus*, 410 *busta*, 751-2 inuerso ordine, 755 om.; errors of V, 499 *preces*, 731 *arbitror*, 893

---

et KQ e d pq; *Agam.* 544 *furibundum* (E P C) S[2mg] Q[2pc]: *-e* S[ac] KQ[ac] l[ac]: *-us* l[2pc] n V d mpq. Several variants involve confusion of t and r (471 *perit/petit*; 732 *timete/timere*); the error is in S, which on my stemma suggests that the script of θ was open to misreading on this point; η may have resolved its doubts by entering double readings.

[1] Note also 267 *cui uenia est opus*] c. u. *opus est* V d p: *est cui uenia opus* m; 481 *nimbis* E P CS V: *membris* d mp.

classe, 963–5 om. V¹, add. rubricator in mg., 932 om., add. manus posterior). I call the parent of Vd σ.

(*e*) The MSS KQ e are distinguished not by unique readings shared by all three, but by the presence of extensive E-branch contamination. The Etonensis stands apart from KQ, containing approximately three times as many E readings; in addition it possesses a number of errors not found in KQ (e.g. 88 *pondera*, 129 *prome*, 145 *certa*, 166 *sacrilegio*, 372 *tu*, 454 om., add. e², 762, 889 -*que* om., etc.). Its numerous unique errors make me reject MacGregor's suggestion that e is the source of KQ's E readings.[1] The only MS which exhibits a close connection to e is Oxford Canon. Class. Lat. 93 (Ox.1), which agrees with e in several variants not found elsewhere (126 *consilium*, 188 *et*, 474 *uentique*, 638 *turba*, 645 *ad aras*, 911 *efuge*). The Oxford MS is not the parent of the Etonensis, since it has its own unique errors (88 *in ipso*, 261 *uocas*, 290 *nubat*, 298 *superbe*, etc.) and its pattern of E-branch borrowing is not identical. The link between these MSS may be significant for tracing the source of E readings in these and other A MSS. The Oxford MS contains the *argumenta* of Albertino Mussato (in their augmented version) in a purer form than is available in any other MS;[2] this suggests the possibility that Ox.1 has a Paduan (or connected) origin. The Σ MSS N and F are also linked to the Paduan circle by containing the metrical notes of Lovato Lovati; it has been suggested that Σ itself was a copy of E made by Lovato.[3] It may be observed that even the most highly contaminated MSS (those I call 'AE'[4]) do not show knowledge of some correct E readings, and that these readings are also absent in the Σ MSS; it is thus likely that the 'AE' MSS derive their E-branch readings from a Σ-source and not directly from E. The Etonensis (and the Oxford MS) do not match the 'AE' MSS precisely in their E-branch readings, but they do agree with the 'AE' MSS in some apparent conjectures not in E: 188 *et* (for *en* E P CS),

[1] *Survey.*   [2] Megas (1969) 1–23.
[3] See above, p. 65.
[4] Harley 2484, Laur. 37.6, Vat. Lat. 1647, Camb. U.L. Nn. 11.35 (see below, pp. 84 ff.).

506 *fracta* (for *trunca* E, *structa* P CS), 519 *pudenda* (for *perdenda* E P CS); in the first case the reading is also in F MN, in the second in M. It appears that a Σ MS connected to the Paduan circle was directly or indirectly responsible for several instances of E-branch contamination in the early and middle fourteenth century.

KQ are considerably less interesting. Their common origin is shown by numerous shared errors (32 *ne*, 33 *fert* om., 177 *tamen*, 393a *cedens*, 400 *aut*, 557 *neque*, 963–5 om.), but neither can be identified as the parent of the other.

(*f*) The MSS ln are connected by the greater influence of Trevet's commentary, readings of which are adopted independently by each (in l: 664 *lacrimis lacrimas*, 705 *regum*] *nurum*, 883 *tremo*] *cerno*; in n: 11 *curie*] *aule regie*, 453 *cursus*, 845 *crudos*] *cruentos*).[1] In addition, the scribe of l comments on the absence of line 694 in his *expositio* – a clear reference to Trevet.

If the conclusions reached in the preceding paragraphs are valid, the consequences for the editor are clear. The agreement of the η MSS (or better, of Vd, the purest of them) with P C will give the reading of θ and isolate a *lectio singularis* of S. In more than twenty places in *Agamemnon* I have used Vd for this purpose, but have not thought it necessary to cite them; the apparatus in such cases is negative, recording only the dissident reading of S. The η MSS can render more important service where C and S differ in a way that leaves the reading of β in doubt (the clearest case will be if neither agrees with P); where Vd side with C (or P against both C and S), this will usually give the reading of β; where they agree with S, that of θ. This occurs in a handful of places in *Agamemnon* (e.g. 216, 731), and here I have cited Vd. It is also theoretically possible that Vd could preserve a reading of A which had been independently lost in P, C, and S; I know of no such case in *Agamemnon*, nor do I think it likely that more than one or two are to be found in the

---

[1] On the end of *Medea* in l, see MacGregor, *Survey*.

entire corpus.[1] The limited use that an editor can make of Vd does not justify citation throughout; the text essentially rests, therefore, on E P CS.

NICHOLAS TREVET

The commentary of Nicholas Trevet, an English Dominican of Blackfriars, Oxford,[2] was composed in the years 1314–16 at the request of Niccolò de' Albertini da Prato, Cardinal Bishop of Ostia and Velletri, a person of importance at the papal court of Avignon.[3] The work was completed by 1317, when payment was authorised by John XXII for the copying of a text of the tragedies with commentary.[4]

The lemmata of Trevet's commentary yield a nearly complete text of the plays; it has been reconstructed for *Thyestes* and, using a more elaborate basis of recension, for *HF, Agamemnon,* and *HO*.[5] Since Trevet's notes are elementary and often quite

---

[1] Philp (163) suggests that at *Med.* 492 d's *minus* may be the reading of A (*mitis* P: *mitius* CS); though V shares d's reading (*minus* V^{ac}: *mitius* V^{pc}), it may be no more than a conjecture.

[2] For Trevet's life cf. Emden, *Biographical register of the University of Oxford to 1500*, III.1902f.; F. Ehrle, *Nikolaus Trevet, sein Leben, seine Quodlibet und Quaestiones Ordinariae* (Münster, 1923). A comprehensive study by R. J.. Dean has long been promised; cf. her articles in *Medium Aevum* x (1941) 161–8 and *Studies in Philology* xlv (1948) 541–64, and for the most recent treatment cf. A. H. MacDonald in *Catalogus Translationum et Commentariorum* II (1970) 340–2.

[3] Niccolò's letter and Trevet's reply are printed by Franceschini 29f.; the *terminus post quem* of 1314 for Niccolò's request was suggested by Ehrle (14f.).

[4] Daniel Williman, *The books of the Avignonese popes and clergy* (diss. Toronto, 1973) 236. Payment was made to Guillelmus de Broa, 'pro libro tragediarum Senece cum expositione' (the MS also contained the Senecan *Declamationes* with a commentary, another work known to have been glossed by Trevet); see now Marco Palma, *IMU* xvi (1973) 317ff., who suggests that Vat. Lat. 1650 may be the MS acquired in 1317.

[5] *Thyestes*, ed. E. Franceschini (Milan, 1938), based on Vat. Lat. 1650 (P), Padua, Bibl. Univ. 896 (T), and Vat. Urb. Lat. 355 (V); *HF*, ed. V. Ussani, Jr (Rome, 1959); *Agamemnon*, ed. P. Meloni (Cagliari, 1961); *HO*, ed. by Meloni (Rome, 1963). To PTV Ussani and Meloni add London Soc. of Antiquaries 63 (Soc), Bologna, Bibl. Univ. 1632 (B), Rome, Vat. Lat. 7611 (S), Milan, Bibl. Trivulziana 809 (Z), and Venice, Marc. Lat. 12.41 (M).

wrong, his importance for students of Seneca derives from the role played by his MS in the history of the transmission. Before the discovery of P and C, Trevet's MS was the earliest known witness to the A-branch; it has long since lost all such claims to pre-eminence, but its precise status is still in dispute.

That Trevet based his commentary on one and only one MS is explicitly attested in a letter he wrote to Niccolò de' Albertini.[1] That this MS was closely related to C is evident from the agreement of Trevet's commentary in numerous errors and omissions found in C but not in E, P, or S; indeed, it is simpler to tabulate the peculiar errors of C *not* found in Trevet, a much smaller number.[2] On the basis of these agreements it has been suggested that C itself was Trevet's MS.[3] This is difficult to prove; even errors in Trevet which result from misreading C's script or abbreviations[4] show only that Trevet's MS was directly descended from C, and do not rule out at least one intermediate MS. In addition, there is positive reason to believe that Trevet did not use C itself. His complaint about the defective condition of his text[5] cannot easily apply to C, which is a clearly legible and carefully written MS. Trevet's commentary also deviates from the readings of C in more than a few places: in addition to unique variants (which would not tell against descent from C itself),[6] there are agreements with E against P CS[7] and with the later A MSS (the branches called θ and η in my stemma)

---

[1] Franceschini 30: 'de textu, quem unicum habui, qualemcumque sensuum explanatione, exculpsi.'

[2] For *Agamemnon* the C errors noted in the apparatus at 251, 441, 482, 487, 505, 550, 640, 731, 883, 896, 916, 943, 963, 974, 1002; more than half of these slips were corrected in C itself. Virtually all other errors of C (e.g. the omission of 694, the transposition of 750 after 760) are found in Trevet.

[3] Stuart, *CQ* vi (1912) 13ff.; MacGregor, *Survey.*

[4] Philp (164–7) cites the misreading of C's *con-* abbreviation as *o* in *Med.* 943 and 979; cf. also Stuart 16.

[5] Franceschini 30: 'me tamen defendit in parte textus diminutio' (wrongly read as *corruptio* in U by Peiper).

[6] In *Agamemnon* cf. e.g. 11 *curie*] *aule*, 20 *fugaces*] *stigias*, 145 *que petit*] *sequi*, 185 *suus* om., 324 *sacris* om., 430 *puppes*] *rates*, 453 *cursus*, 469 *ad*] *et*, 664 *lacrimis lacrimas*, 686 *non*] *nec*, 883 *tremo*] *cerno*, 961 *putas*] *reputas*.

[7] *Agam.* 150 *scelus scelere* (also in P), 213 *immixta*, 273 *ignouit*, 486 *rupto*, 701 *fraterni*, 911 *fuge et*; others, cf. Philp 166.

against P and C;[1] it is also noteworthy that in some of the places where Trevet agrees with E, the η MSS agree with E as well.[2] Some of these deviations from C might be the result of deterioration in the MSS containing Trevet's commentary, but the majority must surely reflect the text which Trevet himself used. Nor can Trevet himself be plausibly considered the source of the readings which his commentary and the θ and η MSS have in common. First, the groups θ and η are distinguished by shared errors not all of which appear in Trevet; then, only a few of these MSS show external signs of influence from Trevet;[3] finally, it seems unlikely that a commentary could have infiltrated readings into so many MSS in such a short time,[4] while so many of its unique variants failed to become widespread. It seems, then, that Trevet's MS was at the nearest a copy of C contaminated from an η-branch source (which was also responsible for most of Trevet's E readings).[5]

The process of contamination almost certainly took place in Italy, since both the E and θ–η strains of tradition are almost entirely restricted to Italian MSS until quite late in the transmission.[6] If Trevet himself is responsible, he may have brought

---

[1] *Agam.* 457 *patent*, 964 *post hec*, *Thy.* 233 *more*, 864 *egloceros* (all θ); *Agam.* 736 *amazonum*, 806 *pectore*, *HF* 528 *exaggeret*, 1037 *occidi*, *Thy.* 370 *dachos*, *Med.* 681 *pestesque*, 744 om. *membra*, *Oed.* 289 *gradu*, 683 *sequi*. Publication of Trevet's commentary for all plays would probably turn up other such agreements.

[2] *Agam.* 258 *mariti* (E²ᵖᶜ), *HF* 1281 *agedum*, *Pho.* 389 *cient*, 477 *matris*. In other cases (e.g. *Thy.* 482 *iungent/-et*, *Pho.* 228 *uerbis/umbris*) the η MSS are divided, but some at least agree with E and Trevet.

[3] Most notably Laur. 24 sin. 4 (see above, p. 80).

[4] The earliest MSS of the θ group fall in the period 1300–30; some may therefore antedate the composition of Trevet's work. The first mention of a Trevet MS (apart from the one in the papal library at Avignon) comes from 1338 (Simone of Arezzo, cf. MacDonald 342 for reference).

[5] Philp (167) and Woesler (51–4) take account of the E readings in Trevet, but not of the agreements with the later A MSS. Philp concludes that Trevet's MS was probably a contaminated copy of C, Woesler only that it was very closely related to C.

[6] The only possible exception is the Cambrai MS (K), and Rouse (118 n.1) has suggested that it was the work of a French scribe copying an Italian MS. Its close textual connection to Q, which is Italian, makes an Italian origin for K's text highly probable.

an English MS with him on a mission to Italy in 1304 or after receiving Niccolò de' Albertini's letter in 1314/15.[1] I consider it more likely, however, that Trevet faithfully reproduced a single MS than that he personally consulted other sources; in the latter case one might expect him to boast of his diligence and concern for a correct text.

The existence of MSS such as the one postulated above may be partially demonstrated by the example of Paris B.N. Lat. 6395.[2] An Italian MS containing a miscellaneous body of Senecan and pseudo-Senecan works, it presents a text (for *Agamemnon* at least)[3] very close to C but with deviations in which it agrees with E, later A MSS, or both together. It lacks the clear signs of agreement with η visible in Trevet, which may mean that the source of its contamination was a MS of a less well-defined character.[4]

THE 'AE' MSS

This convenient label (first used, it seems, by Philp) denotes MSS in which contamination of an A text with E readings appears consistent and deliberate; the MSS so described are learned conflations instead of typical contaminated MSS. Though Philp applied the term 'AE' to the group KQ e, I prefer to restrict its use to the group Harl Laur Vat Cant, in which the use of an E source has progressed much further;[5] so

---

[1] Rouse 119f. The earlier date appears less likely; it would imply a long-standing interest in the plays which does not emerge from Trevet's correspondence with Niccolò or from his glosses.

[2] See above, pp. 37f.

[3] The MS has underonge extensive correction in *HF*, resulting in a much greater proportion of E readings.

[4] I cannot accept MacGregor's description of this MS (*Survey*) as a descendant of V contaminated from Trevet. In *Agam.* it agrees with the peculiar errors of C nearly as often as does Trevet (it contains at least one, 641 *hinc uel*, not in Trevet), and lacks the characteristic readings of the θ or η groups.

[5] MacGregor (*Survey*) provides illuminating figures: of 408 E variants in *Phaedra*, Harl and Laur concur in 175; the Etonensis agrees with E in 103 places, K in 45, Q in 33; a fairly typical contaminated MS, Lond. Brit. Mus. Burney 250, in 35.

far, in fact, as to create doubt regarding the basic affiliation of the MS.[1]

The four MSS named above show several signs of a common origin:[2] the commentary in Harl is reproduced, in abridged form, in Laur;[3] variants not found in other sources are shared by two, three, or all four (suggesting that they derive from a MS in which these readings were present as *uariae lectiones*);[4] in at least one place all four MSS show traces of a single mechanical corruption.[5] The most sophisticated of the group is Harl, whose commentary represents a considerable advance in learning and resourcefulness over Trevet's; Harl is probably the source of Laur,[6] which in turn is the parent, at least in part, of Cant.

The sources of the E and A texts which are combined in these MSS may be tentatively determined. The E readings derive, not from the Etruscus, but from a Σ source: this conclusion may be argued both negatively (the 'AE' group do not show E-branch readings not in F MN) and positively ('AE' MSS share readings of F MN against both E and P CS).[7] The A source must be sought within the η group, as chronology and geography would have suggested;[8] in particular it may be observed that the 'AE' MSS and the Etonensis agree on several variants not found in E, F MN, P CS, Vd, ln, or KQ.[9]

---

[1] Though the 'AE' MSS present the external arrangement (order and titles) of A, MacGregor designates them 'EA', meaning that the basic component of the text is of the E-class (*Survey*).

[2] I cannot speak of the other MSS which MacGregor would assign to this group, e.g. Vat. Lat. 2212.

[3] On this commentary see above, pp. 39f.

[4] *Agam.* 5 *excutit*] *occupat* Harl Cant; 133 *mixtus*] *iustus*; 301 *regi ac* / *regia*] *regio*; 534 *perstrinxit*] *pertransit*; 934 *poscunt fidem secunda et aduersa exigunt* Harl Vat; 987 *demetere*] *diuidere*.

[5] *Agam.* 101 *ruitura*] *natura al. ruitura* Harl: *iratura al. ruitura* Vat: *natura* Cant: *natura* (*al. ruitura*^{su}) Laur.

[6] Philp 169.

[7] *Agam.* 186 *briseida* (MN); 188 *et* (F MN); 382 *triuia nota* (F M); 506 *fracta* (M); 597 *nimias* (MN); 873 *et furor* (F MN).

[8] All four MSS are Italian (central), of the mid-fourteenth century or later; MacGregor (*Survey*) suggests Verona as a home for the group, but on the basis of tenuous links to the Paduan circle of Lovato and Mussato.

[9] *Agam.* 519 *pudenda*, 840 *gerionis*, 845 *crudus* (with K), 863 *dardani* (with Q).

MSS of a learned and eclectic character may have drawn on branches of tradition no longer visible, and the possibility that the unique variants of the 'AE' group have such an origin has recently been raised.[1] Lost branches of tradition, however, are not to be multiplied without necessity; since all the good readings found in the 'AE' MSS can easily be explained as successful emendations,[2] I have treated these MSS solely as *fontes coniecturarum*, citing only those readings which possess critical interest.[3]

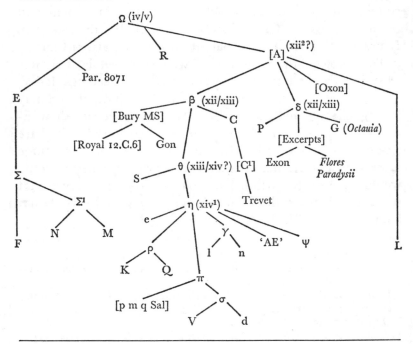

---

[1] Philp 169; MacGregor, *TAPA* cii (1971) 348 (n), now modified in *Survey*.

[2] E.g. *Agam.* 213 *immixtis*, *Oed.* 1047 *fallentes* (*pallentes* E: *fallaces* CS), *Octauia* 495 *ciues* (*uices* CS: *uiros* KQ e).

[3] These MSS are clearly important for the *Textgeschichte*, but have no place as witnesses in an apparatus.

REMARKS

1. The conjectural date of lost MSS is given in parentheses; the dates of surviving sources may be found in the appropriate catalogue-entry.

2. Hypothetical and lost MSS are designated by Greek letters (or by such terms as 'Bury MS'), except that the latest common ancestor of P CS is called A, as elsewhere in the edition. The term [Oxon] designates the source of the fragment in New College 21 (cf. above, p. 50 n.6).

3. Contamination is too widespread in the lower reaches of the stemma to be clearly shown: there is contamination, for example, in both Σ and Σ¹ (probably from an η or θ source), in Trevet (from η/θ and perhaps from an E source), in several members of the η group, in 'AE', and in ψ (from the E branch).

4. The relationships of the η MSS have not been precisely determined; the stemma places closely-related MSS in separate sub-groups, but the specific formations depicted (that of π, for example) are given only *exempli gratia*.

EDITIONS

Seneca's tragedies have not been generally fortunate in their editors. Only two Latinists of great distinction, Gronovius and Leo, have produced texts of the corpus; the contributions of Heinsius and Bentley, though valuable, have been limited in one case to *aduersaria*,[1] in the other to marginal jottings.[2] For the rest, the record has more often been one of stagnation or even of retrogression than of steady advance.

The earliest editions, starting with the *editio princeps* published at Ferrara by Andreas Bellfortis near 1484, are virtually indistinguishable from late MSS. The text, like that of all editions before 1661, was based on contaminated A sources, with no knowledge of the pure E tradition. A somewhat different, but no better, text appears in the Venetian editions of the next decade, now surrounded by a mindless commentary by Marmita and Caietanus.

---

[1] Ed. P. Burman the younger (Haarlem, 1742).
[2] Collected by E. Hedecke in *Studia Bentleiana* fasc. 2 pp. 9ff. (1899). I have gleaned further information from the margins of Bentley's copy of Gronovius in the British Museum (cat. no. 686.f.8).

The first edition in which judgement appears to have played a part is that of Iodocus Badius Ascensius (= Josse Bade), issued at Paris in 1514.[1] The enduring value of the work lies entirely in its commentary, in which Ascensius made a genuine attempt to deal with the problems of the text, showing fair learning and sound literary instincts; both text and commentary cite a number of readings traditionally ascribed to Avantius' Aldine of 1517,[2] which emerges, when reduced to its genuinely new contributions, as the work of a careful but rarely exceptional critic.[3]

The rest of the sixteenth century brought no advance in recension and little in emendation; at its end appeared the learned and diffuse compilations of the Jesuit Del Rio, still the fullest collection of illustrative material for the entire corpus. Del Rio's work is useful as a starting-point for commentators, though more remarkable for diligence than penetration; his material was ably digested by the 'excellent and indefatigable'[4] Thomas Farnaby, whose modest edition with notes went through several printings in the early seventeenth century.

If Gronovius had done nothing but uncover the 'Etruscus', his edition would still mark an epoch in the history of the text; for the first time an editor could draw on a second, and often purer, branch of tradition. Gronovius exploited his discovery in hundreds of passages which had appeared in a corrupt or interpolated form for two centuries. His own corrections are also numerous, but many are either restorations of readings lightly corrupted in E[5] or minor repairs which were still to be done because no skilled critic had yet read the text with care;[6] even

---

[1] Professor and printer at Paris (1462–1535); cf. Marie-Madeleine de la Garanderie, *La correspondance d'Érasme et de Guillaume Budé* (1967) 291; for his Seneca cf. Ph. Renouard, *Bibliographie des impressions et des œuvres de Josse Badius Ascensius* (Paris, 1908) III.252–4.

[2] E.g. *bina* (42), *Spartenne* (281).

[3] Cf. 566, 671, 934, 264; several of these readings might have been taken from *recentiores*.

[4] Housman, Lucan preface p. xxxi.

[5] So, for example, *Eurotan tuum* (281), *Ilio* (577).

[6] Cf. 526, 530, 888, 913.

at their most ingenious,[1] his emendations cannot rival Bentley's for depth or brilliance.[2]

The only other edition before Leo deserving mention is that of F. H. Bothe, issued in an omnibus edition of Latin dramatic poetry. Though not a critic of the first rank, Bothe read his texts attentively, with independent and sane judgement; some of his conjectures are clearly right,[3] others are plausible,[4] and still others call attention to a real, but previously ignored, difficulty.[5]

The modern age of Senecan textual scholarship began with the edition of Friedrich Leo, published by Weidmann in 1878–9. The text was accompanied by a volume of critical observations displaying enormous learning and acumen; the worth of this part of Leo's edition for students of Latin poetry is hardly diminished today.[6]

Leo's principles of recension were Lachmannian in their rigid simplicity: E was the only reliable transmitter of ancient readings, and thus the single basis of recension;[7] M and N were descended from an apograph of E (Σ) and were thus of interest only when E itself had suffered damage after Σ had been copied from it; all other extant MSS stemmed from an interpolated tradition (A) which had its origin in a thorough stylistic re-writing carried out in late antiquity. Leo denied all authority to A, and where E was corrupt he often resorted to conjecture rather than accepting unobjectionable A readings.[8] He did, however, admit that A might in places contain the truth against E, and in practice he often corrected E's errors and corruptions from A.[9]

---

[1] Such as *alio* (500).
[2] Note in particular *domina* (785), *adulterae* (970).
[3] In 636 *ut* must be right; in 146 *quis* is very attractive.
[4] See commentary on 13f. (*accolere*).
[5] Cf. 416, 496.
[6] For an evaluation see Ed. Fraenkel's introduction to Leo's *Ausgewählte kleine Schriften* (Rome, 1960) xixff.
[7] *Obs.* 15: 'itaque in futurum quoque unicum recensionis fundamentum Etruscus habebitur.'
[8] *Obs.* 4.
[9] *Obs.* 5.

Leo might have modified his views of the A group if he had been aware of the best A MSS, P and C. His manuscript research, however, had been conducted almost entirely in Italy, and he based his knowledge of A primarily on two highly contaminated MSS, Laurentianus 37.6 (Laur) and Vaticanus Latinus 1647 (Vat), which attracted attention because they bore secure dates (1368 and 1391/2 respectively). Unfortunately, Leo's uncompromising statement of E's superiority continued to influence the outlook of editors long after it had been invalidated by better knowledge of A.

Although Leo is beyond doubt the greatest Latinist to have edited the tragedies in the modern age, his personal contribution to the emendation of the text was neither large nor lasting. I have adopted two of his proposals in this edition, the deletion of line 548 and the correction of *Dardaniae* to *Dardanidae* in 863 (anticipated in *recentiores*); other suggestions are discussed at 428, 481, 686, 715, 730ff., and 742. Leo was also excessively hospitable to the conjectures of Wilamowitz, few of which show true feeling for or understanding of Senecan style.

The second Teubner text of Peiper and Richter (1902; reprinted 1921, 1937) represented a vast improvement over their eccentric edition of 1867, and remained the standard edition of the plays until 1966. Its importance for recension lies in its attempt to improve upon Leo's account of A by identifying a stage in A's transmission earlier than that embodied in the *recentiores*. This effort was a failure: the four 'early A' MSS used – Rehdigeranus 118 and 122, Augustanus 23, and Sangallensis Vad. 303 – were exposed as typical *recentiores*,[1] and the other source used to represent A, the rext reconstructed from the commentary of Nicholas Trevet, was soon proven to descend at no great distance from a surviving manuscript (C). In the course of the investigation, however, Richter propounded a criterion for assessing A MSS which in other hands was to be of fundamental importance. He observed that many A MSS, among them that used by Trevet, lacked *HF* 125–61, and

---

[1] Düring, *Hermes* xlii (1907) 113ff.; cf. Stuart, *CQ* vi (1912) 1.

rightly concluded that the hyparchetype of the A tradition had contained this lacuna. MSS which preserved this lacuna would therefore provide the most reliable basis for reconstructing the A hyparchetype.[1]

On the comparative authority of E and A Peiper–Richter took a professedly moderate position, while making the important point that many of A's good readings in places where E is corrupt will be those of their common archetype.[2] In practice, however, E's superiority was not often challenged. Richter, who supervised the final form of the edition after the death of Peiper, intelligently pruned the apparatus of the 1867 edition, largely by suppressing the bolder fancies of his late collaborator. Though neither displayed particular genius in emendation, Richter was clearly the more talented; his *Thespias* at 316 solves a small, but real difficulty, and his *cuncta* at 545 would stand in the text were the entire line not suspect. Peiper's only real contribution is the deletion of 934. Other suggestions are recorded at 99, 268, 316f., 481, 531, 534, 592, 596, 765, 811, and 898.

The decade beginning in 1902 saw the greatest advance in knowledge of the MS tradition since the discovery of E by Gronovius. The lacuna-criterion of purity was refined and widely applied by Theodor Düring and Wilhelm Hoffa, pupils of Leo who were preparing a revised edition of his text for Weidmann. The result was the discovery of several 'pure-A' MSS, of which Düring pronounced the datable MSS l, n, and r to be the best.[3] At nearly the same time, however, C. E. Stuart, a Prize Fellow of Trinity College, Cambridge, was conducting the broadest survey of Seneca MSS ever undertaken, in the course of which he subjected more than 300 MSS to an even more sophisticated form of the lacuna-test. Stuart's research uncovered P and C, the oldest complete A MSS (dating from the first half of the thirteenth century), and he added to them an

---

[1] *Kritische Untersuchungen* (1899) 1–13, and preface to 1902 edition, p. xi.
[2] *De corruptis quibusdam Senecae tragoediarum locis* (Jena, 1894), 1ff., and 1902 preface xiv; also R. Peiper, *De Senecae tragoediarum vulgari lectione (A) constituenda* (Breslau, 1893) 131.
[3] *Hermes* xlii (1907) 113ff.; l was called b by Düring.

exceptionally pure Italian MS of the fourteenth century, S. In a still fundamental article,[1] Stuart correctly analysed the relationships of P, C, and S and concluded that their testimony was sufficient to reconstruct the hyparchetype of the A family.[2] Düring and Hoffa were quick to recognise the importance of Stuart's discoveries, and their later work gives proper emphasis to CPS. In a note prefacing the draft apparatus for their revision of Leo, Düring wrote 'mit Absicht habe ich n b r höchst selten einzeln ausgeführt. Sie können in der Tat entbehrt werden. P C S geben A vollständig.'[3] Of Düring's emendations in *Agamemnon* only *regna* for *terga* in 756 (made independently by Damsté) deserves serious consideration; others are recorded in the apparatus at lines 13, 280, 545, 807, and 976. The text which Düring and Hoffa planned to print would have differed little from that of Leo, but because of its improved manuscript basis it would immediately have superseded both Leo and Peiper–Richter. The work was far advanced, and only *Oedipus* and most of *Phaedra* lacked an apparatus, when Düring, Hoffa, and Stuart were called up in 1914.[4] All three died in the war.

While it is proper to regret that these capable scholars did not live to complete their labours, it is also useful to recall that by 1914 they had recorded in accessible publications all the information needed for a satisfactory edition of Seneca's

---

[1] *CQ* vi (1912) 1–20.

[2] Stuart's unpublished papers, now in the library of Trinity College, include collations and descriptions of MSS and his fellowship dissertation on the tragedies. Though useful and instructive, this *Nachlass* contains nothing comparable in importance to the published articles.

[3] *Materialen* iva (Niedersächsische Staats- und Universitätsbibliothek Göttingen, MS 4° Philol. 142ⁿ).

[4] Letter of Hoffa to Düring, 20 September 1914 (*Materialen* iii no. 29): 'Was nun den Seneca angeht, so bitte ich Sie mit der Arbeit ganz so zu verfahren wie Sie es für recht halten und dabei gar keine Rücksicht auf meine Person zu nehmen. Benutzen Sie bitte, was ich Ihnen geschickt habe, ganz als das Ihrige und vollenden Sie die Arbeit so weit es geht. Die Sache ist ja die Hauptsache und meine Person tritt ja selbstverständlich ganz zurück.' In 1917 one might with justice have said οἱ μὲν γὰρ οὐκέτ' εἰσίν, οἱ δ' ὄντες κακοί.

EDITIONS

tragedies. That more than fifty years would pass before such an edition appeared is due not so much to the difficulty of the task as to the abilities of those who carried it out.

Between 1917 and 1965 complete critical editions were produced by U. Moricca (Paravia, 1917–23; second edition, 1946–7), Léon Herrmann (Budé, 1924–6), and G. Viansino (Paravia, 1965; second edition (vol. 1), 1968).[1] Since these editions made no contribution whatever to recension and virtually none to emendation,[2] discussion of their shortcomings would be gratuitous.[3] The same judgement must be made of the editions of single plays by R. Giomini (*Phaedra*: Rome, 1954; *Agamemnon*: 1955) and P. Grimal (*Phaedra*: Paris, 1965). The latter, however, deserves special mention for having stated his devotion to the 'best MS' in almost precisely the form exploded by Housman sixty years before: 'nous avons préféré systématiquement les leçons de E, ne recourant à la tradition A que dans le cas où E donnait un texte évidemment corrompu' (p. 23).

Some progress was made in this half-century. Gunnar Carlsson continued the revaluation of A begun by Richter, demonstrating that E and A must in principle be regarded as of equal weight, and that the intrinsic quality of their readings is the only valid criterion of choice between them.[4] Unfortunately, Carlsson's announced intention to produce an edition (in collaboration with Bertil Axelson) was never fulfilled. In addition, two meritorious editions of single plays appeared: Th. H. Sluiter's *Oedipus* (Groningen, 1941) and W. Woesler's

---

[1] I omit the bilingual editions of F. J. Miller (Loeb series, 1917ff.), essentially a reprint of Leo, and of T. Thomann (Zurich, 1961–9).
[2] For Herrmann cf. 268, 273, 481; Viansino 449, 537f., 556, 970.
[3] On Herrmann's edition cf. G. Carlsson, *Gnomon* iv (1928) 492–8, Woesler 68f.; on Viansino cf. G. C. Giardina in *Boll. Acc. Naz. Lincei* xiv (1966) 65–85, O. Zwierlein in *Gnomon* xxxviii (1966) 678–88, and on the first volume of the second edition (all published to date) cf. E. Courtney in *CR* N.s. xx (1970) 198ff.
[4] 'Die Überlieferung der Seneca-Tragödien', *Lunds Universitets Årsskrift*, N.F. 1 Avd. v. 21 (1925); 'Zu Senecas Tragödien: Lesungen und Deutungen', *Kungl. Humanistiska Vetenskapssamfundet i Lund. Årsberättelse 1928–9*, 39–72. See also Axelson, *Korruptelenkult* 7–25.

93

Phaedra (diss. Münster, 1965). Both embodied accurate accounts of P CS and showed sound judgement in choosing between E and A variants.[1]

By comparison with its immediate predecessors, the most recent complete edition, by G. C. Giardina (Bologna, 1966), seems a monumental achievement.[2] P CS are fully and, in general, accurately reported, and even E was freshly collated;[3] thus in this edition the reader of Seneca possesses for the first time the information needed to grasp the shape of the paradosis. Giardina, however, is vague and inconsistent in his treatment of MSS apart from E P CS: the Σ group[4] is excluded although Giardina regards Σ as independent of E,[5] while on the other hand lnr, Trevet, and KQe are sporadically or even systematically cited although Giardina makes no claim of independence for them.[6] In addition, the apparatus is poorly drafted and needlessly inflated. Giardina's own conjectures are few and modest (see apparatus on 578 and 973) and his choice of variants is fallible, though free of bias toward E or A. For all its shortcomings, Giardina's is the best complete edition now available.[7]

---

[1] The edition of *Troades* by R. L. Wertis (diss. Columbia University, 1970) resembles those of Sluiter and Woesler in being based essentially on E P CS.

[2] See O. Zwierlein, *Gnomon* xli (1969) 759–69; E. Courtney, *CR* N.S. xviii (1968) 173–7.

[3] In my own reports of E P CS I have silently corrected about a score of misstatements.

[4] To the previously known F MN Giardina wished to add Neapolitanus Oratorianus (Biblioteca dei Gerolamini) CF.4.5 (= O); cf. the reservations of Zwierlein 760, and above, p. 63 n.2, 71 n.3.

[5] Preface ix (modified xxvi–xxvii).

[6] Preface xiii (contrast xxvi) on lnr; preface xiv (apparently contradicting *Boll. Acc. Naz. Lincei* xiii (1965) 91–100 and *Vichiana* ii (1965) 63–73) on KQe.

[7] The only edition to appear since Giardina, that of *Medea* by C. D. N. Costa (Oxford, 1973), marks no advance in recension; indeed, the inconsistent citation of both lnr and KQe alongside E P CS is a backward step.

THE APPARATUS CRITICUS

The text is constituted from the testimony of four MSS (E P CS), and only these MSS are fully reported in the apparatus. I have recorded even *lectiones singulares*, since on the one hand the errors of E and P cannot be distinguished from those of their hyparchetypes (see stemma, p. 86), while on the other neither C nor S contains many unique errors; consistency and completeness were thus compatible with brevity. I have, however, excluded trifles (e.g. *negglecta* for *neglecta*) and have segregated orthographical variants, including most of those involving proper names, in an appendix (pp. 363–8). The readings of the major excerpt collections, which are independent of E P CS, are cited in the few relevant passages.

Other witnesses are cited only for specific reasons: the Σ MSS (F MN) where they clarify the reading of their ultimate parent, E (e.g. 76, 306); the best MSS of the η-group (Vd) where the reading of β is not clear from CS (e.g. 216, 731), or to distinguish an error of θ from a *lectio singularis* of S; these and other MSS (including the great mass collectively called *recentiores*) where they offer readings of some critical interest not found in E P CS. In places where the major MSS divide along unusual lines and in a few other passages, I have permitted myself greater flexibility in citing other MSS. Agreement of other witnesses in individual errors of E, P, C, or S is almost never recorded, and I have made no attempt to record even a small sample of the corruptions or conjectures of Σ, η, Trevet or the *recentiores*; my view is that an apparatus cannot portray the complexity of the later MS tradition without damage to its primary function, to record the basis of the editor's text.

The apparatus is negatively drawn wherever this will not cause inconvenience or obscurity, and is elsewhere positive. In general, I have cited substantive differences of the two main branches (E and A) in positive form. When a variant is cited in negative form (e.g. 'iugis P'), this may be taken to mean that the major MSS not named (E CS in this instance) have the reading printed in the text. No conclusions are to be drawn regarding MSS other than E P CS, with this exception: where a variant is cited only from S, it may be assumed that Vd, the best representatives of the η group, agree with E P C (i.e. that the error is one of S, not of θ). A lemma is given as required for ease of reference (e.g. '29 maius] magis P'). I avoid the siglum 'A' in the apparatus, preferring the more precisely informative 'P CS' (so arranged to depict the subdivision of A into δ, represented by P, and β, represented by CS). The siglum *recc.* designates a reading found in a number of late MSS (listed as 'Other MSS' below, pp. 100f.).

TEXT

SIGLA

E-class

E   Laurentianus Mediceus plut. 37.13

F   Parisinus Bibl. Nat. Lat. 11855
M   Ambrosianus D 276 inf.
N   Vaticanus Latinus 1769

A-class

C   Cantabrigiensis Coll. Corp. Christi 406
P   Parisinus Bibl. Nat. Lat. 8260
S   Scorialensis T. III.11
a   Parisinus Bibl. Nat. Lat. 6395
d   Neapolitanus Bibl. Nat. IV.e.1
l   Laurentianus plut. 24 sin. 4
m   Venetus Marcianus xii.25
n   Neapolitanus Bibl. Nat. IV.d.47
p   Patavinus Bibl. Antoniana 1.9
q   Brixianus B.1.13
r   Vaticanus Reginensis Latinus 1500
Sal   Londiniensis B.M. add. MS 11987
V   Vaticanus Latinus 2829

Conflated MSS

e   Etonensis 110
K   Cameracensis 555
Q   Casinensis 392 P
Harl   Londiniensis B.M. Harleianus 2484
Laur   Laurentianus plut. 37.6
Vat   Vaticanus Latinus 1647
Cant   Cantabrigiensis Bibl. Vniu. Nn. II.35

Excerpt collections, etc.

Brux   Excerpta Bruxellensia cod. 20030–32
Gon   Excerpta Cantabrigiensia Coll. de Gonu. et Caius 225
Exon   Excerpta Exoniensia 3459 B
L   Excerpta Leidensia Bibl. Vniu. 191 B
Exc. Par.   Excerpta Parisina Bibl. Nat. Lat. 8049

SIGLA

Hieremias   Hieremias de Montagnone, *Compendium Moralium Notabilium*
Treuet   Nicolai Treuet Expositio *Agamemnonis* (ed. P. Meloni, Cagliari, 1961)
Vincentius Vincentius Bellouacensis, *Speculum Maius*

Other MSS

Bo   Bononiensis Bibl. Vniu. 2485

F1   Laurentianus plut. 37.1
F2   Laurentianus plut. 37.3
F3   Laurentianus plut. 37.9
F4   Laurentianus plut. 37.11
F5   Laurentianus plut. 37.12
F6   Laurentianus plut. 91 sup. 30
F7   Riccardianus 527

For   Foroiuliensis 75

L1   Londiniensis B.M. Arundel 116
L2   Londiniensis B.M. Kings 30
L3   Londiniensis B.M. Burney 250
Leid.1   Leidensis Vossianus F.99
Leid.2   Leidensis Vossianus Q.31

M1   Ambrosianus H.77 inf.
M2   Ambrosianus G.89 inf.
M3   Ambrosianus A.118 inf.
M4   Triuultianus 809

Ox.1   Oxoniensis Canon. Class. Lat. 93
Ox.2   Oxoniensis Ashmole 1791
Ox.3   Oxoniensis D'Oruille 176
Ox.4   Oxoniensis Laud. Lat. 71
Ox.5   Oxoniensis Bodleianus 292
Ox.6   Oxoniensis Canon. Class. Lat. 88
Ox.7   Oxoniensis Canon. Class. Lat. 89
Ox.8   Oxoniensis Canon. Class. Lat. 90
Ox.9   Oxoniensis Digby 142
Ox.10   Oxoniensis D'Orville 21
Ox.11   Oxoniensis D'Orville 22
Ox.12   Oxoniensis D'Orville 23

R1	Vaticanus Ottobonianus Lat. 1749
R2	Vaticanus Vrbinas Lat. 356
R3	Vaticanus Latinus 1642
R4	Vaticanus Latinus 1649
R5	Vaticanus Latinus 2827
R6	Vaticanus Latinus 2828
R7	Vaticanus Latinus 7319
R8	Vaticanus Latinus 7620
V1	Venetus Marcianus xii.26
Vi.1	Vindobonensis Palatinus 61
Vi.2	Vindobonensis Palatinus 122
η	Consensus of Vd lnr KQ e mpq Sal
codd.	Consensus of all MSS.

In addition the following signs are used; they have been adapted from those employed by R. D. Dawe (*Collation and investigation of manuscripts of Aeschylus* (1964) 197).

E^{ac}	The reading of E before correction
E^{pc}	The reading of E after correction, no conclusion to be drawn about
E^{1pc}	the author of the correction. E^{1pc} is used to designate corrections by
E^{2pc}	the scribe, E^{2pc} for those in any hand other than that of the scribe.
E^{c}	E *ex correctione*, where E^{ac} is not legible. The letter or letters which are due to the corrector are italicised.
E^{ul}	A reading entered in E as a *uaria lectio*
mg	*In margine*

TESTIMONIA

1. *Inscriptio Pompeiana* (*C.I.L.* IV *Supp*. 2.6698): idai cernu nemura (cf. 730).

2. *Priscianus* (*G.L.K.* VI.264): Seneca in Phaedra: 'Hippolyte, nunc me compotem uoti facis' (= *Pha*. 710); in eadem: 'compote uoto' (cf. *Agam*. 379).

3. *Aldhelmus* (*M.G.H. Auct. Ant.* xv *p*. 194.27): d littera in t transmutatur ut Lucius Anneus Seneca in sexto uolumine tetrametro brachycatalecto sic ait 'geminumque duplices Argos attollit domus' et infra 'dubia labat ceruice? famuli attollite' (cf. 729, 787).

AGAMEMNON

PERSONAE

THYESTAE VMBRA

CLYTEMESTRA

NVTRIX

AEGISTHVS

EVRYBATES

CASSANDRA

AGAMEMNON

ELECTRA

ORESTES (tacitus)

STROPHIVS

PYLADES (tacitus)

CHORVS MYCENAEARVM uel ARGIVARVM

CHORVS ILIADVM

Scaena Mycenis uel Argis ante regiam

AGAMEMNON

ACTVS PRIMVS

THYESTAE VMBRA

Opaca linquens Ditis inferni loca
adsum, profundo Tartari emissus specu.
incertus utras oderim sedes magis:
fugio Thyestes inferos, superos fugo.
En horret animus et pauor membra excutit: 5
uideo paternos, immo fraternos lares.
hoc est uetustum Pelopiae limen domus,
hinc auspicari regium capiti decus
mos est Pelasgis, hoc sedent alti toro
quibus superba sceptra gestantur manu,   10
locus hic habendae curiae, hic epulis locus.
Libet reuerti. nonne uel tristes lacus
†incolere satius, nonne custodem Stygis
trigemina nigris colla iactantem iubis?
ubi ille celeri corpus euinctus rotae   15
in se refertur, ubi per aduersum irritus
redeunte totiens luditur saxo labor,
ubi tondet ales auida fecundum iecur
et inter undas feruida exustus siti
aquas fugaces ore decepto appetit   20
poenas daturus caelitum dapibus graues –
sed ille nostrae pars quota est culpae senex?
reputemus omnes quos ob infandas manus
quaesitor urna Cnosius uersat reos:

Inscriptionem scaenae om. P CS (notam personae, i.e. Thiestes, habet C, om. P S)
5 inhorret *Gronouius (non E, ut ipse putauit)* et] en *Vi.1* membra] mentem
Bentleius 9 alti *P CS*: alte *E*: alto *M^c recc.* 13f. *locus nondum sanatus*
13 incolere] accolere *Bothe*: uidere *fort.* agnoscit *Ascensius*: tolerare *Bentleius*
nonne *saepe sed frustra temptatum* (nosse *Koetschau* (*Philologus lxi.145*): *e.g.*
tremere *Düring*: pone *Weber* (*Philologus lxvii.307*)) stygis] pati *Bentleius*
14 trigemina *E S*: ter- *P C* nigris *P CS*: nimis *E* iugis *P* *u.* 14 *cum*
sequenti sic coniungere uoluit Withofius: iactantem iubis | uidere? celeri corpus
ubi uinctus rotae eqs. *post u.* 14 *unum uersum excidisse putat* Zwierlein (*e.g.*
uidere et atras Ditis inuisi domus) 15 aduinctus *Grotius* rote *P CS*: rota
E 23 repetamus *Treuet 'AE' recc.*

uincam Thyestes sceleribus cunctos meis. 25
a fratre uincar, liberis plenus tribus
in me sepultis? uiscera exedi mea.
  Nec hactenus Fortuna maculauit patrem,
sed maius aliud ausa commisso scelus
natae nefandos petere concubitus iubet. 30
non pauidus hausi dicta, †sed cepi nefas.
ergo ut per omnes liberos irem parens
coacta fatis nata fert uterum grauem
me patre dignum. uersa natura est retro:
auo parentem (pro nefas!), patri uirum, 35
natis nepotes miscui, nocti diem.
  Sed sera tandem respicit fessos malis
post fata demum sortis incertae fides:
rex ille regum, ductor Agamemnon ducum,
cuius secutae mille uexillum rates 40
Iliaca uelis maria texerunt suis,
post decima Phoebi lustra deuicto Ilio
adest, daturus coniugi iugulum suae.
  Iam iam natabit sanguine alterno domus.
enses secures tela, diuisum graui 45
ictu bipennis regium uideo caput.
iam scelera prope sunt, iam dolus caedes cruor –
parantur epulae. causa natalis tui,
Aegisthe, uenit. quid pudor uultus grauat?
quid dextra dubio trepida consilio labat? 50
quid ipse temet consulis torques rogas
an deceat hoc te? respice ad matrem: decet.

---

27 sepultis?] *interpunxit* M. *Müller* (*diss.*, *p. 38*)   29 maius] magis *P*
31 ausi *S*^{ac} sed cepi *uix sanum*: suscepi *Koetschau* (*Philologus lxi.145*), *fort.*
recte: concepi *Siegmund* (*1907, 11*): sed coepi *ed. 1492*   33 uterum grauem]
fort. utero genus (*uel sim.*)?   34 me] et *N* digna *Viansino*   35 parentem
E: nepotem *P CS*   36 miscui *E*: miscuit (*sc.* natura) *P CS*   38 facta *M*,
cod. Lipsii incertę *E*: inceste *P CS*   42 decima *E*: dena *P CS*: bina *agnoscit*
Ascensius: gemina *Bentleius* (*ad Lucani Bell. Ciu. 2.568*)   44 sanguine
alterno] *inu. ord.* P   45 secures *P CS*: -em *E*: -im *Vat*   48 parentur *d*
51 temet *P CS*: timet *E*   52 ad *E*: an *P CS*: at *Auantius* (*i.e.* respice:
at matrem decet) decet] dē *S*

Sed cur repente noctis aestiuae uices
hiberna longa spatia producunt mora,
aut quid cadentes detinet stellas polo?   55
Phoebum moramur: redde iam mundo diem.

CHORVS

O regnorum magnis fallax
Fortuna bonis, in praecipiti
dubioque locas nimis excelsos.
   Numquam placidam sceptra quietem   60
certumue sui tenuere diem:
alia ex aliis cura fatigat
uexatque animos noua tempestas.
non sic Libycis Syrtibus aequor
furit alternos uoluere fluctus,   65
non Euxini turget ab imis
commota uadis unda niuali
uicina polo,
ubi caeruleis immunis aquis
lucida uersat plaustra Bootes,   70
ut praecipites regum casus
Fortuna rotat. metui cupiunt
metuique timent, non nox illis
alma recessus praebet tutos,
non curarum somnus domitor   75
pectora soluit.
   Quas non arces scelus alternum
dedit in praeceps? impia quas non
arma fatigant? iura pudorque

---

55 aud *E* quid] qui *Harl Vi.1 R4*   56 moramur? *interpunxit Leo* reddo
Gronouius   57 O *habent E L: om. P CS*   59 locas nimis excelsos *Bentleius,*
necnon Withofius (*cf. W. V. Clausen, Mnemos.1955.50*) ac *Luc. Müller* (*de re*
metrica² 187): locas excelsos nimis *E*: nimis excelsa loco *P CS L*: nimis excelsa
locas *eᵃᶜ* (*et e³ᵐᵍ*) *Ox.1*: nimis excelsos locas '*AE*'   62 aliis] alia *Fabricius*
(*e codice*)   63 uexatque *P CS*: uexat *E* noua] fera *L*   66 *euxini Eᶜ*
72 rotas *Bentleius*   76 soluit *Eᶜ P CS L:* -et *F* (*Eᵃᶜ?*)

et coniugii sacrata fides   80
fugiunt aulas; sequitur tristis
sanguinolenta Bellona manu
quaeque superbos urit Erinys,
nimias semper comitata domos,
quas in planum quaelibet hora   85
tulit ex alto.
  Licet arma uacent cessentque doli,
sidunt ipso pondere magna
ceditque oneri fortuna suo.
uela secundis inflata Notis   90
uentos nimium timuere suos;
nubibus ipsis inserta caput
turris pluuio uapulat Austro,
densasque nemus spargens umbras
annosa uidet robora frangi;   95
feriunt celsos fulmina colles,
corpora morbis maiora patent,
et cum in pastus armenta uagos
uilia currant, placet in uulnus
maxima ceruix. quidquid in altum   100
Fortuna tulit, ruitura leuat.
  Modicis rebus longius aeuum est:
felix mediae quisquis turbae
sorte quietus
aura stringit litora tuta   105
timidusque mari credere cumbam
remo terras propiore legit.

---

80 fides E^c 81 fugiunt P CS: faciunt E 83 urit] urget *Leo* (*testibus
Düring et Hoffa*)   84 nimias E: tumidas P CS 85 qu(a)elibet E P: qualibet CS 87 arma] alma P sidunt E P CS: cadunt L V^c dp e $Ox.1$ $Vi.1$
$Leid.1$ M^1(*mg*)   91 uentos nimium] nimium uentos (*sc.* uela inflata
nimium) *Rossbach* (*B.Ph.W.xxiv.367*)   96 flumina P 97 morbis] maius
Stuart   patent E^c 99 currant E P C Vd: certant S N KQ^{ac} e $Ox.1$: currunt
recc.   placet] patet $Ox.1$ q *For Leid.1* Bo $F1$ $L1$ (*postea coni. Richter*)   103 felix
medie quisquis turbe P L Vd (meduse d): felix medie turbe quisquis CS: felix
quisquis medie turbe E 104 sorte E: parte P CS 106 cimbam P CS
107 terram *Treuet*

ACTVS SECVNDVS
CLYTEMESTRA–NVTRIX

CLYTEMESTRA

Quid, segnis anime, tuta consilia expetis?
quid fluctuaris? clausa iam melior uia est.
licuit pudicos coniugis quondam toros   110
et sceptra casta uidua tutari fide;
periere mores ius decus pietas fides
et, qui redire cum perît nescit, pudor.
da frena et omnem prona nequitiam incita:
per scelera semper sceleribus tutum est iter.   115
  Tecum ipsa nunc euolue femineos dolos,
quod ulla coniunx perfida atque impos sui
amore caeco, quod nouercales manus
ausae, quod ardens impia uirgo face
Phasiaca fugiens regna Thessalica trabe: 120
ferrum, uenena – uel Mycenaeas domos
coniuncta socio profuge furtiua rate.
quid timida loqueris furta et exilium et fugas?
soror ista fecit: te decet maius nefas.

NVTRIX

Regina Danaum et inclitum Ledae genus,   125
quid tacita uersas quidue consilî impotens
tumido feroces impetus animo geris?
licet ipsa sileas, totus in uultu est dolor.

---

108 anim*e* E^c expetis] ex *P*   111 uidua *E*: iuncta *P CS*   tutari] tuta *P*
113 cum perit nescit *E P L*: nescit cum perit *CS*   perît *Ascensius*: perit *codd.*
114 incita] mota *S*   115 tutum *om. P*   117 ulla] illa *N*: nulla *e Ox.1*
Sal recc.   118 caeca *Bentleius*   120 trabe *P CS*: graue *E*: rate *F6 Ox.10*
121 mycenaeas domos *E*: -enas domos *P*: -ena domo *CS Vd*: -enea domo
M F²ᵖᶜ ln Sal   123 et fugas *E CS*: fugas *P*: et fugam *Sal Leid.2 M2*
124 soror *E*: sors *P CS*   125 tegina *P*   126 consilii *P CS*: -ia *E*
127 timido *O (postea coni. Bentleius)*   128 ipse *Gon*

proin quidquid est, da tempus ac spatium tibi:
quod ratio non quit saepe sanauit mora.   130

CLYTEMESTRA

Maiora cruciant quam ut moras possim pati:
flammae medullas et cor exurunt meum;
mixtus dolori subdidit stimulos timor;
inuidia pulsat pectus; hinc animum iugo
premit cupido turpis et uinci uetat;   135
et inter istas mentis obsessae faces
fessus quidem et deuictus et pessumdatus
pudor rebellat. fluctibus uariis agor
ut, cum hinc profundum uentus, hinc aestus rapit,
incerta dubitat unda cui cedat malo.   140
proinde omisi regimen e manibus meis:
quocumque me ira, quo dolor, quo spes feret,
hoc ire pergam; fluctibus dedimus ratem.
ubi animus errat, optimum est casum sequi.

NVTRIX

Caeca est temeritas quae petit casum ducem.   145

CLYTEMESTRA

Cui ultima est fortuna, quid dubiam timet?

---

129 proin $E^{ac}F^{ac}N$: proinde E^{pc} (cf. Leonis Obs. 17, 38) $F^{2pc}PCS$ da tempus
ac spatium E: tempus da ac spatium P: da spatium ac tempus CS 130 non
quit $E\,P\,CS$ (quid $P\,S^{ac}$): non quiuit Exon   131 ut $P\,CS$: om. E quam
moras possim ut pati Heinsius   133 mixtus $P\,CS\,F^{2pc}$: iuxtus E^c: iustus F^{ac}
'AE': istus M^{ac}: mixtos e^{2mg} Bo recc.   subdidit] subdit hinc Heinsius   stimulo
S^{ac} 134 inuidia] uiduumque (sc. pectus) Heinsius   pectus] cecus (sc. cupido,
ut uid.) E 137 deuictus $P\,M\,e$: deuinctus $E\,CS$: deiectus agnoscit Ascensius
143 hoc $E\,C$: huc $P\,S$ dedimus E: dedam $P\,CS$: dedi ed. princeps: credam $R4$
144 casu P 145 ceca] certa Hieremias e^{ac} 146 cui…timet] quîs…
timent Kenney: ubi…times Birt (Rhein. Mus. xxxiv.551)   quid] qui P: quis
Bothe (fort. recte)   dubiam $E\,P\,L$: dubium CS Exc. Par.

NVTRIX

Tuta est latetque culpa, si pateris, tua.

CLYTEMESTRA

Perlucet omne regiae uitium domus.

NVTRIX

Piget prioris et nouum crimen struis?

CLYTEMESTRA

Res est profecto stulta nequitiae modus.   150

NVTRIX

Quod metuit auget qui scelus scelere obruit.

CLYTEMESTRA

Et ferrum et ignis saepe medicinae loco est.

NVTRIX

Extrema primo nemo temptauit loco.

CLYTEMESTRA

Rapienda rebus in malis praeceps uia est.

---

147 tua] uia *P*   150 res] lex *Vi.1*   151 metuit] meruit *recc.* (*teste Delrio*),
Marmita in ed. 1498   scelus scelere *E P L Exon*: scelere scelus *CS Exc. Par.*
154 rapienda *E L d^c*: capienda *P C V d* (*u.l.*): sapienda *S*

NVTRIX

At te reflectat coniugî nomen sacrum. 155

CLYTEMESTRA

Decem per annos uidua respiciam uirum?

NVTRIX

Meminisse debes subolis ex illo tuae.

CLYTEMESTRA

Equidem et iugales filiae memini faces
et generum Achillem: praestitit matri fidem?

NVTRIX

Redemit illa classis immotae moras 160
et maria pigro fixa languore impulit.

CLYTEMESTRA

Pudet pigetque: Tyndaris, caeli genus,
lustrale classi Doricae peperit caput!
reuoluit animus uirginis thalamos meae
quos ille dignos Pelopia fecit domo 165
cum stetit ad aras ore sacrifico pater
quam nuptiales! horruit Calchas suae
responsa uocis et recedentes focos.
o scelera semper sceleribus uincens domus:

---

155 coniugî *ed. princeps*: -ii *codd.*: -is *Lipsius*   158 et quidem *E*   160–
1 *Nutrici tribuit E*: *Clytemestrae dant P CS*   161 pigno *S^{ac}* lango *E*
162 pigetque *P CS*: doletque *E (fort. recte)*   163 peperit *P CS*: peperi *E*
166 sacrifico *E*: sacrilego *P CS*   167 quam *E*: quasi *P CS*

cruore uentos emimus, bellum nece!   170
 Sed uela pariter mille fecerunt rates?
non est soluta prospero classis deo,
eiecit Aulis impias portu rates.
sic auspicatus bella non melius gerit:
amore captae captus, immotus prece   175
Zminthea tenuit spolia Phoebei senis,
ardore sacrae uirginis iam tum furens.
non illum Achilles flexit indomitus minis,
non ille, solus fata qui mundi uidet
(in nos fidelis augur, in captas leuis),   180
non populus aeger et relucentes rogi;
inter ruentis Graeciae stragem ultimam
sine hoste uictus marcet ac Veneri uacat
reparatque amores; neue desertus foret
a paelice umquam barbara caelebs torus,   185
ablatam Achilli diligit Lyrnesida
nec rapere puduit e sinu auulsam uiri –
en Paridis hostem! nunc nouum uulnus gerens
amore Phrygiae uatis incensus furit,
et post tropaea Troica ac uersum Ilium   190
captae maritus remeat et Priami gener.
 Accingere, anime: bella non leuia apparas.
scelus occupandum est; pigra, quem expectas diem?
Pelopia Phrygiae sceptra dum teneant nurus?
an te morantur uirgines uiduae domi   195
patrique Orestes similis? horum te mala
uentura moueant, turbo quîs rerum imminet:

---

170 emimus *CS*: -nus *E P* 171 *Clytemestrae dant E P CS*: *Nutrici tribuunt Treuet e²ᵇᶜ Ox.1 recc.* uela *P CS*: bella *E* 173 aulis *P CS*: alio *E* impia *P*
176 tenuit] renuit *F7 (postea coni. Bentleius)* spolia] dona *Bentleius* senis *E*:
ducis *P CS* 177 ardore *E P*: ardorem *CS* iam tum *E P C*: tantum *S*
furens *E P*: ferens *CS* 182 *habent P CS*: *om. E* 183 ac *E P Vd*: at *CS*:
et *recc.* 184 reparat *P* 185 barbara *E*: uel suus *P CS*: barbara ac
Heinsius 186 lyrnesida *E F*: briseida *MN* 'AE': briseidam *P CS*
187 auulsam *E*: uulsam *P CS*: euulsam 'AE' *Bo M1 F5* 188 en *E P CS*:
et *F Mᵃᶜ N eᵃᶜ Ox.1* 'AE' paridis *P CS*: rapidis *E* 190 troiaca *E* 193
quem *E P S*: quam *C* 194 *habet E*: *om. P CS*

quid, misera, cessas? en adest natis tuis
furens nouerca. per tuum, si aliter nequit,
latus exigatur ensis et perimat duos;   200
misce cruorem, perde pereundo uirum:
mors misera non est commori cum quo uelis.

NVTRIX

Regina, frena temet et siste impetus
et quanta temptes cogita. uictor uenit
Asiae ferocis, ultor Europae; trahit   205
captiua Pergama et diu uictos Phrygas.
hunc fraude nunc conaris et furto aggredi
quem non Achilles ense uiolauit fero,
quamuis procacem toruus armasset manum,
non melior Aiax morte decreta furens,   210
non sola Danais Hector et bello mora,
non tela Paridis certa, non Memnon niger,
non Xanthus armis corpora immixtis ferens
fluctusque Simois caede purpureos agens,
non niuea proles Cycnus aequorei dei,   215
non bellicoso Thressa cum Rheso phalanx,
non picta pharetras et securigera manu
peltata Amazon: hunc domi reducem paras
mactare et aras caede maculare impia.
ultrix inultum Graecia hoc facinus feret?   220
equos et arma classibusque horrens fretum

---

199 aliter *E*: aliquid *P*: aliud *CS*   nequit] nequid *N S*: nequis *e*ᶜ *l*ᵃᶜ *Leid.2*
F7   200 et] ut *Leid.2*   201 pereundo *P CS*: perfunde *E*   202 mors]
sors *Heinsius*   non est *E CS Gon*: est non est *P*   cum quo *E CS Gon*: cum *P*
203 impetum *edd. uett. aliquot*   204 temptes *E*: -as *P CS*   205 *post* asie
distinguit N   trahens *edd. uett.* (*teste Scaligero*)   206 diu uictos] ducit uictos
Sal: diu inuictos *Munro*   207 nunc] num *Madvig* (*Emend. Lat. p. 124*): tu
Bothe   et furto *E*: insana *P CS*   213 immixtis ferens *ego* (immixtis gerens
'*AE*', immersis ferens *Bentleius*): immixta gerens *E*: immixte gerens *P CS*:
immixta aggerens *Gronouius* (aggerans *Peiper*)   216 t(h)ressa *E P S V*:
cressa *C M²ᵖᶜ* '*AE*' *d pq Sal Treuet recc.*   r(h)eso *E P*: theso *S V F N*: theseo *C
M²ᵖᶜ d Treuet ln recc.*   220 ultrix *P CS*: uictrix *E*

propone et alto sanguine exundans solum
et tota captae fata Dardaniae domus
regesta Danais: comprime affectus truces
mentemque tibimet ipsa pacifica tuam.　　　225

AEGISTHVS–CLYTEMESTRA

AEGISTHVS

Quod tempus animo semper ac mente horrui
adest profecto, rebus extremum meis.
quid terga uertis, anime? quid primo impetu
deponis arma? crede perniciem tibi
et dira saeuos fata moliri deos:　　　230
oppone cunctis uile suppliciis caput
ferrumque et ignes pectore aduerso excipe,
Aegisthe: non est poena sic nato mori.
　Tu nos pericli socia, tu, Leda sata,
comitare tantum; sanguinem reddet tibi　　　235
ignauus iste ductor at fortis pater.
sed quid trementes circuit pallor genas
iacensque uultu languido optutus stupet?

CLYTEMESTRA

Amor iugalis uincit ac flectit retro:
remeemus illuc unde non decuit prius　　　240
abire; sed nunc casta repetatur fides:

---

222 propone *E P*: pre- *CS*　　　224 res gesta *P*
Scaen. tit. Egistus. Clytemestra *P CS*: Aegisthus. Clytemestra. Nutrix *E*
(*uide infra uu.* 288 ff.)　　　228 animae *E*　　　229 perniciem *P CS*: permitti *E*
230 deos:] *interpunxit M. Müller* (*Philologus xlv. 268*) : deos. *uulgo*　　　231 cunc-
tis] meritis *Treuet Harl*^su *recc.* (*postea Fabricius*)　　　233 *Aegistho tribuit E*:
Clytemestrae dant P CS　　　234 periclis otia *E*^ac　　　sata] fata *S* (*ut uid.*)
235 comitare] tmitare *P post* comitare *interpungunt F V d recc.*　　　236 iste]
ille *C*　　at *Delrius*: ac *codd.*　　pater *P CS*: pariter *E*　　　238 optutus] obrutus *S*
240 remeemus *P CS*: referemus *E*: referamur *Gronouius*: referemur *Leo* (*ed.*
uol. II.382): referimur *M. Müller* (*Philologus xlv.268*): temere imus *Vincentius*
(*Spec. Hist. ix.114*)　　　241 sed] uel *Gronouius*

nam sera numquam est ad bonos mores uia.
quem paenitet peccasse paene est innocens.

AEGISTHVS

Quo raperis amens? credis, aut speras tibi
Agamemnonis fidele coniugium? ut nihil 245
subesset animo quod graues faceret metus,
tamen superba et impotens flatu nimis
fortuna magno spiritus tumidos daret.
grauis ille sociis stante adhuc Troia fuit:
quid rere ad animum suapte natura trucem 250
Troiam addidisse? rex Mycenarum fuit,
ueniet tyrannus: prospera animos efferunt.
effusa circa paelicum quanto uenit
turba apparatu! sola sed turba eminet
tenetque regem famula ueridici dei. 255
feresne thalami uicta consortem tui?
at illa nolet. ultimum est nuptae malum
palam maritam possidens paelex domum.
nec regna socium ferre nec taedae sciunt.

CLYTEMESTRA

Aegisthe, quid me rursus in praeceps agis 260
iramque flammis iam residentem incitas?
permisit aliquid uictor in captam sibi:

---

242 nam] *omittunt excerpta et florilegia, more suo (i.e. L Brux Exon Gon Hieremias)*
243 p(a)ene est innocens *E P CS L Gon Hieremias*: pene innocens est *Exon*:
fere innocens est *Brux*　　247 impotens *P CS*: innocens *E*　　248 magnos
P^{ac}　　250 rere *E P C Vd*: tere *S N* (terreat *S^{2ul}*)　　quid reris ad suapte
natura trucem *Bothe*　　251 mercennarum *C*　　252 efferunt *E P CS L
Hieremias*: -ant *e a Bo F2 Exc. Par. (postea coni. Buecheler)*: -ent *e F5*　　254
turba *E*: longe *P CS*: turbam *Heinsius*　　255 regem] regnum *cod.
Lipsii*　　257 nolet *P CS*: nollet *E*　　258 maritam *F2 (postea coni.
Heinsius)*: marita *E^{ac} P CS*: mariti *E^{pc} Vd Hieremias Treuet*　　260 aegistae *E*
agis *E*: rapis *P CS*　　262 aliquid *P CS*: aliquis *E*　captas *Treuet Harl^{mg}
recc. (postea coni. Bothe)*

AGAMEMNON

nec coniugem hoc respicere nec dominam decet.
lex alia solio est, alia priuato toro.
quid, quod seueras ferre me leges uiro   265
non patitur animus turpis admissi memor?
det ille ueniam facile cui uenia est opus.

AEGISTHVS

Ita est? pacisci mutuam ueniam licet?
ignota tibi sunt iura regnorum aut noua?
nobis maligni iudices, aequi sibi,   270
id esse regni maximum pignus putant
si quidquid aliis non licet solis licet.

CLYTEMESTRA

Ignouit Helenae; iuncta Menelao redit
quae Europam et Asiam paribus afflixit malis.

AEGISTHVS

Sed nulla Atriden Venere furtiua abstulit   275
nec cepit animum coniugi obstrictum suae.
iam crimen ille quaerit et causas parat.
nil esse crede turpe commissum tibi:
quid honesta prodest uita flagitio uacans?
ubi dominus odit, fit nocens, non quaeritur.   280

---

264 solio *E*: socio *P CS*   priuato *P CS*: -a *E*   toro *M* (*postea coni. Auantius,*
Damsté): in toro *E P CS*   266 non] nunc *P*   267 dat *Bentleius* uenia
est opus *E P CS Gon*: uenia opus est *Exon*: est opus uenia *Hieremias*   268 itane
est *Richter*   pacissi *P*: pacissci *E* (*cf. Viansino, proleg. p. 6 n. 2*)   269 aut *E*:
haut *P CS*   273ff. *locus difficilis et fortasse turbatus*   273 ignouit *E*:
agnouit *P CS*   ignouit helenae *corruptum esse suspicatus est Stuart*: ignotane
helena est? *coni. L. Herrmann*: *nil mutandum censeo, sed u. infra u.* 275; *fortasse*
aliquid de Menelao ante u. 273 *excidit*   275 sed] hunc *Damsté*: *fort.* tunc (*si*
hic de Agamemnone agitur)   276 obstrictum *E*: obstructum *PCS*   279 uita
E: *om. P CS*   uacans *E*: carens *P CS*   280 ubi] *an* quem? fit] sit *Treuet*
l F4² Ox.2 Ox.3 Leid.2 (*postea coni. Düring*): *possis et* fis

Spartamne repetes spreta et Eurotan tuum
patriasque sedes profuga? non dant exitum
repudia regum: spe metus falsa leuas.

CLYTEMESTRA

Delicta nouit nemo nisi fidus mea.

AEGISTHVS

Non intrat umquam regium limen fides.   285

CLYTEMESTRA

Opibus merebor ut fidem pretio obligem.

AEGISTHVS

Pretio parata uincitur pretio fides.

CLYTEMESTRA

Surgit residuus pristinae mentis pudor;
quid obstrepis? quid uoce blandiloqua mala
consilia dictas? scilicet nubet tibi   290
regum relicto rege, generosa exuli?

---

281 spartamne *E*: spartem non *P*: -em num *CS*: -en num *l For Leid.2 R7*:
-en nunc *V d q*: spartenne *Ascensius, fort. recte*   et eurotan tuum *Gronouius*: et
eurotantum *E*: et a tanto uiro *P CS*   283 metus *E*: -um *P CS*   287
parata] -tur *P*   uincitur pretio fides *E P CS Gon*: pretio perit fides *Exon*
288–91, 293b, 295–301 *Clytemestrae tribuunt P CS*: *Nutrici dat E*   289 ob-
strepis] obstupes *P*   290 nubet *fort. uix sanum*: nubam *Sal Leid.2 R1 R7*
(*postea coni. Bentleius*): nubam et *Ox.2*   *post u.* 290 *totum uersum qualis est
u.* 125 *supra* (regina Danaum et inclitum Ledae genus) *excidisse suspicor*
291 generosa *P CS*: -o *E*

AEGISTHVS

Et cur Atrida uideor inferior tibi,
natus Thyestae?

CLYTEMESTRA

Si parum est, adde et nepos.

AEGISTHVS

Auctore Phoebo gignor; haud generis pudet.

CLYTEMESTRA

Phoebum nefandae stirpis auctorem uocas,   295
quem nocte subita frena reuocantem sua
caelo expulistis? quid deos probro addimus?
subripere doctus fraude geniales toros,
quem Venere tantum scimus illicita uirum,
facesse propere ac dedecus clarae domus   300
asporta ab oculis: haec uacat regi ac uiro.

AEGISTHVS

Exilia mihi sunt haud noua: assueui malis.
si tu imperas, regina, non tantum domo
Argisue cedo; nil moror iussu tuo
aperire ferro pectus aerumnis graue.   305

---

293 Thyeste *Bentleius*   297 addimus *E*: aduocas *P CS*   298 subripere
doctus *P C Vd E* (sub rupe reductus): s. doctos *S*: subruere doctus *Heinsius*
toros *P CS*: tori *E*   300 facesse *E*: secede *P CS*   ac *E*: *om. P CS*   clare
P CS: nostrę *E*   301 haec...uiro] regia haec pateat uiro *Gronouius*   uacat]
uacet *possis*   regi ac *P S Vd*: regia *E C*: regio *M*   302 sunt haud noua
E: haud(t) sunt noua *P CS*

CLYTEMESTRA

(Siquidem hoc cruenta Tyndaris fieri sinam!)
quae iuncta peccat debet et culpae fidem.
secede mecum potius ut rerum statum
dubium ac minacem iuncta consilia explicent.

CHORVS

Canite, o pubes inclita, Phoebum!   310
   tibi festa caput
turba coronat, tibi uirgineas
   laurum quatiens
de more comas innuba fudit
   stirps Inachia;   315
tu quoque nostros, Thebais hospes,
   comitare choros,
quaeque Erasini gelidos fontes,
   quaeque Eurotan,
quaeque uirenti tacitum ripa   320
   bibis Ismenon,
quam fatorum praescia Manto
   sata Tiresia
Latonigenas monuit sacris
   celebrare deos.   325
Arcus uinclo, pace relata,
   Phoebe, relaxa

---

306 cruentum F^{ac} (*ut uid.*), *postea coni. Bentleius*   sinam? *ed. 1506*: sinam *P CS F MN*: sin *E* (-am *detersum cum scholiis*)   307 *Aegistho tribuit Scaliger* (308–9 *Aegistho dat P*)   iuncta *Vi.2 cod. Delrii* (*teste Grutero*): inuita *E P CS* 312 coronet *Vi*   314 fudit *E*: fundit *P CS*: fundat *ego olim*   315 stirps inachia *P CS*: stirpis inachiae *E*: stirps inachidum *Bentleius*   316–17 *post* 321 *posuit Bothe*   316 nostros *E C V^{2pc} d S^{2mg}*: nostro *P S^{ac} V^{ac}* thebais hospes *E*: Thespias hospes *Richter*: Oebalis hospes *Heinsius*: thebana manus *P CS*   317 comitata *ed. 1529*: imitare *Leid.2*   thoros *P*   324 sacris *P CS*: sacri *E*   326 uinclo C^{2pc} M^{2mg} *Treuet* n^{2pc} (a uinculo *l*): uicto *P C^{ac} S V*: uictor *E*   pace relata *E*: phebe relata *P C^{ac} S V*: phebe relaxa C^{2pc} *d*: om. *l a M1 M4 ed. princeps, del. Bothe*

umeroque graues leuibus telis
    pone pharetras
resonetque manu pulsa citata   330
    uocale chelys:
nil acre uelim magnumque modis
    intonet altis,
sed quale soles leuiore lyra
    flectere carmen   335
simplex, lusus cum docta tuos
    Musa recenset.
licet et chorda grauiore sones
    quale canebas
cum Titanas fulmine uictos   340
    uidere dei,
uel cum montes montibus altis
    super impositi
struxere gradus trucibus monstris;
    stetit imposita   345
Pelion Ossa, pinifer ambos
    pressit Olympus.
Ades, o magni soror et coniunx,
    consors sceptri
regia Iuno: tua te colimus   350
    turba Mycenae,
tu sollicitum supplexque tui
    numinis Argos
sola tueris, tu bella manu
    pacemque geris;   355
tu nunc laurus Agamemnonias
    accipe uictrix,
tibi multifora tibia buxo
    sollemne canit,

---

336 lusus *E*: usus *P CS*: uersus *e²ᵖᶜ Vᶜ l recc.*   338 sonos *Eᵃᶜ*   340f. uictos
| uidere *E*: misso | fregere *P CS*   348 Aades *E* o] et *P*   350 tua te]
tute *P*   355 geris *M1* (*agnouit Ascensius, coni. Bentleius*): regis *E P CS*
356 laurus *E*: claros *P CS* agamennonias *E*: -ios *P CS*   358 tibi abuxo
E

tibi fila mouent docta puellae   360
    carmine molli,
tibi uotiuam matres Graiae
    lampada iactant:
ad tua coniunx candida tauri
    delubra cadet   365
nescia aratri, nullo collum
    signata iugo.
Tuque, o magni nata Tonantis
    inclita Pallas,
quae Dardanias saepe petisti   370
    cuspide turres,
te permixto matrona minor
    maiorque choro
colit et reserat ueniente dea
    templa sacerdos: 375
tibi nexilibus turba coronis
    redimita uenit,
tibi grandaeui lassique senes
    compote uoto
reddunt grates libantque manu   380
    uina trementi.
Et te Triuiam nota memores
    uoce precamur:
tu maternam sistere Delon
    Lucina iubes,   385
huc atque illuc prius errantem
    Cyclada uentis;
nunc iam stabilis fixa terras
    radice tenet,
respuit auras religatque rates   390
    assueta sequi.

---

361 nulli *P^{ac}*   365 cadet *E*: -it *PCS*   368 tu queo magni *E*   370 sepe
petisti cuspide turres *P CS*: cuspide turres sepe petisti *E*   372 tu *P*
380 reddent *S*   382 triuiam nota *E*: triuia nota *MF* '*AE*': triuia grata
P CS   386 errantem *P CS*: -e *E*   390 respuit] despicit *Delrius,
Bentleius*

tu Tantalidos funera matris
  uictrix numeras:
stat nunc Sipyli uertice summo
  flebile saxum   395
et adhuc lacrimas marmora fundunt
  antiqua nouas.
colit impense femina uirque
  numen geminum.
Tuque ante omnes, pater ac rector   400
  fulmine pollens,
cuius nutu simul extremi
  tremuere poli,
generis nostri, Iuppiter, auctor,
  cape dona libens   405
abauusque tuam non degenerem
  respice prolem.
Sed ecce, uasto concitus miles gradu
manifesta properat signa laetitiae ferens
(namque hasta summo lauream ferro gerit)   410
fidusque regi semper Eurybates adest.

ACTVS TERTIVS
EURYBATES–CLYTEMESTRA
EURYBATES

Delubra et aras caelitum et patrios lares –   392a
post longa fessus spatia, uix credens mihi –
supplex adoro. uota superis soluite:

---

394 sypili *E*: syphili *P*: sisiphi *CS*   395 flebile *E P C*: flexile *S Vd*
post u. 397 *haec praebet E*: lacrimas maesta aeternum | marmora manant:
primum omisit ed. 1498   398 impensae *E*   400 tuque *E*: teque *P CS*
405 cape *P CS*: caede *E*   406 abauoque *S*   409 ferens *E*: gerens
P CS   410 hasta *E CS²ᵖᶜ V* (busta *d*): -am *P Sᵃᶜ*   411 regi *P CS*:
regis *E* semper] *om. P*
Scaen. tit. Euribates. Clytemestra *P CS*: Euribates. Clytemestra. Chorus *E*
392a–411a *hos uersus sic adnotaui ne a Gronouii aliorumque editorum numeris hinc
usque ad finem fabulae recederem*   393a credens *E*: concedens *P S Vd*: con-
credens *C*: cedens *KQᵃᶜ recc.*

telluris altum remeat Argolicae decus 395a
tandem ad penates uictor Agamemnon suos.

CLYTEMESTRA

Felix ad aures nuntius uenit meas.
ubinam petitus per decem coniunx mihi
annos moratur? pelagus an terras premit?

EURYBATES

Incolumis, auctus gloria, laude inclitus 400a
reducem expetito litori impressit pedem.

CLYTEMESTRA

Sacris colamus prosperum tandem diem
et, si propitios, attamen lentos deos.
†tu pande uiuat† coniugis frater mei
et pande teneat quas soror sedes mea. 405a

EURYBATES

Meliora uotis posco et obtestor deos:
nam certa fari sors maris dubii uetat.
ut sparsa tumidum classis excepit mare,
ratis uidere socia non potuit ratem.
quin ipse Atrides aequore immenso uagus 410a
grauiora pelago damna quam bello tulit
remeatque uicto similis, exiguas trahens 412
lacerasque uictor classe de tanta rates.

398a per decem] abesse *P* mihi] *om. P* 399a terram *P* 402a
prospero...die *P* 403a attamen *E*: artamur *P CS* 404a tu pande
uiuat *uix sanum* tu] ubi *Birt* (*Rhein. Mus. xxxiv. 550*) *exempli gratia* edissere
ubi sit coniugis frater mei *uel* ubi nunc, precor, sit c. f. m. *uel simile scribendum
puto* 405a soror sedes] *inu. ord.* P*ac* 413 laceras *P* uictor *om. P*
classa *E*

CLYTEMESTRA

Quis fare nostras hauserit casus rates
aut quae maris fortuna dispulerit duces.   415

EURYBATES

Acerba fatu poscis, infaustum iubes
miscere laeto nuntium. refugit loqui
mens aegra tantis atque inhorrescit malis.

CLYTEMESTRA

Exprome: clades scire qui refugit suas
grauat timorem; dubia plus torquent mala.   420

EURYBATES

Vt Pergamum omne Dorica cecidit face
diuisa praeda est, maria properantes petunt.
iamque ense fessum miles exonerat latus,
neglecta summas scuta per puppes iacent,
ad militares remus aptatur manus   425
omnisque nimium longa properanti mora est.
signum recursus regia ut fulsit rate
et clara lentum remigem monuit tuba,
aurata primas prora designat uias
aperitque cursus mille quos puppes secent.   430
    Hinc aura primo lenis impellit rates

---

414 quis...rates *P CS*: effare casus quis rates hausit meas *E*: eas *pro* meas
coni. Damsté, numeris inuitis; receperunt edd. plerique nostras] uestras *R8*
415 dispulerat *Bothe*   416 iubens *Bothe*   418 mensae gratantis *E*
419 clade *P^{ac}*   421 omne] omnis *Bentleius (falso coll. Tro. 14)*   423
fessum] festum *P d* exornant *P*   424 summas *P CS*: summa *E*
428 lentum] laetum *Leo (Obs. 32)*   remigem monuit *E*: regimen emouit *P*
CS: remigem mouit '*AE*' (*cf. quae collegit Housman in Manil. lib. I pr. p. lvi*)
429 aurata *E*: aurora *P CS*   designat *E*: signauit *P CS*

adlapsa uelis; unda uix actu leui
tranquilla Zephyri mollis afflatu tremit
splendetque classe pelagus et pariter latet.
iuuat uidere nuda Troiae litora,   435
iuuat relicti sola Sigei loca.
properat iuuentus omnis adductos simul
lentare remos, adiuuat uentos manu
et ualida nisu bracchia alterno mouet.
sulcata uibrant aequora et latera increpant,   440
dirimuntque canae caerulum spumae mare.
ut aura plenos fortior tendit sinus,
posuere tonsas, credita est uento ratis
fususque transtris miles aut terras procul
quantum recedunt uela fugientes notat   445
aut bella narrat: Hectoris fortis minas
currusque et empto redditum corpus rogo,
sparsum cruore regis Herceum Iouem.
tunc qui iacente reciprocus ludit salo
tumidumque pando transilit dorso mare   450
Tyrrhenus omni piscis exultat freto
agitatque gyros et comes lateri adnatat,
anteire naues laetus et rursus sequi;
nunc prima tangens rostra lasciuit chorus,
millesimam nunc ambit et lustrat ratem.   455
    Iam litus omne tegitur et campi latent
et dubia pereunt montis Idaei iuga;
et iam, quod unum peruicax acies uidet,
Iliacus atra fumus apparet nota.
iam lassa Titan colla releuabat iugo,   460

---

432 actu leui *E*: tactu leui *P*: tractu leui *M* '*AE*': tactu leuis *CS*
433 tranquilla *E P*: -o *CS*   434 et pariter] et partim *Gronouius*: om. *P*
436 sigea *S*   439 ualidam subracchia *E^{ac}*   441 cane] caue (*ut uid.*) *C*
443 tonsos *P*   444 miles *E*: nauita *P CS*   448 herceum *E* (-ae-):
herculeum *P CS*   449 tunc *E*: tum *P CS*   451 omnis *N e V^c Leid.2*
452 agitatque *E*: agitque *P CS*   453 rursus] cursus *Treuet* '*AE*' *Ox.2 n^{2mg}*
a M1   457 pereunt *Poggius*: parent *E P C*: patent *S Vd*   458 iam *P*
CS: id *E*

126

in alta iam lux prona, iam praeceps dies.
exigua nubes sordido crescens globo
nitidum cadentis inquinat Phoebi iubar;
suspecta uarius occidens fecit freta.
nox prima caelum sparserat stellis, iacent 465
deserta uento uela. tum murmur graue,
maiora minitans, collibus summis cadit
tractuque longo litus ac petrae gemunt;
agitata uentis unda uenturis tumet,
cum subito luna conditur, stellae latent; 470
nec una nox est: densa tenebras obruit 472
caligo et omni luce subducta fretum
caelumque miscet. undique incumbunt simul
rapiuntque pelagus infimo euersum solo 475
aduersus Euro Zephyrus et Boreae Notus.
sua quisque mittit tela et infesti fretum
emoliuntur; turbo conuoluit mare.
Strymonius altas Aquilo contorquet niues
Libycusque harenas Auster ac Syrtes agit; 480
†nec manet in Austro fit† grauis nimbis Notus
imbre auget undas; Eurus orientem mouet
Nabataea quatiens regna et Eoos sinus.

---

461 alta *Damsté* (*Nisbet*): astra *codd.* 462 glebo *P* 463 nitidum]
nondum *C ln recc.* cadentis] cand- *S*: occidentis (*sc.* nondum) *Treuet Harl*[ul]
466 tum] cum *S* 469 uenturis] nocituris *Treuet recc.*: nocturnis *Harl*[ul]
470 stella *P* latent *E*: cadunt *P CS* 471 *post* 489 *collocaui: delere uult*
Kassel (*cf. Zwierlein, Gnomon xxxviii.687*) 472 una nox est *E*: nox una
est *P*: est nox una *CS* 474 undique] uentique *e Ox.1* 475 infimo
euersum solo *P CS*: infimum euerso polo *E*: infimum euerso salo *Peiper*:
infimum euertunt polo *Düring*: infimum uenti polo *Leo* (*deleto u. sequenti*)
476 aduersos *E*[ac] 477 mittit *E*: mittunt *P CS*: miscent *Gronouius* 480
ac *P CS*: ad *E* 481 nec...fit] *aliquid turbatum esse iam fere constat: exempli*
gratia immane turgens et grauis nimbis Notus *Hubbard* (*possis et* adfinis Austro
fit grauis n. N. *uel* madidis et Africo grauis n. N.): *totum uersum del. Richter*
fit] flat '*AE*' (*postea coni. Leo*): res *uel* uis (*sc.* manet) *L. Herrmann: sed Damsté*
fit grauis] grauis enim *Nisbet* nimbus *P* 482 auget undas] *inu. ord. C*
483 et eoos sinus *P CS*: eteoeo sonus *E*[ac]: et eoe sinus *E*[2pc]

quid rabidus ora Corus Oceano exerens?
mundum reuelli sedibus totum suis   485
ipsosque rupto crederes caelo deos
decidere et atrum rebus induci chaos.
uento resistit aestus et uentus retro
aestum reuoluit; non capit sese mare: 489
in astra pontus tollitur, caelum perit   471
undasque miscent imber et fluctus suas.   490
nec hoc leuamen denique aerumnis datur,
uidere saltem et nosse quo pereant malo:
premunt tenebrae lumina et dirae Stygis
inferna nox est. excidunt ignes tamen
et nube dirum fulmen elisa micat;   495
miserisque lucis tanta dulcedo est malae,
hoc lumen optant. ipsa se classis premit
et prora prorae nocuit et lateri latus.
illam dehiscens pontus in praeceps rapit
hauritque et alio redditam reuomit mari;   500
haec onere sidit, illa conuulsum latus
summittit undis, fluctus hanc decimus tegit;
haec lacera et omni decore populato leuis
fluitat; nec illi uela nec tonsae manent
nec rectus altas malus antemnas ferens,   505
sed trunca toto puppis Ionio natat.

---

484 quid] quin (*sc.* reuellit) *Rossbach* (*de Sen. Phil. librorum recensione et
emendatione, p. 136*)   rabidus *E*: rap- *P CS*   exercens *P*   485 reuelli *P
CS*: -it (*sc.* Corus) *E*   totum] motum *P*   486 rupto *E*: -os *P CS*: raptos
Ox.1² L2 F6   487 decedere *E*   indici *Cac*   489 recipit *C*   471 in
astra pontus] nox atra ponto *Bentleius*   perit] petit *KQ ʻAEʼ lrac Bo Vi.1 R7*
491 datur *E*: datum est *P CS*   492 malo] modo *P*   496 est mal(a)e]
est, male *Bothe*: *fortasse* et malae   499 in] im *E*   500 et] *om. P*   alio
Gronouius: alto *codd.*   reuomet *Sac*   mari *Monac. 5343* (*postea coni. Gronouius*):
mare *E P CS*   501 sidit *E*: sedit *P CS*: cedit *Leid.1*   illa] et illa *P*
503 latera *E*   populato *E*: populata *P CS*: populata et *Poggius*   504 illi]
ulli *Heinsius*   505 rectas *Cac*   506 trunca *E*: structa *P CS*: fracta *M
ʻAEʼ e Ox.1ul Leid.1²*   puppis *E*: turpis *P CS*   ionio] in ponto *Housman* (*ad
Manil. 4.767*): icario *Wilamowitz*: iliaco *Damsté*

nil ratio et usus audet, ars cessit malis;
tenet horror artus, omnis officio stupet
nauita relicto, remus effugit manus.
in uota miseros ultimus cogit timor   510
eademque superos Troes et Danai rogant.
quid fata possunt! inuidet Pyrrhus patri,
Aiaci Vlixes, Hectori Atrides minor,
Agamemno Priamo: quisquis ad Troiam iacet
felix uocatur, cadere qui meruit gradu,   515
quem fama seruat, uicta quem tellus tegit.
'Nil nobile ausos pontus atque undae ferunt?
ignaua fortes fata consument uiros?
perdenda mors est? quisquis es, nondum malis
satiate tantis, caelitum, tandem tuum   520
numen serena: cladibus nostris daret
uel Troia lacrimas. odia si durant tua
placetque mitti Doricum exitio genus,
quid hos simul perire nobiscum iuuat,
quibus perimus? sistite infestum mare: 525
uehit ista Danaos classis? et Troas uehit.'
nec plura possunt: occupat uocem mare.
    Ecce alia clades. fulmine irati Iouis
armata Pallas quidquid aut hasta minax
aut aegide et furore Gorgoneo potest   530
†aut igne patrio temptat et caelo nouae
spirant procellae. solus inuictus malis
luctatur Aiax; uela cogentem hunc sua

---

507 usus] ausus *P MN* ars cessit *E*: in magnis *P CS Gon Exc.Par.*
508 omnis] *om. P*: gnauus *Castiglioni*   514 agamemno *Gronouius*: -non
codd.   515 gradu *E*: manu *P CS*   517 ferunt *E*:-ent *P CS*   518 fata]
freta *cod. Mogunt.* (*teste Delrio*) consumunt *KQ e²ᵇᶜ l Sal* 519 pudenda *e*
Ox.1 recc. quisquis] quis *Sᵃᶜ*   520 tantis] malis *P*   521 lumen *P*
525 quibus] quid *P* sistite *CS*: siste *P*: et sistite *E*: sistito *Bentleius, Bothe*
526 classis? et] *interpunxit Gronouius* troias *E* uehit *E*: simul *P CS*   529
aut] haut(d) *MN recc.* (*postea coni. M. Müller*)   530 aut...et *Gronouius*:
aut...aut *codd.*: haut...haut *M. Müller* (*diss. p. 38*) aegidae *E*   531 aut
uix sanum: en *M. Müller*: nunc *Castiglioni*: at *Richter*: an hoc? temptat]
fort. uincit *uel sim.*   531f. nouas | spirat (*sc. Pallas*) procellas *Heinsius*

tento rudente flamma perstrinxit cadens.
libratur aliud fulmen: hoc toto impetu   535
certum reducta Pallas excussit manu,
imitata patrem. transit Aiacis ratem
ratisque partem secum et Aiacem tulit.
nil ille motus, ardua ut cautes, salo
ambustus exstat, dirimit insanum mare   540
fluctusque rumpit pectore et nauem manu
complexus ignes traxit et caeco mari
conlucet Aiax, omne resplendet fretum.
tandem occupata rupe furibundum intonat:
[superasse nunc se pelagus atque ignes. 'iuuat   545
uicisse caelum Palladem fulmen mare.']
'Non me fugauit bellici terror dei,
[et Hectorem una solus et Martem tuli]
Phoebea nec me tela pepulerunt gradu:
cum Phrygibus istos uicimus – tene horream   550
aliena inerti tela mittentem manu?
quid si ipse mittat?' plura cum auderet furens,
tridente rupem subruit pulsam pater
Neptunus imis exerens undis caput
soluitque montem, quem cadens secum tulit   555
terraque et igne uictus et pelago iacet.
    Nos alia maior naufragos pestis uocat.

---

534 tento *E*: tenso *P CS*   perstrinxit] praestrinxit *Richter*: pertransit '*AE*'
536 certum] tortum *R7, cod. Scaligeri*   537–8 *delere uoluit Viansino*
537 aiacis *scripsi*: aiacem et *codd.*   538 ratisque *P CS E^c*: satisque *F MN*
(*E^{ac}?*)   aiacem *l Cant M4 V1 Vi.2 F3 (postea coni. Pontanus, Bentleius)*: aiacis
P CS: magis *E*   541 fluctus rumpitque *S*   542 ignes *Madvig*: in se
codd.: ipse *Bothe*   544 furibundum *E P S^{2mg}*: furibunde *CS^1*: furibundus
Vd l^{2pc} n recc.   545–6 *deleui*   545 nunc se *P CS*: nunc *E*: nunc me *V1*
(*postea coni. Giomini*): me nunc *Düring*: nunc iam *Peiper*: cuncta *Richter (inter
coniecturas optima)*: iuuit *Leo*: noui *Wilamowitz*   548 *deleuit Leo (Obs. 209)*
et] sed *Damsté* haectorem *E*   550 istis *C* tene *E*: tandem *P CS*
551 mittentem manu *Heinsius*: mitti dextera *PCS*: pepulerunt gradu (*iteratum
ex u.* 549) *E*: mittis dextera *Lipsius*: perdentem manu *Gronouius*   552 quid]
quod *P*: quin *Damsté*   mittat – ' *F. J. Miller*   555 soluit *C*   556 tor-
raque *E^{ac}* iacens *Viansino*

est humilis unda, scrupeis mendax uadis,
ubi saxa rapidis clausa uerticibus tegit
fallax Caphereus; aestuat scopulis fretum   560
feruetque semper fluctus alterna uice.
arx imminet praerupta quae spectat mare
utrimque geminum: Pelopis hinc oras tui
et Isthmon, arto qui recuruatus solo
Ionia iungi maria Phrixeis uetat,   565
hinc scelere Lemnon nobilem, hinc et Chalcida
tardamque ratibus Aulida. hanc arcem occupat
Palamedis ille genitor et clarum manu
lumen nefanda uertice e summo efferens
in saxa ducit perfida classem face.   570
haerent acutis rupibus fixae rates;
has inopis undae breuia comminuunt uada;
pars uehitur huius prima, pars scopulo sedet;
hanc alia retro spatia relegentem ferit
et fracta frangit: iam timent terram rates   575
et maria malunt. cecidit in lucem furor:
postquam litatum est Ilio, Phoebus redit
et damna noctis tristis ostendit dies.

CLYTEMESTRA

Vtrumne doleam laeter an reducem uirum?
remeasse laetor, uulnus at regni graue   580
lugere cogor. redde iam Grais, pater

---

560 scopulus *P*   562 arsx *E*: ars *S^{ac}*   564 arto] alto *C*   566 hinc et
chalcida *recc.* (*teste Delrio*), *postea Auantius* (hinc chalcida *Scaliger*): hinc
calchedona *P CS*: et calchedona *E*: h. calidona *Leid.2*: h. chalcodona *I.*
Gronouius: h. anthedona *Gronouius*   567 aulida] aulin *Bentleius*   568 ille
P CS: illi *E*   569 e summo *l Sal Cant. recc.*: ex summo *P CS*: summo *E*
573 huius, prima *interpunxit Damsté*   576 et maria malunt *E*: uoluntque
maria *P CS*: maluntque maria *Monac. 5343, cod. Lipsii*   577 ilio phoebus
Gronouius: illo phoebus *E*: phebus in lucem *P CS*: ilico phoebus *Bessel*
(ilicet *Giardina*)   579 leter an *P CS*: an letaere *E*   580 laetor *E*: leter
P CS   at *P CS*: et *E*

altisona quatiens regna, placatos deos.
nunc omne laeta fronde ueletur caput,
sacrifica dulces tibia effundat modos
et niuea magnas uictima ante aras cadat.   585
  Sed ecce, turba tristis incomptae comas
Iliades adsunt, quas super celso gradu
effrena Phoebas entheas laurus quatit.

CHORVS

Heu quam dulce malum mortalibus additum
uitae dirus amor, cum pateat malis   590
effugium et miseros libera mors uocet
portus aeterna placidus quiete.
nullus hunc terror nec impotentis
procella Fortunae mouet aut iniqui
flamma Tonantis.   595
pax alta nullos ciuium coetus
timet aut minaces uictoris iras,
non maria asperis insana Coris,
non acies feras puluereamue nubem   600
motam barbaricis equitum cateruis,
non urbe cum tota populos cadentes
hostica muros populante flamma
indomitumue bellum.
perrumpet omne seruitium   605
contemptor leuium deorum:
qui uultus Acherontis atri,

---

583 fronde *P CS*: fronte *E*   587 celsa *P*
Scaen. tit. Chorus Iliadum. Cassandra *E*: Chorus. Cassandra *P CS*   590
durus *C*   *post u.* 592 *collocauit uu.* 605–9 *Leo* (*Obs. 117*): *uu.* 605–9 *post*
u. 595 *posuit Richter* (*et uide infra u.* 596): *fortasse uu.* 605–6 *post u.* 592 *ponendi*
(*ut monet Mynors*), *uel lacuna incerti spatii post u.* 595 (*uel u.* 592) *statuenda*
593 impotentis *E*: impotens *P CS*   596 *ita suppleuit Richter*: alta pax
⟨illum tenet, ille⟩ nullos *eqs.*   coetos *E*   597 minaces *P CS*: minas *E*:
nimias *MN recc.*   600 -ue *E*: -que *P CS*   601 mota *E*   604 -ue *E*:
om. P CS   605 seruitium *E*: solus *P CS*

qui Styga tristem non tristis uidet
audetque uitae ponere finem,
par ille regi, par superis erit.   610
O quam miserum est nescire mori!
uidimus patriam ruentem
nocte funesta, cum Dardana tecta
Dorici raperetis ignes.   613a
non illa bello uicta, non armis,
ut quondam Herculea cecidit pharetra;   615
quam non Pelei Thetidisque natus
carusque Pelidae nimium feroci
uicit acceptis cum fulsit armis
fuditque Troas falsus Achilles,
aut cum ipse Pelides animos feroces   620
sustulit luctu celeremque saltu
Troades summis timuere muris.
perdidit in malis
extremum decus, fortiter uinci:
restitit annis Troia bis quinis   625
unius noctis peritura furto.

Vidimus simulata dona
molis immensae Danaumque   627a
fatale munus duximus nostra
creduli dextra tremuitque saepe
limine in primo sonipes cauernis   630
conditos reges bellumque gestans;
et licuit dolos uersare ut ipsi
fraude sua caderent Pelasgi:
saepe commotae sonuere parmae
tacitumque murmur percussit aures,   635
ut fremuit male subdolo

---

610 par et superis *S e recc.*   614 non (2°) *E*: nec *P CS*   617 nimiumque
P   620 pelides *P C Vd*: -dos *E S*   625 annis troia bis quinis *P CS*:
quinis bis annis *E*   626 furto *E* (peritur afurto): fato *P CS*   632 dolos
uersare *E*: *inu. ord. P CS*   633 *post* sua *add.* capti *P CS* caperent *P*
634 commotae] somote *P*   636 ut *Bothe*: et *codd.*

parens Pyrrhus Vlixi.
Secura metus Troica pubes
sacros gaudet tangere funes.
hinc aequaeui gregis Astyanax,   640
hinc Haemonio desponsa rogo
ducunt turmas, haec femineas, ille uiriles.   642–643
festae matres uotiua ferunt munera diuis,
festi patres adeunt aras;   645
unus tota est uultus in urbe;
et, quod numquam post Hectoreos uidimus ignes,
laeta est Hecabe.

Quid nunc primum, dolor infelix,
quidue extremum deflere paras?   650
moenia, diuum fabricata manu,
diruta nostra?
an templa deos super usta suos?
non uacat istis lacrimare malis:
te, magne parens, flent Iliades.   655
uidi, uidi senis in iugulo
telum Pyrrhi uix exiguo
sanguine tingui.

ACTVS QVARTVS
CASSANDRA–CHORVS

CASSANDRA

Cohibete lacrimas omne quas tempus petet,
Troades, et ipsae uestra lamentabili   660
lugete gemitu funera: aerumnae meae

---

637 pyrr(h)us *om. P*   641 hinc uel *C*   rogo] uiro *Cant Vi.1*   647 haec-
toreos *E*   650 deflere *P CS*: deferre *E*   652 nostra] graia *Bentleius*
655 flent *PCS*: flectent *E* (flectenti liades *E^{ac}*): flemus *Gronouius*   656 senes
P   658 tingui *E^{ac} P CS MN*: tingi *E^{2pc} F*
Scaen. tit. addidi (cf. ante u. 589)   659 quas tempus petet *E*: q. t. petit
P CS: quîs tempus patet *Heinsius, Garrod*: quae tempus petant *uel* petent
malim

134

socium recusant. cladibus questus meis
remouete: nostris ipsa sufficiam malis.

CHORVS

Lacrimas lacrimis miscere iuuat;
magis exurunt quos secretae   665
lacerant curae;
iuuat in medium deflere suos.
nec tu, quamuis dura uirago
patiensque mali,   668a
poteris tantas flere ruinas.
non quae uerno mobile carmen   670
ramo cantat tristis aedon
Ityn in uarios modulata sonos,
non quae tectis Bistonis ales
residens summis impia diri
furta mariti garrula narrat   675
lugere tuam poterit digne
conquesta domum.
licet ipse uelit clarus niueos   677a
inter olores
Histrum Cycnus Tanainque colens
extrema loqui, licet alcyones   680
Ceyca suum fluctu leuiter
plangente sonent,
cum tranquillo male confisae
credunt iterum pelago audaces
fetusque suos nido pauidae   685
titubante fouent;   685a

---

662 sociunt *P*   664 lacrimas lacrimis *E*: -as -as *P CS*: -is -as *Treuet*
(*praeter codd. T Soc B*) *l²ᵇᶜ Sal recc.*   667 tu *E*: enim *P CS*   670 mobile *E*:
no- *P CS*   671 aedon *Auantius*: edom *E*: edonis *P CS*   672 ityn] ytim
S NF   673 bistonis *P CS*: bis tonos *E*   674 summis *E P*: siluis *CS*
675 narrat *E*: deflet *P CS*   676f. digne | conquesta] condigne (*om.* con-
questa) *C*   677a ipse *P CS*: ipsa *E*   683 malae *E*   684 credunt se
iterum *Viansino*   685 foetusque *E*

non si molles imitata uiros
tristis laceret bracchia tecum
quae turritae turba parenti
pectora rauco concita buxo
ferit ut Phrygium lugeat Attin.   690
non est lacrimis, Cassandra, modus,
quia quae patimur uicere modum.
   Sed cur sacratas deripis capiti infulas?
miseris colendos maxime superos putem.

CASSANDRA

Vicere nostra iam metus omnes mala.   695
equidem nec ulla caelites placo prece
nec si uelint saeuire quo noceant habent:
Fortuna uires ipsa consumpsit suas.
quae patria restat, quis pater, quae iam soror?
bibere tumuli sanguinem atque arae meum.   700
quid illa felix turba fraterni gregis?
exhausta nempe: regia miseri senes
uacua relicti, totque per thalamos uident
praeter Lacaenam ceteras uiduas nurus.
tot illa regum mater et regimen Phrygum   705
fecunda in ignes Hecuba fatorum nouas
experta leges induit uultus feros:
circa ruinas rabida latrauit suas,
Troiae superstes, Hectori, Priamo, sibi.

---

686 imitata] comitata *Leo*   689 pectora *E*: pectore *P CS* concita *P CS*
(conscita *P*): concitata *E* buxo *E*: -um *P CS*   690 ferit *P CS*: fur- *E*
693 deripis *E*: dir- *P CS* (dirr- *P*)   694 *choro tribuunt P S*: *Cassandrae dat E*:
om. C putem *E*: reor *P S*   696 equitem *P*   701 fraterni *E*: fratrum
P CS: tot fratrum *Poggius*   702 exhausta *P CS*: -stu *E*: exusta '*AE*' (*cp.*
Ed. Fraenkel, Gnomon ii.512f.) regia *E C*: -am *P S* senes *E*: -is *P CS*
703 uacua *E*: -am *CS*: -i *P* per] post *Viansino*   705 regum] nurum
regum *C* (*et C²ᵐᵍ*)   708 latrabit *Cant*

CHORVS

Silet repente Phoebas et pallor genas   710
creberque totum possidet corpus tremor;
stetere uittae, mollis horrescit coma,
anhela corda murmure incluso fremunt,
incerta nutant lumina et uersi retro
torquentur oculi, rursus immites rigent.   715
nunc leuat in auras altior solito caput
graditurque celsa, nunc reluctantes parat
reserare fauces, uerba nunc clauso male
custodit ore maenas impatiens dei.

CASSANDRA

Quid me furoris incitam stimulis noui,   720
quid mentis inopem, sacra Parnasi iuga,
rapitis? recede, Phoebe: iam non sum tua,
extingue flammas pectori infixas meo.
cui nunc uagor uesana? cui bacchor furens?
iam Troia cecidit – falsa quid uates ago?   725
  Vbi sum? fugit lux alma et obscurat genas
nox alta et aether abditus tenebris latet.
sed ecce, gemino sole praefulget dies
geminumque duplices Argos attollit domus.
Idaea cerno nemora? fatalis sedet   730
inter potentes arbiter pastor deas?
timete, reges, moneo, furtiuum genus:
agrestis iste alumnus euertet domum.

---

710 phoeba *E*   711 possidet totum *C^{ac}*   712 uicte *S*   715 immites]
immoti *Bentleius, Leo*   722 phoebae *E*   725 agor ' *AE*' *Q^{2bc}* (*postea coni.*
Heinsius)   727 abditus *E*: -is *P CS*   tenebris] membris *C*   729 domus
E Aldhelmus (*cf. Testimonia, p. 101 supra*): -os *P CS*   730-3 *delere uoluit Leo*:
post u. 729 *uersus aliquot de Troiae fatis excidisse suspicatus est Wilamowitz*
730 idea *P CS*: idae *E*: idai *nescioquis Pompeianus* (*cf. Testimonia, p. 101 supra*)
731 potentes] petentes *e* (*non male*): patentes *D. Heinsius*   deas *E P Vd*:
deos *C*: deus *S*   732 timere *S N e l*   furtiuum] fugitiuum *P*   733 iste
E: ille *P CS*

quid ista uecors tela feminea manu
destricta praefert? quem petit dextra uirum   735
Lacaena cultu, ferrum Amazonium gerens?
quae uersat oculos alia nunc facies meos?
uictor ferarum colla sublimis iacet
ignobili sub dente Marmaricus leo,
morsus cruentos passus audacis leae.   740
    Quid me uocatis sospitem solam e meis,
umbrae meorum? te sequor, tota pater
Troia sepulte; frater, auxilium Phrygum
terrorque Danaum, non ego antiquum decus
uideo aut calentes ratibus ambustis manus,   745
sed lacera membra et saucios uinclo graui
illos lacertos; te sequor, nimium cito
congresse Achilli Troile; incertos geris,
Deiphobe, uultus, coniugis munus nouae.
iuuat per ipsos ingredi Stygios lacus,   750
iuuat uidere Tartari saeuum canem
auidique regna Ditis. haec hodie ratis
Phlegethontis atri regias animas uehet,
uictamque uictricemque. uos, umbrae, precor,
[iurata superis unda, te pariter precor,]   755
reserate paulum terga nigrantis poli,
leuis ut Mycenas turba prospiciat Phrygum.
spectate, miseri: fata se uertunt retro.

---

734 feminea *om. P*   735 destricta *E*: dist- *P CS*   736 cultu *P CS*: uultu
E   737 alia *P CS*: alta *E*   738 uictor *E C^{mg} V^c d*: uicto *P S*: uicta *C*:
rector *Bentleius*   sublimis *E*: uexatus *P CS*: subcisus *Gronouius*   740 leae
E: dee *P CS*   742 te sequor tota pater *P CS*: testis uel tota pater *E*: te
sequor, testis pater | Troiae sepultae *Leo (Obs. 5)*   745 aut] ut *P*   ratibus
ambustis *M. Müller (diss. p. 40)*: ruptas bustis *E*: ratibus exustis *P C^{1pc}*
(exustas *C^{ac}*) *S*   746 menbra *E*   saucios uinclo *P CS*: connectens uinculo *E*
747 illos lacerto *E*: fortes lacertos *P CS*   sequor nimium *P CS*: sequitur
tuum *E*   748 troile *P CS*: troia *E*   750 *post* 760 *habet C*   751 *s*euum
E^c   752 rates *E*   753 uehet *P CS*: uehit *E*: uehat *M2*   754 uictamque *P CS*: uit- *E*   uictricem *P*   755 *deleui*: *om. P N d*   756 terga] regna
Damsté, Düring (fort. recte): claustra *Bentleius*   nigrantis *E*: mig- *P CS*
758 spectare *S d*

Instant sorores squalidae,
anguinea iactant uerbera, 760
fert laeua semustas faces
turgentque pallentes genae
et uestis atri funeris
exesa cingit ilia,
strepuntque nocturni metus 765
et ossa uasti corporis
corrupta longinquo situ
palude limosa iacent.
et ecce, defessus senex
ad ora ludentes aquas 770
non captat, oblitus sitim,
maestus futuro funere;
exultat et ponit gradus
pater decoros Dardanus.

CHORVS

Iam peruagatus ipse se fregit furor, 775
caditque flexo qualis ante aras genu
ceruice taurus uulnus incisa gerens.
releuemus artus. – En deos tandem suos
uictrice lauru cinctus Agamemnon adit,
et festa coniunx obuios illi tulit 780
gressus reditque iuncta concordi gradu.

---

760 anguinea *Heinsius*: sanguinea *codd.*   uerbera *E*: uerba *P CS*   761
semustas *Eac P CSac*: semi- *E2bc S2bc Treuet recc.* (*cp. Tro. 1085*)   762 turgentque *E*: ardentque *P CS*   763 atri funeris] arcte funebris *Heinsius*
764 exesa *P CS*: excisa *E*   cingit] tingit *C*   765–8 *uersus nondum satis
enarrati: lacunam post u.* 764 *statuit Peiper*: uu. 766–8 *post* 772 *posuit Richter*
768 linosa *S*   771 captat] capud *P*   sitim *E*: -is *P CS*   772 futuro]
furore *Eac* (*ut uid.*)   *ante* 775 chorus *E*: chorus troyanus *P*: chorus
troianorum *CS*   775 se] si *S*   fregit *bis P*   776 genu *E*: gradu *P CS*
777 incisa *P CS*: incertum *E*   778 en deos *E*: entheos *P CS*   779 lauru
E: -o *P CS*   780 et festa coniunx *E*: coniunxque pariter *P CS*   obuius *Eac*
781 reditque *e2bc Harl*: ridetque *E*: redit *P CS*

139

AGAMEMNON-CASSANDRA

AGAMEMNON

Tandem reuertor sospes ad patrios lares;
o cara salue terra! tibi tot barbarae
dedere gentes spolia, tibi felix diu
potentis Asiae domina summisit manus.   785
   Quid ista uates corpus effusa ac tremens
dubia labat ceruice? famuli, attollite,
refouete gelido latice. iam recipit diem
marcente uisu. suscita sensus tuos:
optatus ille portus aerumnis adest.   790
festus dies est.

CASSANDRA

Festus et Troiae fuit.

AGAMEMNON

Veneremur aras.

CASSANDRA

Cecidit ante aras pater.

AGAMEMNON

Iouem precemur pariter.

CASSANDRA

Herceum Iouem?

---

784 felix] phenix *Damsté* (*parum apte coll. Sen. Epist. 42.1*)   785 domina
Bentleius: troia *codd.*   summisit] sumpsit *P*   786 quid *E*: cur *P CS*   ista]
illa *P^{ac}*   789 marcentem *P*   793 precemur. Pariter *sic diuidit M.*
Müller (*diss. p. 41*)   pariter] pater ut *Damsté*   hercaeum *E*: herculeum *P*
CS (*cf.* 448 *supra*)

AGAMEMNON
Credis uidere te Ilium?

CASSANDRA
Et Priamum simul.

AGAMEMNON
Hic Troia non est.

CASSANDRA
Helena ubi est, Troiam puto.   795

AGAMEMNON
Ne metue dominam famula.

CASSANDRA
Libertas adest.

AGAMEMNON
Secura uiue.

CASSANDRA
Mihi mori est securitas.

AGAMEMNON
Nullum est periclum tibimet.

---

794 Priamum et *possis*   795 helena ubi *B. Schmidt* (*Obs. 51*): ubi helena *codd.*
796 metuae *E*   797 secure *C* uiues *Bothe* mihi mori *E*: mors mihi *P*
CS securitas est *P*   798 hullum *P*

CASSANDRA

At magnum tibi.

AGAMEMNON

Victor timere quid potest?

CASSANDRA

Quod non timet.

AGAMEMNON

Hanc, fida famuli turba, dum excutiat deum   800
retinete, ne quid impotens peccet furor.
At te pater, qui saeua torques fulmina
pellisque nubes, sidera et terras regis,
ad quem triumphi spolia uictores ferunt,
et te, sororem cuncta pollentis uiri,   805
Argolica Iuno, pecore uotiuo libens
Arabumque donis supplici et fibra colam.

CHORVS

Argos nobilibus nobile ciuibus,
Argos iratae carum nouercae,
semper ingentes educas alumnos;   810
imparem aequasti numerum deorum:
tuus ille bis seno meruit labore
adlegi caelo magnus Alcides,
cui lege mundi Iuppiter rupta

---

at] dat *P*   tibi *E*: tibi est *P CS*   806 pectore *Vd Treuet (codd. V P* S Q)*
807 supplici *V1 F3 (cf. Neue–Wagener II.46)*: supplice *E P CS*   supplici et
fibra] supplici et uitta *Düring*: supplex et fibris *Q²ᵖᶜ r Cant F2*   *Ante*
808 chorus *P CS*: chorus. cassandra *E*   811 deorum] laborum *Peiper*
813 *bis scriptum in* *Pᵃᶜ*   814 munda *P*   ippiter *E*

roscidae noctis geminauit horas 815
iussitque Phoebum
tardius celeres agitare currus
et tuas lente remeare bigas,
pallida Phoebe. 818a
rettulit pedem nomen alternis
stella quae mutat seque mirata est 820
Hesperum dici; Aurora mouit
ad solitas uices caput et relabens
imposuit seni collum marito.
sensit ortus, sensit occasus
Herculem nasci: uiolentus ille 825
nocte non una poterat creari.
tibi concitatus substitit mundus,
o puer subiture caelum.

Te sensit Nemeaeus arto
pressus lacerto fulmineus leo, 830
ceruaque Parrhasis,
sensit Arcadii populator agri
gemuitque taurus Dictaea linquens
horridus arua.
morte fecundum domuit draconem 835
uetuitque collo pereunte nasci
geminosque fratres
pectore ex uno tria monstra natos
stipite incusso fregit insultans
duxitque ad ortus Hesperium pecus, 839a
Geryonae spolium triformis. 840
egit Threicium gregem
quem non Strymonii gramine fluminis
Hebriue ripis pauit tyrannus:

---

817 radius *P*   818 lentes *P*   818a pallida *E*: candida *P CS*   819 retulit
E: retulitque *PCS* (rett- *P*)   nomen alternis *E*: *inu. ord. PCS*   821 mouet *E*
823 seni collum marito *E*: senis umero mariti *P CS*   824 occasum *P*
826 non] etiam *P*   828 o puer ⟨magnum⟩ s. c. *Fabricius*   832 agri *om.*
P, add. post linquens (*u.* 833)   838 ex uno *E*: ab uno *P CS*

hospitum dirus stabulis cruorem
praebuit saeuis tinxitque crudos 845
ultimus rictus sanguis aurigae.
uidit Hippolyte ferox
pectore e medio rapi
spolium et sagittis
nube percussa Stymphalis alto 850
decidit caelo
arborque pomis fertilis aureis
extimuit manus insueta carpi
fugitque in auras leuiore ramo;
audiuit sonitum crepitante lamna 855
frigidus custos nescius somni
linqueret cum iam nemus [omne] fuluo
plenus Alcides uacuum metallo.
tractus ad caelum canis inferorum
triplici catena tacuit nec ullo 860
latrauit ore,
lucis ignotae metuens colorem.

Te duce succidit
mendax Dardanidae domus
et sensit arcus iterum timendos; 864a
te duce concidit totidem diebus 865
Troia quot annis.

---

844 hospitium *P N e recc.* dixus *P* stabilis *P* 845 seuistrinxitque *E*
846 ultimus *P CS*: -os *E* 848 medio] uiduo *Heinsius* 849 sagittis *E*:
-as *P CS* 851 decidit *P CS*: ce- *E* 855 lamna *E*: lamina *P*: flamma
CS 857 omne *deleuit M. Müller* fuluo *om.* E^{ac}
863 succidit] succedit *E*: dux cadit *D. Heinsius* 864 dardanidae *Cant,
ed. princeps (postea coni. Leo)*: dardani(a)e *E P CS*: dardani *KQ 'AE' F4 R1
(postea coni. Peiper)* 864a timendo *E*

ACTVS QVINTVS

CASSANDRA

Res agitur intus magna, par annis decem.
eheu quid hoc est? anime, consurge et cape
pretium furoris: uicimus uicti Phryges.
bene est, resurgis, Troia; traxisti iacens   870
pares Mycenas, terga dat uictor tuus.
tam clara numquam prouidae mentis furor
ostendit oculis; uideo et intersum et fruor,
imago uisus dubia non fallit meos:
spectemus. epulae regia instructae domo   875
quales fuerunt ultimae Phrygibus dapes
celebrantur; ostro lectus Iliaco nitet;
merumque in auro ueteris Assaraci trahunt,
et ipse picta ueste sublimis iacet,
Priami superbas corpore exuuias gerens.   880
detrahere cultus uxor hostiles iubet,
induere potius coniugis fidae manu
textos amictus – horreo atque animo tremo:
regemne perimet exul et adulter uirum?
uenere fata: sanguinem extremae dapes   885
domini uidebunt et cruor Baccho incidet.
mortifera uinctum perfidae tradit neci
induta uestis: exitum manibus negant
caputque laxi et inuii claudunt sinus.
haurit trementi semiuir dextra latus,   890

Scaen. tit. Cassandra *P S*: *om.* (*i.e. solam notam personae praebent*) *E C*   867 par
annis *P CS*: per annos *E*   868 eheu *E P C V*: heu *S d*   anime *P CS*: -a *E*
et *om. P*   870 resurgis *P CS*: -it *E*   traxistis *P^{ac}*   871 pares *CS*: partes
P: parens *E*   872 furor *E*: pudor *P CS*   873 ostende *S^{ac}* et fruor
P CS: fruor *E*: furor *F MN 'AE'*: et furor *Q e Ox.1 d^{2pc}*   875 spectemus
E: -amus *P CS* regio *P*   877 lectus *om. P*   879 et] en *Heinsius*
883 amictos *C^{ac}*   885 uenere] uertere *Bothe*   886 bacha *P*   887
perfidae *ed. 1498, E^{ac}(?)*: perfide *E^{1pc} P CS*   tradit *E*: -et *P CS*
888 exicium *P* negant *Gronouius*: negat *codd.*   889 inuii *P S*: inuli *E*:
nimii *C M*: niuei *ed. 1529* (*u.l.*)

nec penitus egit: uulnere in medio stupet.
at ille, ut altis hispidus siluis aper
cum casse uinctus temptat egressus tamen
artatque motu uincla et in cassum furit,
cupit fluentes undique et caecos sinus   895
dissicere et hostem quaerit implicitus suum.
armat bipenni Tyndaris dextram furens,
qualisque ad aras colla taurorum popa
designat oculis antequam ferro petat,
sic huc et illuc impiam librat manum.   900
habet, peractum est. pendet exigua male
caput amputatum parte et hinc trunco cruor
exundat, illinc ora cum fremitu iacent.
nondum recedunt: ille iam exanimem petit
laceratque corpus, illa fodientem adiuuat.   905
uterque tanto scelere respondet suis:
est hic Thyestae natus, haec Helenae soror.
stat ecce Titan, dubius e medio die
suane currat an Thyestea uia.

ELECTRA

Fuge, o paternae mortis auxilium unicum,   910
fuge et scelestas hostium euita manus.
euersa domus est funditus, regna occidunt.
   Quis iste celeres concitus currus agit?

---

891 hec *P*   egit *E*: agit *P CS*   893 dum *P*   898 qualis qui *Peiper*
tauror *P*   popa *Bentleius* (*ad Lucani Bell. Ciu. 1.612*), *Wilamowitz*: prius *codd.*,
quod seruauerunt multi: pius (*sc. mactator hostiarum*) *Ascensius*: *lacunam unius uersus*
post u. 898 *statuit Rossbach* (*B. Ph. W. 1904.363*)   903 illic *Vd*   904
recedent *S* exanimem *P CS*: exanimę *E*: exanimum *Nisbet* (*recte?*): exanime
impetit *Heinsius*: -e expetit *Bentleius*   905 laceratque] lacerat autem *P*
907 est hic *E*: *inu. ord. P CS* thyestae *ed. 1563*: -e *codd.* soror] furor E^{2pc}
908 e medio *scripsi*: emerito *E P CS*: emerso V^{ul}: emenso *recc.*, *Bentleius*
909 suane *P CS*: sua nec *E* thyeste auia *E* tyesta *P*   *ante* 910: Electra
P CS: Electra. fugiens. Orestes. tacitus *E*   910 fuge o] fugito *P*   911
fuge et *E*: fugito *P CS* euita *P CS*: uita *E*   912 est domus est C^{ac}
913 quis iste celeres *P CS* (scel- *P*): hospes quis iste *E* concitus] -os *Gronouius*

germane, uultus ueste furabor tuos.
quid, anime demens, refugis? externos times?   915
domus timenda est. pone iam trepidos metus,
Oresta: amici fida praesidia intuor.

STROPHIVS–ELECTRA

STROPHIVS

Phocide relicta Strophius Elea inclitus
palma reuertor. causa ueniendi fuit
gratari amico cuius impulsum manu   920
cecidit decenni Marte concussum Ilium.
quaenam ista lacrimis lugubrem uultum rigat
pauetque maesta? regium agnosco genus.
Electra, fletus causa quae laeta in domo est?

ELECTRA

Pater peremptus scelere materno iacet;   925
comes paternae quaeritur natus neci;
Aegisthus arces Venere quaesitas tenet.

STROPHIVS

O nulla longi temporis felicitas!

ELECTRA

Per te parentis memoriam obtestor mei,
per sceptra terris nota, per dubios deos: 930
recipe hunc Oresten ac pium furtum occule.

---

915 quid *E*: quos *P CS*   times *E*: fugis *P CS*: metus *M, cod. Lipsii*   *ante*
918: Strophius. Electra *P CS*: Strophius. Electra. Orestes *E*   922 uultu
P   923 regum *P*   924 fletus *E*: luctus *P CS*

STROPHIVS

Etsi timendum caesus Agamemnon docet,
aggrediar et te, Oresta, furabor libens.
[fidem secunda poscunt, aduersa exigunt.]
cape hoc decorum ludicri certaminis   935
insigne frontis; laeua uictricem tenens
frondem uirenti protegat ramo caput,
et ista donum palma Pisaei Iouis
uelamen eadem praestet atque omen tibi.
tuque, o paternis assidens frenis comes,   940
condisce, Pylade, patris exemplo fidem.
uos Graecia nunc teste ueloces equi,
infida cursu fugite praecipiti loca.

ELECTRA

Excessit, abiit, currus effreno impetu
effugit aciem. tuta iam opperiar meos   945
hostes et ultro uulneri opponam caput.
  Adest cruenta coniugis uictrix sui
et signa caedis ueste maculata gerit;
manus recenti sanguine etiamnunc madent
uultusque prae se scelera truculenti ferunt.   950
concedam ad aras. patere me uittis tuis,
Cassandra, iungi, paria metuentem tibi.

CLYTEMESTRA–ELECTRA

CLYTEMESTRA

Hostis parentis, impium atque audax caput,
quo more coetus publicos uirgo petis?

---

932 cesus *P CS*: quid sit *E*   934 *deleuit Peiper*: poscunt fidem secunda et
aduersa exigunt *Harl Vat Poggius* (at *pro* et *coni. Auantius*)   secundam *E*
938 donum *E*: demum *P CS*   943 lora *C^{ac}*   946 uulneri] uultum *S*
950 pre sae *E*   951 uictis *P CS*   *ante* 953 Clytemestra. Electra.
(A)Egistus. Cassandra *codd.*

.

ELECTRA

Adulterorum uirgo deserui domum. 955

CLYTEMESTRA

Quis esse credat uirginem –

ELECTRA

natam tuam?

CLYTEMESTRA

Modestius cum matre.

ELECTRA

Pietatem doces?

CLYTEMESTRA

Animos uiriles corde tumefacto geris,
sed agere domita feminam disces malo.

ELECTRA

Nisi forte fallor, feminas ferrum decet. 960

CLYTEMESTRA

Et esse demens te parem nobis putas?

---

955 adulatorum *P*   957 pietatem *E*: eia tandem *P CS*: me tandem
Poggius   959 feminam *P CS*: semitam *E*   960 nisi *E*: ni *P CS*   961
demens te parem nobis *E*: parem nobis demens te *P CS*: nobis te parem
demens *Poggius*

ELECTRA

Vobis? quis iste est alter Agamemnon tuus?
ut uidua loquere: uir caret uita tuus.

CLYTEMESTRA

Indomita posthac uirginis uerba impiae
regina frangam; citius interea mihi   965
edissere ubi sit natus, ubi frater tuus.

ELECTRA

Extra Mycenas.

CLYTEMESTRA

Redde nunc natum mihi.

ELECTRA

Et tu parentem redde.

CLYTEMESTRA

Quo latitat loco?

ELECTRA

Tuto quietus, regna non metuens noua:
iustae parenti satis; adulterae parum?   970

---

962 uobis *E*: nobis *P CS*   963 *suo loco praebet E*: *post* 965 *P CS*: *om. Treuet*
Harl F recc.: 963–5 *om.* *V*^{ac} (*add. rubricator in mg.*) *KQ*^{ac} ut *E*: tu *P CS* (*cf.*
HO 852)   tuus uita *C*^{ac} 964 post hec *S Vd*   965 regin^a *E*^{c} 966
om. P   967 extra *E*: exiit *P CS*   970 *uersum Electrae tribuunt P CS*:
Clytemestrae dat E: ἀντιλαβὴν *post* satis *statuerunt Poggius, Bothe*   iuste *P CS*:
dixi *E*: dixti *W. Morel*   adulterae *Bentleius*: at irat(a)e *E P*: ac i. *CS*: an i.
Viansino

CLYTEMESTRA

Morieris hodie.

ELECTRA

Dummodo hac moriar manu.
recedo ab aris. siue te iugulo iuuat
mersisse ferrum, praebeo iugulum uolens;
seu more pecudum colla resecari placet,
intenta ceruix uulnus expectat tuum.   975
scelus paratum est: caede respersam uiri
atque obsoletam sanguine hoc dextram ablue.

CLYTEMESTRA

Consors pericli pariter ac regni mei,
Aegisthe, gradere: nata genetricem impie
probris lacessit, occulit fratrem abditum.   980

AEGISTHVS–ELECTRA–CLYTEMESTRA

AEGISTHVS

Furibunda uirgo, uocis infandae sonum
et aure uerba indigna materna opprime.

ELECTRA

Etiam monebit sceleris infandi artifex,
per scelera natus, nomen ambiguum suis,
idem sororis natus et patris nepos?   985

---

972 iugulum *S Vd*   973 uolens *P CS*: tibi *E*: libens *F1 R7, postea coni.*
Giardina   974 reserari *C*   975 intenta] interea *P*   976 paratum *E*:
peractum *P CS*: piandum *Düring* (*cf. Thy. 824, Pho. 457*)   977 obsoletam
E: ab- *P CS*   979 gradere *E*: grandes *P*: gaudes *CS* gnatam *E*   980
occulit fratrem abditum *E*: abditum fratrem occulit *P CS* (oculum *S^{ac}*)
ante 981 *scaenae titulum addidi* (*cf. ante* 953 *supra*)

CLYTEMESTRA

Aegisthe, cessas impium ferro caput
demetere? fratrem reddat aut animam statim.

AEGISTHVS

Abstrusa caeco carcere et saxo exigat
aeuum; per omnes torta poenarum modos
referre quem nunc occulit forsan uolet.   990
inops, egens, inclusa, paedore obsita,
uidua ante thalamos, exul, inuisa omnibus,
aethere negato sero succumbet malis.

ELECTRA

Concede mortem.

AEGISTHVS

                    Si recusares, darem:
rudis est tyrannus morte qui poenam exigit.   995

ELECTRA

Mortem aliquid ultra est?

AEGISTHVS

                    Vita, si cupias mori.
abripite, famuli, monstrum et auectam procul
ultra Mycenas ultimo in regni angulo
uincite saeptam nocte tenebrosi specus,
ut inquietam uirginem carcer domet.   1000

---

987 fratrem] fremit *P*   988–1000 *loquitur Aegisthus cum Electra in E*:
loquitur Clytemestra in P CS   988 obstrusa *P*   989 euum. per *P CS*:
aeuum et per *E*   990 que *P*   991 poedore *E*   obsita *P CS*: obruta *E*
995 paenam *E*   996 mortem *P CS*: -e *E*

CLYTEMESTRA–CASSANDRA

CLYTEMESTRA

At ista poenas capite persoluet suo
captiua coniunx, regii paelex tori:
trahite ut sequatur coniugem ereptum mihi.

CASSANDRA

Ne trahite, uestros ipsa praecedam gradus.
perferre prima nuntium Phrygibus meis   1005
propero: repletum ratibus euersis mare,
captas Mycenas, mille ductorem ducum,
ut paria fata Troicis lueret malis,
perisse dono, feminae stupro, dolo.
nihil moramur, rapite; quin grates ago.   1010
iam iam iuuat uixisse post Troiam, iuuat.

CLYTEMESTRA

Furiosa, morere.

CASSANDRA

Veniet et uobis furor.

---

ante 1001 *scaenae titulum addidi* (*cf. ante* 953 *supra*)   1001 ast *C*   ista *P CS*:
ipsa *E*   persoluet] -it *P*^{ac}: -at *e Cant q Leid.2 recc.*   1002 coniunx *om.* *C*^{ac}
1008 lueret *E*: tulerit *P CS*   1009 dono, feminae *sic interpunxi*: dono
feminae, stupro *uulgo* strupo *S* (*cf., e.g., HF 488, Thy. 222*)   1011 nam
iam *P*   1012 furiosa *E*: furibunda *P CS*   *post* 1012 MARCI.LVCII.
ANNEI.SENECAE.AGAMENNON.EXPLICIT.INCIPIT.THYESTES.FELICITER *E*:
L(ucii) Annei Senece Agamenon explicit (feliciter). incipit Octauia
eiusdem *P CS*

COMMENTARY

COMMENTARY

To keep the commentary within tolerable limits some information has been omitted or presented in abbreviated form. Books and articles listed in the bibliography are usually cited by author's name alone; bare references to illustrative parallels are often used when the full text is not required; a reference to a discussion elsewhere sometimes takes the place of a complete statement of evidence; commonplaces have been selectively illustrated, and some of the most ubiquitous ones have been taken as read. It has not been possible to refer to every discussion of *Agamemnon* in the abundant interpretative literature of the last half-century; I have in particular generally refrained from mentioning views which I think are mistaken, except when they contribute to the discussion of a genuine difficulty. I have cited my source for an illustrative parallel only when the passage is especially telling; some part of every commentary is tralatitious, and I must be content to acknowledge here in a general way the significant fraction of my material which I owe to my predecessors: Del Rio and Gronovius above all, and also Ascensius, Farnaby, Lemaire, and Giomini.

COMMENTARY

PROLOGUE (1-56)

The opening section of the play comprises an expository monologue, an arrangement used also in *HF*, *Tro.*, and *Med.* and imitated by the author of *HO*. In *Oed.* and *Thy.*, the opening monologue introduces a dialogue which fills the rest of the act, while the first scene of *Pho.* (1-319) is throughout in ostensible dialogue-form. The first act of *Pha.* is doubly remarkable: it begins with a monody, and contains two distinct scenes (1-84, 85-273).[1] Finally, the author of *Octauia* departs from Senecan practice in this, as in other respects: the long opening scene (1-272) between Octavia and her nurse mingles lyric and dialogue sections in a way that has no parallel in the authentic plays.[2]

Senecca's predilection for the introductory monologue is 'Euripidean',[3] as is the preliminary character of his opening scenes in general: only in *Pha.* does the action proper begin before the first choral song.[4]

The prologue-speakers of Seneca's plays form three groups, each of them with Euripidean counterparts. The protagonist begins the play in *Tro.*, *Med.*, *Pha.*, and *Oed.*, for which one may compare Euripides' *Andromache*, *Helen*, *Phoenissae*, and *IT*; in *HF* and *Thy.*, as in Euripides' *Hippolytus* and *Bacchae*, the prologue is delivered by a non-human agent who has a part in causing the action or catastrophe. In *Agamemnon* the prologue-speaker is a non-human character chosen because he knows the background of the action; his function may be compared with that of Hermes in *Ion* and the ghost of Polydorus in *Hecuba*. These speakers, like the ghost of Thyestes, have extensive knowledge of both past and future events, but are powerless to influence them.[5]

It has been asserted that the prologues of Seneca differ from their Euripidean ancestors in predicting the catastrophe.[6] The case is in reality more complex. In some plays the audience's foreknowledge is presumed and used for ironic effect, as when Oedipus urges himself *linque lacrimas, funera | tabifica caeli uitia quae tecum inuehis | infaustus hospes, profuge iamdudum ocius –* |

---

[1] For other views of *Phaedra* cf. Heldmann 67ff.
[2] All other instances of lyric portions within an act involve only one actor or the chorus (assuming that *HO* 1863–939 belong to Alcmena). On 'act' and *actus* see Anliker, *Prologe und Akteinteilung* 49–51.
[3] For Euripidean practice cf. J. von Arnim, *De Euripidis prologorum arte et interpolatione* (diss. Greifswald, 1882), W. Nestle, *Die Struktur des Eingangs in der griechischen Tragödie* (Stuttgart, 1930) 83ff.
[4] Cf. von Arnim 84; for Seneca cf. F. Leo, *Plautinische Forschungen*[2] (1912) 188ff.
[5] Cf. *Hec.* 43ff., *Ion* 77f.; *Agam.* 37ff.
[6] C. Lindskog, *Studien zum antiken Drama* II (Lund, 1897) 18.

uel ad parentes (*Oed.* 78ff.) ;[1] in others, the more explicit forward references are due to Seneca's preference for protagonists as prologue-speakers (compare, for example, *Med.* 25f. and 53f. with Eur. *Med.* 36f.); and where Seneca's divine or infernal figures make unambiguous predictions of the outcome, they are only taking a step further a function already discharged by their Euripidean counterparts.[2]

In the techniques used to convey essential information, Seneca's prologues again appear as a further development of a Euripidean pattern. The prologue-speakers of Euripides are far from being the featureless retailers of facts whom Aristophanes wittily mocked in the *Frogs*; the gods among them in particular are often linked to the drama they initiate by powerful emotional ties. Their feelings, however, are not permitted to obstruct their narrative function; if their predictions prove incomplete or inaccurate, this is not because of an excess of passion. In Seneca, the *affectus* of the speaker rather than the information he can impart is the centre of interest. Prediction is provoked and shaped by emotion, and as a result is often imperfect or distorted: in *HF* Juno dwells fondly on Hercules' coming madness, but fails to mention the release he obtains at the play's end; Thyestes sees the death of Agamemnon as a requital of his own sufferings to be effected by Aegisthus, and so reduces Clytemestra to an instrument and ignores Cassandra.[3] The narrative function of the prologue is not forgotten, though more is demanded of the listener than in Greek drama, but the emphasis and outlook are determined by rhetorical considerations.[4] The *Agamemnon* prologue deals at length with Thyestes' misdeeds not for the meagre light they shed on the action, but because Seneca found Thyestes a vehicle for the rhetorical expression of character which most interested him as a dramatist.

Dramatists of the Renaissance generally knew the ghost-prologue only in its Senecan form, and so took the prologues of *Agamemnon* and *Thyestes* as models for scores of later plays.[5] The Senecan ghost, however, conforms to a well-established convention of the ancient theatre, whose essential patterns are already visible in the earliest extant tragedy, Aeschylus' *Persae*. The belief that ghosts could be released from the Underworld only for a limited time restricted their dramatic appearances to single episodes and may have

---

[1] On the uses to which Seneca puts his audience's familiarity with his material see Seidensticker 156ff.

[2] Cf. *Hipp.* 21f., 48f., *Hec.* 43ff.; some predictions are false or misleading, cf. *Ion* 69ff., *Ba.* 50ff. (with Dodds's note on 52). See also von Arnim 87 and M. Imhof, *Bemerkungen zu den Prologen des Sophokles und Euripides* (diss. Bern 1953 (1957) 66ff., 77f.

[3] Cf. F. Frenzel, *Die Prologe der Tragödien des Seneca* (diss. Leipzig, 1914) 52.

[4] Leo, 'Monolog' 91.

[5] For English imitations see G. Dahinten, *Die Geisterszene in der Tragödie vor Shakespeare* (Göttingen, 1958).

encouraged their use as prologue-speakers.[1] It is therefore unlikely that the ghost of Polydorus in Euripides' *Hecuba* was the first prologue-ghost, and it has been plausibly argued that the *Hecuba* prologue was inspired by the appearance of Achilles' spirit in Sophocles' *Polyxena*.[2] Furthermore, it cannot be forgotten that the two Senecan ghost-prologues themselves may be based on lost Greek tragedies.[3] Roman tragedy of the Republic contained at least one memorable ghost-scene, the appearance of Deiphilus in Pacuvius' *Iliona*, and Cicero reveals that a means for the sudden entrance of a ghost on stage as if from beneath the earth existed in the temporary theatres in use before 55 B.C.[4] Although the fragments of Republican tragedy provide no clear evidence of a ghost-prologue, it is improbable that this role of the ghost was neglected.[5]

In this light the often-repeated assertion that the speech of Thyestes is a free adaptation of the speech of Polydorus in Euripides' *Hecuba* seems questionable.[6] The parallels are limited to the opening lines, and even here consist of conventional formulae (*linquens...adsum* – ἥκω...λιπών) and expressions which arise naturally from the similar contexts (*profundo specu* – σκότου πύλας). It is also worth noting that Thyestes displays characteristics of the traditional revenge-ghost as well as those of the prologue-ghost.[7] The influence of Euripides' *Hecuba* is negligible.

Extended speeches in Seneca are usually divided by editors into sections marked by spacing or indentation, but the result is not usually consistent or

---

[1] See note on 55f. below.

[2] Cf. Wilamowitz, *Griechische Tragödien* III[2] (1906) 268 n.1, and more recently Friedrich, *Untersuchungen* 104ff. and W. M. Calder III, *GRBS* vii (1966) 43ff. and 53ff.

[3] A. Lesky, *WS* xliii (1923) 189ff. suggests a Euripidean original for *Thyestes*.

[4] *Sest.* 126 *emergebat subito cum sub tabulas subrepserat, ut 'mater, te appello' dicturus uideretur*; the same scene is recalled in *Tusc.* 1.106, *Acad. Pr.* 2.88, Hor. *S.* 2.3.60.

[5] The lines

> Adsum atque aduenio Acherunte uix uia alta atque ardua
> per speluncas saxis structas asperis pendentibus
> maxumis, ubi rigida constat crassa caligo inferum...

(*inc. inc. trag.* 73ff. R[2]) were assigned to the prologue of Accius' *Troades* by Ribbeck, and Jocelyn (305) considers the prologue to Ennius' *Hecuba* a possible source; the metre, however, does not suit a prologue-speech, and the stress on the hardship of the ascent is odd in a ghost's mouth. Hercules or Theseus might speak thus on returning to the upper world.

[6] Cf. Frenzel 49; C. Brakman, *Mnemos.* N.S. xlii (1914) 392; Anliker 11.

[7] For these types cf. M. V. Braginton, *The supernatural in Seneca's tragedies* (diss. Yale, 1933) 78, R. M. Hickman, *Ghostly etiquette on the classical stage* (Iowa Studies in Classical Philology vii (1938)).

instructive. For example, Giardina's text of the *Agamemnon* prologue shows indentation at lines 1, 37, and 53, but the actual divisions of thought and tone are far more frequent. A proper approach to this part of the editor's task begins with the fact that the Senecan unit of division is the *sententia*; as Quintilian observed, *subsistit omnis sententia ideoque post eam utique aliud est initium*.[1] In Thyestes' speech such climactic *sententiae* occur at the following points: *fugio...fugo* (4), *hic epulis locus* (11), *uiscera exedi mea* (27), *nocti diem* (36), *daturus coniugi iugulum suae* (43), *respice ad matrem: decet* (52), and *redde iam mundo diem* (56). The new starts to which Quintilian alludes are also evident (e.g. 12 *nonne uel tristes lacus...*, 5 *en horret*). In a highly wrought speech such as this, the *sententiae* do more than give an air of finality to the last lines of a section;[2] to a considerable degree the speech is constructed around its *sententiae* and is shaped to set them off to best effect.[3]

In *Agamemnon*, as in *Thyestes*, Seneca designates the setting as both Argos and Mycenae. In *Ag.* 729, Cassandra's vision of a twofold Argos is clearly a distortion of her actual surroundings, and the invocation to Argos in 808ff. is addressed to the native city of Agamemnon (808–10, cf. 782ff.) and thus to the scene of the action.[4] The use of Mycenae is equally well attested: in 121 Clytemestra meditates flight from *Mycenaeas domos*; in 351 the chorus, in a prayer to Juno, calls itself *tua turba, Mycenae*; in 967 and 998 characters who have left or are about to leave the city are *extra Mycenas*.[5] Of the two, Mycenae is the more common, but a degree of inconsistency is ineradicable.

Seneca's procedure is not derived from Aeschylus, who avoids in the *Oresteia* all mention of Mycenae and places the home of the Atreidae in Argos.[6] In the prologue of *Electra*, Sophocles calls the place Mycenae (9 Μυκήνας τὰς πολυχρύσους, recalling Homer), but his description draws as well on Argos and the surrounding countryside; elsewhere in the play Agamemnon's subjects are called both Argives and Mycenaeans.[7] Seneca's practice, however, corresponds most closely to that of Euripides, in whose

---

[1] *Inst.* 8.5.27.

[2] For this use of 'terminal *sententia*' in Lucan, cf. S. F. Bonner, *AJPh* lxxxvii (1966) 264ff., M. P. O. Morford, *The poet Lucan* (1967) 17f., 50; in Sophocles, cf. E. Wolf, *Sentenz und Reflexion bei Sophokles* (diss. Tübingen, 1910).

[3] Cf. J. de Decker, *Iuuenalis declamans* (1913) 168ff.

[4] *Thy.* 404ff. *optata patriae tecta et Argolicas opes...cerno* suggest an apostrophe to Argos, but the city has the Cyclopean walls of Mycenae; for the conjunction cf. Eur. *Her.* 15.

[5] See also *Thy.* 188, 561, 1010f.

[6] *Ag.* 23, 810, *Cho.* 676, 680, *Eum.* 654 (Ἀργεία χθών in *Ag.* 503, 506); in some of these passages Ἄργος may denote the Argolid. For possible motives in excluding Mycenae see Fraenkel on *Ag.* 23.

[7] *El.* 161, 423, and especially 1459f.

plays (as Elmsley noted) Ἄργος and Μυκῆναι are not more clearly distinguished than Τροία and Ἴλιον.[1]

Seneca also uses the wider sense of *Argos*, referring to the Argolid or the area under the control of Argos–Mycenae; this use of Ἄργος is dominant in Homer and archaic Greek literature and often found in tragedy.[2] In *Agamemnon* it is present in 395a *telluris Argolicae decus* (*tellus Argolica* also in *Thy.* 185) and perhaps in 806 *Argolica Iuno*. In 350ff. *Argos* refers to Juno's patronage of the Argolid, while *tua turba Mycenae* identifies a specific group of worshippers within that demesne; for the distinction cf. Eur. *I.T.* 508ff. Ἄργος πατρίδ᾽ ἐμὴν ἐπεύχομαι...ἐκ τῶν Μυκηνῶν, fr. 228.6 N² ἐλθὼν ἐς Ἄργος ᾤκισ᾽ Ἰνάχου πόλιν.[3]

In *Agamemnon*, where Seneca insists on the power and humiliation of Troy's conqueror, *Mycenae* might be used with conscious reference to its epic background, exploiting its elevated tone for pathetic effect: compare Ovid, *Met.* 15.426ff. *clara fuit Sparte, magnae uiguere Mycenae...uile solum Sparte est, altae cecidere Mycenae* and *Ag.* 870f. *resurgis Troia: traxisti iacens | pares Mycenas*. Seneca might also have been influenced by other Latin poets: Virgil and Ovid associate Agamemnon with Mycenae, never with Argos.[4]

The particular setting of the action is more consistently described; as in Aeschylus' *Agamemnon* and Sophocles' *Electra*, the play is set before the palace of the Pelopidae (6ff. with commentary). Although the public character of the place is largely forgotten during the intrigue of the second act, Clytemestra's concluding command to Aegisthus, *secede mecum potius* (308), suggests withdrawal to more private areas. The second choral song invests the place with sacral significance, and it becomes clear from the opening words of Eurybates (392aff.) that the open space before the palace is thought of, in accordance with Greek practice, as containing an altar or altars; these remain prominent through the rest of the play (cf. 585, 778ff., 951f., 972f.).

1 **opaca...adsum** Such an announcement is normal for visitors from the Underworld, cf. Aesch. *Pers.* 688ff., Soph. fr. 523 P (Polyxena) ἀκτὰς ἀπαίωνάς τε καὶ μελαμβαθεῖς | λιποῦσα λίμνης ἦλθον ἄρσενας χοὰς | Ἀχέροντος ὀξυπῆγας ἠχούσας γόους, Eur. *Hec.* 1f. ἥκω νεκρῶν κευθμῶνα καὶ σκότου

---

1 Elmsley on *Heracl.* 188; cf. Strabo 8.6.19 (p. 377), schol. Soph. *El.* 4, H. Hennig, *de Iphigeniae Aulidensis forma et condicione* (diss. Berlin, 1870) 49–52.

2 C. P. Bill, *TAPA* lxi (1930) 118–29 (though his attempt to show that no Attic tragedian deviated from the Homeric association of Agamemnon with Mycenae is misguided).

3 In *Ag.* 304 and *Thy.* 122ff., 298f., 627ff., *Argos* could be taken in either sense.

4 *Aen.* 11.266, 6.838; Ovid, *Am.* 2.8.12, *Her.* 3.109, *Tr.* 2.400, *Met.* 6.414, *F.* 3.83; cf. Sen. *Epist.* 66.26. Other poets also distinguish Argos and Mycenae: Hor. *C.* 1.7.9, Virg. *Aen.* 6.838, Ovid, *Met.* 6.414, *F.* 6.47.

πύλας | λιπών, ἵν' "Αιδης χωρὶς ᾤκισται θεῶν, *fr. inc. inc. fab.* 73ff. R² *adsum atque aduenio Acherunte* eqs.; note also *adsum* of Jupiter's arrival from heaven in Pl. *Amph.* 1131. Our passage may be echoed in Chapman's *Revenge of Bussy d'Ambois* (v. 1): 'Up from the chaos of eternal night... once more I ascend.'

opaca Darkness was not merely a characteristic of the ancient Underworld, but constituted one of its terrors, cf. Lucr. 3.1011 *Cerberus et Furiae iam uero et lucis egestas,* Hor. *C.* 1.4.16 *iam te premet nox,* Sen. *Epist.* 24.18 *nemo tam puer est ut Cerberum timeat et tenebras.*

Ditis inferni The phrase is not precisely paralleled, but cf. *Med.* 741 *opacam Ditis umbrosi domum, Tro.* 432 *ab imo...Dite,* Luc. 1.455 *Ditisque profundi, C.I.L.* III.2197 (=*Carm. Epigr.* 1534) *inferi Ditis specus,* Auson. *opusc.* 343.3 Peiper *Tartareus Dis.* Dis is more commonly named by a periphrasis such as *inferni Iouis* (*HF* 47; cf. Aesch. *Supp.* 157f., 231, *Ag.* 1386f.), *inferno tyranno* (Ov. *Met.* 5.508, *Pha.* 1153), *inferni regis* (Virg. *Aen.* 6.106, Ov. *Met.* 2.261, *Pha.* 95, 952), or *inferno Tonanti* (Stat. *Th.* 11.209).

2 adsum *Adesse* is regularly used in Senecan entry-announcements, even where motion is specified or implied, cf. *Tro.* 522f. *adest Vlixes, et quidem dubio gradu | uultuque, Pha.* 834 *en ipse Theseus redditus terris adest*; verbs of explicit motion (*propero, gressus ferre*) are often reserved for solemn or excited entrances, cf. 408ff. below. In Greek tragedy, on the other hand, verbs such as ἥκω, στείχω, etc. are more commonly used than πάρειμι (for which, however, see Soph. *O.T.* 513ff., Eur. *Tro.* 36f., *Rhesus* 892f.). For *adsum* in Republican tragedy, cf. Acc. 277, 498 R².

linquens...adsum An equivalent of the Greek tragic entrance-formula ἥκω...λιπών generally applied to divine, supernatural, or kingly figures, cf. Soph. *Phil.* 1413ff., Eur. *Hec.* 1f., *Tro.* 1, *Ba.* 1ff. (1 ἥκω; 13 λιπών...20 ἦλθον); cf. Aesch. *Pers.* 159 λιποῦσ' ἱκάνω (Queen), *Eum.* 9ff. λιπών...ἦλθε (Phoebus), probably Euripides [*Phrixus*] *ap.* Arist. *Frogs* 1225f. ἐκλιπών (Cadmus); Anliker 104 n.4. This is its only appearance in Seneca.

emissus Ghosts generally leave the Underworld for a stated purpose, for example revenge or honourable burial (cf. Aesch. *Pers.* 686ff., *Eum.* 95ff., Eur. *Hec.* 49ff., Sen. *Thy.* 1ff.), but Thyestes is simply *emissus.* The word here carries no indication of motive, as in *Oed.* 394 *emissus Erebo ut caedis auctorem indicet,* Val. Fl. 4.258f. *Tartarus umbras...ad meritae spectacula poenae | emittit* (cf. *Hamlet* II.i.83f. 'as if he had been looséd out of hell | to speak of horrors'), but means only 'released, let loose', as in Virg. *G.* 3.551f. *in lucem Stygiis emissa tenebris | pallida Tisiphone morbos agit,* Sen. *Contr.* 9.1.8 *emissusque sede sua Miltiades maiestate refulsit,* Ov. *Met.* 5.321, Sen. *HF* 79f., *Thy.* 671f., Stat. *Th.* 8.376f., *S.* 2.1.227. When so used *emittere* may suggest unleashing a wild or unruly animal (*Rhet. ad Her.* 4.51 *sicut cauea leo emissus*) or a violent wind (cf. Ov. *Met.* 1.264 with Bömer's note); see Cic. *Pis.* 95 and Nisbet *ad loc.*

specu   *Specus* of the Underworld is found in Ennius, *sc.* 155 R² = 152 J *inferum uastos specus*, and in Virgil, *Aen.* 7.568f. (note also *alta spelunca* in *Aen.* 6.237 and *specus* in *Aen.* 8.241). Seneca uses *specus* in this sense often, adding such qualifiers as *ingens* (*HF* 94, *Tro.* 198), *uastus* (*HF* 718, *Thy.* 9), *immensus* (*HF* 665, *Tro.* 178; *HO* 262), *obscurus* (*Tro.* 430), etc.; see further J. Kroll, *Gott und Hölle* (1932) 390f.

3 incertus...magis   The *dubitatio* has more rhetorical than emotional force; its function is to prepare for and heighten the effect of the following *sententia*. For the device compare Naevius, *Com.* 115 R², Cic. *Pis.* 22 *in quo nemo potest dicere utrum iste plus biberit an effuderit* (with Nisbet's note), *Cluent.* 26, Sall. *Jug.* 24.3 *ferro an fame acrius urgear incertus sum*, 95.4, *Hist.* IV fr. 1, Hor. *Epist.* 1.16.27f. (cf. *OGIS* 458.3ff. Dittenberger), Ov. *Met.* 1.578 *nescia gratentur consolenturne parentem*, and see note on 140 below.

4 fugio...fugo   'Th' infernall fiendes I fly, the foalke of earth I chase about' (Studley). To an inhabitant of Tartarus, *superi* are not the gods of heaven but the people who dwell on earth, cf. *fr. pall. inc. inc.* 51 R² *si nunc redire posset ad superos pater*, Virg. *Aen.* 6.481, 680 *animas superumque ad lumen ituras* (and cf. Henry, *Aeneidea* III.326), Prop. 2.1.37, Sen. *Pha.* 145, *Thy.* 82f. *quando contingget mihi | effugere superos?* Lucan's Erictho speaks of a world *cuius uos [sc. Manes] estis superi* (6.478f.).

The *sententia* is expertly phrased, but it depicts Thyestes' equivocal status more successfully than his psychological condition. The similar antithesis in ps.-Quint. *decl. mai.* 12.8 is less brilliant but more expressive: *quos tester deos? superosne quos per tantum nefas fugauimus an inferos quos nobis permiscuimus?*

Thyestes   In prologues spoken by figures outside the action Seneca derives rhetorical advantage from the necessity of identifying the speaker; *HF* 1f. *Soror Tonantis – hoc enim solum mihi | nomen relictum est*, *Thy.* 3f. *quis male deorum Tantalo uisas domos | ostendit iterum?* Ben Jonson strives for a similar effect in the prologue of *Catiline*, but without Seneca's characteristic compression: 'Do'st thou not feele me, Rome? not yet? Is night | so heavy on thee, and my weight so light? | Can SYLLA's ghost arise within thy walls, | lesse threatening than an earthquake, the quick falls | of thee and thine?'

5 en horret   The reading of the paradosis (*inhorret* was wrongly attributed to E by Gronovius and many subsequent editors) involves a slight irregularity. *En* is nowhere else in Seneca used of a mental event; where it does not indicate physical objects it calls attention to situations which can be visualised, and does so in dialogue, cf. *Pha.* 91 *profugus en coniunx abest*, *Oen.* 797 *tangis en ipsos metus*, *Thy.* 1050f. *Horret animus* without interjection occurs at *Med.* 670, cf. Pac. 294 R² *horrescit animus*, 883 below, *horreo atque animo tremo*; on the inverted word-order cf. Seidler 108.

Inhorret is a slight alteration that removes the abnormality. The change is palaeographically plausible; although *en* is corrupted to *in-* four times in

Seneca and *in-* to *en* only once (Zwierlein 70), the single example is one in which a rare verb is altered to *en* followed by a familiar verb (*Tro.* 625 *intremuit* E PCS: *en tremuit* l²n: *en timuit* recc.). *Inhorret*, however, is not otherwise attested for Seneca and is itself anomalous, since the inceptive of *horreo* is properly *inhorresco* (cf. Housman, *CQ* vii (1913) 25–7, a reference I owe to G. P. Goold). Of the three certain occurrences of *inhorreo* before A.D. 200, none appears in a context similar to that of the *Agamemnon* passage. (Livy 8.8.10, cited in *T.L.L.* vii¹.1600.59ff., is emended by Housman). On the other hand, it is not implausible that Seneca should have used the rare but real verb *inhorreo* and extended its range to include mental phenomena, particularly since he may have been the first to extend the range of *inhorresco* in just this direction (cf. 418 below, *T.L.L.* vii¹.1600.82ff.).

With arguments so evenly balanced, it is best to retain the transmitted *en*; it may be supported by Ovid, *Pont.* 3.7.33f. *torqueor en grauius, repetitaque forma locorum | exilium renouat triste recensque facit.* Furthermore, in our passage *en* is given its normal force by *pauor membra excutit*; for the combination *animus–membra* compare Pl. *Cas.* 622 *cor metu mortuomst, membra miserae tremunt.*

et pauor membra excutit *Animus* and *membra* are similarly linked in *Tro.* 168 *pauet animus, artus horridus quassat tremor.* Bentley's *mentem* is misguided; Senecan ghosts are thoroughly corporeal in their ability to feel distress (compare *Thy.* 97ff.). Limbs shaken by fear were a cliché before Seneca, ¦cf. Bömer on Ov. *Fasti* 3.331, Zwierlein, *Gnomon* xxxviii (1966) 684f.; Senecan examples are collected by Canter 76ff.

6 uideo...lares 'I see my father's – or rather my brother's house.' *Immo* appears in the tragedies only here and, again corrective, in *HF* 314, cf. Cic. *Att.* 6.2.7 *uenio ad Brutum tuum, immo nostrum*, Sen. *Epist.* 120.17 *nihil satis est morituris, immo morientibus.* (Professor Jocelyn refers me to Pl. *Rud.* 1206 *mi liberte, mi patrone potius, immo mi pater.*) S. often uses self-correction for point, cf. *HF* 643f. *Lycus Creonti debitas poenas dabit. | lentum est dabit: dat. hoc quoque est lentum: dedit, Thy.* 411f. *occurret Argos, populus occurret frequens – | sed nempe et Atreus*; Marx, *Chorlieder* 62f.

7–11 hoc...locus Detailed description of the setting is uncommon in both Greek and Senecan tragedy. Greek poets generally provide brief and allusive indications, cf. Soph. *Ajax* 3, *O.T.* 15, *O.C.* 14ff., Eur. *Tro.* 36, *Ba.* 5f., except where the setting is dramatically significant, as for example in Soph. *Phil.* 1ff., 27ff. Roman tragedy, however, may point to lost Greek examples: Ennius' lines *asta atque Athenas anticum opulentum oppidum | contempla et templum Cereris ad laeuam aspice* (242f. R² = 239f. J) may come from the prologue to a non-Euripidean *Medea* (Jocelyn 344–6), and the descriptions of Mycenae in Seneca's *Thyestes* (404ff., 641ff.) have been taken as derivations from a Greek, perhaps Euripidean account (cf. A. Lesky, *WS* xliii (1922/3) 194ff.).

At first the *Agamemnon* passage might appear to be a reworking of the prologue to Sophocles' *Electra* (4–10). But despite verbal similarities (the reference to the Pelopid house in lines 6 and 10 of Seneca and Sophocles, the demonstrative adjectives in anaphora) Seneca derives nothing essential from Sophocles, and the resemblances may be due to simple coincidence. In its details the Senecan account is clearly and directly inspired by Virgil, *Aeneid* 7.170–6:

> tectum augustum, ingens, centum sublime columnis,
> urbe fuit summa, Laurentis regia Pici,
> horrendum siluis et religione parentum.
> hic sceptra accipere et primos attollere fascis
> regibus omen erat, hoc illis curia templum,
> hae sacris sedes epulis; hic ariete caeso
> perpetuis soliti patres considere mensis.

Hence come Seneca's *regia*, his *sceptra*, his *curia*, his anaphora of *hic*, and the inspiration for his climactic *hic epulis locus*; the apparently haphazard order in which Thyestes indicates the leading sights of Argos is derived from Virgil, and Seneca could have relied on his audience to applaud the cleverness with which he adapted Virgil's *hae sacris sedes epulis* to a Mycenaean context.

8 hinc auspicari...Pelasgis Seneca preserves the religious overtones of *omen erat* by referring to the Roman practice of taking auspices at the investiture of the old kings (cf. Livy 1.6.4ff., Enn. *Ann.* 77–96 V³, Cic. *Rep.* 2.16, *de Or.* 2.17, *Epist. ad Brut.* 1.5.4). The *fasces*, however, were too patently Italian to remain, and in their place stands the anachronistic diadem (*capiti decus*). Virgil's neutral *sceptra accipere* is expanded to suggest the arrogance of the Pelopidae (9 *alti toro*, 10 *superba manu*).

auspicari...Pelasgis 'Here it is the custom for the Argive kings solemnly to begin their reigns.' The phrase seems somewhat strained, but is not to be suspected.

The sense is closely paralleled by *Thy.* 657 *hinc auspicari regna Tantalidae solent*, where *auspicor* in the sense 'begin solemnly, with the taking of auspices' governs its expected object (cf. 174 below *bella*, also Varro, *ling. Lat.* 6.16 *uindemia*, Apul. *Met.* 8.9 *nuptias*). Here the diadem represents the reign of its wearer; the phrase is thus a less obvious variant of such expressions as *nondum ullum honorem auspicatus* (Val. Max. 8.15.8) or *senatorium per militiam auspicantes gradum* (Sen. *Epist.* 47.10), and the synecdoche is comparable to, though bolder than, the use of *torus* to signify the marriage of those who occupy it (cf. *Med.* 285 *per auspicatos regii thalami toros*).

For *capiti decus* (nearly = *capitis decus*), cf. *HF* 257f. *uidi regium capiti decus | cum capite raptum* (*capiti* Eᵃᶜ: *-is* E²ᵖᶜ P CS) and *Thy.* 701f. *regium capiti decus | bis terque lapsum est*; other instances of *capiti decus*, as in Livy 1.34.9 *humana manu* [Stroth: *humano* codd.] *superpositum capiti decus* and Stat. *Th.*

11.160f. *ut...induerem capiti decus* are not parallels in the strict sense, since in them *capiti* is clearly influenced by the verbs *superpositum* and *induerem*.

9 Pelasgis The interpretation of *auspicari decus* advanced above requires that *Pelasgis = regibus Pelasgis*, for it is they, not their subjects, who begin reigns or don crowns. This is not the obvious reading of the text, but it is supported by *Thy.* 657, where *Tantalidae* clearly refers to the royal house, and by Virg. *Aen.* 7.174 *regibus omen erat*.

10 gestantur For *sceptra gestare* cf. Virg. *Aen.* 12.210f. *(sceptrum) aere decoro | inclusit patribusque dedit gestare Latinis*, Sen. *Tro.* 772.

11 locus hic habendae curiae S. has transferred Virgil's reference to the primitive *curia* of Picus (*hoc illis curia templum*) unchanged into an Argive setting. Anliker rightly remarks (p. 105 n.21) that the style of government practised by Atreus and Aegisthus leaves little room for a *curia* (it was otherwise in Aeschylus, cf. *Ag.* 844f. with Fraenkel's note).

habendae curiae Although both *curia* with the sense of *senatus* and *senatum habere* meaning 'to hold a meeting of the senate' are familiar expressions, *curiam habere* in this sense seems unparalleled.

hic epulis locus This rhetorical device, by which an apparent anti-climax is paradoxically a true climax, is effective in *Pho.* 313ff. *hic Oedipus Aegaea transnabit freta | iubente te, ...iubente te praebebit alitibus iecur, | iubente te uel uiuet* and in *Oed.* 8of. *profuge iamdudum ocius – | uel ad parentes*; there is, however, some straining for effect in *HF* 1259ff. *cuncta iam amisi bona, | mentem arma famam coniugem natos manus, | etiam furorem* and in *Pho.* 240 *lacrimae supererant, has quoque eripui mihi*; see further Morford, *The poet Lucan* (1967) 50f., and now Costa on *Med.* 19.

12 libet reuerti The outburst lacks the force of similar threats to leave the stage made by the ghost of Tantalus (*Thy.* 70f.) and Oedipus (*Oed.* 8of.); unlike these figures, Thyestes is extraneous to the drama and his departure would leave the action unaffected.

12ff. nonne...iubis The thought is similar to that expressed later in the play by Cassandra (750ff.), but the expression is clearly influenced by Virg. *Ecl.* 2.14f. *nonne fuit satius tristis Amaryllidis iras | atque superba pati fastidia? nonne Menalcan...?* (and cf. Prop. 2.25.11f.). *Nonne* appears only here and in *Pha.* 880, *satius* only here; on *nonne* cf. Axelson, *Unpoetische Wörter* 89f.

13f. incolere...iubis Although the general sense of these words is clear, the text contains a corruption for which no certain remedy has yet been found. The transmitted text requires *incolere* to govern both *lacus* and *custodem Stygis*; *incolere custodem*, however, seems intolerable. It could only be defended as a brachylogy of *incolere Styga a Cerbero custoditam*, on the analogy of *Med.* 86 *tripoda mouere* for *mouere Pythiam in tripode sedentem*, but this comparison reveals how much more violent the present passage is.

Since Leo, those who have recognised a problem have set about replacing the second *nonne* with a verb suitable for governing *custodem* (see apparatus for details). Quite apart from the quality of the proposals, this line of attack cannot succeed: the repetition of *nonne* is required by the rhetorical structure and is guaranteed by the close parallel with *Ecl.* 2.14f.

An approach first suggested by Withof (*Praemetium Crucium Criticarum* (1749) 197f.) introduces an appropriate verb after verse 14, Withof accomplished this by recasting the lines as follows: *custodem . . . colla iactantem iubis | uidere? celeri corpus ubi uinctus rotae | in se refertur.* A far more plausible refinement of Withof's solution is proposed by Zwierlein (not yet published), namely the assumption of a lacuna after verse 14 to be filled by some such line as *uidere et atras Ditis inuisi domus* or *uidere, nonne Ditis inuisi domus.* This gives *ubi* (15) a more precise antecedent, preserves the unobjectionable *incolere lacus* (cf. Cic. *Verr.* 2.5.188, *T.L.L.* vii¹.978.41ff.; compare Virg. *Aen.* 6.133ff. *innare lacus . . . uidere | Tartara*) and produces a tripartite structure exactly parallel to that of 750ff. below.

The last attempt at emendation deserving mention regards *incolere* as the locus of corruption. Bentley replaced it with *tolerare* (and *Stygis* with *pati*); limpid, but unbearably flat. It is better to introduce the unarguably apt *uidere* (perhaps adumbrated by Ascensius in his gloss 'incolere aut uidere custodem Stygis'). *Videre* governs *lacus* and *custodem* equally well, and produces a proper contrast to line 6 *uideo . . . fraternos lares.* Nor is *uidere* a weak word, since looking upon hell or its inhabitants was thought to unnerve all but the hardiest, cf. Virg. *Aen.* 6.133ff., Ov. *Met.* 10.64ff., ps.-Sen. *HO* 22; for *uidere* in this sense of 'have the courage to look at' cf. Hor. *C.* 1.3.18ff., 1.37.25f., Shackleton Bailey, *Propertiana* 3, 612 below with note. The admittedly valid objection to *uidere* is the improbability of its having been ousted by the less common *incolere*. The change becomes palaeographically plausible only in the minuscule period, and minuscule errors common to E and A are too few and slight to make this a likely explanation. The last conjecture to be noted involves the least physical alteration: *accolere* for *incolere* (Bothe). While *accolere* more comfortably governs *lacus* than *custodem*, its use with a personal object is demonstrated by a strikingly similar passage of Statius: *Maeonium Ascraeumque senem non segnior umbra | accolis* (*S.* 5.3.27f.).

14 trigemina Seneca's Cerberus is consistently three-headed, cf. 860 below, *HF* 62, 795f., *Oed.* 581; in *Apocol.* 13.3 mild fun is made of Horace's *belua centiceps* (*C.* 2.13.34). On the topic see Frazer on ps.-Apollodorus, *Bibl.* 2.5.12, West on Hes. *Theog.* 311f., Immisch in Roscher s.v. 'Kerberos'.

iubis The hound's 'mane' is formed by the snakes that ring its head, cf. Virg. *Aen.* 6.419 *uates horrere uidens iam colla colubris*, Hor. *C.* 3.11.17f., Tib. 1.3.71f., Lygd. 4.87, Ov. *Met.* 10.21f., *HF* 785ff. The metaphor in *iubis* may have been suggested by the use of *iuba* and *iubatus* of snakes, cf. Naev. *sc.* 21 R², Virg. *Aen.* 2.206 (with Austin's note), Val. Fl. 3.228, 8.88,

Claud. *Ruf.* 1 *pr.* 4. With *colla iactantem iubis* compare Calp. Sic. 7.61 *quibus hirtae | iactantur per colla iubae.*

15ff. Seneca's descriptions of hell invariably include a catalogue of the famous sinners (cf. *HF* 750ff., *Med.* 744ff., *Pha.* 1229ff., *Thy.* 4ff.; cf. *HO* 938ff.); here they engross almost the entire scene, doubtless because Thyestes feels a kinship with them in guilt. The writer of the *Octauia* has the ghost of Agrippina call down traditional torments on Nero (619ff.). This form of the commonplace also appears in poetic invective (cf. Ovid, *Ibis* 173ff., 189ff., Claud. *Ruf.* 2.506ff.) and may have a proverbial origin (cf. *Paroem. Gr.* II.680.10 Leutsch Τιτυοῦ σε περιμένει καὶ 'Ιξίονος κολαστήρια); it survives as well in neo-Senecan drama, cf. Kyd, *Spanish Tragedy* IV.v.31ff.

The trinity of Tityos, Sisyphos, and Tantalos goes back to the *Odyssey* (11.576ff., cf. Plato, *Gorg.* 525E), and the doom of Ixion was familiar to several older writers, although Apollonius Rhodius is the earliest surviving author who clearly places him in the Underword (3.62). The first explicit evidence connecting Ixion with the three Homeric figures is in the scholia on Demosth. 24.10.4 (pp. 771.24ff. Dindorf); the statement of Pindar (*Ol.* 1.60ff.) that Tantalos has μετὰ τριῶν τέταρτον πόνον could mean that he suffers with three other offenders, but also (and perhaps more naturally) that he suffers a fourth torment along with three others (cf. Wilamowitz, *Pindaros* 236 n.4, G. Tarditi, *Parola del Passato* ix (1954) 204–11). These four form the canon of sinners here and in other Senecan passages (*Thy.* 4ff., *Pha.* 1229ff., *Apocol.* 14.5), cf. also *Octauia* 621ff., Stat. *Th.* 4.537ff., Lucian, *Necyomant.* 14; Ovid shows a preference for this group augmented by the Danaidae (*Met.* 4.457ff., 10.41ff., *Ibis* 173ff.). Other variations and partial lists are also common, cf. Waser in Roscher v.1042, Smith on Tib. 1.3.73ff. On the sinners in Latin poetry see A. Zingerle, *Kleine Philol. Abhandl.* (Innsbruck, 1871ff.) III. 69ff.; for their survival in later English tragedy cf. Dahinten 55–60.

The omission of the offenders' names is characteristic of Senecan style (compare *Tro.* 975ff. with Eur. *Tro.* 248ff.), but in this case his allusiveness has a precedent in Virg. *G.* 3.39 *immanemque rotam et non exsuperabile saxum* and *Aen.* 6.616ff. *saxum ingens uoluunt alii, radiisque rotarum | districti pendent*; note also Prop. 3.5.42 *num rota, num scopuli, num sitis inter aquas*, ps.-Virg. *Culex* 241ff., Stat. *Th.* 4.537ff., Juv. 13.51f.; the generalising plural is also used by Lucian, *Luct.* 8.

15f. ubi...refertur The story of Ixion was told by Pherecydes (*FGrHist* 3 F 51 a–b) and was the subject of tragedies by Aeschylus and Euripides. The punishment of the wheel was familiar to Pindar (*P.* 2.21f.) and Sophocles (*Phil.* 676ff.), but Pindar places it in the air rather than in the Underworld (cf. also schol. Eur. *Phoen.* 1185, ps.-Apoll. *Epit.* 1.20, Philostratus, *Vit. Apoll.* 7.12).

celeri The speed of the wheel is mentioned by Pindar (πτερόεντι) and Sophocles (δρομάδα); *celeris* (or *rapida*) *rota* becomes the stereotypical Latin epithet, cf. Tib. 1.3.74, Ov. *Ibis* 174, 190, Sen. *Thy.* 8, cf. Claud. *Rapt.* 2.335

(*praeceps*). In other passages Seneca's efforts to elaborate the commonplace also heighten the violence of the punishment, cf. *HF* 750 *rapitur uolucri tortus...rota, Pha.* 1236f. *haec incitatis turbinibus ferat | nusquam resistens orbe reuoluto rota*; here the original touch consists of the picturesque *in se refertur* perhaps inspired by Ov. *Met.* 4.461 *uoluitur Ixion et se sequiturque fugitque.*

euinctus rotae *Euinctus* is a stronger variation on *uinctus*, as in, e.g., Ov. *Ibis* 174 *quique agitur rapidae uinctus ab orbe rotae.* For the 'Greek' accusative *corpus* cf. Virg. *Aen.* 5.269 *euincti tempora taenis*, Sil. 2.341 *artis post terga catenis euinctus palmas*, Hofmann–Szantyr 36; for *euincio* with the object to which a person or thing is affixed cf. Gell. 14.1.3 *omnia rerum humanarum...tamquam stellis... euincta duci et regi*, 20.1.54 *binis quadrigis euinctus in diuersa nitentibus laceratus est.*

16f. ubi...labor The stone of Sisyphus was proverbial to Euripides (*Her.* 1103) and Aristotle (*Rhet.* 1412a6); note as well Ter. *Eun.* 1085 *satis diu hoc iam saxum uorso* (Donatus: 'prouerbium in eos qui inextricabili labore afflicti sunt'), Prop. 2.20.32 *tumque ego Sisyphio saxa labore geram.*

16 per aduersum labor 'the effort of pushing the stone uphill' ('*per aduersum* = contra montem' Ascensius), cf. *Epist.* 24.18 *saxum trudi in aduersum*, Lucr. 3.1000f. *aduerso...trudere monte | saxum* (*Culex* 243), Hyg. *fab.* 60 *aduersus montem*; *in aduersum* (*-a*) generally of an uphill progress, Quint. *Inst.* 12.16.78, Sil. 1.495.

17 redeunte...saxo S.'s tendency to abstract language produces a lifeless distillation of the scene vividly described by Homer (*Od.* 11.598) and Lucretius (3.1000ff.). Elsewhere he permits himself an epithet denoting the stone's elusiveness (*lubricus, Med.* 747, *Thy.* 7; cf. *reuolubilis*, Ov. *Ib.* 189, Sil. 11.474; *ruiturus*, Ov. *Met.* 4.460; *remeabilis* Stat. *Th.* 4.537) or its size (*grande HF* 751; cf. πελώριον *Od.* 11.594, *ingens* Virg. *Aen.* 6.616).

totiens An allusive reference to Sisyphus' eternal failure to complete his task; in *Pha.* 1231 *perennis* expresses the idea more conventionally (compare *longus* Hor. *C.* 2.14.20, *perpetuus* Ov. *Met.* 4.467, ἀνήνυτος ps.-Plato, *Axiochus* 371E), while the author of *Octauia* lamely speaks of *dirum laborem* (622).

18 tondet A direct borrowing from Virg. *Aen.* 6.597ff. *rostroque immanis uultur obunco | immortale iecur tondens fecundaque poenis | uiscera*; the emphatic position of *tondet* saves Seneca's otherwise featureless picture (*ales auida, fecundum iecur*) from dullness.

ales Homer afflicted Tityos with two vultures (*Od.* 11.578f.), and other Greek sources retain the plural number (cf. Lucian, *dial. mort.* 30.1, *luct.* 8, ps.-Apoll. *Bibl.* 1.4.1); in Latin, however, Virgil's impressive picture of a single *uultur* may have led later authors to speak, though not consistently, of a single bird (for details cf. Zingerle 69ff., Waser in Roscher v.1037f.). The unspecified *ales* is common in Latin accounts before Virgil (Lucr. 3.984, Hor. *C.* 3.4.78, Prop. 2.20.31, Tib. 1.3.76).

fecundum The picture of Tityos who 'with the still-growing liver feeds the vulture' (Massinger, *Virgin Martyr* 3.1) is of uncertain origin, though perhaps best explained as a conflation of the Homeric description of Tityos and the account of Prometheus given by Hesiod (*Theog.* 524f.) and Aeschylus (*P.V.* 1021ff., *apud* Cic. *Tusc.* 2.24). This aspect of Tityos' torment is mentioned in the pseudo-Platonic *Axiochus*, but this work has been variously dated (cf. Überweg–Praechter 89*); Lucretius names it as a popular error in need of refutation (3.984ff.); and the details given in Sen. *Thy.* 9ff. and Hyg. *fab.* 55 might, but need not, derive from lost sources. What seems certain is that Virgil's account made the regeneration of the liver canonical for later writers.

19ff. The vague reference to *caelitum dapes* can be supplemented by the fuller account of the murder of Pelops in *Thy.* 144ff.; the story is first found in Pindar, *Ol.* 1.40ff. and is mentioned in Eur. *I.T.* 387ff.; it was apparently a favourite tragic plot (Lucian, *salt.* 54).

The punishment of Tantalus assumes two forms in the literary sources. The earliest appears to be the torment of an overhanging rock, constantly threatening to fall; first found in Archilochus (fr. 5 Diehl[3] = fr. 91.14f. West), this is virtually the only form attested in Greek lyric, tragedy, and prose until the Hellenistic period (cf. *Anth. Plan.* 131.10 (Antipater); *P. Sorbonn. inv.* 2254.4ff., on which cf. H. Lloyd-Jones and J. W. B. Barns, *SIFC* xxxv (1963) 205ff.; *inc. inc. fab.* 110 R[2] *apud* Cic. *Tusc.* 4.35). The second punishment is that of the *Odyssey* (11.583ff.), where Tantalus is placed in a pool with water up to his chin and fruit-trees over his head, but can neither drink nor eat; although a variant of these torments was combined with the overhanging rock in a famous painting by Polygnotus (Paus. 10.31.12), other Greek references to the Odyssean conception are considerably later (cf. Polybius 4.45, ps.-Lucian, *Amores* 53, ps.-Apollod. *Epit.* 2.1, Palladas in *Anth. Pal.* 9.377). The form of punishment in our passage, in which only the retreating water is mentioned, appears in ps.-Plato, *Axiochus* 371E and might have been in the Greek source of the tragic line *mento summam amnem attingens, enectus siti* (*inc. inc. fab.* 111 R[2]).

Latin writers generally follow the Homeric account, either naming both hunger and thirst or thirst alone. The former is found often in Ovid (cf. *Met.* 4.458f., *Am.* 2.2.43f., 3.7.51f., *Ars* 2.605f., *Her.* 16.211f., 18.181f., *Ibis* 177f., 191), and its later uses may owe something to his influence (cf. Sen. *HF* 752ff., ps.-Sen. *HO* 1075ff., Petr. *Sat.* 82.5, Stat. *Th.* 6.280, and perhaps *Aetna* 81f., though the text is corrupt). The latter is Seneca's own preferred version (cf. 769 below, *Med.* 745, *Pha.* 1232; cf. *HO* 943f., *Oct.* 621), with the exception of *Thyestes*, which consistently follows Homer (1ff., 68f., 149ff.); it is also by far the most widespread form of the myth in Latin, cf. Hor. *S.* 1.1.68, Tib. 1.3.77ff., Prop. 2.17.5, 4.11.24, Ov. *Met.* 10.41, Stat. *Th.* 4.538, 8.51, Mart. 10.5.16, ps.-Virg. *Culex* 240ff., Claud. *Ruf.* 2.509f., *Rapt.* 2.336f., Boethius, *Cons.* 3.12.36f.

19 exustus siti Cf. Lucr. 3.917, Cic. *Brut.* 16 *exustusque siti flos ueteris ubertatis exaruit,* Ov. *Met.* 11.129, and compare Sen. *Thy.* 98f.

20 aquas fugaces ore decepto Both phrases are conventional in descriptions of Tantalus. For *aquas fugaces* compare Hor. *S.* 1.1.68, Ov. *Am.* 2.2.45, *Her.* 18.182, Sen. *Thy.* 2, 68. For the idea of deception note Prop. 2.17.6, Sen. *HF* 754f., *Thy.* 259, Claud. *Ruf.* 2.510. Seneca's studied plainness saves the lines from banality.

22 pars quota 'Yet how small is his crime when compared with mine!' (perhaps Thyestes recalls that Tantalus served only one son to the gods, compared to his own consumption of three children); *pars quota* often occurs in rhetorical questions or exclamations to which a negative answer is expected, cf. Ov. *Met.* 9.68f. *ut uincas alios, Acheloe, dracones,* | *pars quota Lernaeae serpens eris unus echidnae?, Pont.* 3.6.29f., Luc. 1.283f., Claud. *Ruf.* 2.512f. The device is used sparingly by Seneca (*HF* 383, 1191, *Med.* 896, *Oed.* 67), but with less restraint by the author of *HO* (51, 95, 96, 164, 640). For *senex* = Tantalus, cf. also 769 below.

24 quaesitor...reos A direct borrowing from Virg. *Aen.* 6.432f. *quaesitor Minos urnam mouet; ille silentum* | *conciliumque uocat uitasque et crimina discit.* Besides indulging his tendency towards periphrasis (*quaesitor Cnosius* for *Minos*), S. introduces a bold metonymy (*uersat reos* for *uersat sortes reorum*) which both compresses and enlivens the allusion. Horace's *omne capax mouet urna nomen* (*C.* 3.1.14) may have suggested the phrase. It is possible that Seneca himself was imitated by Statius (*Th.* 4.530ff.): *arbiter hos dura uersat Gortynius urna* | *uera minis poscens* (cf. *Th.* 8.101f. *iudicis urna* | *Dictaei*). Propertius similarly assumes familiarity with this passage of Virgil in 4.11.19f. *si quis posita iudex sedet Aeacus urna,* | *in mea sortita uindicet ossa pila* (*is* (Heinsius)...*iudicet* (LP); cf. G. P. Goold, *HSCP* lxxi (1966) 84ff.).

quaesitor With this term Seneca, following Virgil, gives a specifically Roman touch to the judicial terminology traditionally used of Minos (cf. *Od.* 11.569, Plato, *Gorgias* 524A, Lucian, *dial. mort.* 12); cf. ps.-Asconius in Cic. *Verr.* 2.1 p. 224 Stangl. *Quaesitor* may designate any magistrate with the power of conducting a *quaestio,* cf. Mommsen, *Strafrecht* 208, *Rhet. ad Her.* 4.47, Cic. *Font.* 21, *Vat.* 30; of Minos, cf. Claud. *Ruf.* 2.476.

urna uersat reos In the passages of Virgil and Propertius cited above, the function of the urn has been variously interpreted as determining the order of cases or the composition of the jury, receiving the votes of the judges, and containing the sentences to be imposed (cf. Shackleton Bailey, *Propertiana* 264, Sandbach, *CQ* n.s. xii (1962) 274, Williams, *Tradition and originality* 396ff.). Here *reos* makes it almost certain that the guilt of the shades is known and that the urn establishes either the order of their sentencing or the sentences themselves; the latter is the judges' function in

HF 731f. and that of the urn in Stat. *Th.* 4.530f., 11.571f. and Claud. *Rapt.* 2.332 (cf. Sen. *Tro.* 981f.).

25 uincam...cunctos Thyestes is exceptionally confident; other Senecan characters assert their ability simply to hold their own among the famous sinners, cf. *Med.* 743ff., *Pha.* 1230ff., *Thy.* 18ff.; *HO* 948. K. Trabert (*Darstellung des Pathologischen* 54) has well described this attitude as the inversion of αἰὲν ἀριστεύειν; the theme, however, is not Seneca's invention, cf. Sall. *Hist.* 2.47.3 *quin omnia memorata apud inferos supplicia scelere meo uici,* Cic. *Pis.* 18 *edicere est ausus cum illo suo pari quem tamen omnibus uitiis superare cupiebat.*

Thyestes Awareness of one's mythical reputation is characteristic of Senecan people, the best example being Medea, cf. 166 *Medea superest,* 171 *Medea fiam,* 566f. *incipe quidquid potest* | *Medea,* 933f. *scelus est Iason genitor et maius scelus* | *Medea mater,* cf. *Tro.* 867ff. This self-awareness at times makes possible an effective compression, as in *Thy.* 476 *amat Thyesten frater?*

26–7 a fratre uincar...exedi mea The punctuation found in all modern editions requires Thyestes to retract his boast *uincam Thyesten...cunctos* when it has barely been uttered, and tamely to concede defeat to Atreus. Michael Müller was clearly right to punctuate 26–7 *a fratre... sepultis* as an indignant question, to which *uiscera exedi mea* supplies the negative answer (cf. also Anliker 105 n.31). This necessary alteration also makes the thought consistent with that of *Thyestes,* where Atreus plans the crime to be that of his brother (285 *hoc ipse faciet*), and Thyestes accepts full responsibility for the guilt (1087ff.).

Family rivalry in crime is a theme frequent in Seneca (cf. *Pho.* 335ff.) and particularly prominent in *Agamemnon* (cf. 44, 77ff., 124, 169 below) and *Thyestes* (18ff., 193ff., 1104ff.). Similar rhetoric is applied to affection, cf. *Anth. Lat.* 441 Riese (= *Epigr.* 49 Prato) *sic illos uincam, sic uincar rursus amando;* | *mutuus inter nos sic bene certet amor,* and to virtue, cf. Claud. *Pan. Prob.* 61f. *sed nati uicere patrem solique merentur* | *uictores audire Probi.*

26 plenus S. grotesquely plays on the meaning 'filled to satiety' with food or drink (cf. Ov. *Am.* 2.6.29, Cels. 3.20); compare *Ira* 3.15.2 *deinde ut satis illum plenum malis suis uidit* (of the Persian king who forced a father to consume his children), *Thy.* 890f. *pergam et implebo patrem* | *funere suorum.*

tribus The figure corresponds to that given in *Thyestes* 717ff., where Atreus' victims are Tantalus, Plisthenes, and a nameless *puer* (731f.); three children are also mentioned in schol. *ad* Eur. *Or.* 812 and ps.-Apoll. *Epit.* 2.13, though the latter source provides other names (Aglaos, Callileon, Orchomenos); Hyginus (*fab.* 88) names only Tantalus and Plisthenes. The reference to thirteen children in Aesch. *Ag.* 1605, if sound, is unique.

27 in me sepultis The commonplace is more straightforwardly treated in *Thy.* 1045ff., 1090ff. *si natos pater* | *humare et igni tradere extremo*

172

uolo, | *ego sum cremandus*; for other applications to Thyestes cf. Acc. *Atreus* 226 R² *natis sepulchro ipse est parens,* Manilius 5.461f. *uix una trium memorare sepulchra* | *ructantemque patrem natos* (with Housman's note); in Ov. *Met.* 6.665 it is used of Tereus: *seque uocat bustum miserabile nati.* The metaphor has been traced to Gorgias' γῦπες ἔμψυχοι τάφοι (*apud* anon. *de sublim.* 3.2, cf. Hermogenes p. 292.15, Sen. *Contr.* 10 *pr.* 9, Norden, *Antike Kunstprosa* 384f., 989), and is frequently transferred to other birds and beasts, cf. Enn. *Ann.* 138f. V³, Lucr. 5.993.

uiscera 'my own flesh' (*uiscera* is the poetic equivalent of *carnem,* cf. Axelson, *Unpoetische Wörter* 52); for *uiscera* = 'offspring' see Ovid, *Her.* 1.90 with Palmer's note, *Met.* 6.651, 10.465, Quint. *Inst.* 6 *pr.* 3 *infaustum opus . . . super immaturum funus consumpturis mea uiscera flammis inicere*; this may be the sense of *uiscera* in *Med.* 40 *per uiscera ipsa quaere supplicio uiam,* but see Costa *ad loc.*

28 nec hactenus *Hactenus* means 'so far (and no farther'), cf. *Thy.* 744f. *hactenus si stat nefas,* | *pius est* (Zwierlein, *Gnomon* xli (1969) 769), *Oed.* 954f., Housman, *CQ* xvii (1923) 169 (= *Classical Papers* iii.1081); for *nec hactenus* used as here cf. Val. Max. 4.7.3 *nec hactenus animum egisse contentus, etiam fugae eius comes accessit,* 6.8.7, Stat. *Th.* 3.96f.

maculauit The metaphorical force of *maculo* is somewhat weakened by the absence of an instrumental ablative, as in, e.g., Cic. *Rep.* 2.45 *rex ille . . . regis caede maculatus,* Livy 1.13.2 *ne parricidio macularent partus suos,* Virg. *Aen.* 10.850 *tuum maculaui crimine nomen,* Val. Max. 2.7.1 *exercitus . . . se foederis ictu maculauerat.* For the tropical use of *macula* and *maculare,* see E. Fantham, *Comparative studies in Republican Latin imagery* (1972) 60; the distinctions imposed by Dietzfelbinger in *T.L.L.* viii.28.61–29.60 are more than usually artificial. Note the similar use of *commaculo,* e.g. in Cic. *Cael.* 16, Sall. *Jug.* 102.5, *Hist.* 1.55.21.

29 maius aliud ausa . . . scelus Cf. *Cons. Pol.* 16.5 *hoc fuit in rebus humanis Fortuna, hoc erit: nihil inausum sibi reliquit, Epist.* 91.15 *sciat nihil inausum esse Fortunae.* The un-Senecan phrase *maius ausa matre mortifera malum* of the interpolated verse *Pha.* 688 (on which cf. Zwierlein, *Gnomon* xxxviii (1966) 686) may have been inspired by *maius ausa scelus* here.

30 natae . . . iubet This is the play's clearest reference to the oracle which directed Thyestes to produce an avenger by incest with his daughter (cf. ps.-Apoll. *Epit.* 2.14 with Frazer's note, Hyg. *fab.* 88, 254; Pearson on Soph. fr. 247 P, Ribbeck, *Römische Tragödie* 457ff.); it is alluded to in *sortis incertae* (38), *causa natalis tui* (48), and *auctore Phoebo gignor* (294).

nefandos petere concubitus For the phrase cf. Aesch. *P.V.* 858 θηρεύοντες οὐ θηρασίμους | γάμους (the sons of Aegyptus), Ov. *Met.* 6.540f. *utinam fecisse ante nefandos* | *concubitus,* 3.123f., 10.352f., Val. Max. 1.8 *ext.* 3 *illi nefarium concubitum uoluntaria morte pensarunt.*

31 non...nefas The transmitted text has been interpreted in three senses, none of which is entirely satisfactory.

The natural meaning of the words is 'I accepted the oracle's words fearlessly (*non pauidus = impauidus*), but in doing so I committed evil' (so Giomini and F. J. Miller). It is coherent only if Thyestes was unaware of the oracle's meaning when he heard its words; but the previous lines suggest that the oracle was unequivocal in its command. Also, *cepi* is hardly the right word for the proposed rendering: *feci* would be better, as in *Tro.* 1119 *fleuitque Achiuum turba quod fecit nefas.*

L. Herrmann seems to take *sed* as intensive: 'loin d'être épouvanté à l'annonce de ce forfait, je l'ai accepté'. *Sed*, however, is so used only to introduce an addition to a statement considered ambiguous or incomplete (as in the *Musterbeispiel*, Mart. 1.117.5 *et scalis habito tribus, sed altis*) or to strengthen and make more explicit the preceding statement (cf. *Anth. Lat.* 435 Riese = *Epigr.* 43 Prato *quaedam me (si credis) amat – sed dissilit, ardet,* Sen. *Pho.* 106f.), and neither condition is present here. (On intensive *sed* see Burman on Petr. *Sat.* 128, Mayor on Juv. 5.147, Friedländer on Mart. 1.117.5, Kroll, *Glotta* v (1914) 361, Löfstedt, *Peregrinatio Aetheriae* 179f.)

An acceptable sense might be obtained if *non* were taken, not with *pauidus*, but with *hausi*: 'I did not drink in the words timidly, but took hold of the crime.' This may be the view of Viansino (in the apparatus *ad loc.*) and of *T.L.L.* III.323.46ff. The normal use of *haurio* with *dicta*, etc., however, is against it: the verb implies that the subject 'takes in' the object of hearing or sight without reservation, whatever emotional reaction it provokes in him (this may indeed be terror, as in Virg. *Aen.* 6.559 *constitit Aeneas strepitumque exterritus hausit*). This emerges clearly from Stat. *Th.* 10.769ff.: *si uos placita hostia iuui, | si non attonitis uatis consulta recepi | auribus et (Thebis nondum credentibus) hausi,* where *hausi* must be stronger than the neutral *recepi (non attonitis auribus* is instructive as a parallel for *non pauidus*; cf. also *Oed.* 385 *uoces aure non timida hauriam*).

The transmitted text, then, cannot be satisfactorily interpreted. The clear source of trouble is *sed*; all difficulties vanish if *sed cepi* is replaced by a verb parallel in syntax and meaning to *hausi*. Koetschau's *suscepi* and Siegmund's *concepi* are therefore both on the right lines. Neither is perhaps certain, but *suscepi* fits the context better: *concipere nefas* is 'to plan or devise a crime' (Virg. *Aen.* 4.502, Hor. *C.* 2.13.8ff., Sen. *Pha.* 343), while Thyestes merely 'took up' an obligation laid on him by the oracle.

32 ergo ut *Vt* or *ne* often introduces rhetorical or ironic rather than true motives (see 185 below, with note); for *ergo* in such a context cf. Sen. *Suas.* 6.27 *ergo ut librum uelitis usque ad umbilicum reuoluere, adiciam suasoriam proximae similem* (Ovid uses the formula *ergo ne* in *Met.* 11.224ff., 15.173ff., *Tr.* 5.8.33f., but the motives mentioned are at least possible).

ut...parens 'that therefore I through all my stocke should parent still proceede' (Studley). *Ire per aliquem* has two senses, each of which aptly describes Thyestes' behaviour toward some of his offspring. The first is 'to devour', illustrated by Stat. *Th.* 8.474f. *primo tigris gauisa cruore | per totum cupit ire pecus*; the second is similar to the sexual sense of *inire*, cf. *Priapea* 74.1f. *per medios ibit pueros mediasque puellas* (with a play on the innocent meaning of *ire per medios*, 'to go through the midst of', as in Hor. *C.* 3.16.9f.), Martial 11.61.6 *modo qui per omnes uiscerum tubos ibat*. Thyestes has 'gone through' his children in two senses; hence the emphatic position of *omnes*. The meaning behind the words was grasped by Ascensius: 'filios ingessi in aluum meum et me in uterum filiae'.

parens The juxtaposition *liberos–parens* is intended to stress the violation of nature involved in Thyestes' acts; cf. *Thy.* 89f. *ducam in horrendum nefas | auus nepotes*, *Tro.* 248f. *at tuam natam parens | Helenae immolasti*, 28 above, 166 below with note.

33 nata...dignum The MS text requires *uterum grauem* to signify *natum*, since only the offspring of the union can be ironically called 'worthy to have Thyestes for a father'. The use of *uterus* to refer to the womb's product is not in itself difficult, cf. Ov. *Met.* 6.192f. *illa duorum | facta parens: uteri pars haec est septima nostri*, Celsus 2.10 *feminae uterum gerentes*, Tac. *Ann.* 1.59.1 *Arminium...rapta uxor, subiectus seruitio uxoris uterus uaecordem agebant*, but the addition of *grauis* poses real difficulties for this interpretation (*T.L.L.*'s parallels are illusory, since in Ov. *Met.* 9.684f. and *Octauia* 937f. *uterus grauis* must be taken literally).

Attempts at correction apparently begin with the scribe of N, who wrote *uterum grauem | et patre dignum* (i.e. the womb is worthy of its parent in being incestuous); *grauem* and *patre dignum*, however, form an impossibly ill-assorted pair. Viansino's *digna* has only its palaeographical plausibility to commend it, and is disastrous to the sense. Both lines of approach remove the ironic reference to Aegisthus as a fit descendant of Thyestes, which is surely the point of the lines. If emendation is required, something along the lines of *nata fert utero genus | me patre dignum* should be considered (*ferre utero*, cf. Ov. *Met.* 3.269, 8.133).

34 me patre dignum The sarcastic use of *dignus* or equivalent words is not limited to Seneca or to Latin, cf. Soph. *El.* 1487f., Cic. *Verr.* 4.37 *hominem dignissimum tuis moribus*, *Pis.* 8, *T.L.L.* v¹.1147.7ff., Lucian, *Cat.* 28. What merits notice is that Seneca's people often direct this sarcasm against themselves, as Thyestes does here; cf. *HF* 112f. *facere si quicquam apparo | dignum nouerca*, *Tro.* 861ff., *Pho.* 333, *Oed.* 879, *Thy.* 271. This self-consciousness is perhaps a deliberate reversal of the ancient concern with acting rightly for the sake of one's *dignitas*, cf. Sall. *Cat.* 51.6, 55.6, *Jug.* 31.18, 33.3, 63.8, etc.

35f. auo...diem Seneca's tetracolon is based on one by the declaimer

Murredius (Sen. *Contr.* 9.2.27): *seruiebat forum cubiculo, praetor meretrici, carcer conuiuio, dies nocti,* condemned by the elder Seneca as *tumidissime dictum: nouissima pars sine sensu dicta est, ut impleretur numerus.* In the Thyestean context *nocti diem* is not *sine sensu,* and it effectively raises the repercussions of Thyestes' crime from the human to the cosmic level; for a comparable widening of focus in the last member of a series cf. C. Gracchus fr. 43 (*ORF*[3] p. 187) *pueritia tua adulescentiae tuae inhonestamentum fuit, adulescentia senectuti dedecoramentum, senectus rei publicae flagitium.* Seneca may, however, be criticised for capping a tricolon on Thyestes' incest (cf. Soph. *O.T.* 1405ff.) with a climax that refers to a different crime.

miscui   The verb is often used of incestuous relations or their consequences, cf. Acc. fr. 207f. R[2] (*Atreus*) *matres conquinari regias,* | *contaminari stirpem ac misceri genus,* Manilius 5.463f., Sen. *Pha.* 171f. *miscere thalamos patris et nati apparas* | *uteroque prolem capere confusam impio?,* Rut. Nam. 2.44, Sid. Apoll. *C.* 9.107.

36 nocti diem   It is revealing that the first of the three references made in the play to the sun's reversal should be the most allusive (cf. 297f. and 908f. with note); on this feature of Senecan style see Seidensticker 156ff. The demand on the listener is slight, since the banquet and its consequences were a familiar theme (as early as Pl. *Rud.* 508f., on which cf. Ed. Fraenkel, *Elementi Plautini* 72), cf. Venini on Stat. *Th.* 11.129, adding Manil. 3.18f., 5.464, Luc. 7.451, Sen. *Thy.* 51, 123f., 1035, Mart. 3.45); it figured prominently in tragedies by Accius (223ff. R[2]) and Varius, and perhaps in the *Thyestes* of Pacuvius and the satiric *Oedipothyestes* of Varro; the account in Hyg. *fab.* 88 may derive from a lost Greek source, perhaps dramatic.

37f. sed...fides   'But now at last, after I am dead, the promise of the doubtful oracle looks with favour on us, worn out by griefs.'
Sera tandem respicit fessos malis recalls Virg. *Ecl.* 1.27ff. *libertas quae sera tamen respexit inertem...respexit tamen et longo post tempore uenit;* S. replaces Virgil's elliptical *sera tamen respexit* with an unequivocal *tandem,* which confirms the idea already present in *demum* and *post fata* (= *post mortem,* cf. Virg. *Aen.* 4.20, Prop. 4.11.63, Sen. *HF* 612). The Virgilian reminiscence may help to account for S.'s bold use of *respicio* in its providential sense with *fides;* the expression is more easily understood if one has been reminded of Virgil's half-personified *libertas.*

sortis...fides   'The promise made by the oracle', cf. Cic. *Att.* 9.19.3 *pacis fides nulla est,* Sen. *Tro.* 529f. *sollicita Danaos pacis incertae fides* | *semper enebit, Thy.* 327f. *prolis incertae fides* | *ex hoc petatur scelere; fides* might also = 'fulfilment', cf. Ovid, *Met.* 3.527 *dicta fides sequitur, responsaque uatis aguntur,* 8.711.
It remains to decide between *incertae* (E) and *incestae* (A). Since the oracle was not uncertain in its terms (cf. 31 above), *sortis incertae fides* would mean

'the oracle's uncertain promise' (i.e. uncertain because not yet fulfilled), as in *Tro.* 529 *pacis incertae fides* means 'untrustworthy assurance of peace'. *Sors incesta* would be 'an oracle which commanded incest', on the analogy of *Pha.* 1195 *crimine incesto, Octauia* 521 *incestus Aegyptus,* Stat. *Th.* 2.464 *incesti thalami. Incestus* is the more easily corrupted word, and it has in fact been altered to *incertus* in several passages (*Pha.* 1195, *Oed.* 645, 1026; *Oct.* 260); indeed, *incestus* has been preserved only where the context clearly rules out the substitution of *incertus* (*Pha.* 1185, 560; *Oct.* 521, 536, 854). The present passage offers no such protection. The corruption of *incertae* to *incestae* could only be the result of interpolation, specifically an attempt to improve on the colourless *incertae*. The vagueness of this reading is, however, a strong point in its favour, since Seneca's style often shows a preference for the abstract over the particular (see note on 340ff. below). The uncertainty caused by the oracle's slow fulfilment is also more suited to this context (note *tandem, demum, post fata*) than the incestuous nature of its command, about which enough has been said in the preceding lines.

39 rex ille regum The title is applied to Agamemnon by Cicero, *Att.* 14.17A.2 and by Livy 45.27.9 (in later writers cf. Auson. *opusc.* 218.1 Peiper, Dracontius, *Orest.* 25); elsewhere in Seneca the idea appears in the expressions *regum...maximus rector* (*Tro.* 978) and *regum tyranne* (*Tro.* 303 – a taunt by Pyrrhus). *Rex regum* could describe Agamemnon's status in Homer, but Cicero and Livy may have been thinking as well of its honorific use by Eastern potentates (cf. F. Bilabel, *Geschichte der Vorderasiens und Ägyptens* (1927) 207–14, A. S. F. Gow, *JHS* xlviii (1928) 133f.).

ductor...ducum This expression recurs in 1007 below, where it is again used to gloat over Agamemnon's downfall. In Cicero, *Sen.* 31 Agamemnon is *dux ille Graeciae,* but Ovid's phrases *dux erat ille ducum* (*Her.* 8.46) and *summa ducum* (*Am.* 1.9.37) are closer to Seneca's; the elevated, and mainly poetic, *ductor* (cf. Virg. *Aen.* 2.14 and Servius *ad loc.*; in prose, e.g., Cic. *Tusc.* 1.89, Livy 1.28.6) may have been suggested by Virg. *Aen.* 11.266ff., perhaps Seneca's source for the entire passage: *ipse Mycenaeus magnorum ductor Achiuum | coniugis infandae prima inter limina dextra | oppetiit, deuictam Asiam subsedit adulter.* Seneca was himself imitated by the author of *Octauia* (41–4); there may also be a faint echo of these lines in Dracontius, *Orest.* 25f. *ductorum ductor, regum rex dux Agamemnon | post duo lustra redux et post duo bella triumphans.*

41 Iliaca...suis The hyperbole was originally connected with the fleet of Xerxes (Herodotus 7.45) but was later applied to any large group of ships; for examples see Reid on Cic. *Fin.* 2.112, Pease on Virg. *Aen.* 4.582 *latet sub classibus aequor,* Mayor on Juv. 10.173ff., Miniconi 210. *Tegere maria* (or a similar expression) appears in Sen. *Suas.* 2.3, *Eleg. in Maec.* 45, *Octauia* 42, ps.-Sen. *Epigr.* 69.7 Prato, Claud. *Ruf.* 2.123, Sidon. Apoll. *C.* 5.449;

other writers prefer the more vivid *sterno* or *consterno*, cf. Manil. 1.776, Juv. 10.173ff., D. A. Kidd, *CQ* N.S. xix (1969) 196f.

42 post decima Phoebi lustra *Phoebi* makes it clear that *lustra* cannot here mean 'a period of five years'; expressions like Ovid's *nondum Troia fuit lustris obsessa duobus* (*Am.* 3.6.26; cf. *Ars* 3.15) or Lucan's *bellantem geminis tenuit te Gallia lustris* (1.283) are therefore not comparable, and the emendations *bina* and *gemina* are misguided. *Phoebi lustrum* must mean, as Farnaby recognised, *annuus solis cursus*; an exact parallel is given by Manilius 3.580 *lustra decem...solis*, and note also Lucr. 5.931 *multaque per caelum solis uoluentia lustra*; *lustra* is similarly used, though without a qualifying word, in Manilius 3.321 *per singula lustra* and Stat. *S.* 3.1.45 *annua ueloci peragunt certamina lustro*. (It is possible that *lustrum* = *annus* in Sil. 13.558f.: souls there are purified *mille peractis | lustris*, while in Virg. *Aen.* 6.748 the same process takes place *mille...per annos*.)

Post decima lustra blends *post decem lustra* and *post decimum lustrum* as in *Iliad* 8.404f. ἐς δεκάτους...ἐνιαυτούς combines ἐς δέκα ἐνιαυτούς and ἐς δέκατον ἐνιαυτόν. This use of the plural ordinal in place of a whole number seems to have no Latin parallel before Seneca, a circumstance which may account for the variant *dena* found in A. E's text is, however, supported by a good parallel in Martial 12.31.7f. *post septima lustra reuerso | has Marcella domos paruaque regna dedit*, cf. also Juv. 4.92 *sic multas hiemes atque octogesima uidit | solstitia*, Hofmann–Szantyr 213, B. Löfstedt, *Eranos* lvi (1958) 206f., O. Zwierlein, *Philologus* cxiii (1969) 263.

deuicto Ilio Though perhaps inspired by Virg. *Aen.* 11.268 *deuictam Asiam*, Seneca's language also recalls that of a Roman triumph, cf. Pl. *Pers.* 753 *hostibus uictis, ciuibus saluis, re placida*, *Truc.* 75 (cf. Ed. Fraenkel, *Elementi Plautini* 228), Livy 38.42.12 *nunc certe, perfecto Aetolico bello, recepta ab Antiocho Asia, deuictis Gallis* (and 8.31.5, 38.50.3, 45.13.17, etc.), Suet. *Cal.* 1.

43 daturus 'only to yield his neck'. The primary stress of the future participle, as in *daturus* (23) and *subiture* (828), is on the inevitability of the action (cf. Hor. *C.* 4.7.9f. *aestas | interitura*, Luc. 1.12 *bella...nullos habitura triumphos*), but in this passage there is as well an ironic suggestion of purpose (see on 185 below).

Dare iugulum suggests either a defeated gladiator (cf. Cic. *Mil.* 11, Sen. *Epist.* 30.8, *Tranq.* 11.5, Tac. *Hist.* 2.41, ps.-Quint. *Decl. mai.* 9.21) or a sacrificial animal, as in Juv. 10.268 (of Priam) *ut uetulus bos, | qui domini cultris tenue et miserabile collum | praebet*. The recurrent use of sacrificial language in the play (cf. 219f., 898f.) makes the second interpretation more likely.

44 iam iam 'at any moment now', cf. Virg. *Aen.* 6.602 *silex iam iam lapsura*, Ov. *Met.* 1.535f. *alter inhaesuro similis iam iamque tenere | sperat*, Sen. *Med.* 949, *Tro.* 1141.

natabit Cf. Virg. *Aen.* 3.625f. *sanieque aspersa natarent | limina.*

sanguine alterno 'retributive bloodshed'; the idea had been expressed in different words by Ovid (*Her.* 8.51f.): *iugulo ...Aegisthus aperto | tecta cruentauit quae pater ante tuus.* With this sense of *alternus* the plural is more natural, as in 65 *alternos...fluctus*, Claud. *Ruf.* 1.83 *haec [sc.* Megaera] *Agamemnonios...penates | alternis lusit iugulis*, but for the singular note *nisu... alterno* in 439. Quite different is the force of *alternus* in such passages as Prop. 2.30.21 *spargere et alterna communis caede Penates* or Sen. *Epist.* 95.31 *non pudet homines...gaudere sanguine alterno*, where its meaning is 'mutual' or 'reciprocal'.

45ff. Thyestes' vision of the future is in two parts, each of which moves from an asyndetic series generally suggesting violence (*enses secures tela*; *scelera...dolus caedes cruor*) to a particular foreshadowing of the later action (*diuisum...caput*; *parantur epulae*). In 45 E's *securem* is therefore inappropriately specific, and the plural of A is to be preferred. With the asyndeta compare Petr. *Sat.* 123.215f. *arma cruor caedes incendia totaque bella | ante oculos uolitant* and for Senecan material see Canter 169f. It is a favourite device of Republican drama, cf. Pac. 53, 301 R², Acc. 349, 415, 550, 595 R².

45f. diuisum...caput The picture parallels that recalled by Sophocles' Electra (98f. ὅπως δρῦν ὑλοτόμοι | σχίζουσι κάρα φονίῳ πελέκει) and is slightly at variance with the facts of the murder as presented in 898ff. below: there the head is amputated, while *diuisum...caput* without a qualifying word (e.g. *corpore*) suggests that the head itself is split by the blow (cf. Virg. *Aen.* 9.750f. *mediam ferro...frontem | diuidit*; the discrepancy, however, appears to be without significance.

52 respice ad matrem: decet A similar argument is used in self-address by Atreus (*Thy.* 241ff.): *quid stupes? tandem incipe animosque sume: Tantalum et Pelopem aspice; ad haec manus exempla poscuntur meae,* and in persuasion by Jocasta (*Pho.* 646f.): *regnabit. est haec poena. si dubitas, auo | patrique crede*; compare also Ovid, *Met.* 6.634 *cui sis nupta uide...marito.* Aegisthus' concern to commit only crimes suited to him is typically Senecan, cf. *Med.* 49f. *haec uirgo feci...maiora iam me scelera post partus decent, Tro.* 1002 *perge mactator senum; | et hic decet te sanguis,* 124 below.

53f. sed cur...mora The phenomena described here appear as an *adynaton* in Ovid, *Pont.* 2.4.25f. *longa dies citius brumali sidere noxque | tardior hiberna solstitialis erit.*

sed Prologue speakers in Euripides similarly break off with ἀλλά, cf. *Hipp.* 51, *Med.* 46, *Ion* 76, *Tro.* 45, *Phoen.* 84, *Ba.* 55; note *sed* in Plautus, *Miles* 54.

hiberna...mora The arrangement of the line – two adjectives, a verb, two substantives in chiastic order (a b c B A) – is not uncommon in Seneca, cf. 711, 901 below, *HF* 367, *Thy.* 113; the variant a b c A B is also found, e.g. *Pho.* 95, *Tro.* 240; a more complex form involving two lines (*HF* 457/8) is discussed by Seidensticker 162 n.21. For the construction generally see Norden on *Aeneid* VI, pp. 393ff., also Bömer on Ovid, *Met.* 2.163, Canter 175.

In Greek and Senecan tragedy the action often begins at or just before dawn, cf. Soph. *Ajax* 21, *Ant.* 16, 100, *El.* 17ff., Eur. *El.* 102, *Ion* 82ff., *I.A.* 1ff., Sen. *HF* 123f., *Oed.* 1ff., *Thy.* 120f., *Pha.* 39ff.; *Octauia* 1ff.

56 Phoebum moramur Ghosts are conventionally released for limited periods of time (cf. Aesch. *Persae* 693, Pacuvius, *Iliona* fr. 202 R², Prop. 4.7.89f., Virg. *Aen.* 5.738ff., *Hamlet* 1.5.88ff.), and often must leave the upper world at dawn; Seneca's Juno in *HF*, more demon than goddess, hastens away at daybreak (123f.). With Thyestes, however, the pattern is pointedly reversed, and day refuses to begin until this noisome revenant has vanished. In the prologue of *Thyestes*, the atmosphere of evil generated by Tantalus' visit gives the sun a premonition of the day's event: *en ipse Titan dubitat an iubeat sequi | cogatue habenis ire periturum diem* (120f.; cf. Luc. 7.1ff., Claud. *Ruf.* 2.336f.). Thyestes' words are echoed in May's *Tragedy of Julia Agrippina* (1628), 93ff.: 'Wee must no longer bide, the cocks doe crow...would Titan rise, but that he feares to see | such instruments of Hells impiety. | The Gods themselves forbid our longer stay | for feare our presence should retard the day.'

redde iam mundo diem The command might be taken as addressed to Phoebus (so Ascensius) or as directed to Thyestes himself (for which cf. *Oed.* 1051 *i profuge uade*). Marston's imitation (in *II Antonio and Mellida* III.ii.98ff.) suggests that he read the line in the first sense: 'Darkness, make flight; graves, eat your dead again: | let's repossess our shrouds. Why lags delay? | Mount, sparkling brightness, give the world his day.' So too, perhaps, did the author of *Octauia* 2ff. *surgit Titan...mundoque diem | reddit clarum*. Gronovius' *reddo* perhaps deserves consideration for its greater clarity and apt pomposity. The correption *reddŏ* can be paralleled without difficulty, cf. *Pho.* 304 *quaerŏ maturam uiam*, *Med.* 518 *cedŏ defessus malis*, both in the same position in the line (cf. R. Hartenberger, *De O Finali* 65). In *Med.* 1005 *dedo* appears in A as *dede*, but the structure of the line (first person statement leading to a command addressed to another) rather supports *redde*.

CHORUS (57–107)

Unlike the *parodos* of a Greek tragedy, the first choral song in Seneca need not embody a clear awareness of or reaction to the situation set forth in the opening scene; indeed, such a close connection is found only in *Troades* (67ff.), *Medea* (56ff.), and *Oedipus* (110ff.). The genuine plays of Seneca also fail to distinguish the first from later choral odes by the means usual in

Greek tragedy: self-identification of the chorus, references to the chorus' motive for coming to the scene of the play, and so on.[1] In *Agamemnon* the dramatic isolation of the opening chorus is complete: no line of the ode reveals either a definite *persona* or a specific allusion to the situation revealed by Thyestes' ghost.[2]

Though spoken in a theatrical vacuum, the words of the chorus have obvious relevance to their context; not, perhaps, the crude 'paraphrase' of the prologue detected by some critics,[3] but a set of reflections which permits the audience to comprehend the events of the drama at a level inaccessible to the emotionally involved participants. Those events are not specifically named, but their place in the moral scheme outlined by the chorus is unmistakably indicated (77ff. *quas non arces scelus alternum | dedit in praeceps,* eqs.).[4] The impersonal tone adopted by this and other Senecan choruses suits their function: not to offer sympathy (and thus additional *affectus*) but enlightenment, to render the individual case intelligible by describing the moral facts of which it is a demonstration.[5] The position of the reflective ode between the violent emotions of the first two acts is evidence as well of a sound sense of dramatic (or, perhaps better, of rhetorical) structure.[6]

Given the function of the chorus just described, it is not surprising that the ode on mutability is a hall-mark of Senecan tragedy.[7] A distinct sub-group is made up of odes in which captive women lament the change of fortune which has caused their present misery: 589ff. below, *Tro.* 67ff., and *HO* 104ff. In these choral songs general observations are combined with, and usually overshadowed by, personal expressions of grief. *Agamemnon* alone contains odes of both the generic and the personal type; structure thus reflects content, since the play is built around two related falls from fortune – Troy's and Agamemnon's.

The first ode of *Agamemnon* is remarkable for its merging, under the unifying concept of Fortuna, of several lines of thought which appear separately elsewhere. This is not unusual in the treatment of commonplaces, and the

---

[1] In *Troades*, the chorus is identified and invited to sing by Hecuba (63f.). *Octauia* is notable for its adherence to Greek technique (cf. 273ff. *quae fama modo uenit ad aures?* eqs.).

[2] For the impersonal quality of Senecan choruses, see F. Leo, *Rh. Mus.* lii (1897) 510ff., Zwierlein, *Rezitationsdramen* 74–6.

[3] First, apparently, by Nisard; cf. also Canter 29f., Runchina 190f.

[4] The closest parallel is perhaps *Pha.* 274ff. (but the specific application is made in a more obvious way in 356f.).

[5] Choral odes containing generic observations fulfil this purpose in Greek tragedy as well (Soph. *O.T.* 1186ff., *Ant.* 332ff., and Eur. *Hipp.* 1268ff. are clear examples).

[6] Similar contrast is seen in *HF* 123ff., *Med.* 56ff., *Oed.* 882ff., *Agam.* 310ff., 808ff., etc.

[7] *HF* 524ff., *Pha.* 972ff., 1141ff., *Oed.* 987ff., *Thy.* 546ff.; cf. *HO* 583ff.

following catalogue is bound to be artificial to an extent in its distinctions, but analysis may be useful in demonstrating the ode's exceptional range and diversity. The following ideas may be distinguished:

(*a*) The lives of those enjoying good fortune are attended with anxiety, since they are most vulnerable to sudden reversals. The theme is alluded to in Soph. *Phil.* 178f. and 502f., Eur. *Pho.* 552, and treated explicitly in Eur. *Ion* 621ff.; cf. also Xen. *Ages.* 5.6, Publ. Syr. 162 *excelsos multo facilius casus nocet*, Sall. *Cat.* 51.12, Sen. *Tranq.* 10.6. The dangers of high position (poison, treachery, etc.) are also part of the *locus de diuitiis*.[1] This theme dominates the first section of the ode (57–76).

(*b*) Power and wealth lead to pride and wrongdoing, which are punished by the collapse of power. This view is common in early Greek poetry (cf. Denniston–Page on Aesch. *Ag.* 750ff.) and it is in general that of Aeschylus and Sophocles.[2] The thought enters the ode in the figures of Bellona and Erinys (81ff.), representing the strife and ruin that flow from moral decay. In regarding civil disorder as the punishment of degenerate prosperity Seneca was presumably influenced by the application of this idea to Rome itself in the rhetorical and historiographical tradition; Lucan on the causes of the Civil War (1.158ff.) may serve as another specimen of this outlook.[3]

(*c*) Things which attain a size or state of development far beyond the ordinary risk dissolution from internal pressures (cf. 87–9). Examples of this idea are predominantly Roman; even generic statements such as Sen. *Contr.* 1 *pr.* 7 (*fati*) *maligna perpetuaque in rebus omnibus lex est, ut ad summum perducta rursus ad infimum, uelocius quidem quam ascenderant, relabantur*[4] may be influenced by its application to Rome of the late Republic and Empire, as in, e.g., Livy, *pr.* 4 (*res*) *quae ab exiguis profecta initiis eo creuerit ut iam magnitudine laboret sua*, Hor. *Epod.* 16.2, Prop. 2.15.45f.[5]

(*d*) Whatever is eminent is struck down by a jealous god. A pure statement of this belief is found in Herodotus (7.10 ὁρᾷς τὰ ὑπερέχοντα ζῷα ὡς κεραυνοῖ ὁ θεός... φιλέει γὰρ ὁ θεὸς τὰ ὑπερέχοντα πάντα κολούειν). The unmoralised form of the idea is absent from the outlook of Aeschylus, Sophocles, and Pindar, but prayers to avert φθόνος attest its continuing power.[6] Roman writers do not often speak explicitly of *inuidia deorum*, but

---

[1] Cf. J. de Decker, *Iuuenalis Declamans* (1913) 144ff.

[2] See Fraenkel on Aesch. *Ag.* 757ff.

[3] J. Brisset, *Les idées politiques de Lucain* (1964) 41f. (see also de Decker 36ff.); H. Fuchs, *HSCP* lxiii (1958) 376ff. cites Greek evidence for the belief that prosperity leads to political decline.

[4] Also Sen. *Suas.* 1.3 *quidquid ad summum peruenit, incremento non relinquit locum*, *Epist.* 19.9 (citing Maecenas) *ipsa enim altitudo attonat summa*.

[5] Further examples in E. Dutoit, *REL* xiv (1936) 370, E. Lefèvre, *Hermes* xciv (1966) 487ff.

[6] Cf. Aesch. *Ag.* 904, Soph. *Phil.* 776, Pind. *P.* 10.19f., *I.* 7.39ff.

some of the *exempla* illustrating *sidunt ipso pondere magna* are traditionally linked to ideas of φθόνος θεῶν.

(*e*) Fortuna takes pleasure in casting down those she has placed in her power by raising them to high position (alluded to in *quidquid in altum | Fortuna tulit, ruitura leuat* 100f.). Fortuna's malicious pleasure is more explicit in, e.g., Hor. *C.* 1.34.12ff., 3.29.49ff., Sen. *N.Q.* 3 *pr.* 7 *nescit enim quiescere, gaudet laetis tristia substituere, utique miscere*; the suggestion of purpose in *ruitura* is further developed in *Octauia* 379 *alte extulisti, grauius ut ruerem.*[1]

(*f*) The life of moderation is free of such danger and is thus preferable to that of distinction. This idea is common in Greek tragedy (cf. Aesch. *Ag.* 772ff., Eur. *Med.* 123ff., *Hipp.* 1013ff., *Ion* 625ff.), where it is bound up with the praise of σωφροσύνη in the widest sense (cf. Aesch. *Eum.* 529 παντὶ μέσῳ τὸ κράτος θεὸς ὤπασεν, with Groeneboom's parallels). Idealised pictures of the humble life are also a staple of the declamatory *locus de diuitiis* and are frequent in Seneca's prose and verse;[2] Juvenal's *rarus uenit in cenacula miles* (10.18) memorably encapsulates this aspect of the topic. The attractions of the simple life conclude the ode on a contrasting note; for the technique *Thy.* 391ff. and *Pha.* 1137ff. may be compared.[3]

The concatenation of diverse views on instability which characterises the ode finds a remarkable parallel (cited by Del Rio) in an unassigned fragment of tragic rhesis (*adesp.* 547 N²):

τὰ μεγάλα δῶρα τῆς τύχης ἔχει φόβον
καὶ τὸ πάνυ λαμπρὸν οὐκ ἀκίνδυνον κυρεῖ,
οὐδ' ἀσφαλὲς πᾶν ὕψος ἐν θνητῷ γένει·
ὃ περιέστρεψεν ἢ χρόνος τις ἢ φθόνος,
ἐπὰν ἐπ' ἄκρον τις τοῦ καλῶς πράττειν δράμῃ.
ἡ δὲ μεσότης ἐν πᾶσιν ἀσφαλεστέρα,
τὸ μήτε λίαν ἐν ταπεινῷ τῆς τύχης
μέρει φέρεσθαι μήτ' ἐν ὑψηλῷ πάλιν.
ἢν γὰρ πέσῃ τις ἐξ ἐλάσσονος μέτρου,

---

[1] Later examples in Min. Fel. *Oct.* 37.9 *in hoc altius tolluntur, ut decidant altius*, Claud. *Ruf.* 1.22f. *tolluntur in altum | ut lapsu grauiore ruant*; see further A. Cameron, *Claudian* 331 n.1. In Juv. 10.105ff. ironic purpose is transferred to the victim: *numerosa parabat | excelsae turris tabulata, unde altior esset | casus et impulsae praeceps immane ruinae.*

[2] Cf. *Pha.* 483–539, *Thy.* 449–70, *Epist.* 90.41; note Sen. *Contr.* 2.1.29, where the commonplace nature of the idea is evident: *et illum locum egregie tractauit: omnes cibos suspectos habebo, omnes potiones…non uenenum pauperes timent, non heredem.* Seneca's treatments draw much poetic colouring from Virg. *G.* 2.495ff. and Ov. *Met.* 1.89ff., and are thus closely linked to the topic of the Golden Age (on which cf. Bömer on *F.* 4.395ff., B. Gatz, *Weltalter, goldene Zeit und sinnverwandte Vorstellungen* (1967)).

[3] Giomini 37.

COMMENTARY 57–58f.

εὐπερικάλυπτον ἔσχε τὴν δυσπραξίαν·
ὄγκου δὲ μεγάλου πτῶμα γίγνεται μέγα,
πρὸς γὰρ τὸ λαμπρὸν ὁ φθόνος βιάζεται,
σφάλλει δ' ἐκείνους οὓς ἂν ὑψώσῃ τύχη.

The similarity of sentiments is obvious, but there is no reason to believe that the Greek passage served Seneca as a model. Both are written with the view of a capricious, amoral Tyche which emerges in late Euripides[1] and became commonplace in Hellenistic cult and thought.[2] Though this conception percolated to the Romans through several channels – drama, history,[3] philosophy, rhetoric – Seneca's treatment of the topic is characteristically coloured by sources near to hand, Horatian moralising (*C.* 2.10 and 3.1 in particular) and declamatory rhetoric.[4] Specifically Stoic thinking on Tyche–Fortuna plays no significant part in this ode, but is reserved for the lament of the Trojan captives.

57ff. The hymnic tone of the opening apostrophe is not maintained: by line 72 Fortuna has passed into the third person (on hymns to Fortuna see Nisbet–Hubbard on Hor. *C.* 1.35). The simile beginning *non sic Libycis Syrtibus aequor* (63ff.) is essentially decorative; like other extended comparisons in Seneca, however, it is allowed to develop beyond the needs of the context and must in the end be choked off with an awkward reminder of the object of comparison (*ut praecipites regum casus | Fortuna rotat*, 71f.). On similes in Seneca see Grimal on *Pha.* 764ff., Zwierlein, *Rezitationsdramen* 117ff.

57f. regnorum magnis fallax | Fortuna bonis Fortuna is deceitful toward the riches that accompany rule; for the dative compare Pliny, *N.H.* 3.80 *nauigiis fallax*, Tac. *Hist.* 1.22 *potentibus infidum, sperantibus fallax*, and for *bona regnorum* note *Oed.* 687f. *solutus onere regio | regni bonis fruor*. The moralising strain is similar to that in *Oed.* 6 (*regnum* is a *fallax bonum*) and *Oct.* 34f. (the *fallax aula* deceives with its *facile bonum*).

58f. in praecipiti dubioque *In praecipiti* = 'on the brink', here of

---

[1] Cf. *Ion* 1512ff., *Helen* 412, Seidensticker 74 n.28 with bibliography; note, however, *Helen* 1137ff.

[2] On cults of Tyche see Nilsson, *GGR²* II.200, Rohde, *Griechische Roman²* 296ff.; in literature note, e.g., Chaeremon fr. 19 N², Theophrastus *apud* [Plut.] *Cons. Apoll.* 6, Menander fr. 417b Kock, 463 Körte, Demetrius of Phalerum fr. 79–81 Wehrli, A. Körte, *SB Sächs. Akad. Wiss.*, Phil.-Hist. Klasse lxxxix/3 (1937) 14 n.1.

[3] Cf. Walbank, *Commentary on Polybius* 1.16–26, D. C. Earl, *JRS* lv (1965) 236 on Sallust.

[4] On the *locus de Fortuna* see Nisbet–Hubbard on Hor. *C.* 1.34.12; also Ov. *Tr.* 1.5.25ff., 3.7.41f. (I. Kajanto, *Ovid's conception of Fate* (1961) 31ff.), Juv. 3.38ff.

ruin, elsewhere of death (as a medical term, cf. Hor. *S.* 2.3.292, Cels. 2.6.1, Ov. *Met.* 12.378); cf. Sen. *Epist.* 23.6 *in praecipiti uoluptas stat: ad dolorem uergit nisi modum tenuit*, and compare *in ancipiti* in Sen. *Tranq.* 10.6 *illi rursus, quos sors iniqua in ancipiti posuit, tutiores erunt...fortunam suam quam maxime poterunt in planum deferendo*.

59 locas There may be an echo of Virg. *Aen.* 11.426f. *multos...in solido rursus Fortuna locauit* (note *locare* of *fata* in *Tro.* 656 *illum fata iam in tuto locant*).

nimis excelsos *Nimis* suggests that excessive power or wealth is to be the subject of the ode, cf. Petr. *Sat.* 120.80 *Fors cui nulla placet nimium secura potestas*. The following section, however, states the belief that all those in high position lead uncertain lives (*excelsus* in this sense, Sall. *Cat.* 51.12 *qui magno imperio praediti in excelso aetatem agunt*, Sen. *Thy.* 447 *dum excelsus steti*; of wealth ps.-Sall. *Epist.* 2.1.1, Val. Max. 1.6.12). In the last part of the ode (90–100), the vision extends to natural phenomena for which being *nimis excelsus* means being dangerously conspicuous (cf. Livy 2.9.3 *nihil excelsum, nihil quod supra cetera emineat in ciuitatibus fore*, *Octauia* 471 *quidquid excelsum est, cadat*).

61 tenuere 'have ever obtained': for the generalising perfect cf. 91 below, *Pha.* 1134f. *tremuit telo Iouis altisoni | Caucasus ingens*, Sen. *Suas.* 2.3 *numquam solido stetit superba felicitas*, Juv. 10.7f., Kühner–Stegmann 1.132.9.

certum...sui = *cui credere licet*, cp. Sen. *Epist.* 91.16 *ad omnia patienda pares sumus: nemo altero fragilior est, nemo in crastinum sui certior*.

62 alia ex aliis cura The usual constructions for describing a series of cares, one after another, are *alia ex alia cura* (cf. Lucr. 4.821 *alia ex alia facies aetasque sequatur*, Sen. *de Otio* 1.2) or *aliae ex aliis curae* (cf. Virg. *Aen.* 3.494 *alia ex aliis in fata uocamur*, Ov. *Met.* 15.253, Sen. *Epist.* 19.5, *V.B.* 5.4); the combination of singular and plural is elsewhere found only in distributive constructions which are not parallel. The emendation *alia ex alia* is obvious and old (Fabricius in 1566 cited it from a 'liber uetustus'), but it is better to regard *alia ex aliis cura* as a deliberate variation of the usual construction, emphasising the number of *curae* which have preceded the present one.

64ff. The use of sea- and storm-imagery in describing human emotions is old and widespread (J. Kahlmeyer, *Seesturm und Schiffbruch als Bild im antiken Schrifttum* (diss. Greifswald 1934) 19ff. gives a partial compilation); this passage is close in thought and expression to Prop. 2.5.11ff. *non ita Carpathiae uariant Aquilonibus undae | nec dubio nubes uertitur atra Noto | quam* eqs. and 2.9.33ff. *non sic incerto mutantur flamine Syrtes | nec folia hiberno tam tremefacta Noto, | quam* eqs. (cf. also *Pha.* 764ff.). Like Propertius, Seneca attempts to bring the simile to life with proper names, but with little success. The Syrtes lose much of their evocative power by being placed in a peripheral syntactic position, while the northern scene, perhaps inspired by Ovid's poems of exile, lacks any real point of contact with the object of comparison (note *turget* 66 and *rotat* 72).

64 Libycis Syrtibus On the commonplace cf. Pease on Virg. *Aen.* 4.41, Nisbet–Hubbard on Hor. *C.* 1.22.5; medieval examples in Walther 30948–9.

65 furit...uoluere = *furiose uoluit*, cf. Manil. 5.660 with Housman's note, *T.L.L.* VI. 1.1626.20ff., Nisbet–Hubbard on Hor. *C.* 1.15.27.

alternos...fluctus Cp. Soph. *Tr.* 112ff. τις | κύματ᾽ ἂν εὑρέϊ πόντῳ | βάντ᾽ ἐπιόντα τ᾽ ἴδοι. For *alternus* cf. 439 below.

66ff. non Euxini...polo The geographical details of these lines may owe something to Ovid's poems of exile; cf. *Tr.* 5.10.1f. *ter frigore constitit Hister,* | *facta est Euxini dura ter unda maris, Pont.* 4.9.2, 4.13.39f., *Tr.* 5.2.64.

69f. ubi...Bootes S. departs from the traditional account of Bootes to emphasise the extreme northerly setting of the simile (cf. F. Harder, *Festschrift J. Vahlen* (1900) 449). Bootes is not a circumpolar constellation, and is indeed known to poets from Homer onwards for the slowness of its setting (cf. *Od.* 5.272, Arat. *Phaen.* 581ff., Germ. *Arat.* 139, Manil. 1.314, Sen. *Med.* 315, *Octauia* 234 (with Pedroli's note), Bömer on Ov. *F.* 2.153, Häbler in *RE* III.717f.). Nor does it seem plausible that Seneca has confounded Bootes with the Bear, whose fixed position is equally well attested (cf. *Il.* 18.489f., Cic. *N.D.* 2.105 (with Pease's note), Manil. 5.695, Sen. *Med.* 758f., etc.). The movements of the stars, however, depend upon one's point of vantage (see Haupt on Ov. *Met.* 2.171f.), and, just as Bootes is said by Lucan to set quickly in the shorter nights of the antipodes (3.249ff., with Housman's note), here it is turned into a fixed constellation in the frozen north. In a similar fashion Housman (*CR* xlix (1935) 167f. = *Collected Papers* III.1246f.) emends and explains this fragment of Cornelius Gaetulicus on the Britanni (p. 123 Morel):

> Non aries illum uerno ferit aere cornu,
> Cnosia nec geminos praecedunt cornua, tantum
> sicca Lycaonius resupinat plaustra Bootes.

(MS praecidunt cornua tauri)

Tantum resupinat are taken together: 'Bootes keeps his Wain supreme and shifts it to no other position' (Housman); *sicca...plaustra* corresponds to Seneca's *immunis aquis* and *lucida...plaustra*.

69 immunis Cp. Homer's ἄμμορος, used of the Bear (*Il.* 18.490). S. may have taken the word from Ovid (cf. *Met.* 13.293, *F.* 4.575), replacing Ovid's genitive with the ablative (for which cf. *Pha.* 1054, *Oed.* 52, *Epist.* 85.3; *Octauia* 414).

72 rotat Here *rotat* means 'keeps in motion', and the action of Fortuna is the same as that of Clotho in *Thy.* 617f. *prohibet...Clotho* | *stare fortunam, rotat omne fatum,* of *casus* in *Pha.* 1123 *quanti casus humana rotant,* of the Stoic *series rerum* in *N.Q.* 2.35.2 *sic ordinem fati rerum aeterna series rotat,* and of Isis in

Apul. *Met.* 11.25 *tu rotas orbem* (compare *uersare* in Virg. *Ecl.* 9.5 *quoniam fors omnia uersat*). There is no need to see an allusion to Fortune's wheel, to which the only clear reference in Latin before Seneca occurs in Cic. *Pis.* 22 (see Nisbet *ad loc.*); similarly, Tib. 1.5.70 *uersatur celeri fors leuis orbe rotae* probably refers, not to the wheel, but to the unceasing alternations of fortune in human affairs (cp. κύκλος τὰ ἀνθρώπινα, *Paroem. Gr.* II.492 Leutsch).

72f. metui cupiunt | metuique timent They wish to be feared in order to be obeyed, in the spirit of Accius' much-quoted *oderint, dum metuant* (fr. 203 R²; cf. also Sen. *Oed.* 704 *regna custodit metus*); but they dread being feared because of the retribution their terror may provoke (cf. Enn. *sc.* 379 R² *quem metuunt, oderunt: quem quisque odit, periisse expetit*).

The despot's fear is probably proverbial, cf. Aesch. *P.V.* 226f. (with Groeneboom's note), Publ. Syr. 194 *famulatur dominus ubi timet quibus imperat*. The fear provoked by fear is also a commonplace, cf. Publ. Syr. 338 *multos timere debet quem multi timent*, Laberius *apud* Sen. *Ira* 2.11.3 *necesse est multos timeat quem multi timent*, ps.-Sall. *Epist.* 1.3.2 (and Vretska *ad loc.*), Sen. *Oed.* 705f., *Ira* 2.11.3, *Epist.* 14.10; Otto, *Sprichwörter* 349, *A.L.L.* 11.430, 12.347f. Hence good rulers eschew fear (Pacatus, *Pan. Theod.* 35 *nihil magis timuerat quam timeri*).

The contradictory emotions of our passage are also present in Cic. *Rep.* 2.45, *Off.* 2.23 and Sen. *Clem.* 1.12.3 *nam cum inuisus sit quia timetur, timeri uult quia inuisus est*. The conjunction of *timor* and *cupido* may be meant to recall the emotions forbidden to the *sapiens* (cf. *Epicurea* 495 Usener, *K.D.* 10, Lucr. 6.25, Sen. *Const.* 9.2, *V.B.* 5.1, *Epist.* 5.7, Mart. 10.47.13, Juv. 10.360); this contrast between the tyrant and the *sapiens* is drawn in Hor. *C.* 2.16.10ff. and in the suspect lines *Thy.* 388f. *rex est qui metuet nihil, | rex est qui cupiet nihil* (on which cf. O. Zwierlein, *Gnomon* xxxviii (1966) 684, Seidensticker 106 n.76).

73f. nox...alma The combination seems to occur first in Seneca (also in *Med.* 876, *Tro.* 438; adopted by Statius, *Th.* 1.530); decorative in the other passages, *alma* here exerts its full force, as in the more common *alma lux* (Virg. *Aen.* 1.306, Ov. *Met.* 15.664, etc.).

75f. non...soluit For sound sleep or its absence as an index of moral worth cp. Hor. *C.* 2.16.15f., Sen. *Pha.* 520ff., *Epist.* 56.7, 90.41.

75 domitor The metaphor is old (cf. *Il.* 24.5 ὕπνος πανδαμάτωρ, Soph. *Ajax* 675 ὁ παγκρατὴς ὕπνος), but *domitor* in such contexts is not found before Seneca (cf. also *HF* 1065f. *o domitor | Somne malorum*, Plin. *Pan.* 55.9, *CE* 704.17); *ad rem*, cf. Cic. *Diu.* 2.150 *perfugium uidetur omnium laborum et sollicitudinum esse somnus*. On nouns in *-tor* cf. Brink on Hor. *A.P.* 163; on *dominator* in Seneca cf. Costa on *Med.* 4.

76 pectora soluit Sc. *curis*, as in *Pha.* 100 *non me quies nocturna, non altus sopor | soluere curis*, Lucr. 2.45f., Varro, *Sat.* 36 Buecheler.

77 quas non arces = *quas arces scelus non dedit?* For the position of *non* compare Cic. *Fam.* 15.4.12 *quae non ego benefici loco pono, sed in ueri testimoni* (with Müller's note), Luc. 1.145 *solusque pudor non uincere bello* (and Housman *ad loc.*), cf. Löfstedt, *Syntactica* 11.398.

scelus alternum See on *sanguine alterno*, 44 above.

79ff. The resemblance between these generic statements and the description which Clytemestra later gives of her own moral condition (112f.) may well be intentional. In this passage as well *iura* and *pudor* are, like *fides*, specifically marital virtues (compare, for example, Ov. *Her.* 2.31 *iura, fides ubi nunc, commissaque dextera dextrae?*). On the flight of virtue and its replacement by evil, cp. Eur. *I.A.* 1092ff. ὁπότε τὸ μὲν ἄσεπτον ἔχει | δύνασιν, ἁ δ᾽ Ἀρετὰ κατόπι-|σθεν θνατοῖς ἀμελεῖται, Ἀνομία δὲ νόμων κρατεῖ, Ov. *Met.* 1.128ff *protinus inrupit uenae peioris in aeuum | omne nefas : fugere pudor uerumque fidesque, | in quorum subiere locum fraudesque dolique.*

81 fugiunt aulas *Aula* is often used metonymically to denote the undesirable aspects of high estate, cf. Hor. *C.* 2.10.7f. *inuidenda...aula, Pha.* 982 *fraus sublimi regnat in aula*, Luc. 8.493 *exeat aula, | qui uult esse pius.* The use of *arx* is analogous, cf. *Thy.* 342, Luc. 7.593, Mayor on Juv. 10.307.

81f. tristis | sanguinolenta Bellona manu Bellona is a personification of the spirit of strife, cf. Virg. *Aen.* 7.319, Stat. *Th.* 12.721, Wissowa, *Religion und Kultus* 350, Weinstock, *JRS* xlix (1959) 171ff. Seneca's description is derived from Virg. *Aen.* 8.703 *quam cum sanguineo sequitur Bellona flagello*, perhaps mediated through Seneca's own misquotation of Virgil in *Ira* 2.35.6: *sanguineum quatiens dextra Bellona flagellum.* The *dextra* of Seneca's citation becomes *manu*, and *sanguineum* is replaced by *sanguinolenta* (only here in Seneca, but fifteen times in Ovid; note especially *Her.* 6.45f. *nec Iuno nec Hymen, sed tristis Erinys | praetulit infaustas sanguinolenta faces*). One cannot say whether similar phrases such as Lucan's *sanguineum ueluti quatiens Bellona flagellum* (7.568) and Statius' *sanguinea Bellona manu* (*Th.* 7.73, 9.297) are refashionings of Virgil, Seneca, or both.

83 quaeque superbos urit Erinys The relative phrase suggests that Erinys is an avenging spirit (cf. Aesch. *Ag.* 462ff.; cp. the *deus ultor* of Ov. *Met.* 14.750, *Laus Pis.* 251, Sen. *HF* 385), but the conjunction of Bellona makes it more likely that Erinys here, like Virgil's Allecto (*Aen.* 7.324ff.), is a spirit of conflict rather than of vengeance: 'the madness of war personified' (Austin on *Aen.* 2.337); for this use of *Erinys* see also Ov. *Met.* 1.241 *qua terra patet fera regnat Erinys*, Val. Fl. 3.19, 4.617. Bellona and Erinys form part of a hellish chorus which precedes Discordia in Petr. *Sat.* 124.255ff., and are named as attendants of Fortuna in Amm. Marc. 31.1.1 (on such groups of allegorical figures see Nisbet–Hubbard on Hor. *C.* 1.18.14); note, too, the imitations *HO* 609, 671f., *Octauia* 161f.

84 nimias...domos *Nimius* here nearly = *superbus*, cf. Tac. *Hist.* 1.35

nimii uerbis et lingua feroces, 4.23 *praeferoces initio et rebus secundis nimii*, Claud. *Bell. Goth.* 118 *nec pro successu nimius*.

85 in planum 'into humble estate', cf. *Clem.* 1.5.3 *haec tamen [sc. magnanimitas]...melius in tribunali quam in plano conspicitur, Tranq.* 10.6 *fortunam...in planum deferendo*.

87 licet arma uacent *Vacent* = 'are not in use, are without an owner', cf. *Pha.* 103 *Palladis telae uacant*, 71 *uacuis campis*, 501 *rure uacuo*, *Dig.* 7.4.2.2 *singulorum annorum fructus uacabit*, 7.8.22 *eis quae uacabunt proprietarius non utetur*; the author of *HO* 369f. boldly applies the word to abandoned mistresses: *Thespiades uacant | breuique in illas arsit Alcides face.*

88 sidunt Used by Seneca only here and 501 below, *haec onere sidit [sc. nauis]*; *sido* suggests a slow but steady sinking, cf. Luc. 3.674f. *sidentia pessum | corpora caesa tenent.*

90ff. The same point is made and supported by a similar catalogue of *exempla* in *Epist.* 39.4 (and, with *exempla* first, in *Epist.* 2.3); this technique is also found in didactic poetry, cf. Virg. *G.* 3.242ff., Ov. *Ars* 2.373ff. and see E. J. Kenney, *Ouidiana* (1958) 208. The excessive accumulation of *exempla* is characteristically Senecan (cf., e.g., *Ira* 1.1.6).

90f. uela...suos Metaphorical advice about 'trimming one's sails' is old (cf. Soph. *Ant.* 715ff., Ov. *Tr.* 3.4.32, *Pont.* 1.8.72), but S.'s inspiration is clearly Hor. *C.* 2.10.15f. *contrahes uento nimium secundo | turgida uela* (Horatian reminiscence may in fact be intended to lessen the boldness of *suus* in the sense 'appropriate' being modified by *nimium*).

92f. nubibus ipsis inserta caput | turris Again, the thought is old, cf. *Lib. Prouerb.* 17.16 *qui altam facit domum suam, quaerit ruinam*, but the specific influence is probably to be found in moralising passages connected with the *locus de diuitiis*, e.g. Hor. *C.* 3.29.9f. *fastidiosam desere copiam et | molem propinquam nubibus arduis* (cf. also Sen. *Contr.* 2.1.11, Petr. *Sat.* 120.87, Sen. *Epist.* 89.21, Juv. 10.105ff., Claud. *Ruf.* 2.135f.). The hyperbole is also used in panegyric of Rome, as in Ov. *F.* 1.210 *tetigit summo uertice Roma deos*, Aristides, *ad Romam* 8 (II.93 Keil), Claud. *Cons. Stil.* 3.67f., 133f. (and see W. Gernentz, *Laudes Romae*, diss. Rostock 1918, 53f.), and of other man-made structures (pyramids: Prop. 3.2.19, *Anth. Lat.* 417.3 Riese). The author of *HO* ineptly applies it to the sails of ships (698f.).

The graphic detail in *pluuio uapulat Austro* makes it likely that *turris* is used properly, of towers projecting above an edifice, rather than by synecdoche for an impressive pile (as in Hor. *C.* 1.4.14 *regumque turres*, and perhaps in *C.* 2.10.10f.); compare *Pha.* 1128f. *admota aetheriis culmina sedibus | Euros excipiunt, excipiunt Notos*, and for such towers on palaces and stately homes cf. Virg. *Aen.* 2.460ff., Ovid, *Met.* 1.288ff. (with Bömer's note).

93 pluuio uapulat Austro For the thought compare *Pha.* 1128f. (cited above), *Oed.* 8 *ut alta uentos semper excipiunt iuga*, *Octauia* 897f. Here, however, the expression is enlivened by *pluuio* (cf. *Med.* 311, *Oed.* 632; several times in Horace, *C.* 1.17.4, 3.3.56, *A.P.* 18 and often in technical writers) and the bold transferred use of *uapulo*, for which cp. Lucr. 4.939 *utrimque secus cum corpus uapulet* (by air), Sen. *N.Q.* 6.7.6 *nam apud nos quoque multa quae procul a mari fuerant subito eius accessu uapulauerunt* (Prop. 2.12.20, where *uapulo* is used of an *umbra*, is less daring); on *uapulo* (rare outside *Umgangssprache*) cf. H. Tränkle, *Die Sprachkunst des Properz* (*Hermes* Einzelschriften xv, 1960), 138f.

94f. densasque...frangi The picture is compressed almost to the point of obscurity. The *nemus* probably consists of trees not endangered by their modest size; in Lucan's comparison of Pompeius to an aged oak in 1.136ff., which may owe something to this passage, the *nemus* corresponds to the words *tot circum siluae firmo se robore tollant* in 142. *Frangi* probably signifies the entire tree's being split (rather than the loss of branches as in *Epist.* 39.4 *rami onere franguntur*), and -*que* suggests that the oaks are broken by the winds mentioned in 92f. (as in Luc. 1.141 *primo nutet casura sub Euro*) and not by the lightning of 96.

94 spargens umbras Compare *Carm. Eins.* 2.12 *quae spargit ramos, tremula nos uestiet umbra*, Plin. *N.H.* 16.141 *mas* [*sc.* *cupressus*] *spargit extra se ramos*, 24.76; also *fundere* is used with *umbram* (Sen. *Oed.* 155, Aus. *Opusc.* 346.3 Peiper) as well as with *ramos* (Sil. 13.595; cp. *fundere bracchia, Moretum* 71). This use of *umbra* to denote the leaves or branches which create shade is found in other contexts, cf. Virg. *Ecl.* 5.5 *sub incertas Zephyris motantibus umbras*, *G.* 1.157, Sen. *Med.* 766, Calp. Sic. 5.101, Sil. 12.354.

95 annosa...robora In Virgil and Ovid *annosum robur* qualifies a named species of tree (*Aen.* 4.441 *annoso ualidam cum robore quercum*, Ov. *Met.* 8.743 *annoso robore quercus*), and *annosus* itself is similarly used (*Aen.* 10.766 *annosam...ornum*, Ov. *Met.* 12.357 *annosam pinum*, 13.799 *durior annosa quercu*, cp. Sen. *Oed.* 534f.). Seneca appears to be the first writer to use *annosum robur* independently; after him it occurs in Luc. 9.452 and Stat. *Th.* 1.564 (and note the variation in Calp. Sic. 2.21 *sub annosa medius consederat umbra*).

96 feriunt...colles The idea is familiar from Herodotus (cited above, p. 182) onward; cf. Keller–Holder on Hor. *C.* 2.10.11f. *feriuntque summos | fulgura montis*, S.'s immediate source. The substitution of *celsos...colles* for Horace's *summos...montis* may have for its aim the intertwined alliteration with *feriunt...fulmina*. In *Pha.* 1134f. the commonplace is decorated with proper names (*tremuit telo Iouis altisoni | Caucasus ingens Phrygiumque nemus | matris Cybeles*), for which see also Claudian, *c. min.* 22.36ff.

97 corpora...patent For the vague *corpora maiora* compare Soph. *Aj.* 758f. τὰ γὰρ περισσὰ κἀνόνητα σώματα | πίπτειν βαρείαις πρὸς θεῶν δυσπραξίαις, Florus 1.45 *illa immania corpora, quo maiora erant, eo magis gladiis ferroque patuerunt*. The Florus passage, however, points to a difficulty in Seneca's text, the absence of an explicit comparison between the dangers of greatness and the safety of moderation. Since all bodies are vulnerable to disease (cf. Cic. *Off.* 1.73 *longis morbis senectus, acutis adulescentia magis patet*), S.'s point must be the proportionally greater danger produced by greater size (a proportion is implied in the more abstract imitation *HO* 170 *commoda cladibus | magna magnis patent*). Stuart seems to have seen the problem, but his conjecture *maius* for *morbis* can hardly be the solution: *pateo* in the sense 'be exposed, vulnerable' requires a complement. No other correction suggests itself, and the apparent difficulty may be the result of Seneca's penchant for compression.

98ff. et...ceruix 'And while the common herds run free and wander in search of food, the largest animal is selected for sacrifice.' *Ad rem*, cf. Varro, *r.r.* 2.5.10. *Vagos pastus* might be a bolder variant of Horace's *pecori uago* (*C.* 3.13.12).

99 in uulnus For final *in* cf. Prop. 3.18.18 *stantia...in plausum tota theatra*, 4.7.68, Ov. *Am.* 2.10.12, 1.8.86.

101 ruitura 'intending to overthrow', cf. Gracchus *apud* Gell. 11.10.4 *qui prodeunt dissuasuri*, Cic. *Verr.* 1.56 *Seruilius adest de te sententiam laturus*, Ovid, *Her.* 12.200, Sen. *Ira* 1.3.1, Hofmann–Szantyr 390.

102ff. In the extreme contrasts of this ode the life of moderation is positively *felix*. In other writers the inconspicuous are simply spared the effects of direct divine intervention, cf. Eur. fr. 974 N² τῶν ἄγαν γὰρ ἅπτεται | θεός, τὰ μικρὰ δ' εἰς τύχην ἀφεὶς ἐᾷ, Luc. 5.340ff., Claud. *carm. min.* 22.38f. (above, on 96); a similar lack of qualification is seen in *HO* 697f. *transit tutos Fortuna sinus | medioque rates quaerit in alto*.

103f. mediae...turbae | sorte quietus For *quietus* cf., e.g., Lucr. 5.1129f. *ut satius multo iam sit parere quietum | quam regere imperio res uelle et regna tenere*. For *media turba* compare *Thy.* 533f. *liceat in media mihi | latere turba*, also *medium uulgus* in Ov. *Met.* 7.432, Sen. *Pha.* 212, *media plebs* Ov. *Met.* 5.207. The thought is paralleled in *Anth. Lat.* 433.7 Riese *pars ego sim plebis*, 407.9, *Tranq.* 10.6.

105 aura stringit litora tuta Clearly meant as a counterpart to 90f. *uela secundis...timuere suos*. It is noteworthy that *stringit litora* resembles the excessive timidity rejected by Horace as posing dangers of its own (*C.* 2.10.2ff. *neque...nimium premendo | litus iniquum*). The idea is used both literally and metaphorically: for the first, cf. Virg. *Aen.* 5.162 *litus ama et laeuas stringat sine palmula cautes*, Rut. Nam. 1.219 (1.227 *stringimus*); for the second, cf. Eur. *Her.* 427ff. ἔοιγμεν ναυτίλοισιν, οἵτινες | χειμῶνος ἐκφυγόντες ἄγριον μένος | ἐς χεῖρα γῇ συνῆψαν, *Anth. Lat.* 407.8 Riese *te litoribus cumba propinqua uehat*. *Aura...tuta* may have been inspired by such passages as Hor. *C.* 3.29.62ff. *me...tutum per Aegaeos tumultus | aura feret* and Ov. *Tr.*

3.3.15f. *dum me leuis aura ferebat,* | *haec mea per placidas cumba cucurrit aquas.* Our passage is presumably the source of *HO* 694 *stringat tenuis litora puppis.*

106 cumbam The *cumba*, a small boat used for fishing or pleasure-cruises, could not venture safely into open water (cf. Owen on Ov. *Tr.* 2.330, Helm on Rut. Nam. 1.219). *Mari credere cumbam* suggests embarking on an ambitious enterprise with inadequate forces; thus writers use similar phrases when modestly protesting their limitations (cf. Hor. *C.* 4.15.1 *ne parua Tyrrhenum per aequor* | *uela dare,* Prop. 3.3.22 *non est ingenii cumba grauanda mei,* 3.9.3, Ov. *Tr.* 1.1.85, 2.330f., *Pont.* 2.6.12, Quint. *Inst.* 12.10.37; *T.L.L.* IV.1588.21ff.).

107 remo terras propiore legit For *legere terram, litora,* etc. used of sailing cf. Virg. *Ecl.* 8.7 *siue oram Illyrici legis aequoris,* *Aen.* 3.292, Livy 21.51.7 *nauibus oram Italiae legens,* Ovid, *Met.* 14.89, 15.709, Suet. *Aug.* 16, *Tib.* 11; in metaphors for caution Virg. *G.* 2.44 *ades et primi lege litoris oram,* Sen. *Epist.* 19.9 *hic te exitus manet nisi iam contrahes uela, nisi . . . terram leges.* The detail in *remo propiore* (referring to the oar on the landward side of the *cumba*) recalls Prop. 3.3.23f. *alter remus aquas, alter tibi radat harenas,* | *tutus eris;* compare also *Med.* 331 *sua quisque piger litora tangens,* of men before the invention of navigation.

ACT TWO (108–309)

The opening scene illustrates a dramatic technique much used in Senecan drama: the emotional state of the protagonist is revealed by his or her reaction to the attempts at restraint of a subordinate character.[1] The secondary figure is most often, as in this play, a *Nutrix* (cf. also *Med.* 116ff., *Pha.* 85ff.; cp. *HO* 233ff., *Oct.* 1ff.) or the male equivalent (the *Satelles* of *Thy.* 176ff.); characters of higher status may assume this role in brief scenes where no subordinate is available (Amphitryon in *HF* 1186ff., Jocasta in *Oed.* 81ff.). The prominence of *Nutrices* as confidantes and foils is probably an indirect inheritance from Euripides; the Nurse of the Euripidean *Medea* seems the likeliest source for the stock portrayal (i.e. ineffectual concern).

The present scene departs from the normal pattern in three respects. First: the major speech of the scene, the '*Affektrede*' (Hansen), comes after a lengthy exchange with the *Nutrix* and emerges as the climax of the encounter. In the other genuine plays (*Med.* 116ff., *Pha.* 85ff., and *Thy.* 176ff.), the scene begins with the protagonist's main speech, the *Nutrix* makes a balancing formal reply,[2] and only then does the dialogue

---

[1] Cf. Hansen 2–5; Wanke 83ff.

[2] Omitted in *Thyestes*, where the role of the *Satelles* is not as developed as are those of the *Nutrices* in other plays.

ensue.[1] The plan of this scene thus represents a considerable gain in dramatic realism and power.

The second point of difference is that the *Agamemnon* scene ends with the conflicting views unresolved; in other confrontations (*Thy.* 333ff., *Pha.* 267ff.; cp. *HO* 163ff.) the confidante falls in at last with the protagonist's plan. At *Medea* 174ff. the *Nutrix* and Medea are still bent on opposite courses, but the entrance of Creon at this point creates the impression that the dialogue has been prematurely terminated, and so the impasse is not noticed. Our scene, however, ends with the *Nutrix*'s formal reply to Clytemestra, and nothing indicates that further discussion has been prevented by Aegisthus' unannounced entrance; yet only a few lines later (239ff.) Clytemestra shows no trace of her earlier emotions. The sudden change of attitude is not depicted and so can have no dramatic reality.[2] The proper conclusion appears to be that the Clytemestra–*Nutrix* dialogue and the following scene between Clytemestra and Aegisthus are presented by Seneca as independent dramatic units, each with its own set of premises which are made clear in the opening lines.[3]

The final distinguishing feature of this scene is the lack of relation between its opening speeches. It is clear that the *Nutrix* has not heard Clytemestra's first speech (cf. 126 *quid tacita uersas*, 128 *licet ipsa sileas*), but while calling our attention to this fact Seneca provides no explanation of it. Nothing prevents us from supposing that the *Nutrix* enters after 124, finds her mistress in silent thought, and addresses her (125–6); on receiving no answer, she continues *licet ipsa sileas*, just as characters in Greek tragedy mark the silence of another character with σιγᾷς; or σιγᾷς.[4] Given the vagueness of Seneca's information, this imaginary staging of the scene can be neither proven nor dismissed.[5] Alternatively, one might compare 108–24 with entrance-monologues during which the action is held in suspension and which appear not to be overheard by the other characters on stage.[6] Such

---

[1] The more extended scenes of this sort in *HO* 273–582 and *Octauia* 1–272 cannot be accommodated to the Senecan pattern.

[2] Contrast *Pha.* 250ff. and *HF* 1314ff., where the yielding of the protagonist within the scene is dramatically significant (whether or not Phaedra's change of heart in 250ff. is genuine).

[3] See also on 239ff. below.

[4] Cf. Soph. *Phil.* 951, 804f., *Tr.* 813, *O.C.* 1271, Eur. *Hipp.* 911, *Ion* 582, *I.A.* 1141ff., *Hyps.* fr. 60.7, fr. 126 N² (*Andromeda*).

[5] I cannot agree with Zwierlein (*Rezitationsdramen* 67 n.10) that a delayed entrance here is ruled out by its absence in other *domina–nutrix* encounters.

[6] Leo, *Monolog im Drama* (1908) 89 ('Monolog in der Luft gesprochen'); cf. 226ff., 918ff., and in particular *HF* 332ff. (Zwierlein, *Rezitationsdramen* 67 and n.10). Barrett on *Hipp.* 616ff. discusses passages in Euripides (not restricted to entrance-speeches) in which a character seems to think out loud with no reference to the surrounding situation.

monologues, however, are almost by definition not found at the beginning of an act, and in all cases it is the speaker who causes the action to resume. Finally, Clytemestra's speech might be taken as a quasi-aside, a representation of her inner thoughts which cannot be overheard because it is not really put into speech.[1] The comment of the *Nutrix* (*quid tacita uersas* eqs.), which has no parallel in the Senecan scenes where asides occur,[2] might seem to place intolerable strain on the convention; Shakespeare's handing of Macbeth's aside 'two truths are told...' (1.3.127ff.), however, furnishes a parallel, and indicates that, in his time at least, the artificiality of the technique did not rule out its use by stage-dramatists. On any view, though, the opening of the scene is without an exact parallel in ancient tragedy.[3]

108–15 These lines, which establish Clytemestra's situation and *affectus*, are marked off within the speech by the *sententia* in 115; *tutum* in that line recalls while ironically reversing *tuta consilia* in 108. The eight lines are further divided into four couplets, each beginning with a renewed ictus (contrast the strong verbs *licuit*, *periere*, *da frena* of lines 3, 5, 7 with the weak *et*, *et*, *per* of 4, 6, 8). The opening couplet poses the present dilemma, the middle two gloss it by reference to the past, and the final one suggests the course of future action. The middle four lines are given verbal unity by the repetition of *fides* (111, 112) and *pudor* (110, 113).

108f. quid...fluctuaris Clytemestra cannot extinguish the lingering traces of reason; other Senecan *irati* find that their passion fails them before the critical moment (cf. *Thy.* 283f., 324ff., *Med.* 927f., 989f., *Pha.* 592ff.; cp. *HO* 307f.), a situation which the parody in Aristophanes' *Acharnians* (480ff.) shows to have existed in Euripides. Both difficulties illustrate the principle *affectus cito cadit, aequalis est ratio* (*Ira* 1.17.4; the entire passage is relevant) and the dissatisfaction with self which for Seneca is the mark of a disordered personality (cf. *displicentia sui, Tranq.* 2.10; *aegri animi ista iactatio est: primum argumentum compositae mentis existimo posse consistere et secum morari, Epist.* 2.1).

anime The address is at home in tragedy and elevated poetry, cf. Pac. 284 R², Acc. 489 R², Catull. 63.61; these passages may all reflect the Greek use of θυμέ, καρδία, ψυχή (cf. G. Giangrande, *CQ* n.s. xviii (1968) 59, T. B. L. Webster, *CR* n.s. xv (1965) 17f.; for Euripides cf. *Alc.* 837, *Med.* 1056, 1242, *I.T.* 344, *Ion* 859, *Or.* 466 and P. Rau, *Paratragodia* (1967) 37f.).

---

[1] Zwierlein, *loc. cit.*

[2] E.g. *Pha.* 592ff., *Tro.* 607ff., 625ff., 642ff.

[3] The Senecan aside may have developed from scenes such as Eur. *Hec.* 733ff., but with a diminished sense of physical reality and dramatic continuity. In general Seneca's use of entrance-monologues and asides resembles the technique of New Comedy rather than that of fifth-century tragedy.

Declamation-oratory also affects this usage, cf. Sen. *Contr.* 2.3.6, ps.-Quint. *Decl.* 315 p. 242 Ritter. Its appearances in Senecan drama, however, are remarkably numerous; it is consistently linked with exhortations to action (192 below, *Thy.* 192, *Tro.* 613, 662, *Med.* 40, 976, *Pha.* 592ff.) or protests against inaction (915 below, *Thy.* 324, *Med.* 895, 937, *Pha.* 719, *Oed.* 933, 952, 1024; cp. *HO* 842, 1828); further examples in Leo, *Monolog* 108ff. Philosophical overtones are perhaps not to be ruled out (cf. Pohlenz, *Die Stoa* 1.325f.): S. may be alluding to the assent of the *animus* required to make an instinctive impulse (ὁρμή, *impetus*) into a voluntary act (cf. *Ira* 2.1.3ff., 2.2.2, *Epist.* 16.6, 74.31), a distinction which may be present in Medea's words *quid, anime, cessas? sequere felicem impetum* (895). In seeking *tuta consilia*, Seneca's Clytemestra resembles his Phaedra (179f.): *uadit animus in praeceps sciens | remeatque frustra sana consilia appetens.*

clausa...est Euripides' Clytemestra similarly argues that only one path remained open, *El.* 1046f. ἔκτειν' ἐτρέφθην ἥνπερ ἦν πορεύσιμον, | πρὸς τοὺς ἐκείνῳ πολεμίους. The idea is related to that expressed later in 150 *res est profecto stulta nequitiae modus*, that after a certain point 'returning were as tedious as go o'er' (*Macbeth* III.iv.138).

110 licuit The perfect, together with *quondam*, expresses Clytemestra's awareness that her former state is irretrievably lost (so also Giomini 60); cp. *Oed.* 103f. *quid sera mortis uota nunc demens facis? | licuit perire, Pha.* 1183f. The entire line recalls Virg. *Aen.* 4.550f. *non licuit thalami expertem sine crimine uitam | degere more ferae.*

111 uidua 'bereft of their owner, unattended', cf. Stat. *Th.* 10.13 *uidui moderantibus alni*, 183 *subit ad uidui moderamina claui.*

tutari The force of the verb varies slightly toward its two objects, 'maintain' with the proleptic *pudicos...toros*, 'guard' with *sceptra...uidua.* *Tutari* is more elevated than *seruare*, and is used only here and in *Pha.* 619 *muliebre non est tutari regna urbium*, cp. Virg. *Aen.* 2.677 *hanc primum tutare domum*; it has strong public overtones, cf. Cic. *Rep.* 6.13, *Phil.* 4.2 (*rem publicam*), Hor. *Ep.* 2.1.2 (*res Italas*), Virg. *Aen.* 7.469 (*Italiam*). For the position of Clytemestra as regent cf. Aesch. *Ag.* 259f., 606ff.

112 periere...fides The catalogue of lost virtues is reminiscent of the account of love's effects in Pl. *Most.* 144f.: *nunc simul res, fides, fama, uirtus, decus | deseruerunt.* For the grimmer tone of the Senecan passage compare *Pho.* 237ff. *regnum parentes liberi, uirtus quoque | et...decus | periere, Thy.* 47f. *fratris et fas et fides | iusque omne pereat.*

113 qui...pudor Clytemestra makes use of a common idea about *pudor* (whether in the narrow sense of sexual purity or the wider meaning denoted by αἰδώς), cf. Publ. Syr. 459 *pudor demissus numquam redit in gratiam*, Ov. *Her.* 5.103 *nulla reparabilis arte | laesa pudicitia est, deperit illa semel*, Val. Fl. 7.461f.

114 da frena For the application of the metaphor (on which see Bömer on Ov. *Met.* 1.280) to emotions, cf. Enn. *Ann.* 513 V² *irarum effunde quadrigas*, Virg. *Aen.* 12.499 *irarumque omnis effundit habenas*, Livy 34.2.13, Sen. *Pha.* 449f., Stat. *Th.* 10.703.

prona The metaphor is carried on by *prona*, since S. appears to recall its use of the eager *auriga* by Virgil, *G.* 3.106f. *illi instant uerbere torto | et proni dant lora, Aen.* 5.147 *pronique in uerbera pendent* (cf. also Varro, *r.r.* 2.7.13). The picture is completed by *incita*, cf. Caes. *B.C.* 2.41.4, Otto, *Sprichwörter* 102 s.u. *currere*.

115 per...iter S. expresses this thought more clearly in *Clem.* 1.13.2 *scelera enim sceleribus tuenda sunt*, more compactly in *Pha.* 721 *scelere uelandum est scelus*. For the use of *iter* compare Hor. *C.* 3.16.7f. *fore enim tutum iter ac patens | conuerso in pretium deo*, Prop. 3.16.18, Ov. *Met.* 15.106 *fecit iter sceleri*. The *sententia* was popular with Elizabethan and Jacobean dramatists (cf. J. W. Cunliffe, *Early English classical tragedies* (1912) 332f., adding Kyd, *Spanish Tragedy* iii.xiii.6ff.); the neatest imitation is that of Webster (*White Devil* ii.i), 'small mischiefs are by greater made secure'.

116 euolue The presence of *tecum* sets the passage apart from those where *euoluere* means 'unfold' or 'narrate' (e.g. Pac. 285, Acc. 47 R²); here the meaning is closer to 'ponder', *in mente uolutare* (or *meditare* as in *T.L.L.* viii.1070.17, which cites only Sil. 3.216 and Min. Fel. *Oct.* 40.1 as parallels).

femineos dolos Cf. *Pha.* 828 *instruitur omni fraude feminea [femineus* Gronovius] *dolus*, Eur. *Ion* 843ff. ἐκ τῶνδε δεῖ σε δὴ γυναικεῖόν τι δρᾶν · | ἢ γὰρ ξίφος λαβοῦσαν ἢ δόλῳ τινί | ἢ φαρμάκοισι σὸν κατακτεῖναι πόσιν κτλ. Such unflattering self-characterisations by women are common in Euripides, cf. *Med.* 408f., *Andr.* 181f., 272f., 943ff. (and note Arist. *Thesm.* 518f.).

117ff. Clytemestra's list of models is arranged to include women of various types (*coniunx–nouerca–uirgo*). The *uirgo* must be Medea (who appears as an *exemplum* in another context in Virg. *Ecl.* 8.47f. *saeuus Amor docuit natorum sanguine matrem | commaculare manus*), and an illustrious *nouerca* is easily supplied in Phaedra, but it is more difficult to point to a prototypical *coniunx perfida* apart from Clytemestra herself (as in Ov. *Pont.* 3.1.119). Stheneboea would fit the requirements of the passage (her infatuation with Bellerophon, fr. 664 N²; her willingness to kill her husband, *GLP* 16.7ff. Page (pp. 126ff.); her reputation for immorality, Arist. *Ran.* 1043ff.), but the form of Horace's reference (*C.* 3.7.13ff.) makes one doubt whether she was familiar enough to Seneca's audience to be recognised under such a generically phrased allusion. The passage thus appears to move from a generic reference to one which might be either generic or specific, and to conclude with a purely specific *exemplum* (more fully developed in order to lead Clytemestra back to her own situation; cf. 15ff. above).

117 ulla S. otherwise restricts *ullus* to negative, interrogative, and conditional utterances; here, if sound, it would probably be emphatic ('what *any* unfaithful wife has ever dared'), for which compare Luc. 4.572 *ducibus mirantibus ulli | esse ducem tanti*, 9.595 *quidquid laudamus in ullo | maiorum, fortuna fuit*, Juv. 10.314ff.

impos sui The phrase is common in Plautus in the combination *impos animi* (*Bacch.* 614, *Cas.* 629 etc.); *impos* is found once in Accius (287 R² with *consili*) and has been introduced by conjecture in a fragment of Laevius (fr. 12 Morel: *inops* codd.), then not until Seneca (here and *Epist.* 83.10, where a drunkard is *impos sui*), thereafter not until the second century (Suet. *Aug.* 19.2 with *mentis*, Apul. *Met.* 3.12 with *animi*). See also on *consilî impotens*, 126 below.

nouercales manus The phrase also appears in *HF* 1236. The earliest extant use of *nouercalis* appears to be Sen. *Contr.* 4 *exc.* 6 *quid alterum nouercalibus oculis intueris?* (after S. note Stat. *Th.* 7.177, Juv. 12.71, Tac. *Ann.* 12.2, Apul. *Met.* 10.5).

119 face The cliché is a step nearer abstraction here than in passages like Hor. *C.* 3.9.13 *me torret face mutua* and Prop. 1.13.26 *tibi non tepidas subdidit illa faces*; remarkably similar to Seneca's phrase is Val. Max. 5.7 *ext.* 1 *memor quam improbis facibus arderet*. Our passage may have inspired *HO* 370 *breuique in illas arsit Alcides face*.

120 Phasiaca...regna S. rather overworks *Phasiacus* in references to Medea, cf. *Med.* 44, 211, 451, 672, *Pha.* 907 (and cp. *HO* 850); in this he follows Ovid, who uses both *Phasis* (cf. *Her.* 16.345, 19.176, *F.* 2.42, *Pont.* 4.10.52) and *Phasias* (cf. *Her.* 6.103, *Ars* 2.382, *Met.* 7.298), cf. A. Cattin, *Latomus* xxii (1963) 699. The juxtaposition of *Phasiaca regna* and *Thessalica trabe* is doubtless modelled on Ov. *Her.* 12.10 *turbaque Phasiacam Graia bibistis aquam*; in the present context the accumulation of poeticisms is inappropriately heavy (for *trabs = nauis* cf. Catull. 4.3, Hor. *C.* 1.1.13 *trabe Cypria*, Ovid, *Pont.* 1.3.76 *trabs Colcha*).

124 soror...nefas See note on 26f. above, and 906f. below. The insistence on ever greater, though unspecified, acts of violence is not new in Seneca: there is a distant parallel in Eur. *Med.* 171f. and proximate ones in Cic. *Tusc.* 4.77 *ut facile appareat Atrei filios esse, eius qui meditatur poenam in fratrem nouam: 'maior mihi moles, maius miscendumst malum'* (= Acc. 200 R²), Ov. *Her.* 12.212 *nescio quid certe mens mea maius agit*, *Met.* 6.618f. *magnum quodcumque paraui; | quid sit, adhuc dubito*. In Atreus, however, Seneca has presented the most elaborate and intense specimen of this attitude: *rapior et quo nescio, | sed rapior* (*Thy.* 261f.) *...nescio quid animus maius et solito amplius | supraque fines moris humani tumet |instatque pigris manibus – haud quid sit scio | sed grande quiddam est* (268ff.).

125 regina...genus Compare the first words of the *Nutrix* in *Phaedra* (129): *Thesea coniunx, clara progenies Iouis* and the invocation to Jupiter in

Pacuvius' *Paulus* (fr. 1 R²): *Pater supreme, nostrae progenii patris*; in Greek tragedy cf., e.g., Aesch. *Ag.* 914 Λήδας γένεθλον, δωμάτων ἐμῶν φύλαξ, *Sept.* 39, Soph. *O.T.* 85, Eur. *Med.* 49, 53, *Tro.* 709, ps.-Eur. *Rhes.* 388 χαῖρ' ἐσθλὸς ἐσθλοῦ παῖς, τύραννε τῆσδε γῆς. For the lofty *genus* see Hor. *C.* 1.3.27 with Nisbet–Hubbard's note.

126 consilî impotens Compare *impotens sui* in *Ira* 1.1.2, 3.1.3, *N.Q.* 6.1.3; Atreus is called *nec potens mentis* (*Thy.* 547). The objective genitive with *impotens* is not common, but is frequently used by Livy (note, e.g., 5.37.4, of *ira*).

feroces impetus *Impetus* plays an important role in the Stoic account of emotions (for which see J. M. Rist, *Stoic philosophy* (1969) 22ff.); through Cicero it became the standard Latin equivalent for ὁρμή (cf. *T.L.L.* vii¹.608. 68ff.). It is thus a recurrent idea in *domina–nutrix* scenes, see on 203 below *siste impetus*.

128 licet...dolor It was widely believed that the heart's construction could be read in the face, cf. Otto, *Sprichwörter* s.u. *frons* p. 147 and Cic. *Pis.* 1 *uultus sermo quidam tacitus mentis est* (with Nisbet's note), Ov. *Ars* 1.574 *saepe tacens uocem uerbaque uultus habet*, *Met.* 2.447, Sen. *Contr.* 8 *exc.* 6, Sen. *Ben.* 6.12.1; see also Seyffert–Müller, *Laelius* 421f., T. E. V. Pearce, *C.Q.* N.S. xx (1970) 309. Stoics shared and elaborated this popular notion, cf. Sen. *Ira* 1.1.2–8, *Epist.* 95.65–9, 114.3, E. C. Evans, *Trans. Am. Philos. Soc.* lix.5 (1969). The appearances of the commonplace in Senecan drama have been discussed by Specka 29 and by Trabert 27; see also E. C. Evans, *TAPA* lxxxi (1950) 169ff. The author of *HO* 704f. *licet ipsa neges,* | *uultus loquitur quodcumque tegis* appears to have blended our passage and *Pha.* 362 *quamuis tegatur, proditur uultu furor* (cf. O. Zwierlein, *Gnomon* xlii (1970) 269 n.1).

Although the conventional masks would make such displays of emotion invisible to an audience, ancient stage-drama does allude to tears, blushes, threatening eyebrows, etc., and to gestures (e.g. tearing of clothes, rending of cheeks) which were not performed, cf. Aesch. *Cho.* 731, Soph. *Ant.* 526ff., *O.C.* 319f., Eur. *Med.* 922f., *Hipp.* 174ff. (with Barrett's note), *Andr.* 232f. (and cf. Stevens's note), *Phoen.* 1332f., 1485ff., Ter. *Phorm.* 210 (and Dziatzko–Hauler *ad loc.*), *Ad.* 643; P. R. Löhrer, *Mienenspiel und Maske in der griechischen Tragödie* (diss. Paderborn, 1927).

129 proin Outside Republican tragedy (Naev. 49, 63 R², Acc. 309, 623, *pr.* 32 R², *inc. inc. fab.* 29, 112 R²), comedy, and Lucretius, *proin* and *proinde* are used quite seldom in poetry (twice in Virgil, once each in Silius and Statius). They appear, however, nine times in the Senecan corpus, generally introducing a conclusion (cf. 141 below) or exhortation (cf. *Thy.* 201, *Pha.* 261, on which see Zwierlein, *Rezitationsdramen* 178ff.).

quidquid est 'whatever the trouble may be', cf. *Thy.* 995. The phrase appears to be *sermo cottidianus* (fifteen appearances in Plautus plus seven more of related expressions, seven in Terence); the variant most often used in hexameters, *quidquid id est*, seems Lucretian in origin (3.135, 5.1252, cf. Austin on Virg. *Aen.* 2.49; also Ov. *Her.* 19.203, *Pont.* 1.1.21, 3.3.73, Sen. *Thy.* 827, 963, Pers. 3.95, 6.65, Mart. 3.1.1, 6.68.11, Juv. 7.162, Prud. *Cath. proem.* 30, *Hamart.* 890f.

da...tibi For the advice compare Livy 8.32.14 *orabant ut...irae suae spatium et consilio tempus daret*, Virg. *Aen.* 4.433, Ov. *Her.* 7.73 *da breue saeuitiae spatium*, Sen. *Ira* 3.25.2, Stat. *Th.* 10.704.

130 quod...mora For the commonplace cp. Publ. Syr. 311 *mora omnis odio est, sed facit sapientiam*, Ov. *F.* 3.394 *habent paruae commoda magna morae*, Otto, *Sprichwörter* 227f.; J. de Romilly, *Time in Greek tragedy* (1968) 132ff. For *quod ratio non quit* cf. Sen. *Ira* 3.39.2 *primam iram non audebimus oratione mulcere: surda est et amens. dabimus illi spatium*, also 3.12.4, 3.27.5, 3.41.1, *Epist.* 63.13.

131 maiora...pati For the thought compare *Med.* 155f. *leuis est dolor qui capere consilium potest | et clepere sese*, Eur. *Hipp.* 603f. σίγησον, ὦ παῖ... | – οὐκ ἔστ' ἀκούσας δείν' ὅπως σιγήσομαι. The Euripidean passage also illustrates the repetition of a key word (σίγησον–σιγήσομαι, here *mora–moras*), a feature of Greek dramatic dialogue which is carried further by Seneca, cf. J. C. Hancock, *Studies in stichomythia* (diss. Chicago 1917) 38, Zwierlein, *Rezitationsdramen* 170 n.9, Seidensticker 25ff., 38ff.

132ff. Clytemestra's account of her emotional state is remarkable for its precision and for the complexity of the feelings involved. The combination of emotional chaos and detached intellectual analysis is a distinguishing feature of Seneca's characters (cf. *Tro.* 642ff., *Med.* 893ff., *Pha.* 177ff., 640ff., *Thy.* 26off., 423ff.). In part the technique derives from Ovid, whose characters (especially women) often describe themselves as caught between conflicting forces (*amor* vs *pudor*, *ira* vs *pietas*, etc.); the *Heroides* and *Metamorphoses* are the most significant works in this respect (so Trabert 13ff.; more briefly Zwierlein, *Rezitationsdramen* 66 n.9). Ovid in turn may have been influenced by one or more of the following (some of which may have directly affected Seneca as well): the monologues of New Comedy (note, e.g., Pl. *Epid.* 529, Ter. *And.* 26off. *tot me impediunt curae, quae meum animum diuorsae trahunt: | amor, misericordia huius, nuptiarum sollicitatio, | tum patris pudor*, and Leo, *Monolog* 117ff.); Euripidean monologues such as *Med.* 1019ff. (cf. R. Heinze, 'Ovids elegische Erzählung', in *Vom Geist des Römertums* (1960) 388ff.); Hellenistic poetry, e.g. Apoll. Rhod. 3.648ff. (on Medea's dilemma); rhetorical historiography, e.g. Sall. *Cat.* 46.2, *Jug.* 25.6 *primo commotus metu atque lubidine diuorsus agitabatur*, ps.-Sall. *Epist.* 2.11.1; declamation-oratory, e.g. Sen. *Contr.* 9.4.14 (Montanus) *certamen erat in uno homine, utrum plus posset natura an tyrannus*; Virgilian accounts of emotion,

notably *Aen.* 12.666ff. *aestuat ingens | uno in corde pudor mixtoque insania luctu |
et furiis agitatus amor, et conscia uirtus* (for Statius, note *Th.* 3.18ff., 10.735ff.
and cf. G. Krumbholz, *Glotta* xxxiv (1955) 255ff.); popular philosophical
ideas about emotions, e.g. Sen. *V.B.* 8.6 *uirtutes enim ibi esse debebunt, ubi
consensus atque unitas erit; dissident uitia, Ben.* 1.10.3, Cic. *Fin.* 1.44.

Ovidian accounts of conflicting emotions are marked by a simplicity
verging on schematism, cf. *Am.* 3.10.28f. *hinc pudor, ex illa parte trahebat
amor. | uictus amore pudor,* 3.11.33f., *Her.* 19.173f., 12.61 (Medea), *Met.* 7.19f.
(Medea) *aliudque cupido, | mens aliud suadet,* 8.464f. (Althaea) *pugnant mater-
que sororque | et diuersa trahunt unum duo nomina pectus* (and cp. Hor. *Epist.*
1.2.13, Claud. *Ruf.* 2.197f.). This mode of presentation is also found in some
Senecan monologues, cf. *Tro.* 642f. *animum distrahit geminus timor : | hinc
natus, illinc coniugis cari cinis, Med.* 943f. *ira pietatem fugat | iramque pietas.* These
lines of Clytemestra, however, do not offer a rhetorical amplification of an
essentially simple conflict, but rather a compressed and spare account of a
much more complex situation, for which the closest parallels are to be found
in epic (cf. Virg. *Aen.* 12.666ff., cited above).

132 flammae...meum The fire of love is an old metaphor (cf.
Aesch. *P.V.* 590, 649f. with Groeneboom's note) which becomes common-
place in Hellenistic poetry, cf. Gow on Theoc. 7.55; in Latin cf. Valerius
Aedituus fr. 2 Morel, Lucr. 4.1086ff., Virg. *G.* 3.271, Hor. *C.* 1.25.13ff.,
1.33.6, etc. The flames are conventionally lodged in the victim's bones or
medullae, cf. Archil. fr. 84D, Eur. *Hipp.* 255, Theoc. 3.17 (Gow), Catull. 45.16,
Virg. *Aen.* 4.66 (Pease), Hor. *C.* 1.13.8 (Nisbet–Hubbard), Ov. *Met.* 1.473
(Bömer). In Seneca note *Med.* 836, *Pha.* 282, 640, *Thy.* 97; the author of
HO, as often, betrays himself by over-indulgence (450, 536, 1219, 1226).

133 subdidit...timor For the *stimuli* of *ira, amor, inuidia,* etc., see Acc.
512 R², Lucr. 4.1082f., Cic. *Tusc.* 3.35, *Sest.* 12, Virg. *G.* 3.210, Ov. *F.* 2.779,
Met. 1.244, Sen. *Ira* 1.7.1, Luc. 1.262f., Stat. *Th.* 1.379, 5.489, Juv. 10.328f.,
Claud. *Ruf.* 1.25. *Subdidit* in this context may have been suggested by its
frequent connection with *flamma,* etc. (cf. Virg. *G.* 3.271 *auidis ubi subdita
flamma medullis,* Sen. *Ira* 1.7.1. *nisi hinc flamma subdita est et hic stimulus per-
agitauit*), but cf. Livy 6.34.7 *risus stimulos animo subdidit.*

135 uinci uetat = *se uinci uetat,* 'refusing still to take a foyle' (Studley).
For the omission of the subject of *uinci* compare Stat. *Th.* 3.97 *uetat igne rapi
[sc. corpus],* 6.529 *uetat aequoreus uinci pater*; compare also the use of *nego +*
passive infinitive ('refuses to'), e.g. *HF* 493 *copulari pertinax taedis negat, Tro.*
903f. *quamuis...flecti neget | magnus dolor,* Val. Fl. 5.28f., Claud. *Ruf.* 2.223.
For the thought see Ov. *Met.* 7.10f. *postquam ratione furorem | uincere non
poterat,* Sen. *Pha.* 184, 254f. *qui regi non uult amor | uincatur, Ira* 2.2.1.

136 inter...faces Compare *Oed.* 329 *inter tumultus mentis attonitae*; for
mentis obsessae cp. *HF* 1111f. *pectora tantis | obsessa malis, Tro.* 988f. *cunctis*

mihi | obsessa uideor cladibus, Pha. 559f., Petr. *Sat.* 99.3 (*obsideri aures* in Livy 40.20.5).

137 deuictus *Deuinctus* is better attested, but the confusion is too easy for MS authority to be conclusive. Either word would suit the context: Lucretius says *aeterno deuictus uulnere amoris* of Mars (1.34) and Virgil *aeterno fatur deuinctus amore* of Vulcan (*Aen.* 8.394); note that Lactantius Placidus (*ad* Stat. *Th.* 3.296) cites Lucretius with *deuinctus*, and that several MSS of Virgil read *deuictus*. In our passage *deuictus* would cohere better with the military metaphors in *mentis obsessae* and *rebellat*, and *deuinctus* is normally qualified by an instrumental ablative (cf. Lucr. 4.453, 1027, Catull. 64.122, Cic. *Prou. Cons.* 35, Sen. *Pho.* 39). Hence in *HF* 1078, where the same two readings are transmitted, Woesler (p. 89) argues in favour of *preme deuinctum torpore graui* (which, like *deuictus* here, is the reading with weaker MS support). Some consideration should perhaps be given to *deiectus*, first cited in Ascensius' commentary: it forms a coherent climax with *fessus* and *pessumdatus*, and may be paralleled from *Tro.* 449 *sed fessus ac deiectus et fletu grauis* (though this might itself be the source of the conjecture).

pessumdatus An archaism which appears only here in the plays. *Pessumdare* is found in Comedy and Pacuvius (seven times in Plautus, twice in Terence (*And.* 208 and its repetition in *Phorm.* 181a), Pacuvius 320 R², Caecilius 49 R²), and is rare thereafter in both prose and verse (one appearance each in Lucretius, Cicero, Ovid, Lucan, and Statius), cf. Sall. *Jug.* 1.4, 42.4, Florus 3.12, Sen. *Epist.* 14.13, Apul. *Met.* 5.6, 5.10 (both *pessum deicere*). In Tacitus, *pessum dare* and *ire* are among the 'novelties of the first hexad which are discarded thereafter' (Syme, *Tacitus* 1.352; cf. *Ann.* 1.9, 1.79, 3.66).

138 fluctibus uariis agor Cf. Pl. *Merc.* 890 *quid si mi animus fluctuat*, Catull. 64.97f. *qualibus incensam iactastis mente puellam | fluctibus*, Lucr. 3.1052, 4.1077, ps.-Sall. *Epist.* 2.11.1, Livy 1.27.6 etc., Virg. *Aen.* 4.532, 12.486, Sen. *Epist.* 4.5, 20.1, *T.L.L.* VI¹.942.82ff., 948.26ff., 956.33ff.

139f. ut...malo The comparison is probably based directly on Ovid, *Met.* 8.469ff. *utque carina, | quam uentus uentoque rapit contrarius aestus, | uim geminam sentit paretque incerta duobus* (for which Hollis cites a good parallel in Aristaenetus, *Epist.* 2.11); cf. also *Am.* 2.10.9f. *erro, uelut uentis discordibus acta phaselos, | diuiduumque tenent alter et alter amor, Her.* 21.41f. (cp. Sen. *Thy.* 438f.). The image is further elaborated in *Med.* 939ff.

140 incerta...malo An expansion of Ovid's *paretque incerta duobus* (*Met.* 8.472) perhaps influenced by *Tristia* 1.2.26 *nescit cui domino pareat unda maris.* For other examples of *dubitatio* ascribed to non-human entities, cf. *HF* 685 (Maeander), *Thy.* 697, 723ff. (*cadauer*); nothing in Seneca, however, quite matches Lucan 3.587ff.; cf. 5.602.

141 omisi regimen It may be legitimate to see in *regimen*, alongside the continued nautical metaphor, an allusion to the philosophical use of *regimen*, cf. Lucr. 3.95 [*animus*] *in quo consilium uitae regimenque locatum est*, Sen. *Ira* 3.25.4 *ratio, cui uitam regendam dedi*; metaphorically applied as here, cf. *Epist.* 94.67, 16.3 [*philosophia*] *sedet ad gubernaculum et per ancipitia fluctuantium derigit cursum.*

142 quocumque…feret Compare Medea's *ira, qua ducis, sequor* (933), which probably derives from Ovid, *Her.* 12.209 *quo feret ira, sequor*; cp. also *Oed.* 296, Luc. 1.146.

143 fluctibus dedimus ratem Cf. Sen. *Cons. Marc.* 6.3 *turpis est nauigii rector…qui…permisit tempestati ratem*, Ach. Tat. 3.3.1; for the comparison cf. Luc. 7.124f. *ut uictus uiolento nauita Coro | dat regimen uentis*, Stat. *Th.* 3.28ff.

dedimus The tense suggests that the decision has been taken and cannot be reversed (A's *dedam* is an obvious trivialisation); a similar use of the perfect occurs in Luc. 1.226f. *te, Fortuna, sequor; procul hinc iam foedera sunto; | credidimus fatis, utendum est iudice bello*, 'we have put our trust in fate' (cf. Hofmann–Szantyr 318).

144 ubi animus errat For the *animus* as the locus of passion, cf. Ter. *And.* 260 *curae, quae meum animum diuorsae trahunt*, Sen. *Tro.* 642 *animum distrahit geminus timor*, *Med.* 203f. For *errat* compare Pl. *Merc.* 347 *tantus cum cura meost error animo*, Ennius 187 R² *incerte errat animus*, 360 R², Pacuvius 302 R² *triplici pertimefactus maerore animus incerte errans uagat*, Lucr. 3.1052 *animi incerto fluitans uagaris*, Cic. *Off.* 2.7, Ov. *Met.* 8.473, *Am.* 2.10.9.

145ff. The ensuing stichomythia is notable for a high proportion of gnomai; on this feature of Senecan dialogue see Hancock 23ff., Seidensticker 18off. Similar gnomic stichomythiae are found in the *Octauia* (44off., 572ff.) and in later drama (cf., e.g., Kyd, *Spanish Tragedy* I.iv.8off., Shakespeare, *Richard* I.iii.258ff., Marston, *II Antonio and Mellida* v.ii.82ff.).

145 caeca…ducem Cf. Publ. Syr. 593 *solet esse in dubiis pro consilio temeritas*, 301 *iratus etiam facinus consilium putat.*

146 cui…timet Nowhere else in the tragedies does *cui* precede a vowel. To avoid hiatus, Richter scanned *cui* as a disyllable, a licence defended by Leo (*Obs.* 90) by reference to monosyllabic *meis* (*Tro.* 191) and disyllabic *saxeo* (*Thy.* 233). It could be added that *cui* is disyllabic in *cuicumque* (*Tro.* 852) and that disyllabic *cui* is found four times in Martial (1.104.22, 8.52.3, 11.72.2, 12.49.3) and twice in Juvenal (3.49, 7.211), cf. L. Müller, *de re metrica*² 318, Neue–Wagener II³.453. No other example of disyllabic *cui*, however, involves synaloepha. (J. Soubiran, *L'élision dans la poésie latine* (1966) 404 n.1.)

If emendation is thought necessary, the simplest change is to the plural, *quîs ultima est fortuna, quid dubiam timent* (I owe the suggestion to Professor Kenney); this preserves the unity of the *sententia*, and the corruption of the less common *quîs* is not implausible. Even if the case against *cui* is not thought strong enough to compel emendation, Bothe's *quis* for *quid* merits separate consideration. The MS text gives 'why does one whose fortune is desperate fear an uncertain fortune?', a question which makes best sense when put to a person in *ultima fortuna*. The line would therefore suit the *Nutrix*, but it is less appropriate for Clytemestra. With *quis* the question regains its proper rhetorical status: 'who fears uncertain fortune whose own fortune is desperate?', cf. *HF* 1237, *Thy.* 536, 1103; cp. *HO* 901.

For the thought, cf. Ov. *F.* 2.781 *exitus in dubio est; audebimus ultima, Thy.* 487 *serum est cauendi tempus in mediis malis.*

148 perlucet...domus Seneca similarly advises Nero *tibi non magis quam soli latere contingit. multa circa te lux est, omnium in istam conuersi oculi sunt* (*Clem.* 1.8.4); see also Juv. 8.140f., Pliny, *Paneg.* 83.1, Claud. *IV Cons. Hon.* 271ff., and on 284f. below.

150 res For the apposition see, in prose, Cic. *Fin.* 2.75 *non intellegere nos quam dicatis uoluptatem, rem uidelicet difficilem et obscuram* (with Madvig's note), in poetry Hor. *Epist.* 1.6.1f., Ovid, *Her.* 1.12 with Palmer's note, *Met.* 7.826, *Pont.* 2.7.37; Kühner–Stegmann 1.248 n.7.

profecto A relatively rare word in poetry, cf. Axelson 94. Somewhat like τοι, *profecto* expresses the speaker's confidence in the truth of his statement (cp. English 'surely'); note Cicero, *N.D.* 2.78 *si sunt di (ut profecto sunt)*, and Müller, *Laelius* 14, S. Steinitz, *A.L.L.* 2.334f. For *profecto* in general statements, cf. Pl. *Amph.* 649, *Capt.* 119f. *omnes profecto liberi lubentius* | *sumus quam seruimus*, Sall. *Cat.* 8.1, Ov. *Met.* 8.72f., ps.-Sen. *HO* 713, Quint. *Inst.* 12.7.1.

stulta The adjective appears only here and in *Med.* 919 (in self address); *Tro.* 587 *stulta est fides celare quod prodas statim* was rightly deleted by Leo (cf. Zwierlein, *Gnomon* xxxviii (1966) 685). The word is rare in epic, more often used in elegy, cf. Axelson 100; for *stultitia* see Nisbet–Hubbard on Hor. *C.* 1.3.38.

nequitiae modus *Modus* is here 'limit', as in *Pha.* 141 *pudor est secundus nosse peccandi modum, Thy.* 1052f. *sceleri modus debetur ubi facias scelus,* | *non ubi reponas,* Luc. 1.333f. *quam tamen inueniet tam longa potentia finem?* | *quis scelerum modus est?*, and probably Hor. *C.* 3.15.2 *tandem nequitiae fige modum tuae.* For the thought cp. Ov. *F.* 6.589f. *uiuere debuerant et uir meus et tua coniunx,* | *si nullum ausuri maius eramus opus).*

151 quod metuit The allusion is to the criminal's uneasy conscience; the greater the crimes, the greater will be the fear of discovery they provoke; cf. *Pha.* 162f. *quid poena praesens, conscius mentis pauor,* | *animusque culpa plenus et semet timens, Epist.* 97.13ff., etc. See note on 266 below.

scelus scelere obruit Compare Cato 59 *ORF²* *tuum nefarium facinus peiore facinore operire postulas.*

152 ferrum et ignis 'diseases desperate grown | by desperate appliances are reliev'd | or not at all' (*Hamlet* IV.iii.9ff.). There is a reference to cautery as a form of medical treatment in Aesch. *Ag.* 848ff., but Seneca is rather thinking of later formulations, cf. Prop. 1.1.27 *fortiter et ferrum saeuos patiemur et ignes*, Ov. *Her.* 20.183, *Met.* 1.190f. *cuncta prius temptanda* (= 153 *extrema primo nemo temptauit loco*), *sed immedicabile uulnus | ense recidendum est*, Sen. *Contr.* 4 *exc.* 5, Sen. *Ira* 1.6.2. For the expression see Blomfield's note on Aesch. *Ag.* 822, Welcker, *Kleine Schriften* III.209ff., Otto in *A.L.L.* 4.36, Pease, *HSCP* xxv (1914) 76f.

154 rapienda E's *rapienda* is supported by similar uses of *rapere*, e.g. *uiam* (Ovid, *Her.* 19.74), *iter* (Luc. 4.151), *cursum* (Acc. 123 R², Sen. *Pha.* 449, 738), *fugam* (Val. Fl. 5.271). For the thought cp. Sall. *Cat.* 43.3 *facto non consulto in tali periculo opus esse.*

155 reflectat Cf. Virg. *Aen.* 10.632 *in melius tua, qui potes, orsa reflectas*; note also *flectere mentem* or *animum* in Sen. *HF* 1064, *Pha.* 136, 229, 416, *Clem.* 2.7.5.

157 subolis The word is at times elevated in tone, cf. Cic. *Tusc.* 2.23 *Titanum suboles* (perhaps translating a speech of the lost *Prom. Luomenos* of Aeschylus), Virg. *Aen.* 4.49 *cara deum suboles*; but neither in Seneca nor elsewhere is this tone consistent (cf., e.g., Pl. *Pseud.* 892). In genuine Seneca *suboles* occurs four times (*Tro.* 463, 528, *Pha.* 468), while *Octauia* furnishes three examples (180, 181, 406); for the spelling see Bömer on Ovid, *Met.* 1.251.

ex illo Compare *Med.* 921 *quidquid ex illo tuum est*, *HO* 97 *quis astra natus laudibus meruit suis | ex te et nouerca?*, Ter. *And.* 400. For the appeal to children compare Ovid, *Her.* 12.187f. (Medea) *si tibi sum uilis, communis respice natos: | saeuiet in partus dira nouerca meos.*

158 equidem For *equidem* in a sarcastic retort cp. *Tro.* 310ff.

159 praestitit matri fidem 'Did he [*sc.* Agamemnon] keep faith with her mother?' This must be Clytemestra's reply to 157, but the intervening phrases, and *et generum Achillem* in particular, make the shift of subject to Agamemnon very abrupt; further, the emphasis on *matri* seems pointless without a clear balancing reference to Agamemnon as *pater* (the neutral allusion in *ex illo* seems insufficient for this purpose). Emendation, however, seems impossible, and to assume a line lost after 159 (or between *Achillem* and *praestitit*) would disturb the symmetry of the dialogue (rare in Seneca, and therefore probably deliberate). It is best to retain the transmitted text, noting that here Seneca achieves compression at the expense of point.

161 maria...languore *Piger* of a calm sea Luc. 5.435ff., of the Stygian pool Sen. *HF* 554 *stat pigro* [Bentley: *nigro* codd.] *pelagus gurgite languidum*; of water stilled by magic Sen. *Med.* 764 (*Hister*), Apul. *Met.* 1.3 (*mare*). In Aeschylus the ships are delayed by contrary winds (*Agam.* 190ff.); for a calm, as here, cf. Eur. *I.A.* 9ff.

162–202 Clytemestra's *Affektrede* has elements in common with the *post factum* defence of Clytaemestra in Euripides' *Electra* (1011ff.) and with Ovid's treatment of the story in *Ars* 2.399ff. In contrast to Aeschylus, all three writers make Agamemnon's infidelities and not the sacrifice of Iphigenia the most important cause for Clytemestra's resolve to kill her husband.

162 pudet pigetque *Pudet* and *piget* are the usual components of this expression: cf. Nonius 685 Lindsay (several examples, mainly from Republican tragedy), Pl. *Capt.* 203, Pseud. 281f., *Trin.* 345, Ter. *Ad.* 392, Cic. *Brut.* 88, *Dom.* 29, Sall. *Jug.* 31.10, 95.4, *Hist.* 1.77.14, Tib. 1.1.29, Prud. *Cath. proem.* 11, Rut. Nam. 1.287ff.; alliterative variants include *piget... paenitet* (ps.-Sall. *Epist.* 1.8.9), *piget...paenitet...est pudor* (*Anth. Lat.* 698 Riese (Petronius)). For *dolet* added to *pudet* and *piget* cf. *inc. inc. fab.* 21 R² *Hecuba, hoc dolet pudet piget*; the only parallel for the combination of *dolet* and *pudet*, as in E, is Accius 471 R², and there *piget* follows at the end of the line (*dolet pudetque Graiium me et uero piget*; cf. Pac. 44 R² *dolet pigetque*). A's *piget* might be a normalising interpolation, but on the other hand E's *dolet* might have originated as a gloss on *piget* (note that Donatus on Ter. *Ad.* 391f. used *quod dolet* to gloss *piget*). I have accepted *piget* after some vacillation, but *dolet* cannot be dismissed.

Tyndaris Clytemestra's ancestry is often noticed in Euripides, cf. *El.* 480, 989.

163 lustrale classi...caput Iphigenia became the victim in a *lustratio classis* performed to obtain divine favour for the expedition to Troy (for the custom cf. Livy 29.27.5, 36.42.2, Appian, *B.C.* 5.96; Boehm in *RE* XIII².2035.22ff., R. M. Ogilvie, *JRS* li (1961) 35); compare the sacrifice to Apollo by the Argonauts in Apoll. Rhod. 1.406ff. Human sacrifice for such purposes was seen as exceptional (Livy 1.28.1, Claud. *Eutr.* 1.19ff.) or as barbaric (cf. Lact. Plac. on Stat. *Th.* 10.793 *lustrare ciuitatem humana hostia Gallicus mos est*); hence Clytemestra's outraged tone, with which one should compare Statius, *Th.* 10.793f. *lustralemne feris ego te, puer inclite, Thebis | deuotumque caput uilis ceu mater alebam* (with Williams's note; also Sen. *Tro.* 634f· *lustrale debitum muris puer*, Luc. 6.785f. *Decios...lustrales bellis animas*). Seneca has cast in Roman terms what Aeschylus refers to in *Ag.* 224ff. ἔτλα δ' οὖν θυτὴρ γενέ-|σθαι θυγατρός, γυναικοποί-|νων πολέμων ἀρωγὰν | καὶ προτέλεια ναῶν. The sacrifice of Iphigenia was a common subject in declamation-oratory, cf. Sen. *Suas.* 3 *passim*, Petr. *Sat.* 1, *Rhet. Lat. Min.* p. 508 Halm.

peperit Editors since Leo have preferred E's *peperi*, presumably believing *peperit* to have been inspired by *Tyndaris*. It is no less plausible, however, that *peperi* is the interpolated reading, introduced by a reader who did not grasp the rhetorical force of the third person form of expression (for which see Nisbet–Hubbard on Hor. *C.* 1.7.27).

165 ille Neither Agamemnon nor Cassandra is named in Clytemestra's harangue; both are referred to by contemptuous periphrases (Agamemnon is *Paridis hostis, captae maritus*, and *Priami gener*; Cassandra is *Phrygia uates, Phrygia nurus*, and *furens nouerca*).

166 stetit ad aras Perhaps inspired by Lucr. 1.89f. *at maestum simul ante aras adstare parentem | sensit*, cf. *Thy.* 693 *stat ipse ad aras, inc. inc. fab.* 121 R² *prolem inter aras sacrificas...immolet.* S. uses the plural *arae* forty times but avoids the singular; he is followed by the authors of *HO* and *Octauia* (*ara* is falsely transmitted in *HO* 102, *Octauia* 795). In this preference Seneca agrees with Virgil (cf. Austin on *Aen.* 2.663) rather than Ovid, who uses both forms; see also Löfstedt, *Syntactica* 1².43. The plural *arae* also predominates in Republican tragedy (see Ribbeck's index s.u.).

ore sacrifico *Ore* here = *sermone*, as in Ovid, *F.* 1.130 *sacrifico Clusius ore uocor*; compare the fuller account of an analogous scene in *Thy.* 691f. *ipse est sacerdos, ipse funesta prece | letale carmen ore uiolento canit.* Here *ore sacrifico* refers to Agamemnon's unruffled delivery of the prescribed prayers, cp. Sen. *Cons. Marc.* 13.2 (of a *pontifex*).

pater The word underscores the unnatural character of Agamemnon's act (similarly in Aeschylus, lines 209f., 223ff.); compare *Tro.* 248f. *tuam natam parens | Helenae immolasti, inc. inc. fab.* 214 R², note on *parens* 32 above. Further instances are collected by D. J. Mastronarde, *TAPA* ci (1970) 302.

168 recedentes focos A gruesome detail not present in Aeschylus or Lucretius, since there is no suggestion in those accounts that Iphigenia was to be immolated. Descriptions of ill-omened sacrifice, though not lacking in Greek drama (see Soph. *Ant.* 1007 with Jebb's note), are much more prominent in Seneca, cf. *Oed.* 307ff., and note the use of similar sacrificial language in *Thyestes* 691ff. (*ipse est sacerdos* eqs.), 767ff. *impositas dapes | transiluit ignis inque trepidantes focos | bis ter regestus et pati iussus moram | inuitus ardet*; the motif of retreating flames is absurdly adapted by the author of *HO* 1728ff. (cp. Ovid, *Met.* 8.514 *inuitis correptus ab ignibus arsit*).

169 scelera...domus For the thought, cf. Cic. *Cat.* 1.14 *nonne etiam alio incredibili scelere hoc scelus cumulauit?*, Sall. *Jug.* 14.9 *numquamne ergo familia nostra quieta erit? semperne in sanguine ferro fuga uorsabitur?*, Accius 657–9 R²; for *uincens* compare *Pha.* 687–9 *scelere uincens omne femineum genus, | genetrice peior*, 25 above, *Thy.* 195f. *scelera non ulcisceris | nisi uincis* (a deliberate reversal of the traditional morality expounded in Sall. *Jug.* 42.5 *sed bono uinci satius est quam malo more iniuriam ulcisci*).

170 cruore...nece The two halves of this *sententia* appear to make distinct, if related, points: *cruore uentos emimus* points to the monstrous inequity of the purchase, *bellum nece* (*emimus*) to the madness of the entire venture. It was a commonplace that war is undertaken for the sake of peace, cf. Arist. *Pol.* 1334a15, Cic. *Off.* 1.80, ps.-Sall. *Epist.* 1.6.2; to commit murder for the sake of war, then, is an inversion of sane behaviour (*bellum* here must mean 'an opportunity for making war', not 'a favourable outcome to war'). The shift of emphasis, however, is slightly jarring and the point of *bellum nece* not easily grasped. For comparable arguments cf. Sen. *Suas.* 3.2f.

emimus *Emo* appears only twice in the tragedies, both times in *Agamemnon* (cf. 447 below, *empto redditum corpus rogo*); *redimo* is found in four places. The probable source of this line is Virg. *Aen.* 2.116 *sanguine placastis uentos et uirgine caesa*; the commercial metaphor is Seneca's addition (compare *Tro.* 360f. *dant fata Danais quo solent pretio uiam:* | *mactanda uirgo est*). Boethius (*Cons.* 4 *carm.* 7.4f.) seems to have had our passage in mind: *ille dum Graiae dare uela classi* | *optat, et uentos redimit cruore.*

171 sed...rates The line is assigned to the *Nutrix* in Trevet's commentary and in some *recentiores*; the attribution survived in the early modern vulgate (as reflected in Studley's translation), but has been rightly rejected by all recent editors (L. Herrmann excepted). Apart from the unlikelihood of an interruption in the main speech of the scene, there are rhetorical grounds for preferring the arrangement of the paradosis. If spoken by the *Nutrix*, 171 is an otiose restatement of 160–1; in Clytemestra's mouth it is an effective example of προκατάληψις or *anticipatio* (cf. Volkmann, *Rhetorik der Griechen und der Römer* (1885) 494f.; Seyffert, *Scholae Latinae* 1.140ff.). The following lines contain the *distinctio* with which Clytemestra answers her own question: the ships did sail, but having incurred the enmity of the gods.

pariter 'all together', cf. *Tro.* 1030f. *mille qui ponto pariter carinas* | *obrui uidit*, *Med.* 350ff., Luc. 5.426 *cum pariter soluere rates.*

172 non...deo Cp. Hor. *Epod.* 10.1 *mala soluta nauis exit alite, inc. inc. fab.* 89 R² *soluere imperat secundo rumore aduersaque aui*, Ov. *Met.* 6.433f. *hac aue coniuncti Procne Tereusque, parentes* | *hac aue sunt facti.*

175ff. These lines elaborate with assistance from Euripides and Ovid a motif already present in Aeschylus (*Ag.* 1439 Χρυσηίδων μείλιγμα τῶν ὑπ᾽ Ἰλίῳ). Seneca has not concerned himself with accounting for Clytemestra's knowledge of the affairs she describes.

175 amore captae captus Perhaps derived from Ovid, *Ars* 2.406 *uictor erat praedae praeda pudenda suae* (a more distant echo of Hor. *C.* 2.4.5f. *mouit Aiacem...* | *forma captiuae dominum Tecmessae* is not impossible); cp. Val. Fl. 2.146 *furit et captae indigno famulatur amore.* For this pointed use of *capio* cf. also Enn. *Ann.* 358f. V², Hor. *Epist.* 2.1.156 *Graecia capta...uictorem cepit.*

immotus prece The words, together with *non illum flexit minis* in 178, recall Ovid, *F.* 2.805f. *instat amans hostis precibus pretioque minisque;* | *nec prece nec pretio nec mouet ille minis*; note also Acc. 661 R², Sall. *Cat.* 49.1, Hor. *C.* 3.10.13ff., Prop. 1.16.35ff., Ovid, *Am.* 1.6.61.

176 Zminthea The epithet, extremely rare in Latin (but, characteristically, with Ovidian precedent: cf. *Met.* 12.585, *F.* 6.425), is ultimately derived from Chryses' appeal to Apollo Smintheus in *Iliad* 1.39ff.

tenuit spolia Phoebei senis 'He held on to the spoils taken from Phoebus' old priest': for this genitive with *spolia*, cp. Livy 1.10.6 *spolia ducis hostium caesi...gerens in Capitolium escendit*, 44.45.3, Cic. *Off.* 3.22, Sen. *Pho.* 138 *ego ipse, uictae spolia qui Sphingis tuli*, Tac. *Ann.* 15.52. *Renuit*, the reading of Boccaccio's MS which Bentley later conjectured, is superficially attractive (it fits well with *immotus prece* and *non illum Achilles flexit*) but unnecessary.

177 iam tum A more subtle form of the declamatory *color* in which two allegedly similar events are described as a habitual or constant occurrence; more common formulae are *soleo* (e.g. Sen. *Contr.* 9.6.19 *fauete, ut nullum scelus commissum sit nisi quod solet*, Ovid, *Her.* 4.61f., Sen. *HF* 497 *solita fata*, *Tro.* 249, perhaps 304 (text uncertain), *Med.* 1022, Val. Fl. 8.353f., Claud. *Ruf.* 2.10), and *semper* (cf. 169 above, 810 below). The basic discussion (with further examples) is that of Leo (*Obs.* 149ff.); for another variant note *Med.* 447 *fugimus, Iason, fugimus: hoc non est nouum.*

180 in...leuis 'in our case a trustworthy seer, unimportant when it comes to prisoners'; *fidelis* and *leuis* express the view that Agamemnon took of Calchas' advice, cp. Soph. *O.T.* 435f. (Teiresias to Oedipus) ἡμεῖς τοιοίδ' ἔφυμεν, ὡς μὲν σοὶ δοκεῖ | μῶροι, γονεῦσι δ', οἵ σ' ἔφυσαν, ἔμφρονες. *In nos* may contain an added note of sarcasm ('to our hurt').

182 inter...ultimam Cp. *Tro.* 319f. *interque caedes Graeciae atque ustas rates* | *segnis iacebat belli et armorum immemor* (Agamemnon describing Achilles).

Graeciae The generalising word is often found in Latin accounts of the Trojan War, cf. Prop. 2.6.2, 4.1.116 *natat exuuiis Graecia pressa suis*, Ovid, *Her.* 3.84, *RA* 164 *transtulerat uires Graecia tota suas*, Sen. *Tro.* 193f., 319f. (see above); Ἑλλάς is so used in Euripides, cf. *Hec.* 310, *El.* 917, 1082, *Or.* 574; cp. Accius 464f. R² *quid si ex Graecia* | *omni illius par nemo reperiri potest?*

183 Veneri uacat 'finds time for his amours'; compare Ovid, *Ars* 2.404 (*audierat Clytemestra*) *bellaque per turpis longius isse moras*, Luc. 10.185f. *media inter proelia semper* | *stellarum caelique plagis superisque uacaui*, Claud. *Epith.* 54 *luxuriae Venerique uacat.*

184 reparatque amores 'makes good the loss of his mistress'; *reparare*, cf. Hor. *C.* 4.7.13, Ovid, *Met.* 1.11, Sen. *Pha.* 468 *ut damna semper* *subole repararet noua,* Pet. *Sat.* 119.56f. *detritaque commoda luxu* | *uulneribus reparantur.*

184f. neue...torus For this type of pointed expression, in which an ironic or figurative motive is ascribed to a person or action, cf. Catull. 68.115f. *pluribus ut caeli tereretur ianua diuis,* | *Hebe nec longa uirginitate foret,* Cic. *Phil.* 13.40, Sall. *Cat.* 16.3 *scilicet ne per otium torpescerent manus aut animus, gratuito potius malus atque crudelis erat,* Virg. *Aen.* 8.205f. *ne quid inausum* | *aut intractatum scelerisue doliue fuisset,* Ovid, *Ars* 2.359 *ne sola iaceret* (of Helen), *Her.* 4.61, *Met.* 1.151, Pliny, *N.H.* 19.6, Sen. *HF* 17f. *ne qua pars probro uacet,* | *mundus puellae serta Cnosiacae gerit, Tro.* 431, *Pho.* 121, Luc. 8.603f., Petr. *Sat.* 123.243f., Juv. 10.166f., Claud. *Ruf.* 2.24f., 78; *Eutr.* 1.213f.

185 barbara caelebs torus It is best to accept the prolepsis of *caelebs,* which is softened by the structure of the sentence. If emendation were thought necessary, Heinsius' *barbara ac caelebs* would be the best choice; A's *uel suus caelebs* is a clumsy attempt to remove the prolepsis which sacrifices *barbara,* a further item in Clytemestra's catalogue of offences (compare the evocative force of *barbara* in Hor. *C.* 1.29.6 and see on 189 below).

caelebs torus Compare *in lecto caelibe,* Catull. 68.6, Ovid, *Her.* 13.107.

186f. ablatam...uiri An expansion of Ovid, *Ars* 2.403 *audierat, Lyrnesi, tuos, abducta, dolores. Lyrnesis* is probably a direct borrowing from Ovid; apart from these two passages it appears only in *Ars* 2.711 and *Trist.* 4.1.15 (note also *Lyrnesos,* Sen. *Tro.* 221, and *Lyrnesius,* Ovid, *Her.* 3.45, *Met.* 12.108, 13.176). If Ovid did not coin the word, he may have found it in Latin neoteric poetry.

187 auulsam The word is often used of the forced separation of loved ones, cf. Cic. *Font.* 46 *num etiam de matris hunc complexu...uobis inspectantibus auellet atque abstrahet?,* Catull. 62.21f., Virg. *Aen.* 4.416 (with Pease's note), Sen. *Med.* 949 *iam iam meo rapientur auulsi e sinu,* Val. Max. 5.3.3. Together with *e sinu uiri,* it emphasises the shamelessness of Agamemnon's actions and gives point to the following thrust, *en Paridis hostem!*

188 nouum uulnus gerens S. gives the old poetic cliché of the *uulnera amoris* an ironic force by using it of Agamemnon's affairs at Troy: these were the only *uulnera* he suffered in the war (note what Sophocles' Electra says of Aegisthus (302): ὁ σὺν γυναιξὶ τὰς μάχας ποιούμενος). This ironic use of the commonplace is not rare in Latin, cf. Pl. *Pers.* 24ff., Lucr. 4.1078ff. (with Munro's note), Hor. *C.* 1.27.11f., Ovid, *Ars* 1.165f.

For the taunt in *nouum uulnus,* compare *Tro.* 303f. *iamne flammatum geris* | †*amore subito*† *pectus et Veneris nouae?* [*amore solito,* recc.].

189 amore...furit Certainly a reminiscence of Virg. *Aen.* 2.343 *uenerat insano Cassandrae incensus amore,* with an added note of contempt in *Phrygiae uatis.*

190 post tropaea Troica On the *tropaeum* see Eur. *Phoen.* 1250f., Virg. *Aen.* 11.511, Juv. 10.133ff. (and Mayor *ad loc.*). The line recalls Hor. *C.* 2.4.7f. *arsit Atrides medio in triumpho | uirgine rapta* (and for *post...uersum Ilium* cp. Hor. *A.P.* 141 *captae post tempora Troiae*).

191 Priami gener Compare *Tro.* 934 *leuiora mala sunt cuncta, quam Priami gener | Hecubaeque Pyrrhus*; for a similar juxtaposition cf. *Tro.* 247 *Priamique natam Pelei nato ferum | mactare credis?*, 194 below.

192 accingere, anime A motif of rhetorical self-address which may derive from Euripides, cp. *Med.* 1242 ὁπλίζου, καρδία (imitated by Neophron, 2.12f. N² ὦ χέρες χέρες, πρὸς οἷον ἔργον ἐσοπλιζόμεσθα), Ter. *Phorm.* 318 *tibi omnest exedendum; accingere*, Livy 1.47.4, 2.12.10, Ovid, *Met.* 7.47 *quid tuta times? accingere et omnem | pelle moram*. It would be surprising, in view of Sen. *Med.* 51 *accingere, ira, teque in exitium para*, if Ovid's *Medea* lacked a corresponding use of the phrase.

193 scelus occupandum est That is, if she fails to act first, Agamemnon will put her away in favour of Cassandra. Compare *HO* 435 *scelus occupandum est*, explained by 430ff. *sic coniuges expellit Alcides suas, | haec sunt repudia*, eqs.; Atreus leads himself to the same conclusion (*Thy.* 201ff.): *proinde antequam se firmat aut uires parat, | petatur ultro, ne quiescentem petat. | aut perdet aut peribit: in medio est scelus | positum occupanti.* For the thought compare Pacuvius 148 R² (from *Dulorestes*): *is quis est? – qui te, nisi illum tu occupas, leto dabit.*

194 Pelopia...nurus For the plural, compare *HF* 1284 *matres* (= Megara), *Med.* 279 *nouas...coniuges* (= Glauce), *Pha.* 304 *uirginum* (= Europa), further Leo, *Obs.* 150 n.3. For the periphrasis in *Phrygia nurus* compare Ovid, *Ars* 3.778 *Thebais nupta*, *Met.* 3.129 *Sidonius hospes* (Sen. *Oed.* 713); also Canter 127.

195 uirgines uiduae 'unmarried young girls', cf. Enn. *sc.* 203 R² (Jocelyn compares Eur. *Hipp.* 547 ἄνανδρον τὸ πρὶν καὶ ἄνυμφον), Stat. *S.* 1.2.168, Juv. 4.4, Apul. *Met.* 4.32; compare Sen. *Tro.* 13 *cateruis...uiduis* (= Amazons).

196 patrique Orestes similis The detail seems unrelated to the point at issue, Clytemestra's reluctance to make her children fatherless. Perhaps it is an appeal to pathos, recalling a time when life with Agamemnon was happier; if so, S. may have had in mind Ovid, *Her.* 12.189f., where this idea is more clearly put: *et nimium similes tibi sunt et imagine tangor | et quotiens uideo, lumina nostra madent.* (Professor Sandbach plausibly suggests that the line contains as well an irony visible only to the audience: as Agamemnon killed his daughter, so Orestes will kill his mother.)

197 turbo...rerum Perhaps suggested by Ovid, *Met.* 7.614 *attonitus tanto miserarum turbine rerum*; *turbo rerum* alone in the sense 'a whirlwind of misfortunes' recurs in Statius (*Th.* 3.251, *S.* 2.2.127) and later (Claud. *Ruf.* 1.260, 2.90, Tiberianus 4.10f.). For *res = labores, mala* cf. Ovid, *F.* 2.789 *inscia rerum*, Sen. *Epist.* 76.33f.; cp. πράγματα, Arist. *Ach.* 269, 310, Men. *Dysc.* 28.

198 quid...cessas? Similar exhortations are found in nearly all plays of the corpus (*HF* 75ff., 809ff., *Med.* 26ff., 124ff., 916ff., 976ff., *Pha.* 173, *Oed.* 926ff., 1024ff., *Thy.* 176ff.; cp. *HO* 295ff., 843ff.), cf. Hansen 5. Like the *Affektrede* itself, this motif may descend to Seneca through Ovid from Euripides (cf., e.g., *El.* 757, *Med.* 1242); similar expressions are frequent in Republican drama, as Professor Jocelyn points out to me. Cf. Enn. 182 R² = 194 J, Pac. 385 R², Acc. 302 R².

198f. en...nouerca The argument figures in Medea's deliberations in Ovid, *Her.* 12.188 *saeuiet in partus dira nouerca meos*; Seneca, however, has introduced a further point with *furens*: there is in prospect not merely a *nouerca*, but one given to mad prophecy (cf. Eur. *El.* 1032 ἔχων μοι μαινάδ' ἔνθεον κόρην).

199 si aliter nequit Cp. Catull. 42.16 *quod si non aliud potest*. Synaloepha involving a long vowel in a monosyllabic word is exceptional; cf. *Pho.* 443 (*me*, twice), 488 (*tu*), Zwierlein, *Gnomon* xli (1969) 765.

199f. per...ensis Cp. *Med.* 125f. *est coniunx: in hanc | ferrum exigatur,* 1006 *hac qua recusas, qua doles, ferrum exigam.*

201 perde pereundo uirum Clytemestra's willingness to die while destroying her opponent finds a parallel in Sophocles' Electra (*El.* 1078ff.) and Euripides' Medea (816ff.); cf. also *adesp.* 362 N² ἐρρέτω φίλος σὺν ἐχθρῷ, *inc. inc. fab.* 159 R² *pereant amici dum inimici una intercidant,* Ovid, *F.* 3.638 *et cupit ulta mori,* Sen. *Thy.* 190f. *domus | ruat uel in me, dummodo in fratrem ruat.* It is also the attitude typical of the *iratus*, cf. Sen. *Ira* 3.3.2 and Nisbet–Hubbard on Hor. *C.* 1.16.9.

For the alliterative phrase cf. Pl. *Truc.* 951 *perde et peri, Cist.* 686 *perdita perdidit me,* Ovid, *Her.* 7.61 *perdita ne perdam,* Sen. *Thy.* 203 *aut perdet aut peribit,* ps.-Sen. *HO* 340 *aut pereat aut perimat.*

202 mors...uelis As Leo noted, the line is to be connected with the *sententia* of Vibius Gallus (Sen. *Contr.* 9.6.2) *naturali quodam deploratae mentis adfectu morientibus gratissimum est commori,* cp. *HO* 350 *felix iacet quicumque quos odit premit.* For other expressions of this idea cf. *Tro.* 1013ff. [*dolor*] *gaudet in multos sua fata mitti | seque non solum placuisse poenae, Med.* 426ff. *sola est quies, | mecum ruina cuncta si uideo obruta : | mecum omnia abeant. trahere, cum pereas, libet, Prou.* 5.8, Luc. 7.654f.

For the form of the line compare *Tro.* 869 *optanda mors est sine metu mortis mori. Commori cum aliquo* occurs elsewhere only in Val. Max. 6.8.2, Livy, *perioch.* 3 (afterwards in Tertullian), and *commori* appears only here in Latin poetry after Plautus, cf. *T.L.L.* III.1936.23ff.

203–25 The reply of the *Nutrix* is a *suasoria* in miniature, with a carefully symmetrical structure (cf. Streubel 46f.). The argumentation is declamatory: (*a*) Agamemnon has survived all the dangers of Troy; *a fortiori* he will survive any attack you make; (*b*) even if he could be killed, the revenge Greece would exact should make you hesitate. A similar *diuisio*, but with the arguments in reverse order, occurs in *Suas.* 6.8 (Porcius Latro): *etiamsi impetrare uitam ab Antonio potes, non est tanti rogare; deinde: impetrare non potes.* Other illustrations of the dramatic *suasoria* are *Pha.* 195–217 and *HO* 314–28 (which appears to be based on the present speech); the appeal to restraint is itself of Greek origin (cp. Eur. *Hipp.* 473f. ἀλλ' ὦ φίλη παῖ, λῆγε μὲν κακῶν φρενῶν, | λῆξον δ' ὑβρίζουσ'). See further A. Paul, *Studien zur Eigenart von Senecas Phoenissen* (1953) 28ff.

The first member of the argument elaborates an irony noticed in the Nekyia of the *Odyssey* (11.406ff.), repeated by the dramatists (Soph. *El.* 95f., Eur. *El.* 4ff.), and sharpened by Ovid (*Ars* 1.333f.): *qui Martem terra, Neptunum effugit in undis,* | *coniugis Atrides uictima dira fuit.* Seneca's treatment of this theme is enfeebled by his fondness for catalogues, relevant or not (he offers a comparably swollen catalogue of the exploits of Achilles in *Tro.* 215ff., based on Ovid, *Met.* 13.160ff.).

203 frena...impetus Seneca's *Nutrices* (and other foils) invariably use the language of restraint, cf. *HF* 975 *compesce dementem impetum, Pho.* 347 *mitte uiolentum impetum, Med.* 174 *compesce uerba,* 381 *resiste et iras comprime ac retine impetum* (cp. Acc. 623 R² *animum iratum comprime*), *Pha.* 165 *compesce amoris impii flammas,* 255 *moderare, alumna, mentis effrenae impetus,* | *animos coerce* (cp. Acc. 15 R² *iram infrenes, obstes animis*); compare *HO* 275–7 *pectoris sani parum* [= *HF* 974], | *alumna, questus comprime et flammas doma;* | *frena dolorem,* and *Octauia* 99f. *animi retine uerba furentis,* | *temere emissam comprime uocem.* For *impetus* see on 127 above, and for *frenare,* etc., cf. Cic. *Mil.* 77 *eius furores, quos nullis legibus, nullis iudiciis frenare poteramus,* Sen. *Ira* 3.1.1 *iram...refrenare et impetus eius inhibere,* Nisbet–Hubbard on Hor. 1.16.22.

temet S. uses *-met* at least nine times (this passage is not registered in the *Index Verborum*), six times in *Phaedra* alone; it is a plausible conjecture in *HO* 1246.

206 diu uictos Phrygas 'the slowly conquered Trojans', cp. Sen. *Ira* 1.2.7 *aequo animo tulit diutius Numantiam quam Carthaginem uinci,* Tac. *Germ.* 37 *tam diu Germania uincitur;* for this sense of *diu* in other contexts, cf. *Oed.* 948 *quod saepe fieri non potest, fiat diu, Epist.* 101.13 *quod autem uiuere est diu mori,* *T.L.L.* v².1559.82ff.

207 fraude...furto For the combination cf. Cic. *Q. Rosc.* 26, Ovid, *Met.* 13.32, Sen. *Ira* 2.9.4 (in a catalogue of *publica periuria*), Martial 1.87.7; note also *fraude et insidiis,* Livy 21.34.1, Ovid, *Met.* 15.102, Gratt. *Cyn.* 91, Silius 12.737, Rut. Nam. 1.625.

208ff. The accumulation of negative clauses is a common rhetorical device, cf. Ed. Fraenkel, *MH* xxiii (1966) 194; in poetry cf. Hor. *Epod.* 16.3ff., Virg. *Aen.* 2.197ff., Theocr. 15.137ff.; elsewhere in Seneca, *Tro.* 774ff., *Thy.* 344ff.; cp. *HO* 1202ff. In general see A. Guillemin, *REL* xix (1941) 101ff.

209 procacem...manum The epithet suits the traditional conception of Achilles as rash and impetuous (see on 617 below); it is, however, generally applied to speech (cf. Catull. 61.119, Ovid, *Tr.* 2.435, Sil. 8.248, Tac. *H.* 2.23 *animo ignauus, ore procax*, 4.20).

210 melior...furens *Morte decreta* should be taken with *melior* ('Ajax who was a better man once he had decided to die'), for which compare Horace's description of Cleopatra as *deliberata morte ferocior* (*C.* 1.37.29), and also Luc. 4.533f. *stabat deuota iuuentus | damnata iam luce ferox* (that *morte decreta* refers to Ajax' own death is also suggested by Sen. *Pha.* 258 *decreta mors est*). To take *morte decreta* with *furens* would involve a difficulty: Ajax was no longer mad when he decided to kill himself, and his enmity toward Agamemnon had also passed. *Melior*, therefore, is not a periphrasis for Telamonian Ajax; there is no precedent in Homer or Latin poetry for such an epithet (only Statius, *Ach.* 1.501, uses *Aiax secundus* of Ajax Oileus).

211 sola...mora Leo (*Obs.* 152) noted the close parallel with the *sententia* of Albucius Silo recorded in Sen. *Suas.* 2.19: *ite agite o Danai: magnum paeana canentes, | ite triumphantes, belli mora concidit Hector*; this may in turn be connected with the formulation of Porcius Latro, *erimus certe belli mora* (in the *suasoria* on Thermopylae). Seneca uses the idea again in *Tro.* 124f. *mora fatorum* (Hector), *Pho.* 458 *proinde bellum tollite aut belli moram* (Jocasta).

Behind the declaimers' expression may lie the Homeric descriptions of heroes as walls or bulwarks, cf. *Il.* 1.284 ἕρκος πολέμοιο (Achilles), etc.; see also Pind. *Ol.* 2.89f., Theocr. 22.220, Polemo p. 19.10 Hinck; in Latin, *inc. inc. fab.* 69 R², Cic. *Parad.* 1.12, Ovid, *Met.* 13.281 *Graium murus Achilles*, Sen. *Tro.* 126 *tu murus eras* (Hector), Luc. 6.201; this *color* is in turn related to passages in which Hector and Troy are said to die together, cf. Eur. *Hec.* 21f., *Anth. Pal.* 7.139 (Archias), Hor. *C.* 2.4.9, Sen. *Tro.* 128. See Seidensticker 164 n.29.

212 tela Paridis certa The death of Achilles is foretold in *Il.* 19.416, 22.359ff.; cf. Virg. *Aen.* 6.57f., Ovid, *Met.* 12.604ff. To accommodate the event in his catalogue Seneca gives Paris entire credit for Achilles' death; other authors generally mention Paris and Apollo or Apollo alone.

213f. The motif is epic in origin, cf. *Od.* 21.6ff., Virg. *Aen.* 1.100f. *ubi tot Simois correpta sub undis | scuta uirum galeasque et fortia corpora uoluit*; for later examples see Miniconi 174. S. describes the same scene in *Tro.* 185ff. *aut cum...corporibus amnes clusit et quaerens iter | tardus cruento Xanthus errauit uado* (note also Acc. 322f. R² *Scamandram undam salso sanctam obtexi sanguine*).

The text of the last two words in 213 is uncertain. Gronovius' *immixta aggerens* is attractive for the forceful verb (cf. Cic. *Epist.* fr. 7.5 (Nonius p. 212 M), Pliny, *N.H.* 17.27), but the text found in the 'AE' group of MSS, *armis corpora immixtis gerens*, is preferable for its more elegant arrangement of words (cf. Virg. *Ecl.* 10.55 *mixtis lustrabo Maenala Nymphis*, Luc. 3.518 *senes mixtis armauit ephebis*, Claud. *Ruf.* 1.310). If this arrangement is accepted, *ferens* (Bentley) is the appropriate verb, cf. Virg. *G.* 1.483, Luc. 1.403, Stat. *Ach.* 2.145; for the confusion *fero–gero* compare 409 below, *HF* 757, *Pha.* 994 (Zwierlein, *Gnomon* xxxviii (1966) 682).

215 niuea An aspect of Cycnus mentioned by the earliest writers, cf. schol. *ad* Theocr. 16.49 = Jacoby, *FrGrHist* 1.148 (Hellanicus), Hesiod fr. 119 M–W; compare *Tro.* 183 *Neptunium | cana nitentem perculit iuuenem coma*.

proles aequorei dei The expression is probably derived from Ovid, *Met.* 12.72 *proles Neptunia Cycnus*.

216 bellicoso...phalanx Perhaps adapted from Ovid, *Am.* 1.9.23 *sic fera Threicii ceciderunt agmina Rhesi.*

cum *Vox propria* for *sub duce Rheso*, cf. Cato, *Orig.* fr. 86 Peter, Varro, *ling. Lat.* 5.45, Livy 10.27.11, Virg. *Aen.* 11.467; cp. Ovid, *Ars* 2.140 *abstulit et Rhesi cum duce castra suo.*

217f. non...Amazon Seneca works in the three conventional marks of the Amazon: the painted quivers (cf. Virg. *Aen.* 5.311, Ovid, *Her.* 21.173, Val. Flacc. 5.609ff., Nonnus 37.117f.), the half-moon shield (*peltata*, cf. the above passages and Virg. *Aen.* 1.490f., Ovid, *Am.* 2.14.2, Sen. *HF* 545, *Med.* 214, *Pha.* 402f., Martial 9.101.5, Sueton. *Ner.* 44, Claud. *Nupt. Honor.* 1.32), and the axe (cf. 736 below, Hor. *C.* 4.4.19, Ovid, *Her.* 4.117, Val. Flacc. 5.137). If a single source for such a traditional picture can be named, perhaps it is Ovid, *Her.* 21.119f. *sumpta peltata securi | qualis in Iliaco Penthesilea solo.*

218 domi The word is most closely connected to *reducem*, but may also be construed with *mactare*. It is thus not strictly parallel with the few other cases in which *domi* instead of *domum* is used with words denoting motion; the usage is otherwise Plautine (*Epid.* 361, *Pers.* 731), vulgar (*C.I.L.* iii.4060, iv.2246) or late (Ulpian *ap. Dig.* 13.6.5.14), cf. *T.L.L.* v².1957.53ff., J. Svennung, *Untersuchungen zu Palladius* 388.

219 mactare The word is often used of murder in rhetorical prose, cf. Cic. *Pis.* 16, *Phil.* 13.35, Livy 39.43.4 (*T.L.L.* viii.22.70ff.), usually with a suggestion of the word's sacral associations. Here the sacrificial meaning is uppermost (note the following words); S. may have had in mind the use of *mactare* to describe the sacrifice of Iphigenia (Prop. 3.7.24, Ovid, *Met.* 13.185) or Polyxena (Ovid, *Met.* 13.448, Sen. *Tro.* 196, 248, 943, 1063). A similar use of sacrificial language can be seen at several points in the play (see notes on 43 above, 776f., 898f., 976f. below).

aras caede maculare impia There need be no direct connection to the words of Andromache in Ennius (88 R² = 94 J) *Iouis aram sanguine turpari* [*uidi*]; see the passages cited by Jocelyn, especially Lucr. 1.84f. *aram* | ...*turparunt sanguine foede* | *ductores Danaum*, adding Tac. *Hist.* 3.84, *carmen contra paganos* 36f. (= *PLM* III.288 Baehrens).

220 ultrix inultum A's *ultrix* is preferable on grounds of both thought and style. The argument runs thus: 'Greece has fought a war to avenge a breach of marital fidelity; will she allow a similar insult to the ·army's commander to go unavenged?' It is irrelevant that Greece won the war. Further, *ultrix inultum* illustrates a recurrent feature of Senecan style; compare in this play 327 *graues leuibus*, 397 *antiqua nouas*, 518 *ignaua fortes*, and see further Canter 152f. *Vltrix* and *uictrix* are, of course, frequently confused in manuscripts; *ultrix* is probably to be preferred in these other passages: Sen. *HF* 385, 895, 1103 (cf. Leo, *Obs.* 102), *Octauia* 263, Luc. 7.782, Stat. *Ach.* 1.397.

222 propone The command has a declamatory ring, cf. Sen. *Suas.* 1.4 (Fabianus) *immanes propone beluas, aspice, quibus procellis fluctibusque saeuiat* [sc. *mare*], *quas ad litora undas agat*, Ovid, *Ars* 2.516, Sen. *Pho.* 625f.; compare also Serv. Sulpicius Rufus *ap.* Cic. *Fam.* 4.5.4 *hoc idem...fac ante oculos tibi proponas.*

223f. fata...regesta *Regero* is rare in poetry, and in most of its appearances retains its prose connection with physical objects (cf. Ovid, *Met.* 11.188, Stat. *Th.* 6.621). Seneca, however, uses the word four times in the plays and extends its range from the physical (*Thy.* 769) to the half-literal (*Oed.* 638f. *matri impios* | *fetus regessit*) to the purely metaphorical (here and *Pha.* 720, *crimen*); for the latter I can compare only Hor. *S.* 1.7.29 *expressa arbusto regerit conuicia.*

226ff. Seneca consistently uses in *Agamemnon* a somewhat less artificial form of entrance-monologue than that often found in other plays (on the subject in general see Zwierlein, *Rezitationsdramen* 67–72). In *HF* 332ff., *Med.* 179ff., 431ff., and *Thy.* 491ff., the speaker notes the emotional state of his prospective dialogue-partner within his monologue. Here Aegisthus does not mention Clytemestra's signs of distress until he has completed his reflections and has addressed her. In 786ff. and 918ff. below, the description of the other character is clearly marked off from the monologue proper, although the address still comes at the end; the recognition of the other character is also accompanied by those expressions of surprise (787 *quid ista uates...?*, 922 *quaenam ista...?*) which mark similar points in stage-drama (Zwierlein 69 n.1; add, e.g., Eur. *Ba.* 248, Men. *Dysc.* 167), but which are missing in many Senecan entrance-monologues.

228 terga uertis Used in this metaphorical sense at *Oed.* 86, *Pho.* 188ff., *Epist.* 13.8, 22.8. The combination of *anime* with this physically-based metaphor has been criticised (cf. S. F. Bonner, *Roman declamation* (1949) 166), but here *anime* functions simply as a substitute for *Aegisthe*, without isolating the reasoning faculty.

229 deponis arma Similarly, Seneca in *Prou.* 3.3 depicts Fortuna avoiding a coward with the words '*quid ego istum mihi aduersarium adsumam? statim arma submittet.*'

231 oppone...caput With the exception of the revealing *uile* (cp. *Thy.* 996f. *omnis in uile hoc caput* | *abeat procella*), the words might suit a nobler character; compare Virg. *Aen.* 2.750f. *stat casus renouare omnis omnemque reuerti* | *per Troiam et rursus caput obiectare periclis* (and *Aen.* 8.144f.), Sen. *Cons. Helu.* 19.5 *quae...caput suum periculis pro sepultura obiecit.*

cunctis ...suppliciis Part of an elaborate *uariatio* including *perniciem, dira fata*, and *ferrum et ignes*. The variant (or, rather, conjecture) *meritis* is clearly an attempt to relieve the apparent pointlessness of *cunctis*; the point it makes, however, is already implicit in *uile*, and *meritis* would anticipate and weaken the climactic phrase, *non est poena sic nato mori.*

232 ferrumque...excipe Aegisthus illustrates the freedom from prudential calculation of those whose fortunes cannot worsen, cf. Theogn. 67f., *Rhet. ad Her.* 4.14, Sall. *Cat.* 37.3, Sen. *Clem.* 1.22.1. *impunitatis genus est iam non habere poenae locum, Med.* 163 *qui nil potest sperare, desperet nihil,* [*Oed.* 386], *Oed.* 834 *tuto mouetur quidquid extremo in loco est, Epist.* 5.7.

233 Aegisthe The use of proper names in self-address is a feature of Euripidean monologue (cf. W. Schadewaldt, *Monolog und Selbstgespräch* (1926) 206ff., G. Williams, *Tradition and originality in Roman poetry* (1968) 461ff.) which continued in use in New Comedy; here it also serves to identify the speaker (cf. Friedrich, *Untersuchungen* 9f.).

non est poena sic nato mori A more pointed expression of a thought already present in Accius (193 R²), *cuius sit uita indecoris mortem fugere turpem haut conuenit.* The present formulation may recall the famous words *lex est, non poena, perire* (*Anth. Lat.* 232.7 Riese), for which cf. *Cons. Helu.* 13.2 *si ultimum diem non quasi poenam, sed quasi naturae legem aspicis,* ps.-Quint. *decl. mai.* 11.8 *occidi non est poena, sed exitus.*

234 pericli socia In Dracontius' adaptation this suggestion is elaborated by Clytemestra, who is solely responsible for planning the crime: *communis nos casus habet uitaeque necisque;* | *est nobis commune bonum, commune periclum,* | *sors pariter nos una manet* (*Orest.* 181ff.); cp. Ovid, *Ars* 2.559f. *ubi par fortuna duorum est,* | *in causa damni perstat uterque sui.*

Leda sata The address is given weight by *sata*, perhaps an Ennian word (cf. Norden on Virg. *Aen.* 6.125 *sate sanguine diuom*), which is often used in high poetry by Virgil (also *Aen.* 4.198, 5.244, 7.331, etc.) and Ovid (*Met.* 1.82, 6.157, the source of 323 below, 7.322, 8.363; *F.* 2.419, *Ibis* 468).

This is the only use of the vocative of *satus* in the genuine plays; the author of *HO* 1648f. calls Philoctetes *sate Poeante* to no effect.

Elevated forms of address are typical of Republican drama and high poetry, cf. Enn. *Ann.* 37 V² *Eurydica prognata*, Cic. *Tusc.* 3.26 (quoting a tragedian) *Tantalo prognatus, Pelope natus* (less serious echoes in Cic. *Fam.* 8.15.2, Hor. *S.* 2.1.26f.); Acc. 131 R² *gnato Laerta*, 240 R² *Semela genite* (on which cf. Mariotti, *MH* xxii (1965) 213), *inc. inc. fab.* 102f. R², Furius Bibaculus fr. 11 Morel *Saturno sancte create*, Hor. *C.* 1.12.50 *orte Saturno*.

236 at fortis pater Ironic *fortis* also in *HF* 1283f. *fortis in pueros modo* | *pauidasque matres, Tro.* 755 *fortis in pueri necem*. Del Rio's *at* for *ac* sharpens the sarcasm and seems clearly right. The opposition *rex–pater* was similarly developed by Ovid, cf. *Met.* 12.29f. *postquam pietatem publica causa* | *rexque patrem uicit*, 13.187.

237 circuit 'spread over', cf. Stat. *Th.* 10.115f. *tenuis qui circuit aulam* | *inualidusque nitor, S.* 4.4.26 *sonus geminas mihi circumit aures.*

uultu languido optutus stupet A somewhat mannered reversal of the customary order (i.e. *uultus stupet languido optutu*), cf. Pl. *Bacch.* 668f. *num qui nummi exciderunt, ere, tibi,* | *quod sic terram optuere?*, Virg. *Aen.* 1.495 *stupet optutuque haeret*, 7.249f., 12.665f., Sen. *Ira* 3.4.1 *oculos in uno optutu defixis et haerentibus.*

239ff. Clytemestra's sudden conversion is usually explained as the result of the *Nutrix*'s final appeal. It would be consistent with Senecan dramatic technique for a character stubbornly to resist efforts at persuasion and then suddenly to abandon that position (see on 307 below). Even in Seneca, however, such changes of heart are not delayed and then introduced at a later point without explanation. The dramatic lacuna between the Clytemestra of the earlier scene and the character who speaks these lines is a powerful argument for regarding the scenes as unconnected. For other views, see Streubel 70ff.

It is noteworthy that, apart from the unexpected *amor iugalis*, Clytemestra's words here consist largely of inverted echoes of the first scene: *amor uincit – cupido uinci uetat* (135); *flectit retro – te reflectat coniugî nomen* (155); *casta fides – casta tutari fide* (111); *bonos mores – periere mores* (112).

240 remeemus Editors since Carlsson have rightly accepted A's *remeemus*, although the appearance of the word in *Pha.* 179f. *uadit animus in praeceps sciens* | *remeatque frustra sana consilia appetens* is not as strong an argument as Carlsson claimed. The verb is, however, appropriately used of going back to a starting-point, as in *remeare in patriam* etc.; cf. Virg. *Aen.* 11.793, Ovid, *Met.* 15.480, Stat. *S.* 3.5.12, Tac. *Ann.* 14.25. Note also the use of *redeo* in similar expressions: Naev. *com.* 92 R² *ad uirtutem ut redeatis*, Cato *ap.* Gell. 6.3.14 (*ORF²* fr. 163), Ter. *And.* 190 *ut redeat iam in uiam.* Attempts to emend E's *referemus* have not been convincing (see apparatus;

referemur and *referamur* contain an inappropriate suggestion that Clytemestra is not in control of her actions, cf. Cic. *Tusc.* 1.119). For the thought, cf. Cic. *Att.* 2.16.3 *eo unde discedere non oportuit aliquando reuertamur*, Sen. *Epist.* 98.14 *licet reuerti in uiam, licet in integrum restitui.*

241 sed The adversative force is directed at *non decuit prius abire*; Gronovius' *uel* is unnecessary (Leo, vol. 2 p. 382).

242 sera...uia Cf. R. Greene, *Never Too Late* (1590): 'But this I learned at Vertue's gate, | the way to good is never late.'

243 quem...innocens A proverbial idea, cf. Sen. *Contr.* 7.8.6 *est quaedem proxima innocentiae uerecundia, praebere se legibus*, Publ. Syr. 656 *cito culpam effugias si incurrisse paenitet.*

244 quo raperis amens For the thought cf. Virg. *Aen.* 10.811 *quo moriture ruis*, Claud. *Ruf.* 1.196 *quo, uesane, ruis?* *Raperis*, however, introduces the idea of possession by forces not under one's control, as in *Oed.* 630f. *patria, non ira deum,* | *sed scelere raperis*, *Thy.* 261f. *rapior et quo nescio,* | *sed rapior.*

246 subesset *Subesse* is used of 'underlying' causes or 'hidden' objects, cf. Lucr. 3.273 *nam penitus prorsum latet haec natura subestque*, 4.1081f. *non est pura uoluptas* | *et stimuli subsunt*, Tib. 1.9.8, Ovid, *F.* 5.604 *huic signo fabula nota subest*, Sen. *Thy.* 966f. *subitos fundunt* | *oculi fletus, nec causa subest.*

247ff. The danger of excessive pride was greatest in the moment of triumph, and men who had resisted the temptations of great good fortune were celebrated as models of virtue, cf. Cato, *ORF*² fr. 122, 163 *scio solere plerisque hominibus rebus secundis atque prolixis atque prosperis animum excellere atque superbiam atque ferociam augescere atque crescere*, Cic. *Pis.* 24, Sall. *Cat.* 11.7, *Hist.* 1.55.24, Ovid, *Ars* 2.437 *luxuriant animi rebus plerumque secundis*, Amm. Marc. 26.8.13, Claud. *Ruf.* 2.446, Rut. Nam. 1.497f.; for the example of Aemilius Paullus, cf. Polybius 29.6, Livy 45.8.6f., Vell. Pat. 1.10.4, Plut. *Aem. Paull.* 27.36. The wording of Paullus' speech in Livy may in fact have directly influenced our passage: *is demum uir erit cuius animum neque prosperae res flatu suo efferent nec aduersae infringent.*

In Dracontius this argument is used by Clytemestra: *prospera bellorum quem sic fecere superbum* (175); in *Troades* Agamemnon confesses to this failing: *Troia nos tumidos facit* | *nimium ac feroces?...fateor, aliquando impotens* | *regno ac superbus altius memet tuli* (264ff.).

247 flatu The metaphor is old (cf. Aesch. *Pers.* 601f.); for this use cf., in addition to Livy 45.8.7 (cited above), Cic. *Off.* 2.19 *cum prospero flatu eius* [*sc. Fortunae*] *utimur, ad exitus peruehimur optatos, et, cum reflauit, affligimur*, Sen. *Epist.* 70.3 *alium...uenti segnes ludunt...alium pertinax flatus celerrime perfert* [*sc. ad mortem*], Sil. 7.241, and note the similar use of *aura*, Sen. *Pha.* 488, *Ira* 2.21.7.

spiritus tumidos *Spiritus* here seems not to differ essentially in meaning from *animus* in, e.g., *Tro.* 1096 *animis tumet*, *Pho.* 583, *Thy.* 268, 519, 127 above *tumido...animo* (and cf. Cic. *Tusc.* 3.26 *tumor animi*). There may be Stoic overtones in this use of *tumor*, etc.: compare *Pho.* 352 *tumet animus ira*, *feruet immensus dolor* with Horace, *C.* 1.13.4 *feruens difficili bile tumet iecur* (for literal swelling of the liver, heart, etc., see Nisbet–Hubbard *ad loc.*, H. D. Jocelyn, *PCPS* N.s. xvi (1970) 43).

In the present passage, it might at first appear that *tumidus* describes a person 'puffed up' by success, as in *Tro.* 301f. *o tumide, rerum dum secundarum status | extollit animos*. The presence of *flatu*, however, suggests that the picture of winds swelling the sea is implied; cf. Cic. *Pis.* 89 *rumor inflasset animos* and Sen. *HF* 169ff. *illum populi fauor attonitum | fluctuque magis mobile uulgus | aura tumidum tollit inani*. This is by far the most frequent association of *tumeo* and related words in Seneca, as it is in Ovid (note also *HO* 710ff., where such a comparison is crudely explicit: *ut fractus Austro pontus etiamnunc tumet | ...ita mens adhuc uexatur*).

250 suapte natura A prose construction (cf. Cic. *Fato* 42f., *Fin.* 1.54, etc.; Sen. *Ben.* 4.17.2, *N.Q.* 3.27.8; often in Livy and Tacitus; Apul. *de deo Soc.* 16); Plautus and Terence, though they use the suffix *-pte* in such combinations as *meapte culpa* and *suopte ingenio*, have no example of *suapte natura*; the only other instance I have noted in poetry is Acc. 234 R² *probae...fruges tamen ipsae suapte natura enitent*. The scansion of *suapte* as a disyllable, which Bothe removed by violence, was defended by Leo (*Obs.* 90); see on *cui* in 146 above.

251f. rex...tyrannus Pyrrhus in *Tro.* 303 calls Agamemnon *regum tyranne*.

252 prospera animos efferunt Cf. Cic. *Acad.* 2.135 *sapientis animum numquam cupiditate moueri, laetitia ecferri* (and see Reid on 1.38), *Dom.* 141 *insolentia dominatus extulerat animos*, Sen. *Tro.* 301f. (cited above), *Epist.* 106.9; compare Cicero's portrait of Cato as a failed *sapiens*: *te ipsum...nunc et animi quodam impetu concitatum et ui naturae atque ingeni elatum* eqs. (*Mur.* 65). On the topic cf. H. Fuchs, *HSCP* lxiii (1958) 363ff.

253ff. The picture of Cassandra's position in Agamemnon's entourage may owe something to Ovid, *F.* 3.467f. *inter captiuas facie praestante puellas | grata nimis Baccho filia regis erat*; note also [Virg.] *Aen.* 2.580, in which Aeneas pictures Helen returning home *Iliadum turba et Phrygiis comitata ministris*. The last lines of the speech derive ultimately from Euripides (*El.* 1032ff.): ἀλλ' ἦλθ' ἔχων μοι μαινάδ' ἔνθεον κόρην | ...καὶ νύμφα δύο | ἐν τοῖσιν αὐτοῖς δώμασιν κατείχομεν.

254 apparatu 'pomp', often associated with regal display (cf. *T.L.L.* 11.258.20ff.) and triumphal celebrations (cf. Cic. *Att.* 6.9.2 *nummos mihi opus esse ad apparatum triumphi*). The word is rare in poetry (partly, of course, due to its metrical shape): besides the present passage and Hor. *C.* 1.38.1, *T.L.L.*

lists only Phaedrus 4.25.21 and 5.5.14, both of which differ in sense and stylistic level.

turba eminet E's *turba* is syntactically unusual, since the ablative with *emineo* normally refers to physical emergence, as of objects from water (cf. Ovid, *F*. 2.145, Curt. 4.2.21, Stat. *Ach.* 1.58); Aegisthus, however, must mean that Cassandra overshadows the other *paelices*, not merely that she walks ahead of them. In the sense required here ('excel') *emineo* is regularly used with a preposition (cf. Cic. *Orat.* 104 *unus eminet inter omnis*, Livy 1.17.1 *nemo magnopere eminebat in nouo populo*) or a compound is substituted (cf. Virg. *Aen.* 6.856 *supereminet omnis*). A's *longe*, on the other hand, is unobjectionable; it would mean '(Cassandra) is conspicuous from afar', cf. Livy 27.34.1 *longe ante oculos eminebat C. Claudius Nero*, Val. Fl. 3.337f. *medio rex aggere longe | eminet*. Given A's propensity for interpolation, however, it may be best to retain the more difficult *turba*; the repetition is in S.'s manner (cf., e.g., *Med.* 933f. *scelus est Iason genitor et maius scelus | Medea mater*), though here it seems to lack point.

255 tenetque regem 'holds the king captive'; for the erotic sense of *tenere*, cf. Virg. *Ecl.* 1.31 *dum me Galatea tenebat*, Tib. 1.6.35, 2.6.52, Ovid, *Her.* 2.103, *Am.* 3.7.3. These parallels and the typically Senecan juxtaposition of *regem* and *famula* make Lipsius' *regnum* (from his MS) unnecessary.

256 thalami...consortem A witty variant of the grand Ovidian coinage *consors thalami* (or *tori*) = *uxor*, cf. *Met.* 1.319 with Bömer's note.

257f. ultimum...domum Lamely imitated by the author of *HO* 233f. *o quam cruentus feminas stimulat dolor | cum patuit una paelici et nuptae domus*. The disgrace does not result from the existence of a mistress, but from the status conferred on her by admission to the marital home. For similar indignant reactions, cf. Soph. *Trach.* 545ff., Eur. *El.* 1032ff. (cited above), Amphis fr. 1 Kock, Plut. *Alc.* 8.4, Ter. *Ad.* 747 *meretrix et materfamilias una in domo*, Prop. 3.6.22, Ovid, *Her.* 9.121 *ante meos oculos adducitur aduena paelex* (cf. Pl. *Rud.* 1046f., Ovid, *F.* 3.483f.). Hellenistic marriage-contracts bound the husband 'not to bring another woman into the house' (ἄλλην γυναῖκα ἐπεισάγεσθαι, cf. *Select papyri* 1 nos. 1–3).

258 maritam Heinsius' elegant conjecture neatly accounts for the corrupt *marita* which appears to be the reading of the paradosis (E PCS); *mariti* (E^c FMN) is probably a less successful attempt at emendation. For *maritus* as an adjective, cf. Pl. *Epid.* 180, Hor. *C.S.* 20, Prop. 4.11.33, Ovid, *Ars* 2.381 *uiolataque iura marita*, *Her.* 11.101, Wackernagel, *Indogerm. Forsch.* xxxi (1911/12) 255.

259 nec regna...sciunt Probably a direct borrowing from Ovid, *Ars* 3.564 *non bene cum sociis regna Venusque manent*. The *sententia* is based on the old and common idea that power cannot be easily shared, cf. *Il.* 2.204 οὐκ ἀγαθὸν πολυκοιρανίη, εἶς κοίρανος ἔστω, | εἶς βασιλεύς, Otto, *Sprichwörter* s.u. *regnum* 1 and *Nachträge* 286, Florus 2.13.14, Sen. *Thy.* 444 *non capit regnum duos*, Tac. *Ann.* 13.2. **260 Aegisthe** The use of the proper name aims for an emotional effect; cf. *HF* 654, 1177, *Tro.* 576, 594, *Med.* 892 (compare Eur. *Med.* 1122), etc.

262ff. Two arguments appear to be combined in Clytemestra's apologia for Agamemnon: as a husband, he is permitted occasional intercourse with slaves (263 *nec coniugem hoc respicere nec dominam decet*), and as a public man and a triumphing commander he has prerogatives not granted to ordinary husbands (264).

Clytemestra's toleration of her husband's affairs reflects an attitude commended for different reasons by Plutarch (*Coni. Praec.* p. 140B). Seneca (*Epist.* 94.26, *Ira* 2.28.7) and some of the jurists (cf. Ulpian *apud Dig.* 48.5.14.5) felt it unjust for a husband to be allowed affairs while a wife was held to strict fidelity; Seneca, at least, would have concluded that both parties should be faithful. The inequity of the traditional view was seen by other enlightened writers as well, cf. Menander, *Epitr.* 530ff. (cf. Eur. *El.* 1035ff.).

262 aliquid For the euphemism compare Prop. 2.22.11 *quae si forte aliquid uultu mihi dura negarat*, Ov. *Am.* 3.2.83, *Ars* 1.230, Petr. *Sat.* 100.1 *etiam cum uoluerit aliquid sumere, opus anhelitu prodet*, *T.L.L.* 1.1615.59ff.

263 nec coniugem... nec dominam For the combination cf. ps.-Quint. *Decl. mai.* 2.16; in Ovid, *Her.* 3.5f. Achilles is *uir et dominus*.

264 alia...alia 'There is one law for a king, quite another for a private married man'; for this use of *alius* in drawing distinctions, cf. Cic. *Cael.* 67 *lux denique longe alia est solis, alia lychnarum*, *T.L.L.* 1.1646.54ff.

solio...priuato toro A's *socio* cannot be right, since the primary meaning of *socius torus* would be 'a *torus* shared by two persons' (cf. Ovid, *Ars* 1.566); it is, then, hardly a suitable term to designate Agamemnon's married life as distinguished from his adulterous affairs. With *solio*, *priuato* has its customary association with private as contrasted with public or official things (cf., e.g., Ovid, *F.* 6.597f. *talibus instinctus solio priuatus in alto* | *sederat*, *Am.* 2.18.16 *sceptraque priuata tam cito sumpta manu*, *Trist.* 4.2.74). The *solium* is a commonplace as a symbol of royal status (cf. Cic. *Fin.* 2.69, Virg. *Aen.* 1.506, 10.116 (with Heyne's note); often in Ovid, cf. Bömer on *Met.* 1.178).

It has been observed several times that the line obtains a clearer and more elegant syntax with the deletion of *in*: compare the imitation in Gager's *Ulysses Redux* iii (Boas 209): *lex alia regii, alia priuati est tori*.

265 quid, quod An old rhetorical transition-formula, cf. Pacuvius 143 R², Cic. *Pis.* 89, *Man.* 2, *Tusc.* 1.46, *Fin.* 5.52, *N.D.* 1.108, Hor. *C.*

2.18.23, *Epod.* 8.15, Ovid, *Met.* 5.528, 9.565, 10.616. It occurs only twice in the Senecan tragic corpus (cf. *Tro.* 496), but is frequently found in post-Augustan poetry, cf. Val. Fl. 2.59 (with Langen's note), Martial 4.30.6, de Decker, *Iuuenalis Declamans* 127f., Kühner–Stegmann ii.277 n.4.

266 animus turpis admissi memor The subject was certainly proverbial (Pl. *Most.* 544 *nihil est miserius quam animus hominis conscius*), and was popular with philosophers (cf. Lucr. 5.1152ff., Sen. *Epist.* 97.13ff.) and rhetoricians (ps.-Quint. *Decl. min.* 314 pp. 235f. Ritter, Juv. 13.192ff. with Mayor's notes, de Decker 62f.).

admissi memor The phrase has several Ovidian parallels, cf. *Met.* 11.380 *memor admissi, Ibis* 143 *factorum...memor umbra tuorum, Tr.* 1.8.49 *peccati ne sim memor huius.*

267 det...opus A canon of popular philosophy, cf. Hor. *S.* 1.3.74f. *aequum est | peccatis ueniam poscentem reddere rursus,* Sen. *Ira* 2.34.4, *Ben.* 7.28.3 *ut absoluaris, ignosce*; compare *Euang. Matth.* 6.12.

268 ita est? *Ita* is perhaps less common than *itane* in such questions, but cf. Ter. *Ad.* 642, Sen. *Epist.* 17.8. Richter's *itane* is unnecessary.

pacisci A commercial term, cf. Sall. *Jug.* 26.2 *tantum ab eo uitam paciscatur,* Virg. *Aen.* 5.230 *uitam...uolunt pro laude pacisci* (12.49; cf. Ovid, *Am.* 1.10.47 *pretium pro nocte pacisci*), Sen. *Epist.* 101.15, *Clem.* 1.19.5 *securitas securitate mutua paciscenda* (i.e. between a ruler and his subjects). Elsewhere in the plays only the perfect participle *pactus* is found.

269ff. Aegisthus attempts to weaken Clytemestra's sense of her superior position by associating her with himself among the oppressed victims of power (*nobis* in 270 is a true plural). His indignation over the arbitrary ways of tyrants is richly ironic in view of his own actions after he achieves power (cf. 988ff. below).

269 iura regnorum As a prospective tyrant, Aegisthus has a good grasp of the rules by which power is exercised. For comparable statements cf. *Thy.* 205ff. *maximum hoc regni bonum est, | quod facta domini cogitur populus sui | tam ferre quam laudare,* Pho. 654ff., *Oed.* 703f., cf. *HO* 1591f., *Octauia* 443 (Nero), Sall. *Cat.* 12.5 *quasi iniuriam facere, id demum esset imperio uti.*

271f. id...licet The view is old, cf. Aesch. *P.V.* 52, Soph. *Ant.* 506f. ἀλλ᾽ ἡ τυραννὶς πολλά τ᾽ ἄλλ᾽ εὐδαιμονεῖ | κἄξεστιν αὐτῇ δρᾶν λέγειν θ᾽ ἃ βούλεται, Sall. *Jug.* 31.26 *nam impune quae lubet facere, id est regem esse,* Sen. *Ira* 2.31.3.

273ff. The logic of these lines is difficult to follow, and corruption may justly be suspected. Unfortunately, the obvious imitation in Dracontius (200ff.) is too general to be helpful: *exemplumque recens tibi iam superaddo, Lacaenam, | interfectricem tot regum tot populorum | uiuere felicem post funera tanta quiete.*

The MS text requires Agamemnon to be the subject of *ignouit Helenae*. His tyrannical attitudes have been the subject of the foregoing lines, and the sentence itself offers no other interpretation, given the subordinate position of *iuncta Menelao*. It is not in itself a difficulty that Agamemnon and not Menelaus is credited with Helen's pardon: this is the order of events in Quintus Smyrnaeus (3.385–415), who probably followed a pre-Senecan Greek source. The MS text of the passage as a whole, however, cannot stand, for if Agamemnon is the subject of 273f., then *Atriden* in Aegisthus' reply must also refer to him, and the necessary contrast between 275f. and 277ff. vanishes.

This problem can be met by a change in the text of 275, *tunc* for *sed*. Aegisthus thus responds with a *distinctio*: 'Yes, but at that time secret passion did not steal away his mind' (i.e. Agamemnon could judge Helen with mercy, since he had no personal interest in her condemnation). For *tunc* in a similar disputation cf. *Tro.* 318, 322; here it is answered by *iam* in 277.

This interpretation appears to be the one which involves least change in the MS text. A different approach, which assumes more serious corruption, may lead to a better result. If 275f. can be read as a reference to Menelaus, the contrast between 275f. and 277ff. becomes more effective; in particular the words *animum coniugi obstrictum suae* (which suit Menelaus, not Agamemnon) and *ille* (277) gain in force. But for *Atriden* in 275 to denote Menelaus, we must suppose that an earlier mention of Menelaus has been lost: *Atrides* unqualified appears to be used of Menelaus only where there is no danger of ambiguity, as for example in *Laus Pisonis* 61 *uim Laertiadae, breuitatem uincis Atridae* (a reference to *Il.* 3.213ff.), Ovid, *Ars* 2.371 (note *Menelaus* 359, *Menelae* 361), *Her.* 16.366 (cf. 357 *Atrides...Menelaus*), Petr. *Sat.* 108.14 *decepti pignus Atridae*. On the other hand, Ovid, *Ars* 2.399ff. shows that one may begin to speak of Agamemnon as *Atrides* even when Menelaus has been the subject, perhaps because the primary association of *Atrides* is with Agamemnon (Menelaus is often *Atrides minor*, cf. Ovid, *Ars* 3.11f., *Her.* 5.101, *Met.* 12.623).

If Menelaus must be introduced as the antecedent of *Atriden* in 275, the obvious procedure is to dislodge Agamemnon as subject of *ignouit* in 273. The text of 273, however, has thus far withstood efforts at emendation. The needed reference may be supplied by supposing that a line has dropped out in which Clytemestra put forward Menelaus as a counter-example to Aegisthus' picture of the arbitrary tyrant. The argument might have run: 'But my husband's brother, himself a king, forgave Helen; she returns reunited with Menelaus, the woman who embroiled Europe and Asia in equal woe.'

274 quae *Quae* occurs in synaloepha also in *HF* 674, *Thy.* 978 (cf. Housman on Manilius 4.890 and Addendum); in neither of those passages, though, does *quae* stand first in both the verse and its clause (compare *cum* in *Pho.* 35, *Oed.* 602, and Petr. *Sat.* 89.56, and *qui* in *HF* 593, 604, cf. J. Soubiran, *L'élision dans la poésie latine* 422).

quae...malis The thought is often found in Euripides, cf. Seidensticker 125 n.146. For this formulation, though, the models are Latin, cf. Catull. 68.89 *Troia...commune sepulcrum Asiae Europaeque*, [Virg.] *Aen.* 2.573 *Troiae et patriae communis Erinys*, Ovid, *Am.* 2.12.17f. *nisi rapta fuisset* | *Tyndaris, Europae pax Asiaeque foret*, Sen. *Tro.* 892ff., Val. Fl. 8.395f.

277 crimen...quaerit *Crimen quaerere* is to look for grounds for accusation where none exist, cf. Publ. Syr. 470 *properare in iudicio est crimen quaerere*, Cic. *Cael.* 68 *aut crimen est Caelio quaesitum aut quaestio sublata*, *Cluent.* 174, *Sulla* 67, *Pis.* 74, *de Or.* 2.170, Sen. *Contr.* 7.1.20.

causas parat 'He is getting ready his pretexts', cf. Ter. *Eun.* 138 *fingit causas ne det sedulo*, Tib. 1.6.11 *fingere tunc didicit causas ut sola cubaret*.

278 crede 'assume that' (i.e. for the sake of argument); cf. *Pha.* 147, *HO* 323, also *Pha.* 228 *puta*, 477 *credas*.

279 flagitio uacans For *uacare*, 'to be free of', with *culpa* or a similar word, cf. *HF* 17 *ne qua pars probro uacet*, *Thy.* 321 *ut ipsi culpa et crimine uacent*, also Cic. *Tusc.* 3.19 *sapientis animus semper uacat uitio*, *Fam.* 7.3.4 *uacare culpa magnum est solacium*. Parallels can also be produced for *culpa* (*uel sim.*) *carere*, e.g. *HF* 1201 *casus hic culpa caret*, *Med.* 935 *crimine et culpa carent*. The participle *carens* is often found in such contexts (cf. Hor. *C.* 3.27.39f., Sen. *Pha.* 483 *libera et uitio carens* [*sc. uita*], Petr. *Sat.* 89.15, Juv. 7.56), but I have no other example of *uacans*; A's text probably results from a wish to regularise the expression.

280 ubi...quaeritur The sense was correctly explained by Ascensius: 'fit nocens cui ille nocere uult, licet nihil commiserit, quia non quaeritur, i. e. non fit quaestio aut inquisitio legitima.' For *fieri nocentem* cp. Cic. *Pis.* 99 *te...metuentem uidebo ne reus fias*, Sall. *Jug.* 35.7 *fit reus magis ex aequo bonoque quam ex iure gentium Bomilcar*, Sen. *Med.* 498f., *Oed.* 1019 *nemo fit fato nocens*. Our passage may be the source of *HO* 431f. *nec potest* [*sc. Alcides*] *fieri nocens*. It has been suggested that *fit nocens* here is to be taken impersonally, 'one is declared guilty' (so Zwierlein, *Gnomon* xli (1969) 768); the constructions of this type cited by grammarians, however, are not similar enough to be convincing, cf. Wackernagel, *Vorlesungen* 1.111ff., P. Lejay, *Rev. Phil.* xl (1916) 155ff. Further, the other cases of *fieri nocentem* cited above all involve personal subjects. Only Düring has attempted to remove the syntactical oddity by emendation, and his *sit nocens non quaeritur* (= *non quaeritur an sit nocens*) merely replaces it with another (see below on 404a, to which Düring appeals). One should perhaps think instead of reading *fis* (which might easily have been accommodated to the third person verbs nearby) or, alternatively, *quem dominus odit fit nocens*. The corruption is harder to explain in the second case, but *ubi* is a plausible *Flickwort* (cf. *Oed.* 517 etc.). (It is possible that *nocens* is subject, not complement, of *fit*: 'a criminal is made, not sought'; but this distinction does not stress the arbitrary use of power which Aegisthus is denouncing. Where *fieri* is so distinguished from *nascor*, as in Plin. *N.H.* 17.1 *quae arte et humanis ingeniis fiunt uerius quam nascuntur*, 35.30, Sen. *Ira* 2.10.6, *Thy.* 313f. *ne mali fiant times?* | *nascuntur*, Tert. *Apol.* 18.4, it denotes a conscious effort which is out of place here.)

283 repudia The prosaic legal term (apparently not found elsewhere in poetry after Lucilius) occurs again with pointed effect in *Med.* 52f. *paria narrentur tua* | *repudia thalamis* (and note the imitation in *HO* 431f.).

284ff. The brief stichomythia turns on *fides*, thus reverting to the point of 147f. above, with the position of Clytemestra reversed: her rapid shifting of ground shows her to be the weaker partner in the dialogue (a technique of Greek stichomythia as well, cf. Aesch. *Ag.* 931ff., *P.V.* 36ff.).

284 fidus The only substantival use of the word in Seneca, cf. Enn. *sc.* 182 R² (= 194 J, see Jocelyn *ad loc.*), Livy 8.24.6, Stat. *Th.* 6.402, Tac. *Ann.* 3.46, *Hist.* 3.40. Here the word seems devoid of the emotional force it carries in other authors; Seneca seems to have preferred it to *fidelis* as suited to tragic elevation (Seneca uses *fidus* twenty times, *fidelis* only five times, while the figures for comedy are almost exactly reversed). The 'reliable person' designated by *fidus* must in this context be the *Nutrix* (cf. 147f. above).

285 non...fides For the thought cf. Enn. *sc.* 381 R² *nulla sancta societas nec fides regni est*, Otto, *Sprichwörter* s.u. *regnum* 1.

intrat Cf. ps.-Ovid, *Nux* 137 *intrat et urbanas eadem petulantia portas*, Sen. *Thy.* 451 *scelera non intrant casas*, *HO* 610 (*fraudes cautique doli*), *Octauia* 162f. (*Erinys*).

286 opibus...obligem The suggestion is offensive to generally accepted ideas of *fides* (with *obligem* compare, e.g., Livy 22.22.14 *habita fides ipsa plerumque obligat fidem*) and even more so to the lofty conception of the virtue thus expressed by S. himself: *sanctissimum humani pectoris bonum, nulla necessitate ad fallendum cogitur, nullo corrumpitur praemio* (*Epist.* 88.29). Aegisthus' reply is both rhetorically cogent and morally unobjectionable (cp. *Epist.* 9.9 *placebit aliquod pretium contra amicitiam, si ullum in illa placet praeter ipsam*). For the thought cf. Varius fr. 1 Morel (of Antony) *leges fixit pretio atque refixit*, Prop. 3.13.49 *auro pulsa fides*.

288ff. The lines in question are given to the *Nutrix* by E, to Clytemestra by A. Herrmann and Giardina follow E, and Paratore has written at length in support of this position (*SIFC* xxvii (1956) 347ff.); cf. also Heldmann

120ff. Other editors since Leo give the lines to Clytemestra; this, it seems to me, is the preferable solution.

The internal evidence of the lines points to Clytemestra: Aegisthus' question *et cur Atrida uideor inferior tibi?* takes on added force if addressed to one who has accepted both Agamemnon and Aegisthus as lovers; furthermore, *quem Venere tantum scimus illicita uirum* carries little weight unless *scimus* relates to first-hand experience; finally, the combination of regal status with strong *affectus* in the final lines is unlikely in the mouth of any *Nutrix*, but particularly out of place from the impersonal character of the earlier scene. In addition, the lines are wholly consistent with what we have so far seen of Clytemestra and form in fact an artfully devised climax to Seneca's portrayal of her character. She recognises the evil of Aegisthus' plan (26of.) and her *pudor* is not yet extinct (137f.), but she is not as clever as Aegisthus and so is worsted in argument (244–87). At this point it is quite plausible that she should express her frustrated desire for repentance by denouncing the sophist who stands between her and the *boni mores* she sincerely, though vainly, wishes to recover.

It is also an oddity of dramatic technique for a minor character to interrupt the climax of a dialogue between protagonists, particularly after having remained mute for almost seventy lines. I know of no true parallel from either Greek or Senecan tragedy: in Soph. *O.T.* 924ff. the Corinthian messenger is silent from 964 to 988, and then breaks into a conversation between Oedipus and Jocasta, but he does so to deliver the second part of the message for which Sophocles has brought him on, and in the structure of the entire episode 964–88 count as a digression. The issue is not entirely obvious, since Seneca cannot be bound by the rules of Greek tragic technique and the alternative arrangement produces its own kind of tension (stressing the weakness and passivity of Clytemestra), but I feel that the A attribution of lines is more likely to be right.

The disputed lines, therefore, are probably spoken by Clytemestra; can the MS text of 290 be right? References to oneself in the third person are hardly rare (cf. Nisbet–Hubbard on Hor. *C.* 1.7.27 for some examples), but they are generally protected from ambiguity by the presence of a proper name (e.g. *Il.* 1.240 ἦ ποτ' Ἀχιλλῆος ποθὴ ἵξεται υἷας Ἀχαιῶν) or a demonstrative word (e.g. Ovid, *Her.* 16.155 *hoc caput*, Epict. *Diss.* 1.9.10 τὸν πρεσβύτερον ἐνταῦθα). Here, though, no such aid helps to explain *nubet*. Viansino suggests 'tertia persona quasi pendet ex insequenti uerbo *generosa*', but this will not do: *generosa* is too closely bound to *exuli* to be able to perform double service as the quasi-subject of *nubet*; in the rhetorical structure of the passage *regum relicto rege* and *generosa exuli* must be variations on an irony already expressed.

Emendation seems necessary. The simplest remedy is to read *nubam*; this was known to Coluccio Salutati, and probably formed the basis for the ingenious but impossible *nubam et tibi* found in MS Ashmole 1791. One might object that an original *nubam* would have been altered to *nubet* only in the belief that Clytemestra was not the speaker, whereas the mistaken attribution to the *Nutrix* is only in E and *nubet* is the reading of both E and A. Two explanations are possible. There may have been a stage of transmission at which the entire paradosis gave the lines to the *Nutrix* and so read *nubet*; A may have corrected the distribution without altering the text. More simply, *nubet* could be regarded as a mechanical corruption, by perseveration from *scilicet*.

Alternatively, *nubet* might be retained and explained as an indignant use of the third person, if a line has fallen out after 290 which contained the subject of *nubet* and which provided the basis for the variations *regum relicto rege* and *generosa exuli*. A line similar in thought to 125 above (*regina Danaum et inclitum Ledae genus*) would satisfy the needs of grammar and sense.

288 surgit...pudor Similar statements are made by Hercules (*HF* 1240 *non sic furore cessit extinctus pudor*) and Phaedra (*Pha.* 250 *non omnis animo cessit ingenuo pudor*); note that the latter announces a turning-point in the action of its scene. For *pudor residuus* cf. Sen. *Ben.* 7.28.3.

289 blandiloqua A patent archaism. *Blandiloquus* appears in poetry only in Pl. *Bacch.* 1173 and Sidon. Apoll. *C.* 9.262; related compounds are also characteristic of early and late Latin, cf. *blandidicus* (Pl. *Poen.* 138), *blandificus* (Mart. Capell. 9.888), *blandifluus* (Dracontius, Venantius Fortunatus), *blandiloquens* (Laberius 106 R²), *blandiloquentia* (Enn. *sc.* 227 R² = 226 Jocelyn, who thinks that such words in -*loquentia* 'must have been created by the adapters of tragedy'), *blandiloquentulus* (Pl. *Trin.* 239), *blandiloquium* (first in Augustine). Note, however, that Ovid once uses *magniloquus* (*Met.* 8.396). Adjectives of this type in Seneca are collected by B. Schmidt, *Rh. Mus.* xvi (1861) 589n.

290 dictas *Dicto*, which S. uses only here, may carry a hint of the schoolroom, cf. Hor. *S.* 1.10.74f., *Epist.* 2.1.71, Pers. 1.29f.; note also passages in which sources of inspiration dictate to poets, e.g. Prop. 4.1.133, [Ovid], *Her.* 15.27, 20.29, Martial 8.73.8.

291 exuli Thyestes' incest with Pelopia was sometimes said to have occurred at Sicyon, cf. Frazer on ps.-Apollod. *Epit.* 2.14; *exul* would also suit the Aeschylean account, in which Aegisthus survived the fatal banquet and left Argos with his father (*Agam.* 1605ff.). For the social opprobium of *exul* compare Eur. *Med.* 553f. (Jason) τί τοῦδ' ἂν εὕρημ' ηὗρον εὐτυχέστερον, | ἢ παῖδα γῆμαι βασιλέως φυγὰς γεγώς;

293 adde The pointed use of *adde* is most closely paralleled in the dialogue of comedy, cf. Arist. *Eq.* 336f. – οὐκ αὖ μ' ἐάσεις; – μὰ Δί' ἐπεὶ κἀγὼ πονηρός εἰμι. | – ἐὰν δὲ μὴ ταύτῃ γ' ὑπείκῃ, λέγ' ὅτι κἀκ πονηρῶν. (Professor Jocelyn refers me to Men. *Sic.* 354ff. πρόσθες θυγάτριον and to Pl. *Ps.* 1304, where *hiberna addito* makes a comic point of a different sort.) S.'s immediate source might have been declamatory rhetoric, note Sen. *Contr.* 1.4.12 '*non potui*' inquit '*matrem occidere*'. *quo excusatior sis, adice 'et patrem.*'

297 quid deos probro addimus? Indignant reactions of this kind often occur when divine protection or justification is invoked by the wicked, cf. Soph. *Phil.* 992 θεοὺς προτείνων τοὺς θεοὺς ψευδεῖς τίθης, Eur. *Tro.* 987ff., fr. 254 N², Sen. *HF* 447 *quid uiolas Iouem?* (Lycus to Amphitryon), *Tro.* 753f., *Pha.* 199f.

addimus If E's *addimus* is right (and A's *aduocas* looks like an obvious trivialisation), two interpretations seem possible: (*a*) The plural is universalising, 'why do we (i.e. human beings) involve the gods in our crime?' (for the sense of *addo* cf. Virg. *Aen.* 2.660, Ovid, *Ars* 1.632 *pollicito testes quoslibet adde deos*, Stat. *Th.* 11.706). The construction is not rare (cf. Wackernagel, *Vorlesungen* 1.109, Hofmann–Szantyr 419), but most examples assert or imply that the speaker is part of the group he names (cf. Eur. *Hipp.* 670 ἔχομεν = 'we women', see Barrett *ad loc.*, Hor. *Epist.* 2.1.117 *scribimus indocti doctique poemata passim*, Prop. 3.7.31 *terra parum fuerat fatis, adiecimus undas*, Ovid, *Am.* 3.4.17 *nitimur in uetitum semper cupimusque negata*). A better parallel for our passage is Ter. *And.* 309 *facile omnes quom ualemus recta consilia aegrotis damus*, since the speaker is the *aegrotus* in the situation (note also Arist. *Lys.* 25, 715, in which Lysistrata's generalisations about 'we women' do not describe her own actions).

(*b*) The plural is a pointed way of saying *quid. . .addis?* This 'bedside plural' (so Nisbet in *Critical essays on Roman literature: satire* (1963) 53) is admittedly rare; its use may, however, be illustrated in a passage of Epictetus (*Diss.* 1.2.25) in which an athlete facing a delicate operation is encouraged by his brother, a philosopher: ἄγε, ἀδελφέ, τί μέλλεις ποιεῖν; ἀποκόπτομεν τοῦτο τὸ μέρος καὶ ἔτι εἰς γυμνάσιον προερχόμεθα; A very different passage, Soph. *O.C.* 1627f. (ὦ οὗτος οὗτος Οἰδίπους, τί μέλλομεν | χωρεῖν;) offers something comparable: Schneidewin–Nauck⁸ correctly comment 'τί μέλλομεν hat hier. . .den Sinn eines τί μέλλεις'. The use of this plural is likely to have been more common in colloquial speech; it is perhaps well suited to the openly sarcastic tone of Clytemestra's assault.

299 quem. . .uirum *Tantum* carries the sarcasm: 'whom we know to be a man only in unlawful love'; Hofmannsthal's Elektra makes the same point: 'Ägisth, der tapfre Meuchelmörder, er, der Heldentaten nur im Bett vollführt'. For *esse uirum* in a specifically sexual sense, cf. Ovid, *Am.* 3.7.20 *nec iuuenem nec me sensit amica uirum, Ars* 1.698 *haec illum stupro comperit esse uirum* (possibly the source for the present line), *Met.* 4.385f., Sen. *Pha.* 925f.; perhaps also Hor. *C.* 1.37.9, cf. Nisbet–Hubbard, Brink in *PCPS* 1971, p. 17.

300 facesse propere The phrase has clear archaic overtones. The only exact parallels come from the historians (cf. Livy 4.58.7, 6.17.8, Tac. *Ann.*

16.34.1 (on which see Syme, *Tacitus* II.741)), but both *facesse* in commands to depart and *propere* with an imperative are most common in Republican drama. For *facesse* (which S. uses only here), cf. Pl. *Men.* 249, *Rud.* 1062, Ter. *Phorm.* 635, Afranius 203 R², Titinius 53 R²; in tragedy Ennius, *sc.* 136 R², Pacuvius 326, 342 R²; the word is rare in both prose (cf. Cic. *Leg.* 1.39, *Phil.* fr. 5.49, Livy 1.47.5, Curt. 10.2.27) and poetry (cf. Lucr. 6.957?, Silius 11.107), cf. *T.L.L.* VI¹.39.60ff. The combination of *propere* and an imperative appears four times in Seneca, cf. Pl. *Aul.* 264, *Cas.* 744f., *Curc.* 688, *Rud.* 1323, *Trin.* 1174, Ter. *Hec.* 808, *H.T.* 250 (?), 744, Pac. 16 R², Acc. 301 R², *inc. inc. fab.* 138 R².

clarae If E's *nostrae* were instead the reading of A, it would have been long ago branded a patent gloss. *Dedecus clarae* is another example of Senecan juxtaposition of opposites (see above on *ultrix inultum* 220, below on *grauem leuibus* 323). The process by which *nostrae* could have ousted an original *clarae* is obvious; the reverse hypothesis involves interpolation of a remarkably free nature and is thus less likely (though hardly impossible). It might be objected that *nostrae* suits Clytemestra's resumption of her seigneurial status, but the point of this entire speech (295–301) is the unworthiness of Aegisthus, and this is better advanced by *clarae*.

301 asporta Used only here in the tragedies, and only once (Virg. *Aen.* 2.778) in poetry between Terence and Seneca. It is, however, found in prose (generally historical); compare the use of *portare* (Axelson, *Unpoetische Wörter* 30).

haec...uiro The implication is that Aegisthus is neither *rex* nor *uir*, cf. Livy 24.8.1 *tum uiro et gubernatore opus est*; for the technique cf. Canter 63f. In E and C *regi ac* has been independently corrupted to *regia*, to provide a substantive for *haec*; the unmetrical *regia* was accepted by L. Herrmann and E. Paratore (*SIFC* xxvii (1956) 350). Gronovius incorporated *regia* in a more ambitious rewriting (*regia haec pateat uiro*), of which only the jussive subjunctive needs to be considered (i.e. *uacet* for *uacat*). The indicative, however, better suggests imperious determination.

302ff. Aegisthus skilfully adapts his tactics to Clytemestra's changed mood. In the place of his hectoring superiority comes almost abject recognition of his partner's position (*si tu imperas, regina, iussu tuo*). The offer of suicide is so phrased as to place entire responsibility for it on Clytemestra; Phaedra's threat of suicide similarly overcomes her Nurse's scuples (*Pha.* 250ff.), but for close parallels one must go to later tragedy (cf. T. Legge, *Ricardus III* III.iv, Shakespeare, *Richard III* I.ii, and most strikingly Massinger, *Duke of Milan* III.iii).

302 assueui malis Aegisthus resumes the Stoic indifference to misfortune which marked his entrance-speech; cf. *Epist.* 76.35 *ideo sapiens adsuescit futuris malis*, Val. Fl. 4.449f. *consuetis serum est ex ordine fatis | ingemere.*

304 Argisue The Latin form also appears at *Tro.* 245, *Thy.* 119; the Greek form is more common in Seneca (cf. Nisbet–Hubbard on Hor. *C.* 1.7.9.)

305 pectus aerumnis graue The appeal for pity is saved for last. For the phrase compare *Pha.* 247 *fessumque curis pectus*; *aperire pectus*, cf. Sen. *Ira* 1.2.2 (*iugulum*).

aerumnis S. (and *HO*) use this high-sounding word twenty-three times, more often than any other Latin author. In Republican drama it appears in both tragedy (six times) and comedy (eighteen times in Plautus, four times each in Terence and Caecilius). Persius has it only once, in a probable parody of Pacuvius (1.78 *Antiopa aerumnis cor luctificabile fulta* on which see Bramble, *Persius and the programmatic satire* (1974) 174ff.); it occurs only once in Horace (*Epist.* 2.2.27) and Ovid (*Trist.* 4.6.25).

306 siquidem...sinam Studley and Miller correctly render the sense: 'if only I were to allow this, cruel daughter of Tyndaris that I am'. *Tyndaris*, cf. 162 above.

307 quae...fidem For the thought compare Publ. Syr. 148 *etiam in peccato recte praestatur fides*, Cic. *Off.* 2.40 *quin etiam leges latronum esse dicuntur, quibus pareant, quas obseruent*; compare *HO* 480f.
Clytemestra's sudden change of heart is not unusual in Seneca, cf. *HF* 1301, *Med.* 294f., *Pha.* 250ff., *Thy.* 542, Zwierlein, *Rezitationsdramen* 70f. Indeed, passages in which Seneca depicts a gradual change are rare (*Pho.* 306ff. approximates to such a description; in Greek note, e.g., Soph. *Ant.* 1091ff., *Phil.* 806, 906, 965f.). The artificial character of such sudden alterations should not be taken as merely a sign of poor dramatic technique. Seneca's interest lay more in the rhetorical expression of situations or attitudes than in the realistic depiction of change or development; hence he often takes a situation to its extreme and then abruptly shifts direction. Here this rhetorical interest furthers dramatic tension: in showing the conspiracy of Aegisthus and Clytemestra so close to dissolution he plays against the audience's foreknowledge of its ultimate success.
The use of a gnome to justify a course of action or to underscore a turning-point of narrative or dramatic action is familiar from Greek drama (two examples chosen at random: Soph. *Ant.* 313f., 1031f.); cf. Bömer on Ovid, *Met.* 2.416, and in Seneca cf., e.g., *Med.* 428, *Thy.* 202f. It is typical of Seneca's compressed style that here the gnome is both the statement and the explanation of Clytemestra's decision.

308f. The end of the scene presents several unusual features. First, the exit-formula *secede mecum...ut*, or anything remotely like it, is unparalleled in Seneca. In Senecan drama exits customarily involve only one actor, and are rarely motivated. Where a motive for leaving is given, the one most frequently used is the need to offer sacrifice or perform some other ritual act (cf. 583ff., 805ff. below, *HF* 514, *Med.* 299, *Thy.* 545, *HO* 579f.; also common in Greek drama, cf. Aesch. *Ag.* 1068, Soph. *O.C.* 509, Eur. *Ion* 675). Nor is there another instance of a character commanding another to depart with him (the closest analogous case is *Oed.* 707f., where Oedipus orders Creon to be led away to prison before announcing his own exit).

The command and the formula are, however, found in comedy. For orders to depart (often with an expression such as *sequere tu hac me intro*) cf. Pl. *Trin.* 1109, *Pseud.* 1016, 1230, 1329f., Ter. *Eun.* 506. While *secedere* in comedy is used of withdrawing to another part of the stage rather than of exits (Pl. *Am.* 771, *Asin.* 639, *Capt.* 218, 263, *Curc.* 281, etc.), Plautus and Terence employ *concedere* both of withdrawing (Pl. *Rud.* 1036, 1403, *Pseud.* 414) and of leaving the stage (cf. Pl. *Pseud.* 571 *concedere aliquantisper hinc mi intro lubet*).

The motivation for this exit is also of interest. It is extremely rare in Greek tragedy for two characters to depart with the announced purpose of planning future action (Soph. *O.T.* 861, where Jocasta urges Oedipus ἴωμεν ἐς δόμους, is taken by Jebb as an invitation to converse further, but the text does not require this reading); where such planning is dramatically important, it is normally conducted in the open, as in *Trachiniae*, where Lichas twice enters the palace (334, 496) so that Deianeira's plans may proceed on stage. Conversations which in life would be private are generally brought on to the stage (so in Soph. *O.T.* 697–862) or summarised afterwards (cf. Soph. *Ajax* 91ff., 681, on which cf. Ed. Fraenkel, *MH* xxiv (1967) 79–87).

Once again closer analogies can be found in comedy, in which exits by one or two characters in order to plan or execute action are common, cf. Pl. *Aul.* 694f., *Cas.* 511ff., *Most.* 1036ff., *Pers.* 77f., *Pseud.* 571f., Ter. *Eun.* 921, also K. S. Bennett, *Motivation of exits in Greek and Latin comedy* (diss. Ann Arbor, 1932), M. Johnston, *Exits and entrances in Roman comedy* (diss. Columbia, 1933) 148.

CHORUS II (310–411)

The second choral song, unlike the first, is linked to a specific *persona*, a chorus of Argive maidens. In form it is a hymn of thanksgiving to several gods, sung in celebration of Agamemnon's victory. Its most obvious dramatic function is to provide a variation in tone and outlook from the frenetic and introspective emotions of the first two acts and the brooding pessimism of the first ode.[1]

---

[1] Compare *Oed.* 403ff., *Pha.* 274ff. The attempts of Giomini (91) and Seidensticker (140 n.140) to see ironic connections between the present ode and the events of the play seem to me unpersuasive.

The song corresponds to Menander Rhetor's definition of a ὕμνος κλητικός: κλῆσιν ἔχοντες πολλῶν θεῶν,[1] a type of prayer to which the name *Reihengebet* is often applied and which is found both in the choral odes of Greek drama[2] and in records of genuine cultic observance.[3] It does not declare itself a *Reihengebet* at the start by a general invocation (for which cf. Aesch. *Sept.* 87ff., Hor. *C.* 1.2.25f.), but resembles instead the *parodos* of Sophocles' *Oedipus Tyrannus*, beginning as a paean to Apollo and later invoking several other deities.

Care is obvious in the choice of gods and the order in which they are named. Apollo is awarded first place and the longest invocation because he, as Troy's faithful ally, most needs to be placated and assured of a cult in Argos.[4] He is followed by Juno, who would normally receive the highest honours as the traditional patron of Argos, and then by Pallas, whose services to the Greeks at Troy demand commemoration. The relatively obscure fourth position is occupied by Diana, included perhaps for a symmetrical balance with Apollo.[5] Jupiter comes last (a position of honour, cf. Aesch. *Ag.* 514f.),[6] and the element of petition is more prominent here than elsewhere.

Two features of the opening section deserve notice. The change from command in 310 to description of the chorus' actions in 311–15 led early commentators to postulate an exchange between a chorus leader and the chorus.[7] Such a division is nowhere attested in Seneca, and is here unnecessary: the command *canite* in 310 is addressed by the chorus to its own members, a practice confirmed by numerous parallels.[8] The following lines are also spoken by the chorus, now describing itself in the third person and addressing the god directly (*tibi... tibi*). Seneca may be adapting for a

---

[1] *Rhetores Graeci* III.333.8 Spengel.

[2] Cf. Aesch. *Septem* 87ff., Soph. *Ajax* 693ff., *O.C.* 1085, Arist. *Nub.* 563ff., *Thesm.* 312ff.; Kranz, *Stasimon* 185ff.

[3] Cf. *Acta Fratrum Arualium* fr. 218 Henzen, Varro, *r. rust.* 1.1.5f., *ILS* 5035; Ed. Fraenkel, *Horace* 247.

[4] The prayer of the Herald in Aeschylus (*Ag.* 512ff.) offers a useful (though probably coincidental) parallel. The suggestion of L. Herrmann (*Théâtre de Sénèque* 95) that Phoebus is emphasised out of deference to Nero is unprovable and probably unnecessary.

[5] The invocation to Diana also develops the allusion made in 323ff. to Ovid's story of Niobe.

[6] Note also the position of Zeus in Soph. *O.T.* 200ff.

[7] To this chorus-leader Farnaby attributed 310, Ascensius 310 and 316–25.

[8] Cf. Nisbet–Hubbard on Hor. *C.* 1.21.1 *dicite* (although this passage is of the type dealt with in the following note), adding *Carm. Sal.* fr. 1 Maurenbrecher *diuom patrem cante*, anon. (p. 173 Powell) μέλπετε κοῦραι | Ζῆνα.

dramatic form the conventions of the Hellenistic literary hymn, in which the poet may alternately describe and direct the activities of a chorus.[1]

Less tractable is the problem raised by 316-25, in which the chorus invites the citizens of Thebes and Sparta[2] to join its song. No division of the following prayers among multiple choruses is preserved in the MSS, nor do the contents of the ode suggest that such partitioning was intended.[3] The geographical basis of division is also unusual: where cult-songs are performed by a divided chorus, the semi-choruses are generally composed of boys and girls.[4]

No precise parallel can be found elsewhere in ancient drama. The final scene of Aeschylus' *Septem* (if indeed the chorus of handmaidens is invited to take up the song of the Danaid daughters)[5] is essentially different in that the sentiments of the two groups are clearly distinguished. Perhaps the closest analogue for these lines comes from Aristophanes' *Peace*, in which the chorus is at times panhellenic and is summoned by listing the groups which it comprises.[6] A possible explanation is suggested by the short ὑπόρχημα in Soph. *Trach.* 205ff., which issues orders for a joyful song to be executed by groups of young men and women. This song, however, cannot be literally performed (since Sophocles' chorus consists entirely of women), and the lines calling for it are meant to suggest the joyful state of mind of the chorus. Similarly in our passage, the lines addressed to other Greek cities may be only a rhetorical device for expressing the relief which the defeat of Troy has brought to all Greece.[7]

310 pubes For the collective use cf. *inc. inc. fab.* 33 R² *Attica pubes*, Virg. *Aen.* 5.119 *pubes Dardana*, Tib. 1.1.23 *rustica pubes* (in a sacrificial context), Claud. *Ruf.* 2.283.

Phoebum The statement of the hymn's addressee in the opening line is traditional, cf. *Hymn. Hom.* 1 (*et saepe*), *PMG* 698 Terpander, Alcaeus 308 *PLF*, Catull. 34, Hor. *C.* 1.10, 1.21, etc. Seneca is elsewhere more allusive, cf. *Pha.* 54ff., *Oed.* 403ff.

311 tibi The hymnic use of *tu* in anaphora is too common to require

---

[1] Cf. Callimachus, *Hymn.* 2.8ff., 5 *passim*, Hor. *C.* 1.21, Tib. 2.1; G. Williams, *Tradition and originality* 211ff.
[2] A third city may be invoked in 316, but the text is uncertain.
[3] Cf. 350ff., 400ff.
[4] See Nisbet–Hubbard on Hor. *C.* 1.21 (pp. 253f.); for the dances of the Salii cf. Dion. Hal. *Quaest. Rom.* 2.70.5, and note the description of Trojan thanksgiving in 642f. below (*ducunt turmas, haec femineas, ille uiriles*).
[5] At issue are the words ὑποδέξασθε δ' ὀπαδοὶ | μέλος (1022f.); see most recently A. F. Garvie, *Aeschylus' Supplices: play and trilogy* (1969) 194f.
[6] *Pax* 296ff., 466ff.; for the summoning of the chorus compare *Aues* 227ff.
[7] Compare the purely rhetorical invocations in *HF* 1163ff., *Pho.* 124ff.

illustration (cf. E. Norden, *Agnostos Theos* 143ff., Nisbet–Hubbard on Hor. *C.* 1.10.9); in Seneca cf. Med. 67ff., 797ff., *Pha.* 54ff., *Oed.* 412ff., *Ag.* 829, 862ff.

312ff. uirgineas...comas Seneca insists on the virginal status of the chorus for its sacral significance, cf. Livy 27.37.12, Macr. *Sat.* 1.6.14, Catull. 34.2, Hor. *C.* 1.21.1, *Carm. Saec.* 6ff., *Epist.* 2.1.132.

313 quatiens In other contexts the verb may suggest religious ecstasy, cf. Virg. *G.* 4.64 *Matris quate cymbala circum*, Ovid, *Ibis* 456 *et quatias molli tympana rauca manu.*

314 comas...fudit The liturgical principle is stated by Servius (on *Aen.* 4.518) *in sacris nil solet esse religatum* (cf. Eur. *I.T.* 468f.); cf. Ovid, *F.* 3.257f. *si qua tamen grauida est, resoluto crine precetur | ut* eqs., *Met.* 7.257, 9.772, Tib. 1.5.15 (with Smith's note), Livy 3.7.8, Sen. *Med.* 752f., *Pha.* 371, *Oed.* 230, 403f. *effusam redimite comam*, 416f., Petr. *Sat.* 44, Apul. *Met.* 6.2. For Greek evidence see Nilsson, *GGR* I³.114.

innuba Used only here by Seneca, *innuba* is elsewhere associated with sacred virginity, cf. Ovid, *Met.* 10.567 (Atalanta), 14.142 (the Sibyl); Luc. 9.665, Val. Fl. 1.87, and *Epigr. Bob.* 15.5 Speyer (= *Anth. Pal.* 16.178) (all Pallas), Stat. *Th.* 4.463 (Manto), Prud. *Apoth.* 571 (Mary).

315 Inachia = *Argolica*, cf. Ovid, *Her.* 13.132 *Inachiae...rates*, Sen. *Pho.* 444, *Apocol.* 7.2.12 (*urbs Inachia*, in tragic parody).

316ff. The two references to Thebes in this short catalogue (*Thebais hospes*/*Thebana manus* 316, *quaeque...bibis Ismenon* 320f.) have long troubled editors. Bothe transposed 316–17 to succeed 321, linking the Theban references; the clauses *quaeque...fontes* (318), *quaeque Eurotan* (319), and *quaeque...Ismenon* (320f.) would then naturally be taken as parallel in syntax to *comas...fudit | stirps Inachia*, and the transposed words *tu...choros* would constitute an invitation addressed only to the Thebans. This can hardly be right.

A more promising approach is to remove *Thebais* in 316; it is jarringly direct in this periphrastic context. Heinsius' *Oebalis hospes* is elegant and stylistically apt, since *Oebalius* is a favourite with Ovid (cf. *F.* 1.260, *RA* 458). In this setting, however, *Oebalis hospes* could only suggest Clytemestra: note Soph. *Ant.* 824 τὰν Φρυγίαν ξέναν (of a foreign queen), Juv. 8.218f. *Spartani...coniugii*, Stat. *S.* 3.2.10 *Oebalii fratres* (the Dioscuri). On the other hand Richter's *Thespias* is both geographically and palaeographically unobjectionable. *Thespias* is rare in poetry (cf. Val. Fl. 1.478), but *Thespiades* (Ovid, *Met.* 5.310, Val. Fl. 2.368, Silius 11.19) and *Thespiacus* (Stat. *S.* 2.7.16) are recognised. Only the relative obscurity of the place tells against the change.

Certainty appears out of reach, and the possibility of deeper corruption should not be excluded. The A variant *Thebana manus* might be banalisation of the E text, but might also reflect an early corruption.

318ff. The use of rivers to designate cities, countries, or their inhabitants is an old literary convention, cf. *Il.* 2.825, Aesch. *Ag.* 1157, Hor. *C.* 2.20.20, 3.10.1, 4.15.21, Virg. *Ecl.* 1.62, Ovid, *Tr.* 5.3.24, Sen. *N.Q.* 1 *pr.* 8; cf. *T.L.L.* II.1964.39ff., Levy on Claud. *Ruf.* 1.312. Seneca uses the figure in his other hymns (*Pha.* 57f., *Oed.* 427ff.), and in other contexts, cf. *Med.* 373ff. (adynaton) with Costa's note, *Pho.* 124ff., 602ff., *HF* 1323ff., *Med.* 681ff., 707ff., *Pha.* 505ff.

The rivers described here lacked settled characteristics in Roman poetry. The Erasinus, *gelidus* here and in Stat. *Th.* 1.357, is *ingens* in Ovid, *Met.* 15.276; compare Stat. *Th.* 4.122, 4.713 *numquam in ripis audax Erasinus.* The Eurotas, which Seneca leaves unqualified, is called tree-lined by Catullus (64.89) and Martial (9.75.9), in conformity with Greek tradition (cf. Theogn. 785, Eur. *Hel.* 210, 349, 493, *I.T.* 399, *I.A.* 179); but it is *frigidus* in Ovid (*Am.* 2.17.32) and in Statius it is both *asper* (*Th.* 1.118f.) and *olorifer* (4.227). The Ismenos in our passage has the foliage-lined banks elsewhere attributed to the Eurotas (perhaps derived from Virgil's description of the Mincio in *Ecl.* 7.13 *hic uiridis tenera praetexit harundine ripas | Mincius*); in *Oed.* 42 it is *tenuis* and in *HO* 141 *languidus*, but in *Phoen.* 116 *ubi torua rapidus ducat Ismenos uada* it displays a violence perhaps influenced by Ovid, *Met.* 2.244 (*celer*).

322ff. Seneca's source here is Ovid, *Met.* 6.157ff.: *nam sata Tiresia uenturi praescia Manto | per medias fuerat, diuino concita motu, | uaticinata uias: 'Ismenides, ite frequentes | et date Latonae Latonigenisque duobus | cum prece tura pia lauroque innectite crinem.'* Seneca takes over *sata Tiresia, praescia Manto* and *Latonigenas* (which appears only here and in Ovid). In Ovid, Manto's warning leads to the story of Niobe, which Seneca treats in 392ff. below.

326ff. The prayer to Apollo corresponds to the prayer of the Herald in Aeschylus (*Ag.* 509ff.): ὁ Πύθιός τ' ἄναξ | τόξοις ἰάπτων μηκέτ' εἰς ἡμᾶς βέλη· | ἅλις παρὰ Σκάμανδρον ἦσθ' ἀνάρσιος· | νῦν δ' αὖτε σωτὴρ ἴσθι καὶ παιώνιος. The boys in Horace's *Carmen Saeculare* similarly ask Apollo to hear their prayer *condito mitis placidusque telo* (33). Seneca combines this request with the conventional linking of the bow and the lyre as symbols of Apollo's areas of prowess and patronage; cf. *Hymn. Hom. Apoll.* 131, Call. *Hymn.* 2.18f., Hor. *C.* 2.10.18f., 1.21.11f., Prop. 4.6.69f., Ovid, *R.A.* 705, *Pont.* 4.8.75, [*Her.* 15.23], *Laus Pisonis* 171f.

326 uinclo All editors since Gronovius have accepted E's *uictor*; but how can the Greeks address Apollo as victor? (Ascensius' paraphrase of *uictor*, 'uoti compos cum perfidiam Laomedontis ultus sis' is inappropriate and impossibly obscure.) Furthermore, the Aeschylean parallel makes it clear that Apollo is being asked not to prolong his enmity toward the Greeks beyond the end of the war, and *uictor* has no place in this context. *Vinclo*, though weakly attested, might have been the reading of A (*uicto*, the reading in PS, could more easily be a corruption of *uinclo* than of *uictor*); it removes the difficulty and produces a more elegant word-order. For *uinculum* of the knot which holds the bowstring in place, cf. Ovid, *Pont.* 1.2.19f. *et semel intentus neruo leuis arcus equino | uincula semper habens irresoluta manet*; for the ablative with *relaxo* cf. Cic. *Sen.* 81 [*animi*] *cum se plane corporum uinculis relaxauerint*, *Laus Pis.* 143 *extemplo sed laxat cornua neruo*, cf. Sen. *Med.* 752 *uinculo soluens comam.* The loosening of Apollo's (or Diana's) bow as a sign of benevolence is traditional, cf. *Hymn. Hom.* 3.5f., 27.11ff.

328 graues leuibus The arrows are heavy in the quiver, light when shot from the bow; the juxtaposition is therefore not merely ornamental (for the technique, cf. Ovid, *Met.* 1.551 *uelox pigris*, Sen. *Pha.* 111 *rigida molli*, 309 *obscuri clara*, 653 *mollibus fortes*, 922 *molles dura*, etc. (Seidler 105); for proper adjectives so combined see note on 613 below). S. may have had in mind Horace's *uenenatis grauida sagittis, | Fusce, pharetra* (*C.* 1.22.3f.).

331 uocale here functions like an adverb. The transferred epithet may have been suggested by such passages as Ovid, *Met.* 5.332 *hactenus ad citharam uocalia mouerat ora*, 11.317 *carmine uocali clarus citharaque Philammon*; cf. also Sen. *Thy.* 659 *uocales tubae.*

chelys The word is not securely attested in Latin before the Neronian period; it appears as an equivalent for the older *lyra* or *cithara*; of Apollo, as here, cf. [Ovid], *Her.* 15.181 (in *Carm. Eins.* 1.17 it is played under Apollo's inspiration as a pastoral instrument), cf. Ovid, *Pont.* 4.8.75 *nec ad citharam nec ad arcum segnis Apollo*; of Achilles, Sen. *Tro.* 321 *leui canoram uerberans plectro chelyn*, cf. Stat. *Ach.* 1.575 *digitosque sonanti | infringit citharae*; of Amphion Sen. *Oed.* 611, cf. Stat. *Th.* 8.233; of Orpheus ps.-Sen. *HO* 1033, 1063; in uncertain contexts Pomponius Secundus *inc. fab. fr.* 2 R², Caesius Bassus (*GLK* vi.262).

332 uelim The tone becomes more deferential after the urgent imperatives *relaxa* and *pone* and the commanding *resonet* (for the force of *uelim* see on 694 *putem*). The contrasting forms of song are described in terms often applied in poetry to stylistic discussion: *acre*, *magnum*, *altis modis*, *intonare*, *chorda grauiore sonare* suit the military epic; *leuiore lyra*, *flectere*, *carmen simplex*, *lusus*, *docta Musa*, *recensere* suggest smaller-scale work in an 'Alexandrian' style.

acre 'harsh'; the dominant reference is not to quality of sound (*pace T.L.L.* 1.360.46) but subject matter, cf. *bellum acerrimum* Cic. *Balb.* 14, *Brut.* 76 (of Ennius' *Annales*), *acria bella* Ovid, *Ibis* 642, *acerrima...proelia Laus Pis.* 205f., etc.

332f. modis...altis 'in heroic metres'; the elegists in particular made play with the distinction between the hexameter and the couplet (cf. Ovid, *Am.*

2.17.22), cf. Ovid, *Am.* 1.1.28 *ferrea cum uestris bella ualete modis, R.A.* 381 *Callimachi numeris non est dicendus Achilles.* Epic requires a *grauis numerus* (Ovid, *Am.* 1.1.1), while the *modi* of lyric or elegy are *molles* (Hor. *C.* 2.12.3), *dulces* (*C.* 3.9.10) or *exigui* (Ovid, *F.* 6.22); cf. as well Horace's *exiguos elegos* (*A.P.* 77).

333 intonet As a literary term *intono* refers to the more elevated genres, cf. Prop. 2.1.39f. *neque...Iouis Enceladique tumultus | intonet angusto pectore Callimachus* (cf. Call. *Aetia* fr. 1 Pf. 20 βροντᾶν οὐκ ἐμόν, ἀλλὰ Διός, 35f.), 3.17.40, *Laus Pis.* 239f. *Maecenas alta tonantis* [= *Vergilii*] | *eruit,* Mart. 7.23.1, 8.3.14, Stat. *S.* 5.3.97.

334 leuiore lyra 'in a lighter style', cf. Hor. *C.* 2.1.40 *leuiore plectro,* Ovid, *Am.* 1.1.19 *numeris leuioribus, Met.* 10.152 *leuiore lyra*; for *lyra* of the song sung to it cf. Hor. *C.* 1.6.10 *imbellisque lyrae Musa potens,* 3.3.69 *iocosa lyra,* cf. Prop. 2.10.10 *nunc aliam citharam me mea Musa docet.*

335 flectere *Flectere uocem* is to sing with a florid, ornamented vocal line, cf. Vitruvius 5.4.2 *uox...mutationibus cum flectitur, alias fit acuta, alias grauis,* also Lucr. 5.1406 (with Bailey's note), Tib. 1.7.37, Ovid, *Am.* 2.4.25.

336 lusus *Lusus, ludus,* and *ludere* often denote the lighter genres of poetry, cf. Pliny, *Epist.* 7.9 *carmine...non diu continuo et longo, sed hoc arguto et breui; lusus uocatur,* also Prop. 2.34.85, Hor. *C.* 4.9.9ff., Ovid, *F.* 4.9f., *Carm. Eins.* 1.4, *Culex* 1ff., *Anth. Lat.* 429.1 Riese; H. Wagenvoort, *Studies in Roman literature* 30ff. The Greek equivalent is παίγνιον and παίζειν; cf. *Anth. Pal.* 6.322 (Leonidas), 5.112 (Philodemus), Polybius 16.21.12, Aelian, *H.A.* 15.19.
Apollo is thus invited to amuse himself with literary trifles, as all great poets were thought to do; cf. Stat. *S.* 1 *pr.* 8 *nec quisquam est illustrium poetarum qui non aliquid operibus suis stilo remissiore praeluserit, Culex* 1ff., cf. Ed. Fraenkel, *Kleine Beiträge* (1964) II.192ff. Seneca may well have been thinking of, and adapting, the words of Ovid's Orpheus (*Met.* 10.149ff.): *Iouis est mihi saepe potestas | dicta prius: cecini plectro grauiore Gigantas | sparsaque Phlegraeis uictricia fulmina campis. | nunc opus est leuiore lyra: puerosque canamus | dilectos superis* eqs.

336f. docta...Musa The *doctus poeta* (here Apollo) must be inspired by a *docta puella* or a *docta Musa*; cf. Fordyce on Catull. 35.17, Catull. 65.2, [Tib.] 3.4.5, Ovid, *Met.* 5.255, *Carm. Eins.* 1.35.

337 recenset Used by the historians of inspecting troops (Livy 1.16.1, 2.39.9, Suet. *Calig.* 44), by Gellius (17.10.6) of an author revising his own work.
Seneca here combines two ideas from earlier poetry: that of Apollo practising on his lyre (cf. Virg. *Ecl.* 6.82f. *omnia quae Phoebo quondam meditante... | audiit Eurotas,* cf. Tib. 2.3.19f.), and the Hellenistic theme of the

poet who asks the Muses to review his work, for which compare the opening of the *Seal of Posidippus*: εἴ τι καλόν, Μοῦσαι πολιήτιδες, ἢ παρὰ Φοίβου | χρυσολύρεω καθαροῖς οὔασιν ἐκλύετε | Παρνησοῦ νιφόεντος ἀνὰ πτύχας, κτλ. (on the poem cf. Lloyd-Jones, *JHS* lxxxiii (1963) 75ff.). The first of the Einsiedeln eclogues (which in general seem to owe much to this passage) tastelessly varies the picture by portraying the Muses as rushing to hear Nero perform (35).

338 chorda grauiore Cf. Hor. *C.* 4.2.33 *maiore plectro*, Ovid, *Met.* 10.150. Though *chorda grauiore* is literally true, S. is probably using *grauior* in a transferred sense, cf. *Laus Pis.* 175 *grauis obstreperet...bucina*; in Hor. *A.P.* 348f. *grauis* is applied to the sound produced by the *chorda* (though 349 is suspect).

sones Cf. Hor. *C.* 2.13.26 *te sonantem plenius aureo...plectro*, [Ovid], *Her.* 15.29f. *nec plus Alcaeus... | laudis habet, quamuis grandius ille sonet*, *Laus Pis.* 241, Mart. 9 *pr.* 3 *maiores maiora sonent*.

339 quale canebas I know of no other reference to an epincion sung by Apollo after the Gigantomachy; the first Einsiedeln eclogue, however, portrays Apollo as singing an epinicion at the death of Python (32f.), and this may represent an adaptation of our passage.

340ff. The subject suggested for Apollo's loftier song itself alludes to a Hellenistic literary motif. From Callimachus onwards the Gigantomachy typifies epic, which poets in other genres decline to write since it is unsuited to their talents and interests (cf. Prop. 2.1.19f., 39f., 3.9.47ff., Ovid, *Am.* 2.1.11ff., *Tr.* 2.333f., *Culex* 26ff.; also L. P. Wilkinson in *Entretiens sur l'antiquité classique* II (1953) 241).

Seneca's treatment of the Giants illustrates the tendency to abstraction so often seen in his poetry. The events of the myth are reduced to the most famous, and even this is told in a curiously impersonal manner. The Aloides are not named, and are relegated to a subordinate syntactical position (*trucibus monstris* 344); the verb of action, *struere*, is applied not to the Giants (as in Ovid, *Met.* 1.153, *F.* 5.39) but to the mountains themselves. The mountains are in fact the central figures of the short digression, which concludes by describing them in a calm and motionless tableau; here Seneca permits himself a single graphic word (*pinifer* 346) whose effect is increased by its isolation. The sense of struggle and action conveyed by Horace (*C.* 3.4.42ff.) and (to a lesser extent) by Ovid (*Met.* 1.151ff.) is deliberately avoided, since the event functions here as a memory, not a fact (contrast *Thy.* 804ff.). The indirectness of narration is analogous to that in Ovid, *Am.* 2.1.11ff. *ausus eram, memini, caelestia dicere bella... | cum male se Tellus ulta est ingestaque Olympo | ardua deuexum Pelion Ossa tulit*; the poetic means employed, however, are Seneca's own.

340f. fulmine uictos | uidere dei E/fulmine misso | fregere dei A

238

The A text bears an obvious similarity to Ovid, *Met.* 1.154f. *tum pater omnipotens misso perfregit Olympum | fulmine*, but this is hard to weigh. Senecan imitation of Ovid is endemic, but if Seneca wrote E's version, the Ovidian passage would provide an obvious quarry for an interpolator seeking to improve on the author.

After some vacillation I have retained E's text, primarily because A's version is, in Giomini's words (p. 97), 'innegabilmente più realistico, più animato, più incisivo'. Good qualities in general, but precisely the ones which Seneca seems to have been at pains to avoid in this passage.

342f. montes...impositi Perhaps reminiscent of Manilius 1.425f. [*Iuppiter uidit*] *montibus atque altis aggestos crescere montes.*

344 gradus Cf. *HF* 971f. *uideat sub Ossa Pelion Chiron suum, | in caelum Olympus tertio positus gradu, Tro.* 829f. *tertius caelo gradus* (Pelion).

345ff. stetit...Olympus The order of mountains was subject to variation. In *Odyssey* 11.315f. Olympus stands at the bottom, with Ossa upon it and Pelion on Ossa; in Virgil (*G.* 1.281f.) this order is reversed: *ter sunt conati imponere Pelio Ossam | scilicet atque Ossae frondosum inuoluere Olympum.* Virgil is followed by the author of *Aetna* (49), Homer by Horace (*C.* 3.4.51f.) and Statius (*S.* 3.2.64f.). Ovid and Seneca are not consistent: Seneca adopts the Virgilian order here and in *HF* 970f., but follows Homer in *Tro.* 829f. and *Thy.* 813 (as does the author of *HO* 496, 1152f.); Ovid's account in *Met.* 1.154f. is apparently Virgilian (the phrasing is allusive, but note *subiectae...Ossae*), while *Am.* 2.1.12f., *F.* 1.307f. and 3.441 are clearly Homeric.

346 pinifer More specific than Virgil's *frondosum* (*G.* 1.282, cf. Eur. *Ba.* 560f. ἐν ταῖς πολυδένδρεσ-|ιν Ὀλύμπου | θαλάμαις) and Horace's *opaco* (*C.* 3.4.51); the epithet may have been suggested by Ovid, *F.* 3.389 *summa uirent pinu*, of Pelion (note also Lucan 1.389 *piniferae...Ossae*), though *pinifer* (or *-ger*) of other mountains is not uncommon, cf. Virg. *Ecl.* 10.14f., *Aen.* 4.249, 10.708, Ovid, *F.* 3.84, Stat. *S.* 3.4.12 (of Ida = πιδήεσσα, πολυπίδακος), Val. Fl. 6.392f.

348ff. In the following lines Seneca may be drawing on Ovid, *Am.* 3.13.11ff. *huc, ubi praesonuit sollemni tibia cantu, | it per uelatas annua pompa uias. | ducuntur niueae populo plaudente iuuencae, | ... | et uituli nondum metuenda fronte minaces*, eqs.; though Ovid is describing an Italian festival, he notes its Argive origin and appearance (*Argiua est pompae facies*, 31). It seems unlikely that S. should have sought out Greek accounts of the worship of Argive Hera (as supposed by Nilsson, *Griechische Feste* 43 n.3).

348 ades A formulaic invocation made necessary by the local character of pagan gods. Equivalent Greek expressions (ἐλθέ, ἱκοῦ, μόλε, προφάνητε) are found in epic (*Il.* 23.770), lyric (Alcaeus, *PLF* 34.1, 3) and especially drama (Aesch. *Eum.* 289, *Pers.* 658ff., fr. 255 N², Soph. *Ajax* 697, *O.T.* 167, *O.C.* 1012, Eur. *El.* 680, *Or.* 1231, Arist. *Ach.* 665, *Thesm.* 1136, etc.); cf. W. Kranz, *Stasimon* 186. Latin examples are collected by Bömer on Ovid, *F.* 1.65, Nisbet–Hubbard on Hor. *C.* 1.2.30 *uenias*; for *ades* cf. *Pha.* 54, *Oed.* 405.

soror et coniunx The Latin equivalent of the Homeric κασιγνήτη ἄλοχός τε, cf. Virg. *Aen.* 1.47, Hor. *C.* 3.3.64, Ovid, *Met.* 13.574. Such a commonplace was naturally subject to clever variation: Ovid calls Juno *sui germana mariti* (*F.* 6.17), Valerius Flaccus *regum soror* (3.514); Ovid also calls Jupiter *uir et frater* (*Her.* 4.35). Seneca's *HF* opens with such a variation turned to good dramatic effect (*Soror Tonantis – hoc enim solum mihi | nomen relictum est*, perhaps inspired by Ovid, *Met.* 3.265 *soror et coniunx – certe soror*).

349 consors sceptri The genitive with *consors* is a favourite Ovidian expression; see above on 256 and note *Met.* 6.94 *magni consorte Iouis*. Compare also 978 below, *consors pericli pariter ac regni mei* with Ovid, *Her.* 3.47 *consortes pariter generisque necisque*, *F.* 3.873 *amissa gemini consorte pericli* (and cf. *F.* 3.492 *consors culpae*).

350 regia Iuno Another Ovidian borrowing, cf. *Met.* 9.94, 9.21, 14.829, *Pont.* 1.4.39 (also *regia coniunx* in, e.g., *Met.* 6.332); *regius* is not elsewhere used of a deity in Seneca. *Regia Iuno* may render πότνια Ἥρα (cf. Eur. *Hel.* 1093f., *Pho.* 1365); it also suggests the Roman cult of Iuno Regina, on which see Livy 5.21ff., 31.3 (and Ogilvie *ad locc.*), Bömer on Ovid, *F.* 6.37. For the appositional style of this invocation, see Nisbet–Hubbard on Hor. *C.* 1.10.1.

350f. tua...turba Recalling a close connection with the god is a recurring feature of ancient prayers, cf. *Oed.* 405ff. *uotis | quae tibi nobiles | Thebae, Bacche, tuae...ferunt*, Claud. *Ruf.* 1.338 *Thracas defende tuos* (Ovid plays on the commonplace in *Am.* 2.9.11, of Cupid: *nos tua sentimus, populus tibi deditus, arma*). The association of Hera with Argos was well known, and Seneca need not have looked beyond, e.g., Hor. *C.* 1.7.8, Ovid, *F.* 3.83, *Her.* 14.28, 6.47, *Met.* 6.414.

354 sola The word establishes the god's unique ability to provide for the worshippers' well-being, cf. for examples Norden, *Agnostos Theos* 155 n.1, Nisbet–Hubbard on Hor. *C.* 1.26.9 (*sine te*, a common variant); cf. *Pha.* 406 *regina nemorum, sola quae montes colis*, Eur. *Her.* 770ff.

355 geris The paradosis is *regis*, a word often found in hymns, both of a god's control over a place of cult (so, e.g., Hor. *C.* 1.35.1 *diua gratum quae regis Antium*) or an activity or sphere of influence (cf. Hor. *Epod.* 5.51 *Nox et Diana quae silentium regis*, Caes. *B.G.* 6.17.2 *Martem bella regere* [*u.l. gerere*]); when used with *manu*, however, *regere* normally has a specific physical sense which is not suited to the present context.

The variant *geris* appears, presumably by conjecture, in late MSS and was glossed by Ascensius ('tu geris manu bella et pacem quia regnorum, ob quae bella fiunt, dea est'; this can hardly be right); it was laconically suggested by Bentley ('sic Virgil.' in his edition of Gronovius) and more recently commended by Zwierlein (*Philol.* cxiii (1969) 264).

Bentley's reference was probably to Virg. *Aen.* 7.444 *bella uiri pacemque gerent, quis bella gerenda*; for other instances of *bella pacemque gerere* cf. *Aen.* 9.277, Ovid, *Am.* 3.8.58, Sall. *Jug.* 46.8. The addition of *manu* in our passage, however, raises a slight problem. S. may also have been thinking of another Virgilian line, *Aen.* 7.455 *bella manu letumque gero*, but there *manu* means 'in my hand' and has a precise physical reference, Allecto's torch (this is also the case with similar phrases in Sall. *Cat.* 58.8, Curtius 4.14.25, Manilius 5.302); with *bella pacemque*, however, it is hard to see how *manu* can retain this physical meaning. If, therefore, *geris* is correct, *manu* is best taken to mean 'with strength', cf. Naevius, *com.* 108 R² *qui res magnas manu saepe gessit gloriose*, Enn. *Ann.* 326 V², Sen. *Ben.* 3.29.7 *quae consilio ac manu gero* (see also on 515 below). The sense is thus 'you conduct war and peace with strength', and 'for us, in our interest' is to be understood. If *regis* were retained, *manu* would have to be similarly interpreted; but I have found no instance of *regere manu* in this sense, which leads me to prefer *geris*.

356 Agamemnonias The epithet is found in Euripides (*Andr.* 1034, *Or.* 838) and was perhaps first Latinised by Virgil (*Aen.* 3.54, 4.471, 6.489, 838, 7.723); cf. also Prop. 4.1.111, Livy 45.27.9, Ovid, *Ibis* 525, Sen. *Tro.* 154f., *Anth. Lat.* 411.5, Claud. *Ruf.* 1.82, *Gild.* 1.484.

356f. laurus...accipe uictrix S. may be adapting to an Argive context the Roman custom of placing the *laurus* which had adorned the conqueror's *fasces* on the statue of Iuppiter Optimus Maximus (cf. Pliny, *N.H.* 15.134, Stat. *S.* 4.1.41 *nondum gremio Iouis Indica laurus*); the evidence for dedicating spoils to Argive Hera is slight (cf. Lyc. *Alex.* 1327f. and scholia, Gruppe, *Griech. Myth.* 1117.2b).

358 multifora The adjective occurs only here and Ovid, *Met.* 12.158 *longaue multifori delectat tibia buxi*; Apuleius has *multiforatilis* and *multiforabilis tibia* (*Flor.* 3.4, *Met.* 10.32).

362f. uotiuam...iactant S. need have had no specific ritual in mind; the waving of torches (on *iactant* see Costa's note on *Med.* 112 *excute... ignem*) is not prominent in the worship of Hera or Juno. Gronovius suggested that S. had adapted to a new context a detail derived from the Eleusinian mysteries (compare *HF* 302 *Eleusin tacita iactabit faces*, *Pha.* 106f. *non inter aras, Atthidum mixtam choris, | iactare tacitis conscias sacris faces*, Lact. 1.21 *sacra eius, ardentium taedarum iactatione celebrantur*); for these torches cf. Nilsson, *GGR* 1³.656, P. Stenger, *Griechische Kultusaltertümer* 180. In a somewhat comparable way Statius (*Th.* 10.56ff.) introduces into the cult of Argive Hera the *peplos* normally offered to Athena.

364 coniunx tauri Cows were offered to both Hera and Juno, cf. Pease on Virg. *Aen.* 4.61. For the pompous circumlocution cf. Nisbet–Hubbard on Hor. *C.* 1.17.7, 1.25.14, adding Virg. *G.* 3.218, Ovid, *Am.* 2.12.25 *uidi ego pro niuea pugnantes coniuge tauros*, [3.5.16], *Met.* 10.326 *fit equo sua filia coniunx*, Pliny, *N.H.* 8.43, 10.161, Stat. *Th.* 6.865, Servius on Virg. *Aen.* 4.551.

candida The customary colour of victims offered to *di superi*, cf. Krause in *RE* Suppl. v (1931) 244f., Virg. *Aen.* 4.61, Ovid, *Am.* 3.13.13, *F.* 1.720, Sen. *Med.* 61.

365 cadet The future is to be preferred, both as the reading more likely to have been altered and because the Ovidian parallel (*Am.* 3.13.11ff.) shows that the victims are displayed to the accompaniment of the *tibia* before being slaughtered. *Cadet* may also contain a promise of worship continuing beyond the present occasion, cf. Tib. 1.1.23 *agna cadet uobis*.

366 nescia aratri The victim was required to be both unspotted (*candida* above) and untainted by profane service, cf. Nilsson, *GGR* 1³.433, Bömer on Ovid, *F.* 1.83, also 3.375f. *caesa...iuuenca,* | *quae dederat nulli colla premenda iugo*, 4.335f., Sen. *Med.* 61f., *Oed.* 299 (on which cf. Zwierlein, *Rezitationsdramen* 183f.).

368f. tuque...Pallas The transition is eased by *tuque*, which functions like καὶ σύ or σύ τ' in Greek (cf. Aesch. *Sept.* 127, 135, 140, 145, 150; Arist. *Thesm.* 317, 320, 322); note 382 *et te*, 400 *tuque*.

368 nata Tonantis Cf. *Il.* 5.115 αἰγιόχοιο Διὸς τέκος, Soph. *Ajax* 91, Eur. *Hel.* 25, *Phoen.* 1373, *Or.* 1439, *Cyc.* 350.

369 inclita Of Pallas cf. *Ilias Latina* 1069f. *ipsa tuas depone lyras, ades, inclita Pallas,* | *tuque faue cursu uati iam Phoebe peracto*; of other gods cf. Pl. *Pers.* 251 (Jupiter), Lucr. 1.40 (Venus).

370 quae For the technique of invocation (called 'dynamic predication') see Norden, *Agnostos Theos* 168ff.; in Seneca cf. *HF* 592ff., *Pha.* 960ff., *Oed.* 250ff.; cf. *HO* 1ff.

370f. Dardanias saepe petisti cuspide turres A/Dardanias cuspide turres saepe petisti E The order of A produces a hyperbaton (*Dardanias...turres*) precisely paralleled at several points in the ode, cf. 316f. *nostros...choros*, 324f. *Latonigenas...deos*, 328f. *graues...pharetras*, 348f., 372f., 396f. The effect may be compared to that sometimes produced by a Horatian adonius, e.g. *C.* 1.12.20; 1.22.4, 12; 1.32.4, etc.

petisti Note Virg. *Aen.* 3.603 *bello Iliacos fateor petiise penatis*. For *petere* used of lunging at an opponent (perhaps originally of gladiators) cf. Cic. *Orat.* 228, *Lig.* 9, Virg. *Ecl.* 3.97, Sen. *N.Q.* 2.24.1, 734, 904 below. For Pallas as a war-goddess cf. Hor. *C.* 1.12.21 *proeliis audax*, and Nisbet–Hubbard's note.

371 cuspide The word is applied only to superhuman figures in the Senecan corpus (a restriction not generally observable), cf. *HF* 563 (Dis), *HF* 904 and *Pha.* 755 (Bacchus, cf. Catull. 64.256), *HO* 156 (Hercules); of Pallas also in Ovid, *F.* 6.655, of Mars in Juv. 2.130.

374f. reserat...templa Ancient temples were opened only at times of worship, cf. Wissowa, *Religion und Kultus*[2] 476.

378 grandaeui lassique senes The adjectives combine to suggest infirm old age. Virgil uses *grandaeuus* with proper names (*G.* 4.392 Nereus, *Aen.* 1.121 Aletes) and Ovid twice has *grandaeuus pater* (*Met.* 7.160, 8.520). Seneca uses *grandaeuus senex* (*Oed.* 838), the author of *HO* 1859 *grandaeua anus*. For *lassi* cf. Ovid, *Her.* 1.29 *mirantur lassique* [Riese: *iustique* codd.] *senes trepidaeque puellae*, Luc. 1.324 *ne lassum teneat priuata senectus*, 6.705 *iam, lassate senex* (Charon), Silius 11.323.

379 compote uoto 'their prayer granted'; *T.L.L.* cites no parallel for this use of *compos* until Tertullian. Note, though, that in Ovid, *Met.* 8.745 (*uoti argumenta potentis*), *uoti potentis* may be taken as 'fulfilled prayer', i.e. as a variation on *uoti potens*; the text, however, is uncertain.

380 reddunt grates By comparison with *gratia, grates* is rare and archaic and appears often in prayer and solemn utterance; cf. *T.L.L.* VI[2].2204.16ff., H. Heusch, *Das Archaische in der Sprache Catulls* (1954) 46f., C. P. Jones, *Hermes* xcvi (1968) 380. *Reddere grates* does not occur before Seneca (afterwards in Val. Fl. 4.557, Silius 7.202, Prud. *Cath.* 4.75, *Psych.* 889); the notion of returning thanks is elsewhere expressed by *persoluere* (Virg. *Aen.* 1.600, 2.537), *soluere* (Vell. Pat. 2.25.4), *referre* (Ovid, *Pont.* 2.11.25), and *rependere* (Stat. *Th.* 7.379, etc.). Seneca's other uses of *grates* (1010 below, *Pha.* 926) are with the more common *ago*; the full formula appears to have been *grates ago habeoque* (Pl. *Pers.* 756, Livy 23.11.12, Curtius 9.6.17).

380f. manu...trementi Perhaps based on Ovid, *F.* 5.511 *tremula dat uina rubentia dextra*; the epithet is standard in references to the old (of trembling limbs, Sen. *Contr.* 1.1.8, Juv. 6.622, 10.198, 267; voice, Hor. *C.* 4.13.5, Calp. Sic. 5.4, Quint. 11.3.91; generally, Catull. 61.51, 161; 64.307; 68.142, Ovid, *Met.* 8.660).

381 uina Like other poets, S. avoids the singular *uinum* (*uina* appears three times); cf. Neue–Wagener I[3].600, Maas, *A.L.L.* XII.503 (n.), Löfstedt, *Syntactica* I[2].47f.

382 Triuiam *Triuia* as a cult-title of Diana is illustrated by Catullus 34 (*tu Lucina...tu Triuia...tu Luna*); for *Triuia* as a poetic substitute for *Diana*, cf. Virg. *Aen.* 6.35 *una Phoebi Triuiaeque sacerdos*, 7.774f., Ovid, *Met.* 2.415f., *Pont.* 3.2.71 (perhaps in Ennius, *sc.* 121 V[2] = 363 J). On the connection of

Diana with Trivia and Hecate see Pease on Virg. *Aen.* 4.511, Bömer on Ovid, *F.* 1.141.

nota...uoce *Nota* reminds the deity of past transactions (A's *grata* is either an interpolation inspired by *memores* or a corruption produced by the preceding *grates*).

memores Cf. Cic. *Planc.* 80 *meritam dis immortalibus gratiam iustis honoribus et memori mente persoluunt,* Ovid, *Met.* 9.245 *quod memoris populi dicor rectorque paterque.*

384 maternam...Delon The conventional reference to the god's genealogy is worked in with subtlety (perhaps inspired by Horace's *natalem Delon Apollinis* in *C.* 1.21.10, or *natalem siluam* in *C.* 3.4.63, also of Apollo).

384f. sistere Delon...iubes The story is often told, cf. Williams on Virg. *Aen.* 3.76, adding Ovid, *Her.* 21.85, *Met.* 6.188ff., Sen. *HF* 14f., 453, Lucian, *Dial. Mar.* 9.1, *Anth. Lat.* 707 Riese, Claud. *Pan. Prob.* 185, Dracontius, *Rom.* 10.594f.; its place here may have been suggested by Ovid's brief allusion (*Met.* 6.187ff.) in the story of Niobe. Seneca's account of the event is more extensive than any of its predecessors and owes little to them (an exception is *respuit auras* 390); it is apparently unique in assigning credit to Diana.

385 Lucina For the identification with Diana see Pease on Cic. *N.D.* 2.68, Bömer on Ovid, *F.* 2.255ff., Norden, *Agnostos Theos* 151; as an alternative title, cf. Hor. *C.S.* 15; as a substitute, cf. Virg. *Ecl.* 4.10.

iubes Hymns often use the present of habitual actions, cf. Eur. *Hipp.* 166ff., Aristotle, Εἰς Ἀρετήν 6ff. (= *ALG* 1.117f. Diehl), Cleanthes, *Hymn.* 8ff. (p. 227 Powell). In Horace's hymn to Mercury (*C.* 1.10), the habitual activities of the god are in present tenses (17ff. *reponis...coerces*), the πράξεις in the past (9ff. *risit...fefellit*). Such a distinction, however, cannot be seen here. Rather it is the nature of Diana's deeds which justifies the tense: both actions produced a state which still exists, since Delos still stands firm and Niobe still drips tears (notice *nunc* in 389, 394, and *adhuc* in 396). For this use of the present cf. Virg. *Aen.* 8.141 *tollit* ('sustulit et nunc sustinet', Madvig, *Opusc. Acad.*[2] 582), 8.249f. (in a hymn to Hercules) *Cresia mactas | prodigia,* Ovid, *Met.* 4.23 *sacrilegos mactas.* The abstract *iubes* and *numeras* (393) are characteristic of Senecan style.

387 Cyclada uentis The region was proverbially stormy, cf. Nisbet–Hubbard on Hor. *C.* 1.14.20, Sen. *Thy.* 594f.

390 respuit auras A stronger adaptation of Virgil's *contemnere uentos* (*Aen.* 3.77); for *respuo* of scornful rejection cf. Cic. *Pis.* 45 *qui uos non oculis fugiat, auribus respuat, animo aspernetur?, N.D.* 2.43, Sen. *Contr.* 2.1.29, Ovid, *R.A.* 123f., Sen. *Thy.* 540 *respuere certum est regna consilium mihi, Epist.* 13.12;

compare *despuo* (e.g. Catull. 50.19), πτύω and ἀποπτύω (Aesch. *P.V.* 1069, Soph. *Ant.* 653).

390f. religatque...sequi A Senecan point, cf. *Med.* 358f. *cum... Thracius Orpheus solitam cantu | retinere rates paene coegit | Sirena sequi.*

392ff. The story of Niobe, 'all tears', was a poetic commonplace (cf. Nemes. *Cyn.* 15f. *nam quis non Nioben numeroso funere maestam | iam cecinit?*). Seneca approaches the familiar myth with allusive selectiveness: he avoids specifying the number of offspring (for the variations see Frazer on ps.-Apollod. *Bibl.* 3.5.6) and does not explain the cause for Diana's action; since the power of the god is in point, the lines deal only with the consequences of defiance, cf. Callimachus, *Hymn. Apoll.* 25, Quint. Smyrn. 1.305.

392 Tantalidos funera matris I.e. the deaths she had to endure; cf. Prop. 2.31.14 *altera maerebat funera Tantalidos* and Shackleton Bailey, *Propertiana* 125; for *Tantalis* = Niobe, Ovid, *Met.* 6.211 (*Tantalides matres* appears in *Her.* 8.66); in S. note *Tantalis...parens, HF* 390.

393 numeras Compare Seneca's picture of Niobe in the Underworld (*Oed.* 613ff.) *interque natos Tantalis tandem suos | tuto superba fert caput fastu graue | et numerat umbras.*

394ff. Niobe on Sipylus is an old subject, cf. *Il.* 24.614ff., Soph. *Ant.* 823ff., *El.* 149ff., Callim. *Hymn. Apoll.* 22f., Paus. 1.21.3, Quint. Smyrn. 1.299ff., Cic. *Tusc.* 3.63, Prop. 2.20.7f. (a picture of the rock is provided by Enk, facing back cover), 3.10.8. Seneca's proximate sources appear to be two passages of Ovid, *Her.* 20.105f. *quaeque superba parens saxo per corpus oborto | nunc quoque Mygdonio flebilis adstat humo, Met.* 6.311ff. *in patriam rapta est; ibi fixa cacumine montis | liquitur et lacrimas etiam nunc marmora manant*; apart from the characteristically pointed *antiqua nouas*, every element of Seneca's account has either a direct or nearly direct equivalent in Ovid (a reworking of this material in *HF* 390f. *riget superba Tantalis luctu parens | maestusque Phrygio manat in Sipylo lapis*). The striking phrase *flebile saxum* is used with typical limpness by the author of *HO* 185f. *me uel Sipylum flebile saxum | fingite, superi*; Statius alludes to Niobe as *Phrygium silicem* (*S.* 5.3.87).

396f. These lines are unanimously transmitted as printed; after 397, however, E, Σ, and some *recentiores* contain the unmetrical phrase *lacrimas maesta aeternum marmora manant.* The diagnosis of Grotius, that the addition was the result of Ovid's *et lacrimas etiam nunc marmora manant* (*Met.* 6.312) having been written in the margin, seems the best explanation. The words could only be combined with the text of 396f. in some such form as *et adhuc lacrimas maesta aeternum | marmora manant*, to which two objections can be made: it removes the eminently Senecan *antiqua nouas*, and couples uncomfortably *et adhuc* with adverbial *aeternum.*

396 fundunt Though used of tears, *fundere* is not well suited to describe the oozing of moisture from a stone; *manare*, on the other hand, is applied both to tears (Ovid, *Am.* 1.7.57f., Petr. *Sat.* 89.16, Stat. *S.* 5.2.10, Juv. 15.136f.) and to secretions (Pliny, *N.H.* 37.170 *in attritu purpureo sudore manant*), and generally of slow-moving liquids (e.g. *mella*, Hor. *Epod.* 16.47, *Epist.* 1.19.44; *cruor*, Val. Max. 6.9 *ext.* 5). It may thus be worth considering whether *fundunt* has replaced an original *manant*, perhaps originating as a gloss (*manant* in the phrase added in E after 397 confers no authority whatever on *manant* as a suggested reading in 396).

398f. colit…geminum An adaptation of Ovid, *Met.* 6.313ff.: *tunc uero cuncti manifestam numinis iram | femina uirque timent cultuque impensius omnes | magna gemelliparae uenerantur numina diuae.* Only *femina uirque* (a favourite Ovidian expression, cf. *Am.* 1.10.36, *RA* 814, *Tr.* 2.6, *Ibis* 116) is taken over without change; *impensius* becomes the less obvious *impense* (*impense colere* or *celebrare*, Curtius 6.10.22, Apul. *Apol.* 27), and *numen geminum* is Seneca's own (also in *HF* 905, *Med.* 700).

400 tuque ante omnes 'you above all'; the sun is similarly addressed in *HF* 1057 (also the end of a series). For this use of *ante omnes* cf. *O.L.D.* s.u., *ante* 8.c., Austin on Virg. *Aen.* 1.347. In this context, however, the phrase might evoke unfortunate echoes of its other meaning ('you first of all'), because of the frequent invocation of Zeus or Jupiter at the beginning of a prayer or hymn (on which see Nisbet–Hubbard on Hor. *C.* 1.12.13, Bömer on Ovid, *F.* 5.111). For Zeus in last position, cf. Soph. *Ajax* 694ff., *O.T.* 200ff.

pater ac rector Each of the epithets is quite commonly applied to Jupiter (*rector* is remarkably common in Seneca, cf. *HF* 265, 592, *Pha.* 680, 960, *Thy.* 1077, *HO* 1275); the combination is probably derived from Ovid, cf. *Met.* 2.848 *pater rectorque deum*, 9.245 *dicor rectorque paterque*, 15.860, cf. Sen. *HF* 517 *rector parensque*. The coupling of the two concepts, however, is older, cf. Plat. *Tim.* 28c πατέρα καὶ ποιητὴν τοῦ κόσμου, Hor. *C.* 1.12.49 *pater atque custos* (Augustus, see Nisbet–Hubbard *ad loc.*), Virg. *Aen.* 2.648 *diuum pater atque hominum rex* (with Austin's note), 7.558, Sen. *Epist.* 107.11 (after Cleanthes) *o parens celsique dominator poli*; examples from imperial panegyric are adduced by A. Alföldi, *MH* xi (1954) 143f.

402f. cuius…poli Jupiter's nod is an old commonplace, cf. *Il.* 1.528, Catull. 64.204, Virg. *Aen.* 9.106, 10.115, Hor. *C.* 3.1.8, Ovid, *Met.* 1.179f., 2.849, Stat. *Th.* 7.3, Pliny, *Pan.* 80.4 (of Pallas, Call. *Hymn.* 5.131ff., Neptune, Ovid [?], *Met.* 8.603); these lines, however, seem to owe most to Ovid, *F.* 2.489f. *Iuppiter adnuerat; nutu tremefactus uterque | est polus, et caeli pondera mouit Atlas.*

405 libens Greek equivalent expressions include θέλων (Aesch. *Ag.* 664 with Fraenkel's note), εὐμενῶς (Aesch. *Ag.* 952, Eur. *Suppl.* 630), προφρόνως (Aesch. *Suppl.* 1), ἵλεως (Pind. *P.* 12.4, Soph. *El.* 1376, *Anth. Pal.* 12.131.3), εὔνους (Alcaeus, *PLF* 34.3, 129.9f.). For *libens*, cf. [Tib.] 3.11.9 *magne Geni,* *cape tura libens*; also *uolens* (Hor. *C.* 3.30.16), *lenior* (*C.* 1.19.16 with Nisbet–Hubbard's note), *ames* (Hor. *C.* 1.2.50).

406 abauus Agamemnon is fourth in the line of descent, after Tantalus, Pelops, and Atreus. The precise reckoning is an Ovidian characteristic, cf. *Her.* 8.48 *si medios numeres, a Ioue quintus eris* (to Orestes), and compare *Met.* 13.28 *sic ab Ioue tertius Aiax*, 141ff. *quia rettulit Aiax | esse Iouis pronepos, nostri quoque sanguinis auctor | Iuppiter est* (cf. 404 above *generis nostri, Iuppiter, auctor*).

406f. non degenerem...prolem For the phrase compare Germ. *Arat.* 127f. *suboles oblita priorum, | degeneres semper semperque habitura minores.* The emphasis on fidelity to older standards serves the same ritual purpose as *nota uoce* in 382 above.

407 respice 'look with favour'; in Greek compare ἔπιδε and ἐπίδοι (Aesch. *Sept.* 106, *Suppl.* 1, 1030), ἐπίσκεψαι (Soph. *Ajax* 854), ἄθρησον (Pind. *P.* 2.69f.), Ziegler 71ff. For *respice* cf. Hor. *C.* 1.2.35f. *siue neglectum genus et nepotes | respicis auctor*, Ovid, *F.* 4.161f. *semper ad Aeneadas placido, pulcherrima, uultu | respice totque tuas, diua, tuere nurus*, ps.-Sen. *HO* 1991, Prud. *Cath.* 3.8ff.; also *aspicere*, Catull. 76.19, Virg. *Aen.* 2.690; cf. Hor. *C.S.* 65 *si...uidet* (Ovid, *Met.* 14.729 *si...uidetis*), Ovid, *Met.* 8.482 *aduertite uultus.*

408 sed ecce For the linking of a choral ode to a subsequent dialogue-section cf. *HF* 202, *Pha.* 358, 824, 989, 1154, *Oed.* 911, *Ag.* 693, and compare *HO* 1607.

uasto...gradu A sign of haste, as is clear from *concitus* and *properat* (cf. Luc. 2.100 *quantoque gradu Mors saeua cucurrit*). Descriptions of hasty entrances in Greek tragedy are generally less explicit, cf. Soph. *El.* 871f., 1402, *Tr.* 58 *O.C.* 890, Kassel on Men. *Sic.* 124, but note Eur. *Hec.* 216 (σπουδῇ ποδός). Latin Republican drama provides closer parallels: people in Plautus hasten *grandi gradu* (*Truc.* 286) and *gradibus grandibus* (*Ep.* 13, cf. *Cist.* 378); for tragedy note Acc. 24 R² *celebri gradu | gressum adcelerasse*, Pac. 37 R², *inc. inc. fab.* 25 R², Sen. *Oed.* 1004 *rapido...gradu*. The author of *HO* (509) uses *uasto gradu* of Hercules (cf. Homer's μακρὰ βιβάς, Virg. *Aen.* 10.572 *longe gradientem*). Ovid has *ingens gradus* (*passus*) of Tragoedia (*Am.* 3.1.11) and rustic women (*Ars* 3.303f.), and Polyphemus (*Met.* 13.776).

409f. Aeschylus' herald wears an olive-wreath which probably betokens good news (see Fraenkel on 493f.). In place of the Greek wreath (cf. also Soph. *O.T.* 82f., *Trach.* 178, Eur. *El.* 854) Seneca uses a *laureata hasta*, a victory-sign more familiar to a Roman audience (for *laureatae hastae, litterae*, etc., see Livy 5.28.13, 45.1.6, Ovid, *Am.* 1.11.25, Pliny, *N.H.* 15.133 (with Ernout's note), Persius 6.43f., Mart. 7.6.6, Stat. *Th.* 12.520, *S.* 5.1.92, Juv. 10.65, Tac. *Agr.* 18.6, *Hist.* 2.70, Suet. *Aug.* 58; M. B. Ogle, *AJPh* xxxi (1910) 287ff.).

411 fidusque regi For the dative cf. *HF* 375, *Tro.* 476, *Med.* 978; the

phrase is imitated in *HO* 570 *fidele semper regibus nomen Licha*. The faithfulness
of retainers is a cliché, cf. *Thy.* 344f., *Octauia* 844f.; cf. Eur. *I.A.* 45ff.

Eurybates The Aeschylean herald is nameless. Eurybates and Talthybius are the heralds of Agamemnon in *Il.* 1.320f., Ovid, *Her.* 3.9f., Hyg.
fab. 97.15; they may have been sent to Achilles in Aeschylus' *Myrmidons*
(schol. Aesch. *P.V.* 440), cf. H. Jacobson, *Phoenix* xxv (1971) 334f. The
herald of Seneca's *Troades* is identified as Talthybius in the *personarum notae*,
but is not named in the text (as he is in Euripides, cf. *Tro.* 238).

ACT THREE (392a–588)

The third act in Seneca is most often devoted to a crucial confrontation
which displays the *affectus* of the protagonist at their highest point (so in
Troades, Medea, Phaedra, and *Thyestes*). In *Agamemnon, Hercules Furens*, and
Oedipus, however, this central act is nearly filled by a narration of events of
secondary importance for the plot. In each of these three plays the prominence of the narration throws more traditionally dramatic scenes into
shadow: in *Hercules Furens* the death of Lycus (cf. Sen. 634–44 with Eur.
Her. 701–62); in *Oedipus* the hostility of Oedipus and Creon (cf. Sen. 509–29
and 659–708 with Soph. *O.T.* 512–633); in *Agamemnon* Clytemestra's pre-
tended joy at the news of her husband's return (cf. Sen. 398af., 402af., 579 ff.
with Aesch. *Ag.* 587–614). The inflation of picturesque or horrific messenger-
speeches into centrally-situated scenes may be another sign of Seneca's
freedom from and lack of interest in the theatrical focus of Greek tragedy.

The position of this act in the structure of the entire play should be interpreted in terms of Senecan practice; that a herald reports the return of
Agamemnon at the corresponding point of Aeschylus' play is purely a
coincidence. Apart from a few parallel expressions, easily explicable by the
similarity of situations, the two scenes have little in common. In particular
the report of Eurybates, which dominates the act, owes neither its arrangement nor its contents to its Aeschylean counterpart. The herald in Aeschylus
conveys his information in a mere thirty lines (650–80), of which ten deal
with the storm, ten describe the escape of Agamemnon's ship, and ten
speculate on the fates of the other ships. In Seneca the last two topics are not
handled in the speech, but in the preceding dialogue (cf. 404a–413), while
the storm itself is recounted in exhaustive detail using motifs drawn above
all from Virgil (cf. *Aen.* 1.81ff., 3.192ff.) and Ovid (cf. *Met.* 11.474ff.,
Trist. 1.2 *passim*). The general structure of Seneca's narrative probably
corresponds to that of a lost Greek account of post-Aeschylean date.[1] It
may be represented by the following outline:[2]

---

[1] See above, pp. 19f.
[2] Taken, with modifications, from that of J. Lanowski, 'La Tempête des
"Nostoi" dans la tragédie romaine', *Tragika* (Warsaw, 1952), 1.133ff.

(a) departure from Troy and favourable sailing (421–48)
(b) appearance of dolphins (449–55)
(c) nightfall, with weather-signs suggesting a storm (456–69)
(d) storm (470–527)[1]
  (1) natural phenomena (470–90)
  (2) reaction of men and damage to fleet (491–506)
  (3) fear and indignation of the men (507–27)
(e) punishment of Ajax (528–56)
(f) treachery of Nauplius (557–576a)
(g) dawn: storm subsides (576b–578).

The quality of the speech is best described as uneven.[2] The earlier sections (421–69) are successfully organised and presented: the style is leisurely but not tedious, the action moves briskly, the details are well-chosen; only the lines on weather-signs (462ff.) display invention too baldly. What follows is less impressive, and comparison with Virgil, Ovid, and Lucan is to Seneca's disadvantage. Perhaps the traditional character of the subject and his knowledge of earlier poetic treatments worked to his harm, leading to a comprehensive but uninspired manipulation of familiar topics and inhibiting his own talents for allusiveness and compression.

392a f. The *arae* must be imagined as physically present (note *supplex adoro*); the same altar is mentioned by Clytemestra as a place of sacrifice in 585, is the object of Agamemnon's devotions in 778f., and the refuge sought by Cassandra and Electra (cf. 951f.). All these functions of the stage-altar are derived from Greek drama: for altars saluted by returning exiles, cf. Eur. *Or.* 356, *Phoen.* 631; as places of petition or sacrifice, Soph. *O.T.* 912, *El.* 634ff.; for sanctuary, cf. Aesch. *Sept.* 1ff., *Suppl.* 1ff., Soph. *O.T.* 1ff., Eur. *Her.* 48 (and *passim*), *Andr.* 115 (411), *Ion* 1255, Arist. *Ach.* 332ff. (parodying *Telephus*), Men. *Perinthia* (= P. Oxy. 855), Pl. *Most.* 1114, *Rud.* 688, 761, Ter. *H.T.* 975, *inc. inc. trag.* 31 R², F. Schmidt, *de supplicum ad aram confugientium partibus scaenicis* (diss. Königsberg, 1911).

In no other play does S. make such frequent and varied use of the stage-altar; elsewhere its presence is required for only one act, as in *Pha.* 424f. and 708f. (an exception is *HF*, where Megara takes refuge and Hercules makes sacrifice, cf. 355ff., 503ff., 898ff.).

392a delubra...lares Reminiscent of Accius 593 R² *delubra caelitum, arae, sanctitudines*; such greetings to one's home or its gods on returning are frequent in drama, cf. Aesch. *Ag.* 503, Eur. *Her.* 523, *Pho.* 631, fr. 558 N² (*Oeneus*), P. Mediol. 1 (*Telephus*), GLP 40 (Eupolis, *Demoi*), Menander,

---

[1] Seneca's *diuisio* may be compared to Ovid's handling of the flood in *Met.* 1.262ff.: a description of the natural phenomena (262–90) is followed by an account of the effects on living things (291–312).
[2] See D. Walker and B. Henry, *CP* lviii (1963) 7.

Samia 101, *Aspis* 491(?), fr. 1, 287 Körte, Pl. *Bacch.* 170, *Stich.* 402ff., 649; elsewhere cf. Cato, *Agr.* 2.1, Catull. 31.12, Virg. *Aen.* 7.120, Ovid, *F.* 1.509, Sen. *Thy.* 404ff.

393a uix credens mihi The idea appears in Aesch. *Ag.* 668 οὐ πεποιθότες τύχῃ (in a different context), also Pl. *Amph.* 416, *Rud.* 245; much closer is Catull. 31.4ff. *quam te libenter quamque laetus inuiso, | uix mi ipse credens Thuniam atque Bithunos | liquisse campos et uidere te in tuto,* Ovid, *Met.* 5.213 *credensque parum sibi.*

394a supplex adoro The gesture is that of Homer's Agamemnon (*Od.* 4.521f.); Fraenkel suggests that the Aeschylean herald accompanied his opening words, ἰὼ πατρῷον οὖδας, with a similar action.

uota superis soluite The reference is to *uota publica pro salute (et uictoria) et reditu imperatoris,* for which see Mommsen, *Staatsrecht* 1.166 n.6, Marquardt, *Röm. Staatsverwalt.* III.266; *ActaFratrum Arualium* 114–18 Henzen, Mayor on Juv. 10.284, Dio Cassius 51.19.7, Philostratus, *Vit. Apoll.* 4.44, *CE* 2046.9, 2099.10.

395a altum...decus The expression is more often applied to physical objects, cf. Virg. *Aen.* 1.429 *scaenis decora alta futuris (apta* Bentley), Sen. *Tro.* 15 *alta muri decora,* Amm. Marc. 16.10.14, Rut. Nam. 1.93; the extended use may have been suggested by Virg. *Aen.* 2.448 *auratasque trabes, ueterum decora alta parentum* (cf. Stat. *Th.* 5.424; the Argonauts are *magnorum decora alta parentum*), cf. ps.-Sen. *HO* 391 *uides ut altum famula non perdat decus,* Sil. 3.144. The phrase *telluris...Argolicae decus* may be inspired by Cicero's *O decus Argolicum...Vlixes (carm. fr.* 29.1 Morel); note also *Argiuum decus* of Juno, *inc. inc. fab.* 91 R².

398a ubinam Rare in both prose and poetry after Plautus and Terence; there are three certain appearances in Cicero (the text of *N.D.* 1.24 is variously transmitted), one in Catullus, five in Seneca, and four in Statius. As a rule *ubinam* introduces questions marked by urgency or emotion: surprise (Pl. *Aul.* 821, Ter. *H.T.* 430, *Phorm.* 484; cf. Pl. *Bacch.* 246, Sen. *Thy.* 280), impatience or exasperation (Pl. *As.* 328, *Men.* 434, *Rud.* 391, *Poen.* 468, *Trin.* 1079, Ter. *Phorm.* 827), excitement as shown by a series of questions (Ter. *And.* 965, Cic. *Cat.* 1.9, *Plan.* 33, ps.-Sen. *HO* 1338, 1399, Stat. *Th.* 5.656, *Ach.* 1.127), or rhetorical solemnity (Ter. *H.T.* 256, Catull. 63.55, Cic. *Att.* 1.18.1, Stat. *Th.* 9.385, *S.* 2.1.34). The force of *ubinam* is sometimes paralleled by ποῦ μήν (cf. Denniston s.u. μήν 1.4.ii.a.iii).

Here *ubinam* underscores Clytemestra's sudden change from joy at the news of Agamemnon's return to impatient inquiry about his absence; compare Pl. *Bacch.* 246 *salue. sed ubinamst Mnesilochus?*, Sen. *Thy.* 280ff.

petitus The word can be applied both to lovers (cf. Catull. 61.145f., Prop. 2.20.37) and to enemies (cf. on 371 above, Virg. *Aen.* 3.603, *Laus Pis.*

197), though more often with reference to action than to feeling; both senses may be present here.

399a pelagus an terras premit? *Premere terram* in the sense 'to stand on, set foot on land' is frequent in Ovid, cf. *Am.* 3.6.11f. *si non datur... ulterior nostro ripa premenda pede*, 2.16.19, *Met.* 5.135; *pelagus premere* is much rarer, but note Ovid, *Am.* 1.9.13 *freta pressurus*, Stat. *Ach.* 1.34f. *uideo iam mille carinis | Ionium Aegaeumque premi* (and cf. *premere ratem*, etc., ps.-Sen. *HO* 51f., Val. Fl. 1.203). It is probably too subtle to see in *premit* the sense 'to be a weight on', as in *Pho.* 219 *ego hoc solum, frugifera quo surgit Ceres, | premo?*

400a auctus...inclitus For the thought compare Aesch. *Ag.* 531f. τίεσθαι δ' ἀξιώτατος βροτῶν | τῶν νῦν; *auctus gloria*, cf. Cic. *Planc.* 22, Hor. *S.* 1.6.11 *et uixisse probos, amplis et honoribus auctos*, Ovid, *F.* 4.117, Suet. *Iul.* 52.2.

401a reducem...pedem Cf. Ovid, *Her.* 6.1f. *litora Thessaliae reduci tetigisse carina | diceris*. The use of *pes* may be an attempt at elevated style (see on 780f. below).

403a si propitios attamen lentos deos 'though favourable, yet slow' at first seems an inversion of conventional piety: the gods' punishment is often described as 'slow in coming, but sure to come' (cf. Hes. *Op.* 270ff., *Theog.* 373ff., Solon 1.8ff., 25ff. Diehl, Sappho 92 L.-P, Pind. *P.* 5.1ff., Aesch. *Ag.* 58, *Cho.* 383, Herodotus 1.34.1, Eur. *Ion* 1615, *Ba.* 882, fr. 223, 800 N², *Paroem. Gr.* 1.444.48 Leutsch, Livy 3.56.7, Hor. *C.* 3.2.32, Tib. 1.9.4, Sen. *Contr.* 10 *pr.* 6), and divine favour is occasionally treated with a similar emphasis, as in Virg. *Ecl.* 1.27f. *Libertas quae sera tamen respexit inertem, | respexit tamen et longo post tempore uenit* (see Nisbet–Hubbard on Hor. *C.* 1.15.19). Other examples of this critical attitude, however, are not lacking: Gronovius aptly cited Soph. *Trach.* 201 ἔδωκας ἡμῖν, ἀλλὰ σὺν χρόνῳ, χαράν, and one may add *El.* 1013 αὐτὴ δὲ νοῦν σχὲς ἀλλὰ τῷ χρόνῳ ποτέ, *Phil.* 1041, Eur. *Med.* 912, *Ion* 425, *El.* 411 ὦ θεοὶ πατρῷοι συγγένεσθέ γ' ἀλλὰ νῦν ('be with me now, at least'), Denniston, *GP²* 13, and in Seneca, *HF* 622 *o nate, certa at sera Thebarum salus* and 1203 *oblite nostri, uindica sera manu | saltem nepotes*.

The present passage is also marked by the use of *si...attamen* with contrasting modifiers, a prose construction (cf. Cic. *Planc.* 35, *Brutus* 15, Pliny, *N.H.* 7.100) of which I have observed only one parallel in poetry, Ovid, *Tr.* 2.135 *adde quod edictum, quamuis immite minaxque, | attamen in poenae nomine lene fuit* (the regular function of *attamen* is to introduce an opposing clause). It is tempting to take the opposition between *propitios* and *lentos* in a double sense: Clytemestra is ostensibly reproaching the gods for their slowness in bringing Agamemnon home while secretly expressing gratitude for Agamemnon's prolonged absence ('let us honour the gods who, although they were favourable in the end [i.e. to Agamemnon], at least were slow about it'); for the sense of *attamen* see Housman, *C.Q.* xvi (1922) 88–91. This may, however, be oversubtle, and no similar irony can be seen in the analogous inversions *HF* 975 *pectoris sani parum, magni tamen* and *Thy.* 205f. *tam ferre quam laudare* (cited by B. Schmidt, *Obs. Crit.* 12ff.).

404a †tu pande uiuat† These words are open to three objections, two major and one minor:

(*a*) The omission of an interrogative word after *pande* is extremely harsh (so also Leo, *Obs.* 92). No precise parallel has been adduced: Ovid furnishes examples of *ut* suppressed when it introduces an object clause, e.g. *Ars* 2.398 *ipse querare facit* (= *facit ut ipse queraris*), *Met.* 8.791f. *ea se in praecordia condat...iube* (cf. Kühner–Stegmann II².227ff.); note also the omission of *ut* after *uelim* in 332 above, *H.A. Max.* 31.4, and compressions such as Ovid, *Met.* 8.635 *nec refert dominos...famulosne requiras.*

(*b*) The lamely repeated *pande* has no parallel in such scenes, where Seneca clearly aims for variety: cf. *Tro.* 1065ff. *expone...persequere...ede et enarra omnia*; *Pha.* 993ff. *ne metue...fari...proloquere...effare*; *HF* 647ff. *pande...memorare cogis...fare*; *Oed.* 211ff. *edoce...fare...ede*; 849ff. *effare... fatere...edoce...dic*; *Thy.* 633ff. *effare et istud pande...ede...indica...effare ocius* (640); note even *HO* 1607ff. *effare...edissere.* With the exception of the present line, this scene conforms to the pattern visible elsewhere (*pande* 404a...*fare* 414 (or *effare*: see note *ad loc.*) ...*loqui* 417...*exprome* 419).

(*c*) Clytemestra's question, 'is Menelaus alive?', is in conflict with her knowledge in 273ff. that Helen and Menelaus had survived and were *en route* for Greece. In itself this inconsistency would scarcely be grounds for suspicion (cf. Runchina 189, Zwierlein, *Rezitationsdramen* 105f.).

Objections (*a*) and (*c*) were recognised by Birt, but his suggestion, *ubi pande uiuat*, is stylistically questionable (and still open to objection (*b*)). It seems preferable to allow for a wider corruption. Conjecture in such a case can only be offered *exempli gratia*: as one indication of the required sense, one might propose *edissere ubi sit coniugis frater mei*; this achieves a rhetorical balance, the plain *ubi sit* offset by the periphrasis *coniugis frater mei* as the elaborate *teneat quas...sedes* is by *soror...mea* (for the phrase cf. 965 below). Alternatively, one could assume that the first *pande* has not replaced a comparable imperative and that *pande* in 405a is to be taken ἀπὸ κοινοῦ with both questions. This hypothesis would permit a question of the form *ubi nunc, precor, sit coniugis frater mei* (for *precor*, cf. *Oed.* 773).

406a meliora uotis posco The thought corresponds to γένοιτο δ' ὡς ἄριστα (Aesch. *Ag.* 674), but the expression echoes the common *di meliora* (cf. Pl. *Poen.* 1400, Pac. 112 R², Cic. *Phil.* 8.9, Virg. *G.* 3.456, Ovid, *Met.* 7.37, etc.). For *poscere uotis* see Pease on Virg. *Aen.* 4.158.

407a nam...uetat Compare Aesch. *Ag.* 632f. οὐκ οἶδεν οὐδεὶς ὥστ' ἀπαγγεῖλαι τορῶς | πλὴν τοῦ...Ἡλίου. For *maris dubii*, 'the unsettled sea', cf. Ovid, *Pont.* 4.10.10, Sen. *HF* 1253, *Med.* 942, *Thy.* 292.

408a excepit *Excipere* = 'to withstand a violent attack' (as of an onrushing army); cf. Cic. *Rab. Post.* 42, Caes. *B.G.* 4.17.9, Luc. 1.221 *primus in obliquum sonipes opponitur amnem | excepturus aquas*, Sen. *Pha.* 1128f., *Oed.* 8; cf. *T.L.L.* v².1255.24ff.

412f. The description of Agamemnon's humiliating return probably owes something to the declamatory treatment of Xerxes, cf. Sen. *Suas.* 5.1, Juv. 10.185f. (with Mayor's note), de Decker, *Iuuenalis Declamans* 42ff., Just. *Epit.* 2.13.10 *in exiguo latentem uidere nauigio quem ante uix aequor omne capiebat*. Accounts of Pompey were similarly coloured, cf. Luc. 8.37ff., Florus 2.13.20.

exiguas trahens...rates A bolder version of phrases like *exiguas reliquias trahentem* in *Cons. Helu.* 7.7 (of Aeneas) *uicti exercitus reliquias trahens* in *Epist.* 104.33. For the use of *exiguus* cf. Ovid, *Ars* 1.440 *nec exiguas...adde preces*; the addition of *laceras* saves the passage from ambiguity (*lacera ratis* is an Ovidian favourite, cf. *Ars* 1.412, *Her.* 2.45, *Ibis* 275f., *Pont.* 2.3.28, 3.2.6).

414 quis fare nostras hauserit casus rates A/effare casus quis rates hausit meas E All editors have followed E's text with the exception of L. Herrmann and Viansino, who print the tentative (and unmetrical) suggestion of Damsté, *hausit eas* (cf. B. Axelson, *Korruptelenkult* (1967) 43 for comment, adding P. Hahlbrock, *WS* N.F. ii (1968) 178 n.7). The A version has, to my knowledge, found only two defenders since the time of Gronovius: Bentley and Damsté (*Mnemos.* N.S. xlvii (1919) 112).

Bentley objected in particular to the change of construction in E's text (*hausit...dispulerit*). The only serious attempt to defend it is that of Leo (Bothe's proposal to read *dispulerat* in 415 is clearly unsatisfactory), and Leo himself admits that an exact parallel is lacking (*Obs.* 92); his best examples are Prop. 2.16.29f. *aspice quid donis Eriphyla inuenit amaris, | arserit et quantis nupta Creusa malis* and Val. Fl. 7.119f. *quaerit ut Aeaeis hospes consederit oris | Phrixus, ut aligeri Circen rapuere dracones* (also cited were Prop. 3.5.26ff., Persius 3.66ff., to which may be added Prop. 2.30.29f., 2.34.35ff., *Aetna* 237ff., Val. Fl. 1.278ff. – all of which involve a series of questions). No passage thus far adduced, however, duplicates the awkwardness of E's word-order, which raises the expectation of an imperative with noun-object (*effare casus*) and then reveals an indirect question (*casus quis...hausit*); other commands of this type in Seneca show no trace of ambiguity, cf. *Tro.* 166 *quae causa ratibus faciat et Danais moram | effare*, *Oed.* 798 *effare mersus quis premat mentem timor* (and note also *HO* 1607f. *effare casus, iuuenis, Herculeos, precor, | uultuque quonam tulerit Alcides necem*).

The difficult, though not clearly impossible, syntax of the E text might be thought to betray the hand of the author rather than that of an interpolator. But the A version, besides being syntactically unobjectionable, displays stylistic virtues which seem to exceed the capacities of a mere pedant: the position of *fare* is supported by *Pha.* 894 *quis ede nostri decoris euersor fuit?*;

the hyperbaton *quis...casus* can be taken as expressing emotion (cf. Fraenkel on Aesch. *Ag.* 1448, Nisbet on Cic. *Pis.* 18); *nostras...rates* is a more natural expression than *rates...meas*. The choice is not simple, but the A text seems too good to have resulted from a wish to regularise E's syntax. If, on the other hand, A's *hauserit* had been mechanically corrupted to *hausit* (as *dispulerit* in 415 has been corrupted to *dispulit* in many *recentiores*), an interpolator with a stronger sense of metre than of style might have produced E's text.

416ff. Tragic messengers are conventionally reluctant to reveal bad news; the Aeschylean herald indulges in a short set-piece on the subject (637ff.). The present passage, however, contains the more common brief expression of reluctance, cf. Aesch. *Pers.* 249ff., Soph. *Ant.* 276ff., *O.T.* 1146ff., *Phil.* 329, Sen. *Tro.* 168, 1056, *Pha.* 991; for comic parodies see Ed. Fraenkel, *de Media et Noua Comoedia* (1912) 6ff. Euripidean messengers express horror or sympathy, but not reluctance, cf. *Andr.* 1070, *Her.* 916, *Hel.* 1512, *Or.* 852ff., *Phoen.* 1335ff., *Ba.* 1027; in Sen. *Thy.* 623ff. the messenger expounds his reluctance in fantastic terms. See also Hansen 12ff.

In expression these lines recall Virg. *Aen.* 2.3 *infandum, regina, iubes renouare dolorem* and 2.12 *quamquam animus meminisse horret luctuque refugit*; in the words *infaustum...miscere laeto nuntium* there is a remarkable similarity to Aesch. *Ag.* 648 πῶς κεδνὰ τοῖς κακοῖσι συμμείξω;

418 atque Not a true case of postponed *atque*, since *tantis malis* is to be taken with both *aegra* and *inhorrescit* (*atque* is postponed only once in the genuine plays, at *Thy.* 912, but five times in *Octauia*: 110, 165, 244, 474, 561).

419 exprome Like *pande* (405a), *exprome* aims at solemnity. The absolute use has no precise Senecan parallel; closest are *Pha.* 850f. *quis fremitus aures flebilis pepulit meas? | expromat aliquis*, *Oed.* 384f. *quid ista sacri signa terrifici ferant, | exprome* (other uses of the verb in such contexts, cf. Acc. 499 R², *Tro.* 936, *Pha.* 868, *Oed.* 510).

421f. The brisk opening lines ultimately recall *Od.* 3.130f. αὐτὰρ ἐπεὶ Πριάμοιο πόλιν διεπέρσαμεν αἰπήν, | βῆμεν δ' ἐν νήεσσι; note also the close parallels in Livius Andronicus 2ff. R² [*Aegisthus*] *nam ut Pergama | accensa et praeda per participes aequiter | partita est* and Hyginus, *fab.* 116 *Ilio capto et diuisa praeda* and a number of other comparable passages, e.g. Virg. *Aen.* 3.1ff. *postquam...ceciditque superbum | Ilium*, Ovid, *Met.* 14.466 *postquam alta cremata est | Ilion*, ps.-Apoll. *Epit.* 5.23 (and outside the Trojan context note, e.g., Sall. *Jug.* 91.6 *ceterum oppidum incensum, Numidae puberes interfecti, alii omnes uenumdati, praeda militibus diuisa*). A similar allusion to the sack of Troy outside narrative comes after the *canticum* of Chrysalus in Plautus' *Bacchides* (1053ff.): *fit uasta Troia, scindunt proceres Pergamum...ecfertur praeda ex Troia*, a passage considered by Fraenkel (*Elementi Plautini* 57ff.) to be Plautine invention, perhaps deriving from Roman tragedy.

421 ut At the beginning of a narrative also in *Tro.* 1118, *Med.* 675, *Pha.* 1000, *HO* 1618; *postquam Oed.* 915. The practice is found in tragedy as well as epic, though the use of ἐπεί is particularly characteristic of Euripides (cf. Aesch. *P.V.* 199, Soph. *El.* 893, Eur. *Cyc.* 382, *Med.* 1136, *Hcld.* 800, *Hipp.* 1198, *Andr.* 1085, etc.).

423 ense...latus Cf. *Laus Pis.* 144 *et galea miles caput et latus ense resoluit*; *fessum latus* may recall Hor. *C.* 2.7.18f. *longaque fessum militia latus | depone*. Apart from two occurrences in Ovid, *exonero* is absent from Augustan poetry; other instances of its use with an ablative denoting physical objects come from prose (Livy 5.34.3 *regnum turba*, Sen. *N.Q.* 5.10.3 *terras niue*).

424 neglecta...scuta A sign of the mood of peace prevailing among the men, cf. Smith on Tib. 1.10.49f. The detail has a more elaborate counterpart in Quintus Smyrnaeus (14.374ff.), where the ships are decked out with captured Trojan arms, garlands, and the Greeks' own weapons.

425 ad...remus aptatur manus *Ad* with *apto* is quite rare in poetry; I can cite only Ovid, *Am.* 1.13.14 *miles...aptat ad arma manus* (in prose cf., e.g., Livy 33.5.5, Sen. *Contr.* 10 *pr.* 2, Sen. *Epist.* 107.9 *ad hanc legem animus noster aptandus est*, ps.-Quint. *Decl.* 17.17 *aptatos ad colla nexus*). Seneca does not, however, adopt Ovid's reversal of the action; here, as normally, the implement is fitted to the hand, cf. Hor. *Epod.* 7.2, Virg. *Aen.* 9.364, Ovid, *Met.* 10.381, Sen. *Pha.* 319, 533 and cf. ἀραρίσκω in *Il.* 13.188, 19.370, *Od.* 5.361, 17.4 (so, probably, too, in Soph. *O.C.* 716ff.).

militares A prose word, cf. Livy 7.10.7 (*statura*), Sen. *Prou.* 4.13 (*lacerti*), *Tranq.* 17.4 (*corpus*), Val. Max. 8.8 *ext.* 2 (*militare robur* of Achilles' hands).

426 omnisque...est Perhaps derived from Ovid, *Met.* 11.451 *longa quidem est nobis omnis mora* (in a similar context), note 461ff. *ast iuuenes, quaerente moras Ceyce, reducunt | ordinibus geminis ad fortia pectora remos | aequalique ictu scindunt freta*; cf. also Sall. *Jug.* 64.6 *animo cupienti nihil satis festinatur*. The thought is proverbial of lovers, cf. Pl. *Poen.* 504f., Ovid, *Her.* 19.3, *Met.* 4.350.

427–30 The action described in these lines has not always been correctly understood; a symptom of the trouble is the unjust suspicion of *lentum* in 428. Leo objected that *lentum* was in contradiction with *properantes* (422) and *properanti* (426); his conjecture, *laetum*, is banal and without point (note that in Virg. *Ecl.* 7.48 *laeto* is a trivialisation of *lento*).

These lines describe (with admirable economy) a consecutive sequence of episodes. From 423 onwards the action takes place on board the ships, as the men put aside their arms and prepare to cast off. In 425f. the rowers take their positions and test their oars; there is no reason to take these lines as applying only to some oarsmen, and in the absence of such a direction one naturally regards them as generic. At line 426 the rowers are in position and are waiting for the command to row (the moment described in Ennius, *Ann.* 227ff. V² *tonsas arte tenentes | parerent, obseruarent, portisculus signum | cum dare coepisset*). At this point the focus narrows to the flagship (427 *regia...rate*), where a flare gives the signal for departure; one must assume that both the *tuba* and the *remigem* of the following line are those of Agamemnon's ship (*et* seems to posit a close link between the lines), which immediately departs (429–30). The concision and forward movement of the passage seems to rule out Ker's interpretation of 428 (*CQ* n.s. xii (1962) 49f.) as a reference to oarsmen idling on the quay. The *tuba* is probably not a preliminary signal to board ship (as in Eur. *Tro.* 1266ff., Val. Fl. 1.350ff., probably Virg. *Aen.* 3.519f., Frontinus, *Strat.* 4.1.33), but rather the sign for departure itself, that is, a command to the rowers to begin (so Gronovius); note Livy 29.27.6 *tubaque signum dedit proficiscendi*. (In Ovid, *Met.* 10.652 the *tuba* seems to be the signal for the runners to start.) On this view *lentum* means 'slow to respond' (i.e. the rowing of the men is uncoordinated after ten years' lack of practice).

427 fulsit For the light on the commander's ship cf. Virg. *Aen.* 2.256f. *flammas cum regia puppis | extulerat*, Livy 29.25.11 *in praetoria naue insigne nocturnum trium luminum fore*, C. Torr, *Ancient ships* 99 n.214; cf. Shakespeare, *Henry IV Pt. 1* iii.iii 'thou art our admiral, thou bearest the lantern in the poop'.

429 aurata A sign of regal status, cf. Sen. *Epist.* 76.13 *nauis bona dicitur, non quae pretiosis coloribus picta est, nec cui argenteum aut aureum rostrum est, nec cuius tutela ebore caelata est*; cf. for *aerata prora*, etc. Virg. *Aen.* 8.675, 10.223, Stat. *Th.* 5.335). Comparable expressions include *auratum limen* (ps.-Sen. *HO* 607), *auratae sedis* (*Pha.* 385), *auro nitidae trabes* (*Thy.* 347); see Viansino on *Pha.* 497.

430 secent Of ships, etc., Sen. *Pha.* 88, 530, *Thy.* 590, *Ben.* 6.15.6 *per medios fluctus...secanti uiam*; cf. τέμνειν in, e.g., *Od.* 3.174f. Other terms properly used of ploughing are also applied to sailing, as *sulcare* (see on 440 below, Virg. *Aen.* 5.158, 10.296, Ovid, *Met.* 4.707, Val. Fl. 3.32), *findere* (cf. *T.L.L.* vi.769.31ff.), *arare* (Virg. *Aen.* 2.780, cf. Sen. *Med.* 650 *perarare pontum*); see further Nisbet–Hubbard on Hor. *C.* 1.1.14, 1.7.32 (*iterabimus aequor*).

431ff. The period of calm sailing before the storm is treated expansively, with a number of graphic details; only Quintus Smyrnaeus does likewise (14.403–18). The topic is usually passed over with brief and general comment, cf. *Od.* 3.157f., Eur. *Hel.* 1455f., Pacuvius, *inc. fab.* 409 R² *profectione laeti*, Virg. *Aen.* 1.35, Ovid, *Met.* 13.418 (note also Tac. *Ann.* 1.70, 2.23 *ac primo placidum aequor mille nauium remis strepere aut uelis impelli*).

432 adlapsa The verb suggests a gentle, gliding motion. By applying *adlabor* to the breeze rather than to the water or the ships (the more common uses, cf. Virg. *Aen.* 10.269, 292, Tac. *Ann.* 1.70; Virg. *Aen.* 3.569, Ovid, *Met.* 14.243) S. produces a more striking expression, perhaps recalling Virg. *Aen.* 9.473f. *uolitans pennata per urbem | nuntia Fama ruit matrisque adlabitur auris,* cf. Val. Max. 2 *pr.* 10 *grato...et iucundo introitu animis hominum adlabitur admirationis uelata* [*sc. maiestas*].

actu leui 'with a gentle driving movement', cf. Lucr. 3.192 *mellis... cunctantior actus,* Petr. *Sat.* 135.8 *pocula, quae facili uilis rota finxerat actu,* Luc. 9.472 *pilaque contorsit uiolento spiritus actu.*

433 tremit Perhaps inspired by Ovid, *Her.* 11.75 *ut mare fit tremulum, tenui cum stringitur aura, Met.* 4.135f.; note also Virg. *Aen.* 7.9 *splendet tremulo sub lumine pontus.*

434 splendetque...latet The water is hidden by the vast fleet (cf. 41n.), and at the same time glistens with sunlight reflected either from the *neglecta scuta* of 424 or the metal fittings of the ships. Apollonius Rhodius has a similar picture, cf. 1.544f. στράπτε δ' ὑπ' ἠελίῳ φλογὶ εἴκελα νηὸς ἰούσης | τεύχεα; cf. also Virg. *Aen.* 8.676f. *uideres...auroque effulgere fluctus,* Prop. 4.6.26 *armorum et radiis picta tremebat aqua,* Sil. 6.357f.

435f. The lines may be based on Ovid, *Her.* 1.33f. *hac ibat Simois, haec est Sigeia tellus, | hic steterat Priami regia celsa senis,* but Seneca's tone is different (*nuda* and *sola,* together with the repeated *iuuat,* produce a complex emotional picture).

437 iuuentus omnis The phrase may recall Virgil's *Troiana iuuentus* (*Aen.* 1.467, see Austin on *Aen.* 2.63).

adductos Sc. *ad pectora,* cf. Enn. *Ann.* 230 V² *poste recumbite uestraque pectora pellite tonsis; | pone petunt: exim repetunt ad pectora tonsas,* Ovid, *Met.* 11.462 *reducunt...ad fortia pectora remos,* Luc. 3.543, Sil. 6.362f. For *adductus* cf. Virg. *Aen.* 5.141 *adductis spumant freta uersa lacertis,* also of drawing a bow-string back before shooting, Virg. *Aen.* 5.507, Ovid, *Met.* 1.455 (with Bömer's note), 8.28.

438 lentare remos Ancient oars and spears seem to have been somewhat pliant, cf. Apoll. Rhod. 2.591f., also Catull. 64.183 *quine fugit lentos incuruans gurgite remos,* Virg. *Aen.* 3.384 *Trinacria lentandus remus in unda, Ciris* 461.

adiuuat uentos manu Cf. Ovid, *Ars* 1.368 *uelo remigis addat opem, R.A.* 790 *remis adice uela tuis,* Stat. *Ach.* 1.694.

439 nisu...alterno For the force of *alternus* see on 44 above. When applied to a continuing activity it suggests a steady succession of two distinct actions. Thus Prop. 4.7.18 *alterna ueniens in tua colla manu* describes Cynthia descending from her window by a rope, and in Calp. *Sic.* 2.25 and 6.2 *alternos...cantus* and *alterno carmine* denote amoebaean song. Here the successive action is composed of the two opposite motions of the rowers (in 65 above *alternos...fluctus* refers to the ebb and flow of the waves).

440f. The picture derives ultimately from *Il.* 1.481ff. ἐν δ' ἄνεμος πρῆσεν μέσον ἱστίον, ἀμφὶ δὲ κῦμα | στείρῃ πορφύρεον μεγάλ' ἴαχε νηὸς ἰούσης, but the details are sharper in Apoll. Rhod. 1.542f. ἀφρῷ δ' ἔνθα καὶ ἔνθα κελαινὴ κήκιεν ἅλμη | δεινὸν μορμύρουσα περισθενέων μένει ἀνδρῶν, cf. also Quintus Smyrnaeus 14.416–18.

440 sulcata...aequora Cf. Virg. *Aen.* 10.197 *et longa sulcat maria alta carina* (also *Aen.* 5.158, Ovid, *Met.* 4.707, *Pont.* 1.4.35, 2.10.33); note the *uariatio* in ps.-Ovid, *Hal.* 100f. *tuque, comes ratium tractique per aequora sulci,* | *qui semper spumas sequeris, pompile, nitentes.*

uibrant 'shimmer', cf. Cic. *Acad.* 2.105 [*mare*] *qua a sole collucet, albescit et uibrat,* Luc. 5.446 [*pontus*] *non horrore tremit, non solis imagine uibrat,* Sil. 2.664, 14.566, Claud. *Rapt.* 2.2; cf. Petr. *Sat.* 118.2 (of glittering *sententiolae*), Claud. *Ruf.* 2.356f. (of silk tunics shimmering in a breeze).

latera increpant Cf. Aratus, *Phaen.* 287, Luc. 2.702 *impulsum rostris sonuit mare*; similar language occurs in Ovidian storm-narratives, e.g. *Met.* 11.507 *saepe dat ingentem fluctu latus icta fragorem,* *Tr.* 1.4.24 *increpuit...unda latus.*

441 dirimuntque...mare 'The white trails of foam split the dark-blue water'; such colour-contrasts are often used in speaking of the sea, cf. Eur. *Hel.* 1501f. γλαυκὸν ἔπιτ' οἶδμα κυανόχροά τε κυμάτων | ῥόθια πολιὰ θαλάσσας, Cic. *Prognost.* fr. 3 *saxaque cana salis niueo spumata liquore,* Lucr. 2.766f. *ut mare, cum magni̦ commorunt aequora uenti, uertitur in canos candenti marmore fluctus,* Virg. *Aen.* 8.671f. *haec inter tumidi late maris ibat imago* | *aurea, sed fluctu spumabant caerula cano*; less pointed descriptions in Virg. *Aen.* 3.207, Catull. 64.13, Ovid, *Met.* 11.501, ps.-Quint. *Decl. mai.* 12.16. Lucan may have had this passage in mind when writing 2.701ff.

442ff. The men first row with the sails up, to reach the open sea (cf. Sen. *Tro.* 1045f. *cum simul uentis properante remo* | *prenderint altum fugietque litus*), then allow the stronger winds to carry the ships; so in Quintus Smyrnaeus 14.404f., and see also Catull. 4.4f., Virg. *Aen.* 5.778–7, Ovid, *Tr.* 1.10.3ff.

444 miles A's *nauita* must be a conscious attempt at correction or improvement; the interpolator may have been unfamiliar with the epic practice of warriors rowing their own ships (he need not have been thinking of Ovid, *Met.* 13.418f. *flatuque secundo* | *carbasa mota sonant, iubet uti nauita uentis,* as Giomini suggests (p. 117)).

444f. terras...notat The shipboard illusion that the land is slipping away is common in Latin poetry, cf. Virg. *Aen.* 3.72 *prouehimur portu terraeque urbesque recedunt,* Ovid, *Met.* 6.512 *admotumque fretum remis tellusque repulsa est* (perhaps the inspiration for *Tro.* 1047f. *ubi omnis* | *terra descrescit pelagusque*

COMMENTARY 444-449

crescet), 8.139, 11.466, Luc. 5.467, Val. Fl. 2.8f., 4.645, Sil. 3.157, Stat. *Th.* 1.549. The illusion appears as well in Quintus Smyrnaeus (14.410), where it is seen by the Trojans and takes on pathetic overtones.

446ff. The brief ecphrasis is handled with discrimination and restraint. The sequence is chronological: *Hectoris fortis minas* refers to his expedition to the Greek ships (recalled later by Cassandra, 744 below); the single word *currus* alludes to Hector's mistreatment by Achilles (cf. 746f. below) and *empto rogo* is a pointed reference to *Il.* 24.685. The murder of Priam (for which cf. Eur. *Tro.* 15ff., Ennius, *sc.* 88 R², Virg. *Aen.* 2.550f., Ovid, *Met.* 13.409f., *Ibis* 284; see also on 657 below) is presumably included both because it would be fresh in memory and also as an ominous reminder of the punishment which will follow such a sacrilege.

449ff. The appearance of dolphins as an agreeable event on a sea-voyage is found as early as the Homeric Hymns (3.400, 494; 7.53). The scene described here, in which dolphins gambol around a ship, though present in Eur. *El.* 435ff., is more explicit in Apoll. Rhod. 4.933ff. ὡς δ' ὁπόταν δελφῖνες ὑπὲξ ἁλὸς εὐδιόωντες | σπερχομένην ἀγεληδὸν ἑλίσσωνται περὶ νῆα, | ἄλλοτε μὲν προπάροιθεν ὁρώμενοι, ἄλλοτ' ὄπισθεν, | ἄλλοτε παρβολάδην, ναύτῃσι δὲ χάρμα τέτυκται, also Opp. *Hal.* 1.670ff., Sen. *Oed.* 466 *et sequitur curuus fugientia carbasa delphin.* The topic appears several times in Republican tragedy, apparently related in two cases to the Greeks' return from Troy: Liv. Andr. 5f. R² [*Aegisthus*] *tum autem lasciuum Nerei simum pecus* | *ludens ad cantus classem lustratur*, Pacuvius 408 and 409f. R² *Nerei repandirostrum incuruiceruicum pecus...profectione laeti piscium lasciuiam* | *intuentur, nec tuendi capere satietas potest* (text of last three words doubtful), Acc. 403ff. R² *sicut lasciui atque alacres rostris perfremunt* | *Delphini, item alto mulcta Siluani melo* | *consimilem ad auris cantum et auditum refert* [*lasciui* Ribbeck: *inciti* codd.]. Dolphins presumably figured in an influential Greek account of the νόστοι (no dolphins are to be seen in Quintus Smyrnaeus, though); since dolphins were well-known as harbingers of storms, they would be appropriate in a νόστος poem (cf. Theophrastus, *Sign.* 19, Artemidorus 2.16, Cic. *Diu.* 2.145, Ovid, *Her.* 19.199, Luc. 5.552, Alciphron, *Epist.* 1.10.1, Pliny, *N.H.* 18.361, Isid. *Etym.* 12.6.11). Seneca's immediate source, though, is surely Ovid, *Met.* 3.68off. (the metamorphosis of the Tyrrhenian sailors): note *ludunt* 685 – *ludit* 449; *inque chori...speciem* 685 – *chorus* 454; *lasciuaque...corpora* 685f. – *lasciuit* 454; *truncoque repandus...corpore* 680f. – *pando...dorso* 450; *in undas... desiluit* 680f. – *transilit...mare* 450.

449 iacente...salo For *iaceo* of calm seas cf. Luc. 3.524, 5.434, Val. Fl. 4.712, Sil. 5.583.

reciprocus An extremely rare word in poetry, and far from common in prose (with the exception of the Elder Pliny). Elsewhere it (and *reciprocare*) means 'moving up and down (or back and forth) in a regular motion', and

259

its most common application is to tides, cf. Enn. *sc.* 104 R² (= 116 J) *rursus prorsus reciprocat fluctus*, Sil. 3.60, Tac. *Ann.* 1.70; Cic. *N.D.* 3.24, Livy 28.6.10, Florus 1.24.9 (all three referring to the Euripus); Pliny, *N.H.* 2.212, 213, 219, 9.176, 16.170. Here the word probably describes the regular motion of the dolphins who emerge from the water and then plunge back in again (cf. Ovid, *Met.* 3.684 *emergunt iterum, redeuntque sub aequora rursus*); its use of ships tossed on the waves is comparable, cf. Pacuvius 333 R² *rapide retro citroque percito aestu praecipitem ratem | reciprocare*, Val. Fl. 8.331 *itque reditque ratis lapsoque reciproca fluctu | descendit*.

450 pando...dorso Cf. Lucilius 212 M (with Marx's note), Cic. *Arat.* 91f., Ovid, *Her.* 17.131, *Met.* 2.265, 3.680, *F.* 2.113, *Tr.* 3.10.43, Sen. *Oed.* 464ff., Luc. 5.552, Sil. 14.570, Stat. *Th.* 1.121 (and Heuvel *ad loc.*).

451 Tyrrhenus...piscis An allusion to the Tyrrhenian sailors turned into dolphins by Bacchus (for the background see Bömer on Ovid, *Met.* 3.577–700 (pp. 588f.)); cf. Prop. 3.17.25f., Sen. *Oed.* 457ff. For the generic *piscis* compare Tib. 1.5.46 *uecta est frenato caerula pisce Thetis* with Ovid, *Met.* 11.237 *frenato delphine sedens, | Theti nuda* and Stat. *Ach.* 1.221ff.

452 agitatque gyros Cf. ps.-Arion 939 *PMG*, Opp. *Hal.* 1.676.

lateri adnatat 'swims up to the side in a comradely way'; compare Pliny, *N.H.* 9.24 *obuiam nauigiis uenit, adludit exultans*. Other instances of *adnatare*+dative (Pliny, *N.H.* 8.93, 9.86, 6.99, Sil. 10.610, Stat. *Th.* 7.96) show that the normal meaning is 'swim up to or toward', not 'swim alongside', for which the only evidence is a corrupt passage of Claudian (*Rapt.* 3.444; here Heinsius' *innatat* is the most plausible solution).

454 lasciuit chorus Dolphins (and other fish) are often termed a chorus, cf. Anacr. 55.24, ps.-Arion 939 *PMG*, Soph. fr. 762 P, Eur. *Hel.* 1454f., Theopompus, *Hedychares* fr. 13, Opp. *Hal.* 1.675, Prop. 1.17.25f., Ovid, *Met.* 3.685; note also *lasciuo choro* of the stars accompanying the figure of Night in Tib. 2.1.88.

456ff. iam The fivefold repetition of *iam* is a stylistic device marking successive moments or aspects of the narrative; compare *HF* 125ff., *Anth. Lat.* 465 Riese (Petronius?) *iam nunc ardentes autumnus abegerat umbras | ... | iam platanus iactare comas, iam coeperat uuas | adnumerare suas...uitis*, Stat. *Th.* 1.336ff.; the technique is frequently used in spring-poems (cf. Nisbet–Hubbard on Hor. *C.* 1.4.5) and by Ovid in describing metamorphoses (e.g. *Met.* 2.661f.; S. uses *nunc* for this purpose, cf. 716ff. below).

457 pereunt *Pereunt* is Poggio's conjecture, commended by Leo (*Obs.* 44) but entirely neglected by editors; it is undoubtedly more pointed than *parent*, the reading of the paradosis (*patent*, the variant of S and the *recentiores* which Viansino prints, does not scan). The peaks of Ida are disappearing from sight, and *dubia pereunt...iuga* artfully combines two phases of the action: the *iuga* first become *dubia*, 'hard to distinguish', then vanish utterly. There is similar condensation in Apoll. Rhod. 1.58of. αὐτίκα δ' ἠερίη (= *dubia*) πολυλήιος αἶα Πελασγῶν | δύετο (= *pereunt*), and in Claud. *c. min.* 27.37 *dubio uanescit Cynthia cornu*, Rut. Nam. 1.433f. *sic dubitanda solet gracili uanescere cornu | defessisque oculis luna reperta latet*. For *dubius* of objects fading from sight at dusk cf. Ovid, *Met.* 4.401, 11.596, Juv. 5.22, *T.L.L.* v¹.2109.83ff., and for *pereo* of slowly vanishing objects cf. Ovid, *F.* 3.236 (melting snow, though this literally perishes).

458 iam E's *id* is probably an attempt at improvement; its author thought this line the second subject of *parent* in 457. Seneca does not use *id quod*; it appears only in *Oct.* 454 *id facere laus est quod decet, non quod licet*.

459 Iliacus...fumus The smoke rising from the ruins of Troy is a commonplace, cf. Aesch. *Ag.* 818 καπνῷ δ' ἁλοῦσα νῦν ἔτ' εὔσημος πόλις, Eur. *Tro.* 8 ἣ νῦν καπνοῦται, *Hec.* 1215, Virg. *Aen.* 2.609, 3.3, Sen. *Tro.* 1050ff., Quintus Smyrnaeus 14.393f.

461 in alta iam lux prona The MSS read *in astra*, which is intelligible only if *in astra* can mean *in noctem* (for *pronus in noctem* cf. Luc. 4.29). The best parallels for *astra = nox* which I have found are Luc. 7.451f. *astra Thyestae | intulit* [*sc. Iuppiter*] and Stat. *Th.* 12.48f. *nec dulcibus astris | uicta... coierunt lumina*, and these lack the awkwardness of this passage (I disallow places where *astra = nox* is opposed to *dies*, e.g. Stat. *Th.* 7.471 *hauserat astra dies*, *Ach.* 1.242, Rut. Nam. 1.400; similarly with *sidera*, cf. Ovid, *Met.* 5.444, Luc. 8.202). The alteration of *astra* to *alta* (Damsté, Nisbet) removes the difficulty and restores sense (cf. Luc. 3.40f. *Titan iam pronus in undas | ibat*); for the use of *alta* see, *inter alia*, Virg. *Aen.* 2.203, Ovid, *Ars* 3.390, *F.* 6.498; *T.L.L.* 1.1782.20ff. The two halves of the line thus describe the same moment, but variety is provided by the contrast between *pronus* (cf. Hor. *C.* 3.27.18, Prop. 1.16.23, Ovid, *Met.* 11.257) and the more forceful *praeceps* (for which see Virg. *G.* 3.359, Livy 4.9.13, Ovid, *F.* 1.314).

462 sordido crescens globo Cf. Tac. *Ann.* 2.23 *mox atro nubium globo effusa grando*, cf. Rut. Nam. 1.617 *cum subitis tectus nimbis insorduit aether*, Sid. Apoll. *Epist.* 2.2.16.

463 nitidum...iubar In early Latin *iubar* is most often used of the morning star (cf. Enn. *Ann.* 557 V², *sc.* 337 R², Pac. 347 R², Lucr. 5.697); its range was extended by Ovid, who has it as well of the sun at dawn (*Met.* 7.663, 15.187, *F.* 5.547f.), Aurora (*F.* 4.943f.; cf. Virg. *Aen.* 4.130, the only appearance of *iubar* in Virgil), a star (*Met.* 15.841), and the sun's light generally (*Met.* 1.768 with Bömer's note, cf. Sen. *Pha.* 889 *te, coruscum lucis aetheriae iubar*). Seneca may have been the first writer to use *iubar* of the setting sun, as here (imitated by the author of *HO* 722f., and cf. *Anth. Lat.* 238 Riese *iam nitidum tumidis Phoebus iubar intulit undis*) and of the moon, cf. *Med.* 6 and note Petr. *Sat.* 89.54 *iam plena Phoebe candidum extulerat iubar*. The combination *nitidum iubar* is found twice in Ovid (*Met.* 15.187, *F.* 2.149) and again in *Med.* 100, in all cases referring to morning light.

inquinat Cf. ps.-Sen. *HO* 722 *nulla labe respersus iubar* [*sc. Titan*], Luc. 5.456 *laesum nube dies iubar extulit*, Stat. *Th.* 7.45, Claud. *Ruf.* 1.129.

464 uarius occidens In ancient meteorology a clear sunset forecast fair weather (cf. Theophrastus, *Sign.* 50, Arat. *Phaen.* 825ff., Virg. *G.* 1.458ff.), while any disturbance of the sun's light was a sign of bad weather: black stains on the sun indicate rain; red, wind; and if both black and red appear together (*uarius* in our passage), a severe wind- and rain-storm is to come (cf. Arat. *Phaen.* 102ff., Virg. *G.* 1.450ff.; for *uarius* cf. Claud. *Ruf.* 1.9, Vegetius 4.41). Seneca's compression emerges by comparison with the dissertation Lucan's Caesar receives from Amyclas (5.540ff.); for an ominous sunset see also Stat. *Th.* 1.342ff.

465f. iacent...uela Cf. Virg. *Aen.* 3.568 *fessos uentus cum sole reliquit*, Rut. Nam. 1.343 *sic festinantem uentusque diesque reliquit*.

466–9 The storm-signals in these lines (murmuring on the mountain-tops, groaning sounds along the headlands, swelling of the waves) are connected by Theophrastus (*Sign.* 29) and elaborated by Aratus (*Phaen.* 909ff.), whose Latin imitation by Cicero (*Diu.* 1.13) may have directly influenced Seneca: *atque etiam uentos praemonstrat saepe futuros | inflatum mare, cum subito penitusque tumescit | saxaque cana, salis niueo spumata liquore, | tristificas certant Neptuno reddere uoces | aut densus stridor cum, celso e uertice montis | ortus, adaugescit scopulorum saepe repulsus*. Also relevant are the following Virgilian passages: *G.* 1.356ff. *continuo uentis surgentibus aut freta ponti | incipiunt agitata tumescere et aridus altis | montibus audiri fragor, aut resonantia longe | litora misceri et nemorum increbescere murmur, Aen.* 3.355f., 10.98f. *caeca uolutant | murmura uenturos nautis prodentia uentos* (the probable source for *uentis... uenturis* in 469).

The components of these lines are also found in isolation: for *murmur ponti* see Cic. *Tusc.* 5.116, Luc. 5.571, Val. Fl. 5.121, Quintus Smyrnaeus 14.489f. and for *murmur uentorum* Virg. *Aen.* 1.55, 245, Ovid, *Tr.* 1.2.25, Luc. 10.321, Heliodorus 5.27.2; for the swelling of the waves by wind, cf. Archilochus 56 D, Pac. 411 R², Cic. *Rep.* 1.63, Virg. *G.* 2.479, *Aen.* 3.195, 5.11 (with Williams's note), Sen. *Contr.* 8 *exc.* 7, [Tib.] 4.1.194, Ovid, *Met.* 1.36, *F.* 2.776, *Tr.* 1.4.5, Sen. *Med.* 765f., *Epist.* 53.2, Luc. 5.217f., 565, 10.224, Claud. *Ruf.* 1.70ff.

470 cum subito The suddenness with which storms arise is a traditional motif, cf. Soph. *Ant.* 417, schol. Arat. *Phaen.* p. 509.3 Maass, Lucilius 998 M, Cic. *Diu.* 1.13, Varro, *Sat.* 269 Buecheler, C. Sisenna fr. 104 Peter, Virg. *Aen.* 3.196ff., Sen. *Contr.* 8 *exc.* 7, Ovid, *Pont.* 3.3.9f., Sen. *N.Q.* 2.30.1, *Epist.* 109.18, Petr. *Sat.* 114, Val. Fl. 6.715, Juv. 12.18ff., Ach. Tat. 3.1.1, Heliodorus 5.27.1, Rut. Nam. 1.617f. (for *cum subito* at the start of a line see also Virg. *G.* 4.488, *Aen.* 2.680, Sil. 10.102, Claud. *Ruf.* 2.384; on *cum inuersum* cf. Hofmann–Szantyr 623).

luna conditur The source is surely Hor. *C.* 2.16.1ff. *otium diuos rogat in patenti | prensus Aegaeo, simul atra nubes | condidit lunam neque certa fulgent | sidera nautis.*

stellae latent Cf. Ovid, *Met.* 11.550 *omne latet caelum*, Hor. *Epod.* 10.9f. *nec sidus atra nocte amicum appareat | qua tristis Orion cadit.* In this context A's *cadunt* would have to refer to shooting stars (so Del Rio, followed by Stuart, *CQ* v (1911) 34), another well-known weather sign (cf. Arat. *Phaen.* 926ff., Virg. *G.* 1.365, Manil. 1.826, Luc. 5.562). At this point, however, another sign of an approaching storm is superfluous; in addition, the darkness announced in *luna conditur* would render shooting stars invisible.

471 in astra pontus tollitur, caelum perit Zwierlein (*Gnomon* xxxviii (1966) 687) has shown that the line is unsuited to this context. In ancient storm-descriptions, waves rise to the heavens only when stirred by winds (cf. *Il.* 15.626, *Od.* 3.289f., Apoll. Rhod. 2.169, Virg. *Aen.* 1.101f., Ovid, *Met.* 11.497f., Quintus Smyrnaeus 14.490f.) or by some other force or object which forces the sea upwards (e.g. Scylla and Charybdis in Virg. *Aen.* 3.422ff., Manil. 5.604, cf. Sen. *Med.* 341ff.); this fact appears as a commonplace in *Carm. Eins.* 2.8 *atquin turbari sine uentis non solet aequor* and the exception in Sen. *Pha.* 1007ff. is thought worthy of comment (1010 *placidumque pelagus propria tempestas agit*). In our passage, however, the winds have not yet made their appearance (they enter in 474ff.), and so the action of line 471 is entirely uncaused. The line also fails to cohere with its surroundings (470, 472ff.), which are exclusively concerned with darkness. Finally, it resembles the preceding line in rhythm and structure; it is unlikely that S. would have allowed two such similar lines to stand together.

These arguments may show that 471 is out of place, but they do not convict it of being spurious. In form the line is unobjectionable, and it would be remarkable indeed if this *tour de force* of storm-description omitted one of the most durable of ancient storm-*topoi*, the rising of the waves to hyperbolic height (cf., in addition to the passages cited above, Virg. *Aen.* 3.567, Luc. 1.410ff., 5.563f., 629, 9.313, ps.-Sen. *HO* 817, 1638, *Octauia* 320f., Ach. Tat. 3.2.7, Rut. Nam. 1.644; further material in Zwierlein). A hint of the line's true position may be found in the words *caelum perit* and *fretum | caelumque miscet* in 473f. There are two ways in which sky and sea may be mingled: by darkness so thick that all boundaries of sea and sky disappear (so, too, in *Pha.* 995f. *nunc atra uentis nubila impellentibus | subtexe noctem, sidera et caelum eripe*), or by waves rising to the level of the clouds, where they mix with the falling rain. Line 471 deals with the second of these themes, and has somehow found its way into a handling of the first (perhaps the very words *fretum | caelumque miscet* were instrumental in the dislocation). The proper position of line 471 is therefore in the passage 488ff., which discusses the mingling of sea and sky in the second sense:

uento resistit aestus et uentus retro	488
aestum reuoluit; non capit sese mare;	489
in astra pontus tollitur; caelum perit,	471
undasque miscent imber et fluctus suas.	490

(Note that this collocation not only preserves the sense of 488ff., but nicely clarifies the sequence of events.)

The only other critic to have seen the problems raised by line 471 is Bentley; realising that in its transmitted place the line must deal with darkness and not with winds, he conjectured *nox atra ponto tollitur*. It seems doubtful, however, that *tollitur* can bear the sense required.

472 nec una nox est The combination of night and cloud is traditional (cf. *Od.* 5.293f., Virg. *Aen.* 1.88f., Sall. *Jug.* 38.5, Sen. *Pha.* 955f.; note Juvenal's reference to *densae tenebrae* in his account of the *poetica tempestas*, 12.18ff.); a pointed handling first appears in Pac. 412 R² *tenebrae conduplicantur*, then twice in Ovid (*Met.* 11.521 *caecaque nox premitur tenebris hiemisque suisque*, 550 *duplicataque noctis imago est*).

473 caligo This is the ἀχλύς of Apollonius 2.1103ff., similar to the unnatural darkness seen by Seneca's Thyestes (993ff.) *spissior densis coit | caligo tenebris noxque se in noctem abdidit* or the infernal gloom of Lucan 5.627f. *non caeli nox illa fuit: latet obsitus aer | infernae pallore domus*. Compare Ovid, *Met.* 1.265 [*Notus*] *terribilem picea tectus caligine uultum*, Calp. Sic. 5.47.

474 incumbunt The verb is almost certainly borrowed from Virg. *Aen.* 1.84 *incubuere mari...Eurusque Notusque*; for the force of the word cf. Hor. *C.* 1.3.30f. *noua febrium | terris incubuit cohors* (and see Nisbet–Hubbard *ad loc.*).

475 infimo euersum solo The A text has often been neglected by editors wishing to retain E's *polo*, but it is acceptable without alteration. *T.L.L.* v².1029.59ff. compares Soph. *Ant.* 590f. πόντιον οἶδμα κυλίνδει βυσσόθεν κελαινὰν |θῖνα; the churning up of sand is indeed a commonplace of ancient storms, cf. *Anth. Pal.* 9.290, Theoc. 7.58, Sall. *Jug.* 78.3, Hor. *C.* 3.17.10, Ovid, *Met.* 11.489, *Tr.* 1.4.6, ps.-Quint. *Decl. mai.* 12.16, Quintus Smyrnaeus 14.495f., Rut. Nam. 1.639 (in still other passages the winds expose the sea bed, cf. *Od.* 12.242f., *Anth. Pal.* 13.27, Virg. *Aen.* 1.107, Luc. 5.604). Here, however, *infimo euersum solo* is more accurately taken to mean 'churned up from its bed' (i.e. as an equivalent to *totumque a sedibus imis* in Virg. *Aen.* 1.84), cf. Solon 1.19f. D, Virg. *Aen.* 2.419 *imo Nereus ciet aequora fundo*, Ovid, *F.* 3.591 *imoque a gurgite pontus | uertitur*, *Tr.* 1.2.19, Sen. *N.Q.* 3.27.1 *maria sedibus suis excita...incumbunt*; for *euertere* in this context cf. Virg. *Aen.* 1.43, Ovid, *Her.* 7.42, Sen. *Epist.* 4.7, Petr. *Sat.* 123.234.

infimo In this context the standard word is *imus*, but see Hor. *C.* 4.8.31f. *clarum Tyndaridae sidus ab infimis | quassas eripiunt aequoribus rates.*

476 aduersus...Notus The conventional ἀνέμων στάσις (see Bömer on Ovid, *Met.* 1.58ff., Nisbet–Hubbard on Hor. *C.* 1.3.13) is here introduced in a clever, though mechanical way: four winds in a single line, with opposing directions (East–West, North–South) juxtaposed. Such stylisation, however, is found in the very beginnings of the topic, in *Od.* 5.331f. ἄλλοτε μέν τε Νότος Βορέῃ προβάλεσκε φέρεσθαι, | ἄλλοτε δ' αὖτ' Εὖρος Ζεφύρῳ εἴξασκε διώκειν, and in another passage (*Od.* 5.295f.) Homer comes close to fitting all his winds into one verse: σὺν δ' Εὖρός τε Νότος τ' ἔπεσον Ζέφυρός τε δυσαὴς | καὶ Βορέης (elsewhere in Homer Euros and Notos are the only combatants, cf. *Il.* 2.144, 16.765, so too Theoc. 7.58, Prop. 3.15.32).

The number and identities of the struggling winds were not fixed by convention. Some Greek writers refer to the winds generally without naming any (cf. Alcaeus 326 *PLF*, Aesch. *P.V.* 1085ff.), a practice adopted in several Latin treatments, cf. Pac. 410ff. R², Lucr. 5.647, Virg. *G.* 1.318, Ovid, *Met.* 11.491f., Sen. *B.V.* 7.10; cf. Val. Fl. 2.365 *magnis cum fratribus Eurus.* Virgil in *Aen.* 1.84f. and 2.417f., Horace in *Epod.* 10.3ff., and Silius in 12.617f. name three winds (no two passages agree); two winds appear in Hor. *C.* 1.3.12f. (Africus–Aquilo), Enn. *Ann.* 443ff. V² (Auster–Aquilo), and Stat. *Th.* 1.346ff. (Auster–Boreas). The four winds of the present passage seem to be an Ovidian inheritance, cf. *Met.* 1.61ff., *Ars* 2.431f., *Her.* 11.15f., and in particular *Tr.* 1.2.27ff.

Seneca himself in his capacity as a scientific inquirer in the *Naturales Quaestiones* treated the poetic texts with wry detachment: he cites Ovid, *Met.* 1.61ff., then offers Virg. *Aen.* 1.84f. *si breuius illos complecti mauis*, adding *et, qui locum in illa rixa non habuit, Aquilo* (5.16f.).

478 emoliuntur The word is often rendered by guesses and approximations: 'shake' (Studley), 'stir up' (Miller), 'heave up' (*O.L.D.*, s.u.), *euertere* (Farnaby, W.-H. Friedrich in *T.L.L.* vi¹.518.8ff.); it may, however, here retain its technical sense 'to force out through an aperture', for which cf. Celsus 4.13.2, 7.26.1A, Columella 8.5.21 *per nares emoliri pituitae nauseam*, Apul. *Met.* 4.12 *cuncta rerum nauiter emolitus* [*sc. per fenestram*]. S. thus boldly suggests a picture of winds pressing down on the water and forcing jets to shoot up from the spaces between the masses of wind. The resulting waterspout may be identical with the *turbo* of the second half of the line; cf. Acc. 397 R², Sen. *N.Q.* 7.9.2 *nempe efficit turbinem plurium uentorum inter ipsos luctatio, Epist.* 109.18.

479ff. The following passage illustrates another technique for introducing opposed winds, i.e. singly and with the stateliness of Homeric heroes; compare Manilius 4.592ff., Luc. 5.598ff., Val. Fl. 1.610ff., Silius 17.246ff., Paconianus p. 123 Morel.

479 Strymonius...Aquilo The storm in Aeschylus (*Ag.* 654ff.) is caused by Θρήκιαι πνοαί (cf. 192f. πνοαὶ δ' ἀπὸ Στρυμόνος | μολοῦσαι); for the connection of Aquilo (Boreas) and Thrace cf. *Il.* 9.9, Hes. *Op.* 553, Tyrt. 9.4 D, Ibycus 286.9 *PMG*, Hor. *Epod.* 13.2f., Luc. 5.603 (and compare Ovid, *Met.* 1.64f. *Scythiam...inuasit Boreas*); see further Nisbet–Hubbard on Hor. *C.* 1.25.11.

480 Auster A remarkably protean wind in Latin poetry. Auster is at times hot and dry, as apparently here, cf. Ovid, *Met.* 7.532, Sen. *Oed.* 622f., *N.Q.* 4.2.18, Luc. 9.781, 10.222; alternatively, it may be warm (Sen. *Pha.* 21), or warm and wet (Ovid, *Ars* 3.174); it may also be simply wet (Ovid, *Met.* 1.66, ps.-Sen. *HO* 71, Juv. 5.101, Claud. *Cons. Stil.* 3.103) or, perhaps under the influence of Notus, its neighbour, cold and wet (Virg. *G.* 1.462, 3.278, 4.261, Tib. 1.1.47, Prop. 2.26.36 (on which see Shackleton Bailey, *Propertiana* 116f.), Stat. *Th.* 1.350); cf. Housman's note on Luc. 7.871. For the connection with the Syrtes cf. Silius 17.247 [Auster] *nudauit Syrtim correpta nubilus unda*.

481 †nec manet in Austro: fit† grauis nimbis Notus It has often been recognised that the MS text presents difficulties, but no previous discussion has seen their full extent. Leo objected to *fit* on the ground that Notus, a conventionally wet wind, could not become *grauis nimbis*; he read instead *flat*, a feeble variant found in the *recentiores*. Seneca's *grauis nimbis* is probably derived from Ovid, *Met.* 1.266 *barba grauis nimbis*, a phrase describing Notus' habitual appearance (cf. also Stat. *Th.* 1.160 *madidi... Noti*), but Notus can at times be a detergent wind, cf. Hor. *C.* 1.7.15, with Nisbet–Hubbard's note. Furthermore, Leo's substitution of one verb for another ignores a feature of the passage's arrangement: every other wind controls only one finite verb. Recognising this, Damsté conjectured *sed*; more ingeniously, Nisbet has suggested *grauis enim nimbis Notus* (for the resolution see Strzelecki 59). Of emendations postulating limited corruption this deserves perhaps the highest consideration.

This approach, however, neglects other problems. What, for example, is the subject of *manet*? Del Rio paraphrased 'nec manet procellae dominium penes Austrum', but this is difficult to supply from the context (the theme of struggle for control is elsewhere unambiguous, cf. Hor. *C.* 1.3.15, Luc. 2.454ff., 5.610f., Petr. *Sat.* 114.3, Stat. *Th.* 1.350; Tac. *Ann.* 2.23 *caelum et mare omne in Austrum cessit* comes nearest).

But even if Del Rio's explanation, or something like it, were acceptable, doubts would subsist. The passage as a whole has a clear shape: a general statement (*sua quisque mittit tela* 477) is followed by the appearance of each wind acting on its proper sphere of influence; *nec manet in Austro* is a pointless disruption of this scheme.

These considerations point to deeper corruption (Richter's proposed deletion of the entire line is impossible). The boundaries of the infected area cannot be fixed with certainty, but no doubt attaches to *grauis nimbis Notus | imbre auget undas*. What is required is a fuller description of Notus; note in particular that every other wind has a geographical attribute (*Strymonius, Libycus*) or qualifying phrase (*Eurus orientem mouet* eqs., *ora Corus Oceano exerens*). More precisely, the hyperbolic assumption of the passage is that each wind brings to the scene the disturbance which it produces in its own bailiwick (*altas...niues* 479, *harenas* 480, *Nabataea...regna* 483). Under the corruption in line 481 might lie something along the lines of *madidis et Africo grauis nimbis Notus | imbre auget undas* (a comma after *agit* in 480 would be required).

482f. Eurus...sinus Ovid, *Met.* 1. 61 *Eurus ad auroram Nabataeaque regna recessit* may be the source both of this passage and of Luc. 4.63ff. In Virg. *Aen.* 2.417f. the Eastern colouring is applied with greater economy: *laetus Eois | Eurus equis*.

484 rabidus The choice between E's *rabidus* and A's *rapidus* is not obvious, since *rapidus* in S. can suggest *rapax* as well as *uelox* (cf., e.g., *Med.* 219 *rapida Fortuna ac leuis* [*rapida* P CS: *rabida* R E], and note *rapax* of Corus in *N.Q.* 5.16.5); in most instances of *rabidus* the essential idea is lack of control (of *canes, Med.* 351, *Oed.* 932, cf. 708 below; *rabido ore, Oed.* 561, 626). The principle *utrum in alterum abiturum erat?* cannot be invoked, since the confusion is frequent in both directions (cf. Lachmann on Lucr. 4.712, Housman on Manil. 1.396, 2.211 (vol. v.139), Nisbet–Hubbard on Hor. *C.* 1.28.21) and occurs with reference to Corus in Claud. *fesc.* 2.42, Rut. Nam. 1.463; for *rabidus*, however, *Thy.* 36off. offers a good parallel: *non Eurus rapiens mare | aut saeuo rabidus* [E: *rapidus* P CS] *freto | uentosi tumor Hadriae*.

Corus One of Seneca's favourite winds, almost always violent and stormy, cf. *N.Q.* 5.16.5, also *Tro.* 1032f., *Med.* 411f., *Pha.* 1012f., 1131, *Thy.* 578; *HO* 65of. Our passage may have been imitated by Lucan, 5.598f. *primus ab Oceano caput exeris Atlanteo, | Core, mouens aestus.*

exerens Compare, in addition to Luc, 5.598f., Ovid, *F.* 5.637 *Thybris harundiferum medio caput extulit alueo, Met.* 13.838, Sen. *Pha.* 747.

485 reuelli A's reading is surely correct. E's *reuellit* is based on the misconception that 485 answers the question put in 484. In fact, the reference to Corus completes the catalogue of winds, and the lines that follow describe the effects of their combined exertions.

486 crederes The narrator inserts himself momentarily into the story to soften the hyperbole; for the technique cf. Acc. 395 R² *credas nimbum uoluier*, Virg. *Aen.* 8.691 *pelago credas innare reuolsas | Cyclades* (la Cerda compares the Homeric φαίης κε and οὐδέ κε φαίης), Ovid, *Met.* 11.497f. *caelumque aequare uidetur | pontus*, 503f., 517 *inque fretum credas totum descendere caelum* Luc. 5.634ff., *T.L.L.* iv.1146.71ff.

487 atrum...chaos This apocalyptic vision appears in a storm-narrative only here and in Lucan 5.634ff., but the theme is found outside storms, cf. Ovid, *Met.* 2.299 *in chaos antiquum confundimur* (because of Phaethon), Sen. *Thy.* 831f. *iterumque deos | hominesque premat deforme chaos*, ps.-Sen. *HO* 1134f.

488f. uento...reuoluit For the idea cf. Luc. 3.549f. *quotiens aestus Zephyris Eurisque repugnat, | huc abeant fluctus, illo mare,* and see on 139 above; for *reuoluit* cf. Virg. *Aen.* 10.660, Claud. *Ruf.* 1.532.

489 non capit sese mare Cf. Virg. *Aen.* 7.466 *nec iam se capit unda, uolat uapor ater ad auras,* Manilius 4.830f. *uomit Oceanus pontum... | nec sese ipse capit,* Sen. *N.Q.* 6.20.2.

490 undasque...suas For the mingling of sea and sky in this sense cf. Aesch. *P.V.* 1048ff. (with Groeneboom's note), Aratus, *Phaen.* 936, Virg. *Aen.* 1.129 *fluctibus et caeli ruina,* Ovid, *Met.* 11.519f. *cum caelestibus undis | aequoreae miscentur aquae,* Luc. 5.630 *fluctusque in nubibus accipit imbrem,* Quintus Smyrnaeus 14.518f., 597ff.; see further F. Vian, *Études sur Quinte de Smyrne* (1959) 81ff.

491f. The thought may be compared to *Il.* 17.645ff.; cf. also Luc. 3.416f. *tantum terroribus addit | quos timeant non nosse deos.*

491 aerumnis The dative with *leuamen* regularly names the recipient of the *leuamen* (in most cases a person), the genitive the thing alleviated; a clear parallel for the dative used of the thing relieved is found in *Med.* 548f. *haec causa uitae est, hoc perusti pectoris | curis leuamen*; in other cases the influence of an adjacent phrase accounts for a different construction, cf. *Pho.* 1f. *caeci parentis regimen et fessi unicum | patris leuamen, C.I.L.* VIII.1.251 (*s.* III *in.*) *leuamen hoc doloribus lacrimisque pausam credidit* (see B. Kühler, *A.L.L.* VIII.165, J. Perrot, *Les dérivés latins en -men et -mentum* (1961) 124).

It should also be noted that *leuamen...datur* and *pereant* presuppose an antecedent (*milites, nautae*) which is not in the text and which cannot easily be supplied from the context; the men have not been named since 446 and have not been even indirectly involved in the narrative since 449. Since no emendation seems possible, it is best to supply an antecedent from the wider context of the narrative. Comparison with the parallel account in Quintus Smyrnaeus reveals that the men and their emotions play a much larger and more pervasive part than in Seneca's more schematic arrangement; if these lines correspond closely to lines in the common source of Quintus and Seneca, the slight difficulties they pose may be the result of Seneca's abbreviation or reordering of his material.

493 premunt tenebrae lumina These words, and the *tamen*-clause which follows, are based on Ovid, *Met.* 11.520f. *caret ignibus aether | caecaque nox premitur tenebris hiemisque suisque. | discutiunt tamen has praebentque minantia lumen | fulmina.* In our passage, however, *lumina* are probably the men's eyes, and *premunt* suggests the constraint of the close darkness (cf. Virg. *Aen.* 6.827 *dum nocte premuntur*, Hor. *C.* 1.4.16).

493f. dirae...est Cf. Apoll. Rhod. 4.1697f. οὐρανόθεν δὲ μέλαν χάος, ἠέ τις ἄλλη | ὠρώρει σκοτίη μυχάτων ἀνιοῦσα βερέθρων, Luc. 5.627 *non caeli nox illa fuit.*

494 excidunt ignes tamen Cf. Sen. *N.Q.* 3.27.10 *quod olim fuerat nubilum, nox est et quidem horrida...crebra enim micant fulmina,* more pointedly expressed in Sen. *Contr.* 8 *exc.* 6 *demissa nox caelo est et tantum fulminibus dies redditus* (cf. Sen. *Thy.* 1085f. *lumen ereptum polo | fulminibus exple*). Lucan's handling of this detail is even more effective (5.630f.): *lux etiam metuenda perit, nec fulgura currunt | clara, sed obscurum nimbosus dissilit aer.*

In Homer (*Od.* 12.415, 14.305) and Euripides (*Tro.* 80f.) lightning is not a natural adjunct of a sea-storm, but the weapon of the gods; it does not appear at all in Aeschylus (*Ag.* 654ff.). It appears in Sophocles' *Teucer* (fr. 578 P), but the context is missing. That lightning formed part of an influential Greek storm-description is suggested by its presence in Pacuvius 413 R² *flamma inter nubes coruscat*, Virg. *Aen.* 1.90 *crebris micat ignibus aether*, Chariton 3.10, Ach. Tat. 3.2, and Quintus Smyrnaeus 14.528f. It is a conventional element in Latin storms after Virgil.

495 nube...fulmen elisa In most poetic and scientific descriptions it is the *fulmen* which is squeezed (*elisum*) from the clouds, and not the clouds which are crushed together by the *fulmen*, cf. Arist. *Meteor.* 369a13–b8, Sen. *N.Q.* 1.1.6, 2.12.5, *Prou.* 1.3, Ovid, *Met.* 6.696, 8.339 *excussis elisi nubibus ignes* (although the variant of the lost Spirensis, *excussus elisis nubibus ignis*, is tempting in view of Seneca's similar inversion), 11.435, Luc. 1.151, Petr. *Sat.* 122.123, Val. Fl. 4.663, Claud. *Ruf.* 2.222. The version used here, however, is easily defended, cf. *N.Q.* 6.9.1 *ignis ex hoc collisu nubium cursuque elisi aeris emicuit*, Stat. *Th.* 5.394f. *elisit nubes Ioue tortus ab alto | ignis*, Marius Victor, *Alethias* 3.147f. (*CSEL* xvi.411) *nubibus elisis quod fulmina nuntia signant.*

496f. miserisque...optant The idea that men caught in a storm would be so frightened by darkness as to long for the lightning is characteristically Senecan; the MS text, however, does not seem to convey this idea with the expected point. The difficulty lies in *malae*: without it the line means 'so great is the pleasure of light to the unfortunates (that) they long for *this* light'; with *malae* the meaning must be 'so great is the pleasure afforded by evil light to the wretches (that) they long for this light', which makes the sailors odd fellows indeed. Only Bothe has hitherto seen the problem; his proposal, to read *dulcedo est, male | hoc lumen optant*, is pointless and indeed fatuous, if *male* means 'unwisely'. An equally slight change, to *tanta dulcedo, et malae*, may give a better result: 'so great is the joy of light, even a destructive light...'; *mala lux* may be unexampled, but Lucan has *lux metuenda* (5.630) and Statius uses *sol malus* (*Th.* 7.223) and *ignis malus* (*S.* 5.1.152). I have not, however, adopted any alteration in the text); it seems to me possible that S. himself neglected fully to exploit the rhetorical opportunities of the situation. (The change from *lux* to *lumen* is paralleled in *HF* 669ff.; the paratactic construction of the consecutive clause *hoc lumen optant*, however, is rarely found outside colloquial speech, cf. Hofmann–Szantyr 529.)

497f. Ships collide in *Od.* 10.122 and Aesch. *Ag.* 654f., but the extended treatment here and in Quintus Smyrnaeus 14.516ff. probably points to a lost Greek source; note also Pacuvius 335 R² *flictus nauium*.

499f. This is Seneca's closest approach to another commonplace of storm-narrative, mocked in Shakespeare, *Winter's Tale* iii.iii.89f. 'now the ship boring the moon with her main-mast, and anon swallowed with yeast and froth, as you'ld thrust a cork into a hogshead'; cf. Virg. *Aen.* 1.106f. *hi summo in fluctu pendent; his unda dehiscens | terram inter fluctus aperit*, 3.564f., Ovid, *Met.* 11.502ff., *Tr.* 1.2.19ff., Luc. 5.638ff., Stat. *Th.* 5.371, Ach. Tat. 3.2.5, Quintus Smyrnaeus 14.492ff., 553ff.; in *Od.* 12.242f. only one half of the topic appears.

500 hauritque Often used of objects suddenly sinking, cf. Livy 33.41.7, Ovid, *F.* 3.600, Sen. *Epist.* 30.4, etc.; also *sorbere*, Virg. *Aen.* 3.418, Sen. *Epist.* 4.7; *uorare*, Val. Fl. 8.332; πίνειν, Theogn. 680.

alio...mari The paradosis is *alto redditam reuomit mare*, universally corrected to *alto...mari* by editors. Thus corrected the line presumably means 'the sea swallows the ship and spews it up from the depths of the sea, restored' (*alto mari* ablative, perhaps of source, connected to *reuomit*); the pointlessness of *alto mari* and of *redditam* are obvious. All problems of style and sense are removed by Gronovius' *alio* for *alto*, and a new point is introduced (the ship is spewed up so far from the place at which it disappeared that it can be said to be restored to another sea, cf. Luc. 5.612ff.). The dative form *alio* is attested for Seneca (*Ben.* 4.32.3 *at ego scio alio me istud dare, alio olim debitum soluere*), cf. also Pl. *Pseud.* 1263, Quint. *Inst.* 9.4.23 (though Winterbottom accepts Christ's correction *alii*), *Rhet. ad Her.* 2.19.3, ps.-Quint. *Decl. mai.* 2.9, *Decl.* 347 (p. 367 Ritter). The dative of *alius* (noun or adjective) is not elsewhere used in the tragedies.

501f. conuulsum...undis Allowing the side of the ship to be battered head-on by the waves invariably led to disaster; this is the point of Sen. *Pha.* 1072f. *at ille* [Hippolytus], *qualis turbido rector mari | ratem retentat, ne det obliquum latus*, and the detail occurs in several storm-accounts, cf. Virg. *Aen.* 1.104f. *prora auertit et undis | dat latus*, Ovid, *Met.* 11.507, Luc. 3.628, Val. Fl. 1.619, Silius 17.268.

502 fluctus...decimus The tenth wave seems to play no part in Latin poetic storms before Ovid (*Met.* 11.530 *uastius insurgens decimus ruit* *impetus undae*, *Tr.* 1.2.49f.); Lucan puts the commonplace to novel use, making the wave deposit the ranting Caesar on a cliff (5.672). The Greeks spoke not of tenth waves, but of a τρικυμία (cf. Aesch. *P.V.* 1015, with Blomfield's note, Eur. *Tro.* 83, *Hipp.* 1212 with Barrett's note, Plato, *Resp.* 472A, Menander, fr. 536.8 Körte), and the Romans called other things than waves *decumanus* if they were inordinately large, cf. Paulus *ex* Fest. p. 71 Müller: *decumana oua dicuntur et decumani fluctus, quia sunt magna; nam et ouum decimum maius nascitur et fluctus decimus fieri maximus dicitur.*

504 fluitat Compare Cicero on the ship of state (*Sest.* 46): *rei publicae nauem ereptis senatui gubernaculis fluitantem in alto tempestatibus*; Virgil does not use the word (cf. *Aen.* 1.118f.), and its appearance in this context in Silius 6.685, 14.542 may show the influence of *Culex* 355.

illi Seneca's picture of the fleet's destruction is built up of six individual scenes introduced alternately by *hic* and *ille*, the last four in chiastic order (499 *illam*, 501 *haec*; *illa*, 502 *hanc*; 503 *haec*, 504 *illi*). Heinsius' *ulli* here is therefore out of place.

504f. nec...ferens Similar catalogues of damage are found in Alcaeus 326 *PLF*, Cic. *de Or.* 3.180, Lucr. 2.554 *antemnas proram malos tonsasque natantis*, Varro, *Sat.* 271 Buecheler *uenti...secum trahentes tegulas, ramos, σύρους*, Hor. *C.* 1.14.4ff. (on which see Nisbet–Hubbard), Petr. *Sat.* 114.13 *non arbor erat relicta, non gubernacula, non funis aut remus, sed quasi rudis atque infecta materies ibat cum fluctibus*, Ach. Tat. 3.2.3; a variation appears in Sen. *Contr.* 7.1.2.

Several Greek accounts stress the smashing of the mast and sails, cf. *Od.* 12.409ff., Archil. 43 D, Theog. 671f., Apoll. Rhod. 2.1108, Theoc. 22.12f., Quintus Smyrnaeus 14.594f. (also Luc. 5.594ff., Val. Fl. 1.620f.); other writers single out the groaning of the cables, cf. Pac. 335f. R² *armamentum stridor...strepitus fremitus clamor tonitruum et rudentum sibilus*, Virg. *Aen.* 1.87 *clamorque uirum stridorque rudentum*, Ovid, *Tr.* 1.4.9f., ps.-Quint. *Decl. mai.* 12.16, Silius 17.256; the breaking of oars is included in Hor. *Epod.* 10.5, Virg. *Aen.* 1.104, and Val. Fl. 1.617ff.

506 trunca Cf. Ach. Tat. 3.2.9 γυμνή; perhaps a stronger variant of Horace's *saucia* (*C.* 1.14.5) or Ovid's *lacera* (cf. on 412f. above).

Ionio The MS reading has been unjustifiably suspected. The crux of the matter is not whether *mare Ionium* could be used to mean that part of the Mediterranean near the Ionian coast; Housman himself cites the best proof that it was so used, Ovid, *F.* 4.565ff.: *hinc init Aegaeum, quo Cycladas aspicit omnes,* | *Ioniumque rapax Icariumque legit,* | *perque urbes Asiae longum petit Hellespontum* (of less interest because of its late date is Rut. Nam. 1.320, of the Isthmus: *Ionias bimari litore findit aquas*; cf. Servius *ad Aen.* 3.211 for ideas of *mare Ionium* at this time). The question is rather whether S. can be permitted the loose sense of *mare Ionium* here since the proper sense occurs in

565f. below; I feel that the difference in tone and purpose between the two passages is surely adequate to account for the inconsistency. Here Seneca concludes a description of the helpless ships with an apt hyperbole; accuracy is not relevant, and a proper name is sought for a more highly coloured effect (cf. Prop. 3.11.72 *Caesaris in toto sis memor Ionio*; without the proper name cf. Sen. *Epist.* 109.18 *subitus turbo toto nauem meam mari raperet*). In the later passage Seneca is imparting geographical details, and is alluding in particular to the Isthmus; he is therefore compelled to call things by their correct names (compare the proper use of *mare Ionium* in *Thy.* 142, also geographical in content, and the tragic fragment quoted in Sen. *Epist.* 80.7 *en impero Argis...qua ponto ab Helles atque ab Ionio mari | urguetur Isthmos*).

507ff. Here begins a section describing the helpless reactions of the sailors, another traditional topic, cf. *Il.* 15.624ff., *Od.* 5.297, Eur. *Tro.* 692ff., Apoll. Rhod. 2.561, 4.1699ff., Theoc. 22.18, Virg. *Aen.* 1.91f., Val. Fl. 1.621, Stat. *Th.* 3.29f., 5.383f., Quintus Smyrnaeus 14.491f., 497ff. Seneca's treatment seems to owe most to Ovid, *Met.* 11.539ff. *non tenet hic lacrimas, stupet hic, uocat ille beatos | funera quos maneant; hic uotis numen adorat* (also a possible source of inspiration for Petr. *Sat.* 123.233ff.); the report of a speech made by the desperate crew (517ff.) may have been suggested by Albinovanus Pedo (*apud* Sen. *Suas.* 1.15). (Tacitus transforms the topic with realistic detail in *Ann.* 1.70, 2.23.)

507 ars A recurrent motif in Ovidian storms, cf. *Met.* 11.492 *tanta mali moles, tantoque potentior arte est*, 537, *F.* 3.593 *uincitur ars uento*, *Tr.* 1.2.32 *ambiguis ars stupet ipsa malis*, 1.4.12, 1.11.22; cf. also Luc. 5.645 *artis opem uicere metus*, Stat. *Th.* 3.29 *arte relicta* (cf. 6.451), Claud. *Bell. Gild.* 219 *artem uicere procellae*. The closest parallel to our passage, however, is in Manilius 1.887f. (on a plague): *nec locus artis erat medicae, nec uota ualebant; | cesserat officium morbis* (cf. Sen. *Oed.* 69); *cessit malis*, cf. *Oed.* 1008.

509 remus effugit manus For the detail cf. Quintus Smyrnaeus 14.497f. οὔτ' ἐπ' ἐρετμῷ | χεῖρα βαλεῖν ἐδύναντο τεθηπότες. For this use of *effugio*, cp. *Oed.* 380 *uiscera effugiunt manum*.

510 in uota The vows made by those caught in storms were a traditional motif, cf. Arat. *Phaen.* 426f., Hor. *Epod.* 10.15ff., *C.* 3.29.57ff., Virg. *Aen.* 5.782, Ovid, *Met.* 11.540f., *F.* 3.594, *Tr.* 1.2.59ff., 1.4.25ff., 1.11.22, Luc. 5.450. Here the commonplace introduces a more significant idea, that extremity has reduced the victorious Greeks and the conquered Trojans to the same level (*eademque...rogant* 511). For *in uota* cf. Hor. *C.* 3.29.57f. *ad miseras preces | decurrere*, Virg. *Aen.* 5.782 *descendere in preces* [*cogunt*], Ovid, *Ibis* 206 *cogi in lacrimas*, Sen. *Suas.* 6.7 *Ciceronem in mortem cogi posse, in preces non posse*.

512ff. In *Od.* 5.306ff. and Virg. *Aen.* 1.94ff., which are the obvious sources of these lines, the incidents recalled are suited to the characters of

272

Odysseus and Aeneas; Seneca widens his vision to make a series of ironic points.

514 Agamemno Priamo For the ironic pairing cf. Sen. *Tro.* 308ff. *et nimium diu | a caede nostra regia cessat manus | paremque poscit Priamus*, 794 below. The form *Agamemnŏ* is here required by metre; similarly in Pl. *Bacch.* 946 (*-o* ACD¹; *-on* BD³), Acc. 160 R², Stat. *Ach.* 1.553; see also Cic. *Tusc.* 3.62, 4.17, *Att.* 13.47.1. Similar forms occur elsewhere in *Med.* 201, 276 (*Pelia*), *Oed.* 289 (*Tiresia*), 399 (*Creo*), *Thy.* 783 (*Thyesta*).

514f. quisquis...uocatur The motif has a place outside the present context, cf. Ovid, *Met.* 11.540, *F.* 3.597, Silius 17.260.

ad Troiam iacet For *ad* used to specify location with no discernible suggestion of direction cf. Tib. 1.1.27f. *Canis aestiuos ortus uitare sub umbra | arboris ad riuos praetereuntis aquae*, Prop. 4.7.4 *murmur ad extremae nuper humata uiae*, Sen. *Oed.* 338 *primos ad ortus positus*, *O.L.D.* s.u. *ad* 13.

515 gradu All editors have accepted E's reading, and it is probably right. Although one might have expected *cadere in gradu* for 'to fall at one's place' (cf. Ovid, *Met.* 9.43 *stare in gradu*, also Sen. *Const.* 16.2), there is a good parallel in Silius 16.21 *mansere gradu* (I owe the reference to F. H. Sandbach). A's *manu* would here mean *fortiter*, βιαίως (cf. Pl. *Most.* 479, Virg. *Aen.* 11.116, note on 354 above); the thought would thus resemble Virg. *Aen.* 2.431ff. *Iliaci cineres et flamma extrema meorum, | testor, in occasu uestro nec tela nec ullas | uitauisse uices Danaum et, si fata fuissent, | ut caderem meruisse manu*, and cf. also Sall. *Jug.* 39.1 *quod armatus dedecore potius quam manu salutem quaesiuerat*, 96.3, Silius 2.705 *saepe...optabit cecidisse manu*. While there is no reason for *manu* to have been altered to *gradu*, the reminiscence of the *Aeneid* passage might have prompted A, more prone to interpolation than E, to write *manu* for *gradu*. Furthermore, E's text contains by implication the idea which A's *manu* explicitly states, since *cadere qui meruit gradu* must mean 'who (by his bravery) earned the privilege of falling at his assigned place'.

516 uicta...tegit Aeschylus has this idea in equally pointed form (*Ag.* 451ff.) οἱ δ᾽ αὐτοῦ περὶ τεῖχος | θήκας Ἰλιάδος γᾶς | εὔμορφοι κατέχουσιν· ἐχ-|θρὰ δ᾽ ἔχοντας ἔκρυψεν.

517 nil nobile ausos The reference is to the many persons who have safely crossed the sea with no glorious end in view.

518 ignaua...fata Cf. Ovid, *Met.* 8.518f. *quod tamen ignauo cadat et sine sanguine leto | maeret*, *F.* 6.373 *ignaua...fata timentes*, Sen. *Suas.* 1.15.10f. (Albinovanus Pedo) *seque feris credunt per inertia fata marinis | iam non felici laniandos sorte relinqui*.

519 perdenda 'wasted, expended to no purpose'; the idea appealed to the author of *HO*, cf. 1172 *impendo, ei mihi, | in nulla uitam facta*, 1175f. *Herculis uestri placet | perire mortem* (on which see Housman, *CQ* xvii (1923)

163), 1205 *perdidi mortem*; note also Luc. 3.706f. *non perdere letum | maxima cura fuit*, Silius 4.605f. Seneca similarly couples *perdere* with *uirtutem* (*Med.* 972f.) and *scelus* (*Thy.* 1098, cf. Claud. *Ruf.* 1.244 *perdere nefas*).

quisquis es For the idea cf. Arist. *Frogs* 310 τίν' αἰτιάσομαι θεῶν μ' ἀπολλύναι; The indeterminate *quisquis* also appears in Hor. *C.* 2.1.25f. *Iuno et deorum quisquis amicior | Afris*, Virg. *Aen.* 4.576f. *sequimur te, sancte deorum, | quisquis es* (with Pease's note), Ovid, *Met.* 1.32 *quisquis fuit ille deorum*, 3.613, *Tr.* 3.11.56; see further Bömer on Ovid, *F.* 6.731, Appel 78f.

519f. nondum...satiate The expression is probably modelled on Hor. *C.* 1.2.37 *heu nimis longo satiate ludo* (and see Nisbet–Hubbard on *C.* 1.2.1 *satis* for the cultic background); see also Ovid, *F.* 5.575 *Mars, ades et satia scelerato sanguine ferrum*, Sen. *Med.* 668f., Petr. *Sat.* 123.119, Claud. *Ruf.* 2.204ff. (perhaps inspired by our passage).

521 serena *Numen serena* may be a bolder reminiscence of Virg. *Aen.* 1.255 *uultu quo caelum tempestatesque serenat* (*numen serena = numine placido nubila serena*, cf. Virg. *Aen.* 4.477 *spem fronte serenat*, see Pease *ad loc.*).

521f. cladibus...lacrimas Being in a state so wretched as to move even one's enemy to pity is a common idea, cf. Soph. *Ajax* 924f., *O.T.* 1295f., Enn. *Ann.* 171 V², Ter. *Hec.* 128f., Prop. 4.9.43f., Claud. *Bell. Gild.* 37f. (compare Shakespeare, *Richard II* v.ii.76 'and barbarism itself have pitied him'). For the Greeks pitied by Priam, see Pacuvius 391 R² *Priamus si adesset, commisceresceret* (quite probably from a storm-narrative), Virg. *Aen.* 11.259 *uel Priamo miseranda manus*, Ovid. *Met.* 14.474 *Graecia tum potuit Priamo quoque flenda uideri*.

523 placetque...genus Cf. Luc. 2.56ff. *uel, perdere nomen | si placet Hesperium, superi*, Claud. *Ruf.* 2.207ff.; in a storm-narrative cf. Ach. Tat. 3.5.4 εἰ δὲ ἡμᾶς ἀποκτεῖναι θέλεις, μὴ διαστήσῃς ἡμῶν τὴν τελευτήν.

524f. quid...perimus S. probably has in mind Ovid, *Tr.* 1.2.57f. *fingite me dignum tali nece, non ego solus | hic uehor: immeritos cur mea poena trahit?* (cf. *Her.* 14.63 *finge uiros meruisse mori: quid fecimus ipsae?*, *Met.* 2.290ff.).

sistite Bentley's *sistito* is unnecessary; *quisquis es...caelitum* is adequate preparation for a general appeal (for the shift from singular to plural cf. *Tro.* 1003ff. *et hic decet te sanguis: abreptam trahe. | maculate superos caede funesta deos, | maculate manes*). In addition, the tragedies contain no certain instance of an imperative in -*to* (cf. Zwierlein, *Philologus* cxiii (1969) 262f.).

526 uehit...uehit For the anadiplosis cf. *HF* 638 *differ amplexus parens, coniunxque differ*, Volkmann 471; for Greek tragic examples cf. J. Jackson, *Marginalia Scaenica* (1955) 198f. Here the device has a point only revealed by the punctuation of Gronovius.

527 occupat uocem I.e. the roar of the sea cuts off the men's appeal before it can reach the ears of the gods, cf. Hor. *Epist.* 1.6.32 *caue ne portus occupet alter*, ps.-Sen. *HO* 763 *luctum occupasti*; ad rem, Ovid, *Tr.* 1.2.15f.

528ff. It is remarkable that the transition from natural disaster to divine intervention is made with the brusque *ecce alia clades*. This difficulty does not arise in Quintus Smyrnaeus, who narrates the divine causation of the storm at great length (14.419–84) and who pauses again at the height of the tempest to stress its divine origin (14.505–15). It is possible that Seneca has abbreviated a source in which Athena (or the gods generally) plan to destroy the Greek fleet to avenge the blasphemy of Ajax Oileus (such a plan is clear in Euripides, *Tro.* 69f. and 75ff., and in Virgil, *Aen.* 1.39ff. *Pallasne exurere classem | Argiuum atque ipsos potuit summergere ponto, | unius ob noxam et furias Aiacis Oilei*). Other examples of vague or awkward writing point in the same direction. The words *solus inuictus malis | luctatur Aiax* (532f.) are puzzling in that they suggest that all the other Greeks had been destroyed; the words in Quintus Smyrnaeus which describe Ajax' struggles (14.548ff., cf. also 551f., 556f.) refer to a point in the narrative when Athena has splintered Ajax' ship (532ff.) and when Ajax' crew have been hurled into the water and drowned (539f.), a point at which Seneca's *solus inuictus malis | luctatur Aiax* would make perfect sense. In Seneca the anger of Jupiter is mentioned without being accounted for (*fulmine irati Iouis* 527); in Quintus Smyrnaeus Athena appeals to Zeus for assistance in punishing the Greeks and receives assurances of aid (14.424–48, also 507ff.). Similarly, the intervention of Neptune, abruptly introduced in Seneca (552ff.), is more clearly integrated into the narrative in Quintus Smyrnaeus (14.567f.; Poseidon is active in 14.507ff.).

528 ecce alia clades The transition-formula can be paralleled from Euripides, cf. *Phoen.* 1427 ἄκουε δή νυν καὶ τὰ πρὸς τούτοις κακά, although the immediate inspiration may be declamation-oratory, cf. Sen. *Contr.* 6 *exc.* 7 *audite rem nouam*, Juv. 12.24 *genus ecce aliud discriminis audi*, de Decker 104ff.; compare also Quintus Smyrnaeus 14.513ff. In the Petronian *Bellum Ciuile* (*Sat.* 119.13) the formula *ecce alia clades* is used with deliberate ineptitude.

528f. fulmine...armata Pallas The earliest certain use of this detail is in Eur. *Tro.* 75ff.; it is, however, possible that Athena cast the thunderbolt in Sophocles' *Teucer* (fr. 578 P, parodied in Arist. *Clouds* 583), and in Accius' *Clytemestra*, though the fragments give no definite indication, cf. 34f. R² *pectore incohatum fulmen flammam ostentabat Iouis* (text uncertain), perhaps also Cic. *Top.* 61 *at cum in Aiacis nauem 'crispisulcans igneum | fulmen' iniectum est, inflammatur nauis necessario* (= *inc. inc. fab.* 36 R²). Her role was presumably elaborated in the common source of Seneca and Quintus Smyrnaeus (cf. Hero, *Automatopoetica* 22.6, p. 264 Diels, ps.-Apollod. *Epit.* 6.6, Hyginus 116.2); traces of this account are perhaps also to be seen in Virg. *Aen.* 1.39ff.

529–31 The paradosis is *quidquid aut hasta minax | aut aegide aut furore Gorgoneo potest | aut igne patrio temptat*, which can only mean 'Pallas tries what she can do either threatening with her spear, or with the aegis or the Gorgon's madness, or with her father's fire.'

This can hardly be right. In this context the *fulmen* is not one of several weapons in Pallas' armoury; it is *the* weapon. The entire passage (528–52) is based on the fact that Athena uses the *fulmen* and no other weapons; this is confirmed by the fuller account of Quintus Smyrnaeus. Only the *fulmen* can produce storms (*caelo nouae | spirant procellae* 531f., and Quintus Smyrnaeus 14.530ff.), and Ajax' taunt *tene horream | aliena inerti tela mittentem manu* (550f.) loses its force if Athena has been using her own weapons.

The emendation involving the slightest change is Castiglioni's *nunc* for *aut* in 531 (the corruption is easily imaginable given the thrice repeated *aut* of the preceding lines). This gives an intelligible sense, but it makes Athena's use of the *fulmen* a mere whim; it is also untrue that Athena could raise storms or blast ships with her normal weapons. If *nunc* is adopted, it demands further change, e.g. *uincit* for *temptat*, to make the point that Pallas, when armed with her father's thunderbolt, surpasses her own formidable capabilities. It might be objected that the alterations required are not easily accounted for.

A different approach (perhaps foreshadowed by MN's *haut hasta*) was suggested by M. Müller: *quidquid haut hasta minax, | haut aegide, haut furore Gorgoneo potest, | en igne patrio temptat*. This, too, produces sense (though *quidquid* is somewhat inappropriate), but it is awkward to have this stated at Athena's first appearance, without the slightest hint that other arms have been tried and found wanting. No support is forthcoming from Quintus Smyrnaeus, whose closest approach to these lines is in a description of Pallas arming, where the aegis is named along with the thunderbolt (14.449ff.; the aegis plays no further part in the story). It may be significant, though, that Servius (on *Aen.* 1.42) records it as a common opinion (*multi dicunt*) that Athena used the *fulmen* against Ajax because other weapons were inadequate. The weak point in Müller's proposal is *en* in 531, a clear example of a meaningless filler; Castiglioni's *nunc* is at least somewhat better, though not compelling; *hoc* might be suggested. Müller's is the best solution so far advanced, but it is unlikely that the text of these lines can be restored with complete confidence.

530 aegide et furore The MSS have *aut*, but it seems unlikely that S. would have juxtaposed the aegis and the Gorgon as distinct weapons; Hor. *C.* 1.15.11f. *iam galeam Pallas et aegida | currusque et rabiem parat* does not present comparable difficulty.

536 certum distinguishes Athena's second, more successful, shot from her first. The aim of the gods is conventionally accurate, cf. Hor. *C.* 1.12.23f. (with Nisbet–Hubbard's note); the topic is often applied to Amor, cf. Prop. 2.34.60, Ovid, *Met.* 1.519f. (Phoebus of Amor) *certa quidem nostra est, nostra tamen una sagitta | certior*, Sen. *Pha.* 193, 278.

537–8 transit…tulit The transmitted text of these words involves several difficulties. It is hard to accept that Ajax, having been transfixed by a lightning-bolt, is merely *ambustus* in the following line; it is also unsatisfactory to have *ratis partem* and *partem Aiacis* placed on the same level, as though all 'parts' of Ajax were equally dispensable. Note also that the more circumstantial account of Quintus Smyrnaeus describes Athena's thunderbolt smashing Ajax' ship and hurling its occupants into the water (14.532ff., compare *Od.* 12.415ff.); while Hero of Alexandria and Hyginus do say that Ajax himself was struck by Athena's thunderbolt, their testimony on this point does not carry great weight (Hero for technical reasons may have simplified the events narrated in his source; Hyginus is highly compressed). Seneca's words can be made to conform both to the requirements of sense and to the tradition as preserved in Quintus Smyrnaeus by a simple alteration:

transit Aiacis ratem

ratisque partem secum et Aiacem tulit.

This proposal receives additional support from other accounts of Ajax' death, cf. Hor. *Epod.* 10.13f. *cum Pallas usto uertit iram ab Ilio | in impiam Aiacis ratem*, Virg. *Aen.* 1.43 *disiecitque rates.* Seneca may have been thinking of the fate of Ovid's Phaethon (*Met.* 2.311ff.): [Iuppiter] *intonat et dextra libratum fulmen ab aure | misit in aurigam pariterque animaque rotisque | expulit.*

539 ardua ut cautes The comparison is found in Homer (*Il.* 15.618ff.) and tragedy (Soph. *O.C.* 1240f., Eur. *Med.* 28, *Andr.* 537f.), and often in later literature, cf. Apoll. Rhod. 3.1294f., Virg. *Aen.* 10.693ff., Hor. *C.* 3.7.21, Tib. 2.4.9f., Ovid, *R.A.* 691ff., *Met.* 9.39ff., 11.330, Sen. *Pha.* 580ff., Stat. *Th.* 9.90ff. The present passage owes most to Virg. *Aen.* 7.586 *ille uelut pelagi rupes immota resistit*, 6.471 *quam si dura silex aut stet Marpesia cautes.*

540ff. The details of these lines correspond in general to those in Quintus Smyrnaeus 14.548ff. Αἴας δ᾽ ἄλλοτε μὲν περινήχετο δούρατι νηός, | ἄλλοτε δ᾽ αὖ χείρεσσι διήνυεν ἁλμυρὰ βένθη, | ἀκαμάτῳ Τιτῆνι βίην ὑπέροπλον ἐοικώς. | σχίζετο δ᾽ ἁλμυρὸν οἶδμα περὶ κρατερῇσι χέρεσσιν | ἀνδρὸς ὑπερθύμοιο (grasping the wreckage derives ultimately from *Od.* 14.310f.). Seneca, however, is more successful in lending the scene a preternatural intensity, primarily by adding that the wreckage is in flames (the synecdoche in *nauem manu | complexus* is also suggestive). Compare Philostratus, *Imag.* 2.13 κεχώρηκε τοῖς κύμασι, τῶν μὲν διεκπαίων, τῶν δὲ ἐπισπώμενος, τὰ δὲ ὑπαντλῶν τῷ στέρνῳ, and for Ajax in flames cf. Val. Fl. 1.373 *nato stridente per undas*, Silius 14.480 *ardentibus ulnis.*

542 ignes The MSS have *in se*, which is intolerably weak after *complexus*: 'nihil est nauem, quam iam complexus erat, in se trahere' (Madvig, *Aduersaria Critica* 11.125). Madvig's *ignes* convincingly removes the defect and provides a basis for the following words, *caeco mari | collucet Aiax* (cf. also Zwierlein, *Gnomon* xli (1969) 768).

544 occupata rupe Seneca is as vague as Virgil (*Aen.* 1.45 *scopulo acuto*), Ovid (*Ibis* 337 *aliquis scopulus*), and ps.-Apollodorus (*Epit.* 6.6 πέτρα τις), but Homer (*Od.* 4.500, followed by Philostr. *Imag.* 2.13.1 and Quintus Smyrnaeus 14.569f.) names the place of Ajax' death as the Gyrae. Most ancient sources locate the Gyrae near Myconos (cf. schol. *ad Od.* 1.218, 4.500, Hesychius s.u. Γυραί, Eustathius 1507.7), but Euripides (*Tro.* 84ff.) places them off the coast of Euboea (and note Ovid, *Ibis* 338). F. H. Sandbach (*C.R.* xxxvi (1942) 63ff.) persuasively identifies the ἄκρα Γυρέων of Archilochus 56 D (and possibly the Gyrae of the *Odyssey*) with Tenos.

furibundum intonat Homer gave Ajax one boast, reported in *oratio obliqua* (*Od.* 4.504 φῆ ῥ' ἀέκητι θεῶν φυγέειν μέγα λαῖτμα θαλάσσης), and this is paraphrased in ps.-Apoll. *Epit.* 6.6 and slightly elaborated (still in *oratio obliqua*) in Quintus Smyrnaeus 14.565ff. Other writers allude generally to his boastfulness, Lyc. *Alex.* 395, Philostr. *Imag.* 2.13, Virg. *Aen.* 1.41 *furias*. Sophocles in *Aias Lokros* and Callimachus in the *Aetia* (fr. 35 Pfeiffer) may have given Ajax extended speeches, but we are ignorant of their contents.

545ff. The opening line of Ajax' speech (for *intonat* must introduce Ajax' own words) has been corrupted: E gives a line lacking a syllable, while A (and Σ) read *nunc se*, requiring *superasse* to be governed by *intonat*. The neatest remedy so far offered is Richter's *cuncta*, which, though it adopts A's syntax, has at least palaeographical plausibility. The conjunction *pelagus atque ignes* might be a reference to the traditional opposition of these elements, similar to that in Ovid, *Ibis* 340f. *utque ferox periit et fulmine et aequore raptor,* | *sic te mersuras adiuuet ignis aquas* (for the cooperation of fire and water as an ἀδύνατον, cf. Aesch. *Ag.* 650 with Headlam's note, *inc. inc. fr.* 155 R², Otto, *Sprichwörter* 30, la Penna on Ovid, *Ibis* 341, Sen. *Pha.* 568, *Thy.* 480).

The following line poses even graver problems. While *pelagus atque ignes* may have some point, what is one to make of its inane repetition in the shapeless catalogue *caelum Palladem fulmen mare?* It is also suspicious that Athena, the target of the entire speech from 547 onwards, should here be so casually grouped with dangers already overcome. Finally, there is the accusative *Palladem*, guaranteed by metre. The correct form is, of course, *Pallada*, and this is the only form I have found elsewhere in Latin poetry before the end of the first century A.D. (thirteen times in Ovid, six times in Statius, also Prop. 4.9.57, Mart. 9.3.10; other poets do not use the word in the accusative).

Suspicion may justly be attached to both 545 and 546; without them the speech begins on a more appropriately defiant note with *non me fugauit bellici terror dei* (547). As for the corruption in the earlier line, it is no guarantee of authenticity. I have printed the interpolator's handiwork as it appears in A (*nunc se*), since it seems possible that the lines were intended to be in *oratio obliqua*; E's defective *nunc* would then be best taken as a mechanical corruption (perhaps under the influence of the foregoing *superasse*).

Line 548 was deleted by Leo (cf. *Obs.* 200), whose arguments were restated and elaborated by Zwierlein (*Rezitationsdramen* 184ff.). The most obvious basis for suspicion is the double appearance of Hector, with Mars in 548 and (by implication) as one of the *istos* in 550. The syntax of the line (*et...et*) also disrupts the parallel structure *non me...nec me* in 547 and 549. These objections, however, might be met if 548 were taken as a parenthesis, allowing both thought and syntactical structure to run from 547 to 549.

Two problems remain. First, the god who assisted Hector in his assault on the Greek ships is variously identified as Apollo and Zeus (*Il.* 15.254ff., 594ff.; when describing the struggle of Ajax and Hector, Homer says only ἐπεί ῥ' ἐπέλασσέ γε δαίμων, 418). Second, the line attributes to Ajax Oileus an exploit of his greater namesake. Indeed, whether genuine or spurious, the line clearly recalls Ovid's words on the greater Ajax in *Met.* 13.384f. *Hectora qui solus, qui ferrum ignesque Iouemque | sustinuit totiens, unam non sustinet iram.* Such a confusion is visible in Philostratus (*Imag.* 2.13.2 ὁ αὐχήν τε ἀνέστηκεν οἷος ἐπὶ Ἕκτορα καὶ Τρῶας), but the form it assumes in our passage is far grosser. Del Rio called the line 'mera iactatio et apta furenti', but it is a misconception of modern criticism that ancient poets depicted madness by writing nonsense.

A positive argument for deletion may be offered. With 548 removed, Ajax' boasts mean only that he survived the expedition to Troy and did not fall victim either to the fear of battle or the plague sent by Apollo. A precise parallel is provided by Ovid, *Ars* 1.333, of Agamemnon: *qui Martem terra, Neptunum effugit in undis.* It is a stroke of wit worthy of Seneca that, on this basis, the lesser Ajax should speak as if he had encountered Mars and Apollo in person and could thus scorn the threats of Pallas. (One might compare the claim of Ulysses in Ovid, *Met.* 13.171ff. that the merit of Achilles' deeds rightfully belongs to him, since he brought Achilles from Scyros to Troy.)

549 gradu 'from my position' (see on 515 above), cf. Livy 7.8.3 *primum gradu mouerunt hostem, deinde pepulerunt*, *Bell. Alex.* 76.2, Sen. *Const.* 16.2 [*gladiator*] *premit uulnus et stat in gradu*; for the thought cf. Pl. *Amph.* 238ff.

551 aliena...tela Similarly used in taunts in Ovid, *Met.* 9.75f. *quid fore te credas falsum qui uersus in anguem | arma aliena moues...?*, Sen. *HF* 329f. *uenit | aliena dextra sceptra concutiens Lycus*, Claud. *Rapt.* 2.220; without a mocking tone, cf. Stat. *Th.* 5.396f., Claud. *Ruf.* 1.9f.

mittentem manu E has repeated *pepulerunt gradu* from two lines above, while A's *mitti dextera* does not construe given the correct *tene* in the previous line (A has *tandem*). All editors have accepted Lipsius' easy correction of A to *mittis dextera*, but Heinsius' *mittentem manu*, though farther from the A reading, is rhetorically superior (so also Bentley). It is possible that E here reproduces an archetypal corruption which A has attempted to repair by interpolation; if so, A's reading need not govern the editor's choice. With Heinsius' text the contemptuous *tene horream* is linked to its explanation in the following line; as punctuated by other editors *tene horream* stands as a less pointed independent question.

552 'quid si ipse mittat?' The phrase is complete as printed; for *ipse* alone of Jupiter cf. Ovid, *Met.* 2.390; of the *princeps* etc., see Ovid, *F.* 4.952, *Met.* 15.851, *T.L.L.* vII².343.25ff.; in the language of slaves *ipse* is 'the master', cf. *T.L.L.* vII².344.14ff. For *quid si mittat? = immo mittat*, cf. Virg. *Ecl.* 5.9 *quid si idem certet Phoebum superare canendo?* (with Heyne's note).

plura cum auderet For the interrupted speech cf. Ovid, *F.* 4.385 *plura locuturi subito seducimur imbre*, *Met.* 1.525 *plura locuturum* [*sc. Apollinem*] *timido Peneia cursu | fugit.*

553f. pater | Neptunus For the phrase cf. Lucilius 19ff. Marx, Sen. *Oed.* 266, *inc. poet.* p. 177 Morel; on *pater* with gods other than Jupiter see Servius on Virg. *G.* 2.4, Wissowa, *Religion und Kultus* 26f., Carter, *Epitheta deorum* 65f.

554 imis...caput Probably inspired by Virg. *Aen.* 1.127 [*Neptunus*] *summa prospiciens placidum caput extulit undis*; the ablative of separation with *exero*, however, seems to be Ovidian, cf. *F.* 1.458 [*delphin*] *patriis exerit ora uadis*, *Met.* 2.271 *Neptunus aquis cum toruo bracchia uultu | exerere ausus erat*, Sen. *HF* 594, *Oed.* 532, *T.L.L.* v².1855.16ff.

555 montem A distinction between *montem* here and *rupem* in 553 is not clearly drawn; in Quintus Smyrnaeus, Poseidon not only shatters the Gyrae, but hurls part of the headlands on to Ajax (14.580f.).

556 terra...igne...pelago Cf. *Med.* 661 *fulmine et ponto moriens Oileus* (perhaps based on Ovid, *Ibis* 341 *utque ferox periit et fulmine et aequore raptor*); cf. also Quintus Smyrnaeus 14.588f. ἀμφὶ δέ μιν θανάτοιο μέλας ἐκίχησατ' Ὄλεθρος, | γαίη ὁμῶς δμηθέντα καὶ ἀτρυγέτῳ ἐνὶ πόντῳ.

558ff. est... The ecphrasis on Caphereus stands in the same relationship to the following shipwreck as Homer's description of Gortyne (*Od.* 3.293ff.). On the other hand, the storm in *Aeneid* i is immediately followed by an ecphrasis (159ff. *est in secessu longo locus*, eqs.). A similar promontory plays a part in a fragment of Pacuvius (94ff. R²) *Idae promunturium quoius lingua in altum proicit | ...incipio saxum temptans scandere | uorticem in summum inde in omnes partes prospectum aucupo.*

Seneca's lines use the conventional postposition of the proper name, for which cf. Menander, *Aspis* 23f. ποταμός τις ἐστὶ τῆς Λυκίας καλούμενος | Ξάνθος, Virg. *Aen.* 7.563ff. *est locus Italiae...Amsancti ualles.* The topic is introduced in the regular way, with *est* followed by *ubi* (559); a new beginning, however, is made with *arx imminet* (562), and this is in turn resumed after an interval by *hanc arcem occupat* (567). For details of the commonplace see Zwierlein, *Rezitationsdramen* 116ff., G. Williams, *Tradition and originality* 640f., 651ff. Seneca's *ecphraseis* are at times elaborated beyond the requirements of the narrative, to lengths for which Greek tragedy offers no parallel (ten lines here, eighteen in *Oed.* 530ff.; in Greek it is rare to find ἐστί and its responding word separated by more than five lines, cf. Eur. *El.* 1258–64).

558 humilis = *non profunda*, cf. Virg. *Aen.* 7.157 *humili fossa*, Tac. *Hist.* 1.61, Pliny, *Epist.* 8.20.5.

560 fallax Caphereus The fame of Caphereus as a devourer of ships (whence its modern Greek name, Xylophagos) is mentioned in a fragment of Philodemus (*Rhet.* p. 260 Sudhaus); see also *A.P.* 9.289.1 (Bassus) οὐλόμεναι νήεσσι Καφηρίδες, Pac. 136 R², *ultor Caphereus* in Virg. *Aen.* 11.260, *Culex* 354f., Dio, *Or.* 7.32.

561 alterna uice For the phrase cf. Enn. *sc.* 110 R² (= 123 J); the plural is more common, cf. *HF* 377f. *uicibus alternis fugax* | *Euripus, Pha.* 1028 *spumat uomitque uicibus alternis aquas*, Luc. 1.409f., Manilius 1.258f.

562ff. quae spectat, eqs. The hyperbolic description of the view from Caphereus resembles what is said in jest (or tragic parody?) in Arist. *Knights* 173f. ἔτι νῦν τὸν ὀφθαλμὸν παράβαλλ᾽ εἰς Καρίαν | τὸν δεξιόν, τὸν δ᾽ ἕτερον εἰς Καρχηδόνα. Similar exaggeration is used to describe the range of a sound in Luc. 7.477ff., Claud. *Ruf.* 2.131ff., *Eutr.* 2.160ff.

563 utrimque geminum Strictly interpreted this would mean that Caphereus looks out on two seas on each side, a statement with some basis in fact (the northern and southern halves of the Aegean in one direction, the Ionian and Cretan seas in the other); it also seems possible, though, that *utrimque* is used simply to reiterate *geminum*, and that the reference is to the Thracian and Myrtoan seas only (cf. *HO* 776f. *Phrixeum mare* | *scindit Caphereus*).

The phrase *quae spectat mare* | *utrimque geminum* recalls one of the conventional poetic descriptions of the Isthmus of Corinth (cf., e.g., Eur. *Tro.* 1097, *Med.* 35f., Hor. *C.* 1.7.2, Ovid, *Her.* 12.104, Luc. 2.399ff., *Anth. Lat.* 440.5 Riese, Val. Fl. 5.442, Stat. *Th.* 1.120, 7.106f., Claud. *Ruf.* 2.190, *Eutr.* 1.90f.); Ovid applied this language to Troezen (*Her.* 4.105f.) and to the Propontis (*Tr.* 1.10.32); Seneca extends it further, to Thebes (*Oed.* 266f.) and to Argos (*HF* 1164f., *Thy.* 181).

Pelopis...tui The sudden intrusion of the dramatic circumstances has a jarring effect; this and *nos* in 557 are the only personal touches in the entire narrative.

564f. Isthmon...uetat Perhaps based on Ovid, *F*. 6.495f. *est spatio contracta breui, freta bina repellit,* | *unaque pulsatur terra duabus aquis*; for the idea cf. also Prop. 3.21.22 *Isthmos qua terris arcet utrumque mare*, Sen. *Pho*. 374f., *Thy*. 113, Luc. 1.101.

566 scelere Lemnon nobilem The women of Lemnos slighted Aphrodite and were punished by a noisome smell; their husbands turned to Thracian slave-girls, for which they were murdered by the wives (cf. ps.-Apollod. *Bibl*. 3.6, Hyg. *Fab*. 15). Seneca may have called attention to Lemnos and its history for the sake of a veiled reference to Agamemnon's death.

nobilem 'notorious', cf. Sen. *Pha*. 1023 *scelere petrae nobiles Scironides*; for this sense see also Pl. *Rud*. 619 *qui se scelere fieri nolunt nobiles, Pseud*. 1112, Ter. *H.T*. 227, Cic. *Verr*. 2.82 *accipite nunc aliud eius facinus nobile*, Ovid, *Am*. 2.18.37 *nobile crimen*, Petr. *Sat*. 119.30.

hinc et Chalcida The MSS unanimously read *Calchedona*, but A has *hinc* and E *et* as the preceding word. The arrangement of the passage as a whole shows that *hinc* at least is required: Seneca first describes the view to the south-west, taking in Argos and the Isthmus; then turns to the north-east and names Lemnos; *-que* in 567 shows that the place named at the end of 566 lies in the same direction as Aulis. Therefore a change of direction is needed between Lemnos and the final pair. The same process of reasoning shows that the transmitted *Calchedona* is impossible; it is as well absurdly and pointlessly hyperbolic. The neatest and most satisfying emendation is *hinc et Chalcida*, which is geographically apt; cf. Aesch. *Ag*. 190f. Χαλκίδος πέραν ἔχων παλιρρό|χθοις ἐν Αὐλίδος τόποις. The corruption postulated is of two stages, but not implausible: once *Chalcida* had been replaced by *Calchedona* (perhaps by *interpolatio Christiana*, as Καρχηδόνα has been corrupted to Χαλκηδόνα in Arist. *Eq*. 1304), E and A independently adjusted the text to restore metre. Gronovius' *Anthedona* also deserves mention. It lies in the proper direction from Caphereus, and has a respectable place in Latin poetry as the birthplace of Glaucus (cf. Ovid, *Met*. 7.232, Stat. *Th*. 7.335, *S*. 3.2.28; also *Anthedonius*, Stat. *Th*. 9.291, 327, Aus. *Mos*. 276). It does not, however, account as well for the transmitted text as does *hinc et Chalcida*.

567 Aulida Bentley's *Aulin* would eliminate a rough-sounding elision and avoid homoeoteleuton with *Chalcida*, but the case is not strong enough to justify emendation.

hanc arcem occupat Seneca's wording may be influenced by Ovid, *Met*. 4.525ff. *imminet aequoribus scopulus...occupat hunc – uires insania fecerat – Ino*.

569 efferens A *uox propria* for the hoisting of signals, cf. Livy 10.19.13, 24.46.7, Virg. *Aen*. 2.256f. *flammas cum regia puppis* | *extulerat*.

570 perfida...face A recurring motif in Greek epigrammatic references to Nauplius, cf. *A.P.* 9.429.3f. (Crinagoras) ὁ ψεύστης δ' ὑπὸ νύκτα Καφηρείης ἀπὸ πέτρης | πυρσός, 289.3f. (Bassus) πυρσὸς ὅτε ψεύστας χθονίης δνοφερώτερα νυκτὸς | ἦψε σέλα; cf. Val. Fl. 1.370ff. A different *color* is used in Prop. 4.1.115 *Nauplius ultores sub noctem porrigit ignes*.

571ff. No other surviving author describes the damage done to the Greek ships by Nauplius in such detail: general statements are found in Eur. *Hel.* 1122ff., Pacuvius 136 R², Accius 33 R², Quintus Smyrnaeus 14.624ff. Lost tragedies of Sophocles and Euripides might have contained fuller accounts. It is conceivable that in these lines Seneca is elaborating Virg. *Aen.* 1.108ff. *tris Notus abreptas in saxa latentia torquet,* | ...*tris Eurus ab alto* | *in breuia et syrtis urget, miserabile uisu,* | *inliditque uadis atque aggere cingit harenae.*

572f. has...sedet There may be an echo of these lines in Lucan 9.335ff. *has uada destituunt, atque interrupta profundo* | *terra ferit puppes, dubioque obnoxia fato* | *pars sedet una ratis, pars altera pendet in undis.*

uehitur 'is carried off'; this violent sense of *ueho* may be seen in Ovid's flood (*Met.* 1.304f. *fuluos uehit unda leones,* | *unda uehit tigres*) and in the Virgilian formula *per aequora uectus* (*Aen.* 1.524, 6.356, 692, 7.228, *G.* 1.206).

574 retro spatia relegentem 'traversing the same ground in the opposite direction'. The scene described here is of a ship which has run on to rocks attempting to steer backwards into open water and being rammed by another ship. For *relegere* cf. Hor. *C.* 1.34.5ff. *nunc retrorsum* | *uela dare atque iterare cursus* | *cogar relectos* (Heinsius: *relicto* MSS) and Bentley's note, Virg. *Aen.* 3.690f. *relegens errata retrorsus* | *litora.*

575 fracta frangit Compare Virg. *Aen.* 2.160 *tu modo promissis maneas seruataque serues,* | *Troia, fidem* (imitated by Sil. 14.172 [*nos*] *seruas nondum seruatus ab hoste*), 7.295 *num incensa cremauit* | *Troia uiros*; the closest parallels come from the declaimers, cf. Sen. *Contr.* 9.6.18 *inuenit quomodo damnata accusaret, moriens occideret, torta torqueret* (and cf. J. Morawski, *Ouidiana* (Warsaw, 1903) 313f.).

timent terram rates Seneca claims in *Epist.* 53.2 to have heard this piece of wisdom from a ship-captain: *coepi gubernatorem rogare ut me in aliquo litore exponeret: aiebat ille aspera esse et importuosa nec quicquam se aeque in tempestate timere quam terram*; cf. also Petr. *Sat.* 123.218f. *huic fuga per terras,* | *illi magis unda probatur* | *et patria pontus iam tutior.*

576 et maria malunt E's *malunt* is clearly the right verb, while A's *uoluntque maria* might appear to have a superior word-order. The *recentiores* combined both traditions to produce *maluntque maria*, which is attractive but which has no serious claims to be true.

cecidit in lucem furor The storm in Aeschylus also ends at daybreak (*Ag.* 658); cf. also Apoll. Rhod. 2.1120f., Virg. *Aen.* 1.143, Sen. *Tro.* 197

(on which see Zwierlein, *Philologus* cxiii (1969) 256f.), Shakespeare, *Comedy of Errors* i.i.88ff.

in lucem 'toward dawn', cf. Virg. *G.* 4.190 *siletur | in noctem, Aen.* 7.8 *aspirant aurae in noctem,* Manil. 2.509 [*Capricornus*] *in Augusti cum fulserit ortum,* Cels. 7.27.1, Val. Fl. 2.59; *T.L.L.* vii¹.753.70ff.

577 postquam litatum est Ilio 'after atonement has been made to Troy', i.e. the Greeks are sacrificed (by the gods, presumably, though this is not stated) to appease the offended *manes* of the Trojan dead. Virgil so described the sacrifice of Iphigenia (*Aen.* 2.118f. *sanguine quaerendi reditus animaque litandum | Argolica*), and Roman history offered examples of human victims used for this purpose, e.g. Marius Gratidianus killed at the tomb of Q. Catulus (cf. Sall. *Hist.* 1.44, 1.55.14, Sen. *Ira* 3.18.2, Val. Max. 9.2.1, Lucan 2.173ff. with scholia), cf. T. E. V. Pearce, *CQ* n.s. xx (1970) 310f., 321. On *litatio* see Forbiger on Virg. *Aen.* 4.50; *litatum est* occurs in Livy 8.9.1, 9.14.4, Curt. 7.7.29, Pliny, *N.H.* 10.75 (with *ei deo*). *Ilio* is a certain correction of E's unmetrical *illo*; parallels between Greece and Troy are an important thematic element in the play (see above pp. 4f.), as also in Aeschylus, cf. H. Lloyd-Jones, *CQ* n.s. xi (1961) 187ff.

578 et...dies A successful ending which produces an effect of finality.
Senecan messenger-speeches often end abruptly at a point of tension and excitement, without the moralising summaries of Greek messengers (but note the exceptions *Pha.* 1110ff., *Thy.* 782ff.; 906ff. below).

579 utrumne...uirum 'Should I grieve or rejoice that my husband has returned?' There is a sense in which Clytemestra may ask this question with propriety, and this is expounded in the following lines; but a less innocent meaning is surely intended as well (Streubel 103ff.). It is not likely that Clytemestra's dilemma is really felt, as is that of Sophocles' Clytaemestra in *El.* 766f. ὦ Ζεῦ, τί ταῦτα, πότερον εὐτυχῆ λέγω, | ἢ δεινὰ μέν, κέρδη δέ; or of Ovid's Scylla in the closely parallel passage *Met.* 8.44f. *laeter...doleamne geri lacrimabile bellum | in dubio est.*

utrumne doleam laeter an The word-order is remarkable, and the closest parallel I know is Mart. 12.65.4 *utrumne Cosmi Nicerotis an librum* [*sc. dem?*], which is not as bold. S. might have been influenced by Ovid's juxtaposition of the contrasting verbs in *Met.* 8.44 '*laeter*' *ait* '*doleamne*'. The construction *utrum(ne)...an* is rare in high poetry after Catullus, except for Seneca and Martial (nine times in each), cf. Axelson, *Unpoetische Wörter* 90f.

580 at A's *at* was preferred to E's *et* by Σ, probably rightly; *at* is supported by the Ovidian parallel, *Met.* 8.45f. *doleo, quod Minos hostis amanti est, | sed nisi bella forent, numquam mihi cognitus esset.*

582 altisona An Ennian translation of ὑψηχής, cf. *Ann.* 575 V², *sc.*

82 R² (= 88 J); it is applied to Jupiter himself by Cicero (*Diu.* 1.106) and Seneca (*Pha.* 1134, cf. *HO* 530).

quatiens Jupiter can shake the heavens with his thunderbolt (cf. Ter. *Eun.* 590 *qui templa caeli summa sonitu concutit* (citation or parody of Ennius?), Lucr. 6.387f., Sen. *Pha.* 155; of the earth in *Octauia* 229) or his car (cf. Hor. *C.* 1.12.58 *tu graui curru quaties Olympum*), but here *quatiens* may denote a more general control; compare *Laus Pis.* 231 *ingenti qui nomine pulsat Olympum.*

583ff. The sacrificial details recall the second choral ode, in particular 311f., 358f., and 364ff. In spite of the recurrent imagery of sacrifice, it may be over-subtle to see an allusion to Agamemnon's death in these lines; the ordering of sacrifice is a variation on a common Senecan exit-formula (cf. *HF* 514f., *Thy.* 545). It is generally (and reasonably) believed that Clytemestra leaves the stage after 588, cf. Seidensticker 120 n.120.

585 niuea...cadat Cf. Virg. *Aen.* 1.334 *multa tibi ante aras nostra cadet hostia dextra,* Ovid, *Her.* 1.25 *Argolici rediere duces, altaria fumant* (cf. Silius 12.332f.).

586ff. The close connection between a secondary chorus and a single character is an aspect of Euripidean technique, which may be observed in *Alexander* (schol. Eur. *Hipp.* 58), *Antiopa* (schol. *Hipp.* 58 and Pacuvius 18f. R²), *Bacchae* (1165ff.), *Hippolytus* (58ff.) and *Phaethon* (fr. 781.4f. N² = 227ff. Diggle). Also Euripidean is the limitation of the secondary chorus' activity to a single stasimon and the following episode; what is unusual is that S. allows the Trojan chorus to be ignored and forgotten after 781 while keeping Cassandra in or near the centre of attention until the end of the play.

The terms in which Cassandra is presented, e.g. *celso gradu* (see on 716 below), *effrena*, and *entheas laurus quatit,* all suggest an ecstatic state far removed from the calm self-possession of Cassandra's opening lines (659ff.); contrast the use of similar language of Cassandra at her first entrance in Eur. *Tro.* 173ff., and the comparison of Seneca's Medea to a *maenas* (*Med.* 382ff.). The possibility of influence from a lost play should perhaps be considered (Pacuvius 309ff. R², from *Periboea,* may announce a secondary chorus of maenads, though this is not certain, cf. Leo, *Kleine Schriften* 1.207).

CHORUS III (589–658)

This is the most consistently personal of the odes, and also the ode most closely related to the dramatic context.[1] The bitter recollection of Trojan

---

[1] Note that the entrance of the chorus is announced (586ff.) and that Cassandra reacts to the ode's final lines in 659ff. Both phenomena are exceptional in Seneca: for announcement of a choral entry cf. *HF* 827ff. (the subject of a choral song is announced in *Oed.* 401f., cf. *HO* 581f.); for reaction to an ode cf. *Med.* 116.

folly and defeat finds parallels in Euripides,[1] but there is no extant Greek analogy for such a lament being sung by a subsidiary chorus.[2] The first ode of *Hercules Oetaeus* is obviously inspired by this song: the resemblances include the basic situation (a secondary chorus of captives accompanying a princess) and close verbal parallels.[3]

589 dulce malum The oxymoron is not purely ornamental: love of life is a comforting vice, and it is more pleasant to prolong life than to prepare for death. The paradox is otherwise familiar from erotic contexts, cf. Ovid, *Am.* 2.9.26, *R.A.* 138, Sen. *Pha.* 134, Apul. *Met.* 4.31 (*dulcia uulnera*); Menander, *Sent.* 159 Jaekel γάμος γὰρ ἀνθρώποισιν εὐκταῖον κακόν, 877 (old age).

mortalibus additum *Additum* suggests that *amor uitae* is inextricably linked to man's existence, cf. Pacuvius 269 R² *fletus muliebri ingenio additus est* and Virg. *Aen.* 6.90 *nec Teucris addita Iuno | usquam aberit*, which ancient commentators gloss correctly *infesta et ueluti affixa* (Macrob. *Sat.* 6.4.2) and for which they refer to Lucilius 469 Marx *si mihi non siet praetor additus atque agitet me* and Plaut. *Aul.* 555 *Argus...quem Ioni Iuno custodem addidit* (cf. also *Miles* 146, Hor. *C.* 3.4.77 *custos additus* of the bird which torments Tityus). The close parallel in Stat. *Th.* 2.320ff. *dolor iraque demens | et, qua non grauior mortalibus addita curis, | spes* may have been influenced by the present passage.

590 uitae...amor The urge to cling to even the shortest span of life is often noted in Greek tragedy; the best parallel is Eur. fr. 816.6ff. N² (*Phoenix*): ὦ φιλόζωοι βροτοί, | οἳ τὴν ἐπιστείχουσαν ἡμέραν ἰδεῖν | ποθεῖτ' ἔχοντες μυρίων ἄχθος κακῶν· | οὕτως ἔρως βροτοῖσιν ἔγκειται βίου, eqs. (and cf. also, e.g., Soph. *Ant.* 220, fr. 67 Pearson, Eur. *Alc.* 671, 692f., *Hipp.* 193ff., *Or.* 1509). Seneca himself writes movingly of the *Lebenslust* of the old in *B.V.* 11.1f.

dirus Used of an emotion the strength of which is incomprehensible and thus frightening to the beholder; so of various forms of desire, e.g. *regnandi cupido* (Virg. *G.* 1.37), *lucis cupido* (Virg. *Aen.* 6.721), *cibi cupido* (Manilius 4.539), *flendi cupido* (Sen. *Thy.* 953), *amor ferri* (Luc. 1.355), and of *lubido* Lucr. 4.1046, *uoluptas* Luc. 4.705, *spes* Sen. *Pha.* 131.

590ff. Early Greek literature regarded suicide as a legitimate way of cutting short intolerable grief or disgrace, cf. *Il.* 18.88ff., *Od.* 10.49ff.,

---

[1] Compare in particular *Hec.* 905ff., *Tro.* 511ff.

[2] The choruses of Euripides' *I.T.* and *Helen* consist of captive women, and the former group is given a set-piece lament (*I.T.* 1089ff., cf. also 447ff.). Captives are silent personages in Soph. *Trach.* 241ff. and 298ff.; cf. Men. *Aspis* 36ff.

[3] Compare, for example, *Ag.* 610 *par ille regi, par superis erit* and *HO* 104 *par ille est superis*; *Ag.* 621 *o quam miserum est nescire mori* and *HO* 111 *numquam ille est miser cui facile est mori.*

Theog. 175f. (cf. Plut. *Stoic. Rep.* 1930F); several tragic heroes choose death over a dishonoured life, cf. Aesch. fr. 177 N² (Ajax in Ὅπλων Κρίσις), Soph. *Phil.* 1348f.). To the Cynics, freely chosen suicide was a commendable alternative to painful existence, and Zeno may have adapted their attitude for Stoic purposes by qualifying ἐξαγωγή (Antisthenes *apud* Athen. 157B) with εὔλογος (D.L. 7.130).

To Stoics suicide could be a καθῆκον, cf. Chrysippus *apud* Plut. *Stoic. Rep.* 1042D, Sen. *Epist.* 70.3 *portus est aliquando petendus, numquam recusandus*; it was not, however, justifiable if done without just cause or in a pusillanimous spirit (cf. Cic. *Tusc.* 1.74, Plut. *Cleom.* 31). A recurring idea is the comforting accessibility of suicide, cf. Cic. *Tusc.* 1.118 *portum potius paratum nobis et perfugium putemus*, 2.66, Sen. *Epist.* 70.15 *placet? uiue. non placet? licet eo reuerti unde uenisti*, cf. Plut. *Aem. Paull.* 26.4ff., 34.2.

On ancient views of suicide see in general R. Hirzel, *Arch. f. Religionswissenschaft* xi (1908) 75ff., 243ff., 417ff., H. D. Jocelyn, *YCS* xxiii (1973) 85 n.191; for Stoic attitudes cf. J. M. Rist, *Stoic Philosophy* (1969) 223ff.; on Seneca, H. H. Eckert, *Weltanschauung und Selbstmord bei Seneca* (diss. Tübingen, 1951).

590f. malis | effugium Cf. Sen. *Pha.* 253 *unicum effugium mali*, *Ira* 2.14.9 *effugium seruitutis*, Val. Fl. 7.332, Tac. *Ann.* 6.49.

591 libera mors The phrase suggests (*a*) a death freely chosen, as in Marc. Aur. 10.8, (*b*) a death which sets one free, as often in Seneca, cf. *Prou.* 2.10, *Ira* 3.15.3f., *Epist.* 12.10, 70.14; cf. also Plut. *Cato min.* 71.1, W. Rutz, 'Amor Mortis bei Lucan', *Hermes* lxxxviii (1960) 462ff.

592 portus The metaphor is old, cf. Kamerbeek on Soph. *Ajax* 683, *trag. adesp.* 369 N², *Anth. Pal.* 7.472B (Leonidas), *EG* 67 Kaibel, 'Longinus' 9.7, Marc. Aur. 3.3; in Latin Cic. *Cluent.* 7, *Tusc.* 1.118, Sen. *Epist.* 70.3, ps.-Sen. *HO* 1021, *Anth. Lat.* 415.5 Riese.

593ff. The transmitted order of verses has often been suspected and altered (see apparatus), but no entirely convincing re-arrangement has been proposed; the difficulty of the lines (which centres about *hunc* in 593 and *pax alta* in 596) might be due to Seneca himself. It is natural to assume that the emphatic *hunc* (593) should refer to the man who does not fear death, as described in 605ff. (and cf. Hor. *C.* 3.3.6), but the MS order requires *hunc* to refer instead to the *portus* of death; this, however, is in itself hardly objectionable, and is in fact quite consistent with the storm-imagery of 593–5. The vague and unconnected *pax alta* is a more serious problem: if 596 follows 589–95, *portus* must still be the antecedent, since it seems difficult to supply a personal antecedent from *miseros* in 591 (these are precisely those *not* at peace) or to take *pax alta* as 'the peace of souls at rest in the harbour of death'; yet a personal subject is surely required for most of the clauses which follow (again Horatian parallels are relevant, see following notes). Proposals to transfer 605–9 leave those lines without their clearly intended climax, 610; nor could 605–10 be moved elsewhere, since 610 seems designed to summarise the entire passage from 589 onwards. Mynors' suggestion, which involves only 605–6, resolves all problems except the abruptness of *pax alta*, and this cannot be remedied by transposition alone; Richter may therefore have been correct in supposing the text defective at this point, although his suggested supplement is unattractive. In the absence of a wholly satisfying solution I have left the transmitted text unaltered, but the possibility of a lacuna before 593 (or, perhaps more likely, after 595) should be considered.

594 procella Fortunae Cf. Cic. *Pis.* 21, *Sest.* 101, 140, *Cluent.* 153, *Tusc.* 2.66, Apul. *Met.* 11.25; in Sen. *N.Q.* 6.32.4 the *procellae* are real: *hanc [sc. animam] qui contempsit, securus uidebit maria turbari, securus aspiciet fulminantis caeli trucem atque horridam faciem* (= *flamma Tonantis*). It is a commonplace that the *sapiens* is unaffected by fortune's reversals, cf., e.g., Cic. *Paradox.* 5.34, *Tusc.* 5.30, Hor. *S.* 2.7.88, Sen. *Const.* 8.3, *Cons. Hel.* 13.2, *Epist.* 57.3, 71.30, 82.5, Juv. 13.19f., etc.

iniqui Impiety need not be seen, since *iniquus* hardly differs in force from *iratus*, *saeuus*, *crudelis*, or *aduersus*, cf. *T.L.L.* VII¹.1640.43ff., Opelt, *Schimpfwörter* 253ff., Nisbet–Hubbard on Hor. *C.* 1.2.47; note Virg. *Aen.* 5.809 *nec dis nec uiribus aequis* and Servius *ad loc.* 'dis iniquis, hoc est: aduersis.'

596ff. The enumeration of the perils which do not terrify the wise man is a common subject (cf. Cic. *Tusc.* 5.30, Hor. *S.* 2.7.83ff., *Anth. Lat.* 444.10ff. Riese), but S.'s immediate model can be confidently identified as Hor. *C.* 3.3.1ff. Several correspondences are nearly exact (*ciuium ardor = ciuium coetus*; *uultum instantis tyranni = minaces uictoris iras*; *Auster, dux inquieti turbidus Hadriae = maria asperis insana Coris*; *fulminantis magna manus Iouis = iniqui flamma Tonantis*), involving only slight changes to suit S.'s tastes (Corus is his favourite storm-wind) or to make the images less specific (*coetus* for *ardor*, *uictoris* for *tyranni*). For Horace's final trial, the *fractus orbis*, Seneca substitutes several lines on war and the sack of cities, suiting the circumstances of his chorus and leading to the narrative section which follows.

596 ciuium coetus The expression is so vague that its import is unclear. It may allude to the common theme of *uanus populi fauor*, cf. Hor. *C.* 1.1.7 *mobilium...Quiritium*, 3.3.3, Sen. *HF* 169, *Pha.* 488, *Thy.* 351; *Octauia* 877ff., Stat. *S.* 2.2.123; Otto, *Sprichwörter* 378; on the other hand, since *coetus* were often secret and conspiratorial (cf. Cic. *Leg. Agr.* 2.12, *Cat.* 1.6, Livy 2.28.1, 32.1, 39.14.4, Tac. *Ann.* 1.16, 32, 2.40, 3.40, 4.27, *Hist.* 4.36), a reference to sedition may be intended.

597 minaces uictoris iras The fortitude of the *sapiens* in the face of tyranny was proverbial, cf. Cic. *Tusc.* 2.53, Sen. *Epist.* 28.8, *Ben.* 5.6.2ff.,

Epict. *Diss.* 1.25.22, Philostratus, *Vit. Apoll.* 7.1ff. (with *exempla*), D.L. 10.118. The reigns of the later Julio-Claudians saw the commonplace take on new vigour, cf. J. M. C. Toynbee, *G&R* xiii (1944) 43ff.

600 puluereamue nubem A recurrent feature of epic battles, see Miniconi 167; the juxtaposition of *cateruis* suggests that S. had in mind Virg. *Aen.* 8.593 *puluseram nubem et fulgentis aere cateruas.*

601 barbaricis...cateruis *Cateruae* often consist of barbarians and receive contemptuous treatment from Roman writers, cf. Hor. *C.* 1.8.16, Tib. 1.2.67, Livy 7.26.7, Claud. *Ruf.* 2.36; note Lucan 7.526f. *ciuilia bella | non bene barbaricis umquam commissa cateruis.*

604 indomitumue bellum Cf. Virg. *Aen.* 2.440 *indomitum Martem,* Luc. 5.309 *militis indomiti.*

606 contemptor leuium deorum *Contemptor deorum* is a strong expression, often denoting impiety (cf. Virg. *Aen.* 7.648, Ovid, *Met.* 1.161, 3.514, Suet. *Ner.* 56); for milder uses of *contemptor* cf. Sen. *Epist.* 88.29 *fortitudo contemptrix timendorum est,* 92.31, 93.4 *contemptorem...fortunae.* The strength of the language is comparable to Virg. *G.* 2.491f. [*qui*] *metus omnis et inexorabile fatum | subiecit pedibus strepitumque Acherontis auari* (for which cf. ps.-Sen. *HO* 107f., *CE* 2099.4); cf. also Juv. 10.52f.

leuium deorum All gods are *leues* in that their favour cannot be relied upon (cf. 931 below, *per dubios deos*); cf. *Anth. Lat.* 415.17 Riese [*spes*] *omnia promittit nota leuitate deorum.*

608 non tristis An essential mark of *tranquillitas,* cf. Sen. *Tranq.* 2.4 *quaerimus quomodo animus semper aequalis secundoque cursu eat propitiusque sibi sit et sua laetus aspiciat et hoc gaudium non interrumpat, Epist.* 27.3. Stoic heroes meet death with joy, for example Socrates in *Prou.* 3.12 *at ille uenenum laetus et libens hauriet,* also Astyanax (*Tro.* 1092ff.) and Polyxena (*ib.* 1151ff.).

610 par...erit The comparison *par superis* is a proverbial means of describing felicity (see Nisbet–Hubbard on Hor. *C.* 1.1.6, 35), but in the present context the phrase clearly recalls the claims made for the *sapiens,* cf. *SVF* 1.216, iii.332, 617, Hor. *Epist.* 1.1.106f. *sapiens uno minor est Ioue, diues, | liber, honoratus, pulcher, rex denique regum.* For the first element cf. also Hor. *S.* 1.3.124ff., Sen. *Thy.* 336f. *rex est qui posuit metus, | hoc regnum sibi quisque dat*; for the second, cf. Cic. *N.D.* 2.153 (with Pease's note), Sen. *Suas.* 6.2 of Cato, Vell. Pat. 2.35.2, Sen. *Prou.* 1.5, *Const.* 8.2, *Epist.* 48.11, etc.

611 nescire mori Elsewhere S. refers to *uiuendi et moriendi scientia* (*B.V.* 19.2) and to death as an object of study (*egregia res est mortem condiscere, Epist.* 26.9); for *mori scire* or *nescire* cf. also *Tranq.* 11.4, *HF* 426, 1075f. In Lucan (9.211) *mori scire* is man's best fate, *mori cogi* the next best.

612 uidimus 'we bore the sight of', as in Aesch. *Pers.* 106ff. ἔμαθον... ἐσορᾶν πόντιον ἄλσος, Cic. *poet. fr.* 11.15 Traglia, *Phil.* 14.27, Virg. *G.* 1.471f.,

Hor. 1.2.13 (with Nisbet–Hubbard's note), Prop. 1.1.11f. (and cf. Shackleton Bailey, *Propertiana* 3), 4.2.53, Sen. *Contr.* 7.3.5, *Suas.* 6.6, Sen. *Cons. Marc.* 20.5, *Thy.* 293; *Octauia* 231, Luc. 1.254ff. See also on 656 below.

613f. Dardana tecta | Dorici...ignes For the juxtaposition of proper adjectives cf., e.g., Hor. *C.* 1.15.35f. *uret Achaicus | ignis Iliacas domos*, Prop. 2.8.32 *feruere et Hectorea Dorica castra face*, Ovid, *Her.* 8.14 *cum Danaus Phrygias ureret ignis opes*, Ars 1.54, *R.A.* 66, *Met.* 14.220, Sen. *Tro.* 135f. *bis pulsari Dardana Graio | moenia ferro.*

615 ut...pharetra In *Tro.* 718ff. Andromache similarly contrasts the behaviour of Hercules and Ulysses after taking the city. For Hercules' expedition against Troy cf. *Il.* 5.640ff., Diodorus 4.32, ps.-Apollod. *Bibl.* 2.6.4.

617 Pelidae nimium feroci For Achilles as a typical *iratus*, cf. Arist. *Poet.* 1454b14, Hor. *Ars* 120f. *si forte reponis Achillem, | impiger, iracundus, inexorabilis, acer, | iura neget sibi nata* (with Brink's note), *S.* 1.7.12, *C.* 1.6.6 *Pelidae cedere nescii, Epist.* 2.1.41f., Ovid, *Her.* 8.1 *Pyrrhus Achillides animosus imagine patris*; cf. F. Buffière, *Les mythes d'Homère et la pensée grecque* (1956) 334ff.

619 falsus Achilles Cf. *Tro.* 447 *uera ex Achille spolia simulato tulit* (*sc.* Hector); both passages may recall Ovid, *Her.* 1.17 *Menoetiaden falsis cecidisse sub armis.*

621 sustulit luctu celeremque saltu S. is less careful than Horace in avoiding rhyme between unrelated words in lyrics: Horace's 558 sapphic hendecasyllables contain only three examples, two of which are extenuated by syntactical division, while Seneca's 432 sapphics (not counting those in polymetric choruses, and therefore excluding this example) contain nine such rhymes (cf. O. Skutsch, *BICS* xi (1964) 73–8).

celeremque saltu For the phrase cf. Enn. *Ann.* 129 V² *at Horatius inclutus saltu*; here the pursuit of Hector is in question.

622 Troades summis timuere muris The elements of the traditional τειχοσκοπία (women looking down in fear from the battlements of the besieged city) are handled with Seneca's characteristic compression and abstraction; compare Enn. *Ann.* 419 V² *matronae moeros complent, spectare fauentes* (and the allusion in *sc.* 59 R² [*Alexander*] *qui te sic respectantibus tractauere nobis*), Virg. *Aen.* 8.592 *stant pauidae in muris matres oculisque sequuntur*, 12.131ff., Luc. 7.369f., Val. Fl. 3.247f., Stat. *Th.* 7.240ff.; other examples in Miniconi 168.

626 unius noctis That all could be lost in the space of a day (here a night) is a commonplace (cf. Men. *Dysc.* 187f.) often used in lamentation and rhetorical historiography, cf. Eur. *Phoen.* 1689 ἐν ἦμάρ μ' ὤλβισ', ἐν δ' ἀπώλεσεν, *Hec.* 285, Enn. *Ann.* 287 V² *multa dies in bello conficit unus*, Lucr.

3.898f. *omnia ademit | una dies infesta tibi tot praemia uitae* (with Bailey's note), 5.999ff., Cic. *Phil.* 2.85, Prop. 3.11.70, Sen. *Suas.* 6.26, Sen. *Epist.* 91.2, ps.-Sen. *HO* 422ff., Suet. *Jul.* 79, Plut. *Ant.* 12.1, App. 2.109, D. Cass. 44.11.2f. For a similar rhetorical climax compare Claud. *Ruf.* 2.50ff.

furto E's *furto* is clearly right, and *fato* a trivialisation: *furto* is the necessary antithesis to *fortiter uinci*.

627 simulata dona Cf. Virg. *Aen.* 2.17 *uotum pro reditu simulant*, 183f., Hor. *C.* 4.6.13f. *equo Mineruae | sacra mentito.* Seneca's desire for brevity excludes Epeius or Minerva. After Virgil, all this could be taken as read; even earlier much was familiar, cf. Pl. *Bacch.* 925–73, 987f., perhaps *Pseud.* 1244, Enn. *sc.* 60f. R² (*Alexander*), and the fragments from plays entitled *Equus Troianus* (Liv. And. 20ff. R², Naev. 14f. R², *inc. inc. fab.* 78 R²; cf. E. Fraenkel, *Elementi Plautini* 61ff., G. W. Williams, *Hermes* lxxxv (1957) 447.

molis immensae Cf. Virg. *Aen.* 2.15 *instar montis*, 150 *molem hanc immanis equi* (and see Austin *ad loc.* for details), 185 *hanc...immensam... molem.*

630 limine in primo The reference must be to the outer gates of Troy, cf. Pl. *Bacch.* 955 *quom portae Phrygiae limen superum scinderetur*; in Virgil the walls are breached (234 *moenia pandimus urbis*) and the horse pulled to the temple of Athena, at whose portal it encounters difficulty (242, cf. 245 *monstrum infelix sacrata sistimus arce*).

For the ill-omened striking of the *limen* see Ovid's account of the arrival of the Magna Mater in Rome (*F.* 4.291ff.), also Tib. 1.2.19f., Ovid, *Am.* 1.12.5f., *Met.* 10.452, Luc. 2.359; M. B. Ogle, *AJPh* xxxii (1911) 251ff.

Virgil's *quater* (242) is characteristically replaced by the vague *saepe*; the imprecise word suits the tone of the ode, stressing the many chances for discovery missed by the Trojans.

sonipes A poetic term popular with Virgil (*Aen.* 4.135, 11.600, 638, cf. Sil. 1.222, Stat. *Th.* 5.3), but not applied by him to the Trojan horse; on the contrary, Virgil stresses the unnatural and portentous character of the horse, cf. *fatalis machina* (237) and *monstrum infelix* (245).

cauernis Cf. Virg. *Aen.* 2.19 with Austin's note.

631 reges A select group, like Homer's πάντες ἄριστοι (*Od.* 8.512) and Virgil's nine heroes (*Aen.* 2.261ff.).

gestans 'carrying in its womb', cf. Pl. *Stich.* 159 *nam illa me in aluo menses gestauit decem*, Sen. *Pha.* 1161f. For this application of the metaphor cf. C. Titius *apud* Macrob. *Sat.* 3.13.13 *ut ille Troianus equus grauidus armatis fuit*, Enn. *sc.* 60 R² (= 72 J) *nam maximo saltu superauit grauidus armatis equus | qui suo partu ardua perdat Pergama* (see Jocelyn *ad loc.* for Greek parallels), Virg. *Aen.* 2.238 *feta armis*, 6.516 *grauis*, Ovid, *Ars* 1.364 *militibus* *grauidum laeta recepit equum*; Petr. *Sat.* 89. 20 *uterum notauit* (*sc.* Laocoon), for which cf. Virg. *Aen.* 2.243.

632 dolos uersare 'i.e. in ipsos authores' (Farnaby), or perhaps simply 'dolos exercere' (so Servius on Virg. *Aen.* 2.62). The phrase appears twice in the *Aeneid*: at 2.62 (if *dolos*, not *dolo*, is right) it means 'to deceive successfully', while at 4.563 it = *in animo dolos uersare*.

634 parmae The word is old and generally poetic, cf. Enn. *Ann.* 402 V², Virg. *Aen.* 2.175, 11.693; this is its only appearance in the tragedies. Seneca is here more specific than Virgil, who says only *sonitum quater arma dedere* (243).

635 tacitumque murmur This is more likely to describe low voices than the sound of the weapons (as in *T.L.L.* VIII.1676.30); for *tacitum murmur* in this sense cf. Ovid, *Met.* 6.203. If *tacitum murmur* refers to voices, it is best taken as a generic description of what immediately follows, the grumblings of Pyrrhus when prevented from making a premature assault in daylight. On this view Bothe's *ut* for *et* in 636 is highly attractive, and I have followed Leo in placing it in the text.

636f. ut...Vlixi For the incident cf. *Od.* 11.528ff. The portrayal of Neoptolemus as impetuous but incapable of baseness is at odds with his cowardly murder of Priam, recalled below in 656ff. (after Virg. *Aen.* 2.499ff.).

636 fremuit Often of indignation, as in Cic. *Att.* 4.1.7, Sen. *Contr.* 2.5.4; of eagerness and impatience (as in this passage) in Val. Fl. 1.702 *fremit obice ponti | clausa cohors*, Sil. 8.4 *impatiensque morae fremit*.

male...parens = *uix parens*, nearly *repugnans*, the only example in the plays of *male* used in litotes to produce a near-negative (see notes on 683, 718, 901 below); cf. Hor. *Epist.* 1.20.15 *male parentem...asellum*, Sen. *Epist.* 8.5, Tac. *Agr.* 32.3.

subdolo S. uses the word only here and in *Tro.* 933 *quidquid subdolo uultu tegis*; it was probably felt as an archaism. The use of *subdolus* and *subdole* of persons is found often in Plautus (nine examples) but not at all in Terence, and three times in Sallust (*Cat.* 5.4, *Jug.* 38.1, 108.1). After this the words are generally rare, and the personal application especially so: Cicero has no certain use of *subdolus* (but cf. *Pis.* fr. 9 Nisbet, *homini leui ac subito filiam conlocauit*, where Watt has conjectured *subdolo*), and only one of *subdole* (*Brut.* 35, of Demosthenes: *nihil acute inueniri potuit...nihil, ut ita dicam, subdole, nihil uersute, quod ille non uiderit*); of the eight appearances of *subdolus* in Tacitus, only one (*Ann.* 16.32.12) is personal; poetry shows only non-personal uses (cf. Lucr. 2.559, 1.1003, Prop. 4.3.66, Ovid, *Ars* 1.598, [Tib.] 3.6.46 [*subdola* Heinsius, *sordida* MSS]). This pattern of usage, the word's uncertain formation (cf. Leumann, *Lautlehre* 254), and Cicero's prefatory *ut ita dicam* combine to suggest a colloquial origin or association (so also Douglas, Jahn–Kroll *ad loc.*).

638 secura metus Cf. Eur. *Tro.* 524 πεπαυμένοι πόνων; *secura* here almost = *oblita*, as in Virg. *Aen.* 7.304 *securi pelagi atque mei.* For the scene compare also Claud. *Ruf.* 2.427f. *uacuo plebs undique muro | iam secura fluit* eqs. **Troica pubes** Cf. Eur. *Tro.* 531 πᾶσα δὲ γέννα Φρυγῶν; Virgil's specific *pueri circum innuptaeque puellae* (238) is expanded in the lines which follow.

639 sacros...funes A compression of Virgil's *sacra canunt funemque manu contingere gaudent* (239); Eur. *Tro.* 525 τόδ' ἱερὸν ἀνάγετε ξόανον is more distantly related.

640ff. The introduction of Astyanax and Polyxena is Seneca's modest contribution to the traditional account; in Euripides Astyanax is considerably younger (cf. 749ff., 1171ff.), and in the parallel ode Euripides merely records the presence of young and old (527f. τίς οὐκ ἔβα νεανίδων, | τίς οὐ γεραιὸς ἐκ δόμων;).

640 aequaeui First found in Virgil (*Aen.* 2.561, 5.452), not used by Ovid, and only here by S.

641 Haemonio desponsa rogo The illusion of immediacy created by the present tenses is undermined by this retrospective allusion to Polyxena's death. For *desponsa rogo* cf. *Tro.* 195 *desponsa nostris cineribus*; for *Haemonio = Achilles* cf. Ovid, *F.* 5.400, *Tr.* 3.11.28, 4.1.15f.

644f. festae matres...festi patres *Festus* appears often in the plays, but its application to persons is restricted to *Agamemnon* (cf. also 311 *festa turba*, 780 *festa coniunx*); the closest parallels appear to be Hor. *C.* 3.18.11f. *festus...pagus*, Sil. 11.270 *festam...urbem*; for Seneca's *festa turba* compare Ovid, *Tr.* 5.12.18 *festos...choros*, *festa pompa* Stat. *S.* 1.2.230, *agmina festa* *CE* 1233.20, *festa plebs* Tac. *Ann.* 2.69.

645 adeunt A *uox propria* in contexts of worship (see Servius Auctus on Virg. *Aen.* 4.56; text uncertain); it is applied to the gods themselves in 779 below, *Pha.* 108f., Cic. *N.D.* 1.77, Prop. 2.34.26, 3.21.18, Ovid, *Met.* 15.63, Tac. *Ann.* 3.59, and also to various sacred objects, e.g. *arae* (as here and Stat. *Th.* 7.96), *delubra* (Lucr. 4.75, Virg. *Aen.* 4.56, Aul. Gell. 4.9.9), *templa* (Stat. *Th.* 7.97), *sacra* (Tib. 1.2.83; cf. Ovid, *Ibis* 98 with la Penna's note), *loca* (Catull. 63.3), *libri* (Cic. *Diu.* 1.97, Livy 34.55.3).
The scene described is also found in Soph. *Ant.* 150f.

646 unus...urbe Compare Ovid on the primitive state of nature: *unus erat toto naturae uultus in orbe* (*Met.* 1.6) and on the festivities in honour of Theseus at Athens: *nec tota tristis locus ullus in urbe est* (*Met.* 7.452).

647 Hectoreos The use of the adjective is common in Virgil, cf. *Aen.* 2.543 with Austin's note, also Ovid, *Met.* 12.67, 13.7, Sen. *Tro.* 369, 415, 528, 1087 (and cf. 356 above, *laurus Agamemnonias*).

649f. quid primum...quidue extremum This form of *dubitatio* appears first in *Od.* 9.14 and is common thereafter, cf. Aesch. *Pers.* 253, Soph. *Phil.* 337, *Trach.* 947, Eur. *El.* 907f., *Phoen.* 1524, *I.A.* 442, 1124, Theoc. 2.64f., 17.11, Apoll. Rhod. 3.1011, Cicero, *Rosc. Am.* 28, *Verr.* 5.83, Ter. *Eun.* 1044, Virg. *Aen.* 4.284, 371 (Pease gives later parallels), Prop. 1.18.5, Val. Fl. 7.433ff., Quint. 9.2.19.

651 diuum fabricata manu Inspired by Virg. *Aen.* 9.144f. *moenia Troiae* | *Neptuni fabricata manu*, with characteristic substitution of *diuum* for *Neptuni* (cf. *Tro.* 479 *muris deum*).

fabricata A verb often used when either the product or the maker is remarkable, cf. Virg. *Aen.* 2.46 *in nostros fabricata est machina muros*, Ovid, *Met.* 1.259 *tela reponuntur manibus fabricata Cyclopum*, Pliny, *N.H.* 7.125, Sil. 1.445, Suet. *Nero* 32.

652 nostra Perhaps S. has in mind the breach made to allow the horse to be received (cf. Virg. *Aen.* 2.234 *diuidimus muros et moenia pandimus urbis*). Bentley's *Graia* removes the ambiguity but weakens the contrast with *diuum*; the note of self-reproach is fully consistent with the mood of the ode.

653 templa...suos The source for *HO* 173 *templa suis collapsa deis*; cf. Ovid, *Met.* 1.287 [*flumina*] *tectaque cumque suis rapiunt penetralia sacris*, Sen. *HF* 506f. *templa supplicibus suis* | *iniecta flagrent*, Const. 6.2, cf. Martial 10.51.14, Massinger, *Duke of Milan* i.iii 'the ransacked temples falling on their saints'.

656 uidi, uidi Probably derived from Virg. *Aen.* 2.499ff., which in turn recalls Ennius' *Andromacha*: *uidi, uidere quod me passa aegerrume...haec omnia uidi inflammari*, eqs. (*sc.* 91, 86 R² = 78, 92 J). There is no need to conclude that S. was imitating Ennius; repetition of *uidi* (*uidimus*, etc.) as a sign of emotion is common in Latin poetry, cf. also Ovid, *Her.* 3.45ff., Sen. *HF* 50, *Tro.* 169, Luc. 6.785, ps.-Sen. *HO* 207f., Petr. *Sat.* 89.11; see Hansen 40f.

657f. uix exiguo | sanguine tingui This detail is not found in Euripides (*Hec.* 21ff., *Tro.* 16ff., 481ff.), Ennius (*sc.* 87 R² = 93 J), or Virgil (*Aen.* 2.553); it first appears in Ovid, *Met.* 13.409f. *exiguumque senis...ara cruorem* | *combiberat*) and is taken up by later authors (cf. Sen. *Tro.* 49f., Luc. 2.128f.); it may have a declamatory origin, cf. Bonner 165. Juvenal speaks generally about the *minimus sanguis* of the old (10.217), and Tacitus (*Ann.* 15.63) includes the detail in his account of Seneca's death (*quoniam senile corpus et parco uictu tenuatum lenta effugia sanguini praebebat*).

ACT FOUR (659–807)

The presence of Cassandra is the only unifying factor in a section of unusual formal diversity, including a choral θρῆνος,[1] a virtuoso possession-scene perhaps inspired (directly or indirectly) by analogous scenes in Greek tragedy,[2] and a pointed series of ἀντιλαβαί between Agamemnon and Cassandra. The first of these divisions continues the theme of the foregoing ode, the griefs of the captive Trojans, but the remainder of the act looks forward to Agamemnon's death and so constitutes an elaborate foreshadowing of the *dénouement*.

659ff. Remarks on the content of a preceding choral ode are not common in Greek tragedy (cf. Soph. *O.T.* 216; Aesch. *Ag.* 489ff. are given to Clytaemestra by many editors and commentators, but cf. O. P. Taplin, *HSCP* lxxvi (1972) 11; the closest parallel comes in the *Choephoroe*, in which the arrival of Electra and the chorus is announced (10ff.; cf. 587ff. above), the chorus sings its entrance-song, and Electra addresses the women of the chorus (83). There is nothing similar elsewhere in Seneca (cf. *Tro.* 409f., *Med.* 116).

659 cohibete...petet 'Restrain those tears which all time will seek (to shed)'; that is, do not weep for Priam, since all ages to come will be eager to do so (*petet* more vigorous than, for example, *dabit*), but instead bewail your own losses. If the transmitted text is sound, this is surely its meaning. For Priam as a proverbial figure of misfortune, see Mayor's note on Juv. 10.258ff. The awareness of future reputation thus implied is rare in Greek and Senecan tragedy (but cf. Eur. *Alc.* 445ff., Sen. *Med.* 423 *faciet, hic faciet dies | quod nullus umquam taceat*), though common in Shakespeare (cf. *J.C.* iii.i.111f., *Ham.* v.ii.339f., *Oth.* v.ii.341ff., *Hen. V* iv.iii.57ff.). A more explicit statement of this idea occurs in an epigram of the Senecan corpus (*Anth. Lat.* 429.13 Riese): *non deerit Priamum qui defleat, Hectora narret.*

If, however, Priam is to be left to the mourning of future ages, how can Cassandra arrogate his sorrows to herself (*aerumnae meae | socium recusant*

---

[1] In contrast to monodies of single characters, which are not infrequent (cf. *Tro.* 705ff., *Med.* 740ff., *Pha.* 1ff., *Thy.* 920ff., *Agam.* 759ff.; cf. *HO* 1863ff.), there is no exact Senecan parallel for a choral lyric within one of the five acts: *Oed.* 980–97 may be so interpreted, but in content and tone these lines function better as an act-dividing ode (on the problems of *Oedipus'* structure cf. Anliker 94ff.). The quasi-*kommos* (1131–289) and concluding choral lyric (1983–96) of *Hercules Oetaeus* find no analogies in the genuine plays.

[2] Cf. Eur. *Tro.* 298ff.; a scene of ecstatic prophecy formed part of the lost *Alexander*, cf. B. Snell, *Euripides' Alexandros* (*Hermes* Einzelschriften v (1937)) 25ff.

661f.) or claim to be equal to them (*nostris ipsa sufficiam malis* 663)? The entire passage 659–64 insists on a distinction between Cassandra's griefs and those of the chorus which the transmitted text of 659 fails to make.

The only emendation of 659 known to me, *quîs* for *quas* and *patet* for *petet* (Heinsius, independently suggested by Garrod, *CQ* v (1911) 218), is misguided. The advice 'do not weep, for you will have a long time in which to weep' is appropriate when there is more urgent business to attend to (so, for example, in Ovid, *Met.* 4.695f., Sen. *Pha.* 1244), but not when the alternative to weeping is mourning of another sort. An equally slight alteration, however, may have more success: *cohibete lacrimas omne quae tempus petent* (or perhaps *petant*). Weeping for Priam will engross all time to come; it should not be begun by those with other losses to mourn. Hence Cassandra discourages the chorus while proposing herself as suitable to the task. On any view the logical structure of the passage is to an extent inexplicit, and for that reason I have not ventured to place my suggestion in the text; it does, however, bring 659 into closer coherence with 660–4 and with the chorus' reply.

660 lamentabili Of the seventeen Senecan iambic lines ending in words of five syllables, more than half involve words with similar associations: *lamentatio* (*Pha.* 852), *inlaetabilis* (*Tro.* 861), *detestabilis* (*Thy.* 23), *exsecrabilis* (*Pho.* 223), *implacabile* (*Oed.* 935), *intractabilis* (*Pha.* 229, 271, 580).

661f. aerumnae...recusant The aloofness of Cassandra is even more marked in Quintus Smyrnaeus (14.395ff.), where Cassandra mocks the helplessness of the other Trojans. The author of *HO* has Iole express her separation from the griefs of her fellow-captives in crasser terms: *nullum querimur commune malum* (177); cf. Sen. *Tro.* 412ff.

665f. magis...curae The thought is proverbial of all violent emotions, cf. Publ. Syr. 505 *peiora multo cogitat mutus dolor*, Ovid, *R.A.* 619, *Met.* 4.64 *quoque magis tegitur, tectus magis aestuat ignis*, Sen. *Med.* 153.

665 exurunt Cf. *N.Q.* 4 *praef.* 2 *alias uoluptate lassamus alias sollicitudine exurimus.*

666 lacerant For the metaphor see Nisbet–Hubbard on Hor. *C.* 1.18.4 *mordaces.*

668 dura uirago In this context *dura* probably suggests 'enduring', πολυτλήμων (cf. Williams on Virg. *Aen.* 3.94; cf. also *Aen.* 11.288); the word is thus used of Hercules, cf. Sen. *HF* 1228, ps.-Sen. *HO* 1280, Stat. *Th.* 11.237 *durus adhuc patiensque mali.*

uirago Previously used of *uirgines* with masculine strength (cf. Plaut. *Merc.* 414) or of women or goddesses engaged in masculine occupations, such as hunting or war (cf. Enn. *Ann.* 522 V² (perhaps Discordia), Virg. *Aen.* 12.468, Ovid, *Met.* 6.130 Pallas, Sen. *Pha.* 54 Diana); Seneca extends the word to *uirgines* with male strength of character, cf. also *Tro.* 1151 of Polyxena.

670ff. The elaboration of the notion *quis flere digne poterit...?* (cf. Sen. *HF* 258, 1227f.) by reference to traditional figures of mourning is a topic of consolation-poetry (cf. ps.-Ovid, *Cons. Liu.* 105ff., Stat. *S.* 5.3.80ff., cf. Prop. 3.9.8ff.); the particular combination in our passage has a close parallel in the *Epitaphium Bionis*:

9   ἀδόνες αἱ πυκινοῖσιν ὀδυρόμεναι ποτὶ φύλλοις...
14ff.   Στρυμόνιοι μύρεσθε παρ' ὕδασιν αἴλινα, κύκνοι,
        καὶ γοεροῖς στομάτεσσι μελίσδετε πένθιμον ᾠδάν
        οἵαν ὑμετέροις ποτὶ χείλεσι γῆρυς ἄειδεν.
37ff.   οὐ τόσον εἰναλίαισι παρ' ἀόσι μύρατο Σειρήν,
        οὐδὲ τόσον ποκ' ἄϋσεν ἐνὶ σκοπέλοισιν ἀηδών,
        οὐδὲ τόσον θρήνησεν ἀν' ὤρεα μακρὰ χελιδών,
        'Αλκυόνας δ' οὐ τόσσον ἐπ' ἄλγεσιν ἴαχε Κῆυξ,
        οὐδὲ τόσον γλαυκοῖς ἐνὶ κύμασι κηρύλος ᾆδεν·
46ff.   ἀδονίδες πᾶσαί τε χελιδόνες ἅς ποκ' ἔτερπεν
        ἅς λαλέειν ἐδίδασκε καθεζόμεναι ποτὶ πρέμνοις
        ἀντίον ἀλλάλαισιν ἐκώκυον, αἱ δ' ὑπεφώνευν.

Seneca's imitators (cf. *HO* 185ff., *Octauia* 6ff.) reduce the topic to a bare catalogue.

670ff. The myth of Procne, Philomela, and Tereus is handled with Seneca's customary allusiveness; Procne and Philomela are treated as types of perpetual sorrow (cf. the swallow in Soph. *El.* 1075ff.), and their earlier history thus receives no direct exposition. None of the characters' human names appears, and the identifying phrases are typically vague (*tristis aedon, Bistonis ales, diri...mariti*).

The form of the legend used by S. can, however, be deduced with some confidence (on the various shapes of the myth see the sources cited in Witlox's note on ps.-Ovid, *Cons. Liu.* 105; also Bömer on Ovid, *F.* 2.853f., I. Cazzaniga, *La saga di Itys* (Milano–Varese, 1950)). His nightingale mourns for Itys, which suggests that she was in former life the wife of Tereus and mother of Itys (= Procne), as in most accounts (e.g. *Od.* 19.518ff., Aesch. *Ag.* 1144ff., Virg. *G.* 4.511ff.). S. stresses the nightingale's musical talent, using different language of the swallow (*garrula narrat* 675); it is a plausible inference that the swallow represents the violated sister (=Philomela), who lost her tongue as well as her virginity (cf. Ovid, *Met.* 6.555ff.). In Sen. *HF* 146ff. (*Thracia paelex...summo stridula ramo*), *stridula* is more appropriate to the swallow's song (cf. Hes. *Op.* 568, *Anth. Pal.* 9.70), and *paelex* is appropriately used of the sister (cf. Ovid, *Tr.* 2.389f.). Further, several authors connect the twittering of the swallow with its mutilation (cf. Stat. *Th.* 8.619, 12.479, *S.* 5.3.83, Nonnus 2.134ff., 12.75ff., *Anth. Pal.* 5.237

(Agathias)). Martial (14.75) thus describes the transformation of the sister: *quae | muta puella fuit, garrula fertur auis*, but the poem is entitled *Luscinia*; was Martial confused, or did the name Philomela cause the poem to be wrongly entitled?

Seneca's vagueness may also be an inheritance from Ovid, several of whose references to the myth lack explicit details, cf. *Am.* 2.6.7ff. *quod scelus Ismarii quereris, Philomela, tyranni, | expleta est annis ista querela tuis; | alitis in rarae miserum deuertere funus; | magna sed antiqua est causa doloris Itys, F.* 2.629, *Met.* 6.667ff.

670 uerno Perhaps to be understood of the entire passage to 677, since both birds were often referred to as harbingers of spring; for the nightingale, cf. *Od.* 19.519, Sappho 136 L–P, Arist. *Aues* 683f., Calp. Sic. 5.16, Rut. Nam. 1.111f.; for the swallow, cf. Stesichorus 211 *PMG*, Simonides 599, 606 *PMG*, Arist. *Pax* 800, *Thesm.* 1, *Anth. Pal.* 10.1 (Leonidas), 10.2 (Antipater), 10.4.5f. (Marcus Argentarius), Hor. *C.* 4.12.5ff., Ovid, *F.* 2.853, Columella 10.80, Stat. *S.* 3.5.57.

uerno...ramo...tectis (673) The differing habitats of the birds are also mentioned in *Anth. Pal.* 9.363.17f. (Meleager), Ovid, *Met.* 6.667f. *quarum petit altera siluas, | altera tecta subit*, ps.-Virg. *Aetna* 586ff. For the nightingale cf. *Od.* 19.520 δενδρέων ἐν πετάλοισι καθεζομένη πυκινοῖσιν, Virg. *G.* 4.511 *populea...sub umbra*, Pliny, *N.H.* 10.81, ps.-Sen. *HO* 193; for the swallow cf. *Anth. Pal.* 10.2f. ἤδη δὲ πλάσσει μὲν ὑπώροφα γυρὰ χελιδὼν | οἰκία, Virg. *Ecl.* 6.78ff., Ovid,¹ *Tr.* 3.12.9, Nonnus 2.134, *Anth.Pal.* 5.237 (Agathias), d'Arcy Thompson, *Glossary of Greek birds* 310.

mobile The word suggests vocal agility and variety, cf. Pers. 1.17f., Sen. *Epist.* 76.9 *habet uocem [sc. homo]: sed quanto clariorem canes, acutiorem aquilae, grauiorem tauri, dulciorem mobilioremque luscinii?*, Vitruvius 5.4.5.

672 Ityn in uarios modulata sonos The bird warbles the name 'Itys' in variable tones; in several Greek passages this is indicated by duplication of the name (cf. Aesch. *Ag.* 1144f., Soph. *El.* 148, Eur. fr. 773.23f. N² = *Phaethon* 70, and see Diggle *ad loc.*; cf. *Culex* 252 *uox 'Ityn' edit 'Ityn'*).

modulata *Modulari* is often applied to musical setting of a text, cf. Virg. *Ecl.* 5.14, 10.50, Manil. 2.767 *fata | Pieridum numeris modulata.* In such contexts the word often governs *sonus* or the like (cf. Livy 27.37.14, Silius 11.465), which S. here replaces with the sound itself, 'Itys'. In the present surroundings (note *in uarios...sonos, mobile carmen*) *modulata* suggests the variety of tone and expression characteristic of the nightingale's song and of bird-song generally, cf. Manil. 4.153 *per uarios cantus modulataque uocibus ora*, Fronto p. 149.16 N *fistulae longe auibus modulatiores*; *ad rem* cf. Pliny, *N.H.* 10.81.

673 Bistonis The Thracian setting of the myth is often mentioned by poets, cf. Arist. *Frogs* 681; also Catull. 65.13, Prop. 3.10.10, ps.-Ovid, *Cons.*

Liu. 106, Sen. *HF* 149, *Thy.* 56 (all with *Threicius*); Ovid, *Am.* 3.12.32 (*Odrysius*); Ovid, *Am.* 2.6.7, ps.-Ovid, *Her.* 15.154 (*Ismarius*); ps.-Virg. *Culex* 252, Stat. *S.* 2.4.21 (*Bistonius*).

674f. impia diri | furta mariti If the swallow is the sister violated by Tereus, *mariti* here is 'the husband' and not 'her husband'. In other authors *dirus* is applied to the sisters (cf. *inc. inc. fab.* 240 R²) or specifically to the mother of Itys, cf. Ovid, *Ars* 2.383 *dira parens*, Stat. *S.* 5.3.84 *dirae queritur Philomela sorori* (*dirae* Gronovius: *durae* codd.). In the present context, however, both sisters must be victims and not aggressors.

675 garrula For the chattering of the swallow cf. Nicostratus fr. 27 K, Theophr. *Char.* 6.4, *Anth. Pal.* 10.1 λαλαγεῦσα χελιδών, Nonnus 2.134; *garrulus* is so used by Virgil (*G.* 4.307), *argutus* by Varro Atac. fr. 22.4 Morel, and Virgil, *G.* 1.377. Pliny (*N.H.* 10.81) and perhaps Martial (14.75) use *garrulus* of the nightingale.

narrat E's *narrat* is clearly better suited to follow *garrula*, in both sound and sense; cf. Virg. *Ecl.* 6.78 *aut ut mutatos Terei narrauerit artus*. The weaker reading *deflet* found in A has a parallel, and conceivably a source, in Mart. 14.75 *flet nefas incesti Tereos Philomela*.

676f. lugere...domum For the topic cf. Virg. *Aen.* 2.361f. *quis cladem illius noctis, quis funera fando | explicet aut possit lacrimis aequare labores?*, Vell. Pat. 2.67.1 *totius temporis fortunam ne deflere quidem quisquam satis digne potuit*, Claud. *Ruf.* 1.249f.

679 Histrum...Tanainque colens Hister and Tanais are among Seneca's favourite place-names, cf. A. Cattin, *Latomus* xxii (1963) 686, Canter 8off. The appeal of the names may explain why Seneca locates his swans in north-eastern Europe instead of their more accustomed haunts in Asia Minor (passages in Gossen, *RE* II².783.43ff., Thompson 180); for northern swans, however, see also Arist. *Aues* 769ff., Aristotle, *H.A.* 615a31–b5, Eur. fr. 775.31 N², Hor. *C.* 2.20.16, Pomp. Mela 1.110, Mart. Cap. 9.927.

Cycnus Probably the son of Sthenelus and ruler of Liguria, transformed by his mourning for Phaethon, cf. Phanocles fr. 6 Powell, Virg. *Aen.* 10.189ff., Ovid, *Met.* 2.367ff., Hyg. *fab.* 154.

680 extrema loqui The swan's song was better known for beauty than sadness (cf. for example Sen. *Pha.* 302 *dulcior uocem moriente cycno*), but note *Epit. Bionis* 14f. It is surely coincidental that the earliest extant reference to the swan's song is in Aesch. *Ag.* 1444f., also with reference to Cassandra; cf. also Plat. *Phaedo* 84E, Aristotle, *H.A.* 615b2, Chrysippus *apud* Athen. 618B, Cic. *Tusc.* 1.73, Ovid, *Met.* 14.430, *Tr.* 5.1.10f. (Ovid's *color*, that the swan is the *cantor* at its own funeral, is taken up by Stat. *S.* 2.4.10, Mart. 13.77.2).

alcyones The halcyon is a type of mourning in *Il.* 9.563, Eur. *I.T.* 1089ff. (note the parody in Arist. *Frogs* 1309ff.), but the legend in which they mourn Ceyx is later, cf. *Epit. Bionis* 39, Prop. 3.10.9, Ovid, *Her.* 18.81f., ps.-Sen. *HO* 197, Stat. *Th.* 9.360f., Hyg. *fab.* 65. Ovid's account (*Met.* 11.267–748) ends with the reconciliation of Ceyx and Alcyone.

681f. fluctu leuiter | plangente Conceivably an imitation of Catull. 64.273 *leuiterque sonant plangore cachinni*, but both the *planctus* of the waves Lucr. 2.1155, Ovid, *Her.* 19.121, Luc. 6.691) and the use of *leuis* or *leuiter* of the sound made by water (cf. Virg. *Ecl.* 1.55, Prop. 2.32.15, Ovid, *F.* 2.204) are common elsewhere.

683ff. The halcyons' annual nesting on the sea's surface (for which cf. Sappho 95 L–P, Theoc. 7.57ff. with Gow's note) is described in unexpectedly negative terms: their trust in the sea's calm seems misguided (for *male* with similar verbs cf. Hor. *S.* 2.4.21, Ovid, *Her.* 7.54 *expertae totiens tam male credis aquae?*, and for the folly of trusting the sea cf. Virg. *Aen.* 5.870, Ovid, *Ars* 2.141, Sen. *Pha.* 530), and their fear (*pauidae*) seems to be a result of their *audacia* rather than a sign of a gentle nature (cf. ps.-Ovid, *Hal.* 98 *pauidi...thynni*, Val. Flacc. 8.32 *pauidae...columbae*). The divine protection mentioned by Ovid (*Met.* 11.747f.) plays no part in Seneca's account. The halcyon mourning the destruction of her aquatic nest and the loss of her young appears in similes in Val. Fl. 4.44ff., Stat. *Th.* 9.360ff.

685f. nido...titubante Compare *HF* 778 (of Charon's skiff weighed down by Hercules) *utrumque Lethen latere titubanti bibit*.

686ff. 'Not even if the *turba* of Cybele's worshippers, who normally beat their breasts in mourning for Attis, were to imitate the *Galli* and rend their limbs in company with you...' The distinction between the *Galli* (= *molles* ...*uiros* 686) and the *turba* of 688 seems essential; while our sources convey little information about votaries of Cybele apart from the *Galli* (cf. Lucr. 2.629ff., Ovid, *F.* 4.210ff. for the Curetes and Corybantes), a fragment of Maecenas (6 Morel) *latus horreat flagello, comitum chorus ululet* implies a similar division of activity.

686 molles...uiros Cf. Ovid, *F.* 4.243 *molles...ministri*, also Catull. 63.10 *teneris digitis*, Livy 33.27.2, Mart. 1.96.10, 3.73.4.

imitata The imitation consists in wounding the arm, an action associated with the *Galli*, cf. Prop. 2.22.15f. *cur aliquis sacris laniat sua bracchia cultris | et Phrygis insanos caeditur ad numeros?*, Val. Flacc. 8.239ff., Wissowa, *Religion u. Kultus*[2] 264. Leo's conjecture *comitata* would assign both the beating of breasts and the wounding of arms to the group of *comites*, and is therefore less likely to be right. The distinction between the groups, however, is not complete, since the *Galli* themselves also beat their breasts (cf. Stat. *Th.* 10.171f., Claud. *Eutr.* 1.279f.).

688 turritae...parenti Cybele wears the *turris* either because she is the protector of cities (Lucr. 2.606f.) or because she gave *turres* to the first cities (Ovid, *F.* 4.219f.); for representations in art see Roscher II¹.1670. For the epithet *turrita* cf. Virg. *Aen.* 6.784, Ovid, *Met.* 10.696, Claud. *Rapt.* 3.271; *turrigera* is more common, cf. Varro, *ap.* Aug. *C.D.* 8.24, Virg. *Aen.* 6.785, Prop. 3.17.35, 4.11.52, Ovid, *F.* 4.224, 6.181, 321, Claud. *Rapt.* 1.181. See further J. Perret, *REL* (1935) 322–57 (especially 348–57).

689 rauco...buxo For the Phrygian *tibia* as a standard feature of the Magna Mater's worship cf. Diogenes Atheniensis *apud* Athen. 636, Callimachus fr. 193.34ff. Pfeiffer, Varro *Sat.* 131 Buecheler, Lucr. 2.620, Catull. 63.22, 64.264, Hor. *C.* 3.19.18f., 4.1.22f., Prop. 2.22.16, Tib. 1.4.70, 2.1.86, Ovid, *F.* 4.181, 214, *Ibis* 452, Mart. 11.84.4. The box-wood *tibia* is specified in Virg. *Aen.* 9.619, Ovid, *Pont.* 1.1.45, Val. Flacc. 1.319; see also Nisbet–Hubbard on Hor. *C.* 1.18.13f. For *raucus* compare Lucr. 2.619 *raucisono...cantu*, Catull. 64.264, Prop. 3.10.23. Several writers mention the exciting effect of the instrument (*concita* in this passage), cf. Ovid, *F.* 4.341, Quint. *Inst.* 1.10.33, Juv. 6.314ff., Apul. *Met.* 8.27.

691f. non...modum Cf. Soph. *El.* 231ff., particularly 236 καὶ τί μέτρον κακότατος ἔφυ; The denial of moderation in lamenting losses, however, is conventional, see Nisbet–Hubbard on Hor. *C.* 1.24.1 *quis desiderio sit pudor aut modus...?*

693 sed...infulas? The action is present in Aeschylus (*Ag.* 1264ff.), but Seneca's treatment is closer in spirit to Euripides (*Tro.* 451ff.): ὦ στέφη τοῦ φιλτάτου μοι θεῶν, ἀγάλματ' εὔια, | χαίρετ', ἐκλέλοιφ' ἑορτάς, αἷς πάροιθ' ἠγαλλόμην.

deripis Perhaps imitated by Statius, cf. *Th.* 2.121 *ramos ac uellera fronti | deripit*, 3.566f. *uertice serta | deripit*. A's *diripis* illustrates a common pattern of corruption, cf. 735 below, Ovid, *Am.* 1.5.12, 1.6.8, and the commentators cited by Mulder in his note on Stat. *Th.* 2.121.

694 miseris...putem The thought may be proverbial, cf. Sen. *Contr.* 8 exc. 1 *diligentius di coluntur irati, magis deos miseri quam beati colunt.*

putem Best taken as a polite use of the potential subjunctive, a *Höflichkeitsausdruck* (cf. Kroll, *Glotta* vii (1916) 128ff.) comparable to *uelim*, *malim*, etc. While *putes* in the sense 'one would think' is not uncommon (cf. Ovid, *Met.* 1.242, 3.453, etc., ps.-Sen. *HO* 1744, Juv. 6.41), I have no parallel for *putem* in this construction (it is deliberative in Hor. *Epist.* 1.4.2, Catull. 22.12, ps.-Sen. *HO* 1978). Its use may reflect the conventions of polite debate, cf. Cic. *Brutus* 25 *hoc uero sine ulla dubitatione confirmauerim*, Livy 23.12.10 *respondeam Hamilconi*; see also Fraenkel's note on Aesch. *Ag.* 838 λέγοιμ' ἄν. The expression is probably meant to depict the extreme diffidence with which the chorus reproves Cassandra's violent behaviour; there is no lack of general statements introduced by *puto* or *reor* (cf. *Pha.* 218, 1119, *Pho.* 656,

Oed. 82, *Thy.* 117, *Octauia* 447, 566, 867), which may account for the reading *reor* in A.

696f. nec...habent Cf. *Tro.* 429 *et quas reperiet, ut uelit, clades deus?* The tone of *nec ulla caelites placo prece* is despairing; compare more explicit statements of the futility of prayer, e.g. Eur. (?) *Phoen.* 1749f., Virg. *Aen.* 6.376 *desine fata deum flecti sperare precando*, Sen. *Oed.* 199f., *Pha.* 1242f., *N.Q.* 2.35.2.

698 Fortuna...suas The immunity to misfortune acquired by exhaustion of one's adversary may be compared to Ovid's account of his own situation (*Pont.* 2.7.41f.): *sic ego continuo Fortunae uulneror ictu, | uixque habet in nobis iam noua plaga locum* and to the difficulty encountered by Seneca's Juno in her struggle with Hercules (*HF* 40ff.): *monstra iam desunt mihi | minorque labor est Herculi iussa exequi | quam mihi iubere*; Lucan, too, speaks of Fortuna *tanto lassata periclo* (2.727). The wording of our passage is probably derived from Juno's complaint in Virg. *Aen.* 7.301 *absumptae in Teucros uires caelique marisque.*

699 quae...soror Compare Andromache in *Tro.* 571f. *ubi natus est? ubi Hector? ubi cuncti Phryges? | ubi Priamus? unum quaeris: ego quaero omnia.*

700 tumuli...atque arae For the plural compare *Tro.* 432 *hostes ab imo conditi Dite exeunt* (= Achilles), and for the line cf. *Tro.* 957 *cinis ipse nostrum sanguinem ac tumulus sitit*, 1164 *saeuusque totum sanguinem tumulus bibit* (*bibere* in similar contexts, cf. *HF* 484, *Med.* 778).

701 turba fraterni gregis The phrase *turba gregis* (or *grex turbae*) occurs in other post-Augustan writers, cf. Val. Max. 4.7.7, Silius 11.275, 13.360, but is used here with a specific purpose. In *Tro.* 32 Hecuba addresses her lost children, *et uos meorum liberum magni greges*; it is natural to take the plural as referring to groups of male and female offspring, as seems to have been done by the author of *HO*, who refers to Niobe's *bis...septenos greges* (1849; cf. A. Ker, *CQ* n.s. xii (1962) 51). Here Cassandra is speaking of only one of these *greges*; *turba* stresses the size of the group (fifty in *Il.* 24.495), *grex* the bond of relationship that defines it. For the rhetorical question cf. Eur. (?) *Phoen.* 1688f.; *quid ille* in such a question, cf. *Pha.* 149ff.; *Octauia* 851ff.

702 nempe In reply to a question, *nempe* often indicates that the answer is self-evident or well known, cf. Cic. *Phil.* 10.6 *legiones abductas a Bruto; quas? nempe eas quas ille ab Antonii scelere auertit*, Ovid, *Ars* 1.173, *Tr.* 3.4.23ff. *qui fuit ut tutas agitaret Daedalus alas...? nempe quod hic alte, demissius ille uolebat*, Petr. *Sat.* 115.12, Juv. 8.57, 10.185. In other Senecan passages, *nempe* in a response often brings a pointed modification of the question, cf. *Tro.* 743 *Spiritus genitor facit? – Sed nempe tractus*; cf. *HO* 437 *At Ioue creatum? – Nempe et Alcmena satum.*

miseri senes 'intellige de uilibus senibus quos in Troiae ruinis reliquerant Graeci tanquam inutile pondus' (Gronovius).

705 regimen Phrygum For the personal use of *regimen* cf. *Pho.* 1 *caeci parentis regimen*, also Livy 4.31.5, Val. Max. 1.1.9.

706 fecunda in ignes At first glance, *ignes* suggests an allusion to the famous dream of Hecuba (cf. Pind. *Paean* 8, Eur. *Tro.* 920ff., Virg. *Aen.* 7.319f., 10.704f., Ovid, *Her.* 17.237ff; Jocelyn 206, 214f.). But *fecunda in ignes* cannot mean 'giving birth to a torch'; *fecundus* [*uel sim.*] in is rather 'abundantly fertile in', 'producing quantities of'; cf. Manilius 4.667 *crimina...in poenas fecunda suas* (and the opposite, Sen. *Med.* 956 *sterilis in poenas fui*), 2.557, 4.124, 161, Lucan 9.620 *fertilis in mortes* [*sc. Libycus aer*], Silius 2.498 *fecundum in fraudes* [*sc. humanum genus*]. The phrase, then, does not in the first instance refer to Hecuba's dream but to the meaning of that vision: she is 'fertile in funeral pyres' (*ignes* = *rogos*, cf. 648 above).

706f. fatorum...leges The meaning seems to be 'conditions of existence' (called *iura naturae* in Ovid, *Ars* 2.42); for *leges fatorum* (or *fatales*) cf. Cic. *Tim.* 43 *imposuit commonstrauitque leges fatales ac necessarias* (= νόμους τε τοὺς εἱμαρμένους), Virg. *Aen.* 12.819 *illud...nulla fati quod lege tenetur*, Ovid, *Met.* 3.316, Manilius 2.642, 4.390ff., Sen. *N.Q.* 1 *pr.* 3 *liceat illi* [*sc. deo*] *hodieque decernere et ex lege fatorum aliquid derogare*, 2.38.3.

707f. induit...suas Hecuba's metamorphosis appears as a grotesque climax to Cassandra's sorrows, unexplained by any of the traditional motivations: grief (Pl. *Men.* 714ff., Cic. *Tusc.* 3.63, Tryphiodorus 401f.), rage at Polymestor (Eur. *Hec.* 1265, Ovid, *Met.* 13.558ff.), or death (Ausonius, *Epit.* 25; cf. Roscher 1.ii.1882f.); comparable treatments are found in Juvenal (10.271f.) and Quintus Smyrnaeus (14.347ff.). In form Seneca is clearly dependent on Ovid: *latrauit* recalls *Met.* 13.568f. *rictuque in uerba parato* | *latrauit, conata loqui*, and *circa ruinas... suas* is an adaptation to the context of *Met.* 13.571 *tum quoque Sithonios ululauit maesta per agros*.

induit uultus feros Possibly imitated by Martial 2.41.13f. *uultus indue tu magis seueros* | *quam coniunx Priami nurusque maior.*

709 Troiae...sibi Similarly pointed expressions often occur in political contexts, cf. Plut. *Scip. Apophtheg.* 23 (= *ORF²* p. 132) οὐ γὰρ οἷόν τε τὴν Ῥώμην πεσεῖν Σκιπίωνος ἑστῶτος οὐδὲ ζῆν Σκιπίωνα τῆς Ῥώμης πεσούσης, Cic. *Fam.* 6.2.3 *omnia si interierint, cum superstitem te esse rei publicae ne si liceat quidem uelis*; later they become rhetorical commonplaces, cf. Sen. *Suas.* 6.6 (Arellius Fuscus) *si ad aetatem* [*sc. Ciceronis*] *respicimus, sexaginta supergressus es, nec potes non uideri nimis uixisse qui moreris rei publicae superstes*, 7.9, Sen. *Const.* 2.2, Florus 2.13.51, Rut. Nam. 2.43. The macabre progress from *Troiae* to *sibi* is ineptly imitated by the author of *HO* 198 *sibi Tantalis est facta superstes* (compare as well the smoother progression in Juv. 10.201 *usque adeo grauis uxori natisque sibique*).

710ff. The detached character of the third-person narrative is remarkable (cf. Zwierlein, *Rezitationsdramen* 60); observations of an actor's behaviour in Greek tragedy are regularly directed to him (cf., e.g., Eur. *Andr.* 1076, *Tro.* 749ff., *Hec.* 739ff., *Ba.* 453ff.; for remarks about silences cf. O. P. Taplin, *HSCP* lxxvi (1972) 94ff.). The looser structure of Senecan drama permits the juxtaposition of such narrative elements (here derived from Virgil's description of the Cumaean Sibyl) and more conventionally dramatic material; this dual character betrays itself in the repetition in lines 710ff. and 720ff. of the same progression from fully rational fear of the god's approach to complete possession.

710 pallor Contrast the monochrome *pallor* with Virgil's *non uultus, non color unus* (*Aen.* 6.47), the *flammata facies* of Medea (Sen. *Med.* 387), and Lucan's account of the Pythia (5.214ff.): *stat numquam facies; rubor igneus inficit ora | liuentesque genas; nec, qui solet esse timenti, | terribilis sed pallor inest.*

711 creberque...tremor Another sign of fear: in *Aen.* 6.54f. it is the Trojans who experience a *tremor* at the appearance of the Sibyl (*gelidus Teucris per dura cucurrit | ossa tremor*).

712 stetere...coma Once again, a manifestation of terror and not of possession (material in Pease on Virg. *Aen.* 4.280); the point is made twice, in *horrescit coma* and in the clever, but tasteless, *stetere uittae*. Possessed or ecstatic persons toss the hair, cf. Virg. *Aen.* 6.48 *non comptae mansere comae*, Sen. *Oed.* 230 *incipit Letoa uates spargere horrentes comas*, K. F. Smith on Tib. 2.5.66 (of worshippers of Cybele, cf. Varro, *Sat.* 132 Buecheler, Cat. 63.23, Lucr. 2.631f., Maecenas fr. 6 Morel, Apul. *Met.* 8.27).

713 anhela...fremunt The transition from fear to possession seems to begin here, since *anhelitus* can signify fear (as in Virg. *Aen.* 5.199f., quoted above) or approaching ecstasy, cf. Pl. *Truc.* 600 *traxit ex intimo uentre suspiritum*, Virg. *Aen.* 6.48f. *sed pectus anhelum, | et rabie fera corda tument*, Luc. 5.216f. *nec fessa quiescunt | corda...* (cf. 191 *anhelo...meatu*), Apul. *Met.* 8.27 *unus ex illis bacchatur effusius ac de imis praecordiis anhelitus crebros referens uelut numinis diuino spiritu repletus* eqs.

714f. Cassandra's eyes droop (*nutant lumina*), then are violently rolled upwards (*uersi retro torquentur*) before returning to a fixed stare (*rursus immites rigent*); the phenomenon (διαστροφὴ ὀμμάτων) was observed in ecstatic, epileptic, and other paranormal states (cf. Page on Eur. *Med.* 1174, Dodds on *Ba.* 1123 for medical and tragic parallels). These details do not appear in Virgil's account of the Sibyl, but cf. Lucan 5.211ff. *illa feroces | torquet adhuc oculos totoque uagantia caelo | lumina*, Stat. *Th.* 10.168 *acies huc errat et illuc.*

714 incerta nutant lumina 'Her unsteady eyes droop'; *incerta* because they are governed by no fixed purpose, like the eyes of the curious (Hor. *Epist.* 2.1.188) or the intoxicated (Sen. *Epist.* 83.21; cf. *incertus pes* in Hor. *Epod.* 11.20, Sen. *Epist.* 95.16); for *nutant* compare Stat. *Th.* 1.340f.

iam Somnus auaris | irrepsit curis pronusque ex aethere nutat, 2.687 *nutantque minae et prior ira tepescit*.

715 torquentur So used of a violent shift in the direction of one's glance in Prop. 1.21.3 *quid nostro gemitu turgentia lumina torques?*, Virg. *Aen.* 4.220 *oculosque ad moenia torsit*, Stat. *Ach.* 1.516 *mox igne genas et sanguine torquens*.

rursus...rigent *Rursus* suggests 'they return to a fixed position'; for *oculi rigent* compare Pl. *Men.* 923 *solent tibi umquam oculi duri fieri?*, Sen. *Oed.* 187.

immites The adjective describes the harsh, unblinking stare of the possessed girl; for the phrase *immites oculi* compare Ovid, *Met.* 6.621, Luc. 5.211f. *feroces...oculos*. Bentley's *immoti* deserves consideration; it would, as Professor Brink points out to me, serve as a counterpart to *incerta...lumina* in the previous line (for *immoti rigent* cf. Mart. 5.31.5 *feritas immota riget*, and for *immoti oculi* cf. Virg. *Aen.* 4.331f., Ovid, *Met.* 2.502). It is, however, hard to account for the corruption of *immoti* to *immites*, unless exception was taken to the apparent pleonasm *immoti rigent* and the offending word altered by interpolation.

716f. leuat...celsa An expansion of Virgil's *maiorque uideri (Aen.* 6.49); compare *celso gradu* in 587 above. For the comparative construction with *solito* see Kühner–Stegmann II.480.

717f. reluctantes...fauces The adjective suggests a comparison to horse-taming (see on *impatiens* and *stimulis* below), cf. Virg. *G.* 4.300f. *huic geminae nares et spiritus oris | multa reluctanti obstruitur*, Ovid, *Am.* 3.4.13f. *equum... | ore reluctanti*, Claud. *Ruf.* 2.353.

718 reserare It seems likely that *reserare fauces* is meant to produce a more elevated tone than the more frequent *resoluere fauces* (cf. Ovid, *Met.* 2.282 and cf. *soluere fauces* in Luc. 3.738f.) or *ora soluere*, cf. Ovid, *Met.* 1.181 and often. (Professor Jocelyn suggests that *reserare* may invoke the metaphorical use of *fauces* for gates or doorways, cf. Enn. *Ann.* 86 V², Cic. *Quinct.* 25, Livy 44.31.9.) Two prose passages in which *reserare* is used of parts of the body confirm this suggestion: Livy 40.8.19 *agite conscelerate aures paternas, decernite criminibus mox ferro decreturi: dicite palam quidquid aut ueri potestis aut libet comminisci; reseratae aures sunt, quae posthac secretis alterius ab altero criminibus claudentur*, and Pliny, *Paneg.* 66.5 *at nunc tua dextera tuisque promissis freti et innixi obsaepta diutina seruitute ora reseramus frenatamque tot malis linguam resoluimus*. The effect aimed at may be illustrated by comparing *Hamlet* i.iv.48ff. 'why the sepulchre... | hath ope'd his ponderous and marble jaws | to cast thee up'.

718f. clauso...ore 'She tries unsuccessfully to hold in the words by shutting her mouth'; *male* is here more than a substitute for *non*, since it

305

suggests the failure of efforts at restraint. The usage is common in Ovid, cf. *Am.* 1.14.51 *lacrimas male continet*, [Ovid], *Am.* 3.5.36 *quem tu...uitare uolebas, sed male uitabas, Met.* 4.351, 7.728, 741. *Ad rem* cf. Aesch. *P.V.* 884, Eur. *Hipp.* 882f. τόδε μὲν οὐκέτι στόματος ἐν πύλαις | καθέξω δυσεκπέρατον.

719 maenas A term applied to any woman who acts as though possessed: cf. Ovid, *Her.* 10.47f. (Ariadne), Sen. *Med.* 806, 849 (Medea), Luc. 1.674f. (a *matrona*), Juv. 6.317 (worshippers of the Bona Dea); of Cassandra herself cf. Eur. *Tro.* 173 etc., *El.* 1032, Prop. 3.13.62, Ovid, *Am.* 1.9.37f. In *Med.* 382ff. *maenas* in its Dionysiac sense is applied to Medea in a simile (see Costa *ad loc.*).

impatiens dei Compare Virgil's *at Phoebi nondum patiens* (*Aen.* 6.77), cf. Stat. *Th.* 10.165; for the imagery see Norden *ad loc.*

720ff. quid...rapitis? The echo of Aesch. *Ag.* 1087 ἆ ποῖ ποτ' ἤγαγές με; is coincidental; similar questions are asked by others in states of possession, cf. Hor. *C.* 3.25.1ff. *quo me, Bacche, rapis tui | plenum? quae nemora aut quos agor in specus | uelox mente noua?*, Lucan 1.678f. *quo feror, o Paean? qua me super aethera raptam | constituis terra?* The emphasis here is on Apollo's purpose in forcing Cassandra to prophesy; hence *quid...quid...?*

721 sacra Parnasi iuga The plural alludes to the conventional picture of Parnassus with twin peaks, for which cf. Ovid, *Met.* 1.316 (and Bömer *ad loc.*), 2.221, *Culex* 15f., Sen. *Oed.* 227, Lucan 3.173, 5.72ff. Seneca's *iuga* may be a Virgilian borrowing, cf. *Ecl.* 10.11 *nam neque Parnasi uobis iuga...moram fecere, Aen.* 1.498.

722 iam non sum tua 'sed Agamemnonis' (Farnaby). Cassandra was conventionally reluctant to prophesy, cf. Aesch. *Ag.* 1174ff., Eur. *Tro.* 408ff., *I.A.* 760f., Ennius, *sc.* 43 R² (= 36 J) *me Apollo...inuitam ciet* (with Jocelyn's note); Seneca characteristically renovates the topic by supplying a new motivation.

724 cui nunc uagor uesana? cui bacchor furens? This type of *uariatio* is a Senecan mannerism, cf. *Tro.* 304 *amoris...ac Veneris nouae, Med.* 226 *decus ingens...florem inclitum, Pha.* 100 *non quies nocturna, non altus sopor,* 731 *crinis tractus et lacerae comae*; analogous expressions are found in Ovid (cf., e.g., *Met.* 1.85f., 6.445f., 2.657f. *uetorque | plura loqui, uocisque meae praecluditur usus*) and Lucan (cf. 1.226f. *te, Fortuna, sequor...credidimus fatis,* 5.804f.). Here, however, the variation is more than ornamental: the succession of short phrases and questions in this and the surrounding lines gives a stylised impression of the *sermo praeruptus* which S. elsewhere (*Ira* 1.1.4, 3.4.2) calls characteristic of emotional states; a similar adaptation of style may be seen in *HF* 958–65.

bacchor Similar language in Eur. *Tro.* 408 εἰ μή σ' 'Απόλλων ἐξεβάκχευεν φρένας, *Alexandros* fr. 24 Snell βακχεύει φρένα; on prophetic madness see Nisbet–Hubbard on Hor. *C.* 1.16.5.

726f. fugit...latet Sudden darkness marks the onset of Hercules' madness and hallucinations, cf. *HF* 939ff. *sed quid hoc? medium diem | cinxere tenebrae. Phoebus obscuro meat | sine nube uultu*; cf. also Quintus Smyrnaeus 12.400ff. (Laocoon).

obscurat genas *Genas* here presumably = *oculos*; the meaning of *obscurat* must therefore be 'blinds, covers' instead of the more common 'conceals, prevents from being seen'. The verb appears only here in the tragedies, not at all in Ovid.

728f. gemino...domus The immediate inspiration for Cassandra's double-vision is Virg. *Aen.* 4.469f. *Eumenidum ueluti demens uidet agmina Pentheus | et solem geminum et duplices se ostendere Thebas*, which itself derives from Eur. *Ba.* 918f.; see Pease *ad loc.*

730ff. The suspicions of older scholars concerning this passage need no longer be considered (cf. Housman, *CQ* xvii (1923) 169 for the decisive defence). There is admittedly momentary ambiguity in 730–1, but it is resolved by the pointedly ambivalent phrases which follow. The passage illustrates the predilection of rhetorical poets for forging new connections between familiar myths. Confronted by the awareness that an *agrestis alumnus* (= Aegisthus) will overthrow a royal house, Cassandra rhetorically asks if she can be witnessing the fatal moment in the fall of Troy, Paris' choice of Venus over Pallas and Juno.

730 Idaea cerno nemora? This is the traditional setting for the Judgement, cf. Ovid, *Her.* 16.53 *est locus in mediae nemorosus uallibus Idae*, also *Ars* 1.625, *F.* 6.15 and cf. Virg. *Ecl.* 2.60f. *habitarunt di quoque siluas | Dardaniusque Paris.* In Lucan, however, Caesar's tour of the Troad takes him to a cave *quo iudex sederit antro* (9.971).

The appearance of these words in a Pompeian graffito (above, p. 101) was erroneously used by Moricca and Giomini as an argument for the authenticity of 730–3; at most it proves that the words *Idaea cerno nemora* come from a passage in existence by A.D. 79. It is interesting that the inscription contains the corrupt *Idae* (= IDAI) also found in E.

730f. fatalis...arbiter Compare Hor. *C.* 3.3.19 *fatalis incestusque iudex*, Sen. *Tro.* 65f. *iamdudum sonet | fatalis Ide, iudicis diri domus.*

Poets refer to Paris as both *arbiter* and *iudex* without apparent difference of meaning: for *arbiter* cf. Ovid, *Her.* 16.19, Stat. *Ach.* 1.67, Dracontius, *Rapt. Hel.* 31, 38, 221; for *iudex* cf. Catullus 61.17, Ovid, *F.* 4.121, 6.44, 99, Sen. *Tro.* 931, Petr. *Sat.* 138, Dracontius, *Rapt. Hel.* 39 and see previous note. Similarly, Propertius refers to Minos as an *arbiter* in one passage (3.19.27) and as an associate *iudex* with Aeacus in another (4.11.19ff.). Cicero observes, though perhaps only half-seriously, that the terms were confused even by jurists (*Mur.* 27). It may, therefore, be mere coincidence that Paris does in some respects function as an *arbiter* in the strict sense; for

COMMENTARY 730f.–733

example, that he is appointed by higher authority (Jupiter, cf. Ovid, *Her.* 16.69ff., Apul. *Met.* 10.30) and accepted by the litigants (for the legal position cf. Ulpian in *Dig.* 4.8.3 *neminem praetor coget arbitrium recipere*); Lucian (*Dial. Deorum* 20.1) adds the detail that Paris was chosen because of his expertise in the matter at issue (ἐπειδὴ καλός τε αὐτὸς εἶ καὶ σοφὸς τὰ ἐρωτικά), for which cf. A. H. J. Greenidge, *Legal procedure of Cicero's time* (1901) 62.

sedet A *uox propria* in descriptions of judicial procedure, cf. Cic. *de Or.* 1.168, 2.245, Livy 40.8.7 *sedeo miserrimus iudex inter duos filios*, Prop. 3.19.27 (Minos), 4.11.19 (Aeacus), Ovid, *Pont.* 3.5.23 *sedissem forsitan unus | de centum iudex in tua uerba uiris*, Sen. *HF* 731, *Pha.* 628, ps.-Sen. *HO* 1007, etc.; cf. Colluthus 15. Paris is often seated in artistic depictions of the scene, cf. Roscher III.1.1624–7, Clairmont, *Der Paris-Urteil in der antiken Kunst* (1964) 104f. (n.100) 143.

731 potentes The epithet seems without point; the contrast with *pastor* is produced by *deas*, with which it is juxtaposed. The conjecture of the Etonensis, *petentes*, merits serious consideration, since it adds a further detail to the legal colouring of the scene.

pastor Paris is a herdsman (βουκόλος) in Greek tragic accounts of or allusions to the judgement, cf. Soph. fr. 469 P, Eur. *Andr.* 274ff., *Hec.* 629ff., *Hel.* 23ff., 357ff., *I.A.* 573ff., 1283ff. (cf. T. C. W. Stinton, *Euripides and the judgement of Paris* (1965)), and *pastor*, the Latin equivalent, first appears in an adaptation of Euripides (Accius 610 R² (*Telephus* prologue)); cf. also Cic. *Att.* 1.18.3, Hor. *C.* 1.15.1, Prop. 2.2.13f., Virg. *Aen.* 7.363, ps.-Sen. *Octauia* 774, Stat. *S.* 1.2.43, 214, *Ach.* 1.20f., 2.51, Dracontius, *Or.* 139, 275f.

732 furtiuum genus The phrase has been glossed as 'nati ex furtiuo coitu' (Del Rio), but the words can equally well refer to adulterers (so, rightly, *T.L.L.* VI¹.1644.42), an interpretation which preserves the ambivalent reference to both Paris and Aegisthus; cf. *furtiui uiri* in Ovid, *Pont.* 3.3.56.

733 agrestis iste alumnus An *agrestis alumnus* is one raised *in agris*; the phrase neatly fits both Paris and Aegisthus. Dracontius was straining for the same effect in the parallel passage cited by Housman (*Or.* 469f.): *nonne laborasti, Helenam ne pastor haberet? | ecce tuam nunc pastor habet.* For the legend of Aegisthus' upbringing see Pearson, *Fragments of Sophocles* 1.185ff.

euertet The future is no obstacle to taking the line as referring to both Paris and Aegisthus, since chronology is often disturbed in prophetic speeches: in Ennius (54 R² = 47 J) Cassandra speaks of the judgement of Paris as a past event, though it has not yet taken place (*iudicauit inclitum iudicium inter deas tres aliquis*; cf. Jocelyn 217), and in Aeschylus' *Agamemnon* (1128ff.) Cassandra describes Agamemnon's death in the present before it occurs (on this use of the present cf. Wackernagel, *Vorlesungen über Syntax* 1.161f.).

734 uecors The same word is used to describe the other major Senecan heroines: Medea (123), Phaedra (1155), Jocasta (*Oed.* 1005).

tela For the poetic plural cf. 42 above, Ovid, *Met.* 6.227f. *medioque in pectore fixa | tela gerit*, 15.806, *Her.* 14.76. For *telum = securis* cf. Livy 1.40.7 *elatam securim in caput deicit, relictoque in uulnere telo ambo se foras eiciunt*, Ovid, *Met.* 8.757 *obliquos dum telum librat in ictus* (of Erysicthon).

736 cultu 'appearance', *habitus*, cf. 881 below *cultus hostiles, Tro.* 865f. *cultus...habitusque Graios*, Petr. *Sat.* 89.42 *Phrygioque cultu*. Here S. uses *Lacaena* primarily for the contrast with *Amazonium*; the expression may have been suggested by the use of *Lacaena* to denote Helen (cf., e.g., Hor. *C.* 4.9.16).

737 facies 'apparition'; the word here comes close to the meaning 'sight', *spectaculum* which it has in later poetry and prose, cf. Sil. 9.254 *iuxta terribilis facies*, Stat. *Th.* 1.437, 10.556, 11.744, Tac. *Hist.* 3.83, Plin. *Pan.* 82.3.

738ff. The animal imagery is paralleled in Aeschylus (*Ag.* 1258ff.), where Clytaemestra is called δίπους λέαινα and Agamemnon εὐγενὴς λέων. In Aeschylus, however, the lioness does not directly attack the lion, but instead deceives him with the wolf (συγκοιμωμένη λύκῳ), while Seneca, following the logic of the comparison to its conclusion, depicts the lion overcome by the lioness (*morsus cruentos passus audacis leae*). The action thus contradicts the common belief that animals of the same species refrain from attacking each other; cf. Sen. *Epist.* 95.31, *Clem.* 1.26.4, cf. Hor. *Epod.* 7.11f., Sen. *Contr.* 2.1.10, Pliny, *N.H.* 7.5, Juvenal 12.159ff., *Prou. Gr.* 1.428 Leutsch, de Decker, *Iuuenalis declamans* 151ff. The murder of Agamemnon is thus depicted symbolically as an unnatural act; the emphasis on the lion's normal rank of conqueror (*uictor*) links the image to a central theme of the play (*uictor* of a lion seems unparalleled, but cf. Ovid, *Met.* 7.835 of a hunter, *Ars* 2.406 of Agamemnon).

738 colla sublimis If sound, the words must describe the lion's customary or former state, since they are appropriate to a proud animal at the height of its powers (cf. Enn. *Ann.* 517 V² *celso pectore saepe iubam quassat simul altam*, Virg. *Aen.* 11.496 *emicat arrectisque fremit ceruicibus alte*) but quite out of place if applied to this lion's present condition; compare Hor. *C.* 1.8.3f. *cur apricum | oderit campum patiens pulueris atque solis* (with Nisbet–Hubbard's note), 2.7.11f. *minaces | turpe solum tetigere mento*, Sen. *Pha.* 669 *certa descendi ad preces*. A's *uexatus* is probably a deliberate alteration by a reader who failed to grasp the force of *colla sublimis* and so thought a reference to the lion's mutilation was required.

739 ignobili...leo A lesser animal seems indicated by *ignobilis*, and this makes it impossible that the phrase simply alludes to the lioness under another aspect: a lioness attacking her mate may be *ferox* or *saeua*, but hardly *ignobilis*. A reference to Aegisthus is the only conceivable alternative, though the vagueness of the line and the absence of a distinct animal-shape for the third character in the vision are disturbing. The action of Aegisthus during Agamemnon's murder could aptly be described as *ignobilis* (cf. *Pha.* 492f. *haud illum niger | edaxque liuor dente degeneri petit*), and the sequence of actions in these lines corresponds to that in the later scene: Clytemestra attacks first and strikes the decisive blow (conveyed here by the perfect *passus*), and Aegisthus then abuses his helpless opponent (*iacet...sub dente*).

A second and slighter difficulty concerns the epithet *Marmaricus*; a harmless ornament in another context (e.g. ps.-Sen. *HO* 1057; cf. Virg. *Ecl.* 5.27ff.), its specific character is badly out of place in Cassandra's vision.

The line's combination of obscurity and bombast permits a degree of suspicion regarding its authenticity. It may be observed that lines 738 and 740 cohere without seam, that *uictor ferarum* is a sufficiently clear periphrasis for *leo* in this context, and that deletion of 739 places the responsibility for Agamemnon's death where the last act of the play places it, on Clytemestra. If spurious, the line may have been inserted because of a pedantic insistence that Cassandra's vision should include all the actors who appear in the later scene; if the line is genuine, this pedantry must be laid to Seneca's account.

Marmaricus Not in Augustan poetry (though *Marmaridae* appears in Ovid, *Met.* 5.125); cf. Pliny, *N.H.* 13.127, Lucan 3.293, 6.309; it is, not surprisingly, often found in Silius.

sub dente Cf. Hor. *C.* 4.3.15f. *[caprea] iam lacte depulsum leonem | dente nouo peritura uidit*, Ovid, *F.* 2.800 *parua sub infesto cum iacet agna lupo*, Luc. 1.307f. *quid, si mihi signa iacerent | Marte sub aduerso?*

742 umbrae meorum The phrase may be intended to recall Virg. *Aen.* 2.431 *Iliaci cineres extremaque flamma meorum*, but *meorum* jarringly repeats *e meis* in the preceding line.

742f. te...sepulte Leo attempted to elicit sense from E's corrupt reading *testis uel tota pater | Troia sepulte* by conjecture, with unconvincing results. The parallel with *Tro.* 29f. is decisive support for the A text: *teque rectorem Phrygum | quem Troia toto conditum regno tegit* (adduced by Siegmund). Similar pointed use of *tumulus*, etc., in Prop. 3.7.12 (of a *naufragus*) *nunc tibi pro tumulo Carpathium omne mare est* (cf. *Anth. Pal.* 7.285, 480), Manilius 4.64f. *Priamique in litore truncum | cui nec Troia rogus*, ps.-Sen. *HO* 1826f. *quae tibi sepulcra, nate, quis tumulus sat est? | hic totus orbis* (on this topic cf. Thuc. 2.43.3, *Anth. Pal.* 7.137.3ff., Luc. 8.798, Martial 5.74, *Anth. Lat.* 400–3 Riese), cf. Axelson, *Korruptelenkult* 47f.

743ff. The mutilation of Hector may have been foreseen by Cassandra in a prophetic speech of Euripides' *Alexandros* (cf. Enn. *sc.* 58 R² = 70 J *quid ita cum tuo lacerato corpore miser*), but Seneca's account seems clearly influenced by Virg. *Aen.* 2.270ff., in particular 272–6: *raptatus bigis ut quondam, aterque cruento | puluere perque pedes traiectus lora tumentis. | ei mihi, qualis erat, quantum mutatus ab illo | Hectore qui redit exuuias indutus Achilli, | uel Danaum Phrygios iaculatus puppibus ignis!* As usual, Seneca's adaptation mutes Virgil's expressions of emotion (compare *ei mihi, qualis erat* eqs. with the less involved *non ego antiquum decus | uideo*) and generalises his graphic details (Seneca's *saucios...lacertos* does not convey the specific suggestion in *pedes...tumentis*, for which see Henry *ad loc.* and G. Murray, *Rise of the Greek epic* (1907) 118). The characteristic Senecan allusiveness and compression are evident in the treatment of Hector's remembered exploits: Virgil's two lines are condensed into one by selecting the more picturesque episode, and the reference is reduced from a clause to a descriptive phrase (*calentes... manus*, with *ratibus ambustis* syntactically subordinate) parallel to *antiquum decus.*

745 ratibus ambustis *Ambustis* (conjectured by M. Müller) was quite probably the reading of the E-tradition, to judge from the presence of *bustis* in the garbled readings of E and the Σ-group. The choice between *ambustis* and *exustis* is not obvious, but *ambustis* is the more graphic and the less hackneyed word. For *ambustis* cf. *Culex* 314, for *rates*, etc. *exurere* cf. Virg. *Aen.* 1.39, 5.635, 7.431, 9.115, 10.36.

746f. saucios...lacertos The close parallels with Hector's appearance in the *Aeneid* require these words to refer to Hector's mangling when dragged behind Achilles' chariot; *uinclo graui* is the chain binding Hector to the chariot-rail (cf. Soph. *Ajax* 1028ff.). It is remarkable that Seneca specifies that Hector was dragged by the arms and not the feet.

747 illos 'those well-remembered arms'. Gronovius cites Cic. *Phil.* 2.63 *tu istis faucibus, istis lateribus, ista gladiatoria totius corporis firmitate.* A's *fortes* is a blatant trivialisation.

747f. nimium...Troile Based on another passage of Virgil, *Aen.* 1.474 *infelix puer atque impar congressus Achilli*; perhaps influenced by Virgil's picture of Troilus trying to escape in his chariot, Seneca has replaced the generic *impar* with *nimium cito* (cf. Pearson, *Fragments of Sophocles* II.253).

748f. incertos...nouae A condensation of Virg. *Aen.* 6.494ff.: *incertos...uultus* renders *uix adeo agnouit pauitantem* in 498 (for *incertus* = 'unrecognisable' cf. *T.L.L.* VII.¹880.23ff., Sen. *Med.* 964f. *dispersis uenit | incerta membris*), while *coniugis munus nouae* conveys the essence of the Virgilian narrative *Aen.* 6.511–30, *munus* recalling in particular 526 *scilicet id magnum sperans fore munus amanti.*

750ff. Cassandra's joy is not that of the *sapiens* who faces death *laetus* or *libens* (cf. 589ff. above, 797 below, *Thy.* 367, *Tro.* 945), but is akin to that of the avenger who gladly shares the death of his victim (cf. 202 above, *Thy.* 191, *HO* 344).

750f. iuuat...iuuat Repetition of *iuuat* is an old rhetorical device (cf., e.g., Lucr. 1.927f.) which S. is at times inclined to overwork; in this play it recurs in 435f., 664ff. and 1011. In *Med.* 911ff., however, it contributes to an effective piece of writing: *iuuat, iuuat rapuisse fraternum caput;* | *artus iuuat secuisse et arcano patrem* | *spoliasse sacro, iuuat in exitium senis* | *armasse natas.*

Stygios lacus...regna Ditis The phrasing of the passage recalls Virg. *Aen.* 6.133ff. *si tanta cupido* | *bis Stygios innare lacus, bis nigra uidere* | *Tartara* and 6.269 *domos Ditis uacuas et inania regna.*

752 auidi A common epithet of death or the gods of the dead, cf. Virg. *G.* 3.553 (Tisiphone), Tib. 1.3.4, Sen. *HF* 555, *Oed.* 164, Sil. 14.622 (Mors), *Oed.* 411, Stat. *Th.* 11.410.

753 Phlegethontis Phlegethon is conceived as a river of water, not of fire, and is used by synecdoche for Tartarus. The first licence has no parallel in Seneca (contrast *Pha.* 1227, *Oed.* 164, *Thy.* 73, 1018) but is found twice in Ovid, *Met.* 5.544 *sparsumque caput Phlegethontide lympha*, 15.532 *lacerum foui Phlegethontide corpus in unda*. The second occurs in *Pha.* 848, where *Phlegethonte ab imo = Tartaro ab imo*; cf. also Luxorius (*Anth. Lat.* 301.1 Riese) *Virgo, quam Phlegethon uocat sororem*, R. Greene, *Friar Bacon and Friar Bungay* 2110 'when everie Charmer...calls us from nine-fold trenchèd Phlegethon'; it may have arisen by analogy with the much more common use of *Acheron* for the Underworld, cf. Fraenkel, *Elementi Plautini* 170f., Nisbet–Hubbard on Hor. *C.* 1.3.36. (Note also that in *Med.* 742, if the words *Tartari ripis* are sound, *Tartarus* seems to be used for one of the rivers of the Underworld.)

754 uos, umbrae, precor Cf. Virg. *Aen.* 2.154ff. *uos, aeterni ignes, et non uiolabile uestrum* | *testor numen...uos arae ensesque nefandi,* | *quos fugi, uittaeque deum, quas hostia gessi*, Sen. *Pha.* 604 *uos testor omnes, caelites, hoc quod uolo.*

The *umbrae* thus invoked cannot be the Trojan dead (the *umbrae meorum* of 741), since it is the Trojans on whose behalf hell is to be opened (757); nor, since they have power, can they be the shades in general (as in Virg. *G.* 4.472) or the famous sinners (Sen. *Pha.* 1229 *umbrae nocentes*). They are probably to be identified with the vague but forbidding *Manes* (cf. Virg. *G.* 4.489 *scirent si ignoscere Manes*, Hor. *C.* 1.4.16 and see R. Lattimore, *Themes in Greek and Latin epitaphs* (1962) 93ff.).

755 iurata superis unda, te pariter precor The appeal to Styx is quite out of place here, since the river could hardly grant the request *reserate...terga nigrantis poli* (contrast *Thy.* 665ff., where the allusion to the witnessing function of Styx is harmlessly redundant, and cf. *HO* 1064ff.).

The line is also suspect for the lameness of its style, *te pariter precor* in particular; the deficiency may be clearly seen by comparison of a genuine
Senecan *conuersio*, *HF* 896f.: *tum quisquis comes | fuerit tyranni iacuit et poenae
comes* (other examples in Canter 159). Even the author of *HO* could do
better than this: *testor nitentis flammeam Phoebi rotam | superosque testor* (1022f.).
The combined objections to content and expression seem powerful enough
to authorise deletion. (The omission of the line in P, N, and some *recentiores*
is almost certainly the result of mechanical error or conscious deletion and
not an indication that the line is doubtfully transmitted.)

756 reserate. . . terga nigrantis poli 'Draw back the covering which
conceals the dark pole.' Seneca's Underworld lies beneath the earth, which
must be opened to reveal the upper to the lower realm. A similar conception
is found in *Oed.* 395ff. (395 *reseranda tellus*, 401 where earth = *claustra
Stygis*), *HF* 54 *en retegit Styga*, *Tro.* 198f., cf. Virg. *Aen.* 8.243ff. *non secus ac si
qua penitus ui terra dehiscens | infernas reseret sedes et regna recludat | pallida* (for
recludere see Hor. *C.* 1.24.17 *recludite fata*), Ovid, *Met.* 9.406f., Val. Fl. 3.410.
The identification of the Underworld with the other pole (*nigrantis poli*) is
also a recurrent Senecan idea, cf. *HF* 607, 1107, *Tro.* 354, *Pha.* 835f., cf.
HO 773, 938. On ancient conceptions of the Underworld see generally E.
West, *RE* s.u. 'Unterwelt', ix.a.1.672ff.

The transmitted text is therefore unobjectionable in its depiction of the
relative positions of earth and lower world; the combination *reserate terga
poli*, however, is unusually bold. I have not found a close parallel among
passages in which *tergum* = *superficies*, e.g. of land, Virg. *G.* 1.97, 2.236; of
ice, 3.361; of water (cf. νῶτα θαλάσσης), Ovid, *Pont.* 1.2.82, Sen. *HF* 535,
Luc. 5.565, Stat. *Th.* 5.482; in all of these *tergum* denotes the topmost layer
of a homogeneous substance, not a covering placed over a hollow space.
(Professor Jocelyn points out that Arist. *Thesm.* 1067, in a close citation from
Euripides' *Andromeda*, has νῶτα. . . αἰθέρος; Euripides is indeed fond of periphrases with νῶτα, cf. *El.* 731 of the sky, *I.T.* 46 of earth, but none of these
passages quite matches *terga poli* here.)

The anomaly of expression could be removed by reading *regna* for *terga*;
regna is paralleled in Virg. *Aen.* 8.243ff., which may have influenced
Seneca, as well as by a passage of *HO* (938 *nigrantis regna qui torques poli*)
which might have been influenced by these lines of *Agamemnon*; compare also
Petr. *Sat.* 121.116 *pande, age, terrarum sitientia regna tuarum*. Bentley's *claustra*
fills the needs of the sense equally well (he may have been thinking of *Oed.*
401; cf. also *Oed.* 560, *HO* 1311, Lucan 9.865), but makes the corruption
much harder to explain. I have retained *terga* in the belief that stylistic
uniformity ought not to be imposed by suppressing oddities whose meaning
causes no real problem; the case for *regna*, however, deserves serious
consideration.

757 leuis. . . turba Cf. Hor. *C.* 1.10.18f. *uirgaque leuem coerces | aurea* *turbam* (Nisbet–Hubbard cite Ovid, *Met.* 10.14 *per...leues populos*); κοῦφος is similarly used, cf. Soph. *Ajax* 125f.

758 spectate In Euripides' *Electra* (68off.) Agamemnon and all the Greeks are similarly invited to assist in the murder of Clytaemestra: νῦν πάντα νεκρὸν ἐλθὲ σύμμαχον λαβών, | οἵπερ γε σὺν σοὶ Φρύγας ἀνήλωσαν δορί. Compare also Ovid, *Her.* 12.159f. *laese pater, gaude; Colchi gaudete relicti;* | *inferias umbrae fratris habete mei*, Val. Fl. 4.258, Kyd, *Spanish Tragedy* 1.i.90f. (Revenge) 'here sit we down to see the mystery, | and serve for Chorus in this tragedy' (and compare the ghost of Andrugio in Marston's *II Antonio and Mellida* v.ii.53 'here will I sit, spectator of revenge').

Anliker (n.246) calls attention to the pointed use of such words as *specto*, *spectator*, and *spectaculum* in Seneca's works, and suggests an implausible connection with the contemporary interest in gladiatorial shows. Two specific applications of this imagery may be mentioned. In the first, words such as *spectator* or *spectaculum* suggest a lack of human feeling on the part of the viewer. This usage is not specifically Senecan, cf. Hor. *C.* 1.28.17 *dant alios Furiae toruo spectacula Marti*, Sen. *Tro.* 1078ff. (1087 *tumulo ferus spectator Hectoreo sedet*), 1123ff., *Ira* 2.5.4 *Hannibalem aiunt dixisse, cum fossam sanguine humano plenam uidisset, 'O formosum spectaculum!'*, Luc. 7.797 *ne laeta furens scelerum spectacula perdat*, Val. Fl. 7.190f. *Caucasiis speculatrix Iuno resedit | rupibus*, Stat. *Th.* 11.422f., Claud. *Ruf.* 2.61ff. In the second pointed use of such images, a character wishes to have his actions observed by an appropriate audience: Medea rejoices when Jason appears to see the murder of his children (*Med.* 987f. *derat hoc unum mihi,* | *spectator iste*), and Atreus somewhat reluctantly settles for an audience of one (*Thy.* 893ff. *quod sat est, uideat pater*). This desire to dramatise one's actions may be with some justice termed a Senecan characteristic, although it is to an extent foreshadowed in Ovid (cf. *Her.* 11.9 *ipse necis cuperem nostrae spectator adesset*).

759ff. This is the only certain example in the authentic plays of a change from trimeters to a lyric metre within a speech, but *Pha.* 1199–200 should probably be assigned to Theseus (with E), thus producing a parallel (*pace* Paratore, *SIFC* xxvii–xxviii (1956) 344f.). Two further instances occur in ps.-Seneca: *HO* 1837–939, spoken by Alcmena (E gives 1863–939 to the Chorus, but this is clearly wrong), and *Octauia* 189–221, spoken by the *Nutrix*. In Greek tragedy such a movement may be illustrated from Aesch. *P.V.* 88–127, where the metre changes twice from trimeters to anapaests (cf. Groeneboom *ad loc.* and Wilamowitz, *Interpretationen* 159 for further examples). The monologue of Seneca's Medea in *Med.* 740–848 demonstrates a degree of metrical variety unparalleled outside archaic Latin drama: 740–51 trochaic septenarii, 752–70 trimeters, 771–86 trimeters alternating with dimeters, 787–842 anapaests, 843–8 trimeters.

The Furies whose approach is imagined by Cassandra have little direct connection with the avenging spirits of Aeschylus' *Choephoroe* and *Eumenides* and Euripides' *Orestes*, and are based instead on the picturesque descriptions of earlier Latin poets, in particular that of Virgil's Allecto (*Aen.* 7.445ff.). Here and in *Med.* 958ff. the Furies have no physical reality; only in the prologue of *Thyestes* does the Fury have an objective existence. There is evidence that Republican tragedy presented scenes in which Furies appeared (cf. Cic. *Pis.* 46, *Sex. Rosc.* 67, Jocelyn 192f., Pease on Virg. *Aen.* 4.471), but no indication that Seneca was influenced by them.

759 sorores squalidae The epithet is suggestive; the monstrous appearance of the Greek Erinyes (cf., e.g., Eur. *Or.* 260f. αἱ κυνώπιδες | γοργῶπες) has been replaced with a milder form of unpleasantness.

760 anguinea...uerbera Heinsius' correction of the transmitted *sanguinea* is virtually guaranteed by numerous parallels, cf. Virg. *Aen.* 7.450f. *geminos erexit crinibus anguis | uerberaque insonuit*, Ovid, *Ibis* 157 *uerbera saeua dabunt sonitum nexaeque colubrae*, Sen. *HF* 88 *uiperea saeuae uerbera incutiant manus*, *Med.* 961f., *Thy.* 96f., Val. Fl. 7.149, cf. *HO* 1001ff. The confusion of *anguinea* and *sanguinea* is easy (cf. [Tib.] 3.4.87, *Ilias Latina* 891; *T.L.L.* ii.81.27ff.).

761 semustas faces For the combination cf. Ovid, *F.* 4.167f. *semustamque facem uigilata nocte uiator | ponet*; elsewhere in S. the adjective describes the person or object burned by the torch, cf. *Tro.* 1085, cp. *HO* 1737. In *Thy.* 79f. it is used of those tormented by the Furies: *quisquis immissas faces | semiustus abigis* (cf. Ovid, *Ibis* 632 *membra feras Stygiae semicremata neci*). For the torches of the Furies, cf. Cic. *Sex. Rosc.* 67, Virg. *Aen.* 7.456f., Claud. *Ruf.* 1.48f., Diggle on Eur. *Phaethon* 214f. (p. 143).

762 turgentque pallentes genae The choice between E's *turgent* and A's *ardent* is inseparable from the interpretation of *genae*. If *genae* = 'eyes', *ardent* is supported by *HF* 767 *concauae lucent genae* (*concauae* = 'sunken', cf. Celsus 2.6.1, Suet. *Cal.* 50.1), where A's *lucent* is confirmed by the Virgilian *stant lumina flamma* (*Aen.* 6.300) and Sen. *Pha.* 1040f. *hinc flammam uomunt | oculi, hinc relucent ... insignes nota* (E gives *squalent* for *lucent*); cf. also *Tro.* 1138, *Oed.* 958f. for flashing *genae* = *oculi*. In the present passage, however, *pallentes* strongly suggests that the *genae* are the cheeks: pallor is generally associated with the cheeks (cf. 237, 710 above, *Med.* 859, *Pha.* 832, *HO* 251, 1722), Seneca elsewhere (*Ira* 3.28.7) refers to the pale cheeks of the dead, and Valerius Flaccus (2.205) describes Ira as *atra* with *genis pallentibus*. But if the *genae* are the cheeks, *turgent* is clearly preferable to *ardent*: burning cheeks express shame or emotional distress (cf. *Med.* 858f., *Pha.* 770), while bloated cheeks, suggesting death and corruption, cohere well with the lines that follow.

pallentes For the association of *pallidus*, etc. with death and the dead see Pease on Virg. *Aen.* 4.26, Nisbet–Hubbard on Hor. *C.* 1.4.13.

763 uestis atri funeris 'a garment of mourning', perhaps on the analogy of such phrases as *cena funeris* and *pompa funeris* (cf. *T.L.L.* VI².1603. 66ff.).

764 exesa...ilia The graphic epithet continues the picture of putrefaction suggested by *turgent* in 762, cf. Sen. *Epist.* 114.25 *magis ac magis uires morbus exedit*, ps.-Sen. *HO* 914 *exedit artus uirus...hydrae*, 1226, Stat. *S.* 2.1.155.

765 strepuntque nocturni metus 'things which cause fear by night'; *nocturnus metus* elsewhere denotes an apparition, cf. Val. Max. 1.7 *ext.* 2 *nocturni metus patefacta imagine*, Stat. *Th.* 5.620f. *o dura mei praesagia somni | nocturnique metus*; compare also Horace's *nocturnus occurram furor* (*Epod.* 5.92). There may be expressive hyperbole in *strepunt*, as in Hamlet's citation from an earlier revenge-play, 'the croaking raven doth bellow for revenge' (III.ii.267).

766–8 The owner of the *uastum corpus* described in these lines has thus far resisted identification; among the candidates may be numbered Typhoeus (Trevet), the Giants (Farnaby), Tantalus (Richter), Geryon (Viansino), Tityus (Giardina), and, surprisingly, Priam (Calder, *CP* lxix (1974) 227f.). All the famous sinners, however, must remain incorruptible for the sake of their peculiar torments, and so cannot be called *corrupta longinquo situ*. The lack of detail suggests that the picture may be deliberately anonymous, an item of appropriately gruesome furniture in Cassandra's vision of hell.

769ff. Seneca's picture of Tantalus and Dardanus reacting to the fortunes of their respective descendants may owe something to the words of Ovid's Althaea (*Met.* 8.486ff. *an felix Oeneus nato uictore fruetur, | Thestius orbus erit? melius lugebitis ambo* eqs.); Seneca's use of the idea, however, is unmistakably his own, particularly the grotesque detail of Dardanus dancing a jig of triumph.

770 ad ora ludentes aquas *Ad* here = *circa*, cf. Ovid, *Ibis* 160 *conscia fumabant semper ad ora faces*, Juv. 11.98f. *caput...aselli, | ad quod lasciui ludebant ruris alumni*. For *ludere* of water cf. *HF* 683f. *qualis incertis uagus | Maeander ludit* (cf. Ovid, *Met.* 2.246); in this context, however, the suggestion of deceit is dominant (*ludere* is so used in 17 above, *Pha.* 1232, *Med.* 748).

771 non captat Analogous motifs are applied to the famous sinners in Virg. *G.* 4.484 *atque Ixionii uento rota constitit orbis* (at the sound of Orpheus' lyre, cf. Ovid, *Met.* 10.41ff., ps.-Sen. *HO* 1068ff.), Prop. 4.11.23f. *Sisyphe, mole uaces; taceant Ixionis orbes; | fallax Tantaleus corripiare liquor*, Sen. *Med.* 743ff.

oblitus sitim The rarer accusative with *oblitus* is probably best retained (with E), cf. Virg. *G.* 2.59 *pomaque degenerant sucos oblita priores*.

775ff. As in the case of Hercules (*HF* 1042ff.) and Lucan's anonymous *matrona* (1.674ff.), Cassandra's visions are followed by a fainting-spell. This is described by the chorus in language termed untheatrical by Zwierlein (cf. *GGA* ccxxii (1970) 227 n.77); the formality of 775–7 is indeed far removed from the directness of Arist. *Vesp.* 995f., Naevius, *pall.* 82 R² *caue cadas amabo*, Pl. *Miles* 1330f. *opsecro, tene mulierem, | ne adfligatur, Most.* 324ff., *Trin.* 1091. Some Euripidean scenes demonstrate a comparable immediacy (cf. *Hcld.* 75ff., *Andr.* 1076f.), but others are more formal, cf. *Hcld.* 602ff. ὦ παῖδες, οἰχόμεσθα· λύεται μέλη | λύπη· λάβεσθε κεῖς ἕδραν μ' ἐρείσατε | αὐτοῦ πέπλοισι τοῖσδε κρύψαντες, τέκνα and especially *Tro.* 462ff. Ἑκάβης γεραιᾶς φύλακες, οὐ δεδόρκατε | δέσποιναν ὡς ἄναυδος ἐκτάδην πίτνει; | οὐκ ἀντιλήψεσθ'; ἢ μεθήσετ' ὦ κακαί, | γραῖαν πεσοῦσαν; αἴρετ' εἰς ὀρθὸν δέμας. Two other Senecan fainting-spells are described in terms similar to those used here, *Tro.* 949ff. *at misera luctu mater audito stupet; | labefacta mens succubuit. assurge, alleua | animum et cadentem, misera, firma spiritum* and *Pha.* 585ff. *terrae repente corpus exanimum accidit | et ora morti similis obduxit color. | attolle uultus, dimoue uocis moras.*

776f. qualis...gerens The point of the comparison is the same as that in Ovid, *Met.* 5.122 *procubuit terrae mactati more iuuenci*, but the details of the lines recall Virg. *Aen.* 2.223f. *qualis mugitus, fugit cum saucius aram | taurus et incertam excussit ceruice securim*; the Virgil passage is the probable source of ps.-Sen. *HO* 798ff. *qualis impressa fugax | taurus bipenni uulnus et telum ferens | delubra uasto trepida mugitu replet*). The simile is applied to Cassandra in Aesch. *Ag.* 1296ff., to Agamemnon in *Od.* 4.535, Eur. *El.* 1141ff.; see also 898f., 973ff. below.

incertum (E)/**incisa** (A) The choice between the variants is not obvious, though no hint of difficulty appears in earlier editions, all of which print *incertum*. This produces a clear echo of Virg. *Aen.* 2.223f. Comparison of the supposed model, however, shows an important difference: in Virgil the inconclusive blow allows the beast to flee the altar and shake loose the axe, while in Seneca there is no suggestion that Cassandra's collapse is gradual or marked by resistance. One may contrast Seneca's account of a *uulnus incertum* in *Oed.* 341ff.: *iuuenca ferro semet imposito induit | et uulnere uno cecidit, at taurus duos | perpessus ictus huc et huc dubius ruit | animamque fessus uix reluctantem exprimit*. E's *incertum*, therefore, introduces a detail at variance with the picture presented by the context, while A's *incisa* coheres faultlessly both with the simile and with the actual event to which it is compared. The possibility of interpolation in A must be reckoned with, but the difficulty raised by *incertum* is not so gross as to have provoked alteration. If *incisa* was the original reading, *incertum* may have arisen from a reminiscence of the lines of Virgil cited above, perhaps assisted by their appearance in the margin; the influence of a marginal parallel may be seen in E at 397ff. above, perhaps in A at 340f. The balance of probability thus slightly favours *incisa*.

778f. en...adit Agamemnon's entrance-announcement is surprisingly abrupt and brief, his entrance remarkably lacking in pomp. Aeschylus covers the triumphal progress of Agamemnon's chariot into the theatre with a choral announcement of unusual length (783–809), and Agamemnon's arrival in Accius' *Clytemestra* may have been attended with some pomp, to judge from Cicero's remarks in *Fam.* 7.1.2: *quid enim delectationis habent sescenti muli in 'Clytaemestra' aut in 'Equo Troiano' creterrarum tria milia aut armatura uaria peditus et equitatus in aliqua pugna?* (he is speaking of the gala revivals to celebrate the opening of Pompey's theatre, but a degree of spectacle may have been present in the play's original performance). Seneca's brevity and vagueness may illustrate his lack of interest in a consistent theatrical vision of the action. Hence, too, the difficulty (and, ultimately, the pointlessness) of determining whether 777–81 are spoken by the chorus of Trojans (active since 589) or the Argive chorus (who clearly sing 808ff.): *releuemus artus* demonstrates concern for Cassandra, but *tandem* in the same line suggests a relief at Agamemnon's safe arrival which better suits the Argive group. Seneca may well have neglected to work out the implications for this scene of his introduction of a second chorus.

deos...adit For the reference to the house-gods cf. *Thy.* 263ff. *totis domus | ut fracta tectis crepuit et moti lares | uertere uultum.* In Seneca their existence is never dramatically significant in the manner of the statues of gods outside the houses of Greek tragedy, cf. Soph. *O.T.* 919ff., Eur. *Hipp.* 73ff.

780f. I know of no exact parallel in Greek drama or in Seneca for the 'dumb-show' quality of these lines; the apparent wish to avoid a spoken confrontation between Agamemnon and Clytemestra has been most awkwardly combined with the need to account for her movements at this solemn moment. Lack of concern for traditional theatrical design could not be more clearly manifested, although critics have not been deterred thereby from reconstructing Clytemestra's movements between 583ff. and 780f., cf. Zwierlein, *Rezitationsdramen* 52, Seidensticker 120 n.120). All we are told by the text is that Clytemestra has gone to meet Agamemnon and comes back walking with him; this is easily compatible with a series of movements performed on stage as they are described. Any further conclusions are unsupported and gratuitous. It is to be stressed that the presence or absence of Clytemestra between lines 588 and 770 is irrelevant for the interpretation of these scenes, since there is apparently no place in Senecan drama in which the silent presence of a character has clear dramatic significance (so, rightly, Zwierlein: 'seine Figuren sind da, wenn er sie braucht, und werden als abwesend behandelt, wenn sie ihm lästig sind', p. 56).

tulit | gressus Such expressions are common in Republican drama (cf. Enn. *sc.* 181, 212 R² = 215 J, with Jocelyn's note, Pl. *Men.* 554 *fer pedem, confer gradum, Merc.* 882 *contra pariter fer gradum et confer pedem*);

Seneca may have inherited the usage at second hand from Ovid, who has both *ferre gressus* and *pedem* often. For Senecan examples cf. *Tro.* 518, 616, *Pho.* 120, cf. *HO* 579, 741, and see further Langen on Val. Fl. 2.282.

781 concordi gradu Cf. Pl. *Truc.* 124 *fer contra manum atque pariter gradere,* Ovid, *Met.* 8.692 *ac nostros comitate gradus.*

785 potentis Asiae domina Bentley's *domina* is as certain as a conjecture can be. The genitive which names the larger geographical entity to which a place belongs is a prose construction (cf. Kühner–Gerth II.1 p. 338, Kühner–Stegmann II.1 p. 414 n.3; neither furnishes a specimen of the construction in poetry); a modifier is not applied to the noun in the genitive; the purpose of the genitive is to impart information, a function excluded here ('Troy, in powerful Asia' is merely ludicrous). Troy's primacy in Asia, on the other hand, is well-attested, cf. Virg. *Aen.* 2.554ff. *Pergama tot quondam populis terrisque superbum | regnatorem Asiae,* Sen. *Tro.* 6f.; its fall is virtually synonymous with that of Asia, cf. *Aen.* 3.1f. *postquam res Asiae Priamique euertere gentem | immeritam uisum superis,* Juv. 10.265f. *omnia uidit | euersa et flammis Asiam ferroque cadentem.* The corruption quite probably arose when *Asiae domina* was glossed by *Troia.* (For *potens Asia* cf. Manilius 4.753, Luc. 9.1002.)

786 quid (E)/**cur** (A) The same trivialisation appears in E at *HO* 909.

787 dubia...ceruice Perhaps based on Ovid, *F.* 6.678 *dubii stantque labantque pedes* (the combination with *labo* also in *Her.* 16.178 *in dubio pectora nostra labant*); cf. Luc. 2.204 *procumbunt dubiaque labant ceruice,* Stat. *Th.* 1.98f.

famuli The ever-present servants of Greek tragedy are often found in Latin Republican tragedy and Seneca. As in Greek practice, the word *famuli* (cf. 997 below, *HF* 1053, *inc. inc. fab.* 138 R²) or a periphrasis (cf. *fida famuli turba* 800 below, *fida famularum manus Pha.* 725, *turba famularis Thy.* 901) need not appear: Ulixes (*Tro.* 627ff.) and Theseus (*Pha.* 863) use the simple plural imperative (cf. *HO* 101 *uos...rapite,* Pac. 360 R², Acc. 187 R²), and Oedipus calls on *aliquis* for a firebrand (*Oed.* 862, cf. Acc. 425 R²); compare Aesch. *Septem* 675f. φέρ' ὡς τάχος | κνημῖδας κτλ. At times the convention seems pointless, as when Creon orders his servants to silence Medea just before his dialogue with her (*Med.* 188f.); in *Phaedra,* however, the *famuli* are dramatically important as witnesses of Hippolytus' damning flight (901f. *hi trepidum fuga | uidere famuli concitum celeri pede*). Seneca uses only *famuli,* never *serui*; the only instance of *serua* is *Pha.* 622, where the 'lowly' word is in place dramatically. *Seruus* is noticeably rare in the dignified genres of poetry (Ovid, for example, uses it often in elegiacs, but never in the *Metamorphoses*); cf. however Liv. And. 25 R² (text doubtful), Enn. *pr.* 3.

attollite S. has only one other instance of a quadrisyllable in synaloepha, *Oed.* 823 *propere accersite*; both cases involve excited commands, cf. P. Hahlbrock, *W.S.* N.F. ii (1968) 182.

319

788 refouete gelido latice The realistic detail is found in Greek and Roman comedy (cf. Arist. *Vesp.* 995f., Menander, *Sic.* 364, Pl. *Miles* 1332, *Trin.* 1091, *Truc.* 366) but not elsewhere in extant Greek tragedy or Seneca (the closest approach is in *Pha.* 730f. *hanc maestam prius | recreate*); cf. Eur. *Hec.* 438ff., *Hcld.* 602ff., *Andr.* 1077ff., *Tro.* 462ff. Not only is the specific detail unusual for Seneca, but also the treatment lacks the pedantic thoroughness of other passages describing action (e.g. *Pho.* 467ff., *Pha.* 705ff., *Thy.* 544); the present passage, at least, cannot be called untheatrical (cf. Zwierlein, *Rezitationsdramen* 56ff. and *GGA* ccxxii (1970) 227). The lines were imitated by Mussato (*Ecerinis* 19ff.).

791ff. The technique of the following ἀντιλαβαί, in which one character speaks in terms of the present and the other pointedly replies in terms of the past, is found in other Senecan dialogues: cf. 157f. above, *Med.* 168f. *– Rex est timendus. – Rex meus fuerat pater. | – Non metuis arma? – Sint licet terra edita, Pha.* 244f. *– Aderit maritus. – Nempe Pirithoi comes? | – Aderitque genitor. – Mitis Ariadnae pater*; indeed, by comparison with these and other examples of pointed dialogue, the present passage seems inflated and feeble, hardly justifying the critical attention it has received, cf. Canter 90ff., K. Trabert 41 (who calls it the 'Kernstück' of the play), E. Lefèvre, *Hermes* xciv (1966) 492f., Seidensticker 119ff.; p. 6 above.

793 Iouem precemur pariter In Agamemnon's mouth *pariter* appears to lack point ('let us together pray' is the most likely rendering), which prompted M. Müller to divide the line *Iouem precemur. – Pariter Herceum Iouem?* Müller wished *pariter* to mean 'pariter atque tum cum occidit Priamus', but this seems impossibly strained; it surely would mean 'Hercean Jove *as well*?' (i.e. 'are *you* going to respect Hercean Jove, unlike Pyrrhus?'); the gain in point is not great enough to justify the alteration of the text. Damsté's more drastic conjecture, *pater ut Herceum Iouem?*, produces a neatly phrased reply, but the resemblance to the previous line (*cedidit ante aras pater*) tells against it. Retention of the MS text seems the best course; *pariter* is not itself pointed, but a gesture of benevolence on Agamemnon's part. For the technique of the retort cf. *Thy.* 1102f. *– Piorum praesides testor deos. | – Quin coniugales?*; Cassandra means 'Are you inviting me to pray to Jove the way Priam did'?

794 The transmitted text contains a synaloepha in antilabe, a phenomenon not rare in Greek tragedy or Roman comedy, but in the Senecan corpus found only in two lines of ps.-Seneca, *HO* 892 *– Vitam relinques miseram? – Vt Alciden sequar* and *Octauia* 457 *– Decet timeri Caesarem. – At plus diligi.* In the *HO* passage the rearrangement suggested by Gronovius, *– Vitam relinques? – Miseram, ut Alciden sequar* removes the metrical anomaly and improves the rhetoric of the dialogue, and is surely right. The present line and *Octauia* 457, however, yield less easily to emendation. The deletion of *et* here and *at* in *Octauia* 457 proposed by Richter is clearly unacceptable, and I would have little confidence in the transposition *Priamum et simul*. The anomaly is probably to be accepted in at least these two passages; the presence of proper names in both may be significant.

The sense of the line was accurately expressed by Farnaby: '*Priamum*, te sc. mox interficiendum ut Priamum'.

795 Helena ubi est The MS order, *ubi Helena est*, contains an unparalleled synaloepha between the second and third syllables of a dactyl (Strzelecki 63). Here a simple remedy offers, Schmidt's transposition *Helena ubi*; the metrical flaw was introduced along with the *simplicior ordo*.

The sense is 'wherever there is a Helen, I think it must be Troy'; for the characteristically Senecan awareness of mythic reputation see on 25 above, *Tro.* 861ff. The first half of the line resembles Eur. *Or.* 1508.

976 ne metue On *ne* with the imperative cf. Hofmann–Szantyr 340, adding to the examples cited there Catull. 67.18, Prop. 2.15.49, 2.16.7, Ovid, *Met.* 1.597, Petr. *Sat.* 124.289, *Anth. Lat.* 469 Riese. Seneca uses *ne* twelve times (excluding *HO* 1373 *ne trepida* E: *non trepida* A), *noli(te)* not at all.

libertas adest The response plays upon popular philosophical ideas of freedom and servitude; the liberty referred to is of course that of death, cf. *Tro.* 791 *i, uade liber, liberos Troas uide, Pha.* 139 *fortem facit uicina libertas senem; Prou.* 2.10 (of Cato) *una manu libertati uiam fecit.*

798 tibimet For the non-reflexive use cf. *Pha.* 588 *tuus en, alumna, temet Hippolytus tenet.* Here the enclitic has no point in Agamemnon's statement but finds its explanation in the contrasting *tibi* in the reply.

799 quod non timet 'the fact that he is not afraid', cf. *Pha.* 879f. *Quod sit luendum morte delictum indica. | – Quod uiuo*; *ad rem*, cf. Sen. *Contr.* 1.8.1 '*non timeo*' *inquit. hoc est, cur timeam.*

800 fida famuli turba For the word-order cf. Virg. *G.* 2.146f. *maxima taurus | uictima*, 4.168 *ignauum fucos pecus*, 246 *dirum tineae genus*, Hor. *C.* 1.20.5 *clare Maecenas eques* (further examples in Nisbet–Hubbard *ad loc.*), Sen. *Tro.* 15 *alta muri decora*, Petr. *Sat.* 89.42 *gemina nati pignora*. Two distinct but comparable mannerisms may be noted: the noun may follow the appositive phrase, as in Hor. *C.* 1.3.20 *infamis scopulos Acroceraunia* with the material in Nisbet–Hubbard, or the appositive phrase may itself be enclosed by the noun and its modifier, cf. Virg. *Ecl.* 1.57 *raucae, tua cura, palumbes*, 1.74, 2.3, 7.21, 9.9, *Aen.* 6.842 *geminas, duo fulmina belli, Scipiadas*, Ovid, *Met.* 8.226 *odoratas, pennarum uincula, ceras*, Sen. *Pha.* 305 *perque fraternos, noua regna, fluctus, Anth. Lat.* 400 Riese *fortes, tua pignora, nati* (and Prato *ad loc.*).

fida...turba Cf. *Anth. Lat.* 698.12 Riese (Petronius) *turbaque fida canum.*

excutiat The verb revives the imagery used to describe the onset of Cassandra's prophetic *furor*, cf. 717f. *reluctantes...fauces*, 719 *impatiens dei*; for *excutere* in relation to horses cf. Livy 8.7.10, Pliny, *N.H.* 8.160, Tac. *Ann.* 1.65.

801 retinete...furor Similar concern for Cassandra is shown by the Agamemnon of Aeschylus (950ff.), though without reference to her prophetic frenzy; Ribbeck has interpreted a fragment of Livius Andronicus' *Aegisthus* (8 R² *nemo haece uostrum ruminetur mulieri*) as an order that Cassandra be well treated and not reminded of Troy's fall, but this must remain purely speculative. A closer parallel (though probably not an immediate source) is Eur. *Tro.* 341f. βασίλεια, βακχεύουσαν οὐ λήψῃ κόρην, | μὴ κοῦφον αἴρῃ βῆμ' ἐς 'Αργείων στρατόν;

801 ne quid...peccet 'so that her madness may not cause any offence', i.e. disturb the decorum of sacrifice with ill-omened effect. For the phrase cf. Ovid, *Pont.* 1.7.37f. *nulla potentia uires | praestandi, ne quid peccet amicus, habet,* and for the force of *peccare* ('to offend') cf. *Pont.* 3.9.6 *hoc peccat solum si mea Musa, bene est.*

802ff. The ritual dedication of *spolia* is described in general terms by Ovid, *Her.* 1.25f. *Argolici rediere duces: altaria fumant. | ponitur ad patrios barbara praeda deos.* Seneca specifically names Jupiter and Juno. For the Roman practice of presenting captured arms to Iuppiter Feretrius cf. Ogilvie on Livy 1.10 (pp. 70ff.); the commander's own arms are offered to Iuppiter Redux in Ovid, *Her.* 13.50; in Greek tragedy Zeus is often honoured by τρόπαια on the battlefield (cf., e.g., Soph. *Ant.* 143, Eur. *Her.* 867, *El.* 671). Argive Juno does not often appear in this capacity, but see on 348ff. above.

803 pellisque nubes = αἴθριος; somewhat different is *Pha.* 300 *ipse qui caelum nebulasque ducit* (so A: *fecit* E: *flectit* Koetschau: *cogit* Leo).

806f. pecore uotiuo...fibra The repetition of *pecore uotiuo* in the more specific *supplici fibra* is remarkable in a catalogue of offerings (compare Hor. *C.* 1.19.15f. *turaque | bimi cum patera meri: | mactata ueniet lenior hostia,* 3.23.3f. *si ture placaris et horna | fruge Lares auidaque porca*). The attempt to remove the repetition by taking *fibra* as *chorda lyrae* (so Nelz in *T.L.L.* vi¹.642.72f.) may be dismissed; the only parallel offered is Paulinus of Nola, *C.* 15.26 *surge...cithara et totis intendere fibris.* Emendation has been fruitless: Düring's *uitta* for *fibra* in the unpublished Göttingen material (perhaps inspired by Hor. *C.* 3.14.7ff. *et soror clari ducis et decorae | supplice uitta | uirginum matres iuuenumque nuper | sospitum*) is unacceptable, since *uitta* does not fit a sequence begun by *pecore* and *Arabum...donis.* The only emendation supported by the sense would be the substitution of a word meaning wine for *pecore,* and no plausible candidate has suggested itself.

The text must be presumed sound, and the repetition defended; Seneca splits into separate items what Ovid, his model, had combined, cf. *Met.* 11.247f. *isque deos pelagi uino super aequora fuso | et pecoris fibris et fumo turis adorat,* 13.636f. A comparable structure can be seen in *Pha.* 207f. *non placent suetae dapes, | non tecta sani moris aut uilis cibus,* where *dapes* and *cibus* stand in a relation similar to that of *pecus* and *fibra* (many editors have preferred Jacob Gronovius' *scyphus* for *cibus*, but cf. Axelson, *Korruptelenkult* 55f.); on a larger scale cf. *Pha.* 471ff.: *orbis iacebit squalido turpis situ,* | *uacuum sine ullis classibus stabit mare,* | *alesque caelo derit et siluis fera,* | *solis et aer peruius uentis erit.* (In the present passage repetition is modified, as Professor Sandbach points out to me, by the adjectives *uotiuo* and *supplici,* which suggest that Agamemnon's offerings have two aims.)

807 Arabumque donis = *tus,* cf. Virg. *G.* 1.57, ps.-Sen. *HO* 376, Val. Fl. 6.138.

colam The strong ending is found in the similar exit-lines *HF* 514f. *ego, dum cremandis trabibus accrescit rogus,* | *sacro regentem maria uotiuo colam;* compare also *HF* 898f. *nunc sacra patri uictor et superis feram,* | *caesisque meritas uictimis aras colam.* The extended structure and direct invocation recall the opening of *Medea* (1–12): *Di coniugales tuque genialis tori,* | *Lucina, custos...* | *et tu, profundi saeue dominator maris,* | *...uoce non fausta precor.*

Sacrifice as a motive for an exit occurs several times in Seneca (cf., besides *HF* 514f. and 898f., *Med.* 299f., *Thy.* 545), as in Greek tragedy (cf., e.g., Aesch. *Ag.* 1056ff., Soph. *O.C.* 503, Eur. *Ion* 663ff.).

CHORUS IV (808–866)

This ode is neither programmatic, like the first, nor dramatically important, like the third (and, to a smaller degree, the second); it is, apparently, a mere interlude separating Agamemnon's entry into the palace from Cassandra's report of his death.[1] This function in Aeschylus is served by the Cassandra-scene, but Seneca has placed his version of this episode before Agamemnon's arrival. He is thus able fully to develop the 'Trojan' aspect of the central action, so that even before Agamemnon's entrance his death has been firmly set in a context of retribution for Troy's fall. In the altered dramatic setting there is nothing germane for a chorus, Trojan or Argive, to say; the labours of Hercules (never in any case far from Seneca's mind[2]) provide as apt a topic as any. Seneca creates tenuous connections with the context by presenting the labours as the exploits of another famous Argive (808ff.) and by arranging them to culminate in the first sack of Troy (863ff.); this technique of

---

[1] E. Lefèvre (*Gnomon* xxxvi (1964) 584) exaggerates the dramatic tension between the calm praises of Hercules and the gruesome murder soon to take place inside. The situation does indeed generate opportunities for tension, but S. does not appear to have shaped this ode in order fully to exploit them.

[2] The instances are registered by Runchina (263f.), who plausibly suggests Ovidian influence (cf., e.g., *Her.* 9.85ff., *Met.* 9.182ff.); see also F. Harder, *Festschrift J. Vahlen* (1900) 454.

attaching an essentially irrelevant ode to its surroundings by linking passages at beginning and end can be seen elsewhere.[1]

The ode is sung by the Argive chorus;[2] the chorus of Trojan captives would hardly choose this moment to glorify Hercules and, through him, Argos.

In the treatment of Hercules there is hardly a trace of the Stoic εὐεργέτης[3] or of the long-suffering hero who at length attains the status of a *sapiens*.[4] The only consistent *color* is an emphasis on Hercules' divine position, which is presented as secure and well-established.[5] Any aspect of his myth which would diminish his glory is suppressed or reshaped: the labours are not said to be imposed by Eurystheus, and seem more like triumphs or πράξεις than trials (the clearing of the Augean stables, a mark of *fortitudo* in *HF* 247f., is here simply omitted); the hatred of Juno receives only one oblique reference (809 *iratae...nouercae*) and poses no obstacle to the apotheosis; the prolongation of the night of Hercules' conception, due in most accounts to Jupiter's wish to linger with Alcmena, is here seen as an honour to Hercules himself (814 *cui*, 827 *tibi*) and a tribute to his greatness. Despite this stress on the divine status of Hercules, the ode contains few conventional hymnic elements; perhaps, in light of the extended hymn earlier in the play (310ff.), S. wished to avoid a tediously similar treatment.[6]

809 iratae...nouercae It is natural to see here a reference to Juno's proverbial hatred and persecution of Hercules (cf. *HF* 1200f. *luctus est istic tuus,* | *crimen nouercae, HO* 10, 31, Luc. 4.637f. *numquam saeuae sperare nouercae* | *plus licuit*). Since, however, Hercules has not yet been mentioned, *iratae... nouercae* probably refers to Juno's perennial anger at her consort's affairs with mortal women (perhaps, as Professor Jocelyn suggests, with a specific reference to Niobe, mother of the legendary founder of Argos, cf. Hyg.

---

[1] Cf. Canter 34 n.12. The significance of these linking passages has been overestimated by writers determined to find the ode dramatically relevant, cf. T. Birt, *NJb* xxvii (1911) 359, F. Giancotti, *Saggio sulle tragedie di Seneca* (1953) 117, Anliker 96, 100. On the confusion of superficial cross-references and organic unity see my remarks in *Phoenix* xxvi (1972) 196.
[2] Cf. Zwierlein, *Rezitationsdramen* 84.
[3] Cf. Sen. *Ben.* 1.13.3, ps.-Sen. *HO* 1ff., Epict. *Diss.* 1.6.33ff., 2.26.31; see note on 812 *meruit*.
[4] For the proverbial *aerumnae Herculis* cf. Pl. *Pers.* 2, Mayor on Juv. 10.360f.
[5] There is no sign of the conflict between divine aspirations and human failings which recent studies have seen in *Hercules Furens*, cf. B. Walker and D. Henry, *CP* lx (1965) 11–22, W. H. Owen, *TAPA* xcix (1968) 291–313, Seidensticker 109ff.
[6] The glorification of Hercules resembles that in Eur. *Hcld.* 911ff., but direct influence is not indicated. Seneca's ode may have inspired Boethius, *Cons.* 4 *c.* 7.15ff.

fab. 155); in *Oed.* 418 the phrase is used in reference to Semele (cf. Plato, *Leges* 672 B).

810 semper...alumnos The tone is reminiscent of Homer's βωτιάνειρα Φθίη (*Il.* 1.155), though this epithet is not applied to Argos itself; for countries as *nutrices* see Nisbet–Hubbard on Hor. *C.* 1.22.15f. *Iubae tellus... leonum | arida nutrix.* Semper is a generalisation from the past case of Hercules (actually born in Thebes, though of Argive ancestry) and the present one of Agamemnon.

811 imparem aequasti numerum deorum The precise reference in these words has not been discovered. Only two interpretations seem worth consideration: Del Rio's suggestion that Hercules' marriage to Hebe produced an even number (i.e. the canonical twelve plus two), and Leo's view that Seneca's chorus includes Hercules as the twelfth member of the Olympian canon (*Obs.* 119). Neither interpretation rests on secure parallels; indeed, some Greek evidence suggests that Heracles was added to a group of gods already numbering twelve (cf. Diod. Sic. 4.39.4, Diodorus of Sinope in Kock II.421 = Athenaeus 239D). Leo's suggestion is, however, supported by evidence that Hercules was occasionally included in the worship of the twelve gods (cf. Weinreich in Roscher VI.764–848): so, for example, he appears in a group of twelve gods on the Puteal Albani (Roscher 797–8), in a Pompeian fresco (807) and in provincial reliefs from Marbach and Osterburken (814f.). Seneca has probably combined this association with the worship of the twelve gods with Hercules' late arrival on Olympus to produce the otherwise unknown conclusion that the apotheosis of Hercules raised the number of Olympians to twelve.

812 bis seno...labore The use of *bis* as an elegant periphrasis or to replace metrically inconvenient numbers is common from Virgil onwards; for *bis sex* or *bis seni* cf. Enn. *Ann.* 323 V², Virg. *Ecl.* 1.43, *Aen.* 1.393, Prop. 2.20.7, Ovid, *Met.* 8.243, *F.* 1.28, Sen. *Tro.* 386, *Oed.* 251 (the singular *bis seno*, however, is apparently a novelty, cf. B. Löfstedt, *Eranos* lvi (1958) 196). Greek does not require circumlocution, cf. Theoc. 24.171 χαῖρε δυωδεκάμοχθε, 24.82, but on occasion uses it, as in Call. *Aitia* I fr. 23.19f. Pf. χαῖρε βαρυσκίπων, ἐπίτακτα μὲν ἑξάκι δοιά | ἐκ δ' αὐταγρεσίης πολλάκι πολλὰ καμών.

meruit A passing reference to the theme of Hercules as εὐεργέτης (on which cf. Gruppe, *RE* Suppl. III.1007–15, Nisbet–Hubbard on Hor. *C.* 1.12.25, Jocelyn, *YCS* xxiii (1973) 85 n.188); cf. Cic. *Off.* 3.25, Ovid, *Ars* 2.217f. *ille, fatigata praebendo monstra nouerca, | qui meruit caelum, Met.* 15.39, Manilius 1.784, Sen. *Suas.* 1.1 *intra has terras caelum Hercules meruit*, 2.5, ps.-Sen. *HO* 97, *Octauia* 504f. In Sen. *Epist.* 93.10 the *sapiens* makes a similar claim: *merui quidem admitti* [*sc. ad deos*].

813 adlegi An official term whose transferred meaning appears first here (cf. M. Coffey, *JRS* xlviii (1958) 226); significantly (in view of 811), *adlego* is used of elections held or appointments made to fill a vacancy or to bring a depleted body up to full strength, cf. Vell. Pat. 2.89.3 *imperium magistratuum ad pristinum redactum modum, tantummodo octo praetoribus adlecti duo*, Suet. *Iul.* 41 *senatum suppleuit, patricios adlegit*, Festus 254 Müller *P. Valerius cos. propter inopiam patriciorum ex plebe adlegit in numerum senatorum C et LX et IIII ut expleret numerum senatorum trecentorum*. Other legal terms are also used of Hercules' divine status, cf. Cic. *N.D.* 3.39 *quasi nouos et adscripticios ciues in caelum receptos*, Diod. Sic. 4.39.4, Lucian, *Iup. Trag.* 21; compare Prudentius on the reception of St Laurence into heaven (*Perist.* 2.553f.): *illic inenarrabili | adlectus urbi municeps*.

adlegi caelo The simple dative is less common than *in* or *inter*, but inscriptions furnish several examples, cf. *CIL* v.5738 *allect. eidem coll(egio)*, VIII.937, x.3676, XI.5697, *CE* 411 Buecheler; cf. also Prud. *Perist.* 2.554 (quoted above).

814 cui The lengthened night is here a mark of Hercules' greatness, not the result of Alcmena's attractions (as in Prop. 2.22.25, Ovid, *Am.* 1.13.45f.); for this *color* cf. Ovid, *Her.* 9.9f. [Jupiter] *cui nox (sic creditur) una | non tanti, ut tantus conciperere, fuit* (Housman's conjecture, *breuis cui nox, si creditur, una | luctanti*...does not alter the relevant point), Sen. *HF* 23f. *pariterque natus astra promissa occupet | in cuius ortus mundus impendit diem*, ps.-Sen. *HO* 1864ff. *plangite natum cui concepto | lux una perit noctesque duas | contulit Eos* (and cp. 1696, where Leo's *cui* may be right), Lucian, *Dial. Deorum* 10.1, Aelius Aristides, *Or.* 40.2 Keil.

815 geminauit horas The most popular form of the story, and the one denounced by Seneca in *B.V.* 16.5 *poetarum furor... quibus uisus est Iuppiter uoluptate concubitus delenitus duplicasse noctem*; in a popular variant, the night is tripled, cf. Lycophron, *Alex.* 33, ps.-Apollod. *Bibl.* 2.4.8, Diod. Sic. 4.9.2, Lucian, *Dial. Deorum* 10.1, Aelius Arist. *Or.* 40.2 Keil, schol. Hom. *Il.* 14.323, Stat. *Th.* 6.289, 12.300f.

818 tuas... bigas The two-horsed chariot is the traditional vehicle of the moon-goddess, cf. Eur. *Ion* 1150f., Enn. *sc.* 96 R² = 97 J (with Jocelyn's note), Sen. *Pha.* 312 *nocturnae bigae Lunae*, Manilius 5.3, Luc. 1.77f., Val. Fl. 2.295, Stat. *Th.* 12.297; cf. Virg. *Aen.* 5.721 (of *Nox*).

Jupiter's order to the moon-goddess is recalled by Juno in Stat. *Th.* 12.299ff.: *da mihi poscenti munus breue, Cynthia, si quis | est Iunonis honos; certe Iouis improba iussu | ter noctem Herculeam – ueteres sed mitto querelas.*

pallida The following lines make it clear that the night was allowed to reach its normal limit before being prolonged; *pallida* better suits the moon just before dawn. For the variants *pallida/candida* cf. Ovid, *Met.* 6.576.

819ff. The sun and moon have received direct orders from Jupiter to slow their progress (for this see also *HF* 25f. *tardusque Eoo Phoebus effulsit* *mari | retinere mersum iussus Oceano iubar*, cf. *HO* 150); Seneca now turns to two celestial figures who have not been forewarned of the altered timetable, and who attempt to go about their business as though this were a normal day. The passage has a droll plausibility reminiscent of Ovid (note a possible parallel in *Met.* 2.208f. *inferiusque suis fraternos currere Luna | admiratur equos*).

819 rettulit pedem Usually interpreted in the sense 'retrace its path'; the emphasis on surprise in *seque mirata est | Hesperum dici*, however, may suggest the other sense of *referre pedem*, 'to recoil, draw back', cf. Ovid, *F.* 2.341f. *ut saepe uiator | turbatus uiso rettulit angue pedem*, 502. Venus arrived in time (as she thought) to be greeted as Lucifer and was thus surprised to be saluted as Hesperus. The point depends on the common poetic fiction that Venus can be seen as Hesperus in the evening and as Lucifer on the following morning, for which cf. Meleager, *A.P.* 12.114 (= Gow–Page[I] 4390ff.), Cinna fr. 6 Morel, Catull. 62.35, Manilius 1.177f., Sen. *Med.* 71ff., *Pha.* 749ff.; the belief had already been applied to the night of Hercules' conception by Meleager (*A.P.* 5.172 = Gow–Page[I] 4136ff.): εἴθε πάλιν στρέψας ταχινὸν δρόμον Ἕσπερος εἴης, | ὦ γλυκὺ φῶς βάλλων εἰς ἐμὲ πικρότατον. | ἤδη γὰρ καὶ πρόσθεν ἐπ᾽ Ἀλκμήνην Διὸς ἦλθες | ἀντίος· οὐκ ἀδαής ἐσσι παλινδρομίης (the reference to παλινδρομίη shows that the star's normal course is from Hesperus in the evening to Lucifer in the morning).

821ff. A witty and successful exploitation of the conventional description of Aurora leaving the chamber of Tithonus, cf. *Iliad* 11.1, Virg. *G.* 1.447 *Tithoni croceum linquens Aurora cubile*, etc.

821f. mouit ad solitas uices | caput 'She awoke in time for the customary change of night to day'; for *uices* cf. *Oed.* 689 *nec ulla uicibus surgit alternis dies*, *Tro.* 1141.

823 relabens Similarly used by Ovid (*Met.* 11.619f.) of Somnus trying to awake: *uix oculos tollens, iterumque iterumque relabens | summaque percutiens nutanti pectora mento*.

imposuit seni | collum marito For the expression *collum marito imponere* cf. Prop. 3.13.22 *imponuntque suis ora perusta uiris*, Ovid, *Met.* 6.291 *imposito fratri moribunda relanguit ore*; for the image conveyed compare Ovid, *Her.* 13.105f. *nox grata puellis | quarum suppositus colla lacertus habet*. The singular *collum* is much rarer in Seneca than the plural, but a clear instance of *collum* (acc.) occurs in 366 above. A's text *imposuit senis | umero mariti* requires *caput* to be understood as the object of *imposuit* and also fails to scan without a change in colometry (or emendation of *senis* to *senili*, cf. *Tro.* 50, *HF* 1312); for this reason I have retained E's text, although the clausula *umero mariti* is appropriate (cf. *geminosque fratres* 837) and the detail in *umero* is apt for this realistic vignette. The interpolation in A (if it is indeed such) is unusually bold and successful.

824 sensit ortus, sensit occasus Poetry often uses *sentire* as a rhetorical variation on simple narrative, particularly in hymnic contexts (as here and in 829 below); cf. *Oed.* 471 *regna securigeri Bacchum sensere Lycurgi, HO* 1f. *sator deorum, cuius excussum manu | utraeque Phoebi sentiunt fulmen domus,* and also (e.g.) Hor. *C.* 4.6.1ff., Ovid, *Am.* 1.9.39, 2.9.11, *F.* 2.135, 4.17, *Met.* 6.119f., 12.112, 595, 13.504, 15.823; compare γνώσεται *Iliad* 18.268ff., *nosces* Hor. *C.* 1.15.27.

ortus…occasus A common phrase = *totus orbis terrarum,* cf. Ovid, *Pont.* 1.4.29f., Sen. *HF* 870, 1330, but literally and pointedly true in the case of Hercules.

825 Herculem nasci *Nasci* here is 'to be conceived' and not 'to be born': compare ps.-Sen. *HO* 1500f. *siue nascente Hercule | nox illa certa est* with 1864f. *cui concepto | lux una perit;* other expressions in *HF* 24 (*in cuius ortus*), 1158 (*cuius in fetu*).

827 concitatus…mundus = *mobile caelum.* For *mundus = caelum* see Nisbet–Hubbard on Hor. *C.* 1.12.15 (adding E. Fraenkel, *RFIC* xcvi (1968) 176); in Seneca, *HF* 125f., *Pha.* 332f., 961 *qui sparsa cito sidera mundo…capis, Oed.* 1028 *ipse mundum concitans diuum sator;* the last two passages illustrate the use of words like *concito* and *citus* of the heavens (see also Ovid, *Met.* 2.75f. *ne te citus auferat axis,* Luc. 6.463 *torpuit et praeceps…mundus,* 500 *praecipiti polo*). It was Stoic teaching that the aether, the lightest of the elements, was the fastest-moving, cf. *SVF* ii.642, Cic. *N.D.* 2.42 with Pease's note; Seneca uses *concito* several times in the *Naturales Quaestiones,* always of the lighter elements, cf. 2.6.3, 7.4.1 (*aer*), 2.6.4., 6.18.3, 6.20.4, 6.21.1 (*spiritus*), 2.15 (*ignis*).

828 subiture caelum 'destined to scale heaven', cf. *HO* 1975 *me iam decet subire caelestem plagam* (spoken from halfway), Sen. *Epist.* 31.11 *subsilire in caelum ex angulo licet* (for the *sapiens*); note also Theoc. 24.80 (ἀμβαίνειν).

829f. Nemeaeus…leo The account of the lion's death closely parallels that given in *HF* 224f. *pressus lacertis gemuit Herculeis leo* and *Oed.* 40 *leonis terga Nemeaei premens;* note *HO* 1235f. *hisne ego lacertis colla Nemeaei mali | elisa pressi* (derived from Ovid, *Met.* 9.197 *his elisa iacet moles Nemeaea lacertis*). In keeping with the essentially simple and straightforward character of this narrative, S. eschews such periphrases for *leo* as *malum* (cf. *HO* 1235, 1665), *pestis* (Ovid, *Her.* 9.61, *HO* 1193), *moles* (Ovid, *Met.* 9.197) and *monstrum* (Martial 4.57.6).

830 fulmineus As applied to animals, men, and weapons by Virgil and Ovid, *fulmineus* suggests several characteristics of a *fulmen:* Virgil's *fulmineus ensis* (*Aen.* 4.580, 9.442) or *fulmineus Mnestheus* (*Aen.* 9.812) suggest speed, destructive power, and also the flash of steel or armour; compare Ovid, *Met.* 1.305 *nec uires fulminis apro* [*sc. prosunt*], 10.550 *fulmen habent acres in aduncis dentibus apri, F.* 2.232 *fulmineo ore* (also *Ars* 2.374), all of which suggest the flashing of the teeth, their impact, and their destructive power (perhaps, as well, the sound of the animal's roar and the heat attributed by some writers to the teeth of an enraged boar, cf. Xen. *Cyn.* 10.17, Pollux 5.79f. Bekker; this is apparently the primary force of *fulmen* in Ovid, *Met.* 8.289 *fulmen ab ore uenit, frondes adflatibus ardent,* cf. Val. Fl. 7.582, Quintus Smyrn. 6.237).

831 ceruaque Parrhasis Here the story is barely touched on. The fuller accounts in *HF* 222ff. and *HO* 1238f. mention the golden horns known from Greek sources (cf. Pind. *Ol.* 3.26ff., Eur. *Her.* 375ff.).

Parrhasis This form of the adjective appears only here in Seneca, four times in Ovid (*Her.* 18.152, *F.* 4.577, *Met.* 2.460, *Tr.* 1.3.48).

832 Arcadii populator agri A variation on Ovid, *Met.* 9.192 *Arcadiae uastator aper*; cf. *HF* 228f., *HO* 890 (*Arcadiae nefas*), 1536f., 1888. The only other appearance of *populator* in Seneca is *Tro.* 26, applied to the Greeks at Troy; it is used of a boar by Martial (7.27.1) and of a fisherman by Claudian (*Ruf.* 2.378 *aequoreus populator*). On nouns in *-tor* cf. Brink on Hor. *A.P.* 163.

833f. gemuitque...arua A more suggestive treatment than the bare catalogue-entry in *HF* 230 *taurumque centum non leuem populis metum* (imitated in *HO* 27); *gemuit* continues a succession of graphic verbs (*sensit*; to come are *domuit, uetuitque, fregit*) and *linquens* alludes to the bull's conveyance to Greece (cf. ps.-Apollod. *Bibl.* 2.5.7, Pausanias 1.27.9, Diod. Sic. 4.13.4, Servius Auctus on Virg. *Aen.* 8.294).

835f. morte...nasci Seneca's favourite labour, described or alluded to in *HF* 241f., 529, 780, 1195, *Med.* 701f. (and cf. *HO* 19, 918ff., 1193f., 1534f., 1813). The account here is more imaginative and effective than the others: *morte fecundum* is a pointed way of stating what is more straight-forwardly put in *HF* 781 *fecunda...capita* and *Med.* 702 *caede se reparans sua* (cf. Ovid, *Her.* 9.96 *serpens fertilis*), and the solemn generality in *uetuitque* (*noua colla*) *collo pereunte nasci* (clearly imitated by Martial 9.101.9 *fecundum uetuit reparari mortibus hydram*) is missing in *HF* 241f. *saeua Lernae monstra... non igne demum uicit et docuit mori?*

837 geminosque fratres The use of *geminus* in the sense *trigeminus* appears unparalleled; the passages cited by *T.L.L.* VI².1741.18ff. are not relevant, Hor. *C.* 4.7.5 *Gratia cum Nymphis geminisque sororibus, CE* 1505 C 43. (Ovid, *Met.* 4.774 is ambiguous, since the Graeae were variously described as two or three.) In our passage, as Professor Brink points out to me, the sense of *geminus* is clarified by the following *tria monstra natos*.

839 insultans The graphic detail may have been suggested by Virg. *Aen.* 6.570f. *sontis ultrix accincta flagello | Tisiphone quatit insultans.*

839a duxitque ad ortus Hesperium pecus The feat is expressed in opposite terms in *HF* 233 *acta est praeda ab occasu ultimo, Apocol.* 7.2.11f. *unde* *ab Hesperio mari* | *Inachiam ad urbem nobile aduexi pecus.* For *ad ortus* = 'toward the east' cf. Ovid, *Met.* 14.386 *tum bis ad occasum, bis se conuertit ad ortus.*

840 triformis Cf. *HF* 232 *tergemini...regis, Apocol.* 7.2.10f.

841ff. For the mares of Diomedes cf. *HF* 226f. *quid stabula memorem dira Bistonii gregis* | *suisque regem pabulum armentis datum,* cf. *HO* 20 *cruore pingues hospitum fregi greges* (based on Ovid, *Met.* 9.194f. *Thracis equos humano sanguine pingues* | *plenaque corporibus laceris praesepia uidi*), 1538f.; note also Eur. *Her.* 381ff. In the words *quem non Strymonii gramine fluminis...pauit tyrannus* there may be an echo of Ovid, *Her.* 9.68 *efferus humana qui dape pauit equas,* a passage also recalled by Claudian, *Rapt.* 2 *pr.* 11f. *diraque sanguinei uertit praesepia regis* | *et Diomedeos gramine pauit equos.* The cruelty of Diomedes offered a fixed point by which even greater cruelty might be measured, cf. *Tro.* 1108f. *nec parua gregibus membra Diomedes suis* | *epulanda posuit,* Claud. *Ruf.* 1.254 *o mites Diomedis equi!*

841ff. Threicium...Strymonii...Hebriue The Thracian colouring is applied with a lavish hand, as in Ovid, *Met.* 2.257 *fors eadem Ismarios Hebrum cum Strymone siccat.*

843 Hebriue ripis Hebrus here lacks its customary ice and cold (cf. Alcaeus 48 L–P Ἔβρε, κάλλιστος ποτάμων, Bacchylides 15.4 ἀνθεμόεντι Ἕβρῳ); for its traditional attributes cf. Nisbet–Hubbard on Hor. *C.* 1.25.20, and Virg. *Ecl.* 10.65, *Aen.* 12.331, Hor. *C.* 3.25.10f.; so also in *HO* 1894ff.

844 stabulis For *stabulum* as the operative word in allusions to the story, cf. *HF* 226 *quid stabula memorem...?*, Lucan 2.163f. *scelerum non Thracia tantum* | *uidit Bistonii stabulis pendere tyranni.*

847 uidit In attempting to maintain the dignified tone of the ode in dealing with this delicate labour Seneca falls into a faintly ludicrous compromise between the indirectness of *HF* 245f. *non uicit illum caelibis semper tori* | *regina* (and cf. *HO* 21 *hostique traxi spolia Thermodontiae*) and the extended narrative of *HF* 542ff. *illic quae uiduis gentibus imperat,* | *aurato religans ilia balteo,* | *detraxit spolium nobile corpori* | *et peltam et niuei uincula pectoris,* | *uictorem posito suspiciens genu.* The combination here of brevity and graphic language (*uidit, pectore e medio*) is unfortunate; compare Claud. *Rapt.* 2 *pr.* 37 *soluis Amazonios cinctus.* The comic possibilities of the encounter with Hippolyta seem to have been exploited by Epicharmus (Diels–Kranz 23 A); cf. also Pl. *Men.* 200f. *meo quidem animo ab Hippolyta subcingulum* | *Hercules haud aeque magno umquam apstulit periculo.*

849ff. sagittis...caelo S. does not choose to make as much of this episode here as in *HF* 243f. *solitasque pinnis condere obductis diem* | *petit ab ipsis nubibus Stymphalidas.* The treatments in *HO* range from the perfunctory (17 *Stymphalis icta est*) to the overblown (1236f. *tensus hac arcus manu* | *astris ab ipsis detulit Stymphalidas?* (compare Martial 9.101.7 *Stymphalidas astris* | *abstulit*), 1889f.).

852ff. Senecan accounts of the theft of the apples generally give pride of place to Hercules' dealings with their guardian; this is the only account that devotes more than glancing attention to the prize itself. The emphasis on the snake's watchfulness (*nescius somni* 856) and the detail that it hears the clatter of the golden fruit as Hercules escapes make it clear that Hercules does not kill the snake (as in Eur. *Her.* 398ff., Lucr. 5.37, Hyginus, *fab.* 30, *HO* 18 *sparsit peremptus aureum serpens nemus*) or put it to sleep with drugs (as in *HF* 529ff. *serpentis resecet colla ferocia, | deceptis referat mala sororibus, | cum somno dederit peruigiles genas | pomis diuitibus praepositus draco*), but instead simply escapes its notice until it is too late for the snake to resist (cf. *Pho.* 316f. *seque serpenti offeret, | quae saeua furto nemoris Herculeo furit*).

854 fugitque in auras 'sprang back into the air' (i.e. after being plucked by Hercules); for *leuiore ramo* cf. Lucan 9.358 *Hesperidum pauper spoliatis frondibus hortus* (in which *pauper* may parallel *nemus...uacuum metallo* in 857f.).

855 crepitante lamna *Crepitare* describes the sound made by the rustling of the golden leaves of the tree. S. is probably thinking of Virg. *Aen.* 6.209 *crepitabat brattea uento* (cf. also Ovid, *Met.* 10.647f. *medio nitet arbor in aruo | fulua comam fuluo ramis crepitantibus auro*); cf. Martial 9.22.6 *ut crepet in nostris aurea lamna toris*. The corruption of the uncommon *lamna* into *flamma* may have been aided by the use of *crepito* with flames (cf. Virg. *G.* 1.85 *crepitantibus...flammis, Aen.* 7.74 *flamma crepitante*).

856 frigidus custos S. avoids the explicit word (*serpens*) by mentioning the coldness characteristic of snakes (cf. Theognis 602, Theoc. 15.58, Virg. *Ecl.* 3.93, 8.71, schol. Nic. *Ther.* 291). This snake is also mentioned in Prop. 2.24.26, Ovid, *Met.* 9.190 and Lucan 9.397; for snakes as treasure-guardians see also Cic. *Phil.* 13.12, Pliny, *N.H.* 16.234, Phaedrus 4.20.3, Macrob. *Sat.* 1.20.3.

nescius somni A conventional attribute of such guardians (Wagner's sleepy Fafner is apparently exceptional), cf. Ovid, *Her.* 6.13 *peruigilem... draconem*, 12.49 *lumina custodis succumbere nescia somno, Met.* 9.190 *pomaque ab insomni concustodita dracone*, Lucan 9.397 *insopiti tutela draconis*, cf. Val. Fl. 4.367 *inscius somni* (of Argus).

857 [omne] M. Müller's deletion of *omne* is to be accepted (for the metrical consequences, see below, pp. 380f.); *omne* is otiose and disturbs the careful balance of *nemus...uacuum* and *plenus Alcides*; it is perhaps to be explained as dittography of *somni* directly above.

857f. fuluo...metallo Periphrases of this sort are popular with poets from the time of Seneca onwards (Ovid does not so modify *metallum*), cf. Lucan 9.364 *robora...rutilo curuata metallo*, Val. Fl. 5.230 *ardenti...metallo*, Silius 8.480, Mart. 8.50.5, 9.61.3, Stat. *Th.* 1.144 (and see Heuvel *ad loc.*),

Lactantius, *Phoen.* 131, Prud. *contra Symm.* 2.838, Claud. *Rapt.* 2.291, *Epith.* 56f.

859ff. The catabasis of Heracles was a popular subject in early Greek poetry, cf. Stesichorus 206 *PMG*, Arist. *Frogs* 108ff., 467ff., schol. *Il.* 21.194, P. Oxy. 2622 (on which cf. H. Lloyd-Jones, *Maia* xix (1967) 206–29), and the raising of Cerberus often appears in the climactic final position in catalogues of the labours (so, apparently, in a long hexameter account by Euphorion, edited with bibliography in Page, *GLP* 492; also in ps.-Apollod. *Bibl.* 2.5.12). In Seneca's *HF* the raising of the dog is narrated at length by Theseus (803ff.). The poet of the *HO*, on the other hand, gives no special status to this labour (cf. 23f., 1244f.).

86of. tacuit...ore A pointed reversal of such expressions as *tria Cerberus extulit ora | et tres latratus semel [simul?] edidit* (Ovid, *Met.* 4.450f.) and *fragor | per ora missus terna* (*HF* 795f.).

862 lucis ignotae metuens colorem The narrowing of focus to a single significant point in the exploit – the beast's unnatural silence at the light of the upper world – compensates for the rather bland language in which the scene is described. The material is handled at greater length and with more detail in the narrative of *HF* (813ff.).

The detail on which the passage is based may ultimately derive from Virg. *Aen.* 8.243ff. *non secus ac si...terra dehiscens | infernas reseret sedes... trepidant immisso lumine manes*, though the form in which it appears here is probably indebted to Ovid, *F.* 4.449f. *namque diurnum | lumen inadsueti uix patiuntur equi [sc. Ditis]*; compare *HF* 652 (Theseus) *torpet acies luminum | hebetesque uisus uix diem insuetum ferunt* and *Pha.* 837 (Theseus again) *uix cupitum sufferunt oculi diem.*

863 te duce 'with you as commander'; compare the use of the phrase of Pollio by Virgil (*Ecl.* 4.13), of Caesar's heir by Horace (*C.* 1.2.52), of Vespasian by Valerius Flaccus (1.19).

864 Dardanidae The correction of the transmitted *Dardaniae* is commended on grounds of fact (Hercules' attack was directed against Laomedon) and style: the generic term for the Trojan royal house would be *domus Dardania*, as in 223 above and *Tro.* 871 (note also *domus Herculea* in *HF* 351, 631; *domus Pelopea* in 165 above, *Thy.* 22). In this context 'the house of Laomedon' must be interpreted as referring as well to his descendants, as *domus Pelopis* in Hor. *C.* 1.6.8 or *Assaraci domus* in Virg. *Aen.* 1.284.

864a arcus iterum timendos I.e. when used by Philoctetes, cf. Soph. *Phil.* 1437 τὸ δεύτερον γὰρ τοῖς ἐμοῖς αὐτὴν χρεὼν | τόξοις ἁλῶναι. References to this detail are common in Latin poets, cf. Prop. 3.1.32 *Troia bis Oetaei numine capta dei*, Ovid, *Met.* 9.232 *regnaque uisuras iterum Troiana sagittas*, Sen. *Tro.* 135ff., 824f. *misit infestos Troiae ruinis | non semel arcus*,

Val. Fl. 2.570; even more frequent are general allusions to *bis capta Troia*, etc.; cf. Virg. *Aen.* 3.476, 8.290f., 9.599, 635, Ovid, *F.* 5.389f., *Met.* 11.213ff.

865f. concidit...Troia The phrase appears in Ovid, *Tr.* 2.317f. *cur non Argolicis potius quae concidit armis | uexata est iterum carmine Troia meo?*, but there may be as well an echo of Hor. *C.* 3.16.11ff. *concidit auguris | Argiui domus ob lucrum | demersa exitio*; for *concido* with *domus*, etc., cf. *HO* 221, 1112 (*caeli regia*), *Octauia* 831 (*tecta...urbis*).

totidem diebus...quot annis The protracted expedition to Troy led by Agamemnon provided Greek rhetoricians and biographers with a convenient standard to which other military exploits might be favourably compared: Plutarch (*Pericles* 28.5), citing Ion of Chios, relates that Pericles so glorified his victory over Samos in nine months, and a similar point appears in Nepos' life of Epaminondas (5.6), *quod autem me Agamemnonem aemulari putas, falleris, namque ille cum uniuersa Graecia uix decem annis unam cepit urbem, ego contra ea una urbe nostra dieque uno totam Graeciam Lacedaemoniis fugatis liberaui* (cf. Plut. *Mor.* 542B). The topic was applied to the two conquests of Troy by Isocrates (*Phil.* 112): Heracles was so superior to later generals that οἱ μὲν μετὰ τῆς τῶν Ἑλλήνων δυνάμεως ἐν ἔτεσι δέκα μόλις αὐτὴν ἐξεπολιόρκησαν, ὁ δ' ἐν ἡμέραις ἐλάττοσιν ἢ τοσαύταις καὶ μετ' ὀλίγων στρατεύσας ῥᾳδίως αὐτὴν κατὰ κράτος εἷλεν. (My colleague C. P. Jones refers me to the jibe of Timaeus (*apud* anon. *de Subl.* 4.2) that Alexander conquered all of Asia in fewer years than Isocrates took to compose his *Panegyricus*, and also to a comparable instance of this sort of invidious comparison in Nepos, *Ages.* 4.4.)

ACT FIVE (867–1012)

At the end of the final choral ode Cassandra reappears on stage.[1] The subject of her opening speech is the murder for which Seneca has elaborately prepared his audience by the predictions of Thyestes and of Cassandra herself. More than once in her account Cassandra draws back to set Agamemnon's death in a larger framework: at the start of her vision (867ff.), it is recompense for the sufferings of the Trojans; at the end (906f.), it is the result of the murderers' evil ancestry. Both interpretations are already

---

[1] I assume that Cassandra is led off under guard with Agamemnon (cf. 801f.) and re-enters after the choral interlude. The other places in the corpus in which it seems clear that a character leaves the stage before an ode and returns immediately afterwards are *Pha.* 271ff./358f. (*Nutrix*), *Oed.* 707f./764 (Oedipus), and *HO* 579ff./700 (Deianira); in these passages the movements of the characters are more clearly and coherently described than in this scene.

familiar to the audience;[1] the reminders give an impression of coherence, of the unity of past and present, and of a crude justice.

But with Cassandra's speech the preparation and foreknowledge of the audience have been exhausted, with a single exception (Cassandra's own death, cf. 750ff.) which is not in fact depicted in what follows. In the last hundred lines of the play Seneca introduces one major character (Electra), one minor character (Strophius), and two κωφὰ πρόσωπα (Orestes and Pylades). Five short scenes are fashioned from the encounters of these characters with each other and with Clytemestra and Aegisthus. None of this action has been prepared for or foreshadowed; such an influx of new characters and situations in the final act is without parallel in Seneca. While late entrances of new characters (apart from messengers) are not rare in Greek tragedy,[2] it is difficult to parallel the sudden shift of dramatic attention which takes place in the closing scenes of *Agamemnon*.[3] From line 910 to line 1000 the dominant concern of all characters, old and new, is not Agamemnon, but Orestes. It is significant that Cassandra vanishes abruptly at the end of her long speech (909) and does not regain the centre of the stage until 1001: her part in the play is inextricably linked with the fortunes of Agamemnon, and when he is forgotten she must follow him into obscurity.

Seneca's dramatic intentions in casting the last act in this form are not beyond conjecture. In the prologue Thyestes foretells Agamemnon's death as a straightforward act of family revenge, but Cassandra and the Trojans present a different view of the event, in which Greece, in the person of its greatest leader, is punished for the destruction of Troy. In this act, as in the play as a whole, Seneca allows these two aspects of the central action to unfold for the most part independently of each other, linking them only by Clytemestra's jealous hatred of Cassandra (itself a third motive for Aga-

---

[1] Cf. 756ff., 791ff. (recompense for Troy); 48ff., 123f. (influence of ancestry). On the relation of these themes see now Liebermann 222 n.65.

[2] Cf. Aesch. *Pers.* 910 (Xerxes), Soph. *Trach.* 974 (Heracles), *El.* 1442 (Aegisthus), Eur. *Ba.* 1168 (Agave), all of which are explicitly prepared for; the entrances of Menelaus and Agamemnon in Soph. *Ajax* 1047 and 1226, though not equally central, are well integrated into the structure of the play, and a brief entrance like that of Eurydice in *Ant.* 1183 is exceptional. Euripides is less rigorous: the Evadne–Iphis scene in *Suppl.* 990ff., the Eurystheus-scene in *Hcld.* 982ff., and the Phrygian's monody in *Or.* 1369ff. are well-known examples, and the entrance of Oedipus in *Phoen.* 1539ff. was criticised even by ancient commentators (cf. Pearson xxvii).

[3] It hardly needs saying that the late entrance of Aegisthus in Aesch. *Agam.* 1577 does not constitute a parallel: his appearance has been implicitly prepared for (cf. 1223ff., 1260), and does not turn attention away from Agamemnon's death; its function as a transition to the action of *Choephoroe* is accomplished by allusions to Orestes in 1647 and 1667.

memnon's death) and by Cassandra's delight in the continuing misfortunes of the ruling house of Mycenae.[1] The prominence of Electra is perhaps explained by Seneca's wish to pass moral judgement on Agamemnon's murderers; introducing such an Electra necessarily entailed references to the vengeance of Orestes. Hence the scene with Strophius (who remains on the periphery of Greek accounts),[2] to explain how Orestes avoided his father's fate.

The resulting composition contains much effective character-portrayal, and the dramatic impact of the characteristically stalemated Senecan finale, with its allusive references to the future, is considerable.[3]

Two negative observations, however, must be made. The speed with which the action from line 910 onwards proceeds brings with it some superficiality and awkwardness, especially evident in the Strophius-scene. A more serious problem is the lack of unity between the parts of the act dominated by Cassandra (867–909, 1001–12) and the scenes centred on Electra (910–1000). These sections are noticeably different in dramatic technique: the Cassandra-scenes display a typically Senecan neglect of the details of physical action (e.g. the unexplained contrast between Cassandra's restraint in 801ff. and her unfettered isolation in 867ff., the lack of any indication at 909 that Cassandra withdraws to the stage-altar, her sudden re-appearance at 1001 and the physical vacuum left at 1012), while the intervening lines are unusually rich in entrances, exits, and other stage activities described in circumstantial and realistic detail (cf. 913, 935ff., 942ff., 947ff., 951f., 972, 978f., 997ff.). Seneca has indeed attempted to knit these discrete sections into a coherent action (cf. 951f., 1001ff.), but the sutures are themselves additional evidence for the essential diversity of his material. The hypothesis that Seneca has conflated two earlier treatments would explain these discrepancies, as well as another noteworthy feature of the final scenes, the presence of four speaking actors between 978 and 1012.[4]

867ff. It seems quite probable that Cassandra is relating a clairvoyant vision of Agamemnon's death, not describing what she can see by looking into the palace. The surprised exclamation *eheu quid hoc est?* (868) is better suited to the sudden onset of preternatural vision and the words *tam clara numquam prouidae mentis furor | ostendit oculis* (872f.) border on the ludicrous if they mean 'I can see more clearly by looking through this door than in

---

[1] Note 1007 *captas Mycenas*, 1012 *ueniet et uobis furor*.

[2] Cf. Aesch. *Agam.* 880ff. (with Fraenkel's note on δορύξενος in 880), *Cho.* 674ff., Soph. *El.* 1110f.

[3] Cf. Seidensticker 143.

[4] It is usually said that Seneca preserves the letter of the Horatian precept *nec quarta loqui persona laboret* (*A.P.* 192) by having Electra led off before Clytemestra turns to Cassandra in 1001 (for discussion and bibliography see Zwierlein, *Rezitationsdramen* 50).

my visions'; the distinction is surely between the vague apparitions of the previous scene (cf. 726–40 above) and the absolute clarity of the present vision. The only apparent obstacle to this interpretation is *spectemus* (875), which was plausibly explained by Gronovius: 'nunc age, inquit, ne tam gratum spectaculum uisus cito praetereat, contemplemur intentae'.

The picture of Cassandra peering through the palace door and giving an extended account of what is happening inside would also run counter to the clearly-established conventions of ancient drama for conveying information about interior scenes (see in general A. M. Dale, 'Seen and unseen on the Greek stage' and 'Interior scenes and illusion in Greek drama' = *Collected papers* (1969) 119ff., 259ff.). There seems to be no valid example of looking through the door of the stage-building in Greek or Senecan tragedy (in Eur. *Her.* 748f. ἀλλ' ὦ γεραιοί, καὶ τὰ δωμάτων ἔσω | σκοπῶμεν, εἰ πράσσει τις ὡς ἐγὼ θέλω, σκοπῶμεν refers to mental attention, cf. Wilamowitz *ad loc.*; in Sen. *HF* 995ff. and *Thy.* 901ff., where action occurring indoors is described or seen, it is clear that in one case the stage-building has been damaged and in the other that its doors have been opened). For New Comedy there is at least one case of looking through a door (cf. Pl. *Bacch.* 833ff. *forem hanc pauxillulum aperi; placide, ne crepa;* | *sat est. accede huc tu. uiden conuiuium?*; in analogous spying-scenes, e.g. *Asin.* 876ff., *Most.* 157ff., those being observed are on stage, not indoors), but here too there is a clear convention: a character leaves one of the stage-houses and informs another character or the audience about what he has seen inside, cf. Men. *Epit.* 878ff., *Mis.* 173ff., *Sic.* 383f. (in Pl. *Cas.* 871f. a plan is devised which requires one of the conspirators to observe from outside the stage-door, but it is never put into effect; similarly, in Men. *Mis.* 162 someone speaks of watching from outside (ἔξωθεν θεωρεῖν), but it is not certain that the action was depicted).

Seneca's source for a claivoyant vision of Cassandra cannot be identified, but such a theatrical stroke would suit a post-Euripidean tragedy. Note, for example, the apparent presence of such a scene in P. Oxy. 2746 (cf. R. A. Coles, *BICS* Suppl. xv (1968) 110–18; *Oxyrhynchus Papyri* xxxvi (1970) 7ff.): in a scene set within the walls of Troy, Cassandra gives Priam and a Trojan chorus a probably clairvoyant account of the duel between Hector and Achilles. The poor quality of the writing excludes an attribution to the famous *Hector* of Astydamas, but the influence of that work on the unknown writer cannot be ruled out.

867 res...magna The language may have a judicial ring ('an important case is being decided inside'); compare Pl. *Ps.* 645, *Epid.* 422f. *res magna amici apud forum agitur, ei uolo ire aduocatus*, Ter. *H.T.* 851 (also Pl. *Men.* 587, *Merc.* 608, *Stich.* 129, Ter. *Hec.* 774, *H.T.* 354, *Phorm.* 631, cf. Ovid, *Ars* 1.86); in Arist. *Frogs* 759 and 1099 μέγα πρᾶγμα is similarly used.

par annis decem 'It pays us back for ten years of war'; compare *Tro.* 22ff. *stat auidus irae uictor et lentum Ilium* | *metitur oculis ac decem tandem ferus* |

ignoscit annis, Claud. *Bell. Get.* 633f. *uno...die Romana rependit | quidquid ter denis acies amisimus annis.* Par also stresses the equal importance of the events, cf. Manil. 4.47 *adiacuit Libycis compar iactura ruinis.* E has misread *par* (or possibly p), as also in *HF* 788; here, however, it has interpolated as well, altering *annis* to *annos.*

868 eheu quid hoc est? The exclamation marks Cassandra's first awareness of her clairvoyant vision; it is used of the onset of prophecy in Ennius 54 R² = 47 J (*Alexander*), and see as well Hor. *Epod.* 15.23, *C.* 1.15.9, Virg. *Aen.* 8.537; in Greek cf. Aesch. *Ag.* 1114 ἒ ἒ παπαῖ παπαῖ τί τόδε φαίνεται;. In several Senecan passages *quid hoc est?* or a similar phrase signals a surprising and unwelcome sight, cf. *HF* 939, 976, 1042, *Pha.* 705, *Oed.* 353, *Thy.* 421; Canter 56f. It thus functions as the equivalent of ἔα· τί λεύσσω; (for ἔα see Page on Eur. *Med.* 1004, Fraenkel on Aesch. *Ag.* 1256f. (p. 580 n.4), Dodds on *Ba.* 644); note also Pl. *Men.* 191.

869 uicimus uicti Phryges The ironic reversal is a commonplace, cf. Herodotus 8.102 οὐδέ τι νικῶντες οἱ ῞Ελληνες νικῶσι, Virg. *Aen.* 2.367f. *uictis redit in praecordia uirtus | uictoresque cadunt Danai,* Otto, *Sprichwörter* 371 s.u. *uinco*; Seneca's language owes most to Ovid, *F.* 1.523 *uicta tamen uinces euersaque, Troia, resurges* (on which see Bömer *ad loc.*), and the slight inappropriateness of *resurgis, Troia* in the Senecan context marks it as a borrowing. This is the clearest and most direct statement of the theme in the play (cf. 175, 183, 412a, 757f.).

870f. resurgis...pares Mycenas A's text is correct, as seen by Siegmund (II.8 n.1) and Carlsson (*C et M* x (1948) 51ff.). Coherence with *traxisti* and the imitation of Ovid's *euersaque, Troia, resurges* (see previous note) combine to show the superiority of *resurgis*; *pares* is commended by parallels dealing with the fate of Marius, cf. Luc. 2.91f. *solacia fati | Carthago Mariusque tulit, pariterque iacentes | ignouere deis,* *Anth. Lat.* 415.36f. Riese *quis fuit ille dies, | quo Marium uidit suppar Carthago iacentem* (*suppar* Burman, *supra* MS); to these may be added Manilius 4.47 and Plut. *Mar.* 40.4. Part of E's corrupt text may be the result of a mechanical error of anticipation (*pares iacēs* becoming *parēs iacēs*), but the substitution of *resurgit* for *resurgis* was perhaps a deliberate alteration.

traxisti...Mycenas For the physical image cf. Rut. Nam. 1.398f. (of the Jews) *latius excisae pestis contagia serpunt | uictoresque suos natio uicta premit.*

870 iacens Of cities defeated and sacked, cf. Serv. Sulp. *apud* Cic. *Fam.* 4.5.4 *quae oppida...nunc prostrata et diruta ante oculos iacent,* Ovid, *Met.* 13.505 *iacet Ilion ingens, Her.* 1.3 *Troia iacet certe; T.L.L.* VII¹.26.48ff., Nisbet–Hubbard on Hor. *C.* 1.37.25.

872f. tam clara...oculis Such assurances of clarity are found elsewhere of dream-images, cf. Aesch. *Pers.* 179f. οὔτι πω τοιόνδ' ἐναργὲς εἰδόμην | ὡς τῆς πάροιθεν εὐφρόνης; Seneca's language may be influenced by Virg.

Aen. 2.589f. (of an apparition of Venus) *cum mihi se non ante oculis tam clara uidendam | obtulit.*

873 uideo et intersum For the emphatic combination compare Cic. *Inu.* 1.104 *si ipse interfuerit ac praesens uiderit, Fam.* 6.12.2 *uidi cognoui interfui* (cf. *Sulla* 12).

875ff. The banquet-hall is the setting for the crime in Homer (*Od.* 4.514ff., 11.404ff.) and Sophocles (*El.* 203f.); see also Pausanias 2.16.6f. and Philostratus, *Imag.* 2.10. Aeschylus and Euripides (*El.* 155f.) place the murder in the bath, while Hyginus (117) and Servius Auctus (on Virg. *Aen.* 11.268f. *coniugis infandae prima inter limina dextra | oppetiit*) preserve a version in which Agamemnon was killed while offering sacrifice. Livius Andronicus is generally thought to have used the Homeric setting, on the basis of fr. 10 R² *in sedes conlocat se regias, | Clytemestra iuxtim, tertias natae occupant* (cf., however, the reservations of N. Terzaghi, *Atti dell'Accademia delle Scienze di Torino* lx (1924) 668).

Seneca's description of the banquet-hall is made up of details chosen to hammer home the parallels between Mycenae and Troy and between Agamemnon and Priam: the banquet itself resembles the last celebrations of the Trojans, and the similarity is enhanced by the use of captured Trojan furnishings and plate; Agamemnon's assumption of Priam's clothing is prominently described and becomes the means by which he is fatally attacked.

878 merum Seneca does not use *merum* as a simple alternative to *uina*: cf. *HF* 779 of the Lapiths and Centaurs *multo in bella succensi mero* (probably derived from Hor. *C.* 1.18.8f. *Centaurea monet cum Lapithis rixa super mero | debellata*; see Nisbet–Hubbard for Horatian usage) and compare *HO* 572 of Hercules *uictus mero, Octauia* 701 of libations; in *Thy.* 913 *capaci ducit argento merum* there is special point in calling Thyestes' drink *merum.*

in auro = *in poculis ex auro factis*; for the metonymy cf. Virg. *G.* 2.506 *ut gemma bibat,* Sen. *Pha.* 518f. *sollicito bibunt | auro superbi, Thy.* 453 *uenenum in auro bibitur,* 913.

Golden goblets are a conventional mark of wealth (first in Enn. *Ann.* 624 V²), often mentioned in the moralising context of a *locus de diuitiis,* cf. Virg. *G.* 2.506 *ut gemma bibat et Sarrano dormiat ostro,* Varius fr. 2 Morel *incubet ut Tyriis atque ex solido bibat auro,* Sen. *Contr.* 1 *pr.* 23, 2.1, *exc.* 5.5, 9.2.6, *Anth. Lat.* 444.6 Riese; cf. Rolland 42ff., Juv. 10.27f. with Mayor's notes; compare Massinger, *Virgin-Martyr* 1.i 'yet poison still is poison, though drunk in gold'.

trahunt A poeticism for *bibunt,* cf. Hor. *Epod.* 14.4, Ovid, *Met.* 15.330, Luc. 7.822, Stat. *S.* 4.6.72; there seems to be little difference in force between *trahere* and *ducere* in such contexts (cf. Lee on Ovid, *Met.* 1.219); *trahere* corresponds to ἕλκειν, cf. Eur. *Cyc.* 417, *Ion* 1200.

879 et The transmitted *et* should not be altered in favour of Heinsius' superficially attractive *en*, since the depiction of Agamemnon is the climactic element of the banquet-scene and not the start of a new section.

picta ueste Since this garment is identical with the *Priami superbas...
exuuias* mentioned in the next line, the primary suggestion is of Eastern opulence (cf. *Thy.* 663f. *hic praeda hostium | et de triumpho picta barbarico chlamys*); in view, however, of Agamemnon's status (and his words in 802ff. above), an allusion to the *picta uestis* or *toga picta* of the triumphing Roman commander cannot be excluded (cf. Livy 10.7.10, 30.15.11f., Suet. *Aug.* 94, *Nero* 25, Dio Cass. 63.20.3, Servius on Virg. *Ecl.* 10.27; cf. Mayor on Juv. 10.38ff.). See also Brink's note on Hor. *A.P.* 228f. *regali conspectus in auro...et ostro.*

sublimis iacet An anachronistic detail, perhaps inspired by Ovid, *Met.* 6.650 *sedens solio Tereus sublimis auito* (cf. also 11.610, *Her.* 12.179, *F.* 2.350ff.).

881ff. A fatal exchange of clothes plays a significant part in *Troades* (883ff., the wedding apparel of Polyxena), *Thyestes* (524ff., Thyestes assumes royal robes), and *Hercules Oetaeus* (571, Deianeira's robe). Closest in form to the present passage is *Thy.* 524ff. *squalidam uestem exue, | oculisque nostris parce, et ornatus cape | pares meis.*

884 regemne...uirum The horror of the coming murder lies in its reversal of social and moral hierarchy, a characteristic Senecan conception.

885 uenere fata Compare Lucan 6.415f. *summique grauem discriminis horam | aduentare palam est, propius iam fata moueri*; in this context *fata* might also refer to the personal destiny of Agamemnon.

886 cruor Baccho incidet A picturesque detail absent in *Od.* 11.420 ἐνὶ μεγάρῳ δάπεδον δ᾿ ἅπαν αἵματι θῦεν, but found in Philostratus' account (*Imag.* 2.10.1 τὸ ἀναμὶξ τῷ οἴνῳ αἷμα, 2.10.2 κύλικες πλήρεις αἱ πολλαὶ λύθρου); it was popular in declamatory contexts, cf. Sen. *Contr.* 9.2.4, 5ff., 24 and compare Livy 39.43.4 (*cruore mensam respersam*), and Lucan 10.423f. *poteratque cruor per regia fundi | pocula Caesareus mensaeque incumbere ceruix.* Seneca's own references to the topic, though frequent (cf. *Thy.* 65, 700, 913ff.; cf. *HO* 657), are generally restrained, as in this passage; the gory exuberance of the neo-Senecans has other sources.

Baccho Cf. *Thy.* 987 *admotus ipsis Bacchus a labris fugit*; for the poeticism see Haupt, *Opusc.* II.74, 166ff., III.506; *T.L.L.* II.1665.78ff.

887 mortifera The word is found outside the more elevated genres of poetry, cf. Lucilius 802 M *mortiferum uulnus* (though this might be epic parody), Sen. *Contr.* 1 *pr.* 7 *nihil...tam mortiferum ingeniis quam luxuria est*, Sen. *Epist.* 57.6 *erunt tamen qui hanc ruinam magis timeant, quamuis utraque mortifera aeque sit.*

perfidae The transmitted *perfide* has usually been interpreted by modern editors as the adverb *perfide* and not the adjective *perfidae* (the latter appears in the 1498 edition, the Aldine text of Avantius, and L. Herrmann's Budé); adverbs in *-e* and *-ter*, however, are uncommon in poetry (cf. Axelson, *Unpoetische Wörter* 62f.), and *perfide* in particular is extremely rare in prose or poetry before the second century A.D. (I have found only one certain example, Sen. *Contr.* 9.3.11); *perfidus*, on the other hand, appears eight times in the plays of both persons and things (cf. 570 above *saxa*, *Med.* 302 *freta*, *Thy.* 235 *consorte nostri perfidus thalami auehit*, where it has the force of an adverb).

888 negant A necessary correction of the transmitted *negat*: the folds (*sinus*) of the garment impede Agamemnon's head and hands, as is clear from *-que* in 889.

889 caputque... claudunt sinus The words describe a cloak with no opening for the head. The fatal garment is so described in schol. Lyc. *Alex.* 1099, Servius on Virg. *Aen.* 11.268 *consilio Aegisthi ab uxore uestem accepit clauso capite et manicis qua implicitus... interiit*, Dracontius, *Orest.* 212 *tunica uertice clauso*, 255ff. *callida funereo perfundit corpus amictu, | sed capiti dum quaerit iter tunicaeque fenestram, | illa manum retinens armatum acciuit Egistum* (the garment implied by this account, thrown over the head but leaving the hands free, is that depicted in illuminations of the scene in numerous MSS of Seneca). See also the material in Fraenkel's note on Aesch. *Ag.* 1382 ἄπειρον.

laxi... sinus The phrase is usually applied to the loosened clothing which was a sign of festive indulgence, cf. *Oed.* 422f. *inde tam molles placuere cultus | et sinus laxi*, Ovid, *R.A.* 680 *toga ... laxo conspicienda sinu*.

inuii... sinus Here 'affording no way out', cf. *Pha.* 93f. *fortis per altas inuii retro lacus | uadit tenebras*; for the opposite meaning ('allowing no entry') cf. Ovid, *F.* 5.581f. *gens fuit et campis et equis et tuta sagittis | et circumfusis inuia fluminibus*, *HF* 485f. *ferro inuius... Cycnus*.

Seneca retains the essential feature of Aeschylus' ἄπειρον ἀμφίβληστρον (cf. Soph. fr. 526 P, Eur. *Or.* 25, Philostr. *Imag.* 2.10).

890 haurit The use of *haurio* to describe wounds inflicted by swords, spears, or animal horns or tusks is found from the first century B.C. onwards, cf. Claud. Quad. fr. 10b Peter, Lucr. 5.1324, Virg. *Aen.* 10.314, Ovid, *Met.* 5.126, 8.371 (with Hollis's note), 9.411, Curtius 7.2.27, Silius 5.524. It is customarily related to *haurio* in the sense 'to scoop or draw up' (cf. Virg. *G.* 4.229 *haustus aquarum*, scooping handfuls of water), cf. Haupt on Ovid, *Met.* 5.126, D. A. West, *CR* N.s. iii (1963) 4ff.). The precise image conveyed is of a weapon entering and leaving the body with gouging or tearing effect (note Claudian's use of the verb to describe chopping ice, *Eutr.* 2.414 *duris haurire bipennibus Hebrum*). This precision of meaning sets *haurio* apart from other 'drink' words in the context of wounding; cf., e.g., Virg. *Aen.* 11.804 [*hasta*] *bibit cruorem*, 12.375 *summum degustat uulnere corpus*, Stat. *Th.* 9.804 *arida...hasta.*

trementi semiuir dextra The effeminate cowardice of Aegisthus is clear in the *Oresteia* (cf. *Ag.* 1625 with Fraenkel's note), but he takes no part in the murder; Sophocles combines the Aeschylean characterisation (cf. *El.* 299ff.) with the Homeric tradition that makes Aegisthus the principal agent in the murder (cf. 97ff.). Seneca adds plausible detail to this conflation by making Aegisthus' first thrust a glancing blow; *trementi...dextra* probably implies effeminacy (cf. *tremula dextra* of a *cinaedus*, Juv. 6. O 2, cf. 299 above). The murder of a great man by an effeminate weakling is paralleled in Lucan's account of Pompey's death (8.550ff.): *tanti, Ptolemaee, ruinam | nominis haut metuis, caeloque tonante profanas | inseruisse manus, impure ac semiuir, audes?*

891 egit 'Elegantia praeteriti uicem praesentis, simul enim fit et factum est, dum narratur' (Gronovius). In Greek such a preterite often marks the onset of some strong emotional reaction, cf. Sappho 31 L–P 6 ἐπτόαισεν, Aesch. *P. V.* 145, 181 ἐμὰς δὲ φρένας ἠρέθισε διάτορος φόβος, 245, Arist. *Eq.* 696. The Latin equivalent is generally called the perfect of instantaneous action or result (cf. Virg. *G.* 1.330f. *terra tremit, fugere ferae et mortalia corda | per gentis humilis strauit pauor*, Hor. *C.* 1.34.14ff. *hinc apicem rapax | Fortuna... | sustulit*, Virg. *Aen.* 1.82ff). Its use produces a *Steigerung* of excitement by momentarily quickening the pace of the narrative: 'the pansy gashes his side with trembling hands – *but he hasn't driven it home* – and stops, dazed, in the act of wounding him'.

892ff. The comparison of beleaguered warriors to wild boars is traditional, cf. *Iliad* 11.324f. (Agamemnon), 13.471ff., [Hes.] *Scutum* 386ff., Virg. *Aen.* 10.707ff., Ovid, *F.* 2.231ff., Stat. *Th.* 2.323ff., 469ff., Sil. 1.421ff. (for other animals in such similes cf. Miniconi 203).

894 artatque motu uincla A neater phrase for the process described in *Pha.* 1085f. *quanto magis | pugnat, sequaces hoc magis nodos ligat*; ad rem, cf. Ovid, *Ars* 1.392 *non bene de laxis cassibus exit aper*, Stat. *Ach.* 1.460 *admotis paulatim cassibus artat.*

895 caecos sinus *Caecus* here has the active sense ('inhibiting sight, blinding'), cf. Virg. *Aen.* 5.589 *caecis parietibus*, 12.444 *caeco puluere campus miscetur*, Mela 1.110 *cum caeca tempestate agerentur.*

897 bipenni Aegisthus has presumably used a sword; Aegisthus wields a sword in *Od.* 11.424 and Eur. *El.* 164f., an axe in Soph. *El.* 97ff. The axe, on the other hand, has twice before in the play been prophetically linked with Clytemestra (cf. 43ff., 935f.), a connection which Seneca may have derived from Euripides (cf. *El.* 160, 278f., *Tro.* 361, *Hec.* 1278f.), though by his day it was a commonplace (cf. Hor. *S.* 1.1.99f.). Aeschylus is deliberately vague about Clytemestra's weapon (see Fraenkel's Appendix B, pp. 806ff.); her use of an axe may be as old as Stesichorus, cf. 219 *PMG* and K. Kunst, *WS* 1924/5, 149 n.1.

898 popa The transmitted reading *prius*, accepted by most recent editors, involves two difficulties: the pleonasm of *prius...antequam* and the absence of a subject in the comparison. The Latin parallels that have been alleged to defend the pleonasm merely make the artless redundancy of the MS text more obvious: Virg. *Aen.* 4.24ff. *sed mihi uel tellus optem prius ima dehiscat | uel pater omnipotens adigat me fulmine ad umbras, | pallentis umbras Erebo noctemque profundam, | ante, pudor, quam te uiolo aut tua iura resoluo,* Prop. 2.25.25f. *aut prius infecto deposcit praemia cursu, | septima quam metam triuerit ante rota?* (text doubtful: *arte* recc.). The only close parallels so far produced are in Jordanes (cf. Wölfflin in *A.L.L.* xi.368) – hardly an encouraging sign. No convincing parallel or defence has yet been produced for the absence of a subject in the *qualis*-clause.

Either of these anomalies in isolation would suffice to render a reading suspect; together they make emendation unavoidable. Ascensius (and later Bothe) suggested the palaeographically neat *pius*, intending it as an equivalent of *sacerdos* (more properly, *mactator hostiarum*), but such a usage appears unattested and unlikely (it may have been an edition with this conjecture which prompted Studley's accurate rendering: 'and as the priest to sacrifice to th'altar side doth stande...'). Peiper's *qualis qui* is clever, but *-que* is needed for the flow of the lines (it links the parallel phrases *armat...dextram* and *librat manum*). Rossbach postulated the loss of a line after 898, but one fails to see what this imaginary line might have contained, save the subject of *designat*. Only Bentley's *popa* for *prius* removes all difficulty without raising new objections; while lacking total conviction (the cause and process of corruption remain obscure), it satisfies the needs of the context so well as to deserve a place in the text.

Roman literature fails to present a sharply defined picture of the *popa*'s function; *popae* are shadowy creatures of low social status (cf. Cic. *Mil.* 65), known for their distinctive dress (cf. Suet. *Cal.* 32, Gell. 12.3.3, Servius on Virg. *Aen.* 12.120) and grasping ways (cf. Prop. 4.3.62, Persius 6.74). The poetic periphrasis *succincti ministri* covers both *popae* and *cultrarii*, their fellows in the *collegium uictimariorum* (cf. Wissowa, *Rel. und Kultus*[2] 427), making the precise functions of each difficult to determine.

Religious art is fortunately more helpful. Numerous reliefs of the first and second century A.D. depicting *suouetaurilia* or *uota publica* show *uictimarii* wearing the *limus* and carrying *mallei* or *secures*, and these figures are generally identified by scholars as *popae* (cf. I. S. Ryberg, 'Rites of the state religion in Roman art', *Memoirs of the American Academy in Rome* xxii (1955) 82, 104–15, 129; also R. M. Ogilvie, *JRS* li (1961) 36). One recurrent scene found in Augustan, Julio-Claudian, and Hadrianic reliefs shows an animal being despatched by several *uictimarii*; of these two usually hold the animal in place (one often holds a *culter* at its throat), while a third is shown with an axe lifted over his head, preparing to strike (cf. Ryberg, fig. 36b, pl. 21; fig. 39a, pl. 25; fig. 71, pl. 46; fig. 77d, pl. 50). The present passage, as well as Lucan 1.612f. *cornua succincti premerent cum torua ministri,* | *deposito uictum praebebat poplite collum,* might have been written to illustrate just such a scene.

Other descriptions of the moment before the fatal blow make a priest the actor, cf. Eur. *I.A.* 1578f. ἱερεὺς δὲ φάσγανον λαβὼν ἐπεύξατο | λαιμόν τ' ἐπε-σκοπεῖθ' ἵνα πλήξειεν ἄν, Sen. *Oed.* 135ff. *colla tacturus steterat sacerdos:* | *dum manus certum parat alta uulnus,* | *aureo taurus rutilante cornu* | *labitur segnis;* in other contexts compare Virg. *Aen.* 11.747f., Ovid, *Met.* 8.757, 12.248f.

901 habet, peractum est 'He's got it [i.e. the mortal blow], it's all over with him'; *habet* (or *hoc habet*) is gladiatorial language, used several times in Comedy (e.g. Pl. *Most.* 715, Ter. *Andr.* 82f.) and once in Virgil (*Aen.* 12.296). In *HO* 1457 the phrase *habet, peractum est* is ineptly used by Hyllus to tell Hercules of Deianeira's death; in *HO* 1472 the MSS have corrupted *bene est, peractum est* (cf. *Oed.* 988) into *habet, peractum est* because of a lingering memory of 1457 (cf. Axelson, *Korruptelenkult* 35ff.).

901f. pendet...parte Seneca does little in this passage to justify his reputation for indiscriminate gore. The physical precision of the brief description is matched on the stylistic level by an approximation of a golden line (*exigua male caput amputatum parte* = a b C B A, cf. Canter 175).

male...amputatum 'imperfectly cut off'; for the use of *male* cf. Nisbet–Hubbard on Hor. *C.* 1.9.24, and in similar contexts cf. *Oed.* 973 *effossis male oculis,* Luc. 10.518 *heu facinus! ceruix gladio male caesa pependit* (deleted by Heinsius, see Housman's note; defended by A. Hudson-Williams, *CR* N.s. xix (1969) 138); cf. Dracontius, *Orest.* 728f. *ossibus ecfractis minuunt per mille secures* | *et male partitos per uulnera palpitat artus.*

903 ora cum fremitu Cf. *Thy.* 728f. *ceruice caesa truncus in pronum ruit,* | *querulum cucurrit murmure incerto caput,* Silius 15.467ff.; note also passages in which tongues continue to move after being cut out, e.g. Ovid, *Met.* 6.557ff., Luc. 2.181f. *exsectaque lingua* | *palpitat.* That parts of the body continue to function for a moment after sudden death is a commonplace of Latin epic; abundant material is collected by O. Zwierlein, *A.u.A.* xvi.2 (1970) 154–7.

904f. exanimem...corpus The change of object has been found awkward, and several remedies proposed. The neatest is Nisbet's *exanimum*; this passage apart, Seneca uses *exanimis* and *exanimus* three times each (the figures given for Seneca in *T.L.L.* v.1172.46ff. are wrong, probably because in *Tro.* 604 *exanimis* has been mistaken for nom. sing. instead of dat. plur.; cf. Virg. *Aen.* 11.110), *exanimum corpus* appearing in *Pha.* 585 and *Thy.* 1059. The conjectures of Heinsius and Bentley take E's *exanime* as a starting-point, but this may be no more than an unmetrical interpolation to bring the adjective into concord with *corpus*. The MS text can be defended, and *exanimem* [*sc. Agamemnona*] *petit* yields an appropriately ironic point ('now that Agamemnon is dead, Aegisthus attacks him') which is lost if *petit* and *lacerat* both govern *exanimum...corpus*.

905 laceratque corpus Attacking a dead enemy is traditionally the act of the timid or cowardly, cf. *Iliad* 22.371 (the Greeks and Hector), schol. Soph. *Phil.* 445, Eustathius p. 208.2ff. (Thersites and Penthesilea), Soph. *Ant.* 1029f. (Creon and Polyneices), Ovid, *Met.* 8.422ff. (the heroes and the Calydonian boar), *Pont.* 4.3.27f. *uix equidem credo: subito insultare iacenti | te mihi nec uerbis parcere fama refert* (cf. *Trist.* 2.571). It is also a commonplace that men most gladly abuse in death those whom they most feared in life, cf. Aesch. *Ag.* 884 with the notes of Fraenkel and Blomfield, Lucr. 5.1140, Juvenal 10.85, Plut. *Dem.* 22.4.

906f. The idea that propensity for crime is a family characteristic plays an important role in several Senecan tragedies (some material is collected by D. J. Mastronarde, *TAPA* ci (1970) 310–12), but the rhetorical exploitation of this notion is hardly peculiar to him, cf. for example Cic. *Tusc.* 4.77 *ut facile appareat Atrei filios esse*, Ovid, *Her.* 4.61f. *en, ego nunc, ne forte parum Minoia credar, | in socias leges ultima gentis eo*. The resemblance of Clytemestra and Helen is a Euripidean motif, cf. *El.* 1062ff. τὸ μὲν γὰρ εἶδος αἶνον ἄξιον φέρειν | Ἑλένης τε καὶ σοῦ, δύο δ᾽ ἔφυτε συγγόνω | ἄμφω ματαίω Κάστορός τ᾽ οὐκ ἀξίω.

respondet suis 'resembles his relations'; for the dative cf. Lucr. 4.166 (of objects reflected in a mirror) *res sibi respondent simili forma atque colore*.

908f. Great crimes in Seneca often set off repercussions in the celestial sphere, cf. *HF* 1202ff., *Pha.* 671ff., *Oed.* 1ff., 868ff., and, of course, the extensive use of this theme in *Thyestes*. Whatever the general validity of Regenbogen's suggestion ('Schmerz und Tod in den Tragödien Senecas' = *Kleine Schriften* (1961) 437f.) that such passages are to be interpreted in the light of the Stoic doctrine of συμπάθεια, this approach would clearly be wide of the mark here: Seneca is undoubtedly borrowing the motif from the Thyestes-myth, where it is well-established as early as Euripides (denied in *El.* 726ff., cf. also *I.T.* 816, *Or.* 1001ff., fr. 861 N²); by Seneca's own time it was a poetic commonplace, cf. Plato, *Pol.* 269A, Accius 223ff. R² *sed quid tonitru turbida toruo | concussa repente aequora caeli | sensimus sonere?*, Ovid, *Am.* 3.12.39, *Ars* 1.329f., *Pont.* 4.6.47, Manilius 3.18f., 5.463f. (later cf. Luc. 1.543, Stat. *Th.* 4.307, *S.* 5.3.96, *Aetna* 20, Claud. *Gild.* 1.399f.).

908 Titan A poeticism used once each by Cicero and Virgil (cf. Pease on *Aen.* 4.119), and popularised by Ovid; in Ovid, however, *Titan* is used only a fraction as often as *Sol*, while in Seneca it predominates by a wide margin (*Titan* seventeen times, *Sol* eight). The author of *HO* carries this Senecan mannerism to typically extreme lengths (twenty-one instances).

e medio die The MSS give *emerito die*, which no editor has questioned, but which can hardly be right: it would mean that the day was over, and the Sun's dilemma would in that case be meaningless, since his *cursus* would be complete (for this use of *emeritus* cf. Ovid, *F.* 4.688, Sen. *Thy.* 797, *Anth. Lat.* 238 Riese, Stat. *Th.* 1.336). Such a conception of the sun's reversal is found in none of the parallel treatments of the topic; several, indeed, explicitly state that the sun was at the zenith when it turned back: cf. Ovid, *Ars* 1.329 *non medium rupisset iter*, Luc. 1.543 *caput medio...cum ferret Olympo*, Stat. *Th.* 4.307 *mediique recursus | solis* (more allusively Claud. *Pan. Prob. et Olyb.* 172 *intercisa dies*). The best evidence comes from S. himself, in the most elaborate of all handlings, *Thy.* 791ff. *quo uertis iter | medioque diem perdis Olympo? | ... | nondum serae nuntius horae | nocturna uocat lumina Vesper; | nondum Hesperiae flexura rotae | iubet emeritos soluere currus; | nondum in noctem uergente die | tertia misit bucina signum; | stupet ad subitae tempora cenae | nondum fessis bubus arator* (and note the forward reference by the *Nuntius* (776ff.): *O Phoebe patiens, fugeris retro licet | medioque raptum merseris caelo diem, | sero occidisti*; it is clear from the *Thyestes* passages that the Thyestean *cena* took place at mid-day and that drinking was not postponed until sunset; an argument from Roman custom in favour of *emerito* here is, therefore, of doubtful weight). These parallels not only indicate the error of the transmitted reading, but suggest a correction: *e medio* for *emerito*. The Sun pauses at the zenith, uncertain whether to continue on his normal course or to turn back as he did on that famous earlier occasion (note *retro* in *Thy.* 776, *frena reuocare* in 296 above). The use of *dies = caelum* is well-attested, cf. Ovid, *Met.* 1.603 *sub nitido die*, Sen. *Thy.* 263 *tonat dies serenus*, Luc. 7.189 *suo quocumque die*, *T.L.L.* v[1].1028.51ff.; *medius dies* of a place rather than a time is also well-known, though other examples refer to a terrestrial region (= *Mezzogiorno*), cf. Sen. *HF* 236, Luc. 1.16 (with Housman's note).

Ante 910 The *inscriptiones scaenae* in E are frequently fuller than those of A, but also less consistent. Thus A omits both silent characters (Orestes and Pylades), while E names Orestes and neglects Pylades. For silent children cf. *HF* 627f., *Med.* 945ff., *Thy.* 485ff., 520ff. (only in *Thyestes* do E's *inscriptiones* acknowledge their presence).

910ff. Giomini notes the similarity of Electra's opening lines to Virg. *Aen.* 2.289f. *heu fuge, nate dea, teque his, ait, eripe flammis. | hostis habet muros: ruit alto a culmine Troia.* The imitation is not entirely fortunate, for the infant Orestes is hardly able to respond to Electra's warnings as Aeneas could to Hector's.

910 auxilium 'remedy', perhaps with medical overtones, cf. Enn. *sc.* 314 R[2], Ovid, *R.A.* 528 *auxilium multis sucus et herba fuit*, Cels. 2.11 *nec posse* *uehementi malo nisi aeque uehemens auxilium succurrere*, Sen. *Oed.* 70 *morbus auxilium trahit*, Luc. 8.333f.

912 euersa...occidunt A similar picture of total ruin is given in *Medea*, cf. 879 *periere cuncta, concidit regni status*, 886 *iam domus tota occidit* (perhaps derived from Ovid, *Met.* 1.240 *occidit una domus*, though the emphasis is different in this passage). It is more common in Seneca to have tyrants or *irati* express the wish or intention of bringing about such destruction, cf. *HF* 351 (Lycus) *stat tollere omnem penitus Herculeam domum, Tro.* 685 (Ulixes), *Pho.* 345 (Oedipus) *ab imo tota considat domus, Med.* 426ff., *Thy.* 190f. (Atreus) *haec ipsa...domus | ruat uel in me, dummodo in fratrem ruat.* The seeds of this outlook are Euripidean, cf. *Med.* 114 πᾶς δόμος ἔρροι; it passes to Seneca via Ovid, cf. *Met.* 8.485 (Althaea) *per coaceruatos pereat domus impia luctus.*

913 concitos currus agit Such entries are not rare in early Greek tragedy, cf. Aesch. *Pers.* 150ff., 607f., 909ff., *Ag.* 753ff.; possibly also in *Memnon*, cf. Arist. *Ran.* 963 Μέμνονας κωδωνοφαλαροπώλους (*Eum.* 405, which is clearly incompatible with Athena's entrance on her aegis in 404, is bracketed by most editors; it may have been substituted for 404 at a later performance, cf. E. Bodensteiner, *Jahrb. d. Class. Phil.* Suppl. XIX (1893) 667). In Euripides as well entrances on chariots often have a scenic or emotional effect, cf. *El.* 998ff. (a sign of Clytaemestra's opulence), *Tro.* 568ff. (Andromache with Astyanax and Hector's armour), *I.A.* 607ff. (Clytaemestra). It is also likely that chariot-entrances appeared in new tragedies written after the fifth century, and it may be significant that Strophius' entrance finds its closest Greek parallel in the *Rhesus* (342ff., note in particular 373ff. πώλους ἐρεθί-| ζων δίβολόν τ᾽ ἄκοντα πάλ-|λων).

quis iste celeres Rossbach (*BPhW* 1904, 367) suggested that A's *quis iste celeres* had grown from *celeres*, entered as a gloss on *concitus* (or *-os*); he adduced *Pho.* 403, where E has *perge, o parens, perge et concita cursu celerem gradum*, A the correct *perge, o parens, et concita celerem gradum.* The comparison thus works in A's favour, suggesting that the juxtaposition *celeres concitus* is quite acceptable (and rendering Gronovius' *concitos* superfluous); note *concitus* of an entering character in 408 above. E may have thought *quis iste...concitus* stood in need of an expressed noun subject, and so inserted *hospes* and removed the apparently otiose *celeres*; all that can be said in support of *hospes* is that it prepares for the paradox *externos fugis? | domus timenda est*, but the point is perfectly clear without it. On balance A's text seems marginally superior, more closely resembling other such announcements (for *quis iste...concitus* compare, for example, 922 below *quaenam ista...maesta*; on the other hand, *hospes* is not elsewhere so used).

914 uultus ueste furabor tuos *Furor* is here 'to conceal' (the passage was missed by *T.L.L.* VI¹.1640.42ff.), cf. Sil. 10.74 *in densis furantem membra* *maniplis*, Stat. *Th.* 11.355, 12.292; in *HO* 1890 the MSS give *totum pinna uelata diem* (of the Stymphalian birds), and *furata* for *uelata* has been proposed by Giardina (*in app.*) and Axelson (*Korruptelenkult* 71f.). The only other appearance of *furor* in the plays is in 933 below (see note).

915 anime demens Self-address; Seneca does not use *anime* as a term of endearment. Electra's suspicion of strangers was revealed in the previous line (*uultus ueste furabor tuos*) and is now rejected as misguided.

917 amici...praesidia Seneca does not avoid this 'unpoetic' word (cf. Axelson 98); it appears seven times in the genuine plays, with three instances in *HO* and *Octauia*. For this genitive cf. *Octauia* 782f. *trepidi cohortes ecce praefecti trahunt | praesidia ad urbis*; elsewhere the genitive specifies the person or thing protected, cf. Ovid, *Pont.* 4.12.46, Sen. *Med.* 227, *Thy.* 523.

918ff. Strophius does not notice Electra until 922; his opening lines are, therefore, 'in der Luft gesprochen' (Leo, *Monolog* 92). The short speech resembles the brief accounts which characters in New Comedy give out at large on entry (cf., e.g., Men. *Dysc.* 153ff., Pl. *Aul.* 178ff., *Capt.* 998ff.), but this is perhaps not to be pressed, since Euripides offers parallels for such bald entrance-announcements. For the circumstances of Strophius' appearance (i.e. paying a courtesy visit to a friend on his way back from a more formal engagement) cf. Eur. *Med.* 663ff. (Aegeus), *Andr.* 884ff. (Orestes). See Leo, *Monolog* 15ff.

918f. Elea inclitus | palma Two anachronisms in three words: Olympic contests are being held at the time of the Trojan war, and palm branches are given as prizes. (Compare *Thy.* 409f. *celebrata iuueni stadia, per quae nobilis | palmam paterno non semel curru tuli.*) For the first of these anachronisms Seneca had ample Greek precedent: Sophocles describes the games at which Orestes is reported to have died with thoroughly contemporary detail (*El.* 681ff.), and Euripides twice alludes to the length of the δρόμος at Olympia (*Med.* 1181 with Page's note, *El.* 880ff.). The plots of *Hypsipyle* and *Alexander* also provided scope for a messenger's report of the games, which was probably couched in fifth-century terms. Ovid, too, introduces the great games with little regard for precise chronology, once as an unexpected periphrasis to describe the age of Picus (*Met.* 14.324f. *nec adhuc spectasse per annos | quinquennem poterat Grais quater Elide pugnam*), in another context as material for simile (*Her.* 18.166; so too Sen. *HF* 840ff.), for which see Ed. Fraenkel, *Elementi Plautini* 88ff., M. Coffey, *Lustrum* ii (1957) 145.

For the Olympic palm cf. Virg. *G.* 1.59, 3.49f., Hor. *C.* 1.1.4 (with Nisbet–Hubbard *ad loc.*), 4.2.17f. *siue quos Elea domum reducit | palma caelestis*, Prop. 3.9.17, Ovid, *F.* 4.392, Stat. *Th.* 10.234.

Seneca's anachronisms are thus quite traditional. It is quite another thing when Dracontius (*Orest.* 287) has Electra carry Orestes off to Athens and enrol him in the Academy. (On anachronisms in S. see generally Herrmann, *Théâtre de Sénèque* 330.)

920f. cuius...Ilium Strophius presents a version of events highly complimentary to Agamemnon: Troy was shaken (*concussum*) by the ten years' war and finally toppled (*impulsum*, cf. Luc. 3.440 *nodosa impellitur ilex*) by Agamemnon; for these successive stages cf. Virg. *Aen.* 4.22f. *animumque labantem | impulit.* Pyrrhus in *Troades* naturally sees matters in a different light: *excidit Achilles, cuius unius manu | impulsa Troia* (204f.); *Ilium uicit pater, | uos diruistis* (235f.).

921 decenni Marte Cf. Petr. *Sat.* 89.8 *decenni proelio | irata uirtus*, Quint. 8.4.22 *rex decenni bello exhaustus* [*sc.* Priam].

922 lugubrem uultum rigat Cf. Virg. *Aen.* 9.251, Ovid, *Met.* 11.419, Sen. *Med.* 388, *Pha.* 990.

925–7 pater...tenet Compare *HF*, where Hercules, newly returned from the Underworld, asks Amphitryon why he and Megara are mourning and receives the answer (629f.) *socer est peremptus, regna possedit Lycus, | natos parentem coniugem leto petit.* In both passages the economic expression of calamity recalls (and may derive from) the tendency of messengers in Greek tragedy to deliver the essence of their news first and only under questioning to embark on a detailed account; cf., e.g., Aesch. *Pers.* 255, Soph. *Ant.* 245ff., *El.* 673ff., Eur. (?) *Phoen.* 1339, *Ion* 1110; in Latin cf. Pacuvius 320 R² *periere Danai, plera pars pessum datast* (perhaps followed by an extended narrative), 213 R² *occidisti, ut multa paucis uerba unose obnuntiem*, Sen. *Tro.* 1003f., *Pha.* 997, ps.-Sen. *HO* 1607ff. For comic use of the device see Ed. Fraenkel, *De media et noua comoedia quaestiones* 6–12.

926 comes paternae...neci For the pointed use of *comes* cf. Ovid, *Met.* 4.151f. *letique miserrima dicar | causa comesque tui, Ibis* 628 *comites Rhesi tum necis, ante uiae* (a possible source for Sen. *HF* 896f. *quisquis comes | fuerat tyranni iacuit et poenae comes*), Sen. *Const.* 2.2, Val. Max. 5.5.4 *comes fraternae necis non defuit*, Tac. *Ann.* 3.15; cf. *T.L.L.* III.1774.57ff.

929f. per...deos Such appeals are often arranged in climactic order, cf. *Med.* 285f. *per ego auspicatos regii thalami toros, | per spes futuras perque regnorum status,* 478ff., *Pha.* 868ff. *per tui sceptrum imperi, | ...perque natorum indolem | tuosque reditus perque iam cineres meos, Oed.* 1021ff. The ironic ambiguity which Seidensticker (pp. 142, 146) attempts to see in *Med.* 285ff. and *Pha.* 868ff. is not present here to the same degree, since the catastrophe of the drama is past; *per dubios deos*, however, strikes a note of uncertainty comparable to *Med.* 286f. *perque regnorum status, | Fortuna uaria dubia quos agitat uice.*

929 per te The position of *te* illustrates the tendency of unemphatic pronouns to assume the second place in the sentence or colon (cf. J. Wackernagel, *Indogermanische Forschungen* i (1892) 333ff. = *Kleine Schriften*

1.1–104; Ed. Fraenkel, 'Kolon und Satz', *Kleine Beiträge* 1.73ff., Kühner–Stegmann 1.584f., ii.593). For examples of this phenomenon in supplicatory expressions, cf. the formulae *sub uos placo* and *ob uos sacro* (Festus p. 190ᵇ2, 309ᵃ30, Wackernagel 74), also Ter. *Andr.* 834 *per ego te deos oro*, Hor. *C.* 1.8.1f. *Lydia, dic per omnes | te deos oro*, Tib. 1.5.7 *per te furtiui foedera lecti, | per Venerem quaeso compositumque caput* (with Smith's note), Virg. *Aen.* 12.56ff. *per has ego te lacrimas... | unum oro*, Sen. *HF* 1183 *per te meorum facinorum laudem precor*, *Med.* 285f.

931 pium furtum Compare Andromache addressing the tomb of Hector in *Tro.* 501f. *coniugis furtum piae | serua et fideli cinere uicturum excipe*; also Ovid, *Met.* 9.711 *inde incepta pia mendacia fraude latebant* (of Iphis being disguised as a boy).

932 timendum *Sc. esse*, cf. Cic. *Verr.* 1.38 *nemo umquam sapiens proditori credendum putauit.* For *timendum est* used absolutely, like *cauendum est*, cf. *Thy.* 473 *rogat? timendum est. errat hic aliquis dolus.*

caesus E's *quid sit* is clearly an intruded grammatical gloss, of a kind found elsewhere in E: cf. 970 below *dixi*, *Tro.* 135 *uidit*, *Thy.* 907 *uirum*, *HO* 538 *ad*, 960 *cum*, 1007 *sede*.

933 furabor Here 'to spirit away' rather than 'to conceal' (for which see note on 914 above), cf. Sil. 14.561 *exigua sese furatus Himilco carina.*

934 fidem secunda poscunt, aduersa exigunt As transmitted by the paradosis and printed by many editors, the line neither scans nor makes sense. The metre was repaired by Poggio, who wrote *poscunt fidem secunda et aduersa exigunt*; *et* was improved to *at* by Avantius, and in this form the line appeared in editions up to and including that of Gronovius. The addition of a particle, though metrically necessary, is stylistically unfortunate, since symmetrically opposed statements of this kind in Seneca are normally asyndetic, cf. *Med.* 159 *Fortuna fortes metuit, ignauos premit*, *Tro.* 497 *miser occupet praesidia, securus legat.*

Though the metrical flaw can be mended, the problem of sense is less easily resolved. Most interpretations require *poscunt* and *exigunt* to denote essentially different actions, yet a sharp distinction between such closely related words is quite improbable (an objection to which, for example, *occupet* and *legat* in *Tro.* 497 are not open).

The line, then, fails to make its point clearly. It may be doubted whether *amicus certus in re incerta cernitur* is indeed the intended meaning, since expressions of that commonplace do not normally mention prosperity as well as misfortune (cf. Eur. *Hec.* 1226, *Or.* 454f., 665ff., esp. 667 ὅταν δ' ὁ δαίμων εὖ διδῷ, τί δεῖ φίλων;, ps.-Sen. *HO* 603f., Otto, *Sprichwörter* s.u. *ignis*, p. 170). The force of the *sententia* is probably nearer to 'loyalty is always in season, but never more welcome than in time of trouble', i.e. that there is always an obligation of *fides* to friends, but that it is more pressing in adversity, cf. Rut. Nam. 1.23f. *securos leuius crimen contemnere ciues; | priuatam repetunt publica damna fidem.* The obscurity of the language and the defective metre make it virtually impossible that the gnome is Senecan; it may have been inserted by a reader who felt that Strophius' decision required a suitably sententious explanation, and its source might have been a *liber sententiarum* (cf. Axelson, *Korruptelenkult* 46 n.35) or possibly a Republican drama.

936 laeua The specific detail is added for vividness, cf. Ovid, *Am.* 2.15.11f. *tunc ego te cupiam, domina, et tetigisse papillas | et laeuam tunicis inseruisse manum*, 3.1.13 *laeua manus sceptrum late regale mouebat, Ars* 2.706, Sen. *Pha.* 707f. *en impudicum crine contorto caput | laeua reflexi* (where the right hand holds the sword); see further Zwierlein, *Philol.* cxiii (1969) 265f.

938 palma Pisaei Iouis *Pisaeus* is used in many periphrases relating to the Olympian games, cf. *Pisaea praemia* Acc. 196 R², *Pisaeasque domos curribus inclitas* Sen. *Thy.* 123, *Pisaeus annus* Stat. *Th.* 1.421, *S.* 1.3.8, *Pisaeae ramus oliuae* Juv. 13.99; note also *Anth. Pal.* 16.54.4 Πισαίου...στεφάνου.

939 omen 'sign of future good fortune'; *omen* unqualified can have positive (Cic. *Diu.* 1.103) or negative (Virg. *Aen.* 2.190) meaning.

940 tuque, o...comes Formal shift of addressee in the manner of Greek tragedy (σὺ δέ).

paternis assidens frenis = *assidens patri frenos tenenti*; compare 951f. below *patere me uittis tuis, | ...iungi* = *patere me iungi tibi uittas gerenti.*

941 condisce...fidem The loyalty of Pylades was proverbial, cf. Eur. *Or.* 1155ff., *Anth. Pal.* 11.362 (Callimachus), Cic. *Fin.* 2.84 *Pyladea amicitia*, Ovid, *Am.* 2.6.15f., *R.A.* 389 *semper habe Pyladen aliquem qui curet Oresten*, Mart. 6.11.9 *ut praestem Pyladen, aliquis mihi praestet Oresten*; to present it as the result of Strophius' *uirtus* provides a known fact with a new context, in the manner cultivated by rhetorical poetry, and also furnishes another instance of a common Senecan motif, the inheritance of virtue and vice.

943 infida...loca Cf. Ovid, *Her.* 11.102f. *fuge turbato tecta nefanda pede.*

944f. excessit, abiit...effugit Compare Acc. 592 R² *egredere exi ecfer te, elimina urbe*, Cic. *Cat.* 2.1 *abiit, excessit, euasit, erupit*; Volkmann, *Rhetorik* 451, 472.

945 opperiar The verb is most often found in Comedy, where it frequently describes actions of the stage-characters, cf. Ter. *Andr.* 523 *immo abi intro: ibi me opperire et quod parato opus est para*, 234f. *sed quidnam Pamphilum exanimatum uideo? uereor quid siet. | opperiar, ut sciam num quid nam haec turba tristitiae adferat.* The word occurs only here in Seneca.

946 ultro uulneri opponam caput Cf. 231 above (Aegisthus) *oppone cunctis uile suppliciis caput*; for different reasons, Aegisthus and Electra have both lost cause to fear.

350

949 manus...madent Cf. Ovid, *Met.* 14.199 *uultus etiamnunc caede madentes.*

950 uultusque...ferunt Cf. *Med.* 446 *fert odia prae se; totus in uultu est dolor,* and note on 127f. above.

truculenti 'fierce, maddened', cf. *Oed.* 958 *ardent minaces igne truculento genae, Thy.* 546f. *ferus ille et acer | nec potens mentis truculentus Atreus*; often used of harsh tyrants, cf. Val. Max. 5.3.3 *truculento uictori iugulandum tradere non exhorruit,* Sen. *HF* 254f.

951 concedam ad aras 'I shall withdraw to the altar'; for examples of *concedo* in Comedy see on *secede* in 308 above.

951f. uittis...iungi The elliptical construction is more than ornamental; Electra wishes not only to join Cassandra at her place of sanctuary but also to share in the protection of her sacred emblems (cf. Daremberg–Saglio s.u. '*uitta*', 950ff.).

953ff. The scene is clearly influenced, though probably indirectly, by the encounter between Electra and her mother in Sophocles (*El.* 516–633). Sophocles' Clytaemestra begins by upbraiding Electra for appearing in public (516ff.), provokes a debate which Electra decisively wins, and feebly threatens her daughter with Aegisthus (626f.). The brevity of Seneca's dialogue, however, and the new position of the scene immediately after Agamemnon's murder, preclude any subtlety of characterisation. In Sophocles both women are flawed and vulnerable, and their relationship is shown to be mutually degrading; Seneca's Electra is a blameless heroine who defies with wit and courage an hysterical and murderous adulteress.

953 impium atque audax caput *Caput* is most often a term of affection, e.g. Hor. *C.* 1.24.1f. *quis desiderio sit pudor aut modus | tam cari capitis?*; for its negative use cf., e.g., Virg. *Aen.* 4.613 (*infandum*), Sen. *Med.* 465 (*ingratum*), also Gaheis 50. The same ambivalence is found with κάρα and κεφαλή, see Barrett on Eur. *Hipp.* 651, T. Wendel, 'Die Gesprächsanrede', *Tübinger Beiträge* vi (1929) 112.

954 quo more 'in accordance with what custom', an expression several times used by Cicero; for examples see R. G. M. Nisbet, *C.R.* n.s. x (1960) 103, and compare as well *more* in such combinations as (*Dom.* 134) *nihil rite, nihil caste, nihil more institutoque perfecit* and (*Sex. Rosc.* 143) *omnia... more iure lege gentium facta.*

coetus publicos uirgo petis Though *coetus publicos* is an obvious exaggeration, Clytemestra's objection is authentically Greek; Jocelyn, *Tragedies of Ennius* 188 n.1, gives numerous tragic and comic examples, to which may be added Aesch. *P.V.* 130f., Soph. *El.* 871f., Arist. *Thesm.* 792ff., ps.-Phocylides 216 *PMG*, Naevius 7 R² *desubito famam tollunt, si quam solam uidere in uia*; cf. L. A. Post, *TAPhA* lxxii (1940) 437ff.

956 quis...uirginem The question must be taken together with Clytemestra's first lines: 'If you will loiter in public, who will believe you are a virgin?'

natam tuam? Electra pretends not to see the point of her mother's question, and completes it in her own sense; for the idea in this context cf. Soph. *El.* 307ff. and especially 608f. εἰ γὰρ πέφυκα τῶνδε τῶν ἔργων ἴδρις, | σχεδόν τι τὴν σὴν οὐ καταισχύνω φύσιν, in general cf. Eur. *Andr.* 622f. ἐκφέρουσι γάρ | μητρῷ' ὀνείδη, Juv. 6.239f. *scilicet expectas ut tradat mater honestos | atque alios mores quam quos habet?*, Ambrose, *de Virgin.* 16 *quid potuit filia de adultera matre discere nisi damnum pudoris?*

958f. animos uiriles...geris Sophocles' Electra and Antigone are accused of forgetting the properly submissive role of women by their weaker sisters (*Ant.* 61f., *El.* 997f.), and Seneca's Creon claims that Medea possesses *feminae nequitia* but *robur uirile* (*Med.* 267f.). In Ovid, *F.* 2.847, however, *matrona uirilis* compliments Lucretia; note too Seneca's phrase *uirilis sapientia* in *Cons. Helu.* 12.4, *Epist.* 115.2. Clytemestra's description is accurate, but we are not to accept her valuation.

corde tumefacto The phrasing may be Virgilian, cf. *Aen.* 6.49 *rabie fera corda tument*, 407 *tumida ex ira tum corda residunt* (*tumefactus* is not used in this sense by Ovid, and appears only here in Seneca), but the concept of emotions as swellings is Stoic (see note on 248 above).

959 agere...feminam 'to play a woman's role'; for *agere* in the theatrical sense cf. Ter. *Phorm.* 27 *primas partis qui aget, is erit Phormio*, Cic. *Rosc. Com.* 20, *Fam.* 7.6.2, Livy 45.25.1 *lenem mitemque senatorem egit*, Ovid, *F.* 6.70, *Ars* 2.294, Pacatus, *Pan. Theod.* 25.2 *miseri uetabamur agere miseros*.

domita...malo *Domare malo* is a euphemism for using torture to wear down resistance, cf. *Tro.* 349f. *compescere equidem uerba et audacem malo | poteram domare*, *Oed.* 518f. *audita fare, uel malo domitus graui | quid arma possint regis irati scies*, Acc. 683–4 R².

960 nisi...decet Electra uses Clytemestra's own actions as the basis for a quibble over the meaning of *agere feminam*; the reference to a sword may be a veiled threat (cf. Soph. *El.* 582f. εἰ γὰρ κτενοῦμεν ἄλλον ἀντ' ἄλλου, σύ τοι | πρώτη θάνοις ἄν, εἰ δίκης γε τυγχάνοις).

nisi forte fallor The expression is clearly sarcastic; cf. Cic. *Pis.* 65, *de Fato* 37, *Senec.* 32, cf. Müller–Seyffert on *Laelius*, p. 55, Sall. *Hist.* 1.77.14; irony may also be present with the related formula *aut ego fallor*, cf. Hor. *A.P.* 42 (with Brink's note), Ovid, *Met.* 1.607f., ps.-Virg. *Ciris* 227f., less clearly so with *ni* (or *nisi*) *fallor*.

961 et...putas? Clytemestra responds to the implied threat of violence in Electra's words by asserting her superior position; *parem nobis* is perhaps 'a match for us', cf. Hor. *C.* 1.6.16 *superis parem*. The line is rhetorically flat, but this weakness is surely intended by Seneca to slant the argument in Electra's favour.

962 uobis...tuus? Electra deliberately misunderstands Clytemestra's *nobis* (probably meant as an equivalent for *mihi*) as a reference to her and Aegisthus, and objects to the idea that Aegisthus has assumed Agamemnon's place. Her sarcasm in *quis iste est alter Agamemnon tuus?* suggests that Aegisthus is unfit for the epithet *alter Agamemnon*, and it seems at least possible that the jibe *uir caret uita tuus* may apply both to Agamemnon's death and to Aegisthus' lack of manhood.

964f. indomita...frangam The words are spoken to no one in particular and are a kind of thinking out loud; for Greek examples cf. Soph. *Ant.* 740, *O.T.* 1160, *Phil.* 910f. (all with ἀνὴρ ὅδε). Here the meaning seems to be 'I shall use my royal power to deal with her later', cf. Massinger, *Roman actor* 1.ii 'as for you, minion, I shall hereafter treat...'; *posthac* in such contexts more often means 'from now onwards, next time', cf., e.g., Pl. *Poen.* 460f. *ego faxo posthac di deaeque ceteri | contentiores mage erunt atque auidi minus*, Ter. *Ad.* 565, Virg. *Ecl.* 3.51, Tib. 1.5.5f.; compare the ironic use of ἐκ τοῦδε in Soph. *Ant.* 578f.

965f. citius...tuus Like Neptune in Virg. *Aen.* 1.134f., Clytemestra postpones punishment to attend to more urgent matters; compare also Agamemnon in Sen. *Tro.* 349f. *compescere equidem uerba et audacem malo | poteram domare; sed...potius interpres deum | Calchas uocetur.*

citius Only here and *Med.* 548, where it is a true comparative; in our passage it is a stronger *cito*, cf. *Apocol.* 7.1 *citius mihi uerum.* In Seneca, as in other poets, *ocius* is far more often used for this purpose (cf. Leo, *Obs.* 90ff.).

966 edissere The word appears in poetry before Virgil only in comedy (Pl. *As.* 325, *Capt.* 967) and Horace's satires (2.3.306), each time with deliberately pompous effect. Its use in high poetry is rare and apparently restricted to the imperative *edissere*; it usually betokens excited interrogation, cf. Virg. *Aen.* 2.149 (Priam questioning Sinon), Sen. *Oed.* 787 (feebly imitated by the author of *HO* 1617), Luc. 10.178, Sil. 10.516.

ubi sit natus, ubi frater tuus An unusually bald example of *uariatio*; if self-correction is intended ('my child, or should I rather say your brother?'), it is obscurely expressed.

967f. redde...redde The epanalepsis is rather feeble; for a more effective variation on this theme cf. *Thy.* 997f. *Redde iam natos mihi. | – Reddam, et tibi illos nullus eripiet dies.*

968 latitat Cf. Ulysses in *Tro.* 627ff. *abditum | hostem... | ubicumque latitat, erutam in medium date.*

969 regna A word associated with the kings of Rome (cf. Ovid, *F.* 2.668, 852) which frequently connotes tyranny and dictatorial use of power, cf. Cic. *Amic.* 41 *Ti. Gracchus regnum occupare conatus est, Sulla* 21, Sall. *Cat.* 5.6, *Jug.* 31.5, Ovid, *Met.* 1.152 *affectasse ferunt regnum caeleste Gigantas,* Luc. 4.691f., Quint. *Inst.* 3.8.47, Suet. *Diu. Iul.* 9.

970 iustae parenti satis; adulterae parum? The MSS differ over the speaker and the first word of the line. On neither point does the testimony of E carry weight: its *dixi* has been long recognised as a grammatical gloss (*pace* W. Morel, *AJPh* lxiv (1943) 94ff.), and the attribution to Clytemestra is irreconcilable with either of the transmitted forms of the verse.

The A text, then (*iustae parenti satis at iratae parum*), must be the starting-point for discussion. An obvious difficulty is *at*, which seems intolerably weak in Electra's mouth. To meet this problem all editors since Leo (except Viansino) have accepted a suggestion made independently by Poggio and Bothe, and have introduced ἀντιλαβή after *satis,* giving *iustae parenti satis* to Electra and the rejoinder *at iratae parum* to Clytemestra. Rhetorical considerations apart, this course is open to a technical objection: Seneca admits ἀντιλαβή neither at the sixth position in the line nor after the two short syllables of a dactyl or the first two syllables of a tribrach (cf. L. Strzelecki 7, 10; E. Harrison, *CR* liv (1940) 152–4). In the only place where the rule is broken by the MS text, *HO* 892 – *Vitam relinques misera? – Vt Alciden sequar,* Gronovius both removed the metrical anomaly and restored rhetorical point by the division – *Vitam relinques? – Miseram, ut Alciden sequar.*

If Electra speaks the whole line, the difficulty raised by *at* remains. Viansino's *an iratae parum?* is neat, and the sarcastic question suits Electra's attitude during this scene (cf. *natam tuam?* 956, *pietatem doces?* 957, *uobis?* 962). A further problem, however, now poses itself: *iratae* is hardly the proper contrast for *iustae,* least of all from Electra's taunting point of view. A moral term is clearly needed to express the point: a parent whose conscience is clear can be satisfied with knowing that her child is in good hands, while the guilty parent, whose crime may be avenged by her offspring, cannot rest until her children are dead as well (for this dilemma cf. Soph. *El.* 767f.). Bentley alone appears to have grasped this difficulty; his *adulterae parum?* solves it brilliantly.

971 morieris The threat is that of the typical stage despot, cf. Cic. *Rab. post.* 29 *regum autem sunt...illae minae:* ' *si te secundo lumine hic offendero, moriere*', probably from Ennius' *Medea,* cf. Eur. *Med.* 352ff., Sen. *Med.* 297ff. (Jocelyn 349; possibly imitated by Ter. *Eun.* 1064ff.), note also Livy 1.58.2 (Tarquin to Lucretia) *moriere, si emiseris uocem.* In Seneca such threats are issued by tyrants and confidants, and are consistently defied, cf. *HF* 429, *Med.* 170, cf. *HO* 332, 1012 below; see further Seidensticker 94 and n.38, Wanke 86.

hodie An emphatic particle expressing emotion. This usage, of probably colloquial origin (cf. Hofmann, *Lateinische Umgangssprache*² 41f.), is frequently found with threats and imprecations in Republican drama, cf. Pl. *As.* 630, 936 *ecastor cenabis hodie, ut dignus es, magnum malum, Men.* 1013, Ter. *Phorm.* 805ff. (cf. Hor. *S.* 2.7.21f.), *Ad.* 570, Naevius 13 R² *numquam hodie effugies quin mea manu moriare* (perhaps the source for Virg. *Ecl.* 3.49 *numquam hodie effugies* and *Aen.* 2.670 *numquam omnes hodie moriemur inulti*, see Austin *ad loc.*). Greek comedy uses τήμερον (or σήμερον) in similar contexts, cf., e.g., Cratinus 123 K, Hermippus 80 K, Arist. *Nub.* 699, 1308, 1491, *Eq.* 68, *Vesp.* 643, *Pax* 243, *Aues* 1045, *Plut.* 433, fr. 597 K, Menander fr. 798 Körte.

dummodo…manu 'as long as I die at your hands'. For *hac manu* = 'this hand of yours' cf. *HF* 1319 *hanc manum amplector libens*; *hic* is generally so used to express affection (see also Pl. *Pers.* 229, Ovid, *Her.* 16.136) or in supplications (e.g. Pl. *Rud.* 627, Ovid, *Met.* 14.373), cf. *T.L.L.* vi³.2704.35ff.

972 recedo ab aris Strikingly similar to Eur. *Andr.* 411f. ἰδοὺ προλείπω βωμὸν ἤδη χειρία | σφάζειν, φονεύειν, δεῖν, ἀπαρτῆσαι δέρην (compare Amphitryon in Eur. *Her.* 319f. ἰδοὺ πάρεστιν ἤδε φασγάνῳ δέρη | κεντεῖν φονεύειν, ἰέναι πέτρας ἄπο).

972ff. siue…praebeo; seu…exspectat The construction is discussed in detail by Leo (*Obs.* 94ff.), who notes that it is generally avoided by good poets with the notable exception of Ovid (more than thirty examples, mostly in the amatory poems); to his examples may be added Calp. Sic. 6.70f., Auson. *Prof. Burd.* 2.39ff. Seneca has the arrangement in prose (cf., e.g., *Ira* 3.1.5, *Epist.* 117.22), but admits it to the tragedies only here.

972ff. siue…iugulo…seu…colla Offering one's opponent a choice of methods may be a Euripidean motif (see the passages cited above on 972), but the specific alternatives mentioned here may derive from Ovid, *Met.* 13.457ff. (Polyxena) '*utere iamdudum generoso sanguine*', *dixit*, | '*nulla mora est; aut tu iugulo uel pectore telum* | *conde meo*' (*iugulumque simul pectusque retexit*); for Ovid's *pectus* Seneca substitutes the less noble *colla* (the place offered Hercules by Amphitryon in *HF* 1040f.). Deliberation over the proper place for the fatal blow also forms part of the topic in which possible methods of suicide are enumerated, cf. *Oed.* 1036ff. (in general Ed. Fraenkel, *Philologus* lxxxvii (1932) 470ff.; to his material may be added Sen. *Pho.* 64ff., *Pha.* 259f., Lucan 8.653, 9.106). The author of *HO* 991ff. has conflated the present passage and *Oed.* 1036ff. (cf. Axelson, *Korruptelenkult* 93f.).

973 uolens E's *tibi* is a manifest syntactical gloss, but objection has also been made to A's *uolens* on the grounds that it is inappropriately emphatic, while *libens* is the proper term for 'willingly, gladly' (cf. Zwierlein, *Gnomon* xli (1969) 765). It is quite true that the two certain appearances of *uolens* in Seneca involve an emphasis on the unforced quality of an action, i.e. *HF* 1300f. *ecce iam facies scelus* | *uolens sciensque, Pha.* 441 *si quis ultro se malis* *offert uolens*; this, however, is no objection to *uolens* here, since Electra may with justice call attention to her voluntary sacrifice (invoking, perhaps, sacral associations). A further point is that there is no visible reason for the corruption of the banal and familiar *libens* (ten instances in the plays, all in this position in the line) into the rarer *uolens*.

975 intenta... ceruix *Intenta* suggests both eagerness (cf. Virg. *Aen.* 5.137 *intenti exspectabant signum*) and physical distension (cf. Ter. *Eun.* 312 *intendam neruos*). For the thought cf. *HF* 1040 and the imitation in *HO* 976f. *si potes letum dare, | animose coniunx, dexteram exspecto tuam.*

976 paratum (E)/**peractum** (A) Del Rio's explanation of *peractum*, 'restat ut impuratam manum sanguine maritali filiali cruore abluas. tunc facinus patrasti, nunc eris misericors', was given new currency by Stuart (*C.Q.* v (1911) 34) and has caused *peractum* to be adopted by more than one modern editor. The ironic use of *ablue* is beyond question (see following note), but it does not depend on reading *peractum*: the crime which Electra has prepared for her mother (*scelus paratum*) can equally well be spoken of in this light. What seems doubtful is that *scelus* in 976, after several lines turning on Electra's impending death, could refer to another criminal act. (It should be noted that *scelus peractum* occurs in *HO* 994f., that is, in a passage clearly modelled on *Agam.* 972ff.; the phrase in *HO*, however, has its normal meaning, and its value as evidence is doubtful.)

E's *paratum*, on the other hand, raises no difficulties, and sums up the four preceding lines in an appropriately sarcastic tone: Electra has made all the preparations, her mother need only strike the blow. For *paratus* in the sense 'at hand' (cf. Hor. *C.* 1.31.17 *frui paratis* with Nisbet–Hubbard's note) in such contexts, cf. *Pho.* 456f. *si placuit scelus, | maius paratum est, HF* 1027 *si piget luctus, habes | mortem paratam, Oed.* 76f. *negatur uni nempe in hoc populo mihi | mors tam parata?*, also Ovid, *Met.* 10.384f. *mortisque paratae | instrumenta uidens*, Lucan 8.34f. *quisquamne secundis | tradere se fatis audet nisi morte parata?*

977 sanguine hoc dextram ablue For the pointed use of words like *piare* and *expiare*, cf. Prop. 3.19.18 *iram natorum caede piauit amor* [*sc. Medeae*], Ovid, *Met.* 8.483 *mors morte pianda est*, ps.-Sall. *Epist. ad Caes.* 1.3.4, *Anth. Lat.* 462.23f. Riese, Juv. 13.54. Electra's words contain the added irony that the purification is not to take place through the death of the criminal (as in all the passages cited), but through the slaughter of another victim.

979 gradere Cf. Pac. 47 R² *gradere atque atrocem coerce confidentiam.*

981 uocis infandae Perhaps the first use of this bold combination; Lucan has it (9.1013) together with *infandum murmur* (6.448) and *infandum carmen* (6.682), cf. *T.L.L.* VII¹.1345.22ff. The repetition of *infandus* in 983 (*sceleris infandi artifex*) may be without significance, though Electra might be using Aegisthus' own term of moral disapprobation against him.

983 etiam monebit *Etiam* expresses shocked surprise, 'does the craftsman of this crime really intend to offer instruction?' The usage may be colloquial in origin, cf. Naevius, *com.* 87 R², Pl. *Aul.* 633 *uerberabilissume, etiam rogitas?*, Ter. *Eun.* 1017 *ehem quid dixti, pessuma? an mentita es? etiam rides?*, cf. Liv. And. *sc.* 19 R² *etiam minitas?*, but it is used twice in the *Aeneid* of indignant or astonished questions, cf. *Aen.* 3.247f. *bellum etiam pro caede boum...* | *Laomedontiadae, bellumne inferre paratis?*, 4.305f. *dissimulare etiam sperasti, perfide, tantum* | *posse nefas?*; cf. also Cic. *Sex. Rosc.* 102 *alter, si dis placet, testimonium etiam dicturus est, Pis.* 2, 23, 31, Sen. *Oed.* 678, *Pha.* 705 *quid hoc est? etiam in amplexus ruit?*

sceleris...artifex Similar expressions are used of Aegisthus in Greek (cf. *Od.* 11.409 τεύξας θάνατόν τε μόρον τε, Aesch. *Ag.* 1604 τοῦδε τοῦ φόνου ῥαφεύς), but Seneca's immediate source may be Ovid, cf. *Ars* 1.656 *necis artifices, Met.* 13.551 *uadit ad artificem dirae...caedis.* Seneca uses *scelerum artifex*, with greater emphasis on connotations of technical expertise, of Medea (734) and of women generally (*Pha.* 559); note also Theseus describing himself as *crudus...leti artifex* | *exitia machinatus insolita* (*Pha.* 1220f.).

984 nomen ambiguum suis 'whose proper name (i.e. relationship) is unclear even to his own'; for *nomen* in similar contexts cf. Cic. *Cluent.* 199 *atque etiam nomen necessitudinum, non solum naturae nomen et iura mutauit, uxor generi, nouerca filii, filiae paelex,* Ovid, *Met.* 10.346ff. *et quot confundas et iura et nomina, sentis?* | *tune eris et matris paelex et adultera patris,* | *tune soror nati, genetrixque uocabere fratris?* The irregularity of Aegisthus' descent was a commonplace of Greek oratory, cf. Andoc. *Myst.* 128f., *in Alcib.* 22.

987 demetere Used only here in the plays, and apparently first applied to human decapitation by Ovid in *Met.* 5.104 *demetit ense caput* (so Heinsius, recc.: *decutit* MSS uett.); common in this sense in Silver epic.

fratrem reddat aut animam Compare *Pha.* 670 *finem hic dolori faciet aut uitae dies,* Sen. *Contr. exc.* 2.4 *in sinu meo et filium et animam deposuit*; cf. Canter 163 n.22.

988ff. abstrusa...malis Aegisthus twice describes the fate in store for Electra. Here, torture and confinement with starvation; in 997–1000 no mention of torture, only chaining in a remote rocky dungeon. Threats of torture and imprisonment are often issued by Senecan despots, in most cases, as here, with a view to obtaining information (cf. *Pha.* 882ff., *Tro.* 573, 578ff., *Oed.* 852, 862 (cf. Soph. *O.T.* 1152, 1154)) or quelling a rebellious spirit (cf. *HF* 426, *Oed.* 518, 707). The richness of detail in the present passage, however, sets it apart from other instances of the topic; only *Tro.* 578f. approaches it (*uerberibus igni* †morte† *cruciatu eloqui* | *quodcumque celas adiget inuitam dolor*).

The origins of this part of the scene may be sought in Greek tragedy. In

Aeschylus' *Agamemnon* (1639ff.) Aegisthus threatens to subdue the recalcitrant chorus-members with chains, confinement in darkness, and starvation. In Sophocles' *Electra* 379ff. a threat of confinement is directed at Electra alone; the details emphasised – the darkness and remoteness of the rocky prison – correspond almost exactly to 997–1000 in Seneca. The prominence of torture in Seneca's lines (989ff.), not accounted for by the Greek scenes adduced, finds a parallel in a fragment of Pacuvius' *Dulorestes* which has been plausibly referred to a scene in which Electra is threatened by Aegisthus (or Clytemestra): *nam te in tenebrica saepe lacerabo fame | clausam* [O. Jahn: *clausum* MSS] *et fatigans artus torto distraham* (158f. R²). Direct Pacuvian influence on Seneca, however, is not thereby demonstrated; declamation-oratory furnishes abundant and graphic references to torture, cf. Sen. *Contr.* 2.5.4ff., 9.6.18, 10.5 *passim*, and S. F. Bonner, *Roman declamation* (1949) 59.

988 caeco carcere In addition to the passages cited above cf. Sall. *Jug.* 14.15 *pauci, quibus relicta est anima, clausi in tenebris cum maerore et luctu morte grauiorem uitam exigunt.*

saxo The rocky prison figures also in Soph. *Ant.* 774 κρύψω πετρώδει ζῶσαν ἐν κατώρυχι, 885f. κατηρεφεῖ | τύμβῳ, Accius 81 R² *sed angustitate inclusam saxi, squalidam...*, Sen. *Oed.* 707 *seruata sontem saxeo inclusum specu.*

990 forsan Typical of the cruel indifference of the despot, cf. Soph. *Ant.* 777f. κἀκεῖ τὸν "Αιδην... αἰτουμένη που τεύξεται τὸ μὴ θανεῖν, *Phil.* 1078f. χοὖτος τάχ' ἂν φρόνησιν ἐν τούτῳ λάβοι | λῴω τιν' ἡμῖν.

991 inops, egens Cf. Acc. 415 R² *exul inter hostis, exspes expers desertus uagus*, Cic. *Tusc.* 3.39 *Telamonem pulsum patria exsulantem atque egentem*, *Auct. ad Her.* 4.52 *inopem atque egentem nunc uidemus*, Ovid, *Met.* 14.217 *solus, inops, exspes, leto poenaeque relictus*; the words may here suggest the starvation which often accompanies the threat of imprisonment (cf. Pl. *Asin.* 145 *reddam ego te ex fera fame mansuetam*).

paedore obsita A's *obsita* is confirmed by the parallel *HF* 627f. *unde tam foedo obsiti | paedore nati?*, cf. also Livy 1.23 *uestis obsita squalore*, 29.16 *obsiti squalore et sordibus*, Tac. *Ann.* 4.28 *obsitus illuuie ac squalore*, Val. Max. 2.9.5; for *paedor* as a concomitant of languishing in prison, cf. Lucan 2.72f., Silius 6.475f.

992 exul, inuisa omnibus The similarity to *Med.* 21 *exul, pauens, inuisus, incerti laris* is striking, and the words are indeed less appropriate to the imprisoned Electra than to Medea's imaginary picture of Jason.

994 concede mortem The life of torment threatened by Aegisthus makes death seem preferable. Electra's sudden collapse is remarkable, since in Seneca resistance to evil is often implausibly unshakable; it is further testimony to the increased stature and effectiveness with which Seneca has endowed Aegisthus.

994f. si...exigit Thus Theseus in Eur. *Hipp.* 1045ff. denies Hippolytus' request for a sentence of death instead of banishment: οὐχ οὕτω θανῇ, | ὥσπερ σὺ σαυτῷ τόνδε προύθηκας νόμον· | ταχὺς γὰρ "Αιδης ῥᾷστος ἀνδρὶ δυστυχεῖ. Typically Senecan is the appended *sententia*; all Senecan tyrants have consulted the same handbook, cf. *HF* 511ff. *qui morte cunctos luere supplicium iubet, | nescit tyrannus esse. diuersa irroga: | miserum ueta perire, felicem iube, Thy.* 246f. *perimat tyrannus lenis: in regno meo | mors impetratur* (as it was under Gaius, according to Sen. *N.Q.* 4.1.17); see also Luc. 2.511f., Claud. *Ruf.* 1.234ff.

996 mortem...mori A common thought, cf. Aesch. *P.V.* 750ff., Soph. *El.* 1007f. οὐ γὰρ θανεῖν ἔχθιστον, ἀλλ' ὅταν θανεῖν | χρῄζων τις εἶτα μηδὲ τοῦτ' ἔχῃ λαβεῖν (cf. Vahlen, *Opusc. Acad.* II.159ff.), Publ. Syr. 504 *quam miserum est mortem cupere nec posse emori,* Hor. *A.P.* 467, Sen. *Contr. exc.* 8.4 *quid est in uita miserius quam mori uelle?,* Ovid, *Her.* 10.82 *mors...minus poenae quam mora mortis habet,* Sen. *Pho.* 98ff.

997 abripite Having clearly got the better of the exchange with Electra, Aegisthus turns brusquely to business; for *abripite...trahite* (1003), cf. *Tro.* 1003 *abreptam trahe.* For similar commands in Greek tragedy cf. Eur. *Cret.* 45ff., *Hipp.* 1084, cf. Acc. 383 R².

monstrum Compare the order of Creon (*Med.* 190f.) *uade ueloci uia | monstrumque saeuum horribile iamdudum auehe*; for such abuse directed by tyrants toward their subjects cf. Opelt, *Schimpfwörter* 165 n.94.

998 ultimo in regni angulo Cf. *Med.* 250f. *urbe si pelli placet, | detur remotus aliquis in regnis locus.* The phrase *ultimus regni angulus* may betray a conception of the kingdom of Argos along Roman lines, cf. Cic. *Cat.* 2.4 *nemo non modo Romae sed nec ullo in angulo Italiae,* Hor. *C.* 2.6.13f. *ille terrarum mihi praeter omnes | angulus ridet,* Prop. 4.9.65f. *angulus hic mundi nunc me mea fata trahentem | accipit.*

999 saeptam Probably a reference to the close confinement of the prison rather than that of the chains; for *saeptus* ('penned in') cf. Enn. *sc.* 254 R² *teneor consaepta,* Virg. *Aen.* 9.398 *inclusus muris hostilique aggere saeptus,* Ovid, *Tr.* 3.11.13f. *sic ego belligeris a gentibus undique saeptus | terreor.*

1000 domet Used euphemistically of death in Ovid, *Met.* 1.311f. *quibus unda pepercit, | illos longa domant inopi ieiunia uictu,* but here probably 'subdue' (cf. note on 959 *domita malo*).

1002 captiua coniunx For *coniunx = paelex,* cf. Prop. 2.8.29 *abrepta desertus coniuge Achilles,* Virg. *Ecl.* 8.18, 66, Ovid, *Ars* 3.331f. *ereptae magno flammatus amore | coniugis...Orestes, Her.* 8.18, 3.37. The addition of *captiua,* however, lends further point; Agamemnon should have regarded Cassandra as a slave, but was preparing to install her in his home with the status of a wife (compare *captae maritus* in 191 above).

359

1003 coniugem ereptum mihi In context this probably means 'the husband she has stolen from me', but there may also be a pointed echo of phrases in which *ereptum mihi* means 'snatched from me by death', e.g. Catull. 68.105ff. *quo tibi tum casu...* | *ereptum est uita dulcius atque anima* | *coniugium*, Lygdamus 2.29f. *dolor huic et cura Neaerae,* | *coniugis ereptae, causa perire fuit*, Sen. *Tro.* 556ff. *utinam...* | *nossemque quis te casus ereptum mihi* | *teneret*.

1004ff. ne trahite...propero Cassandra's eagerness is paralleled by her attitude in Euripides (cf. *Tro.* 460f. ἥξω δ' ἐς νεκροὺς νικηφόρος | καὶ δόμους πέρσασ' 'Ατρειδῶν ὧν ἀπωλόμεσθ' ὕπο, and compare *nihil moramur* in 1010 with 445 στεῖχ' ὅπως τάχιστ' ἐς "Αιδου νυμφίῳ γημώμεθα); a *sapiens* might speak thus (cf. Sen. *Prou.* 5.4 *non trahuntur a fortuna, sequuntur illam et aequant gradus, Tro.* 1147 *Pyrrhum antecedit*, of Polyxena), but the attitude may also be the product of less praiseworthy motives; compare, for example, Hecuba in Sen. *Tro.* 993 *duc, duc, Vlixe, nil moror, dominum sequor*, whose willingness comes from a lively hope for revenge (cf. 994–8). The thought that new arrivals in Hades will inform the dead of events on earth is common, cf. *HF* 639 *nuntiet Diti Lycus* | *me iam redisse, Apocol.* 13 *antecesserat... Narcissus libertus ad patronum excipiendum...'celerius' inquit Mercurius 'et uenire nos nuntia'*; also J. Kroll, *Gott und Hölle* (1932), 381f.

1006ff. repletum...dolo The combination of a summary of the action of the play with allusions to further developments in the myth (1012) is found nowhere else in Seneca, though *Tro.* 1167f. *concidit uirgo ac puer;* | *bellum peractum est* recapitulates part of that play's action and *Thyestes* ends (1110f.) with veiled references to later elements of the myth. In Greek tragedy the only instances of these devices I have noted come from Aeschylean trilogies (summary of action, *Cho.* 1065ff.; forward references, *Agam.* 1646, 1667, *P.V.* 871ff.), where they serve an obvious dramatic purpose. In other Greek plays references in the closing lines to the preceding action are uniformly generic, cf. Soph. *Trach.* 1269, 1276ff., *O.T.* 1525ff., Eur. *Alc.* 1157f. (note reference forward, without specific content), *I.A.* 1621, [Eur.] *Phoen.* 1758ff. It may be significant that the probably non-Aeschylean end of the *Septem* contains forward references, even though the play is the final one of its trilogy (in particular the Herald's speech 1005–25); this evidence, however, is insufficient in itself to justify conclusions about fourth-century taste or techniques (cf. Page, *Actors' interpolations in Greek tragedy* (1934) 32).

1008 paria fata The details of this equality, the last of many references in the play to the congruence of Greek and Trojan destinies, are supplied in the following line: to have died *dono* – the Trojan horse, Clytemestra's robe – *feminae stupro*, and *dolo*. Once the rhetorical point is grasped, the punctuation of 1009 found in all modern editions (*dono feminae, stupro, dolo*) is seen to be erroneous.

1009 feminae stupro Note Prop. 3.19.20f. *Clytemestrae, propter quam tota Mycenis | infamis stupro stat Pelopea domus*; in general, Sen. *Pha.* 560f. [*femina*] *huius incestis stupris | fumant tot urbes*. Seneca uses *stuprum* of all sorts of sexual misbehaviour: here of adultery, in *Pha.* 97 of homosexuality, in 560 of incest, in 726 of rape.

1011 iuuat uixisse post Troiam 'there is pleasure in having survived the fall of Troy'; for comparable pointed joy in defeat (although for a different reason) cf. *Carm. Eins.* 1.40f. *iam tanti cecidisse fuit! gaudete, ruinae | et laudate rogos*. Geminatio of *iam* is somewhat overworked in Seneca (cf. *Med.* 692, 949, 982, *Pha.* 926, *Oed.* 28, 668; Canter 156f.), that of *iuuat* is rarer, cf. *Med.* 911 *iuuat, iuuat rapuisse fraternum caput*; the conjunction of both, and the postposition of the second *iuuat*, effectively express the intensity of Cassandra's *Schadenfreude* (on *iuuat* cf. Seidler 137 n.1). For the ellipse in *post Troiam* see Nisbet–Hubbard on Hor. *C.* 1.18.5 *post uina*.

1012 furiosa Because she has experienced prophetic *furor*, cf. 870 above, Prop. 3.13.65 *ille furor patriae fuit utilis, ille parenti*, Virg. *Aen.* 10.68 *furiis Cassandrae*.

ueniet et uobis furor Cassandra's reply is clearly a reference to the vengeance of Orestes, and *furor* is here 'avenging agent' (= *furia*, ἐρινύς), as perhaps in *Med.* 396 (see Costa *ad loc.*), also Ovid, *Met.* 4.471 *ne...in facinus traherent Athamanta furores*, Val. Fl. 1.796f. *grandaeua furorum | Poena parens*, 7.510 *questus semper furor ultus amantum*, Ruf. *Hist. Eccl.* 3.6.24 *praedonibus furor* (= τοῖς στασιασταῖς ἐρινύς in Eusebius).

APPENDIXES

1. ORTHOGRAPHY

The spelling of a classical author is even more liable than his text to alter in the course of transmission; it cannot, therefore, be restored with even the limited certainty to which a critical text aspires.

Where the MSS of Seneca agree, they yield nothing earlier than the spelling of their late antique archetype, and their agreement on orthographical points does not guarantee even that much. The archetype itself may have deviated from Seneca's spelling; the Ambrosian palimpsest, probably not much later in date than the archetype, contains several clearly un-Senecan spellings: *quaerere* for *querere, suplex, illut, inclytum, execta, adque* fot *atque, at* for *ad, fleuile* for *flebile.* Certainly all MSS agree in spellings which no editor would attribute to Seneca, e.g. *Agamennon, occeano, brachia, littora,*

Where E and A divide, a new problem arises: is E's generally more 'antique' spelling due to genuine tradition, or is it the product of Carolingian archaising which the later medieval A MSS escaped? E, for example, preserves *ae* in many places where it has become *e* in A, but E also inserts *ae* in many places where it is wrong (*haector, hercaeum,* etc.). The same tendency to hypercorrection is visible in E's support of the non-Latin forms *Achillen* (*Tro.* 177) and *Vlixen* (*Tro.* 614). It is clear that the editor can follow neither the MSS generally nor the best single MS without exception.

My general practice has been to preserve a spelling on which all MSS agree unless there is positive reason to correct it; where E and A divide, I have decided each case separately, at times on admittedly arbitrary grounds. Unlike other modern editors of Seneca, I have aimed at consistency on each single point; so I write *natus* everywhere, not *gnatus* or *natus* depending on the MS support in each instance. This has been done mainly to spare the reader distraction; no one can be sure that Seneca was consistent in all such matters, but the MSS are too unsure a guide to justify aping their inconsistencies. In the following lists I record the MS evidence (usually citing only the major MSS, E P CS) and briefly explain, where appropriate, the reasons for my practice. I hope that my choices will seem reasonable ones, not the only reasonable ones.

I. PROPER NAMES

(In each case the form given as the lemma is the one chosen for the text.)

Achilles, acc. *Achillem* (159) E P CS (cf. *Octauia* 815), Housman, *JPhil*

363

xxxi (1910) 236; *CR* v (1891) 293. (Note *Tro.* 177 *-en* E, *-em* PC; *Epist.* 104.31 (citing Virg. *Aen.* 1.458) *-en* codd., printed by Reynolds.)

Agamemnon   The MSS alternate between *Agamennon* and *Agamenon*; only in 39 does E have *Agamemnon* (the name occurs at 245, 396a, 514, 778, and in headings). Similarly *Agamemnonius* (356): E has *Agamenn-*, P CS *Agamen-*.

Assaracus (878)   *Assaraci* E CS: *-ici* P (cf. *Tro.* 17).

Atrides, acc. *Atriden* (275) E P: *-em* CS (cf. *Octauia* 816 *-em* P CS). For *Atriden* cf. Hor. *Epist.* 1.2.12, Ovid, *Her.* 16.366, Sen. *Epist.* 104.31, *Ilias Lat.* 74, Juv. 4.65.

　　　abl. **Atrida** (292) E P CS (cf. *Il. Lat.* 90.327; in Ovid, *Her.* 3.39 the MSS divide between *-a* and *-e*).

Attis, acc. *Attin* (690) E: *atin* Trevet: *atim* C Vd: *athum* P: *arim* S.

Bootes (70)   E PSV: *boetes* C d (cf. *Med.* 315 *boo-* E P: *boe-* CS; *Octauia* 234 *boo-* CS G: *boe-* P; *T.L.L. Onom.* II.2128.31f.).

Calchas (167)   S l recc.: *chalchas* E: *calcas* P C Vd.

Caphereus (560)   *Chapereus* E: *caphareus* P CS (similarly *HO* 777, 804). Cf. Prop. 3.7.39, Ovid, *Tr.* 1.1.83, 5.7.36, Silius 14.143.

Cnosius (24)   Ed. 1506: *gnosius* codd. (cf. Hor. *C.* 1.15.17, Housman, *CQ* xxii (1928) 4f., Kenney on Ovid, *Ars* 1.293, Bömer on Ovid, *Met.* 3.208).

Corus   484 *Corus* edd.: *chorus* codd. 599 *coris* P^{ac}: *ch-* E P^{2pc} CS.

Corus   484 *Corus* edd.: *chorus* codd. 599 *coris* P[ac]: *ch-* E P[2pc] CS.

Cycnus   215 *Cycnus* edd.: *cicnus* E: *cig-* P CS. 679 *cycnus* E: *cig-* P CS.

Deiphobus (749)   *Deiphobe* recc.: *deiphoebe* E: *deiphebe* P CS.

Eurotas (319)   acc. *Eurotan* E: *-am* P CS (cf. *Pho.* 127 *-an* P: *-am* E: *-em* CS, Housman, *JPhil* xxxi (1910) 256).

Geryon (840)   gen. *Geryonae* E: *gerionee* P: *gerionei* CS Vd: *gerionis* e (cf. *HF* 1170 *geryonae* E: *gerionis* P CS); for the form see Housman, *JPhil* xxxi (1910) 253, Virg. *Aen.* 8.202, Silius 3.422; at Prop. 3.22.9 *Gerionis* is the only transmitted reading.

Hecabe (648)   F l^{mg}, *postea coni. Bothe*: *hecube* P CS: *hecubae* E: *hecuba* n² a M3 (cf. *Tro.* 859 *hecuba* E: *hecube* P CS, Housman 261).

Hippolyte (848)   Edd.: *hyppolite* E: *yppolite* P: *ypolite* CS.

Isthmon (564)   Edd.: *istmon* P: *histmon* S: *histhmon* E: *hismon* C (cf. Ovid, *Met.* 6.419f., 7.405, *Her.* 8.69).

Itys, acc. *Ityn* (672) E: *ythin* P: *ytin* C: *ytim* S.

Iuppiter   404 *Iupp-* E: *iup-* P CS. 814 *Iupp-* FN KQ ln: *iup-* P CS: *ipp-* E (cf. *Oed.* 502).

Lemnon (566)   E: *lennon* P CS.

Marmaricus (739)   E CS: *marmoricus* P recc.

Nemeaeus (829)   Ascensius: *nemeus* E P CS (cf. *Oed.* 40 *nemeei* recc.: *nemei* E P CS. *HO* 1193 *nemeaea* Auantius, *nemeaei* Ascensius: *nemaei* E: *nemei* P CS).

Oceanus (484)   Edd.: *occ-* codd. (cf. *Oed.* 504, *HO* 743).

Pallas, acc. *Palladem* (*sic*) (546) E P S: *-en* C. See commentary; the defective form is a sign of the verse's spuriousness.

Parrhasis (831)   Auantius: *parrahsis* E: *parrasis* P CS.

Pelopius   7 *pelopie* E P CS. 165 *pelopia* E: *-ea* CS: *-eia* P (cf. *Thy.* 641, *HF* 997 *Cyclopia* Gronouius: *-ea* E P CS; Leo, *Obs.* 89).

Pyrrhus   512 Edd.: *pirrus* E P C: *pirtus* S (*more suo*). 637 Edd.: *pyrrus* E S: *pirrus* C: *om.* P.

Rhesus (216)   *Rheso* E: *reso* P: *theso* S: *teso* V: *thesso* KQ: *theseo* C recc.

Sipylus (394)   *Sipyli* E: *syphili* P: *sisiphi* CS (cf. *HO* 185 *Sipylum* Gronouius: *syphili* P: *sisiphi* CS: *si syphum* E; also Pliny, *N.H.* 6.34, 39, Stat. *S.* 5.1.33, Florus 1.24.15, Auson. *Epit.* 27).

Sparta (?) (280) acc. *Spartam* E: *-em* P CS: *-en* For Leid.2 d Vi.1 R8 (Ascensius). *Sparten* could be right, but the question cannot be settled with confidence. Seneca has no unanimously transmitted instance of *Sparta* (cf. *Pho.* 128 *-amque* E: *-enque* P: *-emque* CS); *Sparte* is the only form of the nominative in Seneca as in other Latin poets (cf. *Tro.* 854, *Thy.* 627; *Octauia* 773; cf. Palmer on Ovid, *Her.* 1.65). For the oblique cases Virgil uses *Sparta* only (*G.* 3.405, *Aen.* 10.92, also [Virg.] *Aen.* 2.577), but *Sparten* is the only accusative form found in Ovid (*Met.* 10.170, 217, *F.* 6.47, *Her.* 1.65, 15.189), cf. also Statius, *Th.* 1.262.

Strophius (918)   E P CS: *-ilus* d KQ: *-ylus* l: *-us* e.

Tanais, acc. *Tanain* (679) Bothe: *tanayn* F6: *-aim* E P CS.

Threicius (841)   *Threicium* edd.: *treicium* P CS: *threcium* E.

Thressa (216)   E: *tressa* P S: *cressa* C (cf. Ovid, *Her.* 19.100).

Thyestes, gen. *Thyestae* Ante v. 1 *ego*: *thyestis* E: *om.* P CS. 293 edd.: *thiestae* E: *tyeste* P: *thieste* CS. 907 ed. 1563: *-e* codd. For the form *Thyestae* cf. *Tro.* 341, Hor. *A.P.* 91, Ovid, *Ibis* 545, Pers. 5.8, Housman 250.

Thyesteus (909)   *Thyestea* F: *thiestea* E CS: *tyesta* P.

Xanthus (213)   F MN: *santhus* E: *xantus* CS: *xanctus* P: *sanctus* d^ac.

Zmintheus (176)   *Zminthea* E: *zminthe* CS: *et minthe* P (*alii alia*): *Smynthea* Auantius: *fort. Sminthea* (cf. Ovid, *Met.* 12.585, *F.* 6.425; G. P. Goold, *HSCP* lxix (1965) 11).

Clytemestra Thus the MSS generally (*cli-* is common in P CS). The name does not appear in the text; Seneca probably regarded the second syllable as heavy, as do all writers except Ausonius (*Epit. Her.* 1.4). Ritschl (*Opusc.* II.497f.) adduced Livius Andronicus 11 R² *Clytemestra iuxtim, tertias natae occupant* as evidence of an old Latin scansion *Clytĕmestra*, but the shortening could be due to *Iambenkürzung* and so reveals nothing about the normal scansion. Elsewhere both *Clytaemestra* and *Clytemestra* are supported by good MSS and printed by editors: for *Clytemestra* cf. *Rhet. ad Her.* 1.17, 26 (codd. uett. *s.* ix–x), Cic. *Off.* 1.114, *Fat.* 34 (heavy second syllable guaranteed by clausula), Pliny, *N.H.* 35.144 (*Clytemestra* B, *s.* x; *Clytaemnestra* R, ca. 1100), Juv. 6.656 (P, *s.* ix), Apul. *Apol.* 78; on the other hand, *Clytaemestra* is attested by the oldest MS of Cicero's *Ad Familiares* (7.1.2) and by good MSS of Quintilian (2.17.4; 3.11.4, 5, 20; 8.6.53, and cf. Winterbottom, *Problems in Quintilian* (1970) 52). See also *T.L.L., Onom.* II.512.26ff. In light of the parallels for *Clytemestra*, I have not departed from the unanimous testimony of the Seneca MSS; it is noteworthy that E never gives *Clytaemestra*, since it faithfully preserves *-ae-* in other Greek proper names (e.g. *Aegisthus* in several headings and in the text at 262; *Phaedra* in headings before *Pha.* 89, 360, 589, etc.; P CS regularly have *Egist*(*h*)*us* and *Phedra*).

II. OTHER WORDS

aedon (671) Auantius: *edom* E: *edonis* P CS.

alcyones (680) P CS: *altiones* E.

anhelus (713) *anhela* E S: *anela* C: *hanela* P.

bracchia (439) E: *brachia* P CS (cf. *Oed.* 404 *bracch-* E R: *brach-* T P CS).

claudo Forms in *au* are better supported than those in *u*: in 108, 559, 718 forms of *clausus* appear in E P CS; the MSS divide only in 889 *claudunt* P CS: *clu-* E. In other plays *cludo* (*clusus*) appears in E (*Pha.* 47, *Thy.* 916, 1041, *HO* 599), E P (*HF* 281, *Med.* 820), or E P CS (*Tro.* 186, *Pho.* 148, 467, *HO* 1401), but here too *claudo* and *clausus* have numerical superiority.

forsan (990) P C: *forsam* E S^ac.

genetrix (979) Edd.: *geni-* E P CS.

hasta (529) P C S: *asta* E.

hoc, adv. (143) E C: *huc* P S; also *HF* 1225 *hoc* E: *huc* P CS (same division at *Thy.* 710, 1014). The form is found in Seneca's prose, cf. *Epist.* 84.2, *N.Q.* 5.1.1, E. Thomas, *Hermes* xxix (1893) 308f., Rossbach, *de Senecae philosophi librorum recensione et emendatione* (1888) 113–15.

inclitus 125 *inclitum* E P CS; 369 *inclita* P CS: *-uta* E; 918 *inclitus* P CS: *-utus* E.

languor (161) *languore* C: *langore* P S: *lango* E.

litora (435) CS: *littora* E P.

opperior (945) *opperiar* M2 M3: *operiar* E P CS.

periclum 234 *pericli* E: *-uli* P CS. 798 *periclum* P CS: *-ulum* E.

pro, exclam. (35). CS: *proh* E: *proth* P.

semustus (761) E^{ac} P CS^{ac}: *semi-* E^{2pc} S^{2pc} (cf. *Tro.* 1085).

stuprum (1009) *stupro* E P C: *strupo* S (cf. *HF* 488, *Thy.* 222).

suboles (157) *subolis* Peiper: *sob-* codd. Elsewhere E has *suboles* (*Tro.* 463, 528, *Pha.* 468), P CS consistently *soboles* (also *Octauia* 180, 181, 406).

subripere (298) P CS: E's corrupt *sub rupe reductus* might seem to point to *subrupere*, cf. B. Schmidt, *Jb.* xcvii (1868) 878, Housman, *CQ* xvii (1923) 166. Like Housman's other attempts to wrest antique spellings from MS variants, this one is to be resisted (cf. *Tro.* 987f. *ecfluit, Tro.* 69, 146, 551 *graiius, HO* 1219 *reuolsus*).

taedae (259) E CS: *thede* P.

trigeminus (14) E S: *ter-* P C.

tropaea (190) Edd.: *trophea* E P CS.

uitta 712 *uitt(a)e* E P C: *uicte* S. 951 *uittis* E: *uictis* P CS.

III. VARIA

natus In almost all instances of the substantive in *Ag.* E P give *gnatus* and CS *natus* (30, 33, 36, 198, 293, 368, 979, 985; at 616 and 907 all MSS read *natus*); in other plays, however, the picture is somewhat less consistent (cf. Woesler 175). The agreement of E P is striking, and the spelling *gnatus* may be archetypal. I have abandoned it reluctantly in favour of consistency. I regularise to *natus* because this form is six times guaranteed by metre in the genuine plays (*Ag.* 616, *Tro.* 247, *Pho.* 365, *Med.* 507, *Thy.* 354, 1005) and twice in *HO* (896, 1338); note that in *Tro.* 247 E P, in *Thy.* 1005 E gives a mistaken form of *gnatus*. On the other hand, *gnatus* is never shown right by metre: the only apparent exception is *HO* 1415 *si mihi (g)natum inclitum* (*gn-* E: *n-* P CS), but the author of *HO* permits, even cultivates, *mihī* in this position (cf. 7, 311, 1402, 1434, 1444, cf. *Octauia* 150) and so *natum* is acceptable here as well.

Accusative plurals of third declension adjectives In a relatively small number of places the form *-is* is supported by either E alone (32, 400 *omnis*; 167 *nuptialis*; 717 *reluctantis*), E and P (695 *omnis*), or P CS alone

(237 *trementis*; 602 *cadentis*); forms in -*es* are far more commonly given in E P CS (cf., e.g., 246, 328, 425, 445, 518, 584, etc.). I have regularised to -*es*, while admitting a possibility that S. may have retained -*is* in at least some words (notably *omnis*). Some instances of -*is* in MSS, however, are probably due to assimilation to surrounding words (167, 695, perhaps 32); in 298 E's *genialis tori* (for *geniales toros*) probably resulted from mis-interpretation of *genialis toros*. (Compare Woesler 173–5.)

Contraction of -ii- 113 *perît* Ascensius: -*iit* E P CS. 126 *consilî ego*: -*ii* E P CS. 155 *coniugî* ed. princeps: -*ii* E P CS.

Assimilated and non-assimilated prefixes The MSS (i.e. E P CS) agree on the following forms, which I have adopted (except where noted, this agreement extends to all appearances of the word in the corpus): *abripio, accingo, affectus, affligo* (*adf-* in R in *Med.* 209, 255; E in *Oed.* 213; C^{ac} in *Thy.* 941), *afflatus, aggredior, adlego* (813), *admissum* (266), *adnato* (452), *apparatus, apparo, appareo, appeto, assuesco* (*Tro.* 152 *ads-* E: *ass-* P CS, *ut uid.*), *attollo* (729, 787; attested by Aldhelm, see testimonia), *amputo, comminuo, committo* (*Med.* 33 *conm-* C), *commorior, commoueo* (634 *conm-* C, *somote* P), *complector* (*HO* 1340 *comp-* E P: *conp-* CS), *comprimo, effero, effrenus, effugio* (-*ium*), *effundo, immensus* (*Pho.* 22, *Thy.* 1095 *inm-* E: *imm-* P CS), *immineo, immisceo* (*Tro.* 11 *inm-* E P C S), *immotus, immunis, impar, impatiens, impello, impense, impero, impetus, impius, implicitus, impos, impositus, impotens* (*Thy.* 350 *inp-* E: *imp-* P CS), *imprimo* (*Oed.* 1037 *inp-* E P CS), *irritus* (*HF* 659 *inr-* E: *irr-* P CS; *Med.* 748 *inr-* E: *irr-* CS: *def.* P), *opperior, oppono, opprimo*.

The disputed cases are: *adlabor* (432), *adl-* E: *all-* P CS (same division at *Pha.* 667), where I have preferred *adl-* by comparison with *adlego*; *adsum* (2 *ads-* E P: *ass-* CS; 587 *ads-* E S^{pc}: *ass-* P CS^{ac}; cf. *Med.* 699 *ads-* R E P: *ass-* CS);¹ *conluceo* (544), *conl-* E S: *coll-* P C (cf. *Thy.* 908 *conl-* E: *coll-* P CS), where I have adopted *conl-* in accordance with the evidence of the early Virgil MSS (cf. C. D. Buck, *C.R.* xiii (1899) 164); *illicitus* (299), *inl-* E: *ill-* P CS (so also *HF* 595; but *ill-* in E P CS at *Pha.* 97, *HO* 357); *immitis* (715), *imm-* E CS: *inm-* P (and *imm-* generally elsewhere); *succumbo* (993), *subc-* E P: *succ-* CS (cf. *Tro.* 950 *subc-* E: *succ-* P CS); but *succ-* in E P CS at *HF* 776, 1315); *summitto, 502 *summ-* E CS: *subm-* P; 785 *summ-* E C: *subm-* S (*sumpsit* P); E usually gives *summ-* (except at *Tro.* 708, *Pho.* 397), and *summ-* is common in early MSS of other authors (Buck 165); *subripio* (298), *subr-* E (*sub rupe reductus* for *subripere doctus*) S: *surr-* P C.

APPENDIXES

2. COLOMETRY

A. ANAPAESTIC CANTICA

The principles governing Seneca's choral anapaests were known to Bentley, but were first applied to the editing of the text by Leo.[1] The unit is the dimeter κατὰ στίχον, and its most common forms are – ⌣ ⌣ – – (*quaeque Erasini*), ⌣ ⌣ – – – (*gelidos fontes*), – – – – (*non Euxini*), – – ⌣ ⌣ – (*nil acre uelim*), ⌣ ⌣ – ⌣ ⌣ – (*tibi fila mouent*). Hiatus and *syllaba anceps* are generally admitted only at the end of the dimeter; hiatus with *syllaba anceps* is extremely rare even at line-end (but cf. *Ag.* 79 *pudorque | et coniugii*, 646 *uultus in urbe | et quod*).[2] The monometers found in the MSS are not fortuitous, but part of the original structure; Leo thought they functioned like the Greek paroemiac, and could appear only at the end of a sentence, period, or ode.[3] Although scribes occasionally misplace monometers, the transmitted order should be retained when no metrical rule is violated.

The problem for an editor involves the few cases in which part or all of the MS tradition presents exceptions to these rules. Leo attempted to show that all such places were corrupt, and that emendation of the text could repair metre as well.[4] He was unable, however, to account for all the exceptions in this way, and in the case of *Ag.* 68, 88, and 104 was forced to assume that the author of *Agamemnon* had followed looser metrical rules than Seneca.[5] Leo's drastic proposals in other places were motivated in part by his reluctance to accept readings of A, and none has been adopted by later editors.[6]

---

[1] *Obs.* 98–110; cf. J. Mantke, *Eos* xlix (1957/8) 102 n.19, H. Drexler, *Einführung in die römische Metrik* (1967) 140.

[2] According to Mantke's figures, 46 cases of hiatus and 79 of *syllaba anceps* within the dimeter are transmitted in 1,670 verses.

[3] *Obs.* 99f.

[4] *Obs.* 101–10.

[5] A fragment of the Augustan tragedian Gracchus (Non. 202.20 M) admits *syllaba anceps* before the caesura: *sonat impulsa regia cardo*; Del Rio's plausible *impulsu*, however, would remove the exception. All other extant specimens of Augustan anapaests follow the same principles as those of Seneca, cf. Strzelecki, *Eos* liv (1963) 154–70.

[6] Several scholars have endorsed Leo's principles but differed with him in analysis of individual cases, cf. T. Birt, *Rh. Mus.* 1879, 545–7; W. R. Hardie, *CQ* v (1911) 109; K. Prinz, *WS* 1928/9, 185f.; Peiper–Richter (1902) on *HF* 1111, *Pha.* 325, 343ff., *Oed.* 158, 178. Recent editors have been less fastidious: L. Herrmann printed *anceps* at *Pha.* 327 and hiatus at 350; Viansino allowed *anceps* at *HF* 1134, 1136, *Tro.* 102, and *Pha.* 325, and hiatus at *Pha.* 350; Giardina permits all these anomalies and adds hiatus in *HF* 1114.

APPENDIXES

Leo's views were modified by Richter,[1] who pointed out that where E and A agree a close correspondence between metre, syntax, and thought is visible, i.e. that Seneca tends to make the dimeter the unit of thought and syntax, as well as metre. He might have added that this tendency was thought to be characteristic of the anapaestic dimeter in antiquity (cf. Marius Victorinus, *GLK* VI.77.2: *anapaesticum melos binis pedibus amat sensum includere*). Richter plausibly argued that, where colometry is disputed, the text which best preserves this correspondence is to be preferred.

Mantke[2] has confirmed Richter's observations by demonstrating Seneca's fondness for hyperbata of nouns and adjectives within the dimeter: the pattern *Ityn in uarios modulata sonos* occurs in nearly a fourth of Seneca's anapaests (with the adjective placed first in four-fifths of the cases), and the form *durae peragunt pensa sorores* is also common.[3]

Richter also questioned Leo's view of the monometer as an equivalent for the paroemiac, rightly noting that it is often closely linked with the preceding dimeter, with which it forms a trimeter expressing a single idea, as in Eur. *I.A.* 12f. τί δὲ σὺ σκηνῆς ἐκτὸς ἀίσσεις, | Ἀγάμεμνον ἄναξ;, or Sen. *Pha.* 976f. *non sollicitus prodesse bonis,* | *nocuisse malis.* This pattern, too, must be kept in mind when weighing MS colometry.

1. *Ag.* 57–107

At line 68 all MSS give a line with hiatus, *uicina polo, ubi caeruleis*. Following the MS order throughout, and placing monometers at 70 *plaustra Bootes,* 76 *pectora soluit,* 89 *fortuna suo,* and 107 *propiore legit,* also results in two lines with *syllaba anceps* at the caesura, 88 *pondere magna ceditque oneri* and 104 *sorte quietus aura stringit.* Only Moricca has admitted all three lines to the text; recent editors (e.g. Viansino and Giardina) expel the hiatus while allowing the *syllabae ancipites* to remain. But since the Senecan authorship of *Agamemnon* is no longer doubted, there is no justification for permitting a looser metrical practice in this play. I therefore take it as given that both hiatus and *syllaba anceps* should be confined to line-ends. It seems that the placement of monometers has suffered derangement in the entire MS tradition, probably as the result of a single original mistake which inevitably produced further errors; similar misplacements of monometers may be seen in *Med.* 372, 832, *Pha.* 35. I have chosen to place monometers at 68 *uicina polo,* 76 *pectora soluit,* 86 *tulit ex alto,* and 104 *sorte quietus,* an arrangement which seems to avoid metrical irregularities while respecting the claims of sense

---

[1] *Kritische Untersuchungen* (1899) 32–47.
[2] Pp. 105ff.
[3] See also Marx, *Funktion und Form in den Chorliedern Senecas* (diss. Heidelberg, 1932) 29ff.; S. Herzog-Hauser, *Glotta* 1936, 109f.

2 COLOMETRY

and structure. No certainty is possible, however, and a detailed justification of my colometry therefore seems otiose.[1]

2. *Ag.* 310–407

E arranges the chorus in alternating dimeters and monometers, a pattern not elsewhere found in Seneca's anapaests (iambic trimeters and dimeters alternate in *Med.* 771–86); the A MSS give the lines in dimeters throughout, with a monometer at the end. A's colometry results in hiatus at 327 (*relaxa umeroque*) and 395 (*saxum et*), and *syllaba anceps* at 315 (*Inachia*), 347 (*Olympus*), and 368 (*Tonantis*); it has therefore been rightly rejected by all modern editors.

3. *Ag.* 642–58

MS colometry might be less trustworthy here, because of the preceding polymetric section. In particular the trimeters at 642–4 and 651f., in E at 647 and in A at 657f., have been rejected by some or all editors. I have not imposed consistency, but have judged each case separately. The syntactical structure of 642–4 makes reorganisation into dimeters (Leo) or monometer–two dimeters–monometer (Richter) seem artificial and misguided; here I have preserved the MS order. At 647f. A's tetrameter is clearly wrong; I have preferred E's trimeter plus monometer to the dimeters of some editors to preserve the sense-unity of *et...ignes* and the clausulating effect of *laeta est Hecabe* (compare the use of an adoneus in the polymetric cantica). For the same reason, I have ventured to divide the trimeter at 651 and have preferred E's dimeter plus monometer to A's trimeter in 657f.

4. *Ag.* 664–92

In E (and in all modern editions), these lines are printed as dimeters throughout. Thus line 668 appears as *dura uirago patiensque mali*, requiring the scansion *uiragō*. In all its other appearances in Latin poetry known to me, however, *uirago* occurs in metrical positions where its final syllable may be

---

[1] For convenience I list the monometers printed by previous editors: 67 *commota uadis* (Peiper–Richter, Viansino; Mantke 113), 68 *uicina polo* (Gronovius, Leo, L. Herrmann, Giardina), 72 *fortuna rotat* (Gronovius, Peiper–Richter, L. Herrmann), 76 *pectora soluit* (Leo, Viansino, Giardina), 86 *tulit ex alto* (Leo, Peiper–Richter, L. Herrmann), 87 *cessentque doli* (Gronovius), 89 *fortuna suo* (Viansino, Giardina), 90 *uela secundis* (L. Herrmann), 99 *uilia currant* (Peiper–Richter), 100 *maxima ceruix* (Leo), 104 *sorte quietus* (Gronovius, Richter 38), 107 *propiore legit* (Viansino, Giardina).

APPENDIXES

anceps: last in a dactylic hexameter (Virg. *Aen.* 12.468, Ovid, *Met.* 2.765, 6.130, Stat. *Th.* 11.414, Claud. *Rapt.* 2.63, *Cons. Stil.* 3.314) or in the third line of an Alcaic stanza (Stat. *S.* 4.5.23), or in an anapaestic dimeter (Sen. *Pha.* 54), or first in an iambic metron (Sen. *Tro.* 1151). The deviation from normal practice seems greater in the light of Seneca's tendency to shorten final *o* in bacchiac words.[1] The neglected colometry of A offers a solution. A arranges several lines in this section as trimeters, in each case improving the correspondence between sense and metre. I have replaced these trimeters with the equivalent dimeter + monometer (compare A's behaviour in 647f. and 657f.), to produce the arrangement printed in the text. In this way the metrical anomaly in 668 has been removed and the structure of 665f., 676f., 678f., 681f., and 685f. clarified; in addition, the two dimeters brought into being by the new colometry, 683f. *cum...audaces*, correspond better to units of thought and syntax than the lines they replace.

B. POLYMETRIC CANTICA

In striking contrast to the monotonous anapaests and glyconics of most Senecan cantica, *Ag.* 589–637 and 808–66 and *Oed.* 405–15, 472–502, and 710–37 are composed in an astrophic polymetric form without parallel in extant Latin poetry.[2] These cantica present serious problems of colometry for the editor, sine E and A differ in nearly half the lines in either word-order or line-division.

The principles of composition were first expounded by Leo (*Obs.* 110–34); the most valuable later discussions are those of B. Bussfeld (*Die polymetrischen Chorlieder in Senecas Oedipus und Agamemnon*, Diss. Münster, 1935) and L. Strzelecki (*Eos* xlv (1951) 93–107). These studies have shown that Seneca relies basically on Horatian metrical forms, in particular the Alcaic, Sapphic, and Asclepiad, and that he derives new *commata* by the principles of *deriuatio* (i.e. *adiectio, detractio, concinnatio, permutatio*) associated with his younger contemporary Caesius Bassus (*GLK* vi.271).[3] The most remarkable aspect of Seneca's method is the division of the Horatian forms into cola: the Alcaic line *odi profanum uulgus et arceo* consists of independent units (*odi profanum* and *uulgus et arceo*), which may be arranged in numerous ways, e.g. in reverse order (*uulgus et arceo/odi profanum*), or in combination with the

---

[1] R. Hartenberger, *De O finali* (diss. Bonn, 1911) 67, 102; Austin on Virg. *Aen.* 2.735.

[2] On polymetry in Greek poetry cf. P. Maas, *RE* iii.A.2.1232ff.; a Latin specimen may be visible in the Flavian Scaeva (Scaevius?) Memor, cf. L. Strzelecki, *Eos* xlvi (1952) 114f.

[3] The principles of *deriuatio*, however, are considerably older (cf. Leo, *Hermes* xxiv (1889) 280–301), and Seneca need not have learned them from Caesius Bassus.

corresponding Sapphic or Asclepiad *commata* (*odi profanum/decus o colendi, uulgus et arceo/Maecenas atauis*).[1]

Before a detailed analysis can be attempted, questions of method must be considered. Leo gave *a priori* preference to the colometry, as to the text, of E, but often resorted to A where E was clearly defective. Bussfeld's painstaking examination, however, led him to conclude that A was more accurate than E, especially in preserving short lines; he judged that E and A merited equal weight. Strzelecki went a step further: after vindication of A's arrangement in several passages (e.g. *Ag.* 808–19, 862–6), he concluded that A is to be assumed correct unless it can be shown to be wrong. I have followed the same principle here as in the constitution of the text: where E and A differ, their respective merits are weighed without *a priori* bias in either direction. Further, though agreement of E and A must carry a degree of weight, alterations by modern critics are accepted where they result in an improvement.

A more basic question remains: what criteria are to guide the editor's choice? Leo printed pure Horatian lines wherever either MS family offered them, and often introduced them on his own authority where this was possible with simple rearrangement. Bussfeld rejected this approach as a misunderstanding of Seneca's purpose: he saw the aim of *deriuatio* as the generation of new metrical forms (citing Caesius Bassus, *multa ipsi noua excogitare possimus*, *GLK* VI.271). Examination of those lines uniformly transmitted in E and A, however – the only reliable basis for discussion – reveals a high proportion of unaltered Horatian *commata*; moreover, the remaining lines are for the most part relatively simple reshufflings and adaptations of those forms. I therefore conclude that: (1) a pure Horatian form or a simple variant thereof is to be preferred to an anomalous form, (2) in choices between a pure Horatian form and a variant, attention should be paid to units of thought and syntax, (3) pure Horatian lines may be introduced where they are not offered by the MSS only if this also improves the correspondence of metrical form and units of thought and syntax, (4) anomalous metrical forms should not be introduced by conjecture.

The following pages offer a metrical analysis of all lines in the polymetric cantica of *Agamemnon*, with fuller discussion of passages in which E and A differ in colometry. Where the line printed in the text rests on unanimous testimony of E A, only the scansion and a description in Horatian terms are given.

589   $-\,-\,-\,\cup\,\cup\,-\,|\,-\,-\,\cup\,\cup\,-\,\cup\,\times$ (*Maecenas atauis* | − + *edite regibus*)

Lesser Asclepiad with *adiectio* in second colon (so Leo).

---

[1] W. R. Hardie, *Res metrica* 252. For the dissenting view of R. Giomini, cf. Strzelecki in *Gnomon* xxxii (1960) 747–50; for that of G. B. Pighi, cf. E. Paratore in *RCCM* v (1963) 451f.

590   – – – ∪ ∪ – | – ∪ ∪ – ∪ – (*Maecenas atauis* | *edite regibus*)

591   – ∪ ∪ – ∪ ∪ – | – ∪ ∪ – ∪ × (– ∪ ∪ – ∪ ∪ – | *edite regibus*)

Lesser Asclepiad with resolution in first colon.

592   – ∪ – – – | ∪ ∪ – ∪ – × (*lucidum caeli* | *decus o colendi*)

593   – ∪ – – – | ∪ – ∪ – × (*lucidum caeli* | ∪ – ∪ – ×)

The second *comma* may be taken as the second part of a Sapphic hendeca-syllable with substitution of ∪ for ∪ ∪ (Hardie, *Res metrica* 252) or, perhaps better, as the first part of an Alcaic hendecasyllable with an uncommon short first syllable (= *uides ut alta*).

594f. E procella Fortunae mouet aut iniqui
       flamma Tonantis

    A procella Fortunae mouet
      aut iniqui flamma Tonantis

The E order gives a Sapphic hendecasyllable with *adiectio* at the beginning (cf. 602 below, Leo 127), followed by an adoneus with clausulating effect; this is superior to the A arrangement, analysed by Strzelecki as catalectic Alcaic eneasyllable followed by trochaic metron + adoneus.

596   – – ∪ – – | – ∪ – – – (*odi profanum* | *lucidum caeli*)

597   ∪ ∪ – ∪ – – | – – ∪ – – (*decus o colendi* | *odi profanum*)

598   – ∪ ∪ – ∪ – | – – ∪ – – (*uulgus et arceo* | *odi profanum*)

599f.   – ∪ ∪ – ∪ – | – ∪ ∪ – ∪ – × (*uulgus et arceo* | *Lydia dic per omnes*)

There is no need to adopt Leo's rearrangement (*pax alta nullos* | *ciuium*... *minaces* | *uictoris*...*asperis* | *insana*...*feras* | *puluereamue nubem*) which pro-duces one pure Sapphic and two Alcaics by disrupting the correspondence of line and thought-unit.

601   – – – ∪ ∪ – | ∪ ∪ – ∪ – – (*Maecenas atauis* | *decus o colendi*)

602   – – ∪ – – – | ∪ ∪ – ∪ – – (– + *lucidum caeli* | *decus o colendi*)

603   – ∪ – – – | ∪ ∪ – ∪ – – (*lucidum caeli* | *decus o colendi*)

604   – ∪ ∪ – ∪ – × (*Lydia dic per omnes*)

605ff. E perrumpet omne seruitium contemptor
       leuium deorum.
       qui uultus Acherontis atri, qui Styga tristem
       non tristis uidet audetque uitae
       ponere finem, par ille regi par superis erit.

    A perrumpet omne
      solus contemptor leuium deorum.
      qui uultus Acherontis atri,

qui Styga tristem non tristis uidet
audetque uitae ponere finem,
par ille regi par superis erit.

In E the colometry of the entire passage has been disturbed, while in A the damage is confined to the first two lines, which are clearly to be restored *perrumpet omne seruitium | contemptor leuium deorum*. The metrical pattern is thus:

605   – – ∪ – ∪ | – ∪ ∪ –   (*odi profanum | uulgus et ar[ceo]*)

Defective Alcaic hendecasyllable, for which Leo compares *Oed.* 729 *erexit caeruleum caput* (– [– ∪] – – | – ∪ ∪ – ∪ ×).

606   – – – ∪ ∪ – ∪ – ×   (cui flauam religas comam + ×)
607   – – – ∪ ∪ – ∪ – –   (same)
608   – ∪ ∪ – – – – – ∪ ∪   (*soluitur acris hiems grata uice*)
609   – – ∪ – – | – ∪ ∪ – ×   (*odi profanum | fugit inermem*)[1]
610   – – ∪ – – | – ∪ ∪ – ∪ ×   (*odi profanum | uulgus et arceo*)
611   E o quam miserum est
       nescire mori

    A o quam miserum est nescire mori.

An anapaestic dimeter seems more forceful than two monometers.

612f.   E A uidimus patriam ruentem nocte funesta
         cum Dardana tecta Dorici raperetis ignes

Leo interpreted the first line as a truncated Sapphic (*lucidum [caeli] decus o colendi*) + *lucidum caeli*, the second as an anapaestic dimeter catalectic + *decus o colendi*. This is not impossible, but it seems better to begin, as Bussfeld does, with the hipponacteans *uidimus patriam ruentem* and *Dorici raperetis ignes*; this leaves *nocte funesta cum Dardana tecta*, or *lucidum caeli* | – + *fugit inermem* (for the intrusion of a *longum* at this point in the line, cf. 589 above).

614   – – ∪ – – | – ∪ – – –   (*odi profanum | lucidum caeli*)
615   – – – ∪ ∪ – | ∪ ∪ – ∪ – –   (*Maecenas atauis | decus o colendi*)
616   – – – ∪ – | ∪ ∪ – ∪ – ×   (– – – ∪ – | *decus o colendi*)

The first member is treated by Strzelecki as a variant of – ∪ – – –, but it seems less difficult to regard it as – ∪ ∪ – ∪ – with substitution of – for ∪ ∪.

617ff.   E carusque Pelidae nimium feroci uicit
         acceptis cum fulsit armis fuditque Troas
         falsus Achilles

---

[1] Less neatly, *odi profanum | uulgus et arce[o]*.

A carusque Pelidae nimium feroci
uicit acceptis cum fulsit armis
fuditque Troas falsus Achilles

E's colometry is unintelligible, A's wholly acceptable:

617 $--\cup---|\cup\cup-\cup--$ ($-+$ *lucidum caeli* | *decus o colendi*)
618 $-\cup---|--\cup--$ (*lucidum caeli* | *odi profanum*)
619 $--\cup--|-\cup\cup--$ (*odi profanum* | *fugit inermem*)
620 $--\cup---|\cup\cup-\cup--$ ($-+$ *lucidum caeli* | *decus o colendi*)

621ff. E sustulit luctu
celeremque saltu Troades summis
timuere muris. perdidit in malis
extremum decus fortiter uinci.
restitit quinis bis annis unius noctis
peritura furto.

A sustulit luctu celeremque saltu
Troades summis timuere muris.
perdidit in malis extremum decus
fortiter uinci; restitit annis
Troia bis quinis,
unius noctis peritura fato.

The colometry of A yields three pure Sapphic hendecasyllables which are
also coherent units of sense (621–2, 626), and these are to be accepted.
Syntax demands A's *Troia*, and this commends the line *restitit annis Troia bis
quinis* (= *fugit inermem* | *lucidum caeli*). Of the remaining words *extremum decus
fortiter uinci* belong together in sense (*extremum decus* = *quam non Pelei*, 616;
fortiter uinci = *lucidum caeli*), leaving *perdidit in malis* (= *edite regibus*) as an
independent line.

627ff. E Vidimus simulata dona molis immensae
Danaumque fatale munus duximus
nostra creduli dextra tremuitque saepe

A Vidimus simulata dona molis immensae
Danaum fatale munus duximus nostra
creduli dextra tremuitque saepe

The last line in A is a Sapphic hendecasyllable and therefore preferable. The
first line, which is clearly meant to parallel 612 *uidimus patriam ruentem*, is best
printed as another hipponactean, *uidimus simulata dona*. This leaves *molis
immensae Danaumque fatale munus duximus nostra*, in which both *molis immensae*
and *duximus nostra* = *lucidum caeli*. The dominant metre, then, is the Sapphic.
Peiper–Richter suggest *molis immensae Danaumque* (Sapphic with *concinnatio:*

lucidum caeli | *decus o co*[*lendi*] | *fatale munus duximus nostra* (= *odi profanum* | *lucidum caeli*), which has been generally accepted.

630   — ∪ — — — | ∪ ∪ — ∪ — —   (*lucidum caeli* | *decus o colendi*)

631   — ∪ — — — | — — ∪ — —   (*lucidum caeli* | *odi profanum*)

632ff. E   et licuit dolos uersare ut ipsi fraude sua
         caderent Pelasgi; saepe commotae
         sonuere parmae tacitumque murmur
         percussit aures et fremuit male subdolo
         parens Pyrrhus Vlixi.

      A   et licuit uersare dolos ut ipsi
         fraude sua capti caderent Pelasgi;
         saepe commotae sonuere parmae
         tacitumque murmur percussit aures
         et fremuit male subdolo parens Pyrrhus Vlixi.

In general A's colometry and E's text give acceptable results:

632   — ∪ ∪ — ∪ — | — — ∪ — —   (*uulgus et arceo* | *odi profanum*)

633   — ∪ ∪ — ∪ ∪ — ∪ — —   (*flumina constiterint acuto*)

634   — ∪ — — — | ∪ ∪ — ∪ — —   (*lucidum caeli* | *decus o colendi*)

635   ∪ ∪ — ∪ — — | — — ∪ — —   (*decus o colendi* | *odi profanum*)

636   — ∪ ∪ — ∪ ∪ — ∪ —

Glyconic (*cui flauam religas comam*) with second *longum* resolved.

637   — — — ∪ ∪ — —   (*grato Pyrrha sub antro*)

808   — — — ∪ ∪ × | — ∪ ∪ — ∪ ×   (*Maecenas atauis* | *edite regibus*)

809   — ∪ — — — | — — ∪ — —   (*lucidum caeli* | *odi profanum*)

810ff. E   semper ingentes alumnos
         educas; numerum deorum
         imparem aequasti; tuus ille
         bis seno meruit labore
         adlegi caelo
         magnus Alcides, cui lege mundi
         Iuppiter rupta geminauit horas
         roscidae noctis iussitque Phoebum
         tardius celeres agitare currus
         et tuas lente remeare bigas,
         pallida Phoebe

A semper ingentes educas alumnos;
  imparem aequasti numerum deorum;
  tuus ille bis seno meruit labore
  adlegi caelo magnus Alcides,
  cui lege mundi Iuppiter rupta
  roscidae noctis geminauit horas
  iussitque Phoebum tardius celeres
  agitare currus et tuas lente
  remeare bigas, candida Phoebe.

Neither MS arrangement is acceptable throughout. The first verse in E is anomalous (trochaic dimeter or a truncated Sapphic), which argues in A's favour. After this there are no decisive metrical factors except the familiar adonian clausula *pallida Phoebe* in E. The order of A maintains better correspondence of metre and sense as far as *geminauit horas*, but the last three lines in E are preferable on the same grounds. My text is thus analysed:

810 $- \cup - - - \mid - \cup - \cup - -$ (*lucidum caeli* | *ueris et Fauoni*)
811 $- \cup - - - \mid \cup \cup - \cup - \times$ (*lucidum caeli* | *decus o colendi*)
812 $\cup \cup - \cup - - - \mid \cup \cup - \cup - \times$ ($\cup \cup$ + *lucidum caeli* | *decus o colendi*)
813 $- \cup - - - \mid - \cup - - -$ (*lucidum caeli* | *lucidum caeli*)
814 $- - \cup - - \mid - \cup - - -$ (*odi profanum* | *lucidum caeli*)
815 $- \cup - - - \mid \cup \cup - \cup - -$ (*lucidum caeli* | *decus o colendi*)
816 $- - \cup - \times$ (*odi profanum*)
817 $- \cup - \cup \cup - \mid \cup \cup - \cup - -$

Sapphic hendecasyllable with third *longum* resolved (cf. *Med.* 636, with Costa's note).

818 $- \cup - - - \mid \cup \cup - \cup - -$ (*lucidum caeli* | *decus o colendi*)
818a $- \cup \cup - -$ (*fugit inermem*)
819 E retulit pedem nomen alternis (*recte*)

  A retulitque pedem alternis nomen

Greek form of Sapphic penthemimeres + *lucidum caeli*.

820 $- \cup - - - \mid - \cup - - -$ (*lucidum caeli* | *lucidum caeli*)
821 $- \cup - - - \mid - - \cup - \times$ (*lucidum caeli* | *odi profanum*)[1]

---

[1] The hiatus, if authentic, is the most drastic consequence of Seneca's division of Horatian lines into independent units. It may be avoided by writing *Hesperum dici.* | *Aurora mouit ad solitas uices* | *caput et relabens imposuit seni* | *collum marito*, but this produces a short fifth syllable in an Alcaic, a violation of Horatian practice (if *C.* 3.5.17 is emended); in 861 below (*latrauit ore*) the syllable in question occurs at the end of a line (but compare 605 *perrumpet omne* | *seruitium*).

822f. E ad solitas uices
  caput et relabens imposuit seni
  collum marito

A ad solitas uices caput et relabens
  imposuit senis umero mariti

The A text of the last four words is apparently interpolated (see commentary *ad loc.*); A's colometry, however, is superior and when combined with E's text yields:

822 – ∪ ∪ – ∪ – | ∪ ∪ – ∪ – – (*uulgus et arceo* | *decus o colendi*)
823 – ∪ ∪ – ∪ – | – – ∪ – – (*edite regibus* | *odi profanum*)
824 – ∪ – – | – ∪ – – × (trochaic metron | *lucidum caeli*)

Strzelecki suggests that S. may have derived this use of a trochaic metron from Caesius Bassus' analysis of the Phalaecean hendecasyllable (*GLK* VI.261).

825 E Herculem nasci;
  uiolentus ille

A Herculem nasci; uiolentus ille

Nothing is gained by sundering the Sapphic hendecasyllable.

826 – ∪ – – – | ∪ ∪ – ∪ – – (*lucidum caeli* | *decus o colendi*)
827 ∪ ∪ – ∪ – – | – ∪ – – × (*decus o colendi* | *lucidum caeli*)
828 – ∪ – ∪ ∪ – ∪ – × (*cui flauam religas comam* + × , with short second syllable)
829 – – – ∪ ∪ – ∪ – – (*cui flauam religas comam* + ×)
830 – – ∪ – – | – ∪ ∪ – ∪ – (*odi profanum* | *uulgus et arceo*)
831 – ∪ ∪ – ∪ × (*edite regibus*)
832 – ∪ – ∪ ∪ – | ∪ ∪ – ∪ – –

Sapphic with third *longum* resolved (Strzelecki p. 99 n.34).

833 ∪ ∪ – ∪ – – | – – ∪ – – (*decus o colendi* | *odi profanum*)
834 – ∪ ∪ – × (*fugit inermem*)
835 – ∪ – – – | ∪ ∪ – ∪ – × (*lucidum caeli* | *decus o colendi*)
836 ∪ ∪ – ∪ – – | ∪ ∪ – ∪ – – (*decus o colendi* | *decus o colendi*)

837ff. E A geminosque fratres pectore ex uno
  tria monstra natos stipite incusso
  fregit insultans duxitque ad ortus

  Leo geminosque fratres
  pectore ex uno tria monstra natos
  stipite incusso fregit insultans
  duxitque ad ortus

Leo's rearrangement produces improved correspondence of line and sense-unit, and I have adopted it:

837   ∪∪−∪−− (*decus o colendi*)

838   −∪−−− | ∪∪−∪−− (*lucidum caeli* | *decus o colendi*)

839   −∪−−− | −∪−−− (*lucidum caeli* | *lucidum caeli*)

839a   −−∪−− (*odi profanum*)

840   E Hesperium pecus Geryonae
           spolium triformis

       A Hesperium pecus
           Geryonae spolium triformis.

In both sense and metre *Geryonae spolium triformis* belong together (= *flumina constiterint acuto*, cf. 633 above); *Hesperium pecus*, on the other hand, is syntactically and metrically linked to *duxitque ad ortus*, with which it forms a complete Alcaic hendecasyllable.

841ff.   E egit Threicium gregem quem non
             Strymonii gramine fluminis Hebriue
             ripis pauit tyrannus

         A egit Threicium gregem
             quem non Strymonii gramine fluminis
             Hebriue ripis pauit tyrannus.

E's arrangement must be a mere blunder; A's is clearly right:

841   −−−∪∪−∪× (*cui flauam religas comam*)

842   −−−∪∪− | −∪∪−∪× (*Maecenas atauis* | *edite regibus*)

843   −−∪−− | −−∪−× (*odi profanum* | *odi profanum*)

844   −∪−−− | ∪∪−∪−× (*lucidum caeli* | *decus o colendi*)

845   −∪−−− | −−∪−− (*lucidum caeli* | *odi profanum*)

846   −∪−−− | −∪−−− (*lucidum caeli* | *lucidum caeli*)

847   −∪−∪∪−∪− (*cui flauam religas comam*, with short second syllable)

848   −∪−∪∪−∪− (same)

849   ∪∪−∪−− (*decus o colendi*)

850   −∪−−− | −−∪−− (*lucidum caeli* | *odi profanum*)

851   −∪−−− (*lucidum caeli*)

852   −−∪−− | −∪∪−∪− (*odi profanum* | *uulgus et arceo*)

853   −∪∪−∪− | −−∪−− (*uulgus et arceo* | *odi profanum*)

854   −−∪−− | ∪∪−∪−− (*odi profanum* | *decus o colendi*)

855   −−−∪∪− | ∪∪−∪−− (*Maecenas atauis* | *decus o colendi*)

856   −∪−−− | −∪−−− (*lucidum caeli* | *lucidum caeli*)

857   E A linqueret cum iam nemus omne fuluo

2 COLOMETRY

The line as transmitted is a Sapphic hendecasyllable; with Müller's deletion of *omne* (accepted in my text), the metre is trochaic metron + *lucidum caeli*, as in 824 above.

858   – ∪ – – – | ∪ ∪ – ∪ – –   (*lucidum caeli* | *decus o colendi*)
859   – ∪ – – – | ∪ ∪ – ∪ – ×   (same)
860   ∪ ∪ – ∪ – – | ∪ ∪ – ∪ – –   (*decus o colendi* | *decus o colendi*)

861f.   E A latrauit ore lucis ignotae
         metuens colorem

     Leo latrauit ore
        lucis ignotae metuens colorem

Leo's rearrangement is an obvious improvement:

861   – – ∪ – ×   (*odi profanum*)
862   – ∪ – – – | ∪ ∪ – ∪ – ×   (*lucidum caeli* | *decus o colendi*)

863ff.   E te duce succidit mendax
         Dardaniae domus et sensit arcus
         iterum timendos; te duce concidit
         totidem diebus Troia quot annis

     A te duce succidit
        mendax Dardaniae domus
        et sensit arcus iterum timendos;
        te duce concidit totidem diebus
        Troia quot annis.

There can be little doubt that A's colometry is preferable:

863   – ∪ ∪ – ∪ ×   (*edite regibus*)
864   – – – ∪ ∪ – ∪ ×   (*cui flauam religas comam*)
864a   – – ∪ – – | ∪ ∪ – ∪ – –   (*odi profanum* | *decus o colendi*)
865   – ∪ ∪ – ∪ – | ∪ ∪ – ∪ – ×   (*uulgus et arceo* | *decus o colendi*)
866   – ∪ ∪ – –   (*fugit inermem*)

BIBLIOGRAPHY

The first section lists the complete editions which have been consulted at first hand. The second lists editions of single plays if accompanied by a commentary useful for the editing or interpretation of the tragedies, works dealing with points of general interest for the tragedies, and writings specifically concerned with *Agamemnon*. I include some works in the latter two categories which I have not had occasion to cite, in order to distinguish my silence from that of ignorance. Collections of notes on single passages have been included only if relevant to a discussion in the commentary, and reviews only when they make a significant contribution to the subject. Works of reference and general surveys, synthetic works on Seneca, and works dealing with plays other than *Agamemnon* have usually been excluded unless cited elsewhere in the edition. Works which I have not found accessible are enclosed in square brackets. Further bibliographical information for the period 1922–64 may be obtained in the *Lustrum* surveys of M. Coffey and H. J. Mette, and extensive bibliographies of earlier work are given in L. Herrmann's *Le théâtre de Sénèque* and in the Oldfather–Pease–Canter *Index verborum* (qq. uu.).

I. EDITIONS CONSULTED

(The date given is that of the edition consulted; the date or dates of other printings are given in parentheses.)

Editio princeps. Ferrara, Andreas Bellfortis, n.d. (*ca.* 1484?). Hain–Copinger 14662; Reichling VI.153; *British Museum Catalogue of Printed Books to 1500*, pt. VI p.603.

Marmita, Gellius Barnardinus. Lyons, Antonius Lambillon and Marinus Sarazin, 1491. H–C 14665*; *British Museum Catalogue* pt. VII p.307.

Venice, de Soardis, 1492. H–C 14666; *Brit. Mus. Cat.* pt. V. p.491.

and Caietanus (= Galetani), Danielis. Venice, Capcasa, 1493. H–C 14668*; *Brit. Mus. Cat.* pt. V p.484. (The edition published in Venice in 1498 by Tacuinus is virtually identical: H–C 14670*; *Brit. Mus. Cat.* pt. V p.533.)

Benedictus Philologus. Florence, de Giunta, 1506 (1513).

Ascensius, Iodocus Badius. Paris, 1514. With commentaries of Ascensius, Marmita, and Caietanus.

Avantius, Hieronymus. Venice, Aldus, 1517.

Petrus, Henricus. Basle, 1529, 1563 (1550).

Gryphius, Sebastianus. Leiden, 1541 (1536, 1548, 1554, 1584, 1587).

BIBLIOGRAPHY

Fabricius, Georgius. Leipzig, 1566.

Del Rio, Martinus Antonius, S.J. In *Lucii Annaei Senecae tragoedias amplissima adversaria quae loco commentarii esse possunt.* Antwerp, Plantinus, 1576.

Syntagma tragoediae Latinae. Antwerp, Plantinus. 1593/4 (Paris, 1607, 1619).

Raphelengius, Franciscus and Lipsius, Justus. Leiden, 1589 (1601).

Commelinus, Hieronymus. Heidelberg, 1589 (1600, 1604).

Scaliger, Josephus Justus and Heinsius, Danielis. Leiden, 1611.

Scriverius, Petrus. Leiden, 1621 (1651). A convenient edition *cum notis variorum*, with the *adversaria* of Fabricius, Lipsius, Raphelengius, Gruter, Commelinus, Scaliger, D. Heinsius, and Pontanus.

Gronovius, J. Frid. Leiden, 1661 (Amsterdam, 1662).

Gronovius, Iacobus. *Cum notis patris auctis ex chirographo eius et variis aliorum.* Amsterdam, 1682.

Schroeder, Iohannes Casparus. Delft, 2 vols., 1728. With the notes of Gronovius (from the 1682 edition), and selections from those of Del Rio, Farnaby, and others.

Bothe, Friedrich Heinrich. *Poetae scaenici Latini*, III. Halberstad, 1822 (Leipzig, 1819, 1834). With an appendix containing the notes of Torkill Baden (published separately Copenhagen, 1819; Leipzig, 1821).

Lemaire, N. E. Paris (Didot), 1832. Three volumes; text with commentary and 'animadversiones' (textual notes).

Peiper, Rudolf and Richter, Gustav. Leipzig, Teubner, 1867.

Leo, Friedrich. Berlin, 1879 (reprinted Berlin, 1963).

Peiper, Rudolf and Richter, Gustav. Leipzig, Teubner, 1902 (reprinted 1921, 1937).

Miller, Frank Justus. London–Cambridge (U.S.A.). 2 vols., 1917 (reprinted 1927, 1938, 1953, 1960). Leo's text, with an English translation.

Moricca, Umberto. Turin, Paravia, 3 vols., 1917–23 (1947).

Herrmann, Léon. Paris, Collection Budé, 2 vols., 1924–6 (1961). With a French translation.

Thomann, T. Zurich 1961, and 1969. 2 vols., text and German translation with short notes.

Viansino, Giovanni. Turin, Paravia, 3 vols., 1965 (revised ed., vol. 1, 1968). Two volumes of text, one of impenetrable prolegomena.

Giardina, Gian Carlo. Bologna, 2 vols., 1966 (*Studi Pubblicati dall'Istituto di Filologia Classica*, xx).

(Complete editions by O. Zwierlein (Oxford Classical Texts) and G. Brugnoli and V. Ussani, Jr (Bibliotheca Teubneriana) are anticipated.)

II. OTHER WORKS RELATING TO THE TRAGEDIES

Anliker, K. *Prologe und Akteinteilung in den Tragödien Senecas*. Diss. Bern, 1960.

Axelson, Bertil. *Korruptelenkult: Studien zur Textkritik der unechten Seneca-Tragödie Hercules Oetaeus*. Lund, 1967.

Beare, W. 'Plays for performance and recitation', *Hermath*. lxxvii (1945) 8–19.

Billanovich, Giuseppe. 'I primi umanisti e le tradizioni dei classici latini'. *Discorsi Universitari*, N.S. 14. Fribourg (Suisse), 1953.

Billanovich, Guido. 'Veterum Vestigia Vatum', *Italia Medioevale e Umanistica* i (1958) 155–243.

Bishop, John David. *The choral odes of Seneca: theme and development*. Diss. Univ. of Pennsylvania (U.S.A.), 1964.

'The meaning of the choral metres in Senecan tragedy', *RhM* cxi (1968) 197–219.

Bonner, S. F. *Roman declamation*. Berkeley, 1949.

Brady, James F. *Stoicism in the tragedies of Seneca*. Diss. Columbia Univ. (New York), 1958.

Brakman, C. 'De Senecae Agamemnone', *Mnemosyne* N.S. xlii (1914) 392–8.

Brugnoli, Giorgio. 'La tradizione manoscritta di Seneca tragico alla luce delle testimonianze medioevali', *Atti Acc. Naz. d. Lincei*, ser. 8, *Memorie*, vol. 8, fasc. 3 (1957; publ. 1959), 201–87.

'Excerpta Senecana in un manoscritto di Breslavia', *Annali della Facoltà di Lettere, Filosofia e Magistero della Università di Cagliari* xxviii (1960) 155–61.

'Ut patet per Senecam in suis tragoediis', *RCCM* v (1963), 146–63.

Bussfeld, Bernhard. *Die polymetrischen Chorlieder in Senecas Oedipus und Agamemnon*. Diss. Münster. Bochum–Langendreer, 1935.

Calder, W. M. (III). 'The size of the chorus in Seneca's *Agamemnon*', *CP* lxx (1975) 32–5.

'Seneca's Agamemnon', *CP* lxxi (1976) 27–36.

Canter, Howard Vernon. *Rhetorical elements in the tragedies of Seneca*. *University of Illinois studies in language and literature* 10 (1925).

Carlsson, Gunnar. *Die Überlieferung der Seneca-Tragödien* (Lunds Universitets Årsskrift. N.F. avd. 1 bd. 21). Lund, 1926.

Review of the editions of U. Moricca and L. Herrmann, in *Gnomon* iv (1928) 492–9.

'Zu Senecas Tragödien, Lesungen und Deutungen', *Kungl. Humanistiska Vetenskapssamfundet i Lund*. Årsberättelse, 1928–9. Lund, 1929, 39–72.

'Seneca's tragedies, notes and interpretations', *Class. et Med.* x (1948) 39–59.

Cattin, Aurèle. *Les thèmes lyriques dans les tragédies de Sénèque*. Diss. Fribourg (Suisse), 1959. Neuchâtel, 1963.

'La géographie dans les tragédies de Sénèque', *Latomus* xxii (1963) 685–703.

BIBLIOGRAPHY

Charlier, J. *Ovide et Sénèque. Contribution à l'étude de l'influence d'Ovide sur les tragédies de Sénèque.* Diss. Brussels, 1954.

Cleasby, Harold Loomis. *De Seneca tragico Ovidii imitatore.* Diss. Harvard, 1907.

Coffey, Michael. 'Seneca tragedies... report for the years 1922–1955', *Lustrum* ii (1957) 113–86.

Review of R. Giomini, L. *Annaei Senecae Agamemnon,* in *JRS* xlviii (1958) 225–6.

'Seneca and his tragedies', *PACA* iii (1960) 14–20.

Cosenza, M. E. *Dictionary of the Italian Humanists,* 6 vols. Boston, 1962.

Costa, C. D. N. *Seneca: Medea.* Oxford, 1973.

Damsté, P. H. 'Ad Senecae *Agamemnonem'*, *Mnemosyne* N.S. xlvii (1919) 111–15.

Dewey, Ann Reynolds Lawlor. *The chorus in Senecan tragedy exclusive of Hercules Oetaeus and Octavia.* Diss. Columbia Univ. (New York). 1968.

Düring, Theodor. 'Die Überlieferung des interpolirten Textes von Senecas Tragödien', *Hermes* xlii (1907) 113–26, 579–94.

'Zur Überlieferung von Senecas Tragödien', *Hermes* xlvii (1912) 183–98.

Zur Überlieferung von Senecas Tragödien, Ergänzung zu den Abhandlungen in Hermes 1907 und 1912. (1) *37 Handschriften in England.* (2.) τ *und C.* Beilage zum Programm des Königlichen Gymnasium Georgianum zu Lingen (Ems), 1913.

Evans, Elizabeth C. 'A Stoic aspect of Senecan drama, portraiture', *TAPA* lxxxi (1950) 169–84.

Fitch, John G. *Character in Senecan tragedy.* Diss. Cornell, 1974.

Franceschini, Enzo. 'Glosse e commenti medievali a Seneca tragico', *Studi e Note di Filologia Latina Medievale (Pubblicazioni della Università Cattolica del Sacro Cuore,* ser. 4, vol. 30). Milan, 1938, 1–105.

'Gli "Argumenta Tragoediarum Senecae" di Albertino Mussato', *ibid.* 177–97.

Frenzel, Friedrich. *Die Prologe der Tragödien Senecas.* Diss. Leipzig, 1914.

Friedrich, Wolf-Hartmut. *Untersuchungen zu Senecas dramatischer Technik.* Diss. Freiburg-im-Breisgau. Borna–Leipzig, 1933.

'Euripideisches in der lateinischen Literatur', *Hermes* lxix (1934) 300–15.

Gaheis, Alexander. *De troporum in Lucii Annaei Senecae tragoediis generibus potioribus,* Diss. Phil. Vind. v (1895) 3–64.

Garton, Charles. 'The background to character-portrayal in Seneca', *CP* liv (1959) 1–9.

Genius, Adolphus, *De L. A. Senecae poetae tragici usu praepositionum.* Diss. Münster, 1893.

Giancotti, Francesco. *Saggio sulle tragedie di Seneca.* Città di Castello, 1953.

'Note alle tragedie di Seneca', *Riv. di Fil.* N.S. xxx (1952) 149–72.

BIBLIOGRAPHY

Giardina, Gian Carlo. 'Per l'edizione critica di Seneca tragico', *Boll. d. Acc. Naz. dei Lincei* xiii (1965) 61–102.

'La tradizione manoscritta di Seneca tragico', *Vichiana* ii (1965) 31–74.

Review of Viansino, L. *Annaei Senecae tragoediae*, in *Boll. d. Acc. Naz. dei Lincei* xiv (1966) 65–84.

Giomini, Remo. *L. Annaei Senecae Agamemnona edidit et commentario instruxit Remus Giomini.* Rome, 1956.

L. Annaei Senecae Phaedram edidit et commentario instruxit Remus Giomini. Rome, 1955.

De canticis polymetris in Oedipode et Agamemnone Annaeanis. Rome, 1959.

'Ancora sui cori polimetri di Seneca', *RCCM* iii (1961) 249–54.

Grimal, Pierre. *L. Annaei Senecae Phaedra.* Paris, 1965.

Hahlbrock, Peter. 'Beobachtungen zum jambischen Trimeter in den Tragödien des L. Annaeus Seneca', *WS* N.F. ii (1968) 171–82.

Hansen, Ernst. *Die Stellung der Affektreden in den Tragödien Senecas.* Diss. Berlin, 1934.

Harder, Franz. 'Bemerkungen zu den Tragödien des Seneca', *Festschrift für Johannes Vahlen.* Berlin, 1900, 441–63.

Harrison, E. Review of L. Strzelecki, *De Senecae trimetro iambico qu. sel.,* in *C.R.* liv (1940) 152–4.

Heldmann, K. *Untersuchungen zu den Tragödien Senecas.* [*Hermes* Einzelschriften, 31]. Wiesbaden, 1974.

Herington, C. J. 'A thirteenth-century manuscript of the *Octavia Praetexta* in Exeter', *RhM* ci (1958) 353–77.

'The Exeter manuscript of the *Octavia*: a correction', *RhM* ciii (1960) 96.

'Senecan tragedy', *Arion* v (1966) 422–71.

Herrmann, Léon. *Le théâtre de Sénèque.* Paris, 1924.

Hoffa, Wilhelm. 'Textkritische Untersuchungen zu Senecas Tragödien', *Hermes* xlix (1914) 464–75.

Hosius, Carl. 'Seneca und Lucan', *Neue Jahrb.* cxlv (1892) 337–56.

Octavia Praetexta cum elementis commentarii. Bonn, 1922.

Housman, A. E. 'Notes on Seneca's tragedies', *CQ* xvii (1923) 163–9.

Jocelyn, H. D. *The tragedies of Ennius.* Cambridge, 1967.

Kapnukajas, Christos K. *Die Nachahmungstechnik Senecas in den Chorliedern des Hercules Furens und der Medea.* Diss. Leipzig, 1930.

Ker, Alan. 'Notes on some passages of the tragedies of Seneca', *CQ* N.S. xii (1962) 48–51.

Keydell, Rudolf. 'Seneca und Cicero bei Quintus von Smyrna', *WJA* iv (1949/50) 80–8.

Review of F. Vian, *Recherches*, in *Gnomon* xxxiii (1961) 278–84.

Koetschau, Paul. 'Zu Senecas Tragödien', *Philologus* lxi (1902) 133–59.

Kunz, Franz. *Sentenzen in Senecas Tragödien*, Progr. Wiener-Neustadt, 1897.

BIBLIOGRAPHY

Lammers, Joseph. *Die Doppel- und Halb-Chöre in der antiken Tragödie*, Diss. Paderborn, 1931.

Lefèvre, Eckard. Review of A. Cattin, *Les thèmes lyriques*, in *Gnomon* xxxvi (1964) 583–6.

'Schicksal und Selbstverschuldung in Senecas *Agamemnon*', *Hermes* xciv (1966) 482–96.

Review of P. Grimal, L. *Annaei Senecae Phaedra*, in *Gnomon* xxxviii (1966) 689–95.

Review of O. Zwierlein, *Die Rezitationsdramen Senecas*, in *Gnomon* xl (1968) 782–9.

Leo, Friedrich. 'Anecdoton Lugdunense', *Commentationes in honorem F. Buecheleri–H. Useneri*, etc. Bonn, 1873, 37–40, 43ff.

'De recensendis Senecae tragoediis', *Hermes* x (1876) 423–46.

De Senecae tragoediis observationes criticae. Berlin, 1878.

'Die Composition der Chorlieder Senecas', *Rh. Mus.* lii (1897) 509ff.

Review of Peiper, R. and Richter, G., L. *Annaei Senecae tragoediae*, in *GGA* clxv (1903) 1–11 [= *Ausgewählte kleine Schriften*. Rome, 1960, II, 211–22].

'Der Monolog im Drama. Ein Beitrag zur griechisch-römischen Poetik', *Abhandl. der Gött. Ges. d. Wiss.*, Phil.-Hist. Kl., N.F. x no. 5 (1908).

Lesky, Albin. 'Die griechischen Pelopidendramen und Senecas Thyestes', *WS* xliii (1922/3), 172–98.

Liebermann, W.-L. *Studien zu Senecas Tragödien*. Meisenheim, 1974.

Liedloff, Kurt. *De tempestatibus, necyomanteae, inferorum descriptionibus quae apud poetas Romanos primi p. Chr. saeculi leguntur*. Diss. Leipzig, 1884.

'Die Nachbildung griechischer und römischer Muster in Senecas *Troades* und *Agamemnon*', *Jahresbericht der Fürsten- und Landesschule zu Grimma* (1912) 10–19.

Lindskog, Claes. *Studien zum antiken Drama*, Pars II (Lund, 1897) 3–47.

Lohikoski, Klaus Krister. 'Der Parallelismus Mykene–Troja in Senecas *Agamemnon*', *Arctos* N.s. iv (1966) 63–70.

MacGregor, A. P. 'The MS tradition of Seneca's tragedies *ante renatas in Italia litteras*', *TAPA* cii (1971) 327–56.

'The manuscripts of Seneca's tragedies: a survey', *Aufstieg und Niedergang der römischen Welt* II (Berlin, forthcoming).

Maguinness, W. S. 'Seneca and the poets', *Hermathena* lxxxviii (1956) 81–98.

Mantke, Joseph. 'De Senecae anapaesticis canticis', *Eos* xlix (1957/58) 101–22.

Marek, A. *De temporis et loci unitatibus a Seneca tragico observatis*. Diss. Breslau, 1909.

Marti, Berthe M. 'Seneca's tragedies: a new interpretation', *TAPA* lxxvi (1945) 216–45.

'The prototypes of Seneca's tragedies', *CP* xlii (1947) 1–16.

BIBLIOGRAPHY

Marx, Wilhelm. *Funktion und Form der Chorlieder in den Tragödien Senecas.* Diss. Heidelberg. Cologne, 1932.

Mazzoli, G. *Seneca e la poesia.* Milan, 1970.

Megas, Anastasios K. Ο ΠΡΟΟΥΜΑΝΙΣΤΙΚΟΣ ΚΥΚΛΟΣ ΤΗΣ ΠΑΔΟΥΑΣ ΚΑΙ ΟΙ ΤΡΑΓΩΔΙΕΣ ΤΟΥ *L. A. Seneca.* Thessalonica, 1967. ed. ΑΛΒΕΡΤΙΝΟΥ ΜΟΥΣΣΑΤΟΥ. ΟΙ ΥΠΟΘΕΣΕΙΣ ΤΩΝ ΤΡΑΓΩΔΙΩΝ ΤΟΥ ΣΕΝΕΚΑ. ΑΠΟΣΠΑΣΜΑΤΑ ΑΓΝΩΣΤΟΥ ΥΠΟΜΝΗΜΑΤΟΣ ΣΤΙΣ ΤΡΑΓΩΔΙΕΣ ΤΟΥ ΣΕΝΕΚΑ. Thessalonica, 1969.

Meloni, Pietro. ed. *Nicolai Treveti expositio L. Annaei Senecae Agamemnonis.* Cagliari, 1961 (*Pubblicazioni della Facoltà di Lettere e Magistero dell' Università di Cagliari*, 3).

Mendel, Clarence W. *Our Seneca.* New Haven (Conn., U.S.A.), 1941.

Mette, Hans Joachim. 'Die römische Tragödie und die Neufunde zur griechischen Tragödie (insbesondere für die Jahre 1945–1964)', *Lustrum* ix (1964) 5–213.

Mewis, Felix. *De Senecae philosophi studiis litterarum.* Diss. Königsberg, 1908.

Miniconi, Pierre-Jean. *Étude des thèmes 'guerriers' de la poésie épique.* Paris, 1951.

Moricca, Umberto. 'Le tragedie di Seneca IV. Seneca e le regole della tradizione sull'arte drammatica', *Riv. d. Fil.* xlviii (1920) 74–94.

Müller, Michael. *In Senecae tragoedias quaestiones criticae.* Diss. Berlin, 1898. 'Ad Senecae tragoedias', *Philologus* lx (1901) 261–70.

Oldfather, W. A. (with Pease, A. S. and Canter, H. V.), *Index verborum quae in Senecae fabulis necnon in Octavia Praetexta reperiuntur. Univ. of Illinois studies in language and literature*, vol. 4 no. 2. Urbana (Illinois), 1918. (Reprinted Hildesheim, 1964.)

Pack, Roger A. 'On guilt and error in Senecan tragedy', *TAPA* lxxi (1940) 360–71.

Palma, Marco. 'Note sulla storia di un codice di Seneca tragico col commento di Nicola Trevet (Vat. Lat. 1650)', *IMU* xvi (1973) 317–22.

Paratore, Ettore. 'Sulla Phaedra di Seneca', *Dioniso* xv (1952) 195–234. 'Sulle sigle dei personaggi nelle tragedie di Seneca', *SIFC* xxvii–xxviii (1956) 324–60.

Paul, Adolf. *Untersuchungen zur Eigenart von Senecas Phoenissen.* Diss. Bonn, 1953.

Pedroli, Lydia. *Fabularum praetextarum quae extant.* Genoa, 1954. (Contains *Octavia* with commentary.)

Peiper, Rudolf. *Observatorum* [*sic*] *in Senecae tragoedias libellus.* Breslau, 1863. *Praefationis in Senecae tragoedias supplementum.* Breslau, 1870. 'De Senecae tragoediarum vulgari lectione (A) constituenda', *Festschrift zum 250-jährigen Jubelfeier des Gymnasiums zu St. Maria Magdalena zu Breslau am 30. April 1893.* Breslau, 1893.

Philp, Robert H. *The manuscript tradition of Seneca's tragedies.* Diss. Cambridge, 1964.

BIBLIOGRAPHY

'The manuscript tradition of Seneca's tragedies', *C.Q.* N.S. xviii (1968) 150–79.

Pratt, Norman T. *Dramatic suspense in Seneca and in his Greek predecessors.* Diss. Princeton, 1939.

'The Stoic base of Senecan drama', *TAPA* lxxix (1948), 1–11.

'Major systems of figurative language in Senecan melodrama', *TAPA* xciii (1963) 199–234.

Preising, August. *L. A. Senecae poetae tragici casuum usu ratione potissimum habita Vergili, Ovidi, Lucani.* Diss. Münster, 1891.

Regenbogen, Otto. 'Schmerz und Tod in den Tragödien des Seneca', *Vorträge der Bibliothek Warburg* 1927/8, 167–218 (= *Kleine Schriften.* Munich, 1961, 411–64).

Richter, Gustav. *De Senecae tragoediarum auctore commentatio philologica.* Bonn, 1862.

De corruptis quibusdam Senecae tragoediarum locis. Symbola Doctorum Ienensis Gymnasii in honorem Isenacensis collecta. Jena, 1894.

Kritische Untersuchungen zu Senecas Tragödien. Progr. Jena, 1899.

Rolland, E. *L'influence de Sénèque le père et des rhéteurs sur Sénèque le philosophe.* Ghent, 1906.

Rossbach, Otto. *De Senecae philosophi librorum recensione et emendatione.* Breslau, 1888.

Rouse, Richard H. 'The *A* text of Seneca's tragedies in the thirteenth century', *Revue d'Histoire des Textes* i (1971) 93–121.

Runchina, Giovanni. 'Tecnica drammatica e retorica nelle tragedie di Seneca', *Annali della Facoltà di Lettere, Filosofia e Magistero della Università di Cagliari* xxviii (1960) 165–324.

Sandström, C. E. *De Lucii Annaei Senecae tragoediis commentatio.* Uppsala Universitets Årsskrift. Uppsala, 1872.

Schmidt, Bernhard. *De emendandarum Senecae tragoediarum rationibus prosodiacis et metricis.* Diss. Berlin, 1860.

Observationes criticae in L. A. Senecae tragoedias. Habilitationsschrift. Jena, 1865.

Review of *L. Annaei Senecae tragoedias recensuerunt R. Peiper et G. Richter,* in *Fleck. Jahrb.* xcvii (1868) 781–800, 855–80.

Schreiner, Rupert. *Seneca als Tragödiendichter in seiner Beziehung zu den griechischen Originalen.* Diss. Munich, 1909.

Schulze, W. *Untersuchungen zur Eigenart der Tragödien Senecas.* Diss. Halle, 1937.

Seidensticker, Bernd. *Die Gesprächsverdichtung in den Tragödien Senecas.* Heidelberg, 1969.

Seidler, Brigitte. *Studien zur Wortstellung in den Tragödien Senecas.* Diss. Vienna, 1955.

Siegmund, Anton. *Zur Textkritik der Tragödie Octavia.* I Leipzig–Wien, 1907; II Progr. Bohm–Leipa, 1910/11; III Progr. Bohm–Leipa, 1911.

Sluiter, Th. H. *L. A. Senecae Oedipus, specimen editionis criticae.* Groningen, 1941.

'Studia critica in Senecae Phaedram de codicibus interpolatis P et C', *Mnemosyne* ser. iv.1 (1948), 139–60.

Smith, Richard M. *De arte rhetorica in L. A. Senecae tragoediis perspicua.* Diss. Leipzig, 1885.

Snell, Bruno. 'Stemmatologie zu Senecas Tragödien', *Philologus* xcvi (1944) 160.

Specka, Alfred. *Der hohe Stil der Dichtungen Senecas und Lucans.* Diss. Königsberg, 1937.

Spika, Josef. *De imitatione Horatiana in Senecae canticis chori.* Progr. Vienna, 1890.

Stackmann, Karl. 'Senecas *Agamemnon*: Untersuchungen zur Geschichte des Agamemnon-Stoffes nach Aischylos', *Class. et Med.* xi (1950) 180–221.

Steinmetz, Peter. 'Ein metrisches Experiment Senecas?', *MH* xxvii (1970) 97–103.

Strauss, Friedrich. *De ratione inter Senecam et antiquas fabulas Romanas intercedente.* Diss. Rostock, 1887.

Streubel, G. *Senecas Agamemnon.* Diss. Vienna, 1963.

Strzelecki, Wladislaw. *De Senecae trimetro iambico quaestiones selectae.* Kraków, 1938.

De Senecae Agamemnone Euripidisque Alexandro. Prace Wrocławskiego Towarzystwa Naukowego, Travaux de la Société des Sciences et des Lettres de Varsovie. Series A, no. xxxiii (1949).

'De polymetris Senecae canticis quaestiones', *Eos* xlv (1951) 93–107.

Review of R. Giomini, *De canticis polymetris,* in *Gnomon* xxxii (1960) 747–50.

'De rei metricae Annaeanae origine quaestiones', *Eos* liii (1963) 157–70.

Stuart, Charles Erskine. 'The tragedies of Seneca'. Diss. Cambridge, 1907 (Trinity College Library, Add. MS. b.67).

'The tragedies of Seneca. Notes and emendations', *CQ* v (1911) 32–41.

'The MSS of the interpolated (A) tradition of the tragedies of Seneca', *CQ* vi (1912) 1–20.

Studley, John. 'The Eighth Tragedye of L. Annaeus Seneca / Entituled Agamemnon / Translated out of Latin into Englishe / by John Studley', in *Seneca His Tenne Tragedies / Translated into English / Edited by / Thomas Newton / Anno 1581.* Two vols., London, 1927 (Tudor Translations, ser. 2, 11, 12).

Tarrant, R. J. Review of B. Seidensticker, *Die Gesprächsverdichtung,* in *Phoenix* xxvi (1972) 194–9.

Ter Haar Romeny, B. *De auctore tragoediarum quae sub Senecae nomine feruntur, Vergilii imitatore.* Diss. Leiden, 1877.

BIBLIOGRAPHY

Trabert, Karlheinz. *Studien zur Darstellung des Pathologischen in den Tragödien des Seneca*. Diss. Erlangen, 1953.

Ussani, Vincenzo, Jr. 'Per il testo delle tragedie di Seneca', *Atti Acc. Naz. d. Lincei*, ser. 8, *Memorie*, vol. 8 fasc. 7 (1959) 489–552.

Vian, Francis. *Recherches sur les Posthomerica de Quintus de Smyrne. Études et Commentaires* xxx (Paris, 1959).

ed. *Quintus de Smyrne. La Suite d'Homère III. Livres X–XIV* (Paris, 1969), 155–75.

Viansino, Giovanni. *La Fedra di Seneca*. Naples, 1968.

Walker, B. and Henry, Denis. 'Seneca and the *Agamemnon*: some thoughts on tragic doom', *CP* lviii (1963) 1–10.

Wanke, Christiane. *Seneca, Lucan, Corneille: Studien zum Manierismus. Studia Romanica* vi (Heidelberg, 1964).

Weil, Henry. 'La règle des trois acteurs dans les tragédies de Sénèque', *Rev. Arch.* 2° ser. xi (1865) 21–35.

Westman, Rolf. *Das Futurpartizip als Ausdrucksmittel bei Seneca*. Helsinki, 1960.

Wirth, Hermann. *De Vergili apud Senecam philosophum usu*. Diss. Freiburg-im-Breisgau, 1900.

Woesler, Winfried. *Senecas Tragödien, Die Überlieferung der α-Klasse dargestellt am Beispiel der Phaedra*. Diss. Münster. Neuwied, 1965.

Zwierlein, Otto. *Die Rezitationsdramen Senecas*. Diss. Berlin. Meisenheim-am-Glan, 1966.

Review of G. Viansino, *L. Annaei Senecae tragoediae*, in *Gnomon* xxxviii (1966) 679–88.

Review of G. C. Giardina, *L. Annaei Senecae tragoediae*, in *Gnomon* xli (1969) 759–69.

'Kritisches und Exegetisches zu den Tragödien Senecas', *Philologus* cxiii (1969) 254–67.

Review of B. Axelson, *Korruptelenkult*, in *Gnomon* xlii (1970) 266–73.

ADDENDA

Page 23 n. 4. Collation of Paris B.N. Lat. 8031 for *Agamemnon* shows that the MS is indeed a member of the δ-group. The basic text is pure A, with the large *lacunae* intact, and in the great majority of places where P agrees with E against CS, Par. 8031 agrees with E P; if these agreements were the result of contamination from E, one would expect many more errors of P C S to have been replaced by good readings of E. It remains to determine whether Par. 8031 is a direct descendant of P, the only complete δ-MS so far identified, or an independent descendant of δ. Par. 8031 cannot be a mere copy of P: while it shares a number of P's unique errors (e.g., 129 *tempus da ac spatium*, 176 *et minthe*, 432 *tactu leui*, 472 *nec nox una est*, 826 *etiam*, 923 *regum*, 979 *grandes*), it avoids an even greater number of P's blunders, including some omissions (such as 434 *et pariter*, 734 *feminea*, and all of 755) which no copyist could have supplied by conjecture. Par. 8031 is therefore either a descendant of P in which many P errors have been removed by consultation of another MS, or it is independent of P. If an ancestor of Par. 8031 had removed errors of P with the aid of a MS of a different branch of the tradition, traces of this contamination should be visible in Par. 8031. There are in fact a number of readings in Par. 8031 which do not appear in PCS, but are found in E or in later branches of the A group (23 *repetamus*, 117 *nulla*, 130 *nequit*, 213 *immixta*, 403a *attamen*, 486 *rupto*, 664 *lacrimis lacrimas*, 829 *ueniens*); in other places Par. 8031 agrees with CS in a wrong, but plausible reading against E P (and, presumably, δ): 85 *qualibet*, 146 *dubium*, 199 *aliud*, 222 *prepone*, 855 *flamma*. These probable non-δ readings lend plausibility to the suggestion that Par. 8031 is a descendant of P in which contamination has removed many of P's errors. The manuscript itself shows clear signs of a further stage of contamination and correction: in a number of places in *Agamemnon*, errors of P in the first hand have been erased or corrected (14(?), 394(?), 423, 443, 472, 484, 508, 588(?), 738, 798, 844, 886(?)), and in several other passages a second hand has altered the original PCS reading to agree with E or a later branch of A (57 *O*, 120 *rate*, 120 *micenea domo*, 326 *uictor*, 727 *abditus*, 738 *uictor*, 838 *imo*, 840 *gerionis*). This or a similar correcting hand has appended critical notes to the large A *lacunae* (cf., e.g., f. 129^r 'hic desunt xix uersus quorum primus ita incipit *si posset una cede* quos requiras ante principium prime tragedie').

The evidence of *Agamemnon* leads me to regard Par. 8031 as a skilfully corrected descendant of P. Even if readings elsewhere in the MS should establish it as independent of P, the clear evidence of contamination and correction in it would make Par. 8031 an unreliable instrument for the reconstruction of δ. The MS contains no new reading in the text of *Agamemnon* which is worth reporting in the critical apparatus. (A full discussion

ADDENDA

of Par. 8031 arguing for its independence from P is promised by A. P. MacGregor.)

Page 26 n. 1   See B. L. Ullman and P. A. Stadter, *The Public Library of Renaissance Florence* (1972) 232 no. 912.

Page 34   The *Architrenius* of John of Hautville has recently been edited by P. G. Schmidt (1974).

Page 35 n. 1   Professor A. P. MacGregor has kindly allowed me to see the typescript of his survey of Seneca MSS, to appear in a forthcoming volume of *Aufstieg und Niedergang der römischen Welt*; page-references to this volume are not yet available, and so are not included in my citations.

Page 43   For a full description of Leiden Voss. F 99 see K. A. de Meyier, *Codices Vossiani Latini* I (1973) 217–19; for Q 31 see the same, II (1975) 82f.

Page 45   For a description of Vat. Ottobon. Lat. 1749 see E. Pellegrin *et al.*, *Manuscrits classiques latins de la Bibliothèque Vaticane* I (1975) 667–9.

Page 191   100 maxima ceruix   The phrase can be used metaphorically (cf. Claud. *Ruf.* 2.446f. *adspiciat quisquis nimium sublata secundis | colla gerit*), but S. need not be making a tasteless allusion to Agamemnon (as suggested by Seidensticker 122 n.130, following Pratt.) There may be a verbal echo of Virg. *G.* 2.146f. *maxima taurus | uictima*, but the point of that passage is different.

Page 238   399 quale canebas   A closer parallel may be Tib. 2.5.9f., where Apollo sings the praises of Jupiter after Saturn has been overthrown.

Page 251   399a premit   For *premere ratem*, etc. see also Luc. 5.585f. *hanc* [sc. *puppem*] *Caesare pressam | a fluctu defendet onus.*

Page 279   The rhetorical point suggested for Ajax' speech if 545f. and 548 are removed may also be compared to that in *Anth. Pal.* 9.109.5f. (Julius Diocles, to a shield): Ἄρεος ἐν πολέμοις ἔφυγον χόλον, ἔν τε θαλάσσῃ | Νηρῆος.

Page 300   683ff.   The halcyon as a perennial mourner also appears in a simile in *Anth. Pal.* 9.151 (Antipater of Sidon), 262.

Page 321   795 Helena   The awareness of mythic reputation by Seneca's characters has Ovidian precedent, cf. *Her.* 6.151 (spoken by Hypsipyle) *Medeae Medea forem.*

INDEXES

Indexes 1–4 are selective: they do not register all matters mentioned in the book, but only those on which specific comment is offered. The numbers refer to pages.

1 WORDS

dare iugulum, 178
decennis, 348
decet, 179
decus, 250
demetere, 357
deuincere, 178, 201
deuincire, 201
dictare, 227
dignus (sarcastic), 175
dirus, 286, 299
diu, 212
domare, 352, 359
domi, 214
domitor, 187
ductor, 177
durus, 296

edisserere, 353
efferre, 219, 282
emere, 207
emeritus, 345
eminere, 220
emissus, 162
emoliri, 265
en, 163
errare, 202
est..., 280
etiam, 357
euertere, 264
euoluere, 196
excelsus, 185
excipere, 253
excutere, 321
exerere, 280
exesus, 316
exonerare, 255
expromere, 254

fabricare, 294
facessere, 228f.
facies, 309
fallax, 184
fecundus in, 303
ferre/gerere, 214
festus, 293
fides, 176f.
fidus, 225
flatus, 218

flectere, 237
fluitare, 271
fremere, 292
frena, 196, 212
fulmineus, 328f.
fundere, 190, 245f.
furari, 346f., 349
furor = ἐρινύς, 361
furtiuum genus, 308

garrulus, 299
geminus = *trigeminus*, 329
genae, 307, 315
genus, 198
Geryon, 364
gestare, 291
gradu 'at/from one's place'), 273, 279
Graecia, 208
grandaeuus, 243
grates reddere, 243

habet!, 343
hactenus, 173
haurire (*dicta*), 174; (*ratem*), 270; (*latus*), 340f.
Hecabe (orth.), 364
Hectoreus, 293
hic ('of yours'), 355
hoc (adv.), 366
hodie, 354f.
humilis, 281

iacere, 259, 337
iam repeated, 260, 361
iam iam, 178
immitis, 305
immo, 164
immunis, 186
impos+gen., 197
in final, 191; *in lucem*, 284; *in planum*, 189; *in praecipiti*, 184
Inachius, 234
incertus, 176f., 304, 311
incestus, 177
inclitus, 242
increpare, 258
incumbere 264

2 PASSAGES

3 SUBJECTS

abstractness of Seneca's style, 177,
  197, 238f., 244, 260, 288, 290, 294,
  329
Accius, 13f., 18, 19, 21, 275, 318
Aegisthus, 4, 6, 11, 14, 15, 18, 341,
  358
Aeschylus, *Agamemnon*, 4f., 20, 248;
  not S.'s source, 10, 19, 248;
  Persae, 158
Affektrede, 192, 205, 211
Agamemnon, 6, 11, 13; insignificance of in S., 3f.
Ajax Oileus, 19ff.
Alcaeus, 19f.
alliteration, 190, 211
allusiveness of S.'s style, 168, 176,
  245, 297, 311, 332f.
altars on stage, 249
Amazons, 214
anachronism, 339, 347f.
'analyst' approach to S., 3
anapaestic *cantica*, 369ff.
animus, 202
ἀντιλαβή, *see* dialogue-technique
ps.-Apollodorus, 19 n.7, 22 n.1
apparatus criticus, 95f., 99ff., Addenda
archaism in S.'s style, 198, 201, 219,
  227, 228f., 230, 243, 292
asides, 12, 194 n.3
Astydamas, 20, 336
asyndeton, 179, 349
Atreus, 4, 197
Augustan tragedy, 14
Auster, 266
axe as murder-weapon, 341f.

'bedside plural', 228
Bellona, 188
Boethius, imitates S., 207, 324 n.6

Bootes, 186
brachylogy, 166, 350, 351, 361

Caesius Bassus, 372ff.
Callimachus, storm-narrative in, 21,
  23
Caphereus, 280f.
Cassandra, 4, 10, 18, 285, 306, 360
catalogues, fondness of S. for, 212, 271
chariots in theatre, 346
chorus in S., 12, 180f., 231ff.; of
  captives, 181, 285ff., 318; outlook of, 4
Cicero, 9
clairvoyant visions, 335f.
Clytemestra, 4, 6, 11, 14, 15f., 17,
  18, 226
colloquialism in S.'s style, 198f.,
  228, 270, 292f., 355, 357
colometry, 369ff.
compression in S.'s style, 191, 200,
  204, 230, 262, 268, 275, 290, 291,
  311, 318, 330, 351; *see also* abstractness; allusiveness
conscience, guilty, 222
consolation, themes of, 297
contemptor deorum, 289
Corus, 267, 288
Cybele, worship of, 300f.

dating of S.'s plays, 6f.
declamation-oratory, influence of,
  184, 199, 208, 211, 213, 215, 228,
  275, 283, 294, 303, 339, 358
Delos, 244
dialogue-technique, 199, 202, 225,
  320, 354
distinctio, 207, 223
diuisio, 212, 249 n.1

4 MODERN SCHOLARS

5 MANUSCRIPTS

6 MEDIEVAL COMMENTATORS, OWNERS, SCRIBES, SCRIPTORIA